Centre for Human Rights
Geneva

XL

UNITED NATIONS ACTION
IN THE FIELD
OF HUMAN RIGHTS

D1416211

UNITED NATIONS
New York, 1988

NOTE

The 1988 edition of *Human Rights: A Compilation of International Instruments* (ST/HR/1/Rev.3, United Nations publication, Sales No. E.88.XIV.1) contains the full texts of the international instruments relating to human rights, including conventions, declarations, and certain recommendations, adopted by organizations within the United Nations system up to 31 December 1987. Most of the instruments referred to in the present publication will be found in the Compilation.

The 1987 edition of *Multilateral Treaties Deposited with the Secretary-General as at 31 December 1986* (ST/LEG/SER.E/5, United Nations publication, Sales No. E.87.V.6), contains a comprehensive list of signatures, ratifications, accessions, etc., relating to multilateral treaties deposited with the Secretary-General.

A booklet entitled *Human Rights: Status of International Instruments* (ST/HR/5, United Nations publication, Sales No. E.87.XIV.2) provides information as at 1 September 1987 on signatures, ratifications, accessions, etc., relating to 22 international instruments in the field of human rights.

* * *

Symbols of United Nations documents are composed of capital letters combined with figures. Mention of such a symbol indicates a reference to a United Nations document.

The designations employed and the presentation of the material in this publication do not imply the expression of any opinion whatsoever on the part of the Secretariat of the United Nations concerning the legal status of any country, territory, city or area, or of its authorities, or concerning the delimitation of its frontiers or boundaries.

ST/HR/2/Rev.3

UNITED NATIONS PUBLICATION

Sales No. E.88.XIV.2

ISBN 92-1-154067-4

08000P

PREFACE

This 1988 edition of *United Nations Action in the Field of Human Rights* presents a detailed summary of developments relating to human rights that have taken place within the United Nations system since its inception and up to 31 December 1987. It is issued in commemoration of the fortieth anniversary of the Universal Declaration of Human Rights, which was adopted and proclaimed by the General Assembly of the United Nations on 10 December 1948.

Major achievements of these years, as will be seen, include the drafting of a series of international instruments aimed at defining and elaborating human rights and fundamental freedoms, establishing the international machinery required to supervise and monitor their realization, and developing greater public consciousness of the importance of the international protection of human rights.

The Universal Declaration of Human Rights has clearly earned its place of honour as the basic international code of conduct by which performance in promoting and protecting human rights is to be measured. The International Covenants on Human Rights have added supervisory procedures to control the implementation of the international precepts on human rights. Moreover, after many years, torture has finally been banned on a world-wide basis with the entry into force of the Convention against Torture and Other Cruel, Inhuman or Degrading Treatment or Punishment and the establishment of the Committee against Torture. The pages of the present publication provide some of the essential facts upon which evaluation of the extent of acceptance of and compliance with, such instruments can be made.

The international community has recognized, over this 40-year period, that human rights are of deep concern to all humanity. It has recognized that discrimination on any ground, such as race, sex, religion or social status, is an abomination which the world can no longer tolerate. It has also recognized that colonialism, exploitation, foreign domination and occupation are anachronistic relics of the past and that the full equality of men and women is not only possible but also eminently desirable.

While we have made great steps in elaborating international principles and standards in accordance with the Charter of the United Nations, we have not always been able to put a stop to flagrant violations of human rights. Regrettably, mass poverty, widespread illiteracy, summary executions, involuntary disappearances and terrorism still occur in various parts of the globe. The struggle to put an end to *apartheid* continues even after 40 years. In short, the world has found that the task of translating principles into performance, in the very sensitive and complex field of human rights, still presents us with a considerable challenge for future action.

Long-term solutions require the establishment of equitable international conditions—including a just international economic order and real disarmament—which would enable individuals and peoples to realize their human rights and fudamental freedoms. They also require the enhancement of social justice and larger freedom at both the national and international levels.

A rededication of public and private interest in the promotion and protection of human rights and fundamental freedoms is now more than ever needed. Clearly such concern may be stimulated and reinforced through effective programmes of teaching, education and information.

The present publication provides the texts and data needed as a basis for such programmes. It contains material on which more searching studies, books and scholarly evaluations may be prepared.

To the extent that it is used for purposes like these, its wide circulation is amply justified and timely.

Javier PÉREZ DE CUÉLLAR
Secretary-General

SUMMARY OF CONTENTS

Part One

Part Two

CONTENTS

INTRODUCTION

The present publication reviews the activities of the United Nations in the field of human rights from the establishment of the Organization in 1945 up to 31 December 1987. It is issued in commemoration of the fortieth anniversary of the Universal Declaration of Human Rights: 10 December 1988.

It is in two parts: part one describes the numerous bodies within the United Nations system which are concerned with human rights and briefly summarizes their activities and accomplishments; part two outlines the procedural arrangements whereby these bodies endeavour to attain their objectives, namely the setting and implementation of international standards in the field of human rights and the promotion of respect for, and observance of, all human rights and fundamental freedoms.

Chapters I and II outline the impressive development of international concern for these rights and freedoms over a period of four decades, in the course of which many new international organs and agencies were created, and many new international instruments brought into force, with a view to attaining one of the principal purposes of the United Nations: "to achieve international co-operation . . . in promoting and encouraging respect for human rights and for fundamental freedoms for all without distinction as to race, sex, language or religion". *Chapter I* describes the organs and agencies concerned, which number more than twenty-five, while *chapter II* enumerates the relevant international declarations and conventions, of which there are over fifty.

The remaining chapters of part one show how all these varied organs and agencies function and co-ordinate in the complicated process of reaching towards the goals established in the instruments. *Chapter III* is concerned with the realization of the right of peoples and nations to self-determination, *chapter IV* with the elimination of racism, racial discrimination, and intolerance or discrimination based on religion or belief, and *chapter V* with the elimination of *apartheid* and the provision of assistance to its victims.

The advancement of women, one of the key human rights issues of our times, is the subject of *chapter VI,* which spells out what the international community has done, and what remains unfinished, in many areas of special concern, including the achievement of equality of men and women in the enjoyment of each and every human right and fundamental freedom, the improvement of the role of women in development and in society, and the involvement of women in the strengthening of international peace and security.

Chapters VII and VIII deal *seriatim* with each human right set out in the International Bill of Human Rights, and describe both the general and the specific measures taken for the realization of those rights. *Chapter VII* is concerned primarily with the rights elaborated in the In-

ternational Covenant on Economic, Social and Cultural Rights; *chapter VIII* with those elaborated in the International Covenant on Civil and Political Rights.

Chapter IX deals with measures taken to assist the most vulnerable and disadvantaged groups of persons, including children, persons belonging to ethnic, religious or linguistic minorities, aliens, migrant workers, the aging and the disabled. *Chapter X* relates to still another vulnerable group: refugees, stateless persons, displaced persons and others who are outside their own country and unable to return thereto.

Chapter XI summarizes the measures taken within the United Nations system to put a stop to gross and massive violations of human rights affecting whole areas or countries. It deals with such violations in particular areas, such as southern Africa and the Middle East, and in particular countries. It also refers to the technical assistance offered by international bodies to help requesting Governments guarantee the enjoyment of human rights.

Chapter XII describes the endeavours of the United Nations, the International Committee of the Red Cross, and other international humanitarian organizations to extend the protection of human rights in armed conflicts, and the successful efforts of the Diplomatic Conference on the Reaffirmation and Development of International Humanitarian Law Applicable to Armed Conflicts to improve the coverage and effectiveness of the Geneva Conventions of 12 August 1949. It is also concerned with measures taken with a view to dealing with international crimes, including war crimes and crimes against humanity.

Chapter XIII traces the close interrelationship between human rights and peace, and between human rights and development. It is also concerned with measures aimed at ensuring that science and technology are used in the interests of peace and for the benefit of mankind.

Part two deals with the operations and procedures under which all this work proceeds. *Chapter XIV* indicates the ways and means by which international standards in the field of human rights are set, and later supervised, and how communications alleging violations of those rights are handled by the Secretary-General and the competent organs and agencies. *Chapter XV* indicates the ways and means by which various developments in the field of human rights are made known to the public, including the publicizing of international human rights activities, the publication of the *Yearbook on Human Rights* and other periodical volumes and brochures, the preparation and dissemination of studies on various human rights problems and the operation of the programme of advisory services in the field of human rights. Public information and educational measures, including arrangements for the teaching of human rights and the holding of commemorative observances of important human rights anniversaries, are also described.

PART ONE

I. UNITED NATIONS ORGANS, SPECIALIZED AGENCIES AND OTHER ORGANIZATIONS CONCERNED WITH HUMAN RIGHTS

Introduction

1. The deep concern of the international community for the promotion and protection of human rights is clearly expressed in the Charter of the United Nations, in which the peoples of the United Nations record their determination "to reaffirm faith in fundamental human rights, in the dignity and worth of the human person, in the equal rights of men and women and of nations large and small", and for this purpose "to practise tolerance and live together in peace with one another as good neighbours" and "to employ international machinery for the promotion of the economic and social advancement of all peoples".

2. One of the purposes of the United Nations, under Article 1, is "to develop friendly relations among nations based on respect for the principle of equal rights and self-determination of peoples". Another is "to achieve international co-operation in solving international problems of an economic, social, cultural, or humanitarian character, and in promoting and encouraging respect for human rights and for fundamental freedoms for all without distinction as to race, sex, language, or religion".

3. Under Article 55, the United Nations has the duty to promote "universal respect for, and observance of, human rights and fundamental freedoms for all without distinction as to race, sex, language or religion", with a view to "the creation of conditions of stability and well-being which are necessary for peaceful and friendly relations among nations based on respect for the principle of equal rights and self-determination of peoples". Under Article 56, all Members of the United Nations "pledge themselves to take joint and separate action in co-operation with the Organization for the achievement of the purposes set forth in Article 55".

4. The Charter authorizes a number of organs to deal with questions of human rights. Article 13 states that the General Assembly "shall initiate studies and make recommendations for the purpose of 'promoting international co-operation in the economic, social, cultural, educational and health fields, and assisting in the realization of human rights and fundamental freedoms for all without distinction as to race, sex, language or religion' ". Article 62 states that the Economic and Social Council "may make recommendations for the purpose of promoting respect for, and observance of, human rights and fundamental freedoms for all". Article 60 provides that "Responsibility for the discharge of the functions of the Organization set forth in this Chapter [Chapter IX] shall be vested in the General Assembly and, under the authority of the General Assembly, in the Economic and Social Council". Chapter IX, to which Article 60 refers, includes Articles 55 and 56.

5. Under Article 64, the Economic and Social Council "may make arrangements with the Members of the United Nations and with the specialized agencies to obtain reports on the steps taken to give effect to its own recommendations and to recommendations on matters falling within its competence made by the General Assembly", and "may communicate its observations on these reports to the General Assembly".

6. With regard to dependent territories, Article 73 of the Charter states that "Members of the United Nations which have or assume responsibilities for the administration of territories whose peoples have not yet attained a full measure of self-government recognize the principle that the interests of the inhabitants of these territories are paramount, and accept as a sacred trust the obligation to promote to the utmost, within the system of international peace and security established by the present Charter, the well-being of the inhabitants of these territories, and, to this end: (*a*) to ensure, with due respect for the culture of the peoples concerned, their political, economic, social, and educational advancement, their just treatment, and their protection against abuses; (*b*) to develop self-government, to take due account of the political aspirations of the peoples, and to assist them in the progressive development of their free political institutions, according to the particular circumstances of each territory and its peoples and their varying stages of advancement . . .".

7. One of the basic objectives of the International Trusteeship System, which the United Nations is authorized to establish by Article 75 of the Charter, is, in accordance with the purposes laid down in Article 1, to encourage "respect for human rights and for fundamental freedoms for all without distinction as to race, sex, language or religion". Article 87 provides for supervision of the administration of Trust Territories through a system of reports, examination of petitions, and periodic visits.

8. As regards the primary purpose of the United Nations—the maintenance of international peace and security—the General Assembly is authorized in Article 11 of the Charter to "discuss any questions relating to the maintenance of international peace and security brought before it by any Member of the United Nations", and to make recommendations "with regard to any such questions to the State or States concerned or to the

Security Council or to both''. Further, it may ''call the attention of the Security Council to situations which are likely to endanger international peace and security''. And under Article 14 it ''may recommend measures for the peaceful adjustment of any situation, regardless of origin, which it deems likely to impair the general welfare or friendly relations among nations, including situations resulting from a violation of the provisions of the present Charter setting forth the Purposes and Principles of the United Nations''.

9. In Chapters V, VI and VII, the Charter confers on the Security Council primary responsibility for the maintenance of international peace and security and provides it with special powers, including enforcement measures, for this purpose. The Council has on several occasions invoked these powers in dealing with situations involving gross violations of human rights which threatened international peace and security.

10. The authority of the United Nations to promote and protect human rights is subject to the principle set out in paragraph 7 of Article 2 of the Charter, which states that ''Nothing contained in the present Charter shall authorize the United Nations to intervene in matters which are essentially within the domestic jurisdiction of any State or shall require the Members to submit such matters to settlement under the present Charter'', and adds that ''this principle shall not prejudice the application of enforcement measures under Chapter VII''.

11. However in practice this domestic-jurisdiction interdiction has not been viewed as an insurmountable obstacle to the consideration of human rights questions by the competent United Nations bodies, which have usually proceeded on the assumption that any violation of human rights which arouses serious international concern is not ''essentially within the domestic jurisdiction of any State''.

12. Each of the six principal organs of the United Nations—the General Assembly, the Economic and Social Council, the Security Council, the Trusteeship Council, the International Court of Justice and the Secretariat—plays an active role in the unceasing efforts of the United Nations to promote and protect the realization of human rights and fundamental freedoms throughout the world. Four of the specialized agencies of the United Nations—the International Labour Organisation, the United Nations Educational, Scientific and Cultural Organization, the World Health Organization and the Food and Agriculture Organization—have successfully undertaken extensive activities in this field since their establishment. And in recent years six monitoring bodies have been established—the Committee on the Elimination of Racial Discrimination, the Human Rights Committee, the Committee on the Elimination of Discrimination against Women, the Committee on Economic, Social and Cultural Rights, the Committee against Torture and the Group of Three of the Commission on Human Rights—to supervise the implementation of particular multilateral treaties which endeavour to ensure the enjoyment of human rights and fundamental freedoms by everyone without distinction.

13. The relevant functions and powers, as well as the composition, membership and procedures of these bodies, are summarized below.

A. General Assembly

14. The General Assembly is essentially a deliberative, supervisory and reviewing organ of the United Nations. Under Article 10 of the Charter, it ''may discuss any questions or any matters within the scope of the present Charter or relating to the powers and functions of any organs provided for in the present Charter, and, except as provided in Article 12, may make recommendations to the Members of the United Nations or to the Security Council or to both on any such questions or matters''. Article 12 provides that ''while the Security Council is exercising in respect of any dispute or situation the functions assigned to it in the present Charter, the General Assembly shall not make any recommendation with regard to that dispute or situation unless the Security Council so requests''.

1. HUMAN RIGHTS FUNCTIONS AND PROCEDURES

15. As regards human rights, Article 13 of the Charter provides that the General Assembly shall initiate studies and make recommendations for the purpose of ''assisting in the realization of human rights and fundamental freedoms for all without distinction as to race, sex, language or religion''.

16. Most human rights items on the agenda of the General Assembly originate in decisions of the Assembly at previous sessions to take up particular questions. Others have their origin in reports from the Economic and Social Council or in proposals by Members of the United Nations. Still others are included in accordance with the provisions of international instruments in the field of human rights, such as the International Covenant on Civil and Political Rights.

17. The General Assembly consists of all the Members of the United Nations (Article 9 of the Charter). Each Member has one vote (Article 18).

18. Decisions on certain categories of important questions, listed in Article 18, such as recommendations concerning the maintenance of international peace and security, require a two-thirds majority of the members present and voting. Decisions on other questions require a majority of the members present and voting.

19. The General Assembly meets in regular annual sessions and in such special sessions as occasion may require (Article 20). It adopts its own rules of procedure (Article 21). Its meetings are held at the Headquarters of the United Nations, New York, unless convened elsewhere in pursuance of a decision taken at a previous session or at the request of a majority of the Members of the United Nations (rule 3).

6

20. Under rule 98, the Main Committees of the General Assembly are the following:

(*a*) Political and Security Committee (including the regulation of armaments) (First Committee);

(*b*) Special Political Committee;

(*c*) Economic and Financial Committee (Second Committee);

(*d*) Social, Humanitarian and Cultural Committee (Third Committee);

(*e*) Trusteeship Committee (including Non-Self-Governing Territories) (Fourth Committee);

(*f*) Administrative and Budgetary Committee (Fifth Committee);

(*g*) Legal Committee (Sixth Committee).

Each Member may be represented by one person on each Main Committee (rule 100). Each member of the committee has one vote (rule 124). Decisions of committees are made by a majority of the members present and voting (rule 125).

21. Normally, items relating to human rights are referred to the Third Committee. However, from time to time and for a variety of reasons, such items have also been referred to the First Committee, the Special Political Committee, the Second Committee, the Fourth Committee or the Sixth Committee; or have been considered directly by the General Assembly without reference to a Main Committee.

22. The reports of the Main Committees on each item, which normally contain the texts of all proposals and amendments considered by the Committee, the results of all votes taken, and a draft resolution for approval by the General Assembly, are considered in plenary meetings and adopted, amended or rejected.

23. Under rule 161, the General Assembly may establish such subsidiary organs as it deems necessary for the performance of its functions. Among the organs so established are several which are concerned with human rights issues such as decolonization, *apartheid,* and assistance to vulnerable groups of people. Through such bodies the Assembly's work goes on continuously throughout each year.

2. SUBSIDIARY BODIES

(a) *International Law Commission*

24. The International Law Commission, established by General Assembly resolution 174 (II) of 21 November 1947, has for its object the promotion of the progressive development of international law and its codification. Its work includes, on the one hand, the preparation of draft conventions on subjects which have not yet been regulated by international law or in regard to which the law has not yet been sufficiently developed in the practice of States, and, on the other hand, the more precise formulation and systematization of rules of international law in fields where there has already been extensive State practice, precedent and doctrine.

25. Over the years, the Commission has participated actively in the preparation of a number of international instruments in the field of human rights, including the Convention on the Prevention and Punishment of the Crime of Genocide, the Statute of the Office of the United Nations High Commissioner for Refugees, the Convention relating to the Status of Refugees, the Convention relating to the Status of Stateless Persons, the Convention on the reduction of Statelessness, the Protocol relating to the Status of Refugees and the Declaration on Territorial Asylum.

26. The Commission originally consisted of 15 members. The number was increased to 21 in 1956 and to 25 in 1961. In 1981, the number was further increased, to 34, by General Assembly resolution 36/39 of 18 November 1981.

27. Candidates for membership of the Commission are nominated by Governments of States Members of the United Nations. The members of the Commission sit in their individual capacity and not as representatives of their Governments. They must be persons of recognized competence in international law. Elections are conducted by the General Assembly at five-year intervals. Those candidates, up to the maximum number prescribed for each regional group, who obtain the greatest number of votes and not less than a majority of the votes of the Members present and voting are declared elected and serve for a term of five years. Vacancies which occur between elections are filled by the Commission itself.

28. Members of the Commission are elected according to the following pattern, in accordance with paragraph 3 of General Assembly resolution 36/39:

(*a*) Eight nationals from African States;

(*b*) Seven nationals from Asian States;

(*c*) Three nationals from Eastern European States;

(*d*) Six nationals from Latin-American States;

(*e*) Eight nationals from Western European or other States;

(*f*) One national from African States or Eastern European States in rotation, with the seat being allocated to a national of an African State in the first election held after the adoption of the resolution;

(*g*) One national from Asian States or Latin-American States in rotation, with the seat being allocated to a national of an Asian State in the first election to be held after the adoption of the resolution.

29. Articles 16 and 17 of the Statute of the International Law Commission lay down specific steps to be taken by the Commission in the course of its work on the progressive development of international law, and articles 18 to 23 lay down steps to be taken in the course of its work on codification. In practice, however, the Commission has generally considered that its drafts constitute both progressive development of international law and codification of that law, and has found it impracticable to determine into which category each draft or provision falls.

30. The Commission follows essentially the same method for both types of work. A Special Rapporteur is appointed for each topic, and a plan of work is formulated. Governments are requested to furnish relevant administrative, legislative and judicial decisions, which are studied by the Special Rapporteur. On the basis of the Special Rapporteur's report, a provisional draft is prepared and approved by the Commission. The provi-

sional draft is submitted to the General Assembly and sent to Governments for their observations. The Special Rapporteur studies the replies received, together with any comments made in the General Assembly, and submits a further report. On the basis of that report, the Commission adopts a final draft, which it submits to the General Assembly with its recommendation regarding further action. The Commission may recommend that the Assembly take no action, that it take note of the report, that it recommend the Commission's draft to Members, with a view to the conclusion of a convention, or that it convoke a conference to conclude a convention.

31. From time to time, the General Assembly asks the Commission to deal with particular legal problems. Thus, the Commission submitted reports to the Assembly in 1950 on the formulation of the Nürnberg Principles, in 1951 on the question of defining aggression, and in 1951 and 1954 on the draft Code of Offences against the Peace and Security of Mankind.

32. Sessions of the Commission normally begin in May and last 12 weeks. With the exception of the first session, which was held in New York in 1949, the sixth session, which was held in Paris in 1954, and the second part of the seventeenth session, which was held in Monaco in 1966, all sessions have been held at Geneva. The Commission reports annually to the General Assembly.

33. Article 25 of the Statute of the International Law Commission authorizes the Commission to consult with any of the organs of the United Nations on any subject which is within the competence of that organ.

34. At its second and third sessions, in 1950 and 1951, the Commission was notified of resolutions adopted by the Economic and Social Council on the recommendation of the Commission on the Status of Women and the Commission on Human Rights, in which the Council requested the Commission to deal with (a) the nationality of married women, and (b) the elimination of statelessness. The Commission dealt with these subjects in connection with the topic "nationality, including statelessness", which it had selected for codification in 1949.

35. The secretariat for the Commission is provided by the Codification Division of the Office of Legal Affairs of the United Nations.

(b) Special Committee on Decolonization

36. The Special Committee on the Situation with regard to the Implementation of the Declaration on the Granting of Independence to Colonial Countries and Peoples, popularly known as the Special Committee on Decolonization or the Committee of 24, was established by General Assembly resolution 1654 (XVI) of 27 November 1961. The basic function of the Committee is to monitor implementation of the Declaration, which proclaims that all people have a right to self-determination and that colonialism should be brought to a speedy

and unconditional end. A second function is to inform the Security Council of any developments in the Territories covered by the Declaration which might threaten international peace and security; a third is to determine when a Territory becomes an independent State.

37. The Special Committee normally meets at United Nations Headquarters, New York, begins its work about 1 February of each year and concludes it by the end of August. The Special Committee is, however, authorized to meet elsewhere than at United Nations Headquarters whenever and wherever such meetings may be required for the effective discharge of its duties; it has met on various occasions at Addis Ababa, Belgrade, Algiers, Cairo, Conakry, Dar es Salaam, Kinshasa, Lisbon, Lusaka, Mogadiscio and Tangier.

38. From time to time, the Special Committee has sent its Chairman, a delegation of observers, or a visiting mission to one or more of the Territories with which it is concerned, or to a conference relating to decolonization.

39. At the start of each session, the Special Committee, on the basis of suggestions made by its Chairman, considers the organization of its work. In 1987, it allocated various agenda items for consideration either in plenary meetings of the Committee or by its subsidiary bodies: the Working Group, the Sub-Committee on Petitions, Information and Assistance, and the Sub-Committee on Small Territories.

40. The Working Group functions primarily as a Steering Committee. The Sub-Committee on Petitions, Information and Assistance deals with communications containing requests for hearing by the Special Committee in connection with items on its agenda.[1] The Sub-Committee on Small Territories deals with any items referred to it by the Special Committee. The Working Group and both Sub-Committees hold informal as well as official meetings.

41. The Special Committee itself considers a number of Territories directly in plenary meetings and as a result adopts resolutions, consensuses, decisions, conclusions or recommendations. Up to 1981, it adopted its own resolutions, which were recorded in its report to the General Assembly. In 1982, it decided, in accordance with paragraph 31 of General Assembly decision 34/401 of 29 November 1979, to prepare draft resolutions for consideration by the General Assembly. It requested its Rapporteur to prepare draft texts based on the resolutions and decisions which it had adopted by consensus, and on specified ones which it had adopted by vote. After considering the draft texts, the Special Committee adopted them.

42. The Special Committee invites the representative of the South West Africa People's Organization

---

[1] Reservations concerning certain of the Special Committee's procedures, including those relating to the handling of communications and petitions and those relating to visiting missions, have been expressed by certain members of the Special Committee. See *Official Records of the General Assembly, Seventeenth Session, Annexes,* agenda item 25, addendum, document A/5238, paras 16-111.

(SWAPO), the national liberation movement of Namibia, to participate in an observer capacity in its consideration of the question of Namibia. In response to such an invitation, the representatives of SWAPO took part in the relevant proceedings of the Committee and the representative of the African National Congress of South Africa (ANC) made a statement on one item.

43. The Special Committee also invites—in consultation, as appropriate, with the Organization of African Unity (OAU) and the national liberation movements concerned—the participation of individuals who could furnish it with information on specific aspects of the situation in colonial Territories.

44. In its work, the Special Committee takes into account the provisions of General Assembly resolution 37/35 of 23 November 1982, by which the Assembly requested it "to continue to pay particular attention to the small Territories, including the sending of visiting missions thereto, as appropriate, and to recommend to the General Assembly the most suitable steps to be taken to enable the populations of those Territories to exercise their right to self-determination, freedom and independence".

45. The Special Committee examines at each annual session the implementation, in individual territories, of the Declaration on the Granting of Independence to Colonial Countries and Peoples. To assist in its examination of conditions in each Territory, it normally has before it an information paper prepared by the Secretariat describing recent political and constitutional developments and current economic, social and educational conditions. This information is derived from published sources and from the information transmitted by administering Powers under Article 73 e of the Charter.

46. In order to assist administering Powers in the submission of information, the Special Committee has approved and forwarded to them a questionnaire (A/AC.109/6), on the recommendation of a five-member sub-committee, containing two sections on matters directly relating to human rights. Section IV of the questionnaire calls upon the administering Powers to state whether and to what extent suffrage exists in the Territory concerned, and to explain its statutory and other bases. Section VIII, entitled "Human rights and fundamental freedoms", reads as follows:

(a) Describe the statutory and constitutional safeguards, if any, in regard to the observance of human rights and fundamental freedoms. Describe the restraints, if any, on the exercise of any of these rights (furnish relevant texts or extracts);

(b) Describe the rights of the indigenous inhabitants to establish political parties and the actual existence of political parties, freedom of expression, freedom of assembly and freedom of the Press, etc.;

(c) Describe the rights of the workers to form and join trade unions and to otherwise protect their interests;

(d) Describe the situation with regard to effectively guaranteed security of person and of the community with reference to the foregoing rights and freedoms. What are the restraints, if any, on civil liberties, in particular, the right to form political parties and trade unions and to hold public meetings, etc. (give relevant texts and extracts of statutes and regulations).

47. During its sessions, the Special Committee hears statements from the administering Powers, inviting those which are not members of the Committee to participate in its consideration of the Territories they administer. In its consideration of Territories in Africa, the Special Committee hears statements of the national liberation movements concerned which are recognized by OAU.

48. In its work, the Special Committee takes into account the relevant provisions of resolutions adopted by the Commission on Human Rights, and the reports submitted by the *Ad Hoc* Working Group of Experts of the Commission. It also takes into account relevant reports prepared by Special Rapporteurs appointed by the Sub-Commission on Prevention of Discrimination and Protection of Minorities.

49. In a resolution adopted on 18 June 1965, the Special Committee drew the attention of the Commission on Human Rights to the evidence submitted by petitioners concerning violations of human rights in Territories under Portuguese administration and also in South West Africa and Southern Rhodesia, and expressed its profound shock at the violations of human rights committed in order to stifle the legitimate aspirations of the African population to self-determination.

50. In resolution 2 (XXII) of 25 March 1966, the Commission condemned violations of human rights and fundamental freedoms wherever they occur, supported the measures provided for in the Special Committee's resolution, and requested the Economic and Social Council to recommend to the General Assembly that "it request the Special Committee to apprise the Commission . . . of the relevant information coming to the Committee's attention and of its discussions and decisions on questions of violations of human rights in colonial and dependent countries and territories".

51. The Economic and Social Council, in resolution 1164 (XLI) of 5 August 1966, welcomed the Commission's decision to consider its tasks and functions and its role in relation to violations of human rights in all countries, and concurred in the Commission's view that it would be necessary for the Commission to consider the means by which it might be kept more fully informed of violations of human rights. The General Assembly, in resolution 2144 (XXI) of 26 October 1966, invited the Council and the Commission "to give urgent consideration to ways and means of improving the capacity of the United Nations to put a stop to violations of human rights wherever they may occur".

52. Thus, action by the Special Committee on the Situation with regard to the Implementation of the Declaration on the Granting of Independence to Colonial Countries and Peoples had the effect not only of involving the Commission on Human Rights and the Sub-Commission on Prevention of Discrimination and Protection of Minorities in activities aimed at putting an end to violations of human rights and fundamental freedoms in colonial and other dependent territories, but also provided them with an occasion to seek the authorizations necessary to extend such activities to encompass all countries and territories. Further, it led

eventually to the elaboration of a major revision of the procedure for the handling of communications concerning human rights, set out in Economic and Social Council resolution 1503 (XLVIII) of 27 May 1970.

53. In recent years the General Assembly, on recommendation of the Special Committee, has repeatedly deplored the continued links with, and assistance rendered to, South Africa by certain specialized agencies—including the International Monetary Fund—in contravention of the relevant resolutions of the United Nations, thus enhancing neo-colonialist practices in the system of international relations.

54. In resolutions 41/15 of 31 October 1986 and 42/75 of 4 December 1987 the Assembly affirmed and reaffirmed that the specialized agencies and other organizations and institutions of the United Nations system should continue to be guided by United Nations resolutions in their efforts to contribute to the full and speedy implementation of the Declaration on the Granting of Independence to Colonial Countries and Peoples, and called upon them to take all necessary measures to withhold from South Africa any form of co-operation or assistance in the financial, economic, technical and other fields until the people of Namibia have exercised fully their inalienable right to self-determination, freedom and independence in a united Namibia and until the system of *apartheid* has been totally eradicated.

55. The secretariat of the Special Committee functions within the Department of Political Affairs, Trusteeship and Decolonization, and services all committees, working groups and missions of the Committee.

(c) *Special Committee against* Apartheid

56. In resolution 1761 (XVII) of 6 November 1962, the General Assembly established the Special Committee on the Policies of *Apartheid* of the Government of the Republic of South Africa, with the mandate "to keep the racial policies of the Government of South Africa under review when the Assembly is not in session" and "to report either to the Assembly or to the Security Council or to both, as may be appropriate, from time to time". At its twenty-fifth session, in 1970, the Assembly shortened the name of the Special Committee to "Special Committee on *Apartheid*" and extended its terms of reference so that it could constantly review all aspects of the policies of *Apartheid* in South Africa and their international repercussions. At its twenty-ninth session, in resolution 3324 D (XXIX), of 16 December 1974, the Assembly changed its name to "Special Committee against *Apartheid*".

57. In resolution 35/206 P of 16 December 1980, the Assembly requested the Special Committee to continue and to intensify its activities in accordance with the relevant resolutions of the Assembly and with particular reference to (*a*) promoting campaigns for the total isolation of the racist régime of South Africa, (*b*) promoting increased assistance to the oppressed people of South Africa and their national liberation movement, and (*c*) monitoring the implementation of United Nations resolutions on *apartheid* and exposing all collaboration with South Africa.

58. The Special Committee originally consisted of 11 Member States appointed by the President of the General Assembly. The number of members was increased by Assembly resolution 3324 D (XXIX) of 16 December 1974; and in resolution 34/93 R of 17 December 1979 the Assembly requested its President, in consultation with the regional groups, to expand its membership further. As at 31 December 1982, the Special Committee was composed of 18 Member States.

59. The Special Committee submits annual and special reports to the General Assembly and to the Security Council. The Assembly discusses these reports directly in plenary meeting.

60. The Special Committee is assisted in its work by two sub-committees, the Sub-Committee on the Implementation of United Nations Resolutions and Collaboration with South Africa and the Sub-Committee on Petitions and Information, each consisting of five Member States.

61. Since its inception in 1963, the Special Committee has constantly followed and publicized the situation in South Africa and its international repercussions. It has undertaken or sponsored many studies on the matter, and has sent missions to many Governments—especially those which had opposed sanctions or other concrete measures against South Africa—to persuade them to co-operate in international action. It has organized or co-sponsored international, regional and national conferences to encourage concerted action, and has promoted funds for humanitarian, educational, political and other assistance to the oppressed people of South Africa and their national liberation movement. It has encouraged public action against *apartheid,* and taken many initiatives to obtain the understanding and support of world public opinion—of trade unions, religious leaders, writers and artists, sportsmen, the young and other segments of the population—for the efforts of the United Nations.

62. In a communication dated 15 February 1967 from the Acting Chairman of the Special Committee against *Apartheid,* the Secretary-General was requested to draw the attention of the Commission on Human Rights "to the continuing ill-treatment of prisoners, detainees and persons in police custody in the Republic of South Africa, particularly the numerous opponents of *apartheid* who have been imprisoned under arbitrary laws". The communication indicated that the Special Committee hoped that the Commission would consider the matter urgently and take steps to secure an international investigation.

63. The Commission responded by establishing, under resolution 2 (XXIII) of 6 March 1967, a working group now known as the *Ad Hoc* Working Group of Experts on Human Rights in Southern Africa, which has since examined the policies and practices which violate human rights in South Africa and Namibia.

64. The General Assembly, in resolution 2144 A (XXI) of 26 October 1966, requested the Secretary-General to establish a unit within the Secretariat to deal exclusively with policies of *apartheid,* in consultation with the Special Committee. The Unit on *Apartheid* was accordingly established in 1966.

65. In 1975, the General Assembly, in resolution 3411 F (XXX) of 28 November 1975, in accordance with the recommendations of the Special Committee, requested the Secretary-General to rename the Unit as the Centre against *Apartheid* and to strengthen it adequately.

66. The Centre against *Apartheid* functions within the Department of Political and Security Council Affairs.

(d) *United Nations Council for Namibia*

67. At its fifth special session, the General Assembly in resolution 2248 (S-V) of 19 May 1967, established the United Nations Council for South West Africa, to administer the Territory until independence, and decided that the Council should entrust such executive and administrative tasks as it deemed necessary to a United Nations Commissioner to be appointed by the Assembly on the nomination of the Secretary-General.

68. A year later, by resolution 2372 (XXII) of 12 June 1968, the General Assembly proclaimed that, in accordance with the desires of its people, the Territory of South West Africa should be known as "Namibia". The Council was then renamed the United Nations Council for Namibia and the Commissioner became the United Nations Commissioner for Namibia.

69. Originally, the Council was composed of 11 Member States. It was expanded by General Assembly resolution 3031 (XXVII), 3295 (XXIX), and 33/182 A, and now consists of 31 Members.

70. The General Assembly decided, in resolutions 2679 (XXV) of 9 December 1970 and 2872 (XXVI) of 20 December 1971, to establish a United Nations Fund for Namibia for the purpose of putting into effect a comprehensive programme of assistance to Namibians. Later, by resolution 3112 (XXVIII) of 12 December 1973, the Assembly appointed the United Nations Council for Namibia as trustee of the Fund.

71. In resolution 3296 (XXIX) of 13 December 1974, the General Assembly endorsed the decision of the Council to establish an Institute for Namibia at Lusaka.

72. The activities of the Council have included consultations with Governments to bring about the implementation of United Nations resolutions on Namibia, the representation of Namibia in international organizations and conferences, the provision of material assistance to Namibians and the dissemination of information.

73. In 1987, the Council elected a President and five Vice-Presidents for the calendar year. These officers, together with the Chairmen of the three Standing Committees and the Vice-Chairman and Rapporteur of the Committee on the United Nations Fund for Namibia, constituted its Steering Committee.

74. Standing Committee I deals with the representation of Namibia in international organizations and conferences; considers recommendations relating to consultations with Governments of Member States, OAU, the Movement of Non-Aligned Countries and other regional and international political organizations; and consults with representatives of SWAPO on these matters.

75. Standing Committee II reviews the progress of the liberation struggle in Namibia in its political, military and social aspects; considers the compliance of Member States with United Nations resolutions on Namibia, the activities of foreign economic interests operating in Namibia, all legal issues relating to the liberation struggle of the Namibian people, the nature and scale of South African military installations and operations in Namibia; and holds consultations with representatives of SWAPO on these matters.

76. Standing Committee III considers ways and means of increasing the dissemination of information relating to Namibia, and of acquainting world public opinion with all aspects of the question of Namibia; organizes and co-ordinates contacts made by delegations of the Council with leading representatives of the media, educational institutions and other cultural institutions, as well as action and support groups; and holds consultations with representatives of SWAPO on these matters.

77. The Committee on the United Nations Fund for Namibia formulates and reviews policies on the utilization of the resources of the Fund, on the Nationhood Programme for Namibia, and on the activities of the Institute for Namibia at Lusaka. It also formulates and reviews policies relating to the co-ordination of the work of the Council with that of the specialized agencies and other bodies of the United Nations system. The President of the Council acts as Chairman of the Committee.

78. In resolution 42/14 of 6 November 1987, the General Assembly, after examining the report of the United Nations Council for Namibia[2] and the relevant chapters of the report of the Special Committee on Decolonization,[3] reiterated that Namibia is the direct responsibility of the United Nations until genuine self-determination and national independence are achieved in the Territory and, for this reason, reaffirmed the mandate given to the United Nations Council for Namibia as the legal Administering Authority for Namibia until that time.

79. By resolution 2248 (S-V) of 19 May 1967, the General Assembly decided that the United Nations Council for Namibia should entrust such executive and administrative tasks as it deemed necessary to a United

---

[2] *Official Records of the General Assembly, Forty-second Session, Supplement No. 24* (A/42/24).

[3] *Ibid., Forty-first Session, Supplement No. 23* (A/41/23), chap. VIII.

Nations High Commissioner for Namibia, appointed by the Assembly on the nomination of the Secretary-General. The Assembly further decided that, in the performance of his tasks, the High Commissioner should be responsible to the Council. The Commissioner is appointed with an annual mandate.

80. The secretariat of the Council functions within the Department of Political Affairs, Trusteeship and Decolonization, and services all committees, working groups, seminars and missions of the Council.

(e) *Special Committee to Investigate Israeli Practices Affecting the Human Rights of the Population of the Occupied Territories*

81. In resolution 2443 (XXIII) of 19 December 1968, the General Assembly, mindful of the principle embodied in the Universal Declaration of Human Rights regarding the right of everyone to return to his country and the provisions of the Geneva Convention relative to the Protection of Civilian Persons in Time of War of 12 August 1949,[4] decided to establish a Special Committee to Investigate Israeli Practices Affecting the Human Rights of the Population of the Occupied Territories, to be composed of three Member States appointed by the President of the Assembly.

82. The Government of Israel was requested to receive the Special Committee, co-operate with it and facilitate its work; and the Special Committee was requested to report to the Secretary-General as soon as possible and whenever the need arose thereafter.

83. The death of the President of the General Assembly, before he had appointed the Members of the Special Committee, delayed the work of the Committee for some time. In view of this delay, the Commission on Human Rights set up, in 1969, a Special Working Group of Experts which visited several countries in the Middle East, heard witnesses and collected written information, and submitted a report to the Commission in 1970. The Commission noted Israel's refusal to co-operate with the Group, endorsed the Group's conclusions concerning the applicability of the Geneva Convention relative to the Protection of Civilian Persons in Time of War in the territories militarily occupied by Israel, and condemned Israel's refusal to apply the provisions of that Convention.

84. Members of the Special Committee to Investigate Israeli Practices Affecting the Human Rights of the Population of the Occupied Territories were appointed under an alternative procedure by which a Vice-President of the General Assembly, coming from the geographical area of the President, discharged the responsibility which had been assigned to the President by the Assembly. The establishment of the Special Committee was objected to by Israel, which attacked the legality of the procedure adopted in setting up the Committee, questioned its competence and impartiality, and maintained that the resolution by which the Committee had been established prejudged Israel's conduct by its reference to "violations".

85. The Special Committee requested Israel's co-operation in allowing it to carry out on-the-spot investigations of a number of allegations, including charges of ill-treatment while under detention, inside the occupied territories. The Government of Israel refused such co-operation, and the Special Committee therefore visited countries having borders with Israel, and those having concentrations of Palestinian refugees, where it heard witnesses who had recently left, or had been expelled from, the occupied territories. In recent years, the Special Committee has tended to rely increasingly upon news dispatches appearing in the press of Israel and other countries, and upon statements of policy issued by officials and leaders of Israel; and has repeatedly called upon the General Assembly to find an alternative arrangement whereby a first-hand investigation could be undertaken within the occupied territories. The General Assembly has not found such an arrangement, but has deplored the continued refusal of Israel to allow the Special Committee access to those territories and condemned its refusal to permit persons from the territories to appear as witnesses before the Special Committee.

86. The secretariat of the Committee is provided by the Centre for Human Rights.

(f) *Committee on the Exercise of the Inalienable Rights of the Palestinian People*

87. The Committee was established by the General Assembly in resolution 3376 (XXX) of 10 November 1975, in which the Assembly expressed its grave concern that no progress had been achieved towards the exercise by the Palestinian people of its inalienable rights in Palestine, including the right to self-determination without external interference and the right to national independence and sovereignty, or towards the exercise by Palestinians of their inalienable rights to return to their homes and property from which they had been displaced and uprooted. The Committee, composed of 20 Member States, was called upon to consider and recommend to the General Assembly a programme of implementation designed to enable the Palestinian people to exercise those rights, taking into account all the powers conferred by the Charter upon the principal organs of the United Nations.

88. The first report of the Committee[5] contained specific recommendations designed to enable the Palestinian people to exercise its inalienable rights as previously recognized and defined by the General Assembly. Those recommendations were first endorsed by the Assembly in resolution 31/20 of 24 November 1976 as a basis for the solution of the question of Palestine.

---

[4] United Nations, *Treaty Series,* vol. 75, No. 973, p. 287.

[5] *Official Records of the General Assembly, Thirty-first Session, Supplement No. 35* (A/31/35).

In its subsequent reports to the General Assembly,[6] the Committee retained its original recommendations unchanged. On each occasion they have been firmly endorsed by the Assembly, which has also continued to renew and, as necessary, expand the mandate of the Committee.

89. Despite repeated and urgent appeals by the Committee, however, the Security Council was unable to act on or implement the recommendations of the Committee.

90. The Committee meets throughout the year as necessary to carry out its mandate. All States Members of the United Nations and Permanent Observers to the United Nations desiring to participate in the work of the Committee as observers are welcome to do so. The Committee also invited the Palestine Liberation Organization (PLO) to participate in its work as an observer, to attend all its meetings and to make observations and proposals for the consideration of the Committee.

91. The secretariat of the Committee functions within the Division for Palestinian Rights of the Office of the Under-Secretary-General for Political and General Assembly Affairs and Secretariat Services.

B. Security Council

92. The Security Council is the principal organ of the United Nations on which the Charter, in Article 24, confers primary responsibility for the maintenance of international peace and security. Members of the United Nations have agreed that in carrying out its duties under this responsibility the Security Council acts on their behalf.

93. The Council is composed of 15 members, including five permanent members, China, France, the Union of Soviet Socialist Republics, the United Kingdom and the United States of America; and 10 non-permanent members, elected by the General Assembly for two-years terms and not eligible for immediate re-election. Decisions of the Council on all but procedural matters are made on an affirmative vote of nine members, including the concurring votes of the permanent members. All Member States have undertaken to accept and carry out the Council's decisions.

94. The Council submits an annual report to the General Assembly; the Assembly normally takes note of the report without discussion. However, since 1971, the Assembly has from time to time considered the need to enhance the effectiveness of the Security Council in discharging its principal role of maintaining international peace and security. It has also considered, since 1979, the question of equitable representation on, and an increase in the membership of, the Council.

95. Chapter VII of the Charter specifies the action to be taken with respect to threats to the peace, breaches of the peace, or acts of aggression. Article 39 provides that "the Security Council shall determine the existence of any threat to the peace, breach of the peace, or act of aggression and shall make recommendations, or decide what measures shall be taken in acccordance with Articles 41 and 42, to maintain or restore international peace and security".

96. In the discharge of this responsibility, the Security Council is empowered by the Charter to take appropriate measures, including action aimed at the pacific settlement of disputes and preventive and enforcement action. Allegations of violations or denials of human rights and fundamental freedoms have repeatedly given rise to situations brought to the attention of the Security Council.

97. In discharging its duties, the Security Council is required, under Article 24, to act in accordance with the purposes and principles of the United Nations. One of these purposes, as set out in Article 1, paragraph 3, is "to achieve international co-operation in solving international problems of an economic, social, cultural, or humanitarian character, and in promoting and encouraging respect for human rights and for fundamental freedoms for all without distinction as to race, sex, language or religion".

98. Article 34 of the Charter provides that "the Security Councy may investigate any dispute, or any situation which might lead to international friction or give rise to a dispute, in order to determine whether the continuance of the dispute or situation is likely to endanger the maintenance of international peace and security". Under Article 35, "any Member of the United Nations may bring any dispute, or any situation of the nature referred to in Article 34, to the attention of the Security Council or of the General Assembly. A State which is not a Member of the United Nations may bring to the attention of the Security Council or of the General Assembly any dispute to which it is a party if it accepts in advance, for the purposes of the dispute, the obligations of pacific settlement provided in the . . . Charter".

99. Article 83 of the Charter provides that "all functions of the United Nations relating to strategic areas, including the approval of the terms of the trusteeship agreements and of their alteration or amendment, shall be exercised by the Security Council"; and that the basic objectives set forth in Article 76 are applicable to the people of each strategic area. One of these basic objectives is "to encourage respect for human rights and for fundamental freedoms for all without distinction as to race, sex, language or religion, and to encourage recognition of the independence of the peoples of the world".

100. Among the human rights problems which have been dealt with by the Security Council in recent years are the following:

(a) Reports of torture of political prisoners and the deaths of a number of detainees, as well as a mounting wave of repression against

---

[6] *Ibid.* (A/33/35 and Corr.1, A/34/35 and Corr.1, A/35/35 and Corr.1, A/36/35, A/37/35, A/38/35, A/39/35, A/40/35, A/41/35 and A/42/35).

individuals, organizations and news media, in South Africa (resolution 417 (1977));

(b) The failure of Israel to provide adequate protection to the civilian population in the occupied territories (resolution 471 (1980));

(c) The massive repression of all opponents of *apartheid* in South Africa (resolution 473 (1980));

(d) Death sentences passed on three members of the African National Congress of South Africa (resolutions 473 (1980) and 503 (1982));

(e) Death sentence imposed on Mr. Malasela Benjamin Maloise (resolution 547 (1984));

(f) The so-called "New Constitution" endorsed on 2 November 1983 by the exclusively white electorate of South Africa (resolution 544 (1984));

(g) The continued massacres of the oppressed people of South Africa (resolution 556 (1984));

(h) The heightened violence in certain parts of Lebanon (resolution 564 (1985));

(i) Instances of hostage-taking and abduction (resolution 579 (1985));

(j) The question of South Africa (resolution 591 (1986)); and

(k) The situation in the occupied Arab territories (resolution 592 (1986)).

C. Economic and Social Council

1. HUMAN RIGHTS FUNCTIONS AND PROCEDURES

101. The principal human rights functions of the Council, which operates under the authority of the General Assembly and reports annually to that body, are: (a) to "make or initiate studies and reports with respect to international economic, social, cultural, educational, health and related matters" and to "make recommendations with respect to any such matters to the General Assembly, to the Members of the United Nations and to the specialized agencies concerned"; (b) to "make recommendations for the purpose of promoting respect for, and observance of, human rights and fundamental freedoms for all"; (c) to "prepare draft conventions for submission to the General Assembly, with respect to matters falling within its competence"; and (d) to "call, in accordance with the rules prescribed by the United Nations, international conferences on matters falling within its competence". In addition, the Council is responsible for co-ordinating the activities of the specialized agencies through consultation with, and recommendations to, those agencies and through recommendations to the General Assembly and to the Members of the United Nations. In practice, however, the Council has addressed its recommendations not only to the bodies mentioned but also to non-Member States, to subsidiary bodies of the General Assembly, to international conferences, to intergovernmental and non-governmental organizations, to peoples and to individuals. A large proportion of its resolutions and decisions have been prepared, in the form of drafts, by its functional commissions, including the Commission on Human Rights and the Commission on the Status of Women.

102. Under the Charter, the Economic and Social Council "shall consist of eighteen Members of the United Nations elected by the General Assembly" (Article 61). However, Article 61 has twice been amended: first, by General Assembly resolution 1991 B (XVIII) of 17 December 1963, to increase the number of members to 27; and later, by Assembly resolution 2847 (XXVI) of 20 December 1971, further to increase the number of members to 54. The members are elected according to the following pattern: 14 members from African States, 11 from Asian States, 10 from Latin-American States, 13 from Western European and other States, and 6 from socialist States of Eastern Europe.

103. Under rule 1 of its rules of procedure,[7] the Council normally holds an organizational session and two regular sessions each year. Under rule 4, special sessions are held by decision of the Council; upon the request or with the concurrence of a majority of the members of the Council; or upon the request of the General Assembly or the Security Council. The President of the Council, with the concurrence of the Vice-Presidents and, as appropriate, in consultation with members of the Council, may also call a special session.

104. Under rule 16, "each member of the Council shall be represented by an accredited representative, who may be accompanied by such alternate representatives and advisers as may be required".

105. Rules 72 to 78 provide for the participation of non-members of the Council in the Council's deliberations without the right to vote. Under rule 72, non-member States may be invited by the Council or one of its committees or sessional bodies to participate in its deliberations on any matter of particular concern to that State. Under rule 73, any national liberation movement recognized by or in accordance with resolutions of the General Assembly may be invited by the Council to participate in its deliberations on any matter of particular concern to that movement. Rule 74 permits the participation of the President of the Trusteeship Council or his representative in any matter of particular concern to that Council. Rule 75 provides that the specialized agencies shall be entitled (a) to be represented at meetings of the Council, its committees and sessional bodies; and (b) to participate, without the right to vote, through their representatives, in deliberations with respect to items of concern to them and to submit proposals regarding such items, which may be put to the vote at the request of any member of the Council or of the committee or sessional body concerned.

106. Rule 80 establishes a Committee on Non-Governmental Organizations consisting of 19 Members, five from African States, four from Asian States, four from Latin-American States, four from Western European and other States, and two from Eastern European States. The Committee considers applications for the granting of consultative status to non-governmental organizations, and may consult with organizations in categories I and II on matters within their competence. The Committee also makes recommendations to the Council as to which organizations in category I should be heard

---

[7] United Nations publication, Sales No. E.83.I.9.

by the Council or by its sessional committees and on which items they should be heard.

107. The machinery for international economic and social co-operation, which functions within the framework of Chapters IX and X of the Charter of the United Nations, includes the Council itself, its functional commissions, its regional commissions, its standing committees and its expert bodies.

108. Related organs and programmes of the United Nations which constitute the Organization's economic and social machinery include the Office of the United Nations High Commissioner for Refugees (UNHCR), the United Nations Children's Fund (UNICEF), the United Nations Conference on Trade and Development (UNCTAD), the United Nations Development Programme (UNDP), the World Food Programme (WFP), the United Nations Capital Development Fund (UNCDF), the United Nations Environment Programme (UNEP), the United Nations Fund for Population Activities (UNFPA), the United Nations Fund for Drug Abuse Control (UNFDAC), the World Food Council (WFC), and the United Nations Special Fund (UNSF). The Economic and Social Council considers the reports of these bodies on an annual basis.

109. In addition, there are the specialized agencies of the United Nations, and such bodies as the International Atomic Energy Agency (IAEA) and the General Agreement on Tariffs and Trade (GATT). The relations between the United Nations and the specialized agencies are governed by agreements concluded in accordance with Articles 57 and 63 of the Charter.[8]

110. Of the Council's subsidiary bodies, the Commission on Human Rights, the Commission on the Status of Women, the Sub-Commission on Prevention of Discrimination and Protection of Minorities and the Committee on Economic, Social and Cultural Rights are those most directly concerned with human rights questions. Among the related organs and programmes, UNHCR, UNICEF, WFP and UNEP do the most to promote the enjoyment of human rights and fundamental freedoms. Of the specialized agencies, FAO, ILO, UNESCO and WHO are most deeply involved in human rights matters.

111. The Economic and Social Council, at its annual organizational session, held in February, considers and adopts a basic programme of work for the year. The programme indicates the items to be considered in plenary meetings, those to be considered by its First (Economic) Committee, its Second (Social) Committee, and its Third (Programme and Co-ordination) Committee. It also indicates whether the item is to be considered at the Council's first regular session, usually held at United Nations Headquarters, New York, in May; or at its second regular session, usually held at Geneva in July. The Economic Committee meets at both regular sessions; the Social Committee meets only at the first

regular session; and the Programme and Co-ordination Committee meets only at the second regular session.

112. Matters relating to human rights are normally allocated to the Social Committee for consideration. The reports of that Committee including draft resolutions and draft decisions, are submitted to the Council in plenary meetings for its approval.

2. SUBSIDIARY BODIES

(a) Commission on Human Rights

113. Article 68 of the United Nations Charter provides that "the Economic and Social Council shall set up commissions in economic and social fields and for the promotion of human rights, and such other commissions as may be required for the performance of its functions". The Charter does not specify the composition or functions of any of the commissions envisaged in the article.

114. The Commission on Human Rights, a subsidiary of the Economic and Social Council, is one of six functional commissions which the Council established in 1946. The Commission was set up in "nuclear" form by Council resolution 5 (I) of 16 February 1946, and as a full commission by Council resolution 9 (II) of 21 June 1946.

115. Under resolution 9 (II), the commission was directed to submit proposals, recommendations and reports to the Council regarding (a) an international bill of rights; (b) international declarations or conventions on civil liberties, the status of women, freedom of information and similar matters; (c) the protection of minorities; (d) the prevention of discrimination on grounds of race, sex, language or religion; and (e) any other matter concerning human rights not covered by items (a), (b), (c), and (d). Later the Commission was authorized, by Council resolution 1979/36 of 10 May 1979, to assist the Council in the co-ordination of activities concerning human rights in the United Nations system. Under paragraph 3 of Council resolution 9 (II), the Commission was authorized "to call in ad hoc working groups of non-governmental experts in specialized fields or individual experts, without further reference to the Council but with the approval of the President of the Council and the Secretary-General". Under paragraph 8 of that resolution, the Commission was empowered to establish a Sub-Commission on Freedom of Information and of the Press; under paragraph 9, it was empowered to establish a Sub-Commission on the Protection of Minorities; and under paragraph 10, it was empowered to establish a Sub-Commission on the Prevention of Discrimination on the grounds of race, sex, language or religion.

116. The Commission at its first session, in 1947, established the Sub-Commission on Freedom of Information and of the Press and the Sub-Commission on Prevention of Discrimination and Protection of Minori-

---

[8] See *Agreements between the United Nations and the Specialized Agencies and the International Atomic Energy Agency* (United Nations publication, Sales No. E.61.X.1).

ties. The Sub-Commission on Freedom of Information and of the Press was discontinued in 1952.

117. The Commission first made use of the authorization contained in paragraph 3 of resolution 9 (II) at its twenty-third session, in 1967, when by resolution 2 (XXIII) of 6 March 1967 it set up the *Ad Hoc* Working Group of Experts on Human Rights in Southern Africa. Later, the Commission, with the authorization of the Economic and Social Council, set up a number of working groups, including the Working Group on Situations, to examine situations which appear to reveal a consistent pattern of gross violations of human rights, the Working Group on Enforced or Involuntary Disappearances, the Working Group of Governmental Experts on the Right to Development, the Working Group on the draft Convention on the Rights of the Child, the Working Group on the draft Declaration on the Rights of Persons Belonging to National, Ethnic, Religious and Linguistic Minorities, and the Working Group on a draft Declaration on the Right and Responsibility of Individuals, Groups and Organizations of Society to Promote and Protect Universally-Recognized Human Rights and Fundamental Freedoms. In addition, the Chairman of the Commission appointed annually, since 1978, three members of the Commission who are also representatives of States parties to the International Convention on the Suppression and Punishment of the Crime of *Apartheid,* to serve on the Group of Three established in accordance with the Convention.

118. The Commission, further, has entrusted specific tasks to individuals designated as its Special Rapporteurs, or Representatives, usually appointed by the Chairman of the Commission in consultation with other Members. Among these are the Special Rapporteur on the situation of human rights in Afghanistan, the Special Rapporteur on the situation of human rights in Chile, the Special Representative on the situation of human rights in El Salvador, the Special Representative on the situation of human rights in Iran, the Special Rapporteur on Summary or Arbitrary Executions, the Special Rapporteur on Torture, the Special Rapporteur on Religious Intolerance, the Special Rapporteur on Mercenaries, the Expert on the situation of human rights in Guatemala and the Expert on Haiti.

119. The functions and composition of these subsidiary bodies of the Commission on Human Rights, with the exception of the Sub-Commission on Prevention of Discrimination and Protection of Minorities which is dealt with separately below, may be summarized briefly as follows:

Ad Hoc *Working Group of Experts on Human Rights in Southern Africa:* Established by the Commission on Human Rights in resolution 2 (XXIII) of 6 March 1967, the original mandate of the Working Group was to investigate the charges of torture and ill-treatment of prisoners, detainees or persons in police custody in South Africa. This mandate was subsequently extended and enlarged by resolutions of the Commission, the Economic and Social Council and the General Assembly. In resolution 34/24 of 15 November 1979, the Assembly called upon the *Ad Hoc* Working Group of Experts on Southern Africa to study ways and means of implementing international instruments, such as the International Convention on the Suppression and Punishment of the Crime of *Apartheid,* including the establishment of

the international jurisdiction envisaged by the Convention. In resolution 1980/33 of 2 May 1980, the Economic and Social Council invited the Working Group to continue to study the situation of African workers in South Africa, where legislation continued to deny them full and equal trade union rights.

In resolution 1983/9 of 18 February 1983, the Commission decided that the Working Group should continue to study the policies and practices which violate human rights in South Africa and Namibia, bearing in mind the effects of *apartheid* on black women and children and the Group's conclusion that the "criminal effects of *apartheid* amount to a policy bordering on genocide". In resolution 1986/4 of 28 February 1986, the Commission took note of the studies and findings of the Working Group on the relationship between *apartheid* and genocide contained in its report on the subject,[9] and requested the Working Group to continue its investigation of the matter.

The members of the Working Group, who are appointed by the Commission in their personal capacity, are: Mr. Mikuin Leliel Balanda (Zaire), Mr. Humberto Diaz Casanueva (Chile), Mr. Felix Ermacora (Austria), Mr. Branimar Janković (Yugoslavia), Mr. Elly Elikunda E. M'Tango (United Republic of Tanzania), and Mr. Mulka Govinda Reddy (India).

The Working Group normally holds two sessions per year, each of two weeks' duration. In addition, every second year, it visits front-line States for a period of three to four weeks to collect information from individuals who have recently left South Africa or Namibia. In recent years, the Working Group has delegated its Chairman, or one of its members, to conduct hearings outside this cycle.

Working Group on Situations to examine situations which appear to reveal a consistent pattern of gross violations of human rights: Appointed by the Commission on Human Rights within the framework of resolution 1503 (XLVIII) of 27 May 1970 of the Economic and Social Council, the function of the Working Group on Situations is to examine "such particular situations as might be referred to the Commission by the Sub-Commission on Prevention of Discrimination and Protection of Minorities" after the Sub-Commission's consideration of communications relating to human rights. The Working Group also considers those particular situations which the Commission, at the previous session, has decided to keep pending before it under the procedure. The Working Group has been set up by the Commission every year since 1974. It is composed of five members of the Commission appointed in their personal capacity. It meets once a year for one week, immediately before the opening of the Commission's session. Those attending in 1987 were: Mr. Mairegu Bezabih (Ethiopia), Mr. Marc Bossuyt (Belgium), Mr. Todor Ditchev (Bulgaria), Mrs. Victoria Sisante-Bataclan (Philippines) and Mr. Armando Villanueva de Campo (Peru).

Working Group on Enforced or Involuntary Disappearances: In resolution 20 (XXXVI) of 29 February 1980, the Commission on Human Rights decided "to establish for a period of one year a Working Group consisting of five of its Members, to serve as experts in their individual capacities, to examine questions relevant to enforced or involuntary disappearances of persons". The Working Group's mandate has been renewed each year, and since 1986 for two-year periods.

The Working Group is composed of Mr. Toine van Dongen (Netherlands), Mr. Jonas K. D. Foli (Ghana), Mr. Agha Hilaly (Pakistan), Mr. Ivan Tosevski (Yugoslavia), and Mr. Luis Varela Quirós (Costa Rica). Normally it holds three sessions each year, two of five days' duration and one of eight working days. It undertakes field missions from time to time at the invitation of the Government concerned.

Working Group of Governmental Experts on the Right to Development: Established by Commission on Human Rights resolution 36 (XXXVII) of 11 March 1981, the Working Group's mandate is "to study the scope and contents of the right to development and the most effective means to ensure the realization, in all countries, of the economic, social and cultural rights enshrined in various international instruments, paying particular attention to the obstacles encountered by developing countries in their efforts to secure the enjoyment of human rights".

---

[9] E/CN.4/1985/14.

16

After the General Assembly proclaimed the Declaration on the Right to Development in resolution 41/128 of 4 December 1986, the Commission on Human Rights directed the Working Group to study ways and means of implementing the Declaration and to prepare recommendations on that subject. One two-week session of the Working Group is scheduled for 1988.

The Working Group consists of 15 governmental experts appointed by the Chairman of the Commission. At its 1987 session, it was composed of the following members: Mr. Abd-el-Naceur Belaïd (Algeria), Mr. Konstantin Andreev (Bulgaria), Mr. Julio Heredia Pérez (Cuba), Miss Kongit Sinegiorgis (Ethiopia), Mr. Jean-Pierre Le Court (France), Mr. Kantilal Lallubhai Dalal (India), Mr. Riyadh Aziz Hadi (Iraq), Mr. Johannes Zandvliet (Netherlands), Mr. Luis Aguirre Gallardo (Panama), Mr. Juan Alvarez Vita (Peru), Mr. Alioune Sene (Senegal), Mr. Fahd Salim (Syrian Arab Republic), Mr. Grigori Morozov (Union of Soviet Socialist Republics), Mr. Thomas A. Johnson (United States of America) and Mr. Danilo Türk (Yugoslavia).

Working Group on the draft Convention on the Rights of the Child: Open to all participants in the work of the Commission, this informal Working Group is charged with the completion of a draft Convention on the Rights of the Child submitted to the Commission by Poland on 7 February 1978 and subsequently amended. The Working Group meets once a year, prior to the annual session of the Commission, for a period of one week.

Working Group on the draft Declaration of the Rights of Persons Belonging to National, Ethnic, Religious and Linguistic Minorities: Also open to all participants in the work of the Commission, this informal Working Group is charged with the preparation of a draft Declaration on the Rights of Persons Belonging to National, Ethnic, Religious and Linguistic Minorities based on a text submitted to the Commission by Yugoslavia in 1978. The Working Group meets once a year during the annual session of the Commission, for a period of up to four days.

Working Group on a draft Declaration on the Right and Responsibility of Individuals, Groups and Organizations of Society to Promote and Protect Universally-Recognized Human Rights and Fundamental Freedoms: Set up by Commission decision 1984/116 of 16 March 1984 and open to all participants in the work of the Commission, this informal Working Group is mandated to draft a Declaration on the Right and Responsibility of Individuals, Groups and Organizations of Society to Promote and Protect Universally-Recognized Human Rights and Fundamental Freedoms. Since 1986 it met annually prior the Commission's session, for a period of one week.

Tasks entrusted by the Commission to individuals include the following:

Special Rapporteur on the Situation of Human Rights in Afghanistan. The mandate of the Special Rapporteur, Mr. Felix Ermacora (Austria) is to examine the situation of human rights and to report thereon to the General Assembly and the Commission on Human Rights. This mandate was first established by Economic and Social Council resolution 1984/37 of 24 May 1984 and was renewed in 1985 and 1986. The Commission, in resolution 1987/58 of 11 March 1987, called upon the Special Rapporteur to report "on the question of human rights and fundamental freedoms in Afghanistan, taking into consideration the effects on the human rights situation in the country of the announced intention to initiate a process of reconciliation". The Special Rapporteur conducts consultations with the interested parties and travels to the area at the invitation of the Governments concerned for the purpose of collecting information relevant to his mandate.

Special Rapporteur on the Situation of Human Rights in Chile. The mandate of the Special Rapporteur, Mr. F. Volio Jimenez (Costa Rica) is to examine the situation of human rights and to report thereon to the General Assembly and the Commission on Human Rights. This mandate was first established by Commission resolution 11 (XXXV), and was renewed annually. In resolution 1987/60 of 12 March 1987, the Special Rapporteur was requested "to report on the situation of human rights in Chile" for one further year. The Special Rapporteur conducts consultations with the interested parties and travels to the area at the invitation of the Governments concerned for the purpose of collecting information relevant to his mandate.

Special Representative on the Situation of Human Rights in El Salvador. The mandate of the Special Representative, Mr. J. A. Pastor Ridruejo (Spain) is to examine the situation of human rights and to report thereon to the General Assembly and the Commission on Human Rights. First established by the Commission in resolution 37 (XXXVII) of 11 March 1981, this mandate was renewed annually, most recently by Commission resolution 1987/51 of 11 March 1987. The Special Representative conducts consultations with the interested parties and normally visits El Salvador once a year at the invitation of the Government of that country.

Special Representative on the Situation of Human Rights in Iran. The mandate of the Special Representative, Mr. R. Galindo Pohl (El Salvador) is to examine the situation of human rights and to report thereon to the General Assembly and the Commission on Human Rights. First established by the Commission in resolution 1982/27 of 11 March 1982, this mandate was renewed annually, most recently by Commission resolution 1987/55 of 11 March 1987, in which the Special Representative was requested to report "on the human rights situation in the Islamic Republic of Iran, including the situation of minority groups, such as the Baha'is". The Special Representative conducts consultations with the interested parties for the purpose of collecting information relevant to his mandate.

Special Rapporteur on Summary or Arbitrary Executions. The mandate of the Special Rapporteur, Mr. S. Amos Wako (Kenya), is to examine situations involving summary or arbitrary executions, to respond effectively to information on imminent or threatened executions, and to report to the Commission on Human Rights. First established by Economic and Social Council resolution 1982/35 of 7 May 1982, this mandate was renewed annually, most recently by Council resolution 1987/60 of 29 May 1987. The Special Rapporteur conducts consultations with the parties concerned and travels to various areas, at the invitation of the Government concerned, for the purpose of collecting information relevant to his mandate.

Special Rapporteur on Torture. The mandate of the Special Rapporteur, Mr. P. J. Kooijmans (Netherlands) is to examine information on the question of torture, including the occurrence and the extent of its practice, to respond effectively to credible and reliable information that comes to his attention, and to report thereon to the Commission on Human Rights. First established by the Commission in resolution 1985/33 of 13 March 1985, this mandate was renewed annually, most recently by Commission resolution 1987/29 of 10 March 1987. The Special Rapporteur conducts consultations with the parties concerned and travels to various areas, at the invitation of the Governments concerned, for the purpose of collecting information relevant to his mandate.

Special Rapporteur on Religious Intolerance. The mandate of the Special Rapporteur, Mr. A. V. d'Almeida Ribeiro (Portugal), is to examine the level of adherence to the provisions of the Declaration on the Elimination of All Forms of Intolerance and of Discrimination Based on Religion or Belief, to recommend appropriate measures, including the promotion of dialogue between communities of religion or belief and Governments; and to report thereon to the Commission on Human Rights. First established by the Commission in resolution 1986/20 of 10 March 1986, this mandate was renewed by Commission resolution 1987/15 of 4 March 1987. The Special Rapporteur conducts consultations with the interested parties and travels to various areas, at the invitation of the Governments concerned, for the purpose of collecting information relevant to his mandate.

Special Rapporteur on Mercenaries. The mandate of the Special Rapporteur, Mr. Enrique Bernales Ballesteros (Peru), is "to examine the question of the use of mercenaries as a means of violating human rights and of impeding the exercise of the right of peoples to self-determination". The mandate was established by Commission on Human Rights resolution 1987/16 of 9 March 1987. The Special Rapporteur conducts consultations with the interested parties and travels to various areas, at the invitation of the Governments concerned, for the purpose of collecting information relevant to his mandate.

Expert on the Situation of Human Rights in Guatemala. The mandate of the Expert, Mr. H. Gros Espiell (Uruguay) is to assist the Government of Guatemala "through direct contacts, in taking the necessary action for the further restoration of human rights" and "to formulate recommendations for the further restoration of human rights" in Guatemala. Under this mandate, established by resolution

1987/53 of the Commission on Human Rights, the Expert was appointed by the Secretary-General.

Expert on Haiti. The mandate of the Expert, Mr. A. Braunschweig (France), is to assist the Government of Haiti, "through direct contacts, in taking the necessary action for the full restoration of human rights" in Haiti. Under this mandate, established by resolution 1987/13 of 2 March 1987 of the Commission of Human Rights, the Expert was appointed by the Secretary-General.

(b) *Sub-Commission on Prevention of Discrimination and Protection of Minorities*

120. The Sub-Commission is the main subsidiary body of the Commission on Human Rights. It was established by the Commission at its first session, in 1947, under the authority of Economic and Social Council resolution 9 (II) of 21 June 1946. Its functions, as set out in a resolution adopted by the Commission at its fifth session, in 1949, are as follows:[10]

(a) To undertake studies, particularly in the light of the Universal Declaration of Human Rights, and to make recommendations to the Commission on Human Rights concerning the prevention of discrimination of any kind relating to human rights and fundamental freedoms and the protection of racial, national, religious and linguistic minorities;

(b) To perform any other functions which may be entrusted to it by the Economic and Social Council or the Commission on Human Rights.

121. The Sub-Commission was originally composed of 12 experts; the number has been increased progressively over the years and is now 26, including six from African States, six from Asian States, five from Latin-American States, three from Eastern European States and six from Western European and other States. Each member has a single alternate, also meeting the criteria as an expert. Members and alternates act in their personal capacity and not as the representatives of States. Half the membership and the corresponding alternates, if any, are elected every two years, and each serves for a term of four years.

122. In resolution 502 A (XVI) of 3 August 1953,[11] the Economic and Social Council decided that the Sub-Commission should meet at least once a year for a period of three weeks. Up to 1985, sessions were held

---

[10] See E/1371, chap. IV.

[11] In 1950, the Economic and Social Council, by resolution 414 (XIII), decided to discontinue the Sub-Commission after a final session in October 1951, until 31 December 1954, its work to be taken over by the Council, the Commission on Human Rights, the Secretary-General and *ad hoc* bodies as appropriate. The General Assembly, at its sixth session, adopted resolution 532 B (VI) of 4 February 1952, in which, "considering that the prevention of discrimination and the protection of minorities are two of the most important branches of the positive work undertaken by the United Nations", it invited the Council (a) to authorize the Sub-Commission on Prevention of Discrimination and Protection of Minorities "to continue its work so that it may fulfil its mission, and especially to convene a session in 1952", and "(b) to take any practical steps that may be necessary for the continuance, within the framework of the United Nations, of the work on the prevention of discrimination and the protection of minorities". Accordingly a fifth session of the Sub-Commission was held in 1952.

annually at Geneva. However, the thirty-ninth session, scheduled for 1986, was postponed until 1987 owing to the financial situation of the United Nations. As a consequence the Economic and Social Council, on recommendation of the General Assembly, extended the mandates of the experts on the Sub-Commission for one year and postponed the election of new members and their alternates to 1988.

123. In addition to members and alternates, sessions of the Sub-Commission are attended by observers from States Members and non-Members of the United Nations, and from United Nations bodies, specialized agencies, other intergovernmental organizations, national liberation movements and non-governmental organizations in consultative status.

124. The Sub-Commission has three working groups which meet regularly before each of its sessions to assist it with certain tasks: the Working Group on Communications, the Working Group on Indigenous Populations and the Working Group on Slavery. In addition, it sometimes establishes sessional working groups to assist it in particular tasks. It also makes extensive use of members appointed to serve as Special Rapporteurs. The functions and composition of its subsidiary bodies may be summarized as follows:

Working Group on Communications: The Economic and Social Council authorized the Sub-Commission to appoint this Working Group in resolution 1503 (XLVIII) of 27 May 1970 "to consider all communications, including the replies of Governments thereon, received by the Secretary-General under Council resolution 728 F (XXVIII) of 30 July 1959 with a view to bringing to the attention of the Sub-Commission those communications, together with replies of Governments, if any, which appear to reveal a consistent pattern of gross and reliably attested violations of human rights and fundamental freedoms within the terms of reference of the Sub-Commission". The Working Group, consisting of not more than five members of the Sub-Commission, meets once a year for a period of not more than 10 days, immediately before the Sub-Commission's session. Those attending in 1987 were Mr. Murlidhar C. Bhandare, Mr. John Carey, Mr. Martinez-Baez, Mr. Sofinsky and Mr. Yimer.

Working Group on Indigenous Populations: As authorized by Economic and Social Council resolution 1982/34 of 7 May 1982, the Sub-Commission establishes annually a working group on indigenous populations with the mandate of reviewing developments pertaining to the promotion and protection of the human rights and fundamental freedoms of indigenous populations and of drafting new standards on indigenous rights. In this regard, the Group considers information and comments requested by the Secretary-General annually from Governments, specialized agencies, regional intergovernmental organizations and non-governmental organizations in consultative status, particularly those of indigenous peoples, analyses such materials and submits its report to the Sub-Commission. The Working Group is instructed to give special attention to the evolution of standards concerning the rights of indigenous populations, taking account of both the similarities and the differences in the situations and aspirations of indigenous populations throughout the world. To this end, the Group began in 1985 the preparation of a declaration on indigenous rights for eventual adoption by the General Assembly. The Working Group, consisting of five members of the Sub-Commission, meets for five days immediately before the Sub-Commission's session. In 1987 members of the Working Group were: Mr. Miguel Alfonso Martinez, Mrs. Erica-Irene A. Daes, Ms. Gu Yijie, Mr. K. B. S. Simpson and Mr. Danilo Türk.

Working Group on Slavery: Established by Sub-Commission resolution 11 (XXVII) of 21 August 1974 and renewed annually, the Working Group's terms of reference are: "to review developments in the field of slavery and the slave trade in all their practices and manifestations, including the slavery-like practices of *apartheid* and colonialism, the traffic in persons and the exploitation of the prostitution of others as they are defined in the Slavery Convention of 1926, the Supplementary Convention on the Abolition of Slavery, the Slave Trade and Institutions and Practices Similar to Slavery of 1956, and the Convention for the Suppression of the Traffic in Persons and of the Exploitation of the Prostitution of Others of 1949''. The Working Group, consisting of five members of the Sub-Commission appointed by its Chairman, meets for not more than five days immediately before the Sub-Commission's session. In 1987 appointed members of the Working Group were: Mr. Deschênes, Mr. C. L. C. Mubanga-Chipoya, Mr. Uribe Portocarrero, Mr. Masayuki Takemoto and Mr. Whitaker.

Working Group on Detention: This sessional working group, established in accordance with Sub-Commission resolution 1983/23 to draft a Declaration against Unacknowledged Detention of Persons, was convened in 1987 to examine questions relating to the administration of justice and the human rights of detainees. The following members of the Sub-Commission were appointed as members of the Working Group: Mr. Miguel Alfonso Martinez, Mr. John Carey, Mr. Driss Dahak, Mr. Masayuki Takemoto and Mr. Danilo Türk. Two members of the Sub-Commission, although not members of the Working Group, took part in its discussions: Mr. Theo C. van Boven and Mr. Louis Joinet.

Working Group on Traditional Practices Affecting the Health of Women and Children: The Working Group, established in accordance with resolution 1984/48 of the Commission on Human Rights and convened in 1984 and 1985, consisted of two experts designated by the Sub-Commission, Mr. Murlidhar C. Bhandare and Mrs. Halima Embarek Warzazi, and representatives of the United Nations Children's Fund, the United Nations Educational, Scientific and Cultural Organization, the World Health Organization, and of the following non-governmental organizations: International Alliance of Women, World Association for the School as an Instrument of Peace, International Federation of Women Lawyers, International League for the Rights and Liberation of Peoples, International Movement for Fraternal Union among Races and Peoples, Rädda Barnen International, Union of Arab Jurists and World Union of Catholic Women's Organizations.

Working Group on the Rights of Persons Detained on Grounds of Mental Health: This sessional Working Group, open to all participants in the work of the Sub-Commission, was established to elaborate a draft body of guidelines, principles and guarantees for persons detained on the grounds of mental ill-health or suffering from mental disorder. Its mandate is subject to annual review.

125. The following studies, under preparation by members of the Sub-Commission acting in their capacity as Special Rapporteurs, were listed in the report of the Sub-Commission's thirty-ninth (1987) session:[12]

Study on administrative detention without charge or trial, entrusted to Mr. Louis Joinet (Sub-Commission resolution 1987/5);

Study on achievements made and obstacles encountered during the Decade for Action to Combat Racism and Racial Discrimination, entrusted to Mr. Asbjørn Eide (Sub-Commission resolution 1987/24);

Analysis of the current trends and developments regarding the right of everyone to leave any country, including his own, and to return to his country, entrusted to Mr. C. L. C. Mubanga-Chipoya (Sub-Commission resolution 1985/29 and decision 1987/105);

Study on the status of the individual and contemporary international law, entrusted to Mrs. Erica-Irene A. Daes (Sub-Commission resolution 1985/31 and decision 1987/112);

Study on human rights and disability, entrusted to Mr. Leandro Despouy (Sub-Commission resolution 1985/10);

Study on the use of computerized personal files, entrusted to Mr. Louis Joinet (Sub-Commission resolution 1985/14);

Study on the elimination of all forms of intolerance, and of discrimination based on religion or belief: Examination of issues and factors which should be considered before any definitive drafting of a binding international instrument takes place, entrusted to Mr. Theo C. van Boven (Sub-Commission resolution 1987/33).

---

[12] E/CN.4/1988/37, annex III.

(c) *Commission on the Status of Women*

126. The Commission was established by the Economic and Social Council in resolution 11 (II) of 21 June 1946, to "prepare recommendations and reports to the Council on promoting women's rights in political, economic, civil, social and educational fields". The Commission was also called upon to "make recommendations to the Council on urgent problems requiring immediate attention in the field of women's rights with the object of implementing the principle that men and women shall have equal rights, and to develop proposals to give effect to such recommendations".

127. The mandate of the Commission was expanded by Council resolution 1987/22 of 26 May 1986 to include the functions of promoting the objectives of equality, development and peace, monitoring the implementation of measures for the advancement of women, and reviewing and appraising the progress made at the national, subregional, regional, sectoral and global levels. Under that resolution, the Commission's future agendas are to be structured around its four main functions, namely programming, co-ordination, monitoring and policy development.

128. The membership of the Commission was originally 15; it was increased to 18 by Council resolution 414 B.V (XIII), to 21 by resolution 845 (XXXII), and to 32 by resolution 1147 (XLI). In resolution 1987/23 of 26 May 1987, the Council accepted, in principle, the need for a further increase in the membership of Commission, and requested the Commission to submit proposals on the question in 1988.

129. At the close of 1987 the Commission consisted of one representative from each of 32 States Members of the United Nations, selected by the Council on the basis of an equitable geographical distribution and including eight members from African States, six from Asian States, six from Latin-American States, eight from Western European and other States, and four from socialist States of Eastern Europe. With a view to securing a balanced representation in the various fields covered by the Commission, the Secretary-General consults with the Governments selected by the Council before the representatives are finally nominated by those Governments and confirmed by the Council.

130. Up to 1970, the Commission held one regular session each year, although no session was held in 1964. As from 1 January 1971, regular sessions were held on a biennial basis; however, the Commission also held special sessions in its capacity as the preparatory body for international conferences on the advancement of women. Commencing in 1989 and until the year 2000, the Commission will meet annually in accordance with Economic and Social Council resolution 1987/21 of 26 May 1987.

131. Up to 1978, the Commission normally met either in New York or Geneva. Exceptions were its third session, held at Beirut; its 14th, held at Buenos Aires; and its 18th, held at Teheran. From 1980 onwards, however, its normal place of meeting has been Vienna.

132. The Commission operates under the rules of procedure of functional commissions of the Economic and Social Council. Its sessions are attended not only by members and alternates, but also by observers for other States Members of the United Nations, representatives of bodies of the United Nations system, intergovernmental organizations and non-governmental organizations.

133. Representatives of specialized agencies, including FAO, ILO, UNESCO, and WHO, play an active part in the Commission's deliberations. Each of these agencies submits to the Commission at each session a report on its activities of special interest to women. In addition, the Inter-American Commission of Women submits a report on its work to the Commission at each of its sessions.

134. The Commission has emphasized, in resolution 15 (XXIV) of 2 March 1972, the importance of co-ordinating efforts between international organizations and regional and national bodies concerned with the advancement of women. In resolution 2 (XXVII) of 4 April 1978, the Commission recommended the establishment of close co-ordination with regional inter-governmental organizations such as the Inter-American Commission of Women, the Commission of Arab Women and the Pan-African Organization of Women, and requested the Secretary-General to take the measures necessary to ensure such co-ordination.

135. In addition to preparing international instruments and recommendations, supervising the application of such instruments, and preparing international conferences, the Commission adopts a variety of resolutions and decisions, nearly all in the form of draft texts recommended for adoption by the Economic and Social Council.

136. The Commission has no standing subsidiary bodies but establishes informal working groups from time to time to facilitate its deliberations. On one occasion the Economic and Social Council, on recommendation of the Commission, decided to appointed a special rapporteur to prepare a study on the impact of the mass communication media on the changing roles of men and women (resolution 2063 (LXII) of 12 May 1977, para. 8). The report of the Special Rapporteur, Esmeralda Arboleda Cuevas,[13] was considered by the Commission at its twenty-eighth session, and later by the World Conference of the United Nations Decade for Women.

(d) Office of the United Nations High Commissioner for Refugees

137. The Office of the United Nations High Commissioner for Refugees (UNHCR), an organ of the United Nations and an important part of its economic and social machinery, was established originally for a three-year term by General Assembly resolution 319 (IV) of 3 December 1949. In that resolution, further elaborated in the Statute of the Office annexed to Assembly resolution 428 (V) of 14 December 1950, the mandate of the High Commissioner is to provide for the protection of refugees falling under the competence of his Office by:

(a) Promoting the conclusion and ratification of international conventions for the protection of refugees, supervising their application and proposing amendments thereto;

(b) Promoting through special agreements with Governments the execution of any measures calculated to improve the situation of refugees and to reduce the number requiring protection;

(c) Assisting governmental and private efforts to promote voluntary repatriation or assimilation within new national communities;

(d) Promoting the admission of refugees, not excluding those in the most destitute categories, to the territories of States;

(e) Endeavouring to obtain permission for refugees to transfer their assets and especially those necessary for their resettlement;

(f) Obtaining from Governments information concerning the number and conditions of refugees in their territories and the laws and regulations concerning them;

(g) Keeping in close touch with the Governments and intergovernmental organizations concerned;

(h) Establishing contact in such manner as he may think best with private organizations dealing with refugee questions;

(i) Facilitating the co-ordination of the efforts of private organizations concerned with the welfare of refugees.

138. The Statute stipulates that the High Commissioner shall engage in such additional activities, including repatriation and resettlement, as the General Assembly may determine, within the limits of the resources placed at his disposal. Subsequent resolutions of the General Assembly have widened his mandate to include assistance to displaced persons who are in a refugee-like situation. In addition, by resolution 3274 (XXIX) of 10 December 1974, the Assembly requested the Office of the High Commissioner "provisionally to undertake the functions foreseen under the Convention on the Reduction of Statelessness (of 28 August 1961), in accordance with its article 11. . ." and by resolution 31/36 of 30 November 1976, it requested the High Commissioner "to continue to perform these functions".

139. The High Commissioner is elected by the General Assembly on nomination of the Secretary-General, and serves for a term of office specified by the Assembly. He appoints, for the same term of office, a Deputy High Commissioner of a nationality other than his own. The Statute of the Office of the High Commissioner provides that "The work of the High Commissioner shall be of an entirely non-political character; it shall be humanitarian and social. . .".

140. The Office of the High Commissioner is located at Geneva, Switzerland; in addition, representatives are stationed in areas or countries where there are significant refugee problems.

141. The High Commissioner reports annually to the General Assembly through the Economic and Social Council. By a decision of 27 October 1969 the Council retained the report on the agenda of its summer session on the understanding that it would be transmitted to the General Assembly without debate, unless the Council were to decide otherwise, at the specific request of one or more of its members or of the High Commissioner, at the time of the adoption of the agenda.

---

[13] E/CN.6/627.

142. Assistance provided by the High Commissioner is normally channelled through Governments, governmental bodies or non-governmental organizations. Assistance programmes are submitted for authorization to the Executive Committee of the High Commissioner's Programme and a report on the implementation of these programmes is later reviewed by the Committee.

143. Pursuant to paragraph 4 of the Statute, an Advisory Committee on Refugees was established by Economic and Social Council resolution 393 (XIII) B of 10 September 1951. The Committee was reconstituted as the Executive Committee of the United Nations Refugee Fund, which was in turn replaced by the Executive Committee of the Programme of the United Nations High Commissioner for Refugees, established by Council resolution 672 (XXV) of 30 April 1958. The terms of reference of the Executive Committee were set out in General Assembly resolution 1166 (XII) of 26 November 1957 as follows:

(a) To give directives to the High Commissioner for the liquidation of the United Nations Refugee Fund;

(b) To advise the High Commissioner, at his request, in the exercise of his functions under the Statute of his Office;

(c) To advise the High Commissioner as to whether it is appropriate for international assistance to be provided through his Office in order to help to solve specific refugee problems remaining unsolved after 31 December 1958 or arising after that date;

(d) To authorize the High Commissioner to make appeals for funds to enable him to solve the refugee problems referred to in subparagraph (c) above;

(e) To approve projects for assistance to refugees coming within the scope of subparagraph (c) above;

(f) To give directives to the High Commissioner for the use of the emergency fund to be established under the terms set out in paragraph 7 of resolution 1166 (XII).

144. The Executive Committee meets once a year at Geneva. The Committee consists of 40 representatives of States Members of the United Nations or members of any of the specialized agencies, elected by the Economic and Social Council on the widest geographical basis from those States with a demonstrated interest in, and devotion to, the solution of the refugee problem.

(e) Committee on Crime Prevention and Control

145. The Committee, a subsidiary body of the Economic and Social Council consisting of 27 experts, was first established as an *Ad Hoc* Advisory Committee of Experts by General Assembly resolution 415 (V) of 1 December 1950. It was subsequently renamed the Advisory Committee of Experts on the Prevention of Crime and the Treatment of Offenders, and later as the Committee on Crime Prevention and Control. Its functions were specified in resolution 32/60 of the General Assembly and 1979/19 of the Council, whereby the Committee was entrusted with the preparation of the United Nations congresses on the prevention of crime and the treatment of offenders with a view to the introduction of more effective methods and ways of preventing crimes and improving the treatment of offenders. In resolution 31/21 of 9 November 1981, the Assembly called upon the Committee to give particular attention to current and emerging trends in crime prevention and criminal justice with a view to defining new guiding principles for the future course of crime prevention and criminal justice, taking into account the political, economic, social and cultural circumstances and traditions of each country and the need for crime prevention and criminal justice systems to be consonant with the principles of social justice.

146. Members of the Committee are experts, nominated by Member States and elected by the Economic and Social Council for a term of four years. The Committee meets every two years for eight working days; its ninth session was held at Vienna in 1986. It reports direct to the Council and, where appropriate, to other relevant United Nations organs.

147. The Committee elaborated the Code of Conduct for Law Enforcement Officials, adopted by the General Assembly in resolution 34/169 of 17 December 1979.

148. Secretariat services for the Committee are provided by the Crime Prevention and Criminal Justice Branch of the Centre for Social Development and Humanitarian Affairs, located at Vienna.

D. Trusteeship Council

149. In accordance with Article 75 of the Charter, the United Nations established "an international trusteeship system for the administration and supervision of such territories as may be placed thereunder by subsequent individual agreements". The basic objectives of the system are:

(a) To further international peace and security;

(b) To promote the political, economic, social and educational advancement of the inhabitants of the trust territories, and their progressive development towards self-government or independence as may be appropriate to the particular circumstances of each territory and its peoples and the freely expressed wishes of the peoples concerned, and as may be provided by the terms of each trusteeship agreement;

(c) To encourage respect for human rights and for fundamental freedoms for all without distinction as to race, sex, language or religion, and to encourage recognition of the interdependence of the peoples of the world;

(d) To ensure equal treatment in social, economic, and commercial matters for all Members of the United Nations and their nationals, and also equal treatment for the latter in the administration of justice. . .

150. The Trusteeship Council, a principal organ of the United Nations, assists the General Assembly in carrying out the functions of the United Nations relating to the international trusteeship except in areas designated as strategic, for which the Security Council is responsible. Since 1977, however, the trusteeship system includes only one of the original 11 Trust Territories: the strategic Trust Territory of the Pacific Islands, all the others having achieved self-government or independence.

151. The Council considers reports submitted by the Administering Authority of the Trust Territory of the Pacific Islands—the United States of America—and reports thereon to the Security Council. In consultation with the Administering Authority it examines petitions

from individuals and groups on matters relating to the situation in the Territory, provides for periodic visiting missions, and takes other actions in conformity with the Trusteeship Agreement.

152. The membership of the Council reflects a balance between States that administer Trust Territories and those that do not; accordingly the size of the Council has diminished in recent years.

E. International Court of Justice

153. The International Court of Justice is the principle judicial organ of the United Nations. It functions in accordance with its Statute, which forms an integral part of the United Nations Charter. All members of the United Nations are *ipso facto* parties to the Statute of the International Court of Justice. In addition, three States not Members of the United Nations have become parties to the Statute: Switzerland, in 1948; Liechtenstein, in 1950; and San Marino, in 1954. Any non-member State may become a party to the Statute on conditions determined in each case by the General Assembly on recommendation of the Security Council.

154. Article 2 of the Statute of the International Court of Justice provides that the Court is "composed of a body of independent judges, elected regardless of their nationality from among persons of high moral character, who possess the qualifications required in their respective countries for appointment to the highest judicial offices, or are jurisconsults of recognized competence in international law". Under Article 3, paragraph 1, the Court consists of 15 members, no two of whom may be nationals of the same State. Members are elected by the General Assembly and the Security Council for nine years, and may be re-elected. A regular election of five judges is held every three years.

155. Under Article 94 of the Charter, "each Member of the United Nations undertakes to comply with the decision of the International Court of Justice in any case to which it is a party". Article 95 provides that "nothing in the present Charter shall prevent Members of the United Nations from entrusting the solution of their differences to other tribunals by virtue of agreements already in existence or which may be concluded in the future".

156. Under Article 96, "the General Assembly or the Security Council may request the International Court of Justice to give an advisory opinion on any legal question. Other organs of the United Nations and specialized agencies, which may at any time be so authorized by the General Assembly, may also request advisory opinions of the Court on legal questions arising within the scope of their activities".

157. Only States may be parties in cases before the Court. The Court is open to the States parties to its Statute. The conditions under which the Court is to be open to other States are, subject to the special provisions contained in treaties in force, to be laid down by the Security Council, but in no case shall such conditions place the parties in a position of inequality before the Court (Article 35, paragraphs 1 and 2).

158. A number of United Nations human rights instruments contain provisions whereby any dispute between the contracting parties relating to the interpretation, application or fulfilment of the instrument may be submitted to the International Court of Justice at the request of any of the parties to the dispute. Among these are the Convention on the Prevention and Punishment of the Crime of Genocide of 9 December 1948 (article IX), the Convention for the Suppression of the Traffic in Persons and of the Exploitation of the Prostitution of Others of 2 December 1949 (article 22), the Convention relating to the Status of Refugees of 28 July 1951 (article 38), the Convention on the International Right of Correction of 16 December 1952 (article V), the Convention on the Political Rights of Women of 20 December 1952 (article IX), the Slavery Convention signed at Geneva on 25 September 1926 as amended by the Protocol of 23 October 1953 (article 8), the Convention relating to the Status of Stateless Persons of 28 September 1954 (article 34), the Supplementary Convention on the Abolition of Slavery, the Slave Trade, and Institutions and Practices Similar to Slavery of 7 September 1956 (article 10), the Convention on the Nationality of Married Women of 29 January 1957 (article 10), the UNESCO Convention against Discrimination in Education of 14 December 1960 (article 8), the Convention on the Reduction of Statelessness of 30 August 1961 (article 14), the Convention on Consent to Marriage, Minimum Age for Marriage and Registration of Marriages of 7 November 1962 (article 8), the International Convention on the Elimination of All Forms of Racial Discrimination of 21 December 1965 (article 22), the International Convention on the Suppression and Punishment of the Crime of *Apartheid* of 30 November 1973 (article XII), the Convention on the Elimination of All Forms of Discrimination against Women of 18 December 1979 (article 29), and the Convention against Torture and Other Cruel, Inhuman or Degrading Treatment or Punishment of 10 December 1984 (article 30).

159. Neither of the International Covenants on Human Rights specifically provides for adjudication by the International Court of Justice.

160. Only a few contentious cases involving questions of human rights have been dealt with by the International Court of Justice. These have concerned the right of asylum, the rights of aliens, the rights of the child, the question of the continued existence of the mandate for South West Africa, and the question of the seizure and holding as hostages of members of the United States diplomatic and consular staff in Iran.

161. On several occasions, the General Assembly or the Security Council has requested, and received, advisory opinions given by the Court. These have involved the international status of South West Africa, and of Western Sahara, the interpretation of certain peace treaties, reservations concerning the Convention on the Prevention and Punishment of the Crime of Genocide, and the legal consequences of the continued presence of South Africa in Namibia.

F. The Secretariat

162. Under the Charter, the Secretariat is a principal organ of the United Nations, comprising the Secretary-General, who is the chief administrative officer of the Organization, and a staff appointed by him under regulations established by the General Assembly. The Secretary-General and the staff may not seek or receive instructions from any Government or from any other authority external to the Organization, and each Member of the United Nations has undertaken in the Charter to respect the exclusively international character of the responsibilities of the Secretary-General and the staff and not to seek to influence them in the discharge of their responsibilities.

163. Under Article 98 of the Charter, the Secretary-General acts in that capacity in all meetings of the General Assembly, of the Security Council, and of the Trusteeship Council. He performs such other functions as are entrusted to him by these organs. He submits an annual report to the General Assembly on the work of the Organization in accordance with Article 98 of the Charter.

1. Centre for Human Rights

164. From 1946 to 1982, secretariat services for United Nations bodies dealing with human rights were provided by the Division of Human Rights, a unit located first in the Department of Social Affairs, later in the Office of the Under-Secretary-General for Special Political Affairs, and finally in the Office of the Under-Secretary-General for Political and General Assembly Affairs.

165. In resolution 34/47 of 23 November 1979, and again in resolution 35/194 of 15 December 1980, the General Assembly, noting the important contribution which the Division had made to United Nations activities for the promotion and protection of human rights, requested the Secretary-General to consider redesignating the Division as the Centre for Human Rights. The decision of the Secretary-General to do so was announced on 28 July 1982,[14] and was noted by the Assembly in decision 37/437 of 18 December 1982.

166. The Centre, located in the United Nations Office at Geneva with a small Liaison Office at United Nations Headquarters at New York, is headed by the Under-Secretary-General for Human Rights, who is also the Director-General of the United Nations Office at Geneva and whose functions are to co-ordinate the human rights programme with related activities within the Secretariat and the United Nations system, to represent the Secretary-General at meetings of human rights organs and at other human rights events, to promote the ratification and application of international conventions on human rights, to assist in the exercise of the humanitarian good offices of the Secretary-General, and to as-

sure the substantive servicing of the Commission on Human Rights and other human rights bodies.

167. The main functions of the Centre for Human Rights are to assist the General Assembly, the Economic and Social Council, the Commission on Human Rights and other organs of the United Nations in the promotion and protection of human rights and fundamental freedoms as envisaged in the Charter of the United Nations, the Universal Declaration of Human Rights, international conventions on human rights concluded under the auspices of the United Nations and various resolutions of the General Assembly.

168. In general, the Centre serves as a focal point of the United Nations in the field of human rights. It provides secretariat and substantive services to United Nations organs concerned with human rights, including the General Assembly and its Third Committee, the Economic and Social Council and its Social Committee, the Commission on Human Rights, the Sub-Commission on Prevention of Discrimination and Protection of Minorities and their subsidiary bodies, the Committee on the Elimination of Racial Discrimination, the Human Rights Committee, the Committee on Economic, Social and Cultural Rights and the Committee against Torture.

169. The Centre also carries out research and studies on human rights at the request of the organs concerned, follows up and prepares reports on the implementation of human rights, and administers the programme of advisory services and technical assistance in the field of human rights. In addition, it co-ordinates liaison with non-governmental, intergovernmental and governmental organizations active in the field of human rights, and with the media. It collects and disseminates information, and prepares publications, relating to human rights.

170. The Centre includes six sections: the International Instruments Section, which carries out functions and responsibilities relating to the implementation of international human rights treaties of the United Nations; the Communications Section, which processes communications concerning allegations of violations of human rights under established procedures; the Special Procedures Section, which provides substantive services to *ad hoc* or extra-conventional activities such as working groups or special rapporteurs as well as to the Commission on Human Rights; the Research, Studies and Prevention of Discrimination Section, which prepares studies and reports on the promotion and protection of human rights requested by human rights organs and provides substantive services to the Sub-Commission on Prevention of Discrimination and Protection of Minorities; the Advisory Services Section, which administers the programme of advisory services and technical assistance in the field of human rights; and the External Relations, Publications and Documentation Section, which is responsible for ensuring the effective functioning of the external relations aspects of the human rights programmes and policies of the United Nations.

---

[14] ST/SGB/194.

171. In addition, the Centre includes an Administrative Support Unit, which assists in the administration and monitoring of the utilization of the resources available to the Centre; the New York Office, which assists in co-ordinating the activities of the Centre with those of other secretariat units at Headquarters and in servicing sessions of human rights organs meeting at Headquarters; and the secretariat of the Working Group on Enforced or Involuntary Disappearances, which provides secretariat services to the Working Group and assists that Group in operating its procedure of urgent action in cases of reported disappearances.

2. BRANCH FOR THE ADVANCEMENT OF WOMEN, CENTRE FOR SOCIAL DEVELOPMENT AND HUMANITARIAN AFFAIRS

172. The Branch for the Advancement of Women of the Centre for Social Development and Humanitarian Affairs now carries out the functions previously entrusted to the Section on the Status of Women of the Division of Human Rights. The Branch is located in the Vienna International Centre, Vienna, and is headed by a Director.

173. The Branch provides secretariat services to the Third Committee of the General Assembly, the Second (Social) Committee of the Economic and Social Council, and their subsidiary bodies when they deal with questions related to the advancement of women; to the Commission on the Status of Women at all times; and to international conferences and seminars concerning the advancement of women. The Branch prepares the meetings and work programmes of such bodies and carries out, in accordance with their instruction, studies, reports and special assignments. It prepares studies and reports of lasting value for printing by the United Nations. It keeps in touch, through the exchange of documentation and reciprocal representation, with the specialized agencies, intergovernmental and non-governmental organizations, and other organizations concernd with the advancement of women. In addition, it assists in the preparation of international instruments concerning the status and advancement of women, and in the implementation of conventions in this field, and reports on these activities to the General Assembly and other competent bodies. Finally, the Branch, through the Centre for Social Development and Humanitarian Affairs, advises the Secretary-General on all questions falling within its field of competence and keeps him, and through him the interested organs of the United Nations, informed of major developments in this field throughout the world.

3. OTHER SECRETARIAT ELEMENTS

174. The Office of Legal Affairs deals with human rights questions that arise in the International Law Commission and in the Sixth (Legal) Committee of the General Assembly. The Department of Political and Security Council Affairs deals with those that arise in the Security Council and in the First (Political and Security) and Special Political Committees of the General Assembly. The Department of Political Affairs, Trusteeship and Decolonization deals with those that arise in the Trusteeship Council, the Special Committee on the Situation with regard to the Implementation of the Declaration on the Granting of Independence to Colonial Countries and Peoples, and the Fourth (Trusteeship) Committee of the General Assembly. The Office of the United Nations High Commissioner for Namibia deals with those that arise in the United Nations Council for Namibia.

175. The Department of Public Information prepares and disseminates materials of various kinds to acquaint the public with the work and activities of the United Nations in the field of human rights.

G. Treaty-monitoring bodies

176. Whereas the General Assembly, the Economic and Social Council and their subsidiary bodies devote varying amounts of time and attention to supervising the application of human rights standards set out in international declarations, conventions and recommendations, a number of specialized bodies have been established solely to monitor the implementation of particular conventions by States which have ratified or acceded to them. Among these are the Committee on the Elimination of Racial Discrimination, the Human Rights Committee, the Committee on the Elimination of Discrimination against Women, the Committee against Torture, the Committee on Economic, Social and Cultural Rights and the Group of Three.

177. Another such body, the Commission against *Apartheid* in Sports, is to be established six months after the date of the entry into force of the International Convention against *Apartheid* in Sports.

178. The mandates, composition and membership of the established bodies are summarized briefly below. Their activities are recorded in the appropriate chapters which follow.[15]

1. COMMITTEE ON THE ELIMINATION OF RACIAL DISCRIMINATION

179. The Committee monitors the implementation of the International Convention on the Elimination of All Forms of Racial Discrimination,[16] adopted by the Gen-

---

[15] Activities of the Committee on the Elimination of Racial Discrimination are set out in chapter IV, sect. A (5) (*a*); those of the Human Rights Committee in chapter VIII, sect. M (2); those of the Committee on the Elimination of Discrimination against Women in chapter VI, sect. A (3); those of the Committee against Torture in chapter VIII, sect. D (2) (*h*); those of the Committee on Economic, Social and Cultural Rights in chapter VII, sect. K (2); and those of the Group of Three in chapter V, sect. A (4).

[16] For information concerning the Convention, see chapter II, section B (1).

eral Assembly in resolution 2106 A (XX) of 21 December 1965, which entered into force on 4 January 1969.

180. The Committee was established pursuant to article 8 of the Convention at the first meeting of States parties, on 10 July 1969. Its terms of reference, set out in detail in part II of the Convention, may be summarized as follows: to review measures taken by the States parties to implement the Convention, to examine the periodic reports submitted by those States parties on measures taken to give effect to the provisions of the Convention, and to make suggestions and general recommendations to the States parties and to the General Assembly. The Committee is authorized to establish permanent working groups and/or *ad hoc* conciliation commissions to consider respectively communications from individuals and/or inter-State disputes relating to Convention obligations.

181. The Committee is composed of 18 members elected by the States parties for a term of four years. It normally holds two sessions of three weeks' duration each year. It reports annually to the General Assembly, through the Secretary-General, on its activities.

2. HUMAN RIGHTS COMMITTEE

182. The Committee monitors the implementation of the International Covenant on Civil and Political Rights and the Optional Protocol to that Covenant,[17] both adopted by the General Assembly in resolution 2200 A (XXI) of 16 December 1966, which entered into force on 23 March 1976.

183. The Committee was established pursuant to part IV of the Covenant at the first meeting of States parties, on 20 September 1976. Its terms of reference, as set out in the Covenant, may be summarized as follows: to study the reports submitted by States parties on measures taken to give effect to the provisions of the Covenant and to make suggestions and general recommendations to the States parties, and to consider under certain circumstances communications to the effect that a State party claims that another State party is not fulfilling its obligations under the Covenant. It is further authorized, under the Optional Protocol, to consider communications from individuals claiming to be victims of violations of any of the rights set forth in the Covenant, and to forward its views to the State party concerned and to the individual. In the case of inter-State disputes, it may establish *ad hoc* conciliation commissions to consider them with a view to an amicable solution of the matter.

184. The Committee is composed of 18 members elected by the States parties for a term of four years. It normally holds three sessions per year, each of three weeks' duration, one at New York and two at Geneva. It reports annually to the General Assembly, through the Economic and Social Council, on its activities.

3. COMMITTEE ON THE ELIMINATION OF DISCRIMINATION AGAINST WOMEN

185. The Committee monitors the implementation of the Convention on the Elimination of All Forms of Discrimination against Women,[18] adopted by the General Assembly in resolution 34/180 of 18 December 1979, which entered into force on 3 September 1981.

186. The Committee was established pursuant to article 17 of the Convention at the first meeting of States parties, on 16 April 1982. Its terms of reference, as set out in part V of the Convention, may be summarized as follows: to consider the reports of States parties on measures which they have adopted to give effect to the provisions of the Convention, to prepare suggestions and general recommendations based on the reports and other information received from States parties, and to report annually to the General Assembly.

187. The Committee is composed of 23 members, elected by the States parties for a term of four years. It normally meets once a year, for a period of two weeks, at Vienna.

4. COMMITTEE AGAINST TORTURE

188. The Committee monitors the implementation of the Convention against Torture and Other Cruel, Inhuman or Degrading Treatment or Punishment,[19] adopted by the General Assembly in resolution 39/46 of 10 December 1984, which entered into force on 26 June 1987.

189. The Committee was established pursuant to article 17 of the Convention at the first meeting of States parties, on 26 November 1987. Its terms of reference, set out in detail in part II of the Convention, may be summarized as follows: to monitor the progress made in the implementation of the Convention, and in particular to consider the reports submitted by States parties on the measures they have taken to give effect to their undertakings under the Convention; and to make such general comments on the reports as it may consider appropriate.

190. The Committee may also examine "reliable information which appears to it to contain well-founded indications that torture is being systematically practised in the territory of a State party", in co-operation with that State party; may, "if it decides that this is warranted, designate one or more of its members to make a confidential inquiry and to report to the Committee urgently"; may, "in agreement with that State party. . . include a visit to its territory" in such an inquiry; and may, "after examining the findings of its member or members, transmit them to the State party concerned together with any comments or suggestions which seem appropriate in view of the situation".

---

[17] For information concerning the Covenant and Optional Protocol, see chapter II, section A, (2) (*d*) and (*e*).

[18] For information concerning the Convention, see chapter II, section B (3).

[19] For information concerning the Convention, see chapter II, section B (4).

191. The Committee is composed of 10 experts elected by the States parties for a term of four years. After a first session scheduled to convene in April 1988 at Geneva, it will hold one regular session each year. It reports on its activities annually to the States parties and to the General Assembly.

5. COMMITTEE ON ECONOMIC, SOCIAL AND CULTURAL RIGHTS

192. The Committee monitors the implementation of the International Covenant on Economic, Social and Cultural Rights,[20] adopted by the General Assembly in resolution 2200 A (XXI) of 16 December 1966, which entered into force on 3 January 1976.

193. The Economic and Social Council, in resolution 1988 (LX) of 11 May 1976, invited the States parties to the Covenant to submit to it through the Secretary-General reports on the measures that they had adopted and the progress they had made in achieving the observance of the rights recognized in the Covenant and to indicate, when necessary, factors and difficulties affecting the degree of fulfilment of their obligations. The Council also called upon the specialized agencies to submit reports on the progress made in achieving the observance of the provisions of the Covenant falling within the scope of their activities.

194. To assist it in the consideration of such reports, the Council established, by the same resolution, a sessional working group, and invited representatives of the specialized agencies concerned to take part in its proceedings when matters falling within their respective spheres of competence were considered. Later, in decision 1981/158, the Council renamed the working group "Sessional Working Group of Governmental Experts on the Implementation of the International Covenant on Economic, Social and Cultural Rights" and made some changes in its administrative arrangements. Subsequently, by resolution 1985/17 of 28 May 1985, the Council changed the composition of the Working Group to consist of experts serving in their personal capacity, and renamed it "Committee on Economic, Social and Cultural Rights".

195. The Committee's mandate is to assist the Council to fulfil its responsibilities under articles 21 and 22 of the Covenant, which call upon the Council to submit to the General Assembly "reports and recommendations of a general nature and a summary of the information received from the States parties. . . and the specialized agencies on the progress made in achieving general observance of the rights recognized" in the Covenant; and to "bring to the attention of other organs of the United Nations, their subsidiary organs and specialized agencies concerned with furnishing technical assistance any matters arising out of the reports. . . which may assist such bodies in deciding, each within its

field of competence, on the advisability of international measures likely to contribute to the effective progressive implementation of the present Covenant".

196. The Committee is composed of 18 experts nominated by States parties to the Covenant and elected by the Council for a term of four years. It held its first session at Geneva from 9 to 27 March 1987, and is scheduled to meet annually at Geneva for a period of up to three weeks. It reports annually to the Council.

6. GROUP OF THREE

197. The Group monitors the implementation of the International Convention on the Suppression and Punishment of the Crime of *Apartheid*,[21] adopted by the General Assembly in resolution 3068 (XXVIII) of 30 November 1973, which entered into force on 18 July 1976.

198. Pursuant to article IX of the Convention, the Chairman of the Commission on Human Rights appoints at each annual session three members of the Commission who are also representatives of States parties to the Convention, to consider reports submitted by the States parties on the legislative, judicial, administrative or other measures that they have adopted and that give effect to the provisions of the Convention. It held its first session in 1978.

199. The Group of Three meets for a period of not more than five days, usually prior to the annual session of the Commission, to consider the reports received. It reports to the Commission.

H. Specialized agencies

200. The Economic and Social Council is authorized, by Article 63, paragraph 2, of the Charter, to coordinate the activities of the specialized agencies through consultations with and recommendations to such agencies and through recommendations to the General Assembly and to the Members of the United Nations.

201. In accordance with Article 70 of the Charter, arrangements have been made for representatives of the specialized agencies to participate, without vote, in the deliberations of the Council and its commissions, and for Council representatives to participate in the deliberations of the specialized agencies.

202. The Council, by resolution 13 (III) of 21 September 1946, established a standing Administrative Committee on Co-ordination, consisting of the Secretary-General of the United Nations and the Directors-General of the specialized agencies, "for the purpose of taking all appropriate steps, under the leadership of the Secretary-General, to ensure the fullest and most effective implementation of the agreements entered into between the United Nations and the specialized agencies".

---

[20] For information concerning the Covenant, see chapter II, section A (2) (c).

[21] For information concerning the Convention, see chapter II, section B (2).

203. With regard to human rights, the General Assembly, in resolution 33/54 of 14 December 1978, recognized that some of the specialized agencies, especially ILO, UNESCO and WHO, had developed procedures and programmes for the promotion of human rights within their fields of competence, and that the work of these agencies significantly complemented the work done by the United Nations human rights organs. Further, it noted the existence of other human rights organs and programmes which functioned under separate constitutional instruments of intergovernmental organizations and had compiled significant records of human rights actions within their areas of jurisdiction.

204. Considering that the interdependence and indivisibility of human rights and fundamental freedoms demanded renewed efforts to stimulate greater co-operation, co-ordination and communication among all the intergovernmental agencies and institutions involved in protecting and promoting human rights and fundamental freedoms, the Assembly requested the Commission on Human Rights to consult with specialized agencies and other organs and bodies of the United Nations system which are, according to their mandates, concerned with the protection and promotion of human rights and fundamental freedoms and, as appropriate, with other regional intergovernmental bodies related to the United Nations system particularly concerned with human rights, on the various human rights activities and programmes and the existing modes of co-ordination, co-operation and communication among them.

205. The Assembly further requested the Commission to submit a study of the existing modes of co-ordination, co-operation and communication in the field of human rights within the United Nations system, together with its suggestions and proposals, to the Assembly at its thirty-fourth session.

206. The Commission on Human Rights, in resolution 22 (XXXV) of 14 March 1979, decided to carry out the study on the basis of preparatory material to be made available at its thirty-seventh session. The Economic and Social Council, by resolution 1979/36 of 10 May 1979, asked it to proceed, and requested those specialized agencies and other organs and bodies within and related to the United Nations system which are, according to their explicit mandates, concerned with the protection and promotion of human rights and fundamental freedoms, to provide the Secretary-General with a short survey of their human rights activities and programmes. The Secretary-General was requested to compile an analytical presentation of the material received. In the same resolution, the Council further decided to add the following to the terms of reference of the Commission:

The Commission shall assist the Economic and Social Council in the co-ordination of activities concerning human rights in the United Nations system.

207. The Secretary-General's analytical presentation of materials received[22] was presented to the Commission at its thirty-seventh session, in 1981. It was considered

---

[22] E/CN.4/1433.

by the Commission in the context of its overall analysis of the alternative approaches and ways and means within the United Nations system for improving the effective enjoyment of human rights and fundamental freedoms.

1. INTERNATIONAL LABOUR ORGANISATION (ILO)

208. The International Labour Organisation was established on 11 April 1919, as an autonomous institution associated with the League of Nations. The original constitution of the Organisation was adopted as Part XIII of the Treaty of Versailles and formed part of other treaties of peace. Its preamble stated that universal peace "can be established only if it is based upon social justice"; that unjust conditions of labour imperilled the peace and harmony of the world; and that an improvement in such conditions was urgently required.

209. The 26th session of the General Conference of ILO, held at Philadelphia in April and May 1944, adopted a "Declaration concerning the Aims and Purposes of the International Labour Organisation", generally known as the Declaration of Philadelphia. Under an amendment to the Constitution adopted in 1946, the objects set forth in this Declaration are included among those to be promoted by the Organisation, and the text of the Declaration is annexed to the Constitution. The Declaration reaffirms the fundamental principles, upon which the Organisation is based, and in particular that "(a) labour is not a commodity; (b) freedom of expression and of association are essential to sustained progress; (c) poverty anywhere constitutes a danger to prosperity everywhere. . .".

210. The Declaration affirms that "all human beings, irrespective of race, creed or sex, have the right to pursue both their material well-being and their spiritual development in conditions of freedom and dignity, of economic security and equal opportunity", and adds that "the attainment of the conditions in which this shall be possible must constitute the central aim of national and international policy".

211. The Declaration recognizes the solemn obligation of the Organisation to promote programmes to achieve full employment and the raising of standards of living, recognition of the right of collective bargaining, extension of social security, etc. It embodies a pledge that the Organisation will co-operate with other international bodies in the achievement of the objectives it sets forth and in the promotion of the health, education and well-being of all peoples.

212. An Agreement bringing ILO into relationship with the United Nations, in accordance with Article 63 of the Charter, and defining its status as a specialized agency, was unanimously approved by the 29th session of the General Conference on 2 October 1946. The Agreement came into force upon its approval by the General Assembly by resolution 50 (I) of 14 December 1946.

213. Under its Constitution, the International Labour Organisation is concerned both with economic and social rights, such as the right to work, the right to the enjoyment of just and favourable conditions of work, the right to form trade unions and join the trade union of one's choice, the right to social security, and the right to an adequate standard of living; and with civil and political rights, such as freedom of expression, freedom of association, and the right of peaceful assembly.

214. The ILO endeavours to implement the principles of its Constitution by laying down standards, by supervising their application, and by assisting Governments to achieve its objectives.

215. Among the international instruments in the field of human rights prepared by ILO since the establishment of the United Nations are the Freedom of Association and Protection of the Right to Organise Convention, adopted on 9 July 1948; the Right to Organise and Collective Bargaining Convention, adopted on 1 July 1949; the Equal Remuneration Convention, adopted on 29 June 1951; the Abolition of Forced Labour Convention, adopted on 25 June 1957; the Discrimination (Employment and Occupation) Convention, adopted on 25 June 1958; the Employment Policy Convention, adopted on 9 July 1964; the Workers' Representatives Convention, adopted on 23 June 1971; the Labour Relations (Public Service) Convention, adopted on 27 June 1978; the Collective Bargaining Convention, adopted on 19 June 1981; and the Occupational Safety and Health Convention, adopted on 22 June 1981.

216. A distinctive feature of the International Labour Organisation is the tripartite structure which characterizes all its organs, with the exception of organs composed of experts appointed on an individual basis. Under this structure, the delegation of each member State to the International Labour Conference includes two representatives of the Government, one representative of workers and one representative of employers.

217. The International Labour Office, which serves as the secretariat for the International Labour Organisation, is headed by a Director-General. It carries out ILO programmes in accordance with the instructions of the General Conference and the Governing Body.

2. FOOD AND AGRICULTURE ORGANIZATION OF THE UNITED NATIONS (FAO)

218. The Food and Agriculture Organization of the United Nations was the first of the specialized agencies of the United Nations system to be established after the Second World War. At the United Nations Conference on Food and Agriculture, held in May-June 1943 at Hot Springs, Virginia, USA, 44 nations agreed to work together to banish hunger and establish a stable world agriculture. FAO officially came into being with the signing of its Constitution on 16 October 1945.

219. The purpose of creating FAO is set forth in the preamble to its Constitution:

(a) Raising levels of nutrition and standards of living of the peoples under the respective jurisdictions of the nations accepting the Constitution;

(b) Securing improvements in the efficiency of the production and distribution of all food and agricultural products;

(c) Bettering the condition of rural populations;

(d) and thus contributing towards an expanding world economy and ensuring humanity's freedom from hunger.

220. Among the functions of FAO, as described in article 1 of its Constitution, are the collection, analysis, interpretation and dissemination of information relating to nutrition, food and agriculture; the promotion of national and international action to improve education and administration relating to nutrition, food and agriculture; and the furnishing of technical assistance to Governments in these fields.

221. The organs of FAO are the Conference, the Council and the Director-General.

222. FAO was formally brought into relationship with the United Nations as a specialized agency when the United Nations General Assembly approved the Agreement between the two organizations by resolution 50 (I) of 14 December 1946. The Agreement had previously been approved by the FAO Conference on 13 September 1946.

3. UNITED NATIONS EDUCATIONAL, SCIENTIFIC AND CULTURAL ORGANIZATION (UNESCO)

223. The Government of France recommended at the San Francisco Conference that the United Nations should set up an international organization on cultural co-operation. The Conference for the Establishment of an Educational, Scientific and Cultural Organization of the United Nations was convened by the Governments of the United Kingdom and France, and met in London from 1 to 16 November 1945. It drew up the Constitution of UNESCO, and decided that the headquarters of UNESCO should be in Paris. UNESCO came into being on 4 November 1946.

224. The preamble to the UNESCO Constitution recognizes that "since wars begin in the minds of men, it is in the minds of men that the defences of peace must be constructed".

225. The purpose of UNESCO, as stated in article 1 of its Constitution, is "to contribute to peace and security by promoting collaboration among the nations through education, science and culture in order to further universal respect for justice, for the rule of law and for the human rights and fundamental freedoms which are affirmed for the peoples of the world, without distinction of race, sex, language or religion, by the Charter of the United Nations".

226. To achieve its purpose, UNESCO is to accomplish the following:

(*a*) Collaborate in the work of advancing the mutual knowledge and understanding of peoples, through all means of mass communication and to that end recommend such international agreements as may be necessary to promote the free flow of ideas by word and image;

(*b*) Give fresh impulse to popular education and to the spread of culture;

By collaborating with members, at their request, in the development of educational activities:

By instituting collaboration among the nations to advance the ideal of equality of educational opportunity without regard to race, sex, or any distinctions, economic or social;

By suggesting educational methods best suited to prepare the children of the world for the responsibilities of freedom . . .

227.   An agreement establishing the relationship between the United Nations and UNESCO was approved by the first session of the General Conference of UNESCO, held in Paris from 19 November to 10 December 1946, and came into force when approved by the General Assembly of the United Nations by resolution 50 (I) of 14 December 1946.

228.   Within the framework of its standard-setting activity, UNESCO has adopted a number of international instruments aimed at the realization of human rights, including the Convention against Discrimination in Education, adopted on 14 December 1960; the Protocol Instituting a Conciliation and Good Offices Commission to be responsible for seeking a settlement of any disputes which may arise between States parties to the Convention against Discrimination in Education, adopted by the General Conference on 10 December 1962, and which came into force on 24 October 1968; the Declaration on Fundamental Principles Concerning the Contribution of the Mass Media to Strengthening Peace and International Understanding, to the Promotion of Human Rights and to Countering Racialism, *Apartheid* and Incitement to War, adopted on 22 November 1978; and the Declaration on Race and Racial Prejudice, adopted on 27 November 1978.

229.   Under its Constitution, UNESCO contributes to peace and security by promoting collaboration among nations through education, science and culture, with a view to furthering universal respect for justice, for the rule of law, and for the human rights and fundamental freedoms of the peoples of the world without distinction as to race, sex, language or religion.

230.   To achieve these aims, UNESCO establishes and supervises the realization of standards; gathers and disseminates information of educational, scientific or cultural interest; provides advisory services and technical assistance and assists in the establishment of educational, scientific and cultural institutions and centres; organizes congresses, seminars and symposia; and provides subsidies to certain non-governmental organizations.

231.   The main organs of UNESCO are the General Conference, which meets every two years and in which all member States are represented; the Executive Board, elected by the Conference; and the Secretariat, headed by the Director-General.

4. WORLD HEALTH ORGANIZATION (WHO)

232.   The Constitution of the World Health Organization was adopted on 22 July 1946 by the International Health Conference, called for the purpose by the Economic and Social Council. WHO came into being officially on 7 April 1948, 26 Members of the United Nations having accepted its Constitution. In 1987 the Organization was composed of 166 member States.

233.   The objective of WHO, as stated in article 1 of its Constitution, is "the attainment by all peoples of the highest possible level of health". The preamble defines health as "a state of complete physical, mental and social well-being and not merely the absence of disease or infirmity".

234.   The functions of the Organization necessary to attain this objective are enumerated in article 2, the major elements of which can be summarized as follows:

(*a*) WHO's first constitutional function is to act as the directing and co-ordinating authority on international health work. Member States identify collectively priority health problems throughout the world, define health policies and targets to cope with them, and devise strategies, principles and programmes to give effect to these policies and attain the targets.

(*b*) WHO transmits policy decisions on international health matters to other intergovernmental and non-governmental organizations working in the field of health with a view to involving them in a manner that contributes to internationally defined health policy.

(*c*) WHO promotes international agreement on health policies, including the humanitarian dimension of social justice in health matters, particularly through a more equitable distribution of health resources among and within countries. It impresses on policy-makers that health can make a legitimate contribution to development; that it is worthy of investment and is not merely a beneficiary; that appropriate health and socioeconomic policies are closely interlinked and mutually supportive. General Assembly resolution 34/58 of 29 November 1979 recognizes that health is an integral part of development.

(*d*) WHO promotes the rationalization and mobilization of resources for health and supports developing countries in identifying their needs for external resources. It makes available its own collective resources and aims at securing bilateral transfers by more affluent countries and international developmental and financial organizations in a manner commensurate with international health policy.

(*e*) The Organization brings together the world's experts in health matters and serves as a neutral ground for absorbing, distilling, synthesizing and widely disseminating information that has practical value for countries in solving their health problems.

(*f*) WHO identifies or generates health technology that is appropriate in the sense of being scientifically sound, acceptable to local needs, socially acceptable and economically feasible. It promotes research and development with a view to laying the scientific and technical bases for health policies and programmes, including norms and standards in such fields as nutrition, the safety, purity and potency of biological pharmaceutical products, diagnostic procedures, and international nomenclature and classification of diseases. This is achieved by identifying the world's most important health research goals and promoting the collaborative efforts of health research workers throughout the world to attain them—for example, in such particularly relevant fields as human reproduction, the control of tropical diseases and AIDS. In WHO's Global Strategy for the prevention and control of AIDS, the importance of protecting human rights is given great emphasis.

(*g*) The WHO concept of technical co-operation has replaced the technical assistance idea which was based on a donor-recipient relationship and on time-limited assistance projects. Technical co-operation for health implies true partnership to attain national health goals that have been defined *in* countries *by* countries, and that can be sustained and developed further by the country when the involvement of WHO or other member States is no longer required. Such technical co-operation facilitates self-reliant health development.

235.   The Agreement establishing the relationship of WHO with the United Nations was approved by the World Health Assembly on 10 July 1948. This action brought the Agreement into force, since it had previously been approved by the General Assembly on 15 November 1947 by resolution 124 (II).

236.   Although WHO has not adopted international instruments in the field of human rights, it played an important part in the preparation of the Principles of Medical Ethics relevant to the role of health personnel, particularly physicians, in the protection of prisoners and detainees against torture and other cruel, inhuman or degrading treatment or punishment, adopted by the General Assembly in resolution 37/194 on 18 December 1982.

I. Non-governmental organizations

237.   Article 71 of the Charter provides that the Economic and Social Council "may make arrangements for consultation with non-governmental organizations which are concerned with matters within its competence". The arrangements made by the Council for such consultation are set out in resolution 1296 (XLIV) of 23 May 1968, which provides for certain principles to be applied in the establishment of consultative relations, among them:

1. The organization shall be concerned with matters falling within the competence of the Economic and Social Council with respect to international economic, social, cultural, educational, health, scientific, technological and related matters and to questions of human rights;

2. The aims and purposes of the organization shall be in conformity with the spirit, purposes and principles of the Charter of the United Nations;

3. The organization shall undertake to support the work of the United Nations and to promote knowledge of its principles and activities, in accordance with its own aims and purposes and the nature and scope of its competence and activities;

4. The organization shall be of representative character and of recognized international standing; . . .

7. . . . the organization shall be international in its structure . . .

8. The basic resources of the international organization shall be derived in the main part from contributions of the national affiliates or other components or from individual members . . .

238.   In establishing consultative relations with non-governmental organizations, the Council made the following distinctions:

Organizations in category I, in general consultative status, are concerned with most of the activities of the Council and can demonstrate to its satisfaction that they have marked and sustained contributions to make to the achievements of the United Nations;

Organizations in category II, in special consultative status, have a special competence in, and are concerned specifically with, only a few of the fields of activity covered by the Council;

Organizations on the Roster are organizations which can make occasional and useful contributions to the work of the Council or its subsidiary bodies.

239.   Organizations to which consultative status in category II is accorded because of their interest in human rights are those which have a genuine international concern with this question, not restricted to the interests of a particular group of persons, a single nationality or the situation in a particular State or group of States. Special consideration is given to the applications of organizations whose aims place stress on combating colonialism, *apartheid,* racial intolerance and other gross violations of human rights.

240.   Organizations in category I may propose to the Council Committee on Non-Governmental Organizations that the Committee request the Secretary-General to place an item of special interest to the Organization on the provisional agenda of the Council. On the recommendation of the Committee, such organizations may be heard by the Council or by its sessional committees. In special circumstances, an organization in category II may be heard.

241.   Organizations in categories I and II may submit written statements to the Council on subjects in which these organizations have a special competence. Organizations on the Roster may be invited by the Secretary-General, in consultation with the Council or the Committee, to submit such statements.

II. INTERNATIONAL INSTRUMENTS CONCERNED WITH HUMAN RIGHTS

Introduction

1. Although the Charter lists the promotion and encouragement of respect for human rights and for fundamental freedoms among the purposes of the United Nations, and although it calls repeatedly for the observance of those rights and freedoms, it does not endeavour to enumerate or to define them. This task, which the San Francisco Conference on International Organizations did not attempt to undertake, was left to the competent organs of the United Nations: the General Assembly, the Economic and Social Council, the Commission on Human Rights and their subsidiary bodies.

2. In time, these bodies produced an impressive series of international declarations, conventions, protocols and other instruments designed to promote and to protect the enjoyment by everyone of human rights and fundamental freedoms. These instruments, the texts of which are set out in *Human Rights: A Compilation of International Instruments,*[1] are enumerated below.

A. The International Bill of Human Rights

3. In 1946, at the first part of the first session of the General Assembly, in London, the General Committee decided not to include in the Assembly's agenda a proposal by Panama that it should discuss the question of a Declaration on Fundamental Human Rights and the Rights and Duties of Nations. The representative of Panama thereupon submitted a draft Declaration of Fundamental Human Rights and Freedoms and requested that it should be placed on the agenda for the second part of the Assembly's first session.

4. At its 46th plenary meeting, on 31 October 1946, the General Assembly referred the Panamanian draft Declaration of Fundamental Human Rights and Freedoms simultaneously to the First (Political and Security) and Third (Social, Humanitarian and Cultural) Committees. On the basis of their joint recommendation the Assembly, at its 55th plenary meeting, on 11 December 1946, decided to refer the draft Declaration to the Economic and Social Council "for reference to the Commission on Human Rights in its preparation of an international bill of rights". The Assembly expressed the hope that the matter would be referred back to it in time for consideration at its second regular session.

5. The Economic and Social Council had established the Commission on Human Rights in pursuance of Article 68 of the Charter by resolution 5 (I) of 16 February 1946, and had instructed it to submit proposals, recommendations and reports regarding "an international bill of human rights". The Council had further requested the Commission, in resolution 9 (II) of 21 June 1946, to submit "suggestions regarding ways and means for the effective implementation of human rights and fundamental freedoms".

6. The Commission held its first session from 27 January to 10 February 1947. After a general discussion on the form and content of an international bill of human rights, the Commission decided that its Chairman, together with the Vice-Chairman and Rapporteur, should undertake, with the assistance of the Secretariat, the task of formulating a preliminary draft International Bill of Human Rights, to be submitted to the Commission at its second session. This decision was, however, criticized in the Economic and Social Council on the ground that it did not provide for appropriate geographical distribution of members of the informal drafting group.

7. At the request of the Chairman of the Commission the Council, in resolution 46 (IV) of 28 March 1947, altered the procedure for the preparation of the draft International Bill of Human Rights. The Council requested the Secretariat to prepare a documented outline for such an instrument, noted with approval the statement of the Chairman that she intended to appoint a formal drafting committee consisting of members of the Commission from eight States selected with due regard for geographical distribution, and called upon the drafting committee to prepare, on the basis of documentation supplied by the Secretariat, a preliminary draft of an International Bill of Human Rights.

8. Concerning the form which the draft of an international bill of human rights should take, two views were put forward in the Drafting Committee. One was that the draft, in the first instance, should take the form of a declaration; the other that it should be in the form of a convention. It was agreed, however, by those who favoured the declaration form that it should be accompanied or followed by a convention or conventions on specific groups of rights. It was also agreed by those who favoured the convention form that the General Assembly, in recommending a convention to Member States, might make a declaration wider in content and more general in expression. The Drafting Committee therefore decided to attempt to prepare two documents: one in the form of a declaration, which would set forth general principles or standards of human rights; the

---

[1] United Nations publication, Sales No.E.88.XIV.1.

other in the form of a convention which would define specific rights and the limitations or restrictions on their enjoyment. The Committee prepared and submitted to the Commission draft articles of an international declaration on human rights and draft articles of an international convention on human rights. The Committee also considered the question of implementation and transmitted to the Commission a memorandum on the subject prepared by the Secretariat.

9. At its second session, held at Geneva from 2 to 17 December 1947, the Commission on Human Rights decided that the term "international bill of human rights" should be applied to the entire series of documents in preparation, namely, a declaration on human rights, a convention or covenant on human rights, and measures of implementation. The Commission established three working groups: one on the declaration, one on the covenant and one on implementation. On the basis of the reports of the first two working groups the Commission drafted a declaration of human rights and a covenant on human rights. These drafts, together with the report of the working group on implementation, were transmitted to Governments for observations, suggestions and proposals.

10. The Drafting Committee at its second session, from 3 to 21 May 1948, revised the declaration and the covenant, taking into consideration the comments and proposals of Governments.

11. The Commission, at its third session from 24 May to 16 June 1948, once more redrafted the declaration, but did not have time to consider the covenant or the question of implementation. The declaration, thus redrafted, together with the draft covenant and several proposals on implementation, was submitted to the Economic and Social Council and was in turn transmitted by the Council, in resolution 151 (VII) of 26 August 1948, to the General Assembly.

1. THE UNIVERSAL DECLARATION OF HUMAN RIGHTS

12. The General Assembly of the United Nations, meeting in Paris on 10 December 1948, adopted and proclaimed the Universal Declaration of Human Rights "as a common standard of achievement for all peoples and all nations, to the end that every individual and every organ of society, keeping this Declaration constantly in mind, shall strive by teaching and education to promote respect for these rights and freedoms and by progressive measures, national and international, to secure their universal and effective recognition and observance, both among the peoples of Member States themselves and among the peoples of territories under their jurisdiction". Forty-eight States voted in favour of the Declaration, none voted against, while eight abstained.

13. In a statement following the voting the President of the General Assembly pointed out that the adoption of the Declaration, "by a big majority, without any direct opposition, was a remarkable achievement". The

Declaration, he said, only marked a first step, since it was not a convention by which States would be bound to carry out and give effect to the fundamental human rights; nor would it provide for enforcement; yet it was a step forward in the great evolutionary process. It was the first occasion on which the organized community of nations had made a declaration of human rights and fundamental freedoms. The document was backed by the authority of the body of opinion of the United Nations as a whole and millions of people—men, women and children all over the world—would turn to it for help, guidance and inspiration.

14. The Universal Declaration of Human Rights consists of a preamble and 30 articles setting forth the basic human rights and fundamental freedoms to which all men and women everywhere in the world are entitled, without discrimination. The articles deal with civil and political rights (articles 3 to 21) as well as economic, social and cultural rights (articles 22 to 27).

15. In article 1 the philosophical postulates upon which the Declaration is based are laid down. The articles reads:

All human beings are born free and equal in dignity and rights. They are endowed with reason and conscience and should act towards one another in a spirit of brotherhood.

The article thus defines the basic assumptions of the Declaration: (1) that the right to liberty, and equality is man's birthright and cannot be alienated, and (2) that because man is a rational and moral being he is different from other creatures on earth and therefore entitled to certain rights and freedoms which other creatures do not enjoy.

16. Article 2 sets out the basic principle of equality and non-discrimination as regards the enjoyment of human rights and fundamental freedoms, elaborating the Charter provision that the United Nations should promote the observance of those rights and freedoms "for all without distinction as to race, sex, language, or religion". In paragraph 2 it expressly states that the Declaration is applicable to all countries and territories regardless of their status.

17. Article 3 proclaims three fundamental and interrelated rights: the right to life, the right to liberty and the right to security of person. These rights are essential to the enjoyment of all the other rights set forth. Article 3 thus serves as a cornerstone of the Declaration, introducing the series of articles (articles 4 to 21) in which the rights of every person as an individual are elaborated further.

18. The civil and political rights recognized in articles 3 to 21 of the Declaration include: the right to life, liberty and security of person; freedom from slavery and servitude; freedom from torture and cruel, inhuman or degrading treatment or punishment; the right to recognition everywhere as a person before the law; the right to an effective judicial remedy; freedom from arbitrary arrest, detention or exile; the right to a fair trial and public hearing by an independent and impartial tribunal; the right to be presumed innocent until proved guilty; freedom from arbitrary interference with

privacy, family, home or correspondence; freedom of movement; the right of asylum; the right to a nationality; the right to marry and to found a family; the right to own property; freedom of thought, conscience and religion; freedom of opinion and expression; the right of association and of assembly; the right to take part in government; and the right of equal access to public service.

19.   Article 22, the second cornerstone of the Declaration, introduces articles 23 to 27 in which economic, social and cultural rights—the rights to which everyone is entitled "as a member of society"—are set out. The article characterizes these rights as indispensable for human dignity and the free development of personality, and indicates that they are to be realized "through national effort and international co-operation". At the same time it points out the limitations of that realization, the extent of which depends upon the resources of each State and of the international community.

20.   The economic, social and cultural rights recognized in articles 22 to 27 include the right to social security; the right to work; the right to rest and leisure; the right to a standard of living adequate for health and well-being; the right to education; and the right to participate in the cultural life of the community.

21.   The concluding articles—articles 28 to 30—recognize that everyone is entitled to a social and international order in which all human rights and fundamental freedoms can be fully realized, and stress the duties and responsibilities which each individual owes to this community. Article 29 states that "in the exercise of his rights and freedoms, everyone shall be subject only to such limitations as are determined by law solely for the purpose of securing due recognition and respect for the rights and freedoms of others and of meeting the just requirements of morality, public order and the general welfare in a democratic society", and adds that in no case may human rights and fundamental freedoms be exercised contrary to the purposes and principles of the United Nations. Article 30 warns that no State, group or person may claim any right, under the Declaration, "to engage in any activity or to perform any act aimed at the destruction of any of the rights and freedoms set forth" in the Declaration.

22.   The draft Declaration was placed on the agenda of the third session of the General Assembly, held at Paris from 21 September to 12 December 1948, and was considered in detail by the Assembly's Social, Humanitarian and Cultural (Third) Committee. The Committee devoted 85 meetings to the preparation of the Declaration and voted on almost every word, phrase, clause and paragraph—1,400 votes in all. As a result of sustained co-operation and resolve on the part of its dedicated Members, the Committee was able to present a completed draft to the plenary Assembly, which adopted and proclaimed it as the Universal Declaration of Human Rights on 10 December 1948—a little more than three years after the entry into force of the Charter of the United Nations on 24 October 1945.

2. THE INTERNATIONAL COVENANTS ON HUMAN RIGHTS

23.   In resolution 217 E (III) of 10 December 1948, the Assembly requested the Council to ask the Commission to prepare, as a matter of priority, a draft covenant on human rights and draft measures of implementation, and to examine further the question of the right of petition. The Council transmitted these requests to the Commission.

24.   At its fifth session, from 9 May to 20 June 1949, the Commission examined the draft covenant and decided to transmit the text, and several additional articles on economic and social rights which had been proposed, to Governments for comments. At its sixth session, from 27 March to 19 May 1950, it revised the first 18 articles and considered the question of implementation. It decided that a permanent body, a Human Rights Committee, should be established, which would receive any complaint by a State party to the covenant that another State party was not giving effect to any provision thereof, and which would offer its good offices to the States concerned with a view to a friendly solution of the matter. It also decided to secure the co-operation of specialized agencies in the drafting of articles on economic, social and cultural rights.

25.   In resolution 421 E (V) of 4 December 1950 the General Assembly declared that "the enjoyment of civic and political freedoms and of economic, social and cultural rights are interconnected and interdependent", and that "when deprived of economic, social and cultural rights, man does not represent the human person whom the Universal Declaration regards as the ideal of the free man"; and decided "to include in the covenant on human rights economic, social and cultural rights and an explicit recognition of equality of men and women in related rights as set forth in the Charter of the United Nations". The Assembly requested the Commission, in part D of the same resolution, "to study ways and means which would ensure the right of peoples and nations to self-determination".

26.   At its seventh session, from 16 April to 19 May 1951, the Commission drafted 14 articles on economic, social and cultural rights on the basis of proposals made by Governments and suggestions by the specialized agencies. It then formulated 10 articles on measures of implementation of those rights, under which States parties to the Covenant would submit periodic reports concerning the progress made in achieving the observance of human rights.

27.   The draft covenant was discussed by the Economic and Social Council at its thirteenth session, in 1951. The question was raised whether the Human Rights Committee procedure and the periodic reporting procedure should be applied to civil and political rights, or economic, social and cultural rights, or both. Conscious of the difficulties which might result from embodying in one covenant two different categories of rights, and at the same time aware of the importance of both, the Council, in resolution 384 (XIII), invited the General

Assembly to reconsider its earlier decision that there should be only one covenant.

28. The General Assembly responded, after a long debate at its sixth session, in 1952, by requesting the Commission "to draft two covenants on human rights, . . . one to contain civil and political rights and the other to contain economic, social and cultural rights, in order that the General Assembly may approve the two covenants simultaneously and open them at the same time for signature". It specified that the two covenants should contain as many similar provisions as possible in order to emphasize the unity of the aim in view and to ensure respect for and observance of human rights.

29. Further, the General Assembly decided that the two covenants should include an article which would provide that "all peoples shall have the right to self-determination", and stipulate that "all States, including those having responsibility for the administration of Non-Self-Governing Territories, should promote the realization of that right, in conformity with the purposes and principles of the United Nations, and that States having responsibility for the administration of Non-Self-Governing Territories should promote the realization of that right in relation to the peoples of such territories".

30. At its eighth session, from 14 April to 14 June 1952, the Commission began to work on two covenants, one on economic, social and cultural rights and one on civil and political rights. First it drafted an article on the right of peoples and nations to self-determination and decided that that article should be article 1 of each covenant. Then it proceeded to adopt a preamble and 15 articles for the draft covenant on economic, social and cultural rights and a preamble and 18 articles for the draft covenant on civil and political rights. However, it was not able to consider the question of implementation.

31. The Commission completed its preparation of the two draft covenants at its ninth and tenth sessions, held in 1953 and 1954 respectively. At those sessions it concentrated upon measures of implementation and final clauses. It revised the implementation measures contained in both instruments, and discussed, but did not adopt, provisions on the right of petition of individuals, groups, and non-governmental organizations. In forwarding its final texts to the General Assembly, it suggested that the Assembly should give the draft covenants two separate readings at two consecutive sessions.

32. The General Assembly reviewed the draft covenants prepared by the Commission at its ninth session, in 1954, and expressed its gratitude to the Commission for the work accomplished. It decided to give the drafts the widest possible publicity in order that Governments might study them thoroughly and that public opinion might express itself freely. It recommended that its Third Committee start an article-by-article discussion of the texts at the tenth session, with a view to their adoption at the earliest possible date.

33. Although the article-by-article discussion began as scheduled, it was not until the twenty-first session of the General Assembly, in 1966, that the elaboration of the Covenants was completed. In resolution 2200 (XXI) of 16 December 1966, the Assembly adopted and opened for signature, ratification and accession three instruments: (*a*) the International Covenant on Economic, Social and Cultural Rights, (*b*) the International Covenant on Civil and Political Rights, and (*c*) the Optional Protocol to the International Covenant on Civil and Political Rights. The Optional Protocol provides machinery for the handling of complaints from individuals in specified circumstances.

34. Today the International Covenants and the Optional Protocol, together with the Universal Declaration of Human Rights, form the International Bill of Human Rights.

(a) *Similar provisions of the Covenants*

35. In line with the General Assembly's directive in resolution 543 (VI), that the two covenants should contain as many similar provisions as possible, the provisions of the preamble and of articles 1, 3 and 5 of the International Covenant on Civil and Political Rights are almost identical with the provisions of the preamble and of articles 1, 3 and 5 of the International Covenant on Economic, Social and Cultural Rights.

36. The preamble to each covenant serves as an introduction to the articles which follow: it sets forth general principles relating to the inherent dignity of the human person, portrays the ideal of the free man in accordance with the Universal Declaration of Human Rights, reiterates the obligation of States under the Charter of the United Nations to promote human rights, and reminds the individual of his responsibility to strive for the observance of human rights.

37. The first paragraph of each preamble is a statement of the general principle that "recognition of the inherent dignity and of the equal and inalienable rights of all members of the human family is the foundation of freedom, justice and peace in the world". This clause was taken from the first paragraph of the preamble to the Universal Declaration of Human Rights.

38. The second paragraph of each preamble sets out the origin of human rights, stating that they "derive from the inherent dignity of the human person".

39. The third paragraph of each preamble is based on the Universal Declaration of Human Rights as interpreted by the General Assembly in resolution 421 E (V) and reaffirmed in resolution 543 (VI). In those resolutions the General Assembly declared that "the enjoyment of civic and political freedoms and of economic, social and cultural rights are interconnected and interdependent", and that "when deprived of economic, social and cultural rights man does not represent the human person whom the Universal Declaration regards as the ideal of the free man".

40. It is in the third paragraph of the two preambles that a difference in emphasis and wording exists. In the International Covenant on Civil and Political Rights the third paragraph states that "the ideal of free human beings enjoying civil and political freedom and freedom from fear and want can only be achieved if conditions are created whereby everyone may enjoy his civil and political rights as well as his economic, social and cultural rights". In the International Covenant on Economic, Social and Cultural Rights it is declared that "the ideal of free human beings enjoying freedom from fear and want can only be achieved if conditions are created whereby everyone may enjoy his economic, social and cultural rights as well as his civil and political rights". These paragraphs were intended to underline the unity of the two covenants while at the same time maintaining the distinctive character of each.

41. Article 1 of the International Covenant on Civil and Political Rights is identical to article 1 of the International Covenant on Economic, Social and Cultural Rights; both reaffirm the principle that the right of self-determination is universal, and both call upon all States to undertake two obligations: (1) to promote the realization of the right to self-determination in all their territories, and (2) to respect the maintenance of that right in other States. Both Covenants state that "all peoples have the right of self-determination", and add that "by virtue of that right they freely determine their political status and freely pursue their economic, social and cultural development". Both further provide that "all peoples may, for their own ends, freely dispose of their natural wealth and resources . . .".

42. Under article 3 of both Covenants, States parties undertake to ensure the equal right of men and women to the enjoyment of all economic, social and cultural rights, and of all civil and political rights, set out in the respective instrument. The article not only reaffirms the principle of equality of men and women as regards human rights, but also enjoins States to make that principle a reality. The article carries out the General Assembly's instruction, in resolution 421 E (V), that the Covenant should include "an explicit recognition of equality of men and women in related rights, as set forth in the Charter of the United Nations".

43. Under article 5 of both Covenants "saving clauses" are provided to prevent the destruction or limitation of the rights recognized in other articles, and to safeguard rights recognized independently of the Covenants. Paragraph 1 of the article, derived from article 30 of the Universal Declaration of Human Rights, provides protection against misinterpretation of the Covenants to justify infringement of a right or freedom, or restriction of such a right or freedom to a greater extent than provided in the Covenants. Paragraph 2 covers possible conflicts between the Covenant in question and the laws, regulations and customs of contracting States, or agreements other than the Covenants binding upon them; and prevents States from limiting rights already enjoyed within their territories on the ground that such rights are not recognized, or are recognized to a lesser extent, in the Covenant.

(b) *Limitations permitted*

44. The rights and freedoms set out in the International Covenants on Human Rights are not absolute and are in each case subject to limitations. The Covenant on Civil and Political Rights in particular defines the admissible limitations or restrictions on the rights which it sets forth. While the formulation of the limitations clauses differs from article to article, it may be said that in general the Covenant provides that the rights and freedoms with which it deals should not be subject to any restrictions except those which are provided by law, are necessary to protect national security, public order (*ordre public*), public health or morals or the rights and freedoms of others.

45. In this connection the Commission on Human Rights emphasized, in resolution 23 (XXXVI) of 29 February 1980, that in the exercise of his rights and freedoms, everyone should be subject only to such limitations as were determined in the Charter of the United Nations, the Universal Declaration of Human Rights and the International Covenants on Human Rights and other relevant instruments, and that unlawful limitations or persecution of anyone exercising his human rights and fundamental freedoms was at variance with the obligations of States under those instruments to work for the full and effective enjoyment of human rights and fundamental freedoms.

(c) *International Covenant on Economic, Social and Cultural Rights*

46. In article 6 of the Covenant, the States parties recognize the right to work, including the right of everyone to the opportunity to gain his living by work which he freely chooses or accepts, and agree that they will take appropriate steps to safeguard this right, including the establishment of technical and vocational guidance and training programmes, policies and techniques in order to achieve steady economic, social and cultural development and full and productive employment under conditions safeguarding fundamental political and economic freedoms to the individual.

47. In article 7, the States parties recognize the right of everyone to the enjoyment of just and favourable conditions of work which ensure, in particular, fair wages and equal remuneration for work of equal value without distinction of any kind, in particular women being guaranteed conditions of work not inferior to those enjoyed by men, with equal pay for equal work; a decent living for themselves and their families; safe and healthy working conditions; equal opportunity for everyone to be promoted in his employment to an appropriate higher level, subject to no considerations other than those of seniority and competence; and rest,

leisure and reasonable limitation of working hours and periodic holidays with pay, as well as remuneration for public holidays.

48. In article 8, the States parties undertake to ensure the right of everyone to form trade unions and join the trade union of his choice, subject only to the rules of the organization concerned, for the promotion and protection of his economic and social interests; the right of trade unions to establish national federations or confederations and the right of the latter to form or join international trade-union organizations; the right of trade unions to function freely subject to no limitations other than those prescribed by law and which are necessary in a democratic society in the interests of national security or public order or for the protection of the rights and freedoms of others; and the right to strike, provided that it is exercised in conformity with the laws of the particular country.

49. In article 9, the States parties recognize the right of everyone to social security, including social insurance.

50. In article 10, the States parties recognize that the widest possible protection and assistance should be accorded to the family, that special protection should be accorded to mothers during a reasonable period before and after childbirth, and that special measures of protection and assistance should be taken on behalf of all children and young persons without any discrimination for reasons of parentage or other conditions.

51. In article 11, the States parties recognize the right of everyone to an adequate standard of living for himself and his family, including adequate food, clothing and housing, and to the continuous improvement of living conditions and, recognizing the fundamental right of everyone to be free from hunger, agree to improve methods of production, conservation and distribution of food and to ensure an equitable distribution of world food supplies in relation to need.

52. In article 12, the States parties recognize the right of everyone to the enjoyment of the highest attainable standard of physical and mental health, and agree that the steps to be taken to achieve the full realization of this right include those necessary for the reduction of the stillbirth-rate and of infant mortality and for the healthy development of the child, the improvement of all aspects of environmental and industrial hygiene; the prevention, treatment and control of epidemic, endemic, occupational and other diseases; and the creation of conditions which would assure to all medical services and medical attention in the event of sickness.

53. In article 13, the States parties recognize the right of everyone to education, and agree that education shall be directed to the full development of the human personality and the sense of its dignity, and shall strengthen respect for human rights and fundamental freedoms. They further agree that education shall enable all persons to participate effectively in a free society, promote understanding, tolerance and friendship among all nations and all racial, ethnic or religious groups, and further the activities of the United Nations for the maintenance of peace. Further they undertake to have respect for the liberty of parents and, when applicable, legal guardians to choose for their children schools, other than those established by the public authorities, which conform to such minimum educational standards as may be laid down or approved by the State and to ensure the religious and moral education of their children in conformity with their own convictions.

54. In article 14, the States parties undertake to work out and adopt a detailed plan of action to provide compulsory primary education free of charge in all territories under their jurisdiction if they have not already done so.

55. In article 15, the States parties recognize the right of everyone to take part in cultural life, to enjoy the benefits of scientific progress and its applications, and to benefit from the protection of the moral and material interests resulting from any scientific, literary or artistic production of which he is the author.

56. Articles 16 to 25 make up part IV of the Covenant, and provide for the submission by States parties of reports on the measures they have adopted and the progress made in achieving the observance of the rights mentioned above. Specialized agencies also are expected to submit reports on their progress in achieving the observance of the provisions of the Covenant which fall within the scope of their activities. The reports, directed to the Secretary-General of the United Nations, are transmitted by him to the Economic and Social Council and to the specialized agencies concerned.[2]

57. Under article 21, the Council "may submit from time to time to the General Assembly reports with recommendations of a general nature and a summary of the information received from the States Parties . . . and the specialized agencies on the measures taken and the progress made in achieving general observance of the rights recognized in the present Covenant". Under article 22, the Council "may bring to the attention of other organs of the United Nations, their subsidiary organs and specialized agencies concerned with furnishing technical assistance any matters arising out of the reports . . . which may assist such bodies in deciding, each within its field of competence, on the advisability of international measures likely to contribute to the effective progressive implementation of the present Covenant".

58. The Covenant entered into force on 3 January 1976, in accordance with article 27, three months after the date of the deposit with the Secretary-General of the United Nations of the thirty-fifth instrument of ratification or instrument of accession.

---

[2] For information on the establishment and composition of the Council's Committee on Economic, Social and Cultural Rights, see chapter I, section G 5. For information on the activities of the Committee, see chapter VII, section K.

(d) *International Covenant on Civil and Political Rights*

59. Substantive articles of the International Covenant on Civil and Political Rights provide for protection of the right to life (article 6) and lay down that no one shall be subjected to torture or to cruel, inhuman or degrading treatment or punishment (article 7); that no one shall be held in slavery; that slavery and the slave trade shall be prohibited; and that no one shall be held in servitude or required to perform compulsory labour (article 8); that no one shall be subjected to arbitrary arrest or detention (article 9); that all persons deprived of their liberty shall be treated with humanity (article 10); and that no one shall be imprisoned merely on the ground of inability to fulfil a contractual obligation (article 11).

60. These articles further provide for freedom of movement and freedom to choose a residence (article 12), and for limitations to be placed on the expulsion of aliens lawfully in the territory of a State party (article 13). They make provision in considerable detail for equality before the courts and tribunals, and for guarantees in criminal and civil procedure (article 14). They also provide for the prohibition of retroactive criminal legislation (article 15); lay down the right of everyone to recognition everywhere as a person before the law (article 16); and call for the prohibition of arbitrary or unlawful interference with an individual's privacy, family, home or correspondence (article 17).

61. The articles also provide for protection of the right to freedom of thought, conscience and religion (article 18) and to freedom of expression (article 19). They call for the prohibition by law of any propaganda for war and of any advocacy of national, racial or religious hatred that constitutes an incitement to discrimination, hostility or violence (article 20). They recognize the right of peaceful assembly (article 21) and the right to freedom of association (article 22). They also recognize the right of men and women of marriageable age to marry and to found a family, and the principle of equality of rights and responsibilities of spouses as to marriage, during marriage and at its dissolution (article 23). They lay down measures to protect the rights of children (article 24), and recognize the right of every citizen to take part in the government of his country (article 25). They provide that all persons are equal before the law and are entitled to the equal protection of the law (article 26); and they provide measures for the protection of members of such ethnic, religious or linguistic minorities as may exist in the territories of States parties to the Covenant (article 27). Finally the articles provide for the establishment of a Human Rights Committee (article 28),[3] responsible for supervising application of the measures of implementation set out in the Covenant (articles 40 to 45).

---

[3] For information concerning the work of the Committee and its organizational and procedural arrangements, see chapter VIII, section M.

(e) *Optional Protocol to the International Covenant on Civil and Political Rights*

62. The Optional Protocol to the International Covenant on Civil and Political Rights enables the Human Rights Committee, set up under the terms of that Covenant, to receive and consider communications from individuals claiming to be victims of violations of any of the rights set forth in the Covenant.

63. Under articles 1 to 6 of the Optional Protocol, a State party to the Covenant that becomes a party to the Protocol recognizes the Competence of the Human Rights Committee to receive and consider communications from individuals subject to its jurisdiction who claim to be victims of a violation by that State of a right set forth in the Covenant. Individuals who make such a claim, and who have exhausted all available domestic remedies, are entitled to submit written communications to the Committee.

64. Such communications as are determined to be admissible by the Committee are brought to the attention of the State party alleged to be violating a provision of the Covenant. Within six months, that State must submit to the Committee written explanations or statements clarifying the matter and indicating the remedy, if any, that it may have taken.

65. The Human Rights Committee considers the admissible communications, at closed meetings, in the light of all written information made available to it by the individual and the State party concerned. It then forwards its views to the State party and to the individual. A summary of its activities is included in the report which it submits annually to the General Assembly through the Economic and Social Council.

(f) *Entry into force of the Covenants and Optional Protocol*

66. The International Covenant on Economic, Social and Cultural Rights, adopted and opened for signature, ratification and accession by General Assembly resolution 2200 A (XXI) of 16 December 1966, entered into force on 3 January 1976, three months after the date of deposit with the Secretary-General of the thirty-fifth instrument of ratification or accession, as provided in article 27. As at 31 December 1987, the Covenant had been ratified or acceded to by 90 States.

67. The International Covenant on Civil and Political Rights, also adopted by resolution 2200 A (XXI) of 16 December 1966, entered into force on 23 March 976, three months after the date of deposit with the Secretary-General of the thirty-fifth instrument of ratification or accession, as provided in article 49. As at 31 December 1987, the Covenant had been ratified or acceded to by 87 States.

68. As at the same date, 21 States parties to the International Covenant on Civil and Political Rights had made the declaration under its article 41, recognizing

the competence of the Human Rights Committee "to receive and consider communications to the effect that a State Party claims that another State Party is not fulfilling its obligations" under the Covenant. The provisions of article 41 entered into force on 28 March 1979 in accordance with paragraph 2 of that article.

69. The Optional Protocol to the International Covenant on Civil and Political Rights entered into force simultaneously with that Covenant, having received the minimum of ten ratifications or accessions required. As at 31 December 1987, 40 States parties to the International Covenant on Civil and Political Rights had also become parties to the Protocol.

70. In response to the request of the General Assembly in resolution 2200 A (XXI), the Secretary-General has submitted reports on the status of the Covenant and Optional Protocol to the Assembly since 1967. The Assembly has considered the item, "International Covenants on Human Rights" annually since 1976, and has adopted resolutions 31/86, 32/66, 33/51, 34/45, 35/132, 36/58, 37/191, 38/116, 39/136, 40/115, 41/119 and 42/103.

71. In resolution 42/103 of 7 December 1987, the Assembly noted with appreciation the reports of the Committee on Economic, Social and Cultural Rights[4] and of the Human Rights Committee,[5] and noted with satisfaction that the majority of States parties to the International Covenant on Civil and Political Rights and, an increasing number of States parties to the International Covenant on Economic, Social and Cultural Rights, had been represented by experts for the presentation of their reports, thereby assisting the respective monitoring bodies in their work.

72. In the resolution, the Assembly emphasized the importance of the strictest compliance by States parties with their obligations under the Covenants and, where applicable, the Optional Protocol, bearing in mind the need for States parties to provide the fullest possible information during states of emergency, so that the justification and appropriateness of measures taken in these circumstances could be assessed; appealed to the States parties to review whether any reservation made in respect of the provisions of the International Covenants should be upheld; and urged all States parties to pay active attention to the protection and promotion of civil and political rights, as well as economic, social and cultural rights.

B. Human rights instruments monitored by special bodies

73. Four international conventions, in addition to the two Covenants, set human rights standards the implementation of which is monitored by special bodies:

the International Convention on the Elimination of All Forms of Racial Discrimination, monitored by the Committee on the Elimination of Racial Discrimination; the International Convention on the Suppression and Punishment of the Crime of *Apartheid,* monitored by the Group of Three; the Convention on the Elimination of All Forms of Discrimination against Women, monitored by the Committee on the Elimination of Discrimination against Women; and the Convention against Torture and Other Cruel, Inhuman or Degrading Treatment or Punishment, monitored by the Committee against Torture. In addition, a fifth instrument, the International Convention against *Apartheid* in Sports, envisages the establishment of a Commission against *Apartheid* in Sports six months after the Convention enters into force.

74. Basic provisions of these Conventions are summarized below.

1. INTERNATIONAL CONVENTION ON THE ELIMINATION OF ALL FORMS OF RACIAL DISCRIMINATION

75. The Convention was adopted and opened for signature and ratification by the General Assembly of the United Nations in resolution 2106 A (XX) of 21 December 1965, and entered into force on 4 January 1969. As at 31 December 1987, 124 States had become parties to the Convention and 12 of those States had made the declaration under its article 14 recognizing the competence of the Committee on the Elimination of Racial Discrimination[6] to receive and consider communications from individuals or groups of individuals within its jurisdiction claiming to be victims of a violation by hat State party of any of the rights set forth in the Convention.

76. The Convention consists of a preamble, followed by 25 articles, which are divided into three parts. Part I contains the substantive provisions, part II the measures of implementation, and part III the final clauses.

77. The preamble to the Convention sets out a number of considerations which the General Assembly bore in mind in preparing the instrument, among them that:

The Charter of the United Nations is based on the principles of the dignity and equality inherent in all human beings, and that all Member States have pledged themselves to take joint and separate action, in co-operation with the Organization, for the achievement of one of the purposes of the United Nations which is to promote and encourage universal respect for and observance of human rights and fundamental freedoms for all, without distinction as to race, sex, language or religion;

The Universal Declaration of Human Rights proclaims that all human beings are born free and equal in dignity and rights and that everyone is entitled to all the rights and freedoms set out therein, without distinction of any kind, in particular as to race, colour or national origin;

All human beings are equal before the law and are entitled to equal protection of the law against any discrimination and against any incitement to discrimination;

---

[4] *Official Records of the Economic and Social Council, 1987, Supplement No. 17* (E/1987/28).

[5] *Official Records of the General Assembly, Forty-second Session, Supplement No. 40* (A/42/40).

[6] For the mandate, composition and membership of the Committee, see chapter I, section G 1, above. For a summary of its activities, see chapter IV, section A, 5 (b), below.

The United Nations has condemned colonialism and all practices of segregation and discrimination associated therewith, in whatever form and wherever they exist, and that the Declaration on the Granting of Independence to Colonial Countries and Peoples . . . has affirmed and solemnly proclaimed the necessity of bringing them to a speedy and unconditional end;

and

The United Nations Declaration on the Elimination of All Forms of Racial Discrimination . . . solemnly affirms the necessity of speedily eliminating racial discrimination throughout the world in all its forms and manifestations and of securing understanding of and respect for the dignity of the human person.

78. The preamble further expresses the General Assembly's convictions (a) "that any doctrine of superiority based on racial differentiation is scientifically false, morally condemnable, socially unjust and dangerous"; (b) "that there is no justification for racial discrimination, in theory or in practice, anywhere"; and (c) "that the existence of racial barriers is repugnant to the ideals of any human society"; and it reaffirms "that discrimination between human beings on the grounds of race, colour or ethnic origin is an obstacle to friendly and peaceful relations among nations and is capable of disturbing peace and security among peoples and the harmony of persons living side by side within one and the same State". Part I of the Convention (articles 1-7) deals with substantive matters. Article 1 defines the term "racial discrimination" as meaning "any distinction, exclusion, restriction or preference based on race, colour, descent or national or ethnic origin which has the purpose or effect of nullifying or impairing the recognition, enjoyment or exercise, on an equal footing, of human rights and fundamental freedoms . . .". Among other things, the article provides that "special measures taken for the sole purpose of securing adequate advancement of certain racial or ethnic groups or individuals requiring such protection as may be necessary in order to ensure such groups or individuals equal enjoyment or exercise of human rights and fundamental freedoms shall not be deemed racial discrimination, provided, however, that such measures do not, as a consequence, lead to the maintenance of separate rights for different racial groups and that they shall not be continued after the objectives for which they were taken have been achieved".

79. By article 2, paragraph 1, States parties "condemn racial discrimination and undertake to pursue by all appropriate means and without delay a policy of eliminating racial discrimination in all its forms and promoting understanding among all races". In particular they undertake (a) "to engage in no act or practice of racial discrimination against persons, groups of persons or institutions and to ensure that all public authorities and public institutions, national and local, shall act in conformity with this obligation"; (b) "not to sponsor, defend or support racial discrimination by any persons or organizations"; (c) to "take effective measures to review governmental, national and local policies, and to amend, rescind or nullify any laws and regulations which have the effect of creating or perpetuating racial discrimination wherever it exists"; (d) to "prohibit and

bring to an end, by all appropriate means, including legislation as required by circumstances, racial discrimination by any persons, group or organization"; (e) "to encourage, where appropriate, integrationist multiracial organizations and movements and other means of eliminating barriers between races, and to discourage anything which tends to strengthen racial division". Paragraph 2 requires the parties to take "special and concrete measures to ensure the adequate development and protection of certain racial groups or individuals belonging to them, for the purpose of guaranteeing them the full and equal enjoyment of human rights and fundamental freedoms", provided that these measures do not "entail as a consequence the maintenance of unequal or separate rights for different racial groups after the objectives for which they were taken have been achieved".

80. In article 3, States parties "condemn racial segregation and *apartheid* and undertake to prevent, prohibit and eradicate all practices of this nature in territories under their jurisdiction". Under article 4, they "condemn all propaganda and all organizations which are based on ideas or theories of superiority of one race or group of persons of one colour or ethnic origin, or which attempt to justify or promote racial hatred and discrimination in any form, and undertake to adopt immediate and positive measures, designed to eradicate all incitement to, or acts of, such discrimination . . .". Among other things, they are required to "declare an offence punishable by law all dissemination of ideas based on racial superiority or hatred, incitement to racial discrimination, as well as all acts of violence or incitement to such acts against any race or group of persons of another colour or ethnic origin, and also the provision of any assistance to racist activities, including the financing thereof"; to "declare illegal and prohibit organizations, and also organized and all other propaganda activities, which promote and incite racial discrimination", and to "recognize participation in such organization or activities as an offence punishable by law"; and not to "permit public authorities or public institutions, national or local, to promote or incite racial discrimination".

81. By article 5, States parties "undertake to prohibit and to eliminate racial discrimination in all its forms and to guarantee the right to everyone, without distinction as to race, colour, or national or ethnic origin, to equality before the law", notably in the enjoyment of

(a) The right to equal treatment before the tribunals and all other organs administering justice;

(b) The right to security of person and protection by the State against violence or bodily harm, whether inflicted by government officials or by any individual, group or institution;

(c) Political rights, in particular the rights to participate in elections—to vote and to stand for election—on the basis of universal and equal suffrage, to take part in the Government as well as in the conduct of public affairs at any level and to have equal access to public service;

(d) Other civil rights . . .

(e) Economic, social and cultural rights . . .

(*f*) The right of access to any place or service intended for use by the general public, such as transport, hotels, restaurants, cafés, theatres and parks.

82.   In article 6, States parties undertake to "assure to everyone within their jurisdiction effective protection and remedies, through the competent national tribunals and other State institutions, against any acts of racial discrimination which violate his human rights and fundamental freedoms contrary to this Convention, as well as the right to seek from such tribunals just and adequate reparation or satisfaction for any damage suffered as a result of such discrimination". By article 7, they "undertake to adopt immediate and effective measures, particularly in the fields of teaching, education, culture and information, with a view to combating prejudices which lead to racial discrimination and to promoting understanding, tolerance and friendship among nations and racial or ethnical groups, as well as to propagating the purposes and principles of the Charter of the United Nations, the Universal Declaration of Human Rights, the United Nations Declaration on the Elimination of All Forms of Racial Discrimination, and this Convention".

83.   Part II (articles 8-16) sets out measures for the implementation of the Convention. Article 8 provides for the establishment of a Committee on the Elimination of Racial Discrimination, and article 10 authorizes the Committee to adopt its own rules of procedure. Article 9 sets out the undertaking of States parties to the Convention to submit to the Secretary-General of the United Nations, for consideration by the Committee, reports on the legislative, judicial, administrative or other measures which they have adopted and which give effect to the provisions of the Convention. These articles are dealt with in greater detail in chapter IV, section A, below.

84.   Article 11 authorizes a State party, if it considers that another State party is not giving effect to the provisions of the Convention, to bring the matter to the attention of the Committee. The Committee then transmits the communication to the State party concerned, which must submit to the Committee within three months, "written explanations or statements clarifying the matter and the remedy, if any, that may have been taken by that State". If the matter "is not adjusted to the satisfaction of both parties . . . within six months after the receipt by the receiving State of the initial communication", either State has the right "to refer the matter again to the Committee" by notifying it and also the other State.

85.   Article 12 provides that "after the Committee has obtained and collated all the information it deems necessary, the Chairman shall appoint an *ad hoc* Conciliation Commission . . . comprising five persons who may or may not be members of the Committee". The information obtained and collated by the Committee is made available to the Commission. Under article 13, "when the Commission has fully considered the matter, it shall prepare and submit to the Chairman of the Committee a report embodying its findings on all ques-

tions of fact relevant to the issue between the parties and containing such recommendations as it may think proper for the amicable settlement of the dispute". The Chairman of the Committee communicates the report of the Commission to each of the States parties to the dispute and these States must, within three months, inform the Chairman of the Committee whether or not they accept the recommendation of the Commission. If they fail to do so, the Chairman of the Committee shall communicate the report of the Commission and the declarations of the States parties concerned to the other States parties to the Convention.

86.   Under article 14, a State party "may at any time declare that it recognizes the competence of the Committee to receive and consider communications from individuals or groups of individuals within its jurisdiction claiming to be victims of a violation by that State party of any of the rights set forth in this Convention". The Committee may not receive communications concerning a State party which has not made such a declaration. A procedure is established whereby the Committee considers communications in the light of all information made available to it by the State party concerned and by the petitioner, and forwards its suggestions and recommendations, if any, to the State party concerned and to the petitioner.

87.   Paragraph 1 of article 15 stipulates that the provisions of the Convention "shall in no way limit the right of petition granted" to colonial peoples "by other international instruments or by the United Nations and its specialized agencies". Paragraph 2 provides (*a*) that the Committee on the Elimination of Racial Discrimination "shall receive copies of the petitions from, and submit expressions of opinion and recommendations on these petitions to, the bodies of the United Nations which deal with matters directly related to the principles and objectives of this Convention in their consideration of petitions from the inhabitants of Trust and Non-Self-Governing Territories and all other Territories to which General Assembly resolution 1514 (XV) applies, relating to matters covered by this Convention which are before these bodies"; and (*b*) that the Committee "shall receive from the competent bodies of the United Nations copies of the reports concerning the legislative, judicial, administrative or other measures directly related to the principles and objectives of this Convention applied by the administering Powers" within the above-mentioned Territories, "and shall express opinions and make recommendations to these bodies".

88.   Article 16 specifies that the provisions of the Convention concerning the settlement of disputes or complaints "shall be applied without prejudice to other procedures for settling disputes or complaints in the field of discrimination laid down in the constituent instruments of, or in conventions adopted by, the United Nations and its specialized agencies, and shall not prevent the States parties from having recourse to other procedures for settling a dispute in accordance with general or special international agreements in force between them".

89. Part III of the Convention (articles 17 to 25) deals with such matters as: procedures for signing and ratifying the Convention and for depositing instruments of ratification; the date of entry into force of the Convention; the making of reservations to the Convention at the time of ratification or accession; procedure for denunciation of the Convention by a State party; and procedure for revision of the Convention.

2. INTERNATIONAL CONVENTION ON THE SUPPRESSION AND PUNISHMENT OF THE CRIME OF *APARTHEID*

90. In resolution 2922 (XXVII) of 15 November 1972, the General Assembly, recognizing "the urgent need to take further effective measures with a view to the suppression and punishment of *apartheid*", noted with satisfaction "the efforts made in order to elaborate an international document on the suppression and punishment of the crime of *apartheid*" and requested the Secretary-General to transmit to the Special Committee on *Apartheid*, and to States for their comments and views, the revised draft convention which had been submitted to it by Guinea, Nigeria and the Union of Soviet Socialist Republics,[7] and the amendments thereto submitted by Egypt[8]. The Assembly invited the Economic and Social Council to request the Commission on Human Rights to consider the revised draft convention at its twenty-ninth session, in 1973, and to submit the results of its consideration to the General Assembly.

91. The Commission on Human Rights, after examining the documentation made available to it, established a Working Group which agreed on 17 articles for inclusion in the draft convention. The Working Group decided not to consider an article on implementation of the convention, owing to lack of time and because some members believed that there should be specific directives from the Commission on the nature of the implementation machinery. In resolution 16 (XXIX) of 2 April 1973, the Commission approved the preamble and 17 articles of the draft convention and transmitted them, through the Council, to the General Assembly.

92. On 30 November 1973 the General Assembly, in resolution 3068 (XXVIII), adopted and opened for signature and ratification the International Convention on the Suppression and Punishment of the Crime of *Apartheid*, and appealed to all States to sign and ratify the Convention as soon as possible. The Assembly requested all Governments and intergovernmental and non-governmental organizations "to acquaint the public as widely as possible with the text of the Convention, using all the information media at their disposal"; and requested the Secretary-General "to ensure the urgent and wide dissemination of the Convention".

93. The General Assembly, by resolution 3380 (XXX) of 10 November 1975, appealed to the Governments of all States to sign, ratify and implement the Convention without delay, and requested the Secretary-General to submit to it annual reports on the status of the Convention.

94. The Convention entered into force on 18 July 1976, the thirtieth day after the date of the deposit with the Secretary-General of the twentieth instrument of ratification or accession. In resolution 31/80 of 13 December 1976, the Assembly welcomed the entry into force of the Convention, appealed to all States to accede to it, and decided to consider annually the item entitled "Status of the International Convention on the Suppression and Punishment of the Crime of *Apartheid*".

95. Since that time the General Assembly has reviewed at each regular session reports by the Secretary-General on the status of the Convention. Since 1977, the Assembly has annually appealed to those States that have not yet done so to ratify or to accede to the Convention without delay. As at 31 December 1987, 86 States had ratified or acceded to the Convention.

96. In the Convention, the States parties, observing that the General Assembly of the United Nations has adopted a number of resolutions in which the policies and practices of *apartheid* are condemned as a crime against humanity and that the Security Council has emphasized that *apartheid* and its continued intensification and expansion seriously disturb and threaten international peace and security, declare "that *apartheid* is a crime against humanity and that inhuman acts resulting from the policies and practices of *apartheid* and similar policies and practices of racial segregation and discrimination . . . are crimes violating the principles of international law, in particular the purposes and principles of the Charter of the United Nations, and constituting a serious threat to international peace and security". The States parties further declare criminal "those organizations, institutions and individuals committing the crime of *apartheid*".

97. The Convention defines the crime of *apartheid*, in article II, as applying "to the following inhuman acts committed for the purpose of establishing and maintaining domination by one racial group of persons over any other racial group of persons and systematically oppressing them:

(*a*) Denial to a member or members of a racial group or groups of the right to life and liberty of person:

(i) By murder of members of a racial group or group;

(ii) By the infliction upon the members of a racial group or groups of serious bodily or mental harm, by the infringement of their freedom or dignity, or by subjecting them to torture or to cruel, inhuman or degrading treatment or punishment;

(iii) By arbitrary arrest and illegal imprisonment of the members of a racial group or groups:

(*b*) Deliberate imposition on a racial group or groups of living conditions calculated to cause its or their physical destruction in whole or in part;

(*c*) Any legislative measures and other measures calculated to prevent a racial group or groups from participation in the political, social, economic and cultural life of the country and the deliberate creation of conditions preventing the full development of such a group or groups, in particular by denying to members of a racial group or

[7] *Official Records of the General Assembly, Twenty-seventh Session, Annexes,* agenda item 50, document A/8880, para. 42.

[8] *Ibid.,* para. 43.

groups basic human rights and freedoms, including the right to work, the right to form recognized trade unions, the right to education, the right to leave and to return to their country, the right to a nationality, the right to freedom of movement and residence, the right to freedom of opinion and expression, and the right to freedom of peaceful assembly and association;

(d) Any measures, including legislative measures, designed to divide the population along racial lines by the creation of separate reserves and ghettos for the members of a racial group or groups, the prohibition of mixed marriages among members of various racial groups, the expropriation of landed property belonging to a racial group or groups or to members thereof;

(e) Exploitation of the labour of the members of a racial group or groups, in particular by submitting them to forced labour;

(f) Persecution of organizations and persons, by depriving them of their fundamental rights and freedoms, because they oppose *apartheid*."

98. Article III makes it clear that "international criminal responsibility shall apply, irrespective of the motive involved, to individuals, members of organizations and institutions and representatives of the State, whether residing in the territory of the State in which the acts are perpetrated or in some other State, whenever they: (a) commit, participate in, directly incite or conspire in the commission of the acts mentioned in article II . . ., or (b) directly abet, encourage or cooperate in the commission of the crime of *apartheid*."

99. Under article IV, States parties undertake "to adopt any legislative or other measures necessary to suppress as well as to prevent any encouragement of the crime of *apartheid*", and to "bring to trial and punish . . . persons responsible for, or accused of, the acts defined in article II . . . whether or not such persons reside in the territory of the State in which the acts are committed or are nationals of that State or of some other State or are stateless persons".

100. Article V states that "persons charged with the acts enumerated in article II . . . may be tried by a competent tribunal of any State Party to the Convention which may acquire jurisdiction over the person of the accused or by an international penal tribunal having jurisdiction with respect to those States Parties which shall have accepted its jurisdiction".

101. Under article VI, States parties "undertake to accept and carry out . . . the decisions taken by the Security Council aimed at the prevention, suppression and punishment of the crime of *apartheid*, and to co-operate in the implementation of decisions adopted by other competent organs of the United Nations with a view to achieving the purposes of the Convention".

102. Under article VII, they undertake "to submit periodic reports . . . on the legislative, judicial, administrative or other measures that they have adopted and that give effect to the provisions of the Convention". These reports are to be examined by a group consisting of three members of the Commission on Human Rights who are also representatives of States parties to the Convention. The group meets each year for a period of not more than five days either before the opening or after the closing of the session of the Commission.

103. Article VIII provides that "any State Party . . . may call upon any competent organ of the United Nations to take such action under the Charter of the United Nations as it considers appropriate for the prevention and suppression of the crime of *apartheid*". Under article X, the States parties empower the Commission on Human Rights "to prepare, on the basis of reports from competent organs of the United Nations and periodic reports from States Parties to the present Convention, a list of individuals, organizations, institutions and representatives of States which are alleged to be responsible for the crimes enumerated in article II . . . as well as those against whom legal proceedings have been undertaken by States Parties to the Convention". Article XI provides that "acts enumerated in article II . . . shall not be considered political crimes for the purpose of extradition", and that "States Parties . . . undertake in such cases to grant extradition in accordance with their legislation and with the treaties in force."

104. The final clauses of the Convention provide that "disputes between States Parties arising out of the interpretation, application or implementation of the present Convention which have not been settled by negotiation shall, at the request of the States Parties to the dispute, be brought before the International Court of Justice, save where the parties to the dispute have agreed on some other form of settlement".

105. In resolution 31/80 of 13 December 1976, the General Assembly welcomed the entry into force of the International Convention on the Suppression and Punishment of the Crime of *Apartheid* and invited "the Chairman of the thirty-third session of the Commission on Human Rights to appoint a group consisting of three members of the Commission as provided for by article IX of the Convention". The Assembly further invited the Commission "to undertake the functions set out in article X . . . in particular to prepare a list of individuals, organizations, institutions and representatives of States . . . alleged to be responsible for the crimes enumerated in article II . . .".

106. At its thirty-third session, by resolution 13 (XXXIII) of 11 March 1977, the Commission on Human Rights established the three-member group in accordance with article IX of the Convention,[9] and decided that it should meet for a period of five days before the Commission's thirty-fourth session. It invited States parties to the Convention to submit reports on the legislative, judicial, administrative and other measures that they had adopted and that gave effect to the provisions of the Convention and requested United Nations organs, when transmitting copies of petitions to the Committee on the Elimination of Racial Discrimination under article 15 of the International Convention on the Elimination of All Forms of Racial Discrimination, to draw the attention of the Commission to complaints concerning acts enumerated in article II of the International Convention on the Suppression and Punishment of the Crime of *Apartheid*.

---

[9] For information about the establishment and composition of the Group of Three, see chapter I, section G 6. For information about its activities, see chapter V, section A 4.

107. The Commission also requested the competent United Nations organs to provide it with information relevant to the preparation of the list of individuals, organizations, institutions and representatives of States alleged to be responsible for the crimes enumerated in article II of the Convention, as well as those against whom, legal proceedings had been undertaken by States parties to the Convention. It further requested those organs to provide it with information concerning measures taken by the authorities responsible for the administration of Trust and Non-Self-Governing Territories, and all other territories to which General Assembly resolution 1514 (XV) of 14 December 1960 applied, with regard to such individuals alleged to be responsible for crimes under article II of the Convention who were believed to be under their territorial and administrative jurisdiction.

108. At its thirty-fourth session, the Commission received the first report of the Group of Three,[10] and, in resolution 7 (XXXIV) of 22 February 1978, noted the report, in particular the general guidelines proposed by the Group concerning the form and contents of reports to be submitted by States parties under article VII of the Convention. It requested States parties to take the guidelines fully into account in preparing their reports, and called upon them to submit their first report not later than two years after becoming parties to the Convention.

109. As at 31 December 1987, the Group of Three had held 10 sessions, each for a period of no more than five days before the Commission's annual session.[11]

3. CONVENTION ON THE ELIMINATION OF ALL FORMS OF DISCRIMINATION AGAINST WOMEN

110. The General Assembly, by resolution 3521 (XXX) of 15 December 1975, requested the Commission on the Status of Women to complete, in 1976, the elaboration of the draft convention on the elimination of discrimination against women, which had been on the Commission's agenda since 1970. The adoption of such a convention had been envisaged in the Programme for the United Nations Decade for Women prepared by the World Conference of the International Women's Year.

111. The Commission on the Status of Women completed the preparation of the draft convention at its twenty-sixth session and resumed twenty-sixth session held at Geneva from 13 September to 1 October 1976, and from 6 to 17 December 1976, respectively. On the recommendation of the Commission, the Economic and Social Council submitted the draft to the General Assembly.

112. In the Assembly, the draft was considered by Working Groups of the Third Committee at the thirty-second, thirty-third and thirty-fourth sessions. The As-

[10] E/CN.4/1286.
[11] E/CN.4/1988/30.

sembly, by resolution 34/180 of 18 December 1979, adopted and opened for signature, ratification and accession the Convention on the Elimination of All Forms of Discrimination against Women, and expressed the hope that the Convention would be signed and ratified or acceded to without delay and would come into force at an early date.

Provisions of the Convention

113. The Convention consists of 30 articles, and is divided into a preamble and six parts. Part I (articles 1 to 6) contains a number of general provisions; part II (articles 7 to 9) contains provisions relating to political rights; part III (articles 10 to 14) contains provisions relating to social and economic rights; part IV (articles 15 and 16) contains provisions relating to civil and family rights; part V (articles 17 to 22) contains provisions relating to implementation; and part VI (articles 23 to 30) contains a number of final clauses.

114. In the preamble, the States parties to the Convention recall that discrimination against women violates the principles of equality of rights and respect for human dignity, is an obstacle to the participation of women, on equal terms with men, in the political social, economic and cultural life of their countries, hampers the growth of the prosperity of society and the family, and makes more difficult the full development of the potentialities of women in the service of their countries and of humanity; and express their determination to implement the principles set forth in the Declaration on the Elimination of Discrimination against Women. In article 1, the term "discrimination against women" is defined, for the purposes of the Convention, as meaning any distinction, exclusion or restriction made on the basis of sex which has the effect or purpose of impairing or nullifying the recognition, enjoyment or exercise by women, irrespective of their marital status, on a basis of equality of men and women, of human rights and fundamental freedoms in the political, economic, social, cultural, civil or any other field.

115. The Convention contains five articles of a general nature, which are:

Article 2, by which States parties condemn discrimination against women in all its forms and agree to pursue by all appropriate means and without delay a policy of eliminating discrimination against women through legislation and other means;

Article 3, by which States parties agree to take in all fields, in particular in the political, social, economic and cultural fields, all appropriate measures to ensure the full development and advancement of women;

Article 4, which provides that "adoption by States Parties of temporary special measures aimed at accelerating *de facto* equality between men and women shall not be considered discrimination as defined in the present Convention";

Article 5, by which States parties agree to take measures to eliminate prejudices and practices based on the idea of the inferiority or the superiority of either of the sexes or on stereotyped roles for men and women, and to ensure that family education includes a proper understanding of maternity as a social function and the recognition of the common responsibility of men and women in the upbringing and development of their children; and

Article 6, by which States parties undertake to take measures to suppress all forms of traffic in women and exploitation of the prostitution of women.

116. In part II of the Convention, States parties undertake to take all appropriate measures to eliminate discrimination against women in the political and public life of the country and, in particular, to ensure to women, on equal terms with men, the right (*a*) to vote in all elections and public referenda and to be eligible for election to all publicly elected bodies, (*b*) to participate in the formulation of government policy and the implementation thereof and to hold public office and perform all public functions at all levels of government, and (*c*) to participate in non-governmental organizations and associations concerned with the public and political life of the country; as well as the opportunity to represent their Governments at the international level and to participate in the work of international organizations.

117. In addition, in article 9, States parties undertake to grant women equal rights with men to acquire, change or retain their nationality; and to grant women equal rights with men with respect to the nationality of their children.

118. In part III of the Convention, States parties undertake to take all appropriate measures to eliminate discrimination against women in order to ensure them equal rights with men in the fields of education (article 10), employment (article 11), health care (article 12), and other areas of economic and social life (article 13). In addition, they undertake (article 14) to take into account the particular problems faced by rural women and the significant roles which such women play in the economic survival of their families, and to take all appropriate measures to eliminate discrimination against women in rural areas in order to ensure that they participate in and benefit from rural development on a basis of equality with men.

119. In part IV of the Convention, States parties undertake to accord women equality before the law (article 15), and to eliminate discrimination against women in all matters relating to marriage and family relations (article 16).

120. Part V of the Convention sets out measures for the implementation of the Convention. Article 17 provides for the establishment of "a Committee on the Elimination of Discrimination against Women . . . consisting, at the time of entry into force of the Convention, of eighteen and, after ratification or accession to the Convention by the thirty-fifth State Party,

of twenty-three experts of high moral standing and competence in the field covered by the Convention".[12]

121. Article 18 sets out the undertaking of States parties "to submit to the Secretary-General of the United Nations, for consideration by the Committee, a report on the legislative, judicial, administrative or other measures which they have adopted to give effect to the provisions of the present Convention and on the progress made in this respect; (*a*) within one year after the entry into force for the State concerned; (*b*) thereafter at least every four years and further whenever the Committee so requests".

122. Article 19 authorizes the Committee to adopt its own rules of procedure, and specifies that its officers shall be elected for a term of two years. Article 20 provides that the Committee shall normally meet for a period of not more than two weeks annually, and that its meetings shall normally be held at United Nations Headquarters or at any other convenient place as determined by the Committee.

123. Under Article 21 the Committee is to report annually, through the Economic and Social Council, to the General Assembly on its activities. It may make suggestions and general recommendations based on the examination of reports and information received from States parties. The reports are transmitted to the Commission on the Status of Women for its information.

124. Article 22 provides that "the specialized agencies shall be entitled to be represented at the consideration of the implementation of such provisions . . . as fall within the scope of their activities", and further that "the Committee may invite the specialized agencies to submit reports on the implementation of the Convention in areas falling within the scope of their activities".

125. Part VI of the Convention deals with such matters as: procedures for signing and ratifying the Convention and for depositing instruments of ratification (article 25); procedure for revision of the Convention (article 26); the date of entry into force of the Convention (article 27); the making of reservations to the Convention at the time of ratification or accession (article 28); and the procedure for settling any dispute between two or more States parties concerning the interpretation or application of the Convention (article 29).

126. Part VI also contains a provision (article 23) to the effect that nothing in the Convention shall affect any provisions that are more conducive to the achievement of equality between men and women which may be contained (*a*) in the legislation of a State party, or (*b*) in any other international convention, treaty or agreement in force for that State; as well as a provision (article 24) that "States Parties undertake to adopt all necessary measures at the national level aimed at achieving the full realization of the rights recognized in the present Convention".

---

[12] For information concerning the activities of the Committee, see chapter VI, section A, 3.

127. The General Assembly, in resolution 34/180 of 18 December 1979, adopted the Convention and opened it for signature, ratification and accession. The Convention entered into force on 3 September 1981, in accordance with article 27. As at 31 December 1987, 94 States had become parties to the Convention.

4. CONVENTION AGAINST TORTURE AND OTHER CRUEL, INHUMAN OR DEGRADING TREATMENT OR PUNISHMENT

128. The General Assembly, in resolution 3452 (XXX) of 9 December 1975, adopted and proclaimed the Declaration on the Protection of All Persons from Being Subjected to Torture and Other Cruel, Inhuman or Degrading Treatment or Punishment. Two years later, in resolution 32/62 of 8 December 1977, the Assembly requested the Commission on Human Rights to draw up a draft convention against torture and other cruel, inhuman or degrading treatment or punishment in the light of the principles which had been embodied in the Declaration.

129. The Commission carried out the work of preparing the draft convention as a matter of highest priority at each of its annual sessions between 1979 and 1984, entrusting this task to an open-ended Working Group which met for one week prior to each session of the Commission. At its fortieth session the Commission decided, in resolution 1984/21 of 6 March 1984, to transmit to the General Assembly the report of the Working Group containing the draft convention, the comments of Governments on that draft, and the summary records of the Commission's debate on the item.

130. After examining the draft convention and other relevant documentation the Assembly, in resolution 39/46 of 10 December 1984, expressed its appreciation for the work of the Commission and adopted the Convention against Torture and other Cruel, Inhuman or Degrading Treatment or Punishment, opening it for signature, ratification and accession.

131. In adopting the Convention the Assembly called upon all Governments to consider signing and ratifying it as a matter of priority. The Commission on Human Rights also called for early ratification, and invited all States ratifying or acceding to the Convention to consider the possibility of making the declarations provided for in articles 21 and 22, recognizing the competence of the Committee against Torture in certain circumstances.

132. The Convention entered into force on 26 June 1987. As at 31 December 1987 it had been ratified or acceded to by 28 States, 10 of which had made the declarations provided for in articles 21 and 22. Under Article 21, a State party may declare that it recognizes the competence of the Committee against Torture to receive and consider communications to the effect that one State party claims that another State party is not fulfilling its obligations under the Convention. Under article 22, a State party may declare that it recognizes the competence of the Committee to receive and consider communications from or on behalf of victims of a violation by a State party of the provisions of the Convention.

133. The term "torture" is defined in article 1 of the Convention as meaning "any act by which severe pain or suffering, whether physical or mental, is intentionally inflicted on a person for such purposes as obtaining from him or from a third person information or a confession, punishing him for an act he or a third person has committed or is suspected of having committed, or intimidating or coercing him or a third person, or for any reason based on discrimination of any kind, when such pain or suffering is inflicted by or at the instigation of or with the consent or acquiescence of a public official or other person acting in an official capacity. It does not include pain or suffering arising only from, inherent in or incidental to lawful sanctions".

134. Article 2 provides that each State party shall take effective legislative, administrative, judicial or other measures to prevent acts of torture in any territory under its jurisdiction; and that no exceptional circumstances whatsoever, nor an order from a superior officer or a public authority, may be invoked as a justification of torture.

135. Article 3 prohibits the extradition of a person to another State where there are substantial grounds for believing that he would be in danger of being subjected to torture.

136. Under article 4, each State must ensure that all acts of torture are offences under its criminal law, punishable by appropriate penalties which take into account their grave nature. Under article 5, each State must establish its jurisdiction over such offences (a) when committed in any of its territories or on board a ship or aircraft registered by that State; (b) when the alleged offender is a national of that State; and (c) when the victim is a national of that State if that State considers it appropriate. It must also establish its jurisdiction over such offences in cases where the alleged offender is present in any territory under its jurisdiction and it does not extradite him to another State.

137. Articles 6 to 9 deal with procedures to be followed in arresting, detaining or extraditing a person alleged to have committed an act of torture, and provide that the States parties will afford to one another the greatest measure of assistance in connection with related criminal proceedings.

138. Under article 10, each State party undertakes to ensure that education and information regarding the prohibition against torture are fully included in the training of all law enforcement personnel and in the instructions issued to them. Under article 11, each State party agrees to keep under systematic review interrogation rules, instructions, methods and practices, as well as arrangements for the custody and treatment of persons subjected to any form of arrest, detention or im-

prisonment, with a view to preventing any cases of torture.

139. Articles 12 to 15 provide for prompt and impartial investigation whenever there is reasonable ground to believe that an act of torture has been committed, in which the rights of the individual complainant and of witnesses are protected and in which both the complainant and the witnesses are also protected against ill-treatment or intimidation as a consequence of the complaint or of any evidence given. Provision is made under article 14, in particular, for ensuring that the victim of an act of torture obtains redress and has an enforceable right to fair and adequate compensation, including the means for as full rehabilitation as possible.

140. Under article 16, each State party undertakes to prevent, in the territories under its jurisdiction, other acts of cruel, inhuman or degrading treatment or punishment which do not amount to torture as defined in article 1, when such acts are committed by, or at the instigation of, a public official or other person acting in an official capacity.

141. Measures of implementation of the Convention are set out in part II (articles 17 to 24) which provide for the establishment of the Committee against Torture to consider reports submitted by States parties on measures they have taken to give effect to their undertakings under the Convention.[13]

142. In addition to considering these reports, investigating them and forwarding them to the States parties and to the General Assembly with its comments, under article 20 the Committee is authorized to make confidential inquiries which may include on-the-spot inquiries in agreement with the State party concerned when it receives reliable information indicating that torture is being practised systematically in the territory of that State party.

143. The First Meeting of the States parties to the Convention was convened by the Secretary-General at the United Nations Office at Geneva on 26 November 1987 to elect the members of the Committee against Torture. In accordance with article 17 of the Convention, 10 experts were elected as members of the Committee. At that meeting the States parties also took decision relating to their financial responsibilities under article 17, paragraph 7, and article 18, paragraph 5, of the Convention. The first session of the Committee was scheduled to be held at Geneva from 18 to 22 April 1988.

C. OTHER HUMAN RIGHTS INSTRUMENTS PREPARED WITHIN THE UNITED NATIONS SYSTEM

144. In addition to the Universal Declaration of Human Rights, the International Covenants on Human Rights and the international conventions under which special monitoring bodies were established, mentioned above, the United Nations and its specialized agencies developed and put into effect in recent years a wide variety of international instruments aimed at setting standards in the field of human rights and promoting the universal realization of those rights. With a few exceptions, these instruments are either self-executing or rely upon long-established international bodies to perform any necessary supervisory functions.

145. United Nations organs elaborated, and opened for ratification or accession, a surprisingly large number of international human rights conventions between 1948 and 1987, among them the following:[14]

Convention on the Prevention and Punishment of the Crime of Genocide (General Assembly resolution 260 (III) of 9 December 1948). The Convention entered into force on 12 January 1951.

Convention for the Suppression of the Traffic in Persons and of the Exploitation of the Prostitution of Others (General Assembly resolution 317 (IV) of 2 December 1949). The Convention entered into force on 25 July 1951.

Convention relating to the Status of Refugees (adopted on 28 July 1951 by the United Nations Conference of Plenipotentiaries on the Status of Refugees and Stateless Persons convened by General Assembly resolution 429 (V) of 14 December 1950). The Convention entered into force on 22 April 1954.

Convention on the International Right of Correction (General Assembly resolution 630 (VII) of 16 December 1952). The Convention entered into force on 24 August 1962.

Convention on the Political Rights of Women (General Assembly resolution 640 (VII) of 20 December 1952). The Convention entered into force on 7 July 1954.

Protocol amending the Slavery Convention signed at Geneva on 25 September 1926 (General Assembly resolution 794 (VIII) of 23 October 1953). The Protocol entered into force on 7 December 1953.

Convention relating to the Status of Stateless Persons (adopted on 28 September 1954 by a Conference of Plenipotentiaries convened by Economic and Social Council resolution 526 A (XVII) of 26 April 1954). The Convention entered into force on 6 June 1960.

Supplementary Convention on the Abolition of Slavery, the Slave Trade, and Institutions and Practices Similar to Slavery (adopted in 1956 by a Conference of Plenipotentiaries convened by Economic and Social Council resolution 608 (XXI) of 30 April 1956). The Convention entered into force on 30 April 1957.

Convention on the Nationality of Married Women (General Assembly resolution 1040 (XI) of 29 January 1957). The Convention entered into force on 11 August 1958.

---

[13] For the mandate, composition and membership of the Committee, see chapter I, section G, 4, above. For a summary of its activities, see chapter VIII, section D, 2 (h).

[14] The texts of most of the instruments listed here may be found in *Human Rights: A Compilation of International Instruments* (United Nations publication, Sales No. E.88.XIV.1).

Convention on the Reduction of Statelessness (adopted on 30 August 1961 by a Conference of Plenipotentiaries which met in 1959 and reconvened in 1961 in pursuance of General Assembly resolution 896 (IX) of 4 December 1954). The Convention entered into force on 13 December 1975.

Convention on Consent to Marriage, Minimum Age for Marriage and Registration of Marriages (General Assembly resolution 1763 A (XVII) of 7 November 1962). The Convention entered into force on 9 December 1964.

Protocol relating to the Status of Refugees, done at New York on 31 January 1967 (see Economic and Social Council resolution 1186 (XLI) of 18 November 1966 and General Assembly resolution 2198 (XXI) of 16 December 1966). The Protocol entered into force on 4 October 1967.

Convention on the Non-Applicability of Statutory Limitations to War Crimes and Crimes against Humanity (General Assembly resolution 2391 (XXIII) of 26 November 1968). The Convention entered into force on 11 November 1970.

146. Between 1948 and 1987 the General Conference of the International Labour Organisation also adopted a number of human rights conventions, including the following:

The Freedom of Association and Protection of the Right to Organise, Convention (No. 87), adopted on 9 July 1948. The Convention entered into force on 4 July 1950

The Equal Remuneration Convention (No. 100), adopted on 29 June 1951. The Convention entered into force on 23 May 1953.

The Abolition of Forced Labour Convention (No. 105), adopted on 25 June 1957. The Convention entered into force on 17 January 1959.

The Discrimination (Employment and Occupation) Convention (No. 111), adopted on 25 June 1958. The Convention entered into force on 15 June 1960.

The Employment Policy Convention (No. 122), adopted on 9 July 1964. The Convention entered into force on 15 July 1966.

The Workers' Representatives Convention (No. 135), adopted on 23 June 1971. The Convention entered into force on 30 June 1973.

The Rural Workers' Organisations Convention (No. 141) adopted on 23 June 1975. The Convention entered into force on 24 November 1977.

The Migrant Workers (Supplementary Provisions) Convention (No. 143), adopted on 24 June 1975. The Convention entered into force on 9 December 1978.

The Labour Relations (Public Service) Convention (No. 151), adopted on 27 June 1978. The Convention entered into force on 25 February 1981.

The Collective Bargaining Convention (No. 154), adopted on 19 June 1981. The Convention entered into force on 11 August 1983.

The Occupational Safety and Health Convention (No. 155), adopted on 22 June 1981. The Convention entered into force on 11 August 1983.

The Workers with Family Responsibilities Convention (No. 156), adopted on 23 June 1981. The Convention entered into force on 11 August 1983.

147. The General Conference of the United Nations Educational, Scientific and Cultural Organization also adopted human rights conventions between 1948 and 1987, among them:

The Convention against Discrimination in Education, adopted on 14 December 1960. The Convention entered into force on 22 May 1962.

The Protocol Instituting a Conciliation and Good Offices Commission to be responsible for seeking a settlement of any disputes which may arise between States parties to the Convention against Discrimination in Education, adopted on 10 December 1962. The Protocol entered into force on 24 October 1968.

The Universal Copyright Convention and Protocols and Revision, adopted at Geneva on 6 September 1952 and revised at Paris on 24 July 1971. The Convention as revised entered into force on 10 July 1974.

The Convention for the Protection of the World Cultural and Natural Heritage, adopted at Paris on 16 November 1972. The Convention entered into force on 17 December 1975.

148. By the end of 1987, the following declarations and recommendations, dealing exclusively with human rights and fundamental freedoms, had been adopted by the General Assembly of the United Nations:[15]

Universal Declaration of Human Rights (1948);

Declaration of the Rights of the Child (1959);

Declaration on the Granting of Independence to Colonial Countries and Peoples (1960);

Declaration on Permanent Sovereignty over Natural Resources (1962);

United Nations Declaration on the Elimination of All Forms of Racial Discrimination (1963);

Declaration on the Promotion among Youth of the Ideals of Peace, Mutual Respect and Understanding between Peoples (1965);

Recommendation on Consent to Marriage, Minimum Age for Marriage and Registration of Marriages (1965);

Declaration on the Elimination of Discrimination against Women (1967);

Declaration on Territorial Asylum (1967);

Declaration on the Rights of Mentally Retarded Persons (1971);

Declaration of the Principles of international co-operation in the detection, arrest, extradition and punishment of persons guilty of war crimes and crimes against humanity (1973);

---

[15] For the texts of many of the international instruments listed, see *Human Rights: A Compilation of International Instruments* (United Nations publication, Sales No. E.88.XIV.1).

Declaration on the Protection of Women and Children in Emergency and Armed Conflict (1974);

Declaration on the Rights of Disabled Persons (1975);

Declaration on the Protection of All Persons from Being Subjected to Torture and Other Cruel, Inhuman or Degrading Treatment or Punishment (1975);

International Declaration against *Apartheid* in Sports (1977);

Declaration on the Preparation of Societies for Life in Peace (1978);

Declaration on South Africa (1979);

Declaration on the Elimination of All Forms of Intolerance and of Discrimination Based on Religion or Belief (1981); and

Declaration on the Participation of Women in Promoting International Peace and Co-operation (1982).

Declaration on the Human Rights of Individuals Who are not Nationals of the Country in which they Live (1985);

Declaration of Basic Principles of Justice for Victims of Crime and Abuse of Power (1985); and

Declaration on the Right to Development (1986).

149. In addition, the General Assembly had adopted by the end of 1987 the following texts of a general character in which reference is made to the promotion and protection of human rights and fundamental freedoms:

Declaration on Social Progress and Development (1969);

Declaration on the Occasion of the Twenty-fifth Anniversary of the United Nations (1970);

Declaration on Principles of International Law concerning Friendly Relations and Co-operation among States in accordance with the Charter of the United Nations (1970);

Declaration on the Strengthening of International Security (1970);

Declaration on the Use of Scientific and Technological Progress in the Interests of Peace and for the Benefit of Mankind (1975);

Code of Conduct for Law Enforcement Officials (1979);

150. Declarations relating to human rights and fundamental freedoms have also been adopted by international conferences convened by the United Nations or by organizations within the United Nations system. These include:

The Proclamation of Teheran (1968), adopted by the International Conference on Human Rights;

The Declaration of the United Nations Conference on the Human Environment (1972), adopted by the United Nations Conference on the Human Environment;

The Universal Declaration on the Eradication of Hunger and Malnutrition (1974), adopted by the World Food Conference;

The Declaration of Mexico on the Equality of Men and Women and Their Contribution to Development and Peace (1975), adopted by the World Conference of the International Women's Year;

The Declaration of the World Conference to Combat Racism and Racial Discrimination (1978); and

The Declaration of the Second World Conference to Combat Racism and Racial Discrimination (1983).

151. A few texts which are neither declarations, recommendations, conventions or protocols are nevertheless recognized as international instruments in the field of human rights. Among these are the Statute of the Office of the United Nations High Commissioner for Refugees, adopted by General Assembly resolution 428 (V) of 14 December 1950; the Standard Minimum Rules for the Treatment of Prisoners, adopted by the First United Nations Congress on the Prevention of Crime and the Treatment of Offenders, held at Geneva in 1955; the Principles of Medical Ethics relevant to the Role of Health Personnel, particularly Physicians, in the Protection of Prisoners and Detainees against Torture, and Other Cruel, Inhuman or Degrading Treatment or Punishment, adopted by the General Assembly in resolution 37/194 of 18 December 1982; the United Nations Standard Minimum Rules for the Administration of Juvenile Justice, known as the "Beijing Rules", adopted by the General Assembly in resolution 40/33 of 29 November 1985; and the Basic Principles on the Independence of the Judiciary, adopted by the Seventh United Nations Congress on the Prevention of Crime and the Treatment of Offenders at Milan on 5 September 1985 and endorsed by the General Assembly in resolution 40/32 of 29 November 1985.

D. Human Rights Instruments prepared outside the United Nations system

1. INSTRUMENTS PREPARED INDEPENDENTLY

152. Three important international instruments relating to human rights were concluded independently, outside the United Nations system: the Final Act of the Conference on Security and Co-operation in Europe, known as the "Helsinki Accord", signed at Helsinki on 1 August 1975 by 33 European States, Canada and the United States of America; and Protocols I and II Additional to the Geneva Conventions of 12 August 1949, relating to the protection of victims of armed conflicts.

(a) *The Helsinki Final Act*

153. This "Accord" is an agreement signed by the participating States rather than a treaty creating legal obligations and ratified or acceded to by them. One section, headed "Declaration on Principles Guiding Relations between Participating States", provides (para. VII) that

... In the field of human rights and fundamental freedoms, the participating States will act in conformity with the purposes and principles of the Charter of the United Nations and with the Universal

Declaration of Human Rights. They will also fulfil their obligations as set forth in the international declarations and agreements in this field, including *inter alia* the International Covenants on Human Rights, by which they may be bound.

154. In the concluding section of the Final Act, entitled ''Follow-up to the Conference'', the signatory States declare their resolve to continue the multilateral process initiated by the Conference:

(*a*) By proceeding to a thorough exchange of views both on the implementation of the provisions of the Final Act and of the tasks defined by the Conference, as well as, in the context of the questions dealt with by the latter, on the deepening of their mutual relations, the improvement of security and the development of co-operation in Europe, and the development of the process of détente in the future;

(*b*) By organizing to these ends meetings among their representatives, beginning with a meeting at the level of representatives appointed by the Ministers of Foreign Affairs. This meeting will define the appropriate modalities for the holding of other meetings which could include further similar meetings and the possibility of a new Conference . . .

155. The first follow-up meeting was held at Belgrade in 1978. Subsequent meetings were held at Madrid in 1983 and Vienna in 1986. Except for such periodic meetings, no international supervisory body has been established to promote the observance of, and to assess compliance with the provisions of the Final Act. However, a number of unofficial national and international monitoring groups, composed of interested individuals and non-governmental organizations, have endeavoured to perform these functions.

(b) *The Geneva Conventions of 1949 and the Protocols thereto*

156. Geneva Convention No. III, Relative to the Treatment of Prisoners of War, and No. IV, Relative to the Protection of Civilian Persons in Time of War, as well as Protocols I and II additional to those Conventions,[16] are also important international instruments concluded outside the United Nations system. The Conventions were drawn up by the Diplomatic Conference of 1949, convened by the Swiss Federal Council at Geneva from 21 April to 12 August 1949. Protocol I, relating to the protection of victims of international armed conflicts, and Protocol II, relating to the protection of victims of non-international armed conflicts, were adopted at the fourth session of the Diplomatic Conference on the Reaffirmation and Development of International Humanitarian Law Applicable in Armed Conflicts, convened at Geneva from 17 March to 10 June 1977 by the International Committee of the Red Cross with the Government of Switzerland acting as host. Both Protocols were opened for signature at Berne on 12 December 1977.

157. Protocol I reaffirms and develops the provisions of the Geneva Conventions of 1949 protecting the victims of armed conflicts of an international nature,

---

[16] For the texts of the Conventions, see United Nations, *Treaty Series,* Vol. 75, Nos. 970 to 973. For the texts of the Protocols, see International Committee of the Red Cross, *Protocols Additional to the Geneva Conventions of 12 August 1949,* Geneva, 1977.

and supplements the measures intended to secure the application of those provisions. Protocol II does the same with respect to conflicts which are not of an international nature.

158. Part I of Protocol I sets out certain general principles and definitions, and provides (article 5) for the appointment of a Protecting Power, for the purpose of supervising the application of the Conventions and Protocol, by each party to a conflict.

159. Part II contains provisions to ameliorate the condition of the wounded, sick and shipwrecked when an international armed conflict occurs (articles 8 to 34); and provides for the collection and provision of information concerning persons missing or dead as a result of such a conflict (articles 33 and 34).

160. Part III deals with methods and means of warfare (articles 35 to 42) and combatant and prisoner-of-war status (articles 43 to 47). Article 35 prohibits the employment of methods or means of warfare which may cause superfluous injury, unnecessary suffering, or widespread, long-term and severe damage to the environment. Article 44 provides that any combatant who falls into the power of an adverse party shall be considered to be a prisoner of war, and article 45 sets out measures for the protection of such prisoners. Articles 46 and 47 provide that neither spies nor mercenaries shall have the right to the status of prisoner of war.

161. Part IV (articles 48 to 79) provides protection for members of the civilian population who have fallen into the hands of an adverse Party. Articles 48 to 71 supplement the provisions of the Third Geneva Convention relating to the protection of the civilian population and civilian objects against the dangers arising from military operations, and lay down a series of rules, for this purpose, the basic rule being (article 48) that parties to a conflict shall at all times distinguish between the civilian population and combatants and shall direct their operations only against military objectives. Starvation of civilians and attacks against the natural environment, as methods of warfare, are specifically prohibited. Articles 72 to 79 deal with the treatment of persons in the power of a party to the conflict. Articles 76 to 78 set out special measures for the protection of women and children, in particular against rape, forced prostitution and any other form of indecent assault. Article 79 provides that journalists engaged in dangerous professional missions in areas of armed conflict shall be considered as civilians, and shall be protected under the Conventions and Protocol provided that they take no action adversely affecting their civilian status. It further provides for an identity card to be issued to such journalists by their Government, attesting to their status as journalists.

162. Parts V and VI (articles 80 to 102) set out measures for the execution of the Conventions and the Protocol and for repression of breaches of their provisions, including the establishment of an International Fact-Finding Commission (article 90) to inquire into allega-

tions that those provisions have been violated; and include the usual final provisions.

163. Protocol II applies to non-international conflicts, including conflicts between the armed forces of a Government and dissident armed forces or other organized groups which exercise control over part of its territory. It does not, however, apply to situations of internal disturbances and tensions, such as riots and other isolated and sporadic acts of violence.

164. Article 4 calls for humane treatment, without adverse distinction, of all persons who do not take a direct part, or who have ceased to take part, in hostilities, whether or not their liberty has been restricted. It lists a number of acts, such as murder, torture, mutilation and corporal punishment, which are totally prohibited. Article 5 establishes minimum standards with regard to persons deprived of their liberty for reasons related to armed conflict, and lays down rules protecting those prosecuted or punished for criminal offences related to armed conflict.

165. Articles 7 to 12 provide for the protection and care of persons wounded, sick or shipwrecked as a result of a non-international conflict. Articles 13 to 18 set out special measures for the protection of the civilian population against acts or threats of violence (article 13), against starvation as a method of combat (article 14), and against forced movement from their own territory (article 17). In addition, acts of hostility directed against historical monuments, works of art or places of worship—or their use in support of military objectives—are prohibited (article 16).

166. At the request of the General Assembly, the Secretary-General reports periodically on the state of acceptance of the two Protocols.[17] In resolution 34/51 of 23 November 1979, and again in resolutions 37/116 of 16 December 1982, 39/77 of 13 December 1984 and 41/72 of 3 December 1986, the Assembly expressed its appreciation of the virtually universal acceptance of the Geneva Conventions of 1949, but noted that a more limited number of States had become parties to the two additional Protocols. It repeatedly appealed to all States parties to the Geneva Conventions to consider becoming parties also to the Protocols at the earliest possible date, and called upon States parties to Protocol I to make the declaration provided for under article 90 of that Protocol. As at 31 December 1987, 165 States are parties to the Geneva Conventions, 71 States had ratified or acceded to Protocol I, 64 States had ratified or acceded to Protocol II, and 10 States had made the declaration provided for under article 90 of Protocol I.

2. HUMAN RIGHTS INSTRUMENTS PREPARED BY REGIONAL INTERGOVERNMENTAL ORGANIZATIONS

167. Three regional intergovernmental organizations—the Council of Europe, the Organization of African Unity and the Organization of American

---

[17] A/41/535.

States—have adopted international instruments relating to human rights, including conventions establishing special organs to promote the recognition and observance of human rights within their respective regions.

168. Under the auspices of the Council of Europe, the European Convention for the Protection of Human Rights was concluded at Rome on 4 November 1950, and entered into force on 3 September 1953. In accordance with its provisions the European Commission on Human Rights and the European Court of Human Rights were established. States parties to the Convention may make declarations under article 45 accepting the right of individuals to submit a complaint to the Commission, and under article 62 accepting the jurisdiction of the Court.

169. In addition, the following international instruments relating to human rights have been prepared under the auspices of the Council of Europe:

The European Convention on Establishment, concluded at Paris on 13 December 1955, which entered into force on 23 February 1965;

The European Agreement on Regulations Governing the Movement of Persons Between Member States of the Council of Europe, concluded at Paris on 13 December 1957, which entered into force on 1 January 1958;

The European Social Charter, concluded at Turin on 18 October 1961, which entered into force on 26 February 1965;

The European Agreement Relating to Persons Participating in Proceedings of the European Commission and Court of Human Rights, concluded at London on 6 May 1969, which entered into force on 17 April 1971;

The European Convention on Social Security and Supplementary Agreement as to its Application, concluded at Paris on 14 December 1972, which entered into force on 1 March 1977;

The European Convention on the Legal Status of Children Born Out of Wedlock, concluded at Strasbourg on 15 October 1975, which entered into force on 11 August 1978; and

The European Convention on Recognition and Enforcement of Decisions Concerning Custody of Children and on Restoration of Custody of Children, concluded at Luxembourg on 20 May 1980, which entered into force on 1 September 1983.

170. Under the auspices of the Organization of African Unity, the Banjul Charter on Human and Peoples' Rights was concluded at Nairobi, Kenya, on 28 June 1981, and entered into force on 21 October 1986. Under its provisions the establishment of an African Commission on Human and Peoples' Rights is authorized.

171. In addition, the African Convention Concerning the Specific Aspects of Refugee Problems in Africa was adopted on 10 September 1969 by the Assembly of Heads of State and Government of the Organization of

African Unity at Addis Ababa, and entered into force on 20 June 1974.

172. Under the auspices of the Organization of American States, the American Declaration on the Rights and Duties of Man was adopted on 2 May 1948. The American Convention on Human Rights was concluded at San José, Costa Rica, on 22 November 1969, and entered into force on 18 July 1978. In accordance with the provisions of the Convention, the Inter-American Commission on Human Rights and the Inter-American Court of Human Rights were established. Under article 62 of the Convention, a State party may declare that it recognizes as binding the jurisdiction of the Court on all matters relating to the interpretation and application of the Convention.

173. In addition, the following international instruments relating to human rights have been prepared under the auspices of the Organization of American States:

The Inter-American Convention on the Granting of Political Rights to Women, concluded at Bogotá on 2 May 1948, which entered into force on 22 April 1949;

The Inter-American Convention on the Granting of Civil Rights to Women, concluded at Bogotá on 2 May 1948, which entered into force on 22 April 1949;

The Inter-American Convention on Territorial Asylum, concluded at Caracas on 28 March 1954, which entered into force on 29 December 1954;

The Inter-American Convention on Conflict of Laws Concerning the Adoption of Minors, concluded at La Paz on 24 May 1984; and

The Inter-American Convention to Prevent and Punish Torture, concluded at Cartagena, Colombia on 6 December 1985.

E. Human rights instruments under preparation

174. As at 31 December 1987, three new international human rights instruments were in advanced stages of preparation by United Nations organs: the draft international convention against the recruitment, use, financing and training of mercenaries; the draft convention on the rights of the child; and the draft declaration on the rights and responsibilities of individuals, groups and organs of society to promote and protect human rights and fundamental freedoms.

175. The proposed international convention against the recruitment, use, financing and training of mercenaries is intended to provide effective measures to prohibit the recruitment, training, assembly, transit and use of mercenaries and in general to suppress and punish the crime of mercenarism which the Assembly recognized, in resolution 34/140 of 14 December 1979, "as a threat to international peace and security and, like murder, piracy and genocide, is a universal crime against humanity". In that resolution the Assembly called upon all States

... to exercise the utmost vigilance against the menace posed by the activities of mercenaries and to ensure by both administrative and legislative measures that their territory and other territories under their control, as well as their nationals, are not used for the planning of subversion and recruitment, assembly, financing, training and transit of mercenaries designed to subvert or overthrow the Government of any Member State and to fight the national liberation movements which are struggling against colonial domination or alien occupation or racist régimes in the exercise of their right of self-determination ...

176. The convention is under preparation by the *Ad Hoc* Committee on the Drafting of an International Convention against the Recruitment, Use, Financing and Training of Mercenaries, composed of 35 Member States, established in accordance with Assembly resolution 35/48 of 4 December 1980.

177. After examining the 1987 report of the *Ad Hoc* Committee[18] the General Assembly, in resolution 42/155 of 7 December 1987, took account of the progress which had been achieved, renewed the mandate of the *Ad Hoc* Committee, and invited it to make every effort to submit its final report to the Assembly, at its forty-third session, in 1988.

178. The proposed convention on the rights of the child is intended to provide for the continuous improvement in the situation of children throughout the world, as well as their development and education in conditions of peace and security, in order to ensure their full enjoyment of all human rights and fundamental freedoms.

179. The convention has been under consideration since a draft convention on the rights of the child was submitted by Poland to the Commission on Human Rights on 7 February 1978. The General Assembly requested the Commission to give highest priority to the examination of the draft convention first in resolution 33/166 of 20 December 1978 and subsequently in resolutions 34/4, 35/131, 36/57, 37/190, 38/114, 39/135, 40/113, 41/116 and 42/101.

180. The Commission, by resolution 20 (XXXIV) of 8 March 1978 and similar resolutions adopted annually thereafter, authorized meetings of an open-ended working group prior to each session of the Commission to draft the convention. However, as at 31 December 1987 it had not concluded this task.

181. The proposed declaration on the right and responsibility of individuals, groups and organs of society to promote and protect human rights and fundamental freedoms was initiated by the Sub-Commission on Prevention of Discrimination and Protection of Minorities, which in resolution 1982/24 of 8 September 1982 requested one of its members, Mrs. Erica-Irene A. Daes, to prepare draft principles on the subject. Mrs Daes earlier had prepared a study at the request of the Sub-Commission entitled *Study of the Individual's Duties to the Community and the Limitations on Human Rights and Freedoms under article 29 of the Universal Declaration of Human Rights—A Contribution to the Freedom of the Individual Under Law,*[19] in which she had recommended preparation of a draft declaration on the

---

[18] *Official Records of the General Assembly, Forty-second Session, Supplement No. 43* (A/42/43).

[19] United Nations publication, Sales No. E.82.XIV.1.

principles governing the responsibilities of the individual in connection with, in particular, the promotion and observance of human rights and fundamental freedoms in a contemporary community.

182. In authorizing the preparation of the draft principles, the Sub-Commission in resolution 1982/24 reiterated the right and responsibility of individuals, groups and organs of society to promote and protect the rights recognized in the Universal Declaration of Human Rights and other relevant international instruments; deplored all attempts to prevent or punish individuals, groups or organs of society from promoting and protecting the enjoyment of universally-recognized human rights and fundamental freedoms; and emphasized that in the exercise of these rights and freedoms, the individual should be subjected only to such limitations as are determined in article 29 of the Universal Declaration of Human Rights, the International Covenants on Human Rights and other relevant instruments.

183. Having received the draft principles and other relevant documentation prepared by the Sub-Commission, the Commission on Human Rights by decision 1984/52 of 16 March 1984 established an open-ended Working Group to prepare the proposed declaration. The Working Group subsequently held meetings of one week's duration before the 1985, 1986 and 1987 sessions of the Commission, but as at 31 December 1987 had not yet completed the draft declaration.

184. The idea of elaborating a second optional protocol to the International Covenant on Civil and Political Rights has been under consideration by the General Assembly since 1980, when it received documentation on the abolition of the death penalty and requested the views of Governments on that subject. Later, in resolution 37/192 of 18 December 1982, the Assembly transmitted all the relevant documentation to the Commission on Human Rights and asked it to consider the idea of elaborating a draft protocol aiming at the abolition of the death penalty. The Commission in turn sought the views of its Sub-Commission on Prevention of Discrimination and Protection of Minorities, which entrusted the task of preparing an analysis on the subject to one of its members, Mr. Marc Bossuyt, as Special Rapporteur. The analysis[20] was presented to the Sub-Commission at its 1987 session but the Sub-Commission, by decision 1987/109 of 3 September 1987, decided to take no action on a draft resolution by which it would have been forwarded to the Commission on Human Rights for consideration.

F. Outlook for future human rights instruments

185. In 1977 and at each subsequent session, the General Assembly has considered the item, "Alternative approaches and ways and means within the United Nations system for improving the effective enjoyment

---

[20] E/CN.4/Sub.2/1987/20.

of human rights and fundamental freedoms". In resolution 32/130 of 16 December 1977 the Assembly, after acknowledging the progress which had been achieved by the international community in the promotion and protection of human rights and fundamental freedoms, particularly with respect to the standard-setting work within the United Nations system, decided that the approach to the future work within the system with respect to human rights questions should take into account the following concepts:

(a) All human rights and fundamental freedoms are indivisible and interdependent; equal attention and urgent consideration should be given to the implementation, promotion and protection of both civil and political, and economic, social and cultural rights;

(b) "The full realization of civil and political rights without the enjoyment of economic, social and cultural rights is impossible; the achievement of lasting progress in the implementation of human rights is dependent upon sound and effective national and international policies of economic and social development", as recognized by the Proclamation of Teheran of 1968;[21]

(c) All human rights and fundamental freedoms of the human person and of peoples are inalienable;

(d) Consequently, human rights questions should be examined globally, taking into account both the overall context of the various societies in which they present themselves, as well as the need for the promotion of the full dignity of the human person and the development and well-being of the society;

(e) In approaching human rights questions within the United Nations system, the international community should accord, or continue to accord, priority to the search for solutions to the mass and flagrant violations of human rights of peoples and persons affected by situations such as those resulting from apartheid, from all forms of racial discrimination, from colonialism, from foreign domination and occupation, from aggression and threats against national sovereignty, national unity and territorial integrity, as well as from the refusal to recognize the fundamental rights of peoples to self-determination and of every nation to the exercise of full sovereignty over its wealth and natural resources;

(f) The realization of the new international economic order is an essential element for the effective promotion of human rights and fundamental freedoms and should also be accorded priority;

(g) It is of paramount importance for the promotion of human rights and fundamental freedoms that Member States undertake specific obligations through accession to or ratification of international instruments in this field; consequently, the standard-setting work within the United Nations system in the field of human rights and the universal acceptance and implementation of the relevant international instruments should be encouraged; and

---

[21] *Final Act of the International Conference on Human Rights* (United Nations publication, Sales No. E.68.XIV.2), p. 3.

52

(*h*) The experience and contribution of both developed and developing countries should be taken into account by all organs of the United Nations system in their work related to human rights and fundamental freedoms.

186. At each subsequent session, the General Assembly has reaffirmed these concepts, has reaffirmed that it is of paramount importance for the promotion of human rights and fundamental freedoms that Member States should undertake specific obligations through accession to, or ratification of, international instruments in this field and, consequently, that the standard-setting work within the United Nations system in the field of human rights and the universal acceptance and implementation of the relevant international instruments should be encouraged; and has reiterated that the international community should accord, or continue to accord, priority to the search for solutions to mass and flagrant violations of human rights of peoples and individuals affected by situations such as those mentioned in paragraph 1 (*e*) of resolution 32/130, paying due attention also to other situations of violations of human rights.

187. Further, the Assembly has repeatedly expressed concern at the continuing disparity between the established norms and principles and the actual situation of all human rights and fundamental freedoms in the world, has urged all States to co-operate with the Commission on Human Rights in the promotion and protection of human rights and fundamental freedoms; and has reiterated the need to create, at the national and international levels, conditions for the full promotion and protection of the human rights of individuals and peoples.

III. RIGHT OF PEOPLES AND NATIONS TO SELF-DETERMINATION

Introduction

1. Although the Charter of the United Nations refers occasionally to the right to self-determination, it does not define that right. In Article 1, on the Purposes of the United Nations, paragraph 2 refers to "friendly relations among nations based on respect for the principle of equal rights and self-determination of peoples, . . .". In Article 55, on international economic and social co-operation, a similar reference may be found. Article 73, on Non-Self-Governing Territories, declares that:

> Members of the United Nations which have or assure responsibilities for the administration of territories whose peoples have not yet attained a full measure of self-government recognize the principle that the interests of the inhabitants of these territories are paramount, and accept as a sacred trust the obligation to promote to the utmost, within the system of international peace and security established by the present Charter, the well-being of the inhabitants of these territories, and, to this end:
>
> . . .
>
> b. to develop self-government, to take due account of the political aspirations of the peoples, and to assist them in the progressive development of their free political institutions, according to the particular circumstances of each territory and its peoples and their varying stages of advancement;

Article 76, on the International Trusteeship System, sets out as a basic objective of that System:

> b. to promote the political, economic, social, and educational advancement of the inhabitants of the trust territories, and their progressive development towards self-government or independence as may be appropriate to the particular circumstances of each territory and its peoples and the freely expressed wishes of the peoples concerned, and as may be provided by the terms of each trusteeship agreement;
>
> . . .

2. The General Assembly first recognized "the right of peoples and nations to self-determination" as a fundamental human right in resolution 421 D (V) of 4 December 1950, in which it called upon the Economic and Social Council and the Commission on Human Rights to make recommendations on ways and means to ensure the enjoyment of this right.

3. The Assembly, in resolution 545 (VI) of 5 February 1952, decided "to include in the International Covenant or Covenants on Human Rights an article on the right of all peoples and nations to self-determination in reaffirmation of the principle enunciated in the Charter of the United Nations". It further decided that:

> This article shall be drafted in the following terms: "All peoples shall have the right of self-determination", and shall stipulate that all States, including those having responsibility for the administration of Non-Self-Governing Territories, should promote the realization of that right, in conformity with the Purposes and Principles of the United Nations, and that States having responsibility for the administration of Non-Self-Governing Territories should promote the realization of that right in relation to the peoples of such territories.

4. In resolution 637 A (VII) of 16 December 1952, the General Assembly, recognizing that "the right of peoples and nations to self-determination is a prerequisite to the full enjoyment of all fundamental human rights", and that "every Member of the United Nations, in conformity with the Charter, should respect the maintenance of the right of self-determination in other States", adopted a series of recommendations on the subject. To all States Members of the United Nations it recommended that they should "uphold the principle of self-determination of all peoples and nations" and should "recognize and promote the realization of the right of self-determination of the peoples of Non-Self-Governing and Trust Territories who are under their administration . . .". Further, they should "facilitate the exercise of this right by the peoples of such Territories according to the principles and spirit of the Charter of the United Nations in regard to each Territory and to the freely expressed wishes of the peoples concerned, the wishes of the people being ascertained through plebiscites or other recognized democratic means, preferably under the auspices of the United Nations". To States Members of the United Nations responsible for the administration of Non-Self-Governing and Trust Territories it recommended that they should "take practical steps, pending the realization of the right of self-determination and in preparation thereof, to ensure the direct participation of the indigenous populations in the legislative and executive organs of government of those Territories, and to prepare them for complete self-government or independence".

5. In resolution 637 C (VII), the General Assembly requested the Economic and Social Council to ask the Commission on Human Rights "to continue preparing recommendations concerning international respect for the right of peoples to self-determination, and particularly recommendations relating to the steps which might be taken, within the limits of their resources and competence, by the various organs of the United Nations and the specialized agencies to develop international respect" for that right. In recent years the General Assembly has repeatedly affirmed "that, in the absence of a decision by the General Assembly itself that a Non-Self-Governing Territory has attained a full measure of self-government in terms of Chapter XI of the Charter, the administering Power concerned should continue to transmit information under Article 73 e of the Charter with respect to that Territory".

A. Declaration on the Granting of Independence to Colonial Countries and Peoples

6. In resolution 1514 (XV) of 14 December 1960, the General Assembly solemnly proclaimed "the necessity of bringing to a speedy and unconditional end colonialism in all its forms and manifestations", and adopted the Declaration on the Granting of Independence to Colonial Countries and Peoples.

7. In the preamble to the Declaration, the General Assembly referred to "the need for the creation of conditions of stability and well-being and peaceful and friendly relations based on respect for the principles of equal rights and self-determination of all peoples, and of universal respect for, and observance of, human rights and fundamental freedoms for all without distinction as to race, sex, language or religion". It expressed the belief that "the process of liberation is irresistible and irreversible and that, in order to avoid serious crises, an end must be put to colonialism and all practices of segregation and discrimination associated therewith"; recognized "the increasingly powerful trends towards freedom" in territories which had not attained independence; and expressed the conviction "that all peoples have an inalienable right to complete freedom, the exercise of their sovereignty and the integrity of their national territory".

8. The Declaration states that:

1. The subjection of peoples to alien subjugation, domination and exploitation constitutes a denial of fundamental human rights, is contrary to the Charter of the United Nations and is an impediment to the promotion of world peace and co-operation.

2. All peoples have the right to self-determination; by virtue of that right they freely determine their political status and freely pursue their economic, social and cultural development.

3. Inadequacy of political, economic, social or educational preparedness should never serve as a pretext for delaying independence.

4. All armed action or repressive measures of all kinds directed against dependent peoples shall cease in order to enable them to exercise peacefully and freely their right to complete independence, and the integrity of their national territory shall be respected.

5. Immediate steps shall be taken, in Trust and Non-Self-Governing Territories or all other territories which have not yet attained independence, to transfer all powers to the peoples of those territories, without any conditions or reservations, in accordance with their freely expressed will and desire, without any distinction as to race, creed or colour, in order to enable them to enjoy complete independence and freedom.

6. Any attempt aimed at the partial or total disruption of the national unity and the territorial integrity of a country is incompatible with the purposes and principles of the Charter of the United Nations.

7. All States shall observe faithfully and strictly the provisions of the Charter of the United Nations, the Universal Declaration of Human Rights and the present Declaration on the basis of equality, non-interference in the internal affairs of all States, and respect for the sovereign rights of all peoples and their territorial integrity.

B. The principle of equal rights and self-determination of peoples

9. In resolution 2625 (XXV) of 24 October 1970, the General Assembly adopted and proclaimed the Declaration on Principles of International Law concerning Friendly Relations and Co-operation among States in accordance with the Charter of the United Nations and declared that the principles of the Charter embodied in the Declaration constituted basic principles of international law.

10. With regard to the principle of equal rights and self-determination of peoples, the Declaration proclaims that:

By virtue of the principle of equal rights and self-determination of peoples enshrined in the Charter of the United Nations, all peoples have the right freely to determine, without external interference, their political status and to pursue their economic, social and cultural development, and every State has the duty to respect this right in accordance with the provisions of the Charter.

Every State has the duty to promote, through joint and separate action, realization of the principle of equal rights and self-determination of peoples, in accordance with the provisions of the Charter, and to render assistance to the United Nations in carrying out the responsibilities entrusted to it by the Charter regarding the implementation of the principle, in order:

(*a*) To promote friendly relations and co-operation among States; and

(*b*) To bring a speedy end to colonialism, having due regard to the freely expressed will of the peoples concerned;

and bearing in mind that subjection of peoples to alien subjugation, domination and exploitation constitutes a violation of the principle, as well as a denial of fundamental human rights, and is contrary to the Charter.

Every State has the duty to promote through joint and separate action universal respect for and observance of human rights and fundamental freedoms in accordance with the Charter.

The establishment of a sovereign and independent State, the free association or integration with an independent State or the emergence into any other political status freely determined by a people constitute modes of implementing the right of self-determination by that people.

Every State has the duty to refrain from any forcible action which deprives peoples referred to above in the elaboration of the present principle of their right to self-determination and freedom and independence. In their actions against, and resistance to, such forcible action in pursuit of the exercise of their right to self-determination, such peoples are entitled to seek and to receive support in accordance with the purposes and principles of the Charter.

The territory of a colony or other Non-Self-Governing Territory has, under the Charter, a status separate and distinct from the territory of the State administering it; and such separate and distinct status under the Charter shall exist until the people of the colony or Non-Self-Governing Territory have exercised their right of self-determination in accordance with the Charter, and particularly its purposes and principles.

Nothing in the foregoing paragraphs shall be construed as authorizing or encouraging any action which would dismember or impair, totally or in part, the territorial integrity or political unity of sovereign and independent States conducting themselves in compliance with the principle of equal rights and self-determination of peoples as described above and thus possessed of a government representing the whole people belonging to the territory without distinction as to race, creed or colour.

Every State shall refrain from any action aimed at the partial or total disruption of the national unity and territorial integrity of any other State or country.

C. Provisions in the International Covenants on Human Rights on the right of self-determination

11. Article 1 of the International Covenant on Economic, Social and Cultural Rights and article 1 of the International Covenant on Civil and Political Rights are identical; both read as follows:

Article 1

1. All peoples have the right of self-determination. By virtue of that right they freely determine their political status and freely pursue their economic, social and cultural development.

2. All peoples may, for their own ends, freely dispose of their natural wealth and resources without prejudice to any obligations arising out of international economic co-operation, based upon the principle of mutual benefit, and international law. In no case may a people be deprived of its own means of subsistence.

3. The States Parties to the present Covenant, including those having responsibility for the administration of Non-Self-Governing and Trust Territories, shall promote the realization of the right of self-determination, and shall respect that right, in conformity with the provisions of the Charter of the United Nations.

12. As mentioned above, article 1 was included in both Covenants as a result of the decision of the General Assembly in resolution 545 (VI) of 5 February 1952.

13. Under the provisions of each of the Covenants, States parties undertake to submit to the Secretary-General of the United Nations at regular intervals reports on the measures they have adopted which give effect to the rights recognized in that Covenant, and on the progress made in the enjoyment of those rights. The Secretary-General transmits such reports to the competent body—the Committee on Economic, Social and Cultural Rights or the Human Rights Committee—for its consideration. Reports of both Committees are forwarded to the General Assembly.

D. Work of the Special Committee on Decolonization

14. The General Assembly, in resolution 1654 (XVI) of 27 November 1961, established the Special Committee on the Situation with regard to the Implementation of the Declaration on the Granting of Independence to Colonial Countries and Peoples, now commonly referred to as the Special Committee on Decolonization or the Committee of 24.[1]

15. In the resolution establishing the Special Committee, the General Assembly "reiterated and reaffirmed the objectives and principles enshrined in the Declaration" and called upon States "to take action without further delay with a view to the faithful application and implementation of the Declaration". The General Assembly requested the Special Committee "to examine the application of the Declaration" and "to make suggestions and recommendations on the progress and extent" of its implementation. It directed the Committee "to carry out its task by employment of all the means . . . at its disposal . . . for the proper discharge of its functions"; authorized it "to meet elsewhere than at United Nations Headquarters" whenever necessary; invited the authorities concerned to co-operate with the Committee; and requested the Trusteeship Council, the Committee on Information from Non-Self-Governing Territories and the specialized agencies concerned to assist the Committee.

16. In resolution 1810 (XVII), enlarging the Special Committee, the General Assembly invited it:

(*a*) To continue to seek the most suitable ways and means for the speedy and total application of the Declaration to all Territories which had not attained independence;

(*b*) To propose specific measures for the complete application of the Declaration;

(*c*) To submit to the General Assembly . . . a full report containing its suggestions and recommendations on all Territories which had not attained independence;

(*d*) To apprise the Security Council of any developments in those Territories which may threaten international peace and security.

All Member States, especially the Administering Authorities, were requested "to afford the Special Committee their fullest co-operation".

17. By resolutions 1805 and 1807 (XVII) of 14 December 1962 and 1970 (XVIII) of 16 December 1963, the General Assembly entrusted to the Special Committee a series of functions which, up to that time, had been performed by other subsidiary bodies concerned with dependent Territories. The Committees whose functions were taken over by the Special Committee, namely, the Special Committee for South West Africa, the Special Committee on Territories under Portuguese Administration and the Committee on Information from Non-Self-Governing Territories, were dissolved by the Assembly.

18. In resolution 2105 (XX) of 20 December 1965, the General Assembly reiterated the Committee's mandate and requested it, in addition, to pay particular attention to the small Territories and to recommend steps to be taken to enable the populations of those Territories to exercise fully their rights to self-determination and independence.

19. In 1982, the General Assembly, in resolution 37/35 of 23 November 1982, further requested the Special Committee:

to continue to seek suitable means for the immediate and full implementation of General Assembly resolution 1514 (XV) in all Territories that have not yet attained independence and, in particular:

(*a*) To formulate specific proposals for the elimination of the remaining manifestations of colonialism and to report thereon to the General Assembly at its thirty-eighth session;

(*b*) To make concrete suggestions which could assist the Security Council in considering appropriate measures under the Charter with regard to developments in colonial Territories that are likely to threaten international peace and security:

(*c*) To continue to examine the compliance of Member States with the Declaration and with other relevant resolutions on decolonization, particularly those relating to Namibia;

(*d*) To continue to pay particular attention to the small Territories, including the sending of visiting missions thereto, as appropriate, and to recommend to the General Assembly the most suitable steps to be taken to enable the populations of those Territories to exercise their right to self-determination, freedom and independence;

(*e*) To take all necessary steps to enlist world-wide support among Governments, as well as national and international organizations having a special interest in decolonization, in the achievement of the objectives of the Declaration and in the implementation of the relevant resolutions of the United Nations, particularly as concerns the oppressed people of Namibia.

20. On the bases of the information and documentation available to it, the Special Committee has submitted reports to the General Assembly each year since

---

[1] For information concerning the Special Committee, see chapter I, section A, 2 (b).

1963. After examining the reports the Assembly has adopted a number of resolutions and decisions, some relating to general aspects of the right of peoples and nations to self-determination and independence and others to ways and means of implementing the Declaration on the Granting of Independence to Colonial Countries and Peoples. At each regular session the Assembly has renewed the mandate of the Special Committee, has examined its reports, and has called upon it to seek suitable means for the immediate and full application of the Declaration to all Territories which have not yet achieved independence.

21. At recent sessions, the Special Committee has reviewed the situation in each of the Territories to which the Declaration was still applicable; in 1987 the list of those Territories included American Samoa, Anguilla, Bermuda, the British Virgin Islands, the Cayman Islands, East Timor, the Falkland Islands (Malvinas), Gibraltar, Guam, Montserrat, Namibia, New Caledonia, Pitcairn, St. Helena, Tokelau, the Trust Territory of the Pacific Islands, the Turks and Caicos Islands, the United States Virgin Islands and Western Sahara.

22. The delegations of New Zealand (Tokelau), Portugal (East Timor) and the United States of America (American Samoa, the United States Virgin Islands and Guam) participated in the work of the Special Committee; however, the United States delegation did not take part in the Committee's consideration of the Trust Territory of the Pacific Islands, as it maintained that the matter fell within the purview of the Trusteeship Council and the Security Council, not the General Assembly. The delegation of the United Kingdom did not participate in the Committee's consideration of the Territories under its administration.

23. With regard to 13 of the dependent Territories, the Special Committee adopted without vote reports dealing with the political, economic and social development of those Territories and measures for enabling their peoples to achieve self-determination. In most of the reports the Special Committee reiterated that it was the obligation of the administering Powers to create such conditions in the Territories under their administration as would enable their peoples to exercise freely and without interference their right to self-determination and independence. The administering Powers were also urged to promote the economic and social development of the Territories and to safeguard the inalienable right of their peoples to the enjoyment of their natural resources.

24. With respect to Bermuda, Guam, St. Helena and the Trust Territory of the Pacific Islands, the Special Committee reaffirmed its strong conviction that the presence of military bases and installations in those Territories could be a major obstacle to the implementation of the Declaration, and urged the administering Powers to continue to take all necessary measures not to involve those Territories in any offensive acts or interference against other States.

25. With regard to St. Helena, the Special Committee noted with concern the dependency of the Territory on South Africa for trade and transportation, as well as the continued presence of military facilities on the dependency of Ascension Island.

26. With regard to the Trust Territory of the Pacific Islands, the Special Committee noted with satisfaction the assurances given by the Administering Authority that it would continue to fulfil its responsibilities under the Charter and the Trusteeship Agreement. The Special Committee noted with regret that there was no co-operation between the Trusteeship Council and the Special Committee in relation to the Trust Territory, despite the readiness of the Committee to engage in such co-operation.

27. Finally, the Special Committee regretted that the Government of France had not responded to the call to submit information on New Caledonia, as requested in General Assembly resolution 41/41 A of 2 December 1986.

28. The list of Territories which have become self-governing or independent since the Charter of the United Nations came into force on 24 October 1945 is an impressive one, and provides an indication of the success of United Nations activities to promote the realization of the right of peoples to self-determination.

29. That list includes: 1. Indonesia; 2. Libyan Arab Jamahiriya; 3. Eritrea (later federated with Ethiopia); 4. Lao People's Democratic Republic; 5. Democratic Kampuchea; 6. Morocco; 7. Tunisia; 8. Sudan; 9. Ghana; 10. Malaysia; 11. Guinea; 12. United Republic of Cameroon; 13. Senegal; 14. Togo; 15. Madagascar; 16. Zaire; 17. Somalia; 18. Benin; 19. Niger; 20. Upper Volta; 21. Côte d'Ivoire; 22. Chad; 23. Central African Republic; 24. Congo; 25. Cyprus; 26. Gabon; 27. Mali; 28. Nigeria; 29. Mauritania; 30. Sierra Leone; 31. United Republic of Tanzania; 32. Samoa; 33. Burundi; 34. Rwanda; 35. Algeria; 36. Jamaica; 37. Trinidad and Tobago; 38. Uganda; 39. Kenya; 40. Malawi; 41. Malta; 42. Zambia; 43. Gambia; 44. Cook Islands; 45. Singapore; 46. Guyana; 47. Botswana; 48. Lesotho; 49. Barbados; 50. Democratic Yemen; 51. Naurau; 52. Mauritius; 53. Swaziland; 54. Equatorial Guinea; 55. Fiji; 56. Oman; 57. Bahamas; 58. Comoros; 59. Grenada; 60. Guinea-Bissau; 61. Bangladesh; 62. Cape Verde; 63. Sao Tome and Principe; 64. Mozambique; 65. Papua New Guinea; 66. Seychelles; 67. Djibouti; 68. Angola; 69. Bahrain; 70. Bhutan; 71. Kuwait; 72. Maldives; 73. Niue; 74. Qatar; 75. Suriname; 76. United Arab Emirates; 77. Solomon Islands; 78. Dominica; 79. Tuvalu; 80. Kiribati; 81. St. Lucia; 82. Zimbabwe; 83. St. Vincent and the Grenadines; 84. Vanuatu; 85. Belize; 86. Antigua and Barbuda; 87. Brunei Darussalam; and 88. St. Christopher and Nevis.

E. Work of the Trusteeship Council

30. The following Territories had been placed under the trusteeship system of the United Nations by the end

of 1947: the Cameroons under French administration; the Cameroons under British administration; Togoland under French administration; Togoland under British administration; Ruanda-Urundi under Belgian administration; Tanganyika under British administration; Western Samoa under New Zealand administration; New Guinea under Australian administration; Nauru under the joint administration of Australia, New Zealand and the United Kingdom; and the Trust Territory of the Pacific Islands (Marshalls, Marianas and Carolines), designated by the Security Council as a strategic area, under the administration of the United States of America. In 1950 the former Italian colony of Somaliland was placed under trusteeship, with Italy as the Administering Authority.

31. As the result of the plebiscite held in Togoland under British administration, that Territory joined the Gold Coast when the latter became the independent sovereign nation of Ghana on 6 March 1957. Ghana was admitted to membership in the United Nations by General Assembly resolution 1118 (XI) of 8 March 1957.

32. In March 1959 the General Assembly voted to end the Trusteeship Agreement for the Cameroons under French administration; the Republic of Cameroon, now the United Republic of Cameroon, attained independence on 1 January 1960 and was admitted to membership in the United Nations by General Assembly resolution 1476 (XV) of 20 September 1960.

33. On 14 November 1958 the General Assembly, in resolution 1253 (XIII), resolved that the Trusteeship Agreement for Togoland under French administration should be terminated when the Republic of Togoland became independent in 1960. Togo attained independence on 27 April 1960 and was admitted to membership in the United Nations by General Assembly resolution 1477 (XV) of 20 September 1960.

34. The Trusteeship of Somaliland was ended on 1 July 1960 when Italian-administered Somaliland joined British Somaliland, which had acceded to independence a few days earlier. The Republic of Somalia was admitted to membership in the United Nations by General Assembly resolution 1479 (XV) of 20 September 1960.

35. As regards the Cameroons under British administration, the Trusteeship in regard to its northern part came to an end on 1 June 1961 when Northern Cameroons became a part of Nigeria. The Trusteeship in regard to its southern part came to an end on 1 October 1961 when Southern Cameroons became part of Cameroon, now the United Republic of Cameroon.

36. The Trusteeship Agreement for Tanganyika was terminated when that Territory attained independence on 9 December 1961. Tanganyika, now the United Republic of Tanzania, was admitted to membership in the United Nations by General Assembly resolution 1667 (XVI) of 14 December 1961.

37. In the case of Western Samoa, a plebiscite under United Nations supervision, which took place on 9 May 1961, showed that 79 per cent of the people were in favour of independence. The General Assembly endorsed the results of the plebiscite in resolution 1626 (XVI) of 18 October 1961, and resolved that the Trusteeship Agreement should cease to be in force on 1 January 1962, when Western Samoa became an independent sovereign State. Western Samoa was admitted to membership in the United Nations, as Samoa, on 15 December 1976, by General Assembly resolution 31/104 of that date.

38. On 1 July 1962 Ruanda-Urundi achieved independence as Rwanda and Burundi. Rwanda and Burundi were admitted to membership in the United Nations by General Assembly resolutions 1748 and 1749 (XVII) of 18 September 1962.

39. In resolution 2347 (XXII) of 19 December 1967, the General Assembly resolved that the Trusteeship Agreement for Nauru should cease to be in force upon that Territory's accession to independence on 31 January 1968. Nauru did not apply for membership in the United Nations.

40. With regard to New Guinea, the General Assembly, by resolution 2865 (XXVI) of 20 December 1971, decided that "the name to be applied for United Nations purposes to the Non-Self-Governing Territory of Papua and the Trust Territory of New Guinea" should henceforth be "Papua New Guinea". In resolution 3109 (XXVIII) of 12 December 1973, the Assembly welcomed the attainment of self-government by the Territory on 1 December 1973 "as an important step in the progress of Papua New Guinea towards independence". Papua New Guinea was admitted to membership in the United Nations on 10 October 1975, by General Assembly resolution 3368 (XXX) of that date.

41. By 31 December 1982 only one of the eleven Trust Territories had not reached the Charter's goal of independence: the Trust Territory of the Pacific Islands, the only Trust Territory designated a "strategic area" under the Charter.

42. Nevertheless the Trusteeship Council, established to supervise the Territories placed under the International Trusteeship System, continues to function.[2]

F. Work of the specialized agencies and other international organizations

43. Since 1967, the General Assembly has repeatedly recommended that the specialized agencies and international organizations concerned should take urgent and effective measures to assist the peoples struggling for their liberation from colonial rule and work out, in cooperation with the Organization of African Unity, and through it with the national liberation movements, concrete programmes to that end. The question has appeared as a separate item on its agenda since that time.

44. In resolution 42/75 of 4 December 1987 the General Assembly, after reviewing the situation, expressed

---

[2] For information concerning the organizational arrangements and procedures of the Council, see chapter I, section D.

its concern that the assistance extended up to that time by certain specialized agencies and other United Nations organizations to the colonial peoples, particularly the people of Namibia and their national liberation movement, the South West Africa People's Organization, was far from adequate in relation to the actual needs of the peoples concerned. The Assembly regretted that the World Bank continued to maintain certain financial and technical links with the racist régime of Pretoria and expressed the view that those links should be discontinued. It strongly deplored the fact that the International Monetary Fund had been assisting the same racist régime, and expressed the view that the Fund should put an end to such assistance. It strongly condemned the collaboration between the International Monetary Fund and South Africa in disregard of repeated resolutions to the contrary by the Assembly, and called upon the Fund to put an end to such collaboration. And it urged all the specialized agencies and international organizations and institutions within the United Nations system to assist in accelerating progress in all sectors of the national life of the small Territories, particularly in the development of their economies.

45. The Assembly requested the Secretary-General to continue to assist the specialized agencies and other organizations of the United Nations system in working out appropriate measures for implementing the relevant resolutions of the United Nations and to prepare for submission to the relevant bodies, with the assistance of those agencies and organizations, a report on the action taken.

G. Questions relating to the right of peoples and nations to self-determination in particular areas

1. SOUTHERN RHODESIA (ZIMBABWE)

46. In 1923 Southern Rhodesia, a British Territory in central Africa, was granted self-government. In 1961 white settlers, headed by Ian Smith, adopted a new constitution with the concurrence of the United Kingdom Government which effectively excluded the African majority from the exercise of their political rights.

47. In 1962 the General Assembly of the United Nations declared Southern Rhodesia to be a Non-Self-Governing Territory, over the objections of the United Kingdom Government. In 1965 the Ian Smith régime made a unilateral declaration of independence, which the United Kingdom as well as the General Assembly and Security Council of the United Nations condemned.

48. From 1965 to 1980 the international community sought, by every means at its command, to implement the right of the people of Southern Rhodesia to self-determination and true independence.

49. On the day following the unilateral declaration of independence, the Security Council of the United Nations called upon the United Kingdom to quell the "rebellion of the racist minority". It enjoined all States to do their utmost to break relations with the Territory and to stop supplying it with arms, military equipment and petroleum products.

50. In December 1966, for the first time in United Nations history, selective mandatory sanctions were imposed on Southern Rhodesia. Later they were extended so that they included all imports and exports except for medical and education supplies and, in some circumstances, food.

51. Defiant European voters in the Territory approved a new constitution on 20 June 1969, under which a few African representatives could be elected to the legislature but Africans could never attain a majority there. The United Kingdom and the Security Council joined in declaring this act illegal.

52. Proposals for a settlement of the question of Southern Rhodesia, formulated by Ian Smith and the Foreign Secretary of the United Kingdom, were rejected by the United Nations bodies concerned as flagrant violations of the right of the African people of the Territory to self-determination and independence. The General Assembly stipulated that there should be no independence before majority rule on the basis of one man, one vote.

53. In 1976 and 1977 sanctions on the Territory were further expanded to include the interruption of communications and of the transfer of funds from overseas accounts. Nevertheless, European voters in January 1979 approved a new constitution calling for new elections to be held under the old rules—an act which the Security Council condemned as a further attempt to prevent genuine majority rule and independence.

54. The United Kingdom Government convened a Constitutional Conference at Lancaster House in London on 10 September 1979, where arrangements were discussed for a transition period leading to independence which would include the holding of free and fair elections. On 21 December the Conference reached agreement on a Constitution that would provide for genuine majority rule and for a cease-fire between the two opposing factions in the Territory. The Security Council, later that day, called for strict adherence to the Lancaster House Agreement and decided that the international sanctions should be terminated.

55. Elections, observed by United Nations officials, took place in February 1980. On 18 April, Zimbabwe acceded to independence and on 25 August it became a Member of the United Nations.

2. PALESTINE

56. The right of the people of Palestine to self-determination has been emphasized repeatedly in resolutions adopted by the General Assembly. It has also been a matter of concern to the Special Committee to Investigate Israeli Practices Affecting the Human Rights of the Population of the Occupied Territories and the Committee on the Exercise of the Inalienable Rights of the Palestinian People.

57. In resolution 2535 B (XXIV) of 10 December 1969, the General Assembly first noted that "the problem of the Palestine Arab refugees has arisen from the denial of their inalienable rights under the Charter of the United Nations and the Universal Declaration of Human Rights". These views were repeated in Assembly resolutions 2628 (XXV) of 4 November 1970, 2672 (XXV) of 8 December 1970, 2787 and 2792 (XXVI) of 6 December 1971, and 2963 (XXVII) of 13 December 1972.

58. In resolution 3236 (XXIX) of 22 November 1974, the General Assembly recognized that "the Palestinian people is entitled to self-determination in accordance with the Charter of the United Nations" and expressed "its grave concern that the Palestinian people has been prevented from enjoying its inalienable rights, in particular its right to self-determination". Recalling its earlier resolutions affirming the right of the Palestinian people to self-determination, the Assembly reaffirmed "the inalienable rights of the Palestinian people in Palestine", including:

(a) The right to self-determination without external interference;

(b) The right to national independence and sovereignty.

It emphasized that "full respect for and the realization of these inalienable rights . . . are indispensable for the solution of the question of Palestine".

59. In resolution 3376 (XXX) of 10 November 1975, the General Assembly reaffirmed resolution 3236 (XXIX) and expressed its grave concern that no progress had been achieved towards:

(a) The exercise by the Palestinian people of its inalienable rights in Palestine, including the right to self-determination without external interference and the right to national independence and sovereignty;

(b) The exercise by Palestinians of their inalienable right to return to their homes and property from which they have been displaced and uprooted.

The Assembly decided, by that resolution, "to establish a Committee on the Exercise of the Inalienable Rights of the Palestinian People composed of twenty Member States". The Committee was requested "to consider and recommend to the General Assembly a programme of implementation, designed to enable the Palestinian people to exercise the rights recognized in . . . resolution 3236 (XXIX)". In the same resolution the Assembly requested the Security Council "to consider, as soon as possible after 1 June 1976, the question of the exercise by the Palestinian people of the inalienable rights recognized in paragraphs 1 and 2 of resolution 3236 (XXIX)".[3]

60. The Committee's first report[4] contained a series of recommendations designed to enable the Palestinian people to exercise its inalienable rights as previously recognized and defined by the General Assembly. These recommendations were first endorsed by the Assembly in resolution 31/20 of 24 November 1976 as a basis for the solution of the question of Palestine.

61. In its subsequent reports to the General Assembly,[5] the Committee retained its original recommendations unchanged. On each occasion they were again firmly endorsed by the Assembly, which also continued to renew and, as necessary, expand the mandate of the Committee.

62. Despite repeated and urgent appeals by the Committee, however, the Security Council was not able to act on or implement the recommendations of the Committee. The Committee nevertheless remained convinced that positive consideration and action by the Council on those recommendations would advance prospects for the attainment of a comprehensive, just and lasting peace in the Middle East.

63. The General Assembly, in resolution 36/120 C of 10 December 1981, decided to convene under the auspices of the United Nations an International Conference on the Question of Palestine not later than 1984, and authorized the Committee on the Exercise of the Inalienable Rights of the Palestinian People to act as the Preparatory Committee for the Conference and to take all the necessary steps for its organization; it also invited all appropriate United Nations bodies, the specialized agencies and other intergovernmental and non-governmental organizations to co-operate with the Committee in the implementation of that resolution.

64. The International Conference on the Question of Palestine was held at Geneva from 29 August to 7 September 1983. The Conference adopted the Geneva Declaration on Palestine[6] and the Programme of Action for the Achievement of Palestinian Rights.[7] The Declaration, setting out guidelines consistent with the principles of international law which could serve as a basis for concerted international efforts to resolve the question of Palestine, stated in part that:[8]

1. The Conference, having thoroughly considered the question of Palestine in all its aspects, expresses the grave concern of all nations and peoples regarding the international tension that has persisted for several decades in the Middle East, the principal cause of which is the denial by Israel, and those supporting its expansionist policies, of the inalienable legitimate rights of the Palestinian people. The conference reaffirms and stresses that a just solution of the question of Palestine, the core of the problem, is the crucial element in a comprehensive, just and lasting political settlement in the Middle East.

2. The Conference recognizes that, as one of the most acute and complex problems of our time, the question of Palestine—inherited by the United Nations at the time of its establishment—requires a comprehensive, just and lasting political settlement. This settlement must be based on the implementation of the relevant United Nations resolutions concerning the question of Palestine and the attainment of the legitimate, inalienable rights of the Palestinian people, including the right to self-determination and the right to the establishment of its own independent State in Palestine and should also be based on the provision by the Security Council of guarantees for peace and security

---

[3] For information concerning the organizational arrangements and procedures of the Committee, see chapter I, section A, 2 (f).

[4] *Official Records of the General Assembly, Thirty-first Session, Supplement No. 35* (A/31/35).

[5] *Ibid., Forty-second Session, Supplement No. 35* (A/42/35), para. 5.

[6] *Report of the International Conference on the Question of Palestine, Geneva, 29 August-7 September 1983* (United Nations publication, Sales No. E.83.I.21), chap. I, sect. A.

[7] *Ibid.*, chap. I, sect. B.

[8] *Ibid.*, chap. I, sect. A, paras. 1-5.

among all States in the region, including the independent Palestinian State, within secure and internationally recognized boundaries. The Conference is convinced that the attainment by the Palestinian people of their inalienable rights, as defined by General Assembly resolution 3236 (XXIX) of 22 November 1974, will contribute substantially to the achievement of peace and stability in the Middle East.

3. The Conference considers the role of the United Nations in the achievement of a comprehensive, just and lasting peace in the Middle East to be essential and paramount. It emphasizes the need for respect for, and application of the provisions of the Charter of the United Nations, the resolutions of the United Nations relevant to the question of Palestine and the observance of the principles of international law.

4. The Conference considers that the various proposals, consistent with the principles of international law, which have been presented on this question, such as the Arab peace plan adopted unanimously at the twelfth Arab Summit Conference held at Fez, Morocco, in September 1982, should serve as guidelines for concerted international effort to resolve the question of Palestine. These guidelines include the following:

(a) The attainment by the Palestinian people of its legitimate inalienable rights, including the right to return, the right to self-determination and the right to establish its own independent State in Palestine;

(b) The right of the Palestine Liberation Organization, the representative of the Palestinian people, to participate on an equal footing with other parties in all efforts, deliberations and conferences on the Middle East;

(c) The need to put an end to Israel's occupation of the Arab territories, in accordance with the principle of the inadmissibility of the acquisition of territory by force, and consequently, the need to secure Israeli withdrawal from the territories occupied since 1967, including Jerusalem;

(d) The need to oppose and reject such Israeli policies and practices in the occupied territories, including Jerusalem, and any *de facto* situation created by Israel as are contrary to international law and relevant United Nations resolutions, particularly the establishment of settlements, as these policies and practices constitute major obstacles to the achievement of peace in the Middle East;

(e) The need to reaffirm as null and void all legislative and administrative measures and actions taken by Israel, the occupying Power, which have altered or purported to alter the character and status of the Holy City of Jerusalem, including the expropriation of land and property situated thereon, and in particular the so-called "Basic Law" on Jerusalem and the proclamation of Jerusalem as the capital of Israel;

(f) The right of all States in the region to existence within secure and internationally recognized boundaries, with justice and security for all the people, the *sine qua non* of which is the recognition and attainment of the legitimate, inalienable rights of the Palestinian people as stated in paragraph (a) above.

5. In order to give effect to these guidelines, the Conference considers it essential that an international peace conference on the Middle East be convened on the basis of the principles of the Charter of the United Nations and the relevant resolutions of the United Nations, with the aim of achieving a comprehensive, just and lasting solution to the Arab-Israeli conflict, an essential element of which would be the establishment of an independent Palestinian State in Palestine. This peace conference should be convened under the auspices of the United Nations, with the participation of all parties to the Arab-Israeli conflict, including the Palestine Liberation Organization, as well as the United States of America, the Union of Soviet Socialist Republics, and other concerned States, on an equal footing. In this context the Security Council has a primary responsibility to create appropriate institutional arrangements on the basis of relevant United Nations resolutions in order to guarantee and to carry out the accords of the international peace conference.

65. The General Assembly, in resolution 1985/4 of 26 February 1985, noted the outcome of the proceedings of the Conference with satisfaction, supported the Geneva Declaration on Palestine, and welcomed its call to convene an international peace conference on the Middle East under the auspices of the United Nations, in which all parties to the Arab-Israeli conflict, including the Palestine Liberation Organization, the Union of Soviet Socialist Republics and the United States of America, as well as other concerned States, would participate on an equal footing and with equal rights.

66. In the resolution the General Assembly recognized the right of the Palestinian people to regain their rights by all means in accordance with the purposes and principles of the United Nations, and reaffirmed the inalienable right of the Palestinian people to self-determination without external interference and the establishment of a fully independent and sovereign State of Palestine, the basic principle that the future of the Palestinian people can only be decided with its full participation in all efforts, through its legitimate and sole representative, the Palestine Liberation Organization, and its rejection of all partial agreements and separate treaties in so far as they violate the inalienable rights of the Palestinian people and contradict the principles of just and comprehensive solutions to the Middle East problem that ensure the establishment of a just peace in the area, in accordance with the principles of the Charter of the United Nations and with relevant United Nations resolutions. In particular it rejected the plan for "autonomy" within the framework of the "Camp David accords", and declared that those accords have no validity in determining the future of the Palestinian people and of the Palestinian territories occupied by Israel since 1967.

67. In the Introduction to the report which it presented to the forty-second session of the General Assembly, in 1987, the Committee on the Exercise of the Inalienable Rights of the Palestinian People pointed out that:[9]

... the occupation by Israel of Palestinian and other Arab Territories, including Jerusalem, in violation of Security Council and General Assembly resolutions, has continued and is now in its twentieth year. Israel still occupies parts of Lebanon. As a result, the situation relating to the inalienable rights of the Palestinian people has continued to deteriorate. The Committee has repeatedly expressed its grave concern at the policies and practices of Israel in the occupied territories, which are in violation of the Geneva Convention Relative to the Protection of Civilian Persons in Time of War, of 12 August 1949, and the Universal Declaration of Human Rights (General Assembly resolution 217 A (III)). Such policies and practices have continued to pose obstacles to the efforts towards a comprehensive, just and lasting solution, and to exacerbate tension and conflict in the area, further endangering international peace and security. The Committee has therefore repeatedly warned that this situation will continue to prevail as long as the Palestinian people is denied its inalienable rights in Palestine, including those to self-determination without external interference to national independence and sovereignty, to return to its homes and property, and to establish its own independent sovereign State, and as long as the Palestinian and other Arab territories remain occupied. In this connection, the Committee has also been gravely concerned by the violence and destruction directed against Palestinians in refugee camps, for whom the international community has a special responsibility.

---

[9] A/42/35, para. 5.

61

68. In the 1987 report, the Committee expressed its increasing concern at the fact that the situation in the occupied Palestinian territories had continued to deteriorate. It also expressed concern at the continued Israeli policy of confiscating Arab land in the occupied territories and of expanding its settlements, and at the imposition of its iron-fist policy; and at the fact that Israel had continued to take administrative, economic and other measures further to entrench its control over the territories, thereby impeding their autonomous development. At the same time, the Committee noted with appreciation that consensus had been reached on a programme of assistance to the Palestinian people by the United Nations system and that efforts would thenceforth turn to its implementation.

69. The Committee included in its 1987 report a summary of the letters which its Chairman had addressed to the Secretary-General and to the President of the Security Council during the year, drawing their attention to events affecting the inalienable rights of the Palestinian people and urging appropriate action on the basis of United Nations resolutions. The report (section A.2) indicates that on numerous occasions the Chairman expressed grave concern at the persistence and intensification of attacks on Palestinian refugee camps in South Lebanon and at a number of serious incidents in the occupied territories, such as the shooting of Palestinian demonstrators by Israeli troops, arrests, deportations, the closing of schools and universities and the imposition of curfews in several areas.

70. The Committee's report indicated that it had given highest priority, in 1987, to the early convening of an international peace conference. Encouraged by the strong consensus in favour of the urgent convening of the Conference as the most practical and comprehensive approach to a solution of the question and by the fact that none of the members of the Security Council opposed in principle the idea of an international conference under United Nations auspices, the Committee stressed the urgent need for the Security Council and the parties concerned to take positive action towards the convening of the Conference, particularly in the light of the worsening situation in the occupied territories and in the refugee camps.

71. Having considered the Committee's report, the General Assembly, in resolution 42/66 B and C of 2 December 1987, called upon the Secretary-General to continue to assist the Committee in the discharge of its functions. The Assembly also invited all Governments and organizations to co-operate with the Committee, and noted with appreciation the action taken by Member States to observe annually on 29 November the International Day of Solidarity with the Palestinian People.

72. The Commission on Human Rights also examined the right of the people of Palestine to self-determination at recent sessions.

73. In resolution 1986/22 of 10 March 1986, and later in resolution 1987/4 of 19 February 1987, the Commis-sion, bearing in mind the reports and recommendations of the Committee on the Exercise of the Inalienable Rights of the Palestinian People, emphasized repeatedly the right of the Palestinian people to self-determination in accordance with the Charter of the United Nations and the relevant United Nations resolutions, and expressed its grave concern that Israel continued to prevent the Palestinian people by force from enjoying their inalienable rights, in particular their right to self-determination, in defiance of the principles of international law, United Nations resolutions and the will of the international community. In both resolutions the Commission reaffirmed the inalienable right of the Palestinian people to self-determination without external interference and the establishment of their independent and sovereign State on their national soil in accordance with the Charter of the United Nations and General Assembly resolutions, as well as their inalienable right to return to their homeland, Palestine, and their property, from which they have been uprooted by force, and their right to regain their rights by all means in accordance with the purposes and principles of the Charter of the United Nations and with relevant United Nations resolutions. The Commission, further, urged all States, United Nations organs, specialized agencies and other international organizations to extend their support and assistance to the Palestinian people through their representative, the Palestine Liberation Organization, in their struggle to restore their rights.

3. NAMIBIA

74. At the second part of the first session of the General Assembly, a proposal was submitted by the delegation of South Africa calling for the Assembly to approve the annexation by South Africa of the Territory of South West Africa, which had been administered by South Africa since the end of the First World War under a League of Nations Mandate. The South African delegation indicated that the European population of South West Africa had unanimously expressed the wish to be included in the Union of South Africa, and that a majority of the African people who had been consulted also favoured annexation.

75. The General Assembly, in resolution 65 (I) of 14 December 1946, pointed out that "the African inhabitants of South West Africa have not yet secured political autonomy or reached a stage of political development enabling them to express a considered opinion which the Assembly could recognize on such an important question", and therefore declined to accede to the incorporation of the territory in the Union of South Africa. It recommended, instead, "that the mandated territory of South West Africa be placed under the international trusteeship system" and invited the Government of South Africa to propose a trusteeship agreement.

76. On 23 July 1947 the South African Government informed the United Nations that it had decided not to

proceed with the incorporation of South West Africa in the Union. It declared, however, that in view of the wish of the majority of the inhabitants that South West Africa be incorporated in the Union, the Union Government could not act in accordance with the General Assembly's recommendation that the Territory be placed under the International Trusteeship System; and that it considered that it was under no legal obligation to propose a trusteeship agreement for the Territory. The Government indicated that it would maintain the *status quo* and would continue to administer the Territory in the spirit of the existing mandate, and would transmit to the United Nations for its information an annual report on the administration of South West Africa.

77. Since the adoption of resolution 65 (I), the question of Namibia has been on the agenda of every regular session of the General Assembly and of its fifth, ninth and fourteenth special sessions as well as its eighth emergency special session.

78. Between 1969 and 1987 the Security Council adopted more than 20 resolutions on the subject. Several draft resolutions presented for the Council's consideration were not adopted owing to the negative vote of a permanent member of the Council.

79. The International Court of Justice delivered advisory opinions on the question of Namibia, one on 11 July 1950 at the request of the General Assembly and the second on 21 June 1971 at the request of the Security Council.[10]

80. In 1967 the General Assembly established the United Nations Council for South West Africa to administer the Territory until independence, and decided that the Council should entrust such executive and administrative tasks as it deemed necessary to a United Nations Commissioner appointed by the Assembly on nomination by the Secretary-General. Information concerning the organizational and procedural arrangements of the Council appears in chapter I, section A, 2 (d), above.

81. In 1970 and 1971 the General Assembly established a United Nations Fund for the Territory, which it had renamed "Namibia" in accordance with the desires of its people; and in 1973 it appointed the United Nations Council for Namibia as Trustee of the Fund. In 1975, it endorsed the decision of the Council to establish an Institute for Namibia at Lusaka. In 1976, it invited the South West Africa People's Organization (SWAPO) to participate in the sessions and work of the Assembly in the capacity of observer.

82. In its advisory opinion of 21 June 1971,[11] the International Court of Justice informed the Security Council (*a*) that the continued presence of South Africa was illegal and that therefore South Africa was under obligation to withdraw its administration from Namibia immediately; (*b*) that States Members of the United Nations were under obligation to recognize the illegality of South Africa's presence in Namibia and the invalidity of its acts on behalf of or concerning Namibia and to refrain from any acts or dealings with the Government of South Africa implying recognition of the legality of such presence and administration; and (*c*) that it was incumbent on States not Members of the United Nations to co-operate in the action taken by the United Nations with regard to Namibia.

83. Agreeing with the Court's opinion, the Security Council in resolution 301 (1971) of 20 October 1971 declared that any further refusal by South Africa to withdraw from Namibia could create conditions detrimental to the maintenance of peace and security in the region, and called upon States to take a series of measures designed to put end to, or to avoid any recognition of, South Africa's control of the Territory.

84. At a special session in Addis Ababa in February 1972, the Security Council invited the Secretary-General, in consultation with a group of members of the Council, to establish contact as soon as possible with all interested parties with a view to achieving the necessary conditions to enable the Namibian people to exercise their right to self-determination and independence. But in his report to the Council on 30 April 1973 the Secretary-General concluded that the position of the South African Government remained unchanged. The Security Council decided in December 1973 to discontinue the contacts, which had been characterized in the Lusaka Declaration of 14 June 1973, adopted by the United Nations Council for Namibia, as not only unsatisfactory but also counter-productive.

85. On 27 September 1974 the United Nations Council for Namibia enacted a Decree designed to protect the natural resources of the people of Namibia and to ensure that those resources were not exploited without the Council's consent. The Decree was endorsed by the General Assembly in resolution 3295 (XXIX) of 13 December 1974, and all Member States were requested to ensure compliance with the Decree's provisions.

86. The Security Council, in resolutions 366 (1974) of 17 December 1974 and 385 (1976) of 30 January 1976, declared that free elections should be held in Namibia under the supervision and control of the United Nations; and requested South Africa to make a solemn declaration within a six-month period that it would comply with United Nations resolutions and with the advisory opinion of the International Court of Justice, failing which the Council would consider "appropriate action" under the Charter. Although South Africa failed to make such a declaration, the Council was unable to adopt any "appropriate action". On several occasions the negative votes of permanent members of the Council (including France, the United Kingdom and the United States) prevented the adoption of draft resolutions which would have imposed a mandatory arms embargo against South Africa under the terms of Chapter VII of the Charter of the United Nations.

---

[10] *International Status of South West Africa, Advisory Opinion, I.C.J. Reports 1950*, p. 128; and *Legal Consequences for States of the Continued Presence of South Africa in Namibia (South West Africa) notwithstanding Security Council resolution 276 (1970), Advisory Opinion, I.C.J. Reports 1971*, p. 16.

[11] *I.C.J. Reports, 1971, loc. cit.*

87. In 1978 the five Western members of the Security Council—Canada, France, the Federal Republic of Germany, the United Kingdom and the United States—proposed that Territory-wide elections be held under the supervision and control of the United Nations and that a United Nations peace-keeping force be established to maintain order until independence had been attained. The Secretary-General worked out a detailed plan for implementation of the proposal. But the Government of South Africa, after formally accepting the plan, prevented its implementation by conducting "elections" supervised by its own officials.

88. After 35 years of fruitless efforts, the General Assembly in 1978 and again in 1981 recommended that the Security Council impose comprehensive economic sanctions on South Africa, including a trade, oil and complete arms embargo. But in April 1981 a draft resolution by which such sanctions would have been imposed failed to be adopted by the Council because of the negative votes of three of its permanent Members—France, the United Kingdom and the United States.

89. In 1981, negotiations between the Western Contact Group, SWAPO, South Africa and the front-line States (those bordering South Africa) resumed; however, South Africa insisted upon linking any plan for the independence of Namibia to the withdrawal of Cuban troops from Angola. The Security Council declared, on 28 October 1983, that "the independence of Namibia cannot be held hostage to the resolution of issues that are alien" to the 1978 independence plan for Namibia.

90. In 1984, the General Assembly condemned South Africa for sabotaging the independence talks, and declared that attempts to establish a "State Council" to draw up a "Constitution" for Namibia once again made it clear that South Africa had no intention of complying with the United Nations efforts to help the Territory achieve independence.

91. The International Conference for the Immediate Independence of Namibia, held at Vienna from 7 to 11 July 1986, adopted a comprehensive Programme of Action and took note of an appeal for the immediate independence of Namibia signed by eminent persons attending the Conference. In the Programme of Action, the Conference stated that:

1. Namibia summons up the image of a heroic fight against foreign domination and exploitation and of humanity. The achievement of Namibia's independence has been frustrated by the intransigence of the *apartheid* régime as well as by the duplicity of certain members of the international community. Selfish interests have come to the fore, pushing into the background the real issues of decolonization and the people's inalienable right to freedom and independence. The people of Namibia have been subjected to brutal colonialism for more than a century, and 20 years have elapsed since the United Nations terminated South Africa's Mandate over Namibia. In spite of that long passage of time, racist South Africa persists in its illegal occupation of Namibia in violation of the relevant United Nations resolutions, and the agony of the Namibian people continues.

2. The Conference, considering that the fast-deteriorating situation created by the racist régime of South Africa poses a grave danger to peace and security in the region and a growing and direct threat to international peace and security, calls for an immediate, effective and comprehensive response by the international community. The denial of the national rights of the people of Namibia and the continued il-

legal occupation of the Territory by South Africa, in violation of the Charter of the United Nations and the relevant resolutions of the United Nations, constitute a key factor in the growing turmoil in the southern African region. The struggle of the peoples of South Africa and Namibia has reached an acute turning-point. In this twentieth year after the General Assembly terminated South Africa's Mandate over Namibia, the United Nations must take all necessary measures to bring about the immediate independence of Namibia.

3. The Conference calls upon all States to exert every effort towards the immediate and unconditional implementation of Security Council resolutions 385 (1976) and 435 (1978), which remain the only internationally accepted basis for a peaceful settlement of the Namibian question. It further calls upon them to oppose resolutely, in every available forum, the universally and categorically rejected persistent attempts by the United States Administration and racist South Africa to link the implementation of the United Nations plan with irrelevant and extraneous issues, such as the presence of Cuban troops in Angola.

4. The Conference urges the international community to reject all manœuvres aimed at interpreting the present conflict in southern Africa as an East-West confrontation and at diverting attention from the central issue of the decolonization of Namibia, to the detriment of the legitimate aspirations of the Namibian people to self-determination and national independence.

5. The Conference calls upon all Governments, organizations and individuals to exert maximum pressure for the withdrawal of the racist régime from Namibia and to support the actions undertaken by the United Nations in defence of the inalienable right of the Namibian people to self-determination and national independence.

6. The Conference categorically rejects the so-called policy of constructive engagement with South Africa, which has encouraged the intransigence of the Pretoria régime and delayed Namibia's independence, and appeals to the United States to abandon this policy.

7. The Conference condemns the neo-colonialist plans of racist South Africa and the creation in Namibia of the so-called interim government installed in Windhoek in June 1985 and calls upon all States to refrain, in accordance with Security Council resolution 566 (1985) of 19 June 1985, from according any recognition to it or any other régime that South Africa may seek to impose on the Namibian people for the purpose of achieving an "internal settlement". It further calls for the immediate closure of the so-called Namibia Information Offices which the racist Pretoria régime has established in the capitals of certain Western countries to legitimize its puppet institutions in Namibia.

8. The Conference requests the Security Council to selemnly reiterate that Walvis Bay and the offshore islands are an integral part of Namibia and that these should not be the subject of negotiations between South Africa and an independent Namibia.

9. The Conference requests all States to give their full and sincere support to the efforts of the Secretary-General of the United Nations to bring about the immediate and unconditional implementation of Security Council resolution 435 (1978).

10. In view of South Africa's persistent defiance of the resolutions of the United Nations, its brutal suppression of the South African and Namibian peoples, its repeated acts of aggression against neighbouring States, as well as its policies of destabilization of the whole region, the Conference strongly requests the Security Council to immediately adopt and impose comprehensive mandatory sanctions, under Chapter VII of the Charter, against South Africa. The Conference is convinced that the imposition of comprehensive mandatory sanctions is necessary to supplement measures taken by Governments, organizations, the public and individuals to isolate the racist régime and compel it to accept a just settlement of the question of Namibia as well as peaceful change in South Africa itself.

11. The Conference appeals to the United States of America and the United Kingdom of Great Britain and Northern Ireland, permanent members of the Security Council, which have thus far prevented the Council from acting effectively, to reconsider their position in the light of the grave situation in southern Africa and the accumulated evidence of the past 20 years, which irrefutably points to comprehensive mandatory sanctions as the most effective peaceful means of forcing South Africa to terminate its illegal occupation of Namibia.

92. In the Appeal,[12] a number of eminent persons who attended the Conference pointed out that:

Two decades ago, the United Nations assumed direct responsibility for Namibia, having revoked South Africa's Mandate to administer the Territory. Since that time, the Organization has painstakingly established the illegality of South Africa's presence in Namibia. A United Nations plan to grant independence to the Namibian people has for a long time been internationally accepted. To date, however, efforts to implement it have been to no avail. South Africa's continued occupation of Namibia thus stands in open defiance of the united will of the international community. It has consigned yet another generation of Namibians to racial domination, poverty and degradation.

The South African occupation of Namibia is an affront to every principle which civilized people cherish and seek to uphold: self-determination, racial equality and social justice. The leaders of South Africa who perpetuate this ignominious situation have shown by their actions that they are oblivious to moral entreaties and the rule of law. It is therefore clear that stronger pressure most now be exerted on the South African régime. There are several countries, including the United Kingdom, the United States, both permanent members of the Security Council, and the Federal Republic of Germany, which, by virtue of their political and economic prominence, as well as their extensive relations with South Africa, are uniquely qualified to initiate the requisite measures. We profoundly regret that they have failed thus far to do so, out of apparent reluctance to sacrifice the gains that they derive from economic co-operation with South Africa.

Today, southern Africa stands at a crossroad of further and widespread bloodshed or stable peace. The Namibian people, under the inspiring leadership of the South West Africa People's Organization, their sole and authentic representative, have made it clear that they can no longer endure the affront to human dignity and freedom that is their daily fate under the system of *apartheid* and colonial occupation. We urge all members of the international community to grasp this moment to bring independence to Namibia—and an end to *apartheid*—peacefully. The alternative is too bleak to contemplate.

93. The Commission on Human Rights, in a series of resolutions adopted since 1969 on the basis of reports of its *Ad Hoc* Working Group of Experts on Southern Africa, repeatedly expressed its concern at the gross violations of human rights in Namibia and reiterated its affirmation of the inalienable right of the Namibian people to self-determination and independence and the rights enshrined in the Universal Declaration of Human Rights and other relevant international instruments. In resolution 1987/8 of 26 February 1987 the Commission repeated earlier condemnations of South Africa for (*a*) the militarization in Namibia; (*b*) the use of mercenaries to suppress the Namibian people; (*c*) the recruitment and training of Namibians for tribal armies; (*d*) its proclamation of a so-called security zone in Namibia; (*e*) forcible displacement of Namibians from their homes; (*f*) the torture and other forms of brutality meted out to the population and in particular to captured freedom fighters of the South West Africa People's Organization; (*g*) the imposition of military conscription on all Namibian males between 17 and 55 years of age into the occupying colonial army, another sinister attempt to suppress the national liberation struggle of the Namibian people and to force Namibians to kill one another; and (*h*) the exploitation and depletion of natural resources in violation of the decision of the United Nations and Decree No. 1 for the protection of the Natural Resources of Namibia, enacted by the United Nations Council for Namibia on 27 September 1974.

94. The Commission demanded once again, as it had on previous occasions, that South Africa co-operate with the United Nations to bring about the immediate independence of Namibia, without raising extraneous issues, so that the people of Namibia will be enabled to exercise their right to self-determination and enjoy their human rights.

95. The Sub-Commission on Prevention of Discrimination and Protection of Minorities, in resolution 1987/9 of 31 August 1987, expressed its grave concern about the continuing obstacles to the efforts of the United Nations and the international community to bring about the independence of Namibia and requested the Chairman of the Commission on Human Rights to convey that concern to the Secretary-General of the United Nations, the President of the General Assembly and the President of the Economic and Social Council. It condemned in particular the gross violations of human rights of the people of Namibia and the abuse, torture and killing of captured freedom fighters, as well as the continuing atrocities against civilians and ruthless attacks against trade unions and workers; and demanded the immediate and unconditional release of all Namibian political prisoners from detention and concentration camps in Namibia and South Africa as well as the according of prisoner-of-war status to all captured freedom fighters.

96. While continuing to renew the mandate of the Special Committee on Decolonization each year, the General Assembly has also encouraged the Commission on Human Rights to examine human rights aspects of the question of Namibia. The Commission adopted resolutions regarding the violation of the right of peoples to self-determination and other human rights as a result of foreign military intervention, aggression and occupation at its thirty-sixth session, in 1979, and at each subsequent session. In resolution 42/94 of 30 November 1987, the Assembly requested the Commission to continue to give special attention to the violation of human rights, especially the right to self-determination, resulting from foreign military intervention, aggression or occupation.

4. Western Sahara

97. The situation in Western Sahara, a Territory bordered by Morocco, Mauritania and Algeria and administered by Spain until 1976, has been considered by the United Nations since 1963. The General Assembly has repeatedly affirmed the inalienable right of the people of Western Sahara to self-determination and independence in accordance with the Charter of the United Nations, the Charter of the Organization of African Unity and the objectives of Assembly resolution 1514 (XV) and other relevant resolutions of the Assembly and of the Organization of African Unity.

98. In 1975 a United Nations Visiting Mission reported to the Special Committee on the Situation with regard to the Implementation of the Declaration on the Granting of Independence to Colonial Countries and

---

[12] A/41/479, Part III.

Peoples that the Spanish Government wished to decolonize the Territory in conformity with the relevant United Nations resolutions, but that the Governments of Morocco and Mauritania insisted that it should be integrated with their own national territories. The Mission further reported that the population was categorically in favour of independence and rejected the territorial claims of Morocco and Mauritania.

99. In resolution 34/37 of 21 November 1979, the General Assembly deplored the aggravation of the situation resulting from the continued occupation of Western Sahara by Morocco and the extension of that occupation to the territory recently evacuated by Mauritania; and urged Morocco to terminate its occupation of the Territory.

100. At the eighteenth ordinary session of the Assembly of Heads of State and Government of the Organization of African Unity, held at Nairobi from 24 to 27 June 1981, it was decided that a general and free referendum on self-determination should be organized throughout the Territory of Western Sahara.

101. The General Assembly, in resolution 37/28 of 23 November 1982, welcomed the efforts of the Organization of African Unity; appealed for a cease-fire between Morocco and the Frente Popular para la Liberación de Saguia el-Hamra y de Río de Oro (POLISARIO Front) in order to create the objective conditions for peace and to guarantee the fair conduct of a general, free and orderly referendum on self-determination; reaffirmed the determination of the United Nations to co-operate fully with the Organization of African Unity in the fair and impartial organization of the referendum; and requested the Secretary-General to take the necessary steps to ensure effective United Nations participation in the organization and conduct of the referendum.

102. Since 1983, and most recently in resolution 42/78 of 4 December 1987, the General Assembly has repeatedly reaffirmed that the question of Western Sahara is a question of decolonization which remains to be completed on the basis of the exercise by the people of Western Sahara of their inalienable right to self-determination and independence, and has reaffirmed also that the solution of that question lies in the implementation of resolution AHG/Res.104 (XIX) of the Assembly of Heads of State and Government of the Organization of African Unity,[13] which establishes ways and means for a just and definitive political solution to the Western Sahara conflict. The Assembly has requested, again and again, that the two parties to the conflict, the Kingdom of Morocco and the POLISARIO Front, undertake direct negotiations, in the shortest possible time, with a view to bringing about a cease-fire to create the necessary conditions for a peaceful and fair referendum for self-determination of the people of Western Sahara, a referendum without any administrative or military restraints, under the auspices of the Organization of African Unity and the United Nations.

[13] The text of the resolution is reproduced in General Assembly resolution 38/40 of 7 December 1983, para. 1.

103. The Commission on Human Rights, in 1986 and 1987, adopted resolutions along similar lines. In resolutions 1986/21 of 10 March 1986 and 1987/3 of 19 February 1987, the Commission repeated the request of the General Assembly for direct negotiations between the parties to the conflict, expressed its satisfaction at the determination of the United Nations to co-operate fully with the Organization of African Unity in the matter, and decided to follow the development of the situation in Western Sahara as a matter of high priority.

5. EAST TIMOR

104. Prior to the change of Government in April 1974, Portugal maintained that East Timor was an "overseas province" and refused to report to the United Nations on its administration of the Territory as required by Chapter XI of the Charter. Following the change in Government in 1974, however, the new Portuguese Government acknowledged its obligations under Chapter XI as well as the right of the people of the Territory to self-determination, including independence, and, in July 1975, enacted legislation to prepare for the election of a popular assembly in the Territory in October 1976. It was indicated that Portuguese sovereignty would be terminated in October 1978.

105. During the second half of 1975, a civil war erupted in the Territory between Timorese parties desiring independence (notably the Frente Revolucionária de Timor Leste Independente (FRETILIN)) and others preferring integration with Indonesia. In December 1975, Indonesian forces intervened in the Territory and the Portuguese administration withdrew.

106. In August 1976, Indonesia informed the Secretary-General of the United Nations that, at the request of a "Regional Popular Assembly" of East Timor which had been elected the previous May, the Territory had been integrated with Indonesia on 17 July 1976. Indonesia maintained that through integration the people of East Timor had exercised their right to self-determination and acceded to independence, in accordance with the provisions of the Charter of the United Nations and of General Assembly resolution 1514 (XV) of 14 December 1960 and 1541 (XV) of 15 December 1960.

107. In the absence of a decision to the contrary by the General Assembly, the United Nations continues to hold Portugal responsible for the administration of the Territory and the question remains on the agenda of the General Assembly.

108. The Security Council considered the question of East Timor in December 1975 and April 1976, and called upon the Government of Indonesia, in resolutions 384 (1975) of 22 December 1975 and 389 (1976) of 22 April 1976 to withdraw all its forces from the Territory without delay.

109. At its thirty-seventh session, in 1982, the General Assembly heard the statements of the representative of Portugal, as the administering Power, the representative

of Indonesia, and the representatives of FRETILIN, various petitioners and non-governmental organizations. In resolution 37/30 of 23 November 1982 the Assembly, bearing in mind that Portugal, the administering Power, had stated its full and solemn commitment to uphold the right of the people of East Timor to self-determination and independence, expressed its concern about the humanitarian situation prevailing in the Territory and its belief that all efforts should be made by the international community to improve the living conditions of the people of East Timor and to guarantee to those people the effective enjoyment of their fundamental human rights. The Assembly requested the Secretary-General to initiate consultations with all parties directly concerned, with a view to exploring avenues for achieving a comprehensive settlement of the problem; and called upon all organizations of the United Nations system immediately to assist the people of East Timor, in close consultation with Portugal, as the administering Power.

110. The Secretary-General's consultations resulted in contact in June 1983 between Indonesia and Portugal, through their Permanent Representatives at New York. Since that time the two countries have continued the dialogue, and the Secretary-General has reiterated his readiness to assist them in achieving a comprehensive settlement of the problem. The General Assembly, after receiving reports of the Secretary-General each year, has repeatedly deferred further consideration of the question.

111. The Commission on Human Rights, in 1983, considered the question of East Timor and, in resolution 1983/8 of 16 February 1983, called upon all interested parties—namely, Portugal, as the administering Power, and the representatives of the people of East Timor, as well as Indonesia—to co-operate fully with the United Nations with a view to guaranteeing the free and full exercise of the right to self-determination by the people of East Timor.

112. The Sub-Commission on Prevention of Discrimination and Protection of Minorities also considered this question from time to time, and adopted resolutions 1982/20 of 8 September 1982, 1983/26 of 6 September 1983, 1984/24 of 22 August 1984 and 1987/13 of 2 September 1987. In resolution 1987/13 the Sub-Commission, concerned about new allegations regarding the violations of human rights to which the people of East Timor continued to be subjected because of the situation persisting in that country, welcomed the action of the Secretary-General and requested him to continue his efforts to encourage all parties concerned to co-operate in order to achieve a durable solution, taking into full consideration the rights and wishes of the people of East Timor.

6. MAYOTTE

113. In resolution 3161 (XXVIII) of 14 December 1973 the General Assembly reaffirmed the right of the people of the Comoro Archipelago—a group of four

islands between Madagascar and the east coast of Africa—to self-determination and independence, and affirmed the unity and territorial integrity of the Archipelago. In a referendum held in December 1974 three of the islands voted in favour of independence. They became independent, as Comoro, on 6 July 1975 and were admitted to the United Nations as a Member State on 12 November of that year.

114. Because the fourth island, Mayotte, chose not to accede to independence, the Government of France organized two further referendums to ascertain the wishes of the people. The General Assembly subsequently condemned the referendums as null and void, and called upon France to withdraw from the island. Instead, the National Assembly of France granted Mayotte a special status as a "local collectivity" under the administration of the French Minister of the Interior.

115. At the request of the General Assembly the Secretary-General has monitored the situation on Mayotte since 1977, and has maintained continuous contact with the Secretary-General of the Organization of African Unity with regard to this problem, but has not been able to report any substantial progress in the search for a peaceful negotiated settlement. In resolution 41/30 of 3 November 1986, as in several earlier resolutions, the Assembly reaffirmed the sovereignty of the Islamic Federal Republic of the Comoros over the island of Mayotte and requested the Secretary-General to continue to follow developments there.

7. NEW CALEDONIA

116. In resolution 66 (I) of 14 December 1946, the General Assembly noted that information had been transmitted by Member States regarding Non-Self-Governing Territories, including information transmitted by the Government of France on New Caledonia and Dependencies, under Article 73 e of the Charter.

117. On 2 December 1986 the Assembly, aware of the fact that the Government of France had not transmitted any further information on the Territory, and recalling that it had been urged to reinscribe New Caledonia on the list of Non-Self-Governing Territories both by the Heads of Government of the member States of the South Pacific Forum and by the Eighth Conference of Heads of State or Government of Non-Aligned Countries, decided that New Caledonia is a Non-Self-Governing Territory within the meaning of the Charter.

118. The Assembly, in resolution 41/41 A of 2 December 1986, declared that an obligation exists on the part of the Government of France to transmit information on New Caledonia under Chapter XI of the Charter, and requested the Government of France to transmit such information to the Secretary-General. The Assembly further affirmed the inalienable right of the people of New Caledonia to self-determination and independence in accordance with the Declaration on Decolonization.

119. In the debate that preceded the adoption of resolution 41/41 A, the representative of France maintained that New Caledonia in no way could be considered a Non-Self-Governing Territory; its citizens were French and enjoyed fully the rights and freedoms attached to that status. According to him, New Caledonia was therefore fully integrated in the unity of France, with a wide degree of autonomy; if the New Caledonians no longer wished to be French, they had both the right and the possibilities so to determine, but it was for them, and them alone, to make that decision.

H. The right of peoples and nations to permanent sovereignty over their natural wealth and resources

120. The General Assembly, in resolution 523 (VI) of 12 January 1952, expressed the view that developing countries had "the right to determine freely the use of their natural resources", and that they must use such resources for the realization of their economic development plans in accordance with their national interests. These two themes have been reiterated by the Assembly in a number of resolutions. They include resolution 1314 (XIII) of 12 December 1958, by which the Assembly established the Commission on Permanent Sovereignty over Natural Resources and instructed it to conduct a full survey of the status of permanent sovereignty over natural wealth and resources as a basic constituent of the right to self-determination; resolution 1515 (XV) of 15 December 1960, in which it recommended that the sovereign right of every State to dispose of its wealth and natural resources should be respected; and resolution 1803 (XVII) of 14 December 1962, in which it declared that:

1. The right of peoples and nations to permanent sovereignty over their natural wealth and resources must be exercised in the interest of their national development and of the well-being of the people of the State concerned.

. . .

7. Violation of the rights of peoples and nations to sovereignty over their natural wealth and resources is contrary to the spirit and principles of the Charter of the United Nations and hinders the development of international co-operation and the maintenance of peace. . . .

121. The General Assembly dealt further with the question of permanent sovereignty of peoples and nations over their natural wealth and resources in resolutions 2158 (XXI) of 25 November 1966, 2386 (XXIII) of 19 November 1968, 2625 (XXV) of 24 October 1970, 2692 (XXV) of 11 December 1970, 3016 (XXVII) of 18 December 1972 and 3171 (XXVIII) of 17 December 1973. In the latter resolution the Assembly strongly reaffirmed the inalienable rights of States to permanent sovereignty over all their natural resources, on land within their international boundaries as well as those in the sea-bed and the subsoil thereof within their national jurisdiction and in the superjacent waters; supported resolutely the efforts of the developing countries and of the peoples of the territories under colonial and racial domination and foreign occupation in their struggle to regain effective control over their natural resources; and affirmed that the application of the principle of nationalization carried out by States, as an expression of their sovereignty in order to safeguard their natural resources, implies that each State is entitled to determine the amount of possible compensation and the mode of payment, and that any disputes which might arise should be settled in accordance with the national legislation of each State carrying out such measures.

122. In resolution 3175 (XXVIII) of the same date, the Assembly affirmed the right of the Arab States and peoples whose territories are under foreign occupation to permanent sovereignty over all their natural resources; reaffirmed that all measures undertaken by Israel to exploit the human and natural resources of the occupied Arab territories are illegal, and called upon Israel to halt such measures forthwith; affirmed the right of the Arab States and peoples whose territories are under Israeli occupation to the restitution of and compensation for the exploitation and looting of, and damages to, the natural resources, as well as the exploitation and manipulation of the human resources, of the occupied territories; and declared that the above principles apply to all States, territories and peoples under foreign occupation, colonial rule or *apartheid*.

123. The Assembly continued its consideration of this question at its twenty-ninth to thirty-seventh sessions, and adopted resolutions 3336 (XXIX), 3516 (XXX), 31/186, 32/161, 34/136, 35/110, 36/173 and 37/135. At its thirty-eighth session, in resolution 38/144 of 19 December 1983, it took note of the report prepared by the Secretary-General at its request on permanent sovereignty over national resources in the occupied Palestinian and other Arab territories[14] and condemned Israel for its exploitation of those resources. Pointing out that Convention IV of the Hague of 1907 and the Geneva Convention Relative to the Protection of Civilian Persons in Time of War, of 12 August 1949, are applicable to the occupied Palestinian and other Arab territories, the Assembly emphasised the right of the Palestinian and other Arab peoples whose territories are under Israeli occupation to full and effective permanent sovereignty and control over their natural and all other resources, wealth and economic activities.

124. The Assembly also reaffirmed that all measures taken by Israel to exploit the human, natural and all other resources, wealth and economic activities in the occupied territories are illegal, and called upon Israel to desist immediately from such measures. Further, it reaffirmed the right of the Palestinian and other Arab peoples subjected to Israeli aggression and occupation to the restitution of, and full compensation for the exploitation, depletion and loss of and damage to, their natural, human and all other resources, wealth and economic activities, and called upon Israel to meet their just claims.

125. The Assembly called upon all States to support the Palestinian and other Arab peoples in the exercise of

---

[14] A/38/282-E/1983/84.

the above-mentioned rights, and called upon all States, international organizations, specialized agencies, business corporations and all other institutions not to recognize, or co-operate with or assist in any manner, any measures taken by Israel to exploit the national resources of the occupied territories or to effect any changes in the demographic composition, the character and form of use of their natural resources or the institutional structure of those territories.

126. Since 1983 the Secretary-General, at the request of the General Assembly, has endeavoured to elaborate on his report to cover also, in detail, the resources exploited by the Israeli settlements and the Israeli-imposed regulations and policies hampering the economic development of the occupied Palestinian and other Arab territories.

I. Legal status of combatants struggling against colonial and alien domination and racist régimes

127. The struggle of peoples for liberation, for realization of their right to self-determination, and for the elimination of racial prejudice and discrimination has received increasing recognition in the United Nations. The General Assembly first recognized "the legitimacy of the struggle by the peoples under colonial rule to exercise their right to self-determination and independence" in resolution 2105 (XX) of 21 December 1965. In resolution 2326 (XXI) of 11 December 1967 the Assembly declared that the persistence of colonialism, the suppression of liberation movements and the use of armed force against colonial peoples was incompatible not only with the Charter but also with the Universal Declaration of Human Rights.

128. In connection with the tenth anniversary of the Declaration on the Granting of Independence to Colonial Countries and Peoples the General Assembly, in resolution 2621 (XXV) of 12 October 1970, adopted a comprehensive Programme of Action for the full implementation of the Declaration, in which it declared "the further continuation of colonialism in all its forms and manifestations a crime which constitutes a violation of the Charter of the United Nations, the Declaration on the Granting of Independence to Colonial Countries and Peoples, and the principles of international law"; and reaffirmed "the inherent right of colonial peoples to struggle by all necessary means at their disposal against colonial Powers which suppress their aspiration for freedom and independence". The Programme provided for Member States to render all necessary moral and material assistance to the peoples of colonial Territories in their struggle to obtain freedom and independence, for all freedom fighters under detention to be treated in accordance with the relevant provisions of the Geneva Convention Relative to the Treatment of Prisoners of War, and for representatives of liberation movements to be invited by organizations within the United Nations system to participate in an appropriate

capacity in the proceedings of those organs relating to their countries.

129. On 12 December 1973 the General Assembly, noting that the treatment of the combatants struggling against colonial and alien domination and racist régimes captured as prisoners still remained inhuman, solemnly proclaimed, in resolution 3103 (XXVIII), a series of basic principles of the legal status of such combatants in the following terms:

1. The struggle of peoples under colonial and alien domination and racist régimes for the implementation of their right to self-determination and independence is legitimate and in full accordance with the principles of international law.

2. Any attempt to suppress the struggle against colonial and alien domination and racist régimes is incompatible with the Charter of the United Nations, the Declaration on Principles of International Law concerning Friendly Relations and Co-operation among States in accordance with the Charter of the United Nations, the Universal Declaration of Human Rights and the Declaration on the Granting of Independence to Colonial Countries and Peoples and constitutes a threat to international peace and security.

3. The armed conflicts involving the struggle of peoples against colonial and alien domination and racist régimes are to be regarded as international armed conflicts in the sense of the 1949 Geneva Conventions, and the legal status envisaged to apply to the combatants in the 1949 Geneva Conventions and other international instruments is to apply to the persons engaged in armed struggle against colonial and alien domination and racist régimes.

4. The combatants struggling against colonial and alien domination and racist régimes captured as prisoners are to be accorded the status of prisoners of war and their treatment should be in accordance with the provisions of the Geneva Convention Relative to the Treatment of Prisoners of War, of 12 August 1949.

5. The use of mercenaries by colonial and racist régimes against the national liberation movements struggling for their freedom and independence from the yoke of colonialism and alien domination is considered to be a criminal act and the mercenaries should accordingly be punished as criminals.

6. The violation of the legal status of the combatants struggling against colonial and alien domination and racist régimes in the course of armed conflicts entails full responsibility in accordance with the norms of international law.

J. Measures used to suppress or to impede realization of the right of peoples and nations to self-determination

1. ACTS OR THREATS OF MILITARY INTERVENTION OR OCCUPATION

130. Since 1980, both the Commission on Human Rights and the General Assembly have periodically reviewed the question of the universal realization of the right of peoples to self-determination, and have welcomed the progressive exercise of that right by peoples under colonial, foreign or alien occupation and their emergence into sovereign statehood and independence.

131. However, both the Commission and the Assembly have frequently expressed deep concern at the continuation of acts or threats of foreign military intervention or occupation that have threatened to suppress, or have already suppressed, realization of the right to

self-determination by an increasing number of sovereign peoples and nations.

132. In resolution 42/94 of 30 November 1987, the General Assembly most recently expressed its concern that, as a consequence of the persistence of such actions, millions of people have been and are being uprooted from their homes as refugees and displaced persons, and emphasized the urgent need for concerted international action to alleviate their condition.

133. In the resolution, the Assembly reaffirmed that the universal realization of the right of all peoples, including those under colonial, foreign and alien domination, to self-determination is a fundamental condition for the effective guarantee and observance of human rights and for the preservation and promotion of such rights; and declared its firm opposition to acts of foreign military intervention, aggression, and occupation, since these have resulted in the suppression of the right of peoples to self-determination and other human rights in certain parts of the world. It called upon those States responsible to cease immediately their military intervention and occupation of foreign countries and territories and all acts of repression, discrimination, exploitation and maltreatment, particularly the brutal and inhuman methods reportedly employed for the execution of these acts against the peoples concerned.

134. Deploring the plight of millions of refugees and displaced persons who have been uprooted by such acts, and reaffirming their right to return to their homes voluntarily in safety and honour, the Assembly requested the Commission on Human Rights to continue to give special attention to the violation of human rights, especially the right to self-determination, resulting from foreign military intervention, aggression or occupation.

2. USE OF MERCENARIES

135. For many years the Security Council has condemned any State that persisted in permitting or tolerating the recruitment of mercenaries, and the provision of facilities to them, with the objective of overthrowing the Governments of States Members of the United Nations.[15] The General Assembly has also denounced the practice of using mercenaries, in particular against developing countries and national liberation movements, in a number of resolutions.[16]

136. Bearing these decisions in mind the Commission on Human Rights, in resolution 1986/26 of 10 March 1986, condemned the increased recruitment, financing, training, assembly, transit and use of mercenaries, as

well as other forms of support to them, including so-called humanitarian aid, for the purpose of destabilizing and overthrowing the Governments of southern African States and fighting against the national liberation movements of peoples struggling for the exercise of their right to self-determination.

137. The Economic and Social Council, in resolution 1986/43 of 23 May 1986, repeated this condemnation, urged all States to take the necessary measures under their respective domestic laws to prohibit the recruitment, financing, training and transit of mercenaries on their territories and other territories under their control; encouraged the *Ad Hoc* Committee on the Drafting of an International Convention against the Recruitment, Use, Financing and Training of Mercenaries to make every effort to complete its mandate and to submit a draft convention to the General Assembly; and urged the Commission on Human Rights to appoint a special rapporteur on this subject to prepare a report for consideration at the Commission's forty-fourth session, in 1988.

138. Recalling these decisions, the Commission on Human Rights decided, in resolution 1987/16 of 9 March 1987, to appoint for one year a special rapporteur to examine the question of the use of mercenaries as a means of violating human rights and of impeding the exercise of the right of peoples to self-determination. The Chairman of the Commission was requested to appoint an individual of recognized international standing as special rapporteur after consultations with the other members of the Commission's Bureau. The Special Rapporteur was authorized, in carrying out his mandate, to seek and receive credible and reliable information from Governments as well as specialized agencies, intergovernmental organizations and non-governmental organizations.

139. In resolution 42/96 of 7 December 1987, the General Assembly cited "the need for strict observance of the principles of sovereign equality, political independence, territorial integrity of States and self-determination of peoples, as well as scrupulous respect for the principle of the non-use or threat of the use of force in international relations, enshrined in the Charter of the United Nations and developed in the Declaration on Principles of International Law concerning Friendly Relations and Co-operation among States in accordance with the Charter of the United Nations". It expressed its deep concern about the increasing menace that the activities of mercenaries represent for all States, particularly African, Central American and other developing States, and recognized that mercenarism is a threat to international peace and security.

140. The Assembly condemned the increased recruitment, financing, training, assembly, transit and use of mercenaries, as well as all other forms of support to mercenaries for the purpose of destabilizing and overthrowing the Governments of southern Africa and Central America and of other developing States and fighting against the national liberation movements of peoples struggling for the exercise of their right to self-

---

[15] See Council resolutions 239 (1967) of 10 July 1967, 405 (1977) of 14 April 1977, 419 (1977) of 24 November 1977, 496 (1981) of 15 December 1981 and 507 (1982) of 28 May 1982.

[16] See General Assembly resolutions 1514 (XV) of 14 December 1960, 2395 (XXIII) of 29 November 1968, 2465 (XXIII) of 20 December 1968, 2548 (XXIV) of 11 December 1969, 2708 (XXV) of 14 December 1970, 3103 (XXVIII) of 12 December 1973, 34/140 of 14 December 1979, 40/74 of 11 December 1985 and 41/102 of 4 December 1986.

determination. It called upon all States to exercise the utmost vigilance against the menace posed by the activities of mercenaries and to ensure, by both administrative and legislative measures, that the territory of those States and other territories under their control, as well as their nationals, are not used for the recruitment, assembly, financing, training and transit of mercenaries, or the planning of such activities designed to destabilize or overthrow the Government of any State and to fight the liberation movements struggling against racism, *apartheid,* colonial domination and foreign intervention and occupation for their independence, territorial integrity and national unity. Further, it urged all States to take the necessary measures under their respective domestic laws to prohibit the recruitment, financing, training and transit of mercenaries on their territory, and called upon them to extend humanitarian assistance to victims of situations resulting from the use of mercenaries, as well as from colonial or alien domination or foreign occupation. It expressed the view that it is inadmissible to use channels of humanitarian and other assistance to finance, train and arm mercenaries, and welcomed with satisfaction the appointment by the Commission on Human Rights of a Special Rapporteur to study and report on the matter.

3. ACTIVITIES OF FOREIGN ECONOMIC OR OTHER INTERESTS

141.   In 1964, in accordance with General Assembly resolution 1899 (XVIII), the Special Committee on Decolonization undertook a study on the implications of the activities of the mining industry and of the other international companies having interests in Namibia. In 1965 and 1966, the Special Committee, pursuant to a decision which it had taken in 1964, undertook a study of the activities of foreign economic and other interests which are impeding the implementation of the Declaration in the Territories under Portuguese administration, and submitted reports thereon to the Assembly at its twentieth and twenty-first sessions. In 1966 the Special Committee studied the activities of foreign economic and other interests in Southern Rhodesia and their mode of operation in order to assess their economic and political influence, and submitted a report thereon to the General Assembly at its twenty-first session.

142.   The question appeared on the agenda of the Assembly from its twenty-first session onwards; at the thirty-fifth session it was retitled: "Activities of foreign economic and other interests which are impeding the implementation of the Declaration on the Granting of Independence to Colonial Countries and Peoples in Namibia and in all other Territories under colonial domination, and efforts to eliminate colonialism, *apartheid,* and racial discrimination in southern Africa".

143.   Since its twenty-second session, the General Assembly has repeatedly affirmed "the inalienable right of the peoples of dependent Territories to self-determination and independence and to the enjoyment of the natural resources of their Territories, as well as their right to dispose of those resources in their best interests"; has reiterated that "any administering or occupying Power which deprives the colonial peoples of the exercise of their legitimate rights over their natural resources or subordinates the rights and interests of those peoples to foreign economic and financial interests violates the solemn obligations it has assumed under the Charter of the United Nations"; and has reaffirmed that, "by their depletive exploitation of natural resources, the continued accumulation and repatriation of huge profits and the use of those profits for the enrichment of foreign settlers and the entrenchment of colonial domination over the Territories, the activities of foreign economic, financial and other interests operating at present in the colonial Territories, particularly in southern Africa, constitute a major obstacle to political independence and to the enjoyment of the natural resources of those Territories by the indigenous inhabitants".

144.   In resolution 42/74 of 4 December 1987, the Assembly reaffirmed the inalienable right of the peoples of dependent Territories to self-determination and independence and to the enjoyment of the natural resources of their Territories, as well as the right to dispose of those resources in their best interests; reiterated that any administering or occupying Power that deprives the colonial peoples of the exercise of their legitimate rights over their natural resources or subordinates the rights and interests of those peoples to foreign economic and financial interests violates the solemn obligations it has assumed under the Charter of the United Nations; and reaffirmed that, by their depletive exploitation of natural resources, the continued accumulation and repatriation of huge profits and the use of those profits for the enrichment of foreign settlers and the perpetration of colonial domination and racial discrimination in the Territories, the activities of foreign economic, financial and other interests operating at present in the colonial Territories, particularly in Namibia, constitute a major obstacle to political independence and racial equality, as well as to the enjoyment of the natural resources of those Territories by the indigenous inhabitants.

4. ADVERSE CONSEQUENCES OF POLITICAL, MILITARY, ECONOMIC AND OTHER FORMS OF ASSISTANCE

145.   In 1974, the Economic and Social Council, in resolution 1864 (LVI) of 17 May 1974, condemned the activities of States which continued to give political, military, economic and other assistance to the racist and colonial régimes in southern Africa or which refrained from taking any steps to prevent natural or juridical persons within their jurisdiction from assisting those régimes and thus encouraging them to continue violating fundamental human rights; approved the decision of the Commission on Human Rights to authorize the Sub-Commission on Prevention of Discrimination and Protection of Minorities to appoint a Special Rappor-

teur to study the subject; and recommended that the General Assembly should include that item in its agenda.

146. The General Assembly has since considered the item at regular intervals, and has adopted resolutions 3382 and 3383 (XXX) of 10 November 1975, 31/33 of 30 November 1976, 33/23 of 29 November 1978, 35/32 of 14 November 1980, 36/172 A to P of 17 December 1981, 37/39 of 3 December 1982, 39/15 of 23 November 1984 and 41/95 of 4 December 1986 on the subject. Both the Commission on Human Rights and the Sub-Commission on Prevention of Discrimination and Protection of Minorities have also considered the question regularly.

147. The basic documentation for these activities is a report prepared by Mr. Ahmed Khalifa, Special Rapporteur of the Sub-Commission, and updated annually by him,[17] on the adverse consequences for the enjoyment of human rights of political, military, economic and other forms of assistance given to the racist and colonial régime in southern Africa. The General Assembly has on several occasions reaffirmed that the updating of the report is of the greatest importance to the cause of fighting *apartheid* and other violations of human rights in South Africa and Namibia.

148. In resolution 41/95 of 4 December 1986, the General Assembly, after examining the Special Rapporteur's report, vigorously condemned the collaboration of certain Western States, Israel and other States, as well as the transnational corporations and other organizations which maintain or continue to increase their collaboration with the racist régime of South Africa, especially in the political, economic, military and nuclear fields, thus encouraging that régime to persist in its inhuman and criminal policy of brutal oppression of the peoples of southern Africa and denial of their human rights. The Assembly stated again that States and organizations that give assistance to the racist régime of South Africa become accomplices in the inhuman practices of racial discrimination, colonialism and *apartheid* perpetrated by that régime, as well as in the acts of aggression against the liberation movements and neighbouring States.

149. The Assembly, further, called upon the Security Council urgently to consider the imposition of comprehensive and mandatory sanctions under Chapter VII of the Charter of the United Nations against the racist régime of South Africa, in particular:

(a) The prohibition of all technological assistance or collaboration in the manufacture of arms and military supplies in South Africa;

(b) The cessation of all collaboration with South Africa in the nuclear field;

(c) The prohibition of all loans to, and all investments in, South Africa, and the cessation of any trade with South Africa; and

(d) An embargo on the supply of petroleum, petroleum products and other strategic goods to South Africa.

150. The Commission on Human Rights welcomed the Assembly's request to the Security Council in resolution

1987/9 of 26 February 1987, and expressed regret that the Security Council had not been in a position to take binding decisions to prevent any collaboration between South Africa and other States. It condemned in particular the assistance rendered by the major Western countries and Israel to South Africa in the political, economic, financial and military fields, the continuing nuclear collaboration of certain Western States, Israel, and other States with the racist régime of South Africa, and the activities of all foreign economic interests operating in Namibia under the illegal South African administration which are illegally exploiting the resources of the Territory.

151. The Sub-Commission on Prevention of Discrimination and Protection of Minorities, in resolution 1987/7 of 31 August 1987, proposed that the Economic and Social Council should invite the Special Rapporteur to continue to update, subject to annual review, the list of banks, transnational corporations and other organizations assisting the racist régime of South Africa, giving such details regarding the enterprises listed as he may consider necessary and appropriate; and to use all available material in order to indicate the volume, nature and adverse human consequences of the assistance given to the racist régime of South Africa.

K. Study of the implementation of the right of peoples and nations to self-determination

152. By resolution 2649 (XXV) of 30 November 1970, the General Assembly requested the Commission on Human Rights "to study, at its twenty-seventh session, the implementation of the United Nations resolutions relating to the right of peoples under colonial and alien domination to self-determination, and to submit its conclusions and recommendations to the General Assembly, through the Economic and Social Council, as soon as possible".

153. The Commission, in resolution 8 A (XXVII) of 11 March 1971, requested the Secretary-General "to prepare an annotated collection of all the resolutions adopted by the various organs of the United Nations, the specialized agencies and the regional organizations relating to the right of peoples under colonial and alien domination to self-determination"; and decided, "making use of this collection, to continue the consideration of this question with a view to appointing a special rapporteur at its twenty-eighth session".

154. After postponing further consideration of the item at its twenty-eighth and twenty-ninth sessions, the Commission, at its thirtieth session, in 1974, reviewed the report of the Secretary-General[18] and, by resolution 5 (XXX) of 20 February 1974, invited the Sub-Commission on Prevention of Discrimination and Protection of Minorities to appoint a special rapporteur to analyse the Secretary-General's report and to make recommendations to the Commission at its thirty-second session

---

[17] E/CN.4/Sub.2/1987/8 and Add.1.

[18] E/CN.4/1081 and Corr.1 and Add.1 and 2 and Add.2/Corr.1.

"with regard to the implementation of United Nations resolutions relating to the right of peoples under colonial and alien domination to self-determination". The Commission's decisions were approved by the Economic and Social Council in resolution 1866 (LVI) of 17 May 1974.

155. The Sub-Commission, by resolution 4 (XXVII) of 16 August 1974, appointed Mr. Héctor Gros Espiell, one of its members, as Special Rapporteur on the implementation of United Nations resolutions relating to the right of peoples under colonial and alien domination to self-determination. In resolution 32/14 of 7 November 1977, the General Assembly stated that it looked forward to the publication of the study. The final report of the Special Rapporteur[19] was received by the Sub-Commission at its thirty-first session, in 1978. On the recommendation of the Sub-Commission and the Commission on Human Rights, the Economic and Social Council adopted decision 1979/39 of 10 May 1979 to the effect that the study should be printed and given the widest possible distribution, including distribution in Arabic. The printed version of the study was issued in 1980.[20]

156. In the study, the Special Rapporteur considered a number of questions concerning the definition, scope and legal nature of the right of peoples under colonial and alien domination to self-determination, outlined the existing state of implementation of United Nations resolutions relating to that right, and reviewed a number of situations concerning that right which have been or are being dealt with by the United Nations. In addition, he presented his conclusions on future action by the United Nations to implement its resolutions relating to the right of peoples under colonial and alien domination to self-determination, and his recommendations with regard to such future action.

157. The Special Rapporteur found that the action taken by organizations within the United Nations system to secure recognition of the right of peoples under colonial and alien domination to self-determination "has without doubt led to highly positive results as regards the final objective sought . . . However, despite the exceptional importance of what has been done, the problem has not yet been solved entirely, even from the political standpoint alone, nor has the right to self-determination become a reality everywhere. Many colonial situations still exist and there are still many United Nations resolutions on specific cases which have not yet been fully implemented. Hence the need to persevere, to maintain and, if possible, to speed up the process of decolonization, and to consider, systematically and globally, the work done and the procedures employed, in order to determine what new measures are required and what approach should be taken with regard to the implementation of the resolutions already adopted."

L. Study of the historical development of the right of peoples and nations to self-determination

158. The Commission on Human Rights, on recommendation of its Sub-Commission on Prevention of Discrimination and Protection of Minorities, authorized the Sub-Commission to place on its agenda an item entitled "The historical and current development of the right to self-determination on the basis of the Charter of the United Nations and other instruments adopted by United Nations organs, with particular reference to the promotion and protection of human rights and fundamental freedoms", and to designate a special rapporteur to undertake a detailed study on the subject (Commission resolutions 10 (XXIX) of 22 March 1973 and 4 (XXX) of 20 February 1974.

159. The Sub-Commission, by resolution 3 (XXVII) of 16 August 1974, appointed Mr. Aureliu Cristescu, one of its members, as Special Rapporteur for the study. In resolutions 3070 (XXVIII), 3382 (XXX), 31/34 and 32/14, the General Assembly welcomed the decision to carry out the study, and declared that it keenly awaited its completion and publication. The final report of the Special Rapporteur[21] was received by the Sub-Commission at its thirty-first session, in 1978. On the recommendation of the Sub-Commission and of the Commission on Human Rights, the Economic and Social Council decided (decision 1979/39 of 10 May 1979) that the study should be printed and given the widest possible distribution, including distribution in Arabic. The printed version of the study was issued in 1980.[22]

160. In the Study, the Special Rapporteur considers the right to self-determination as developed in the Charter and other major United Nations instruments. After reviewing general legal and political aspects of the principle of equal rights and self-determination of peoples, he surveys such specific aspects as the right of peoples freely to determine their political status, and freely to pursue their economic, social and cultural development.

161. He concludes that the right to self-determination "has become one of the most important and dynamic concepts in contemporary international life", one that "exercises a profound influence on the political, legal, economic, social and cultural planes, in the matter of fundamental human rights and on the life and fate of peoples and of individuals as such". He points out, further, that "the right to self-determination, which is a fundamental human right, plays an important part in the realization of the other human rights and freedoms, by creating the general framework and foundation for the implementation and promotion of human rights. At the same time, respect for each individual human right contributes to the exercise of the right to self-determination."

[19] E/CN.4/Sub.2/405.

[20] *The right to self-determination: implementation of United Nations resolutions* (United Nations publication, Sales No. E.79.XIV.5).

[21] E/CN.4/Sub.2/404.

[22] *The right to self-determination: historical and current development on the basis of United Nations instruments* (United Nations publication, Sales No. E.80.XIV.3).

M. Importance of the universal realization of the right of peoples and nations to self-determination

162. In resolution VIII of 11 May 1968, entitled "The importance of the universal realization of the right of peoples to self-determination and of the speedy granting of independence to colonial countries and peoples for the effective guarantee and observance of human rights", the International Conference on Human Rights pointed out that "the subjugation and oppression of a people by another is a serious violation of the main objectives of the Universal Declaration of Human Rights", and expressed its appreciation to the Special Committee on the Situation with regard to the Implementation of the Declaration on the Granting of Independence to Colonial Countries and Peoples "for its efforts to secure the complete and effective implementation" of that Declaration.

163. The General Assembly has since reviewed periodically the progress achieved in the implementation of the Declaration, and has repeatedly reaffirmed the importance of the universal realization of the right of peoples to self-determination, national sovereignty and territorial integrity, and of the speedy granting of independence to colonial countries and peoples, as imperatives for the full enjoyment of all human rights.

164. In resolution 42/95 of 7 December 1987, the Assembly called upon all States to implement fully and faithfully all the resolutions of the United Nations regarding the exercise of the right to self-determination and independence by peoples under colonial and foreign domination. It called for a substantial increase in all forms of assistance given by all States, United Nations organs, the specialized agencies and non-governmental organizations to the victims of racism, racial discrimination and *apartheid* through national liberation movements recognized by the Organization of African Unity and the United Nations on this question; demanded the immediate and unconditional release of all persons detained or imprisoned as a result of their struggle for self-determination and independence, full respect for their fundamental individual rights in compliance with article 5 of the Universal Declaration of Human Rights, under which no one shall be subjected to torture or to cruel, inhuman or degrading treatment; and urged all States, the specialized agencies and other competent organizations of the United Nations system to do their utmost to ensure the full implementation of the Declaration on the Granting of Independence to Colonial Countries and Peoples.

165. In particular, the Assembly expressed the view "that the denial of the inalienable rights of the Palestinian people to self-determination, sovereignty, independence and return to Palestine, and the repeated acts of aggression by Israel against the people of the region, constitute a serious threat to international peace and security". With regard to southern Africa, it again demanded "the immediate application of the mandatory arms embargo against South Africa, imposed under Security Council resolution 418 (1977) of 4 November 1977, by all countries and more particularly by those countries that maintain military and nuclear co-operation with the racist Pretoria régime and continue to supply it with related *matériel*".

IV. ELIMINATION OF RACISM, RACIAL DISCRIMINATION, AND INTOLERANCE OR DISCRIMINATION BASED ON RELIGION OR BELIEF

Introduction

1. The principles of equality and non-discrimination are set out clearly in the Charter of the United Nations, which repeatedly refers to the realization of human rights and fundamental freedoms "by all without distinction as to race, sex, language or religion". Ideas of equality and non-discrimination also motivate the Universal Declaration of Human Rights, both International Covenants on Human Rights, the Declaration and Convention on the Elimination of All Forms of Racial Discrimination and the Declaration on the Elimination of All Forms of Intolerance and of Discrimination Based on Religion or Belief.

2. This preoccupation of the United Nations with the extirpation of racism, racial discrimination and religious intolerance is not new; it dates back to 2 November 1946, when a draft resolution relating to "religious and so-called racial persecution and discrimination" was submitted to the General Assembly by the representative of Egypt.

3. The draft resolution stated that it appeared from various governmental and unofficial investigations carried out in several States of Central Europe, among both Members and non-Members of the United Nations, that citizens belonging to religious minorities continued, in spite of the victory of the democracies, to be the object of persecution and of discrimination which rendered very difficult life in their native countries, where they had an absolute right to be on an equal footing with all other citizens. Such persecution and discrimination, the draft resolution stated further, constituted a total disregard of the most elementary humanitarian principles and was contrary to the purposes of the United Nations; the General Assembly should therefore call on the Governments and responsible authorities of the areas concerned to put an end to it.

4. The General Committee of the Assembly considered this proposal at its 25th meeting on 6 November 1946. A number of representatives objected to the reference made to Central Europe. Later, the representative of Egypt submitted a revised version of the draft resolution which was worded in general terms and omitted the reference to Central Europe. In this form the draft resolution met with no objection, and it was unanimously adopted at the 48th plenary meeting of the General Assembly as resolution 103 (I) of 19 November 1946. The resolution, as adopted, read as follows:

The General Assembly declares that it is in the higher interests of humanity to put an immediate end to religious and so-called racial persecution and discrimination, and calls on the Governments and responsible authorities to conform both to the letter and to the spirit of the Charter of the United Nations, and to take the most prompt and energetic steps to that end.

5. For many years after the adoption of resolution 103 (1), United Nations bodies confined their consideration of the question of discrimination either to particular areas, such as southern Africa and the Non-Self-Governing and Trust Territories, or to particular fields, such as education, employment and political rights. However, in 1960 an outbreak of manifestations of racial prejudice and religious intolerance occurred in several countries, and these were the subject of broad measures adopted by the Sub-Commission on Prevention of Discrimination and Protection of Minorities, the Commission on Human Rights, the Economic and Social Council and the General Assembly.

6. Early in 1960, both the Sub-Commission on Prevention of Discrimination and the Commission on Human Rights noted with deep concern a series of manifestations of racism and religious intolerance which had occurred in several European countries late in 1959 and which the Sub-Commission characterized as "reminiscent of the crimes and outrages committed by the Nazis prior to and during the Second World War".

7. The General Assembly, in resolution 1510 (XV) of 12 December 1960, shared the concern of the Commission and its Sub-Commission. Affirming that "the United Nations is duty bound to combat these manifestations, to establish the facts and the causes of their origin, and to recommend resolute and effective measures which can be taken against them", the Assembly resolutely condemned "all manifestations and practices of racial, religious and national hatred in the political, economic, social, educational and cultural spheres of the life of society as violations of the Charter of the United Nations and the Universal Declaration of Human Rights"; and called upon "the Governments of all States to take all necessary measures to prevent all manifestations of racial, religious and national hatred".

8. Two years later the Assembly, in resolution 1779 (XVII) of 7 December 1962, indicated that it was deeply disturbed "by the continued existence and manifestations of racial prejudice and of national and religious intolerance in different parts of the world", and recommended further specific measures to eliminate such manifestations. The Assembly:

1. Invited the Governments of all States, the specialized agencies and non-governmental and private organizations to continue to make sustained efforts to educate public opinion with a view to the eradication of racial prejudice and national and religious intolerance and the elimination of all undesirable influences promoting these, and to take appropriate measures so that education may be directed with due regard to article 26 of the Universal Declaration of Human Rights and

to principle 10 of the Declaration of the Rights of the Child adopted by the General Assembly on 20 November 1959;

2. Called upon the Governments of all States to take all necessary steps to rescind discriminatory laws which have the effect of creating and perpetuating racial prejudice and national and religious intolerance wherever they still exist, to adopt legislation if necessary for prohibiting such discrimination, and to take such legislative or other appropriate measures to combat such prejudice and intolerance;

3. Recommended the Governments of all States to discourage actively, through education and all media of information, the creation, propagation and dissemination of such prejudice and intolerance in any form whatever;

4. Invited the specialized agencies and non-governmental organizations to co-operate fully with the Governments of States in their efforts to prevent and eradicate racial prejudice and national and religious intolerance;

5. Invited the Governments of Member States, the specialized agencies and the non-governmental organizations concerned to inform the Secretary-General of action taken by them in compliance with the . . . resolution;

6. Requested the Secretary-General to submit to the General Assembly at its eighteenth session a report on compliance with the . . . resolution.

9. As requested, the Secretary-General submitted further reports on action taken by Member States in compliance with General Assembly resolution 1779 (XVII) to the General Assembly at its eighteenth, nineteenth, twentieth and twenty-first sessions;[1] and the General Assembly, in resolutions 2019 (XX) of 1 November 1965 and 2143 (XXI) of 26 October 1966, took note of those reports.

10. However, in the course of 1967, even more serious manifestations of racism and religious intolerance occurred in some western European countries as a result of the revival of certain groups and organizations professing totalitarian ideologies such as nazism and fascism. Recognizing that firm measures should be taken to halt such activities wherever they occurred, the Assembly, in resolution 2331 (XXII) of 18 December 1967, condemned any ideology, including nazism, which was based on racial intolerance and terror, as a gross violation of human rights and fundamental freedoms and of the purposes and principles of the Charter of the United Nations, and called upon all States to take immediate and effective measures against any such manifestations of nazism and racial intolerance. The Assembly considered the question further at its twenty-third to twenty-fifth sessions, and adopted resolutions 2438 (XXIII), 2545 (XXIV) and 2713 (XXV).

11. The International Conference on Human Rights, held at Teheran from 22 April to 13 May 1968, considered various aspects of the problem of racial discrimination and adopted several resolutions on the subject.[2] In addition it declared, in the Proclamation of Teheran, that:

. . . The peoples of the world must be made fully aware of the evils of racial discrimination and must join in combating them. The implementation of this principle of non-discrimination, embodied in the Charter of the United Nations, the Universal Declaration of Human Rights, and other international instruments in the field of human rights, constitutes a most urgent task of mankind, at the international as well as at the national level. All ideologies based on racial superiority and intolerance must be condemned and resisted.

12. In resolution II, entitled "Measures to be taken against nazism and racial intolerance", the Conference urged "all States, with due regard to the principles contained in the Universal Declaration of Human Rights, to declare illegal and prohibit Nazi and racist organizations and groups and any organized or other activity based on Nazi ideology and any similar ideology that is based on terrorism and racial intolerance and to declare participation in such organizations and activities to be a criminal act punishable by law"; and called upon "all States and peoples and national and international organizations to take all necessary measures for the immediate and final eradication of Nazi and any other similar ideology and practice based on terrorism and racial intolerance".

13. The General Assembly made a major pronouncement on the subject in resolution 2839 (XXVI) of 18 December 1971, in which it confirmed "that nazism and other forms of racial intolerance constitute a serious threat to the realization everywhere of human rights and freedoms and the maintenance of international peace and security". The Assembly called upon States to take steps to bring to light any evidence of the manifestation and dissemination of the ideology and practice of nazism and racial intolerance and to ensure that they were rigorously suppressed and prohibited; and to take immediate and effective measures, including legislative measures, with due regard to the principles contained in the Universal Declaration of Human Rights, to prevent the activities of Nazi and racist organizations and groups.

14. The Assembly also urged those States which had been unable, for serious constitutional or other reasons, to implement immediately and fully the provisions of article 9 of the United Nations Declaration on the Elimination of All Forms of Racial Discrimination and article 4 of the International Convention on the Elimination of All Forms of Racial Discrimination, to take measures designed to ensure the speedy disbandment and disappearance of such organizations, those measures to provide, *inter alia*, that:

(a) Such organizations should not be allowed to receive financial subsidies from organs of the State, private companies or individuals;

(b) Such organizations should not be allowed the use of public premises in which to establish their headquarters or conduct meetings of their members, the use of streets and squares in populated areas for holding demonstrations, or the use of public information media for disseminating propaganda;

(c) Such organizations should not be allowed to form militarized detachments on any pretext, and offenders should be subject to prosecution in the courts;

(d) Persons employed by the State, particularly in the armed forces, should not be permitted to belong to such organizations; and all these measures to be taken only in so far as they are compatible with the principles of the Universal Declaration of Human Rights.

15. The Commission on Human Rights considered the question of measures to be taken against ideologies and practices based on terror or incitement to racial discrimination, or any other form of group hatred, at its

---

[1] A/5473 and Add.1 and Add.1/Corr.1, and Add.2, A/5703 and Add.1 and 2, and A/6347 and Add.1-3.

[2] See *Final Act of the International Conference on Human Rights* (United Nations publication, Sales No. E.68.XIV.2).

thirty-ninth to forty-second sessions, and adopted resolutions 1983/28 of 7 March 1983, 1984/41 of 12 March 1984, 1985/30 of 11 March 1985 and 1986/61 of 13 March 1986. In these resolutions the Commission emphasized that the doctrines of racial or ethnic superiority, on which the totalitarian entities and régimes are based, contradict the spirit and principles of the United Nations and that the realization of such doctrines in practice leads to wars, mass and flagrant violations of human rights and crimes against humanity, such as genocide, and creates obstacles for friendly relations among nations and for social progress in the world.

16.   In resolution 1986/41, the Commission expressed the view that the best defence against all totalitarian ideologies lies in free and effective popular participation in democratic institutions, based on respect for the human rights proclaimed in the Universal Declaration of Human Rights and other relevant international documents. It called upon all States to take the measures necessary to ensure the thorough investigation and the detection, arrest, extradition and punishment of all war criminals and persons guilty of crimes against humanity, who have not yet been brought before a court and paid an appropriate penalty; and called upon the appropriate specialized agencies as well as intergovernmental and international non-governmental organizations to initiate or intensify measures against all totalitarian ideologies and practices.

17.   In 1986 the General Assembly, after considering the problem once more, adopted resolution 41/160 of 4 December 1986, in which it expressed deep alarm at the existence of groups and organizations which still propagate totalitarian ideologies and practices, and concern that the proponents of Fascist, neo-Fascist and other totalitarian ideologies had, in a number of countries, intensified their activities and were increasingly co-ordinating them on an international scale. Once again the Assembly condemned all such ideologies and practices, urged all States to draw attention to the threats to democratic institutions by those ideologies and practices and to consider taking measures to prohibit or otherwise deter activities of groups or organizations or whoever practises those ideologies; and invited Member States to adopt, in accordance with their national constitutional systems and with the provisions of the Universal Declaration of Human Rights, measures declaring punishable by law any dissemination of ideas based on racial superiority or hatred and of war propaganda, including Nazi, Fascist and neo-Fascist ideologies.

A. Racism and racial discrimination

1. RACIAL DISCRIMINATION AND SEGREGATION IN NON-SELF-GOVERNING TERRITORIES

18.   Between 1949 and 1962 attention was focused, in the United Nations bodies concerned, on the question of racial discrimination in Non-Self-Governing Ter-

ritories, with the result that the General Assembly adopted a number of resolutions and decisions on the subject.

19.   In resolution 328 (IV) of 2 December 1949, the General Assembly invited the administering Members "to take steps, where necessary, to establish equal treatment in matters related to education between inhabitants of the Non-Self-Governing Territories under their administration, whether they be indigenous or not".

20.   In resolution 644 (VII) of 10 December 1952, the General Assembly, having regard to "the principles of the Charter and of the Universal Declaration of Human Rights emphasizing the necessity of promoting and encouraging respect for human rights and for fundamental freedoms for all without distinction as to race, sex, language, or religion", recommended to the "Members responsible for the administration of Non-Self-Governing Territories the abolition in those Territories of discriminatory laws and practices contrary to the principles of the Charter and of the Universal Declaration of Human Rights". The General Assembly also recommended that the administering Members should examine all laws, statutes and ordinances in force in the Non-Self-Governing Territories under their administration, as well as their application in the said Territories, with a view to the abolition of any such discriminatory provisions or practices. The General Assembly further recommended that "all public facilities should be open to all inhabitants of the Non-Self-Governing Territories, without distinction of race"; recognized that "the establishment of improved race relations largely depends on the development of educational policies" and commended "all measures designed to improve among all pupils in all schools understanding of the needs and problems of the community as a whole".

21.   In resolution 1328 (XIII) of 12 December 1958, the General Assembly, having regard to "the fundamental importance of race relations, particularly under modern conditions, for the attainment of objectives of Chapter XI of the Charter of the United Nations" and recognizing "the necessity of intensifying the promotion and encouragement of respect for human rights and fundamental freedoms for all, regardless of race, sex, language or religion", reaffirmed resolution 644 (VII). The General Assembly also invited the administering Members "to include in the annual reports submitted under Article 73 e of the Charter of the United Nations information on the measures taken by them for the implementation" of resolutions calling for the elimination of discriminatory practices.

22.   In resolution 1536 (XV) of 15 December 1960, the General Assembly endorsed "the view of the Committee on Information from Non-Self-Governing Territories that not only is racial discrimination a violation of human rights, but it also constitutes a deterrent to progress in all fields of development" in the Territories concerned. The General Assembly also urged the administering Members "to give full and immediate effect to recommendations of the Committee . . . that measures to solve the problem of race relations should include the

extension to all inhabitants of the full exercise of basic political rights, in particular the right to vote, and the establishment of equality among the members of all races inhabiting the Non-Self-Governing Territories''.

23.   In resolution 1698 (XVI) of 19 December 1961, the General Assembly considered ''that racial discrimination and segregation in Non-Self-Governing Territories can be eradicated fully and with the greatest speed by the faithful implementation of the Declaration on the granting of independence to colonial countries and peoples, and that, accordingly, efforts of the United Nations should be concentrated on that task''. In the same resolution the General Assembly condemned resolutely ''the policy and practice of racial discrimination and segregation in Non-Self-Governing Territories'' and urged the administering Members ''to include, among the measures that would contribute to the implementation of the Declaration . . . steps to ensure . . . The immediate rescinding or revocation of all laws and regulations which tend to encourage or sanction, directly or indirectly, discriminatory policies and practices based on racial considerations, the adoption of legislative measures making racial discrimination and segregation punishable by law, and the discouragement of such practices based on racial considerations by all other means possible, including administrative measures''.

24.   In many resolutions adopted later, the General Assembly supported the struggle of the peoples of Non-Self-Governing Territories to obtain racial equality. For example, in resolution 2646 (XXV) of 30 November 1970, the Assembly reaffirmed ''the legitimacy of the struggle of all oppressed peoples everywhere, and in particular those of South Africa, Namibia, Southern Rhodesia and Territories under Portuguese colonial domination, to obtain racial equality by all possible means''. The Assembly, in that resolution, also called for ''increased and continued moral, and in particular material, support to all peoples under colonial and alien domination, struggling for the realization of their right to self-determination and for the elimination of all forms of racial discrimination''.

2. STUDIES ON RACIAL DISCRIMINATION

25.   Two important studies on racial discrimination have been prepared under the auspices of the United Nations. The first, a study of the economic and social consequences of racially discriminatory practices, was originally presented as a report to the fourth session of the Economic Commission for Africa by its Executive Secretary.[3] The second, a study on racial discrimination in the political, economic, social and cultural spheres, prepared by Mr. Hernán Santa Cruz, Special Rapporteur of the Sub-Commission on Prevention of Discrimination and Protection of Minorities, was submitted to the Sub-Commission in 1970 and published in

1971.[4] A revised and updated version of the study, prepared pursuant to a decision taken by the Economic and Social Council at its 1858th meeting, on 18 May 1973, was published in 1976.[5]

(a) Study of the economic and social consequences of racially discriminatory practices

26.   In 1961 the Economic Commission for Africa requested its Executive Secretary to make ''sub-regional studies of the economic and social consequences of racial discriminatory practices on the mobilization of all available resources for the balanced economic development of all territories within the geographical scope of the Commission''. The Executive Secretary's report, entitled *Economic and Social Consequences of Racial Discriminatory Practices,*[3] was submitted to the Commission at its fourth session in 1962.

27.   The study showed that there was clear and deliberate racial discrimination in the distribution and ownership of land, supported by statutes and general government policy overwhelmingly in favour of the ruling racial minorities in many parts of southern Africa. This discrimination in land distribution meant not only the geographical segregation of the different racial groups, but also inequitable distribution of land, racially restrictive practices with regard to property ownership, and differential policies regarding agricultural and extension services and credit and market facilities. Likewise, discriminatory practices obtained in urban areas, where there were severe racial restrictions regarding residence and business property ownership, invariably in favour of the ruling racial group.

28.   The study indicated, further, that in the field of labour, numerous discriminatory laws and practices existed to regulate the geographical and occupational mobility of workers and to bolster the privileged position of distinct racial groups: devices such as racial job reservations, ''pass laws'' to control the movement of labour and channel it to depressed or economically unattractive areas, migratory labour practices, extra-territorial recruitment of labour, racially restrictive trade union laws and practices, and differential wage rates. It indicated, further, that it was in the field of education and training, perhaps more than anywhere else, that the discriminatory practices found their roots and sustaining force; not only was education racially segregated, but European education was compulsory while African education was not, and government expenditure was more than ten times higher per European child than per African child.

29.   The major adverse economic consequences of these racially discriminatory practices were summarized as follows:

---

[3] United Nations publication, Sales No. E.63.II.K.1.

[4] *Special Study on Racial Discrimination in the Political, Economic, Social and Cultural Spheres* (United Nations publication, Sales No. E.71.XIV.2).

[5] *Racial Discrimination* (United Nations publication, Sales No. E.76.XIV.2).

(a) Failure to use human resources fully or efficiently, as a result of racial discrimination in education and training, employment and remuneration;

(b) High production costs entailed by payment of inflated wages in sectors of the economy where job competition is artificially eliminated by racially restrictive trade union practices and officially supported job reservations to protect the ruling racial group; failure to respond to normal forces of supply and demand; reliance on imported skilled labour while at the same time neglecting the training of local manpower;

(c) Waste of land resources, and concentration of masses of the population in overpopulated or impoverished areas, while uncultivated tracts of land lie idle and reserved for the dominant ruling European group, as in South Africa; conversely, over-protection of land rights for Africans, tending in turn to prevent the entry of private non-African capital and the economic exploitation of such resources by non-Africans under appropriate government control;

(d) Combined crippling effects of restrictive labour and land policies on the geographical mobility of labour; perpetuation of migratory, unskilled, inefficient labour;

(e) Separate racial development, which tends to perpetuate dual economies—disintegrated economies in which the subsistence sector is predominantly African and the monetary predominantly European;

(f) Limiting effects on levels of production of discriminatory policies with regard to property ownership, credit policies, extension services and marketing facilities;

(g) Waste of resources involved in administering the instruments of discrimination, particularly in the form of duplication of services and fixed capital;

(h) Large disparities in incomes accruing to different racial groups, and the resulting wide gaps in standards of living;

(i) Narrow internal markets resulting significantly from the small purchasing power of the mass of the population, which in turn is associated with an inequitable distribution of national income within the complex of the racially restrictive policies and practices.

30. The report concluded that:

The existing situation is obviously one that cries out for change and cannot be connived at. Where government action, through legislation or other means, has been the instrument of racial discrimination, government action can be equally the instrument for undoing the system and creating non-racial conditions in the various fields of economic and social activity. Equally, where discrimination is conventional, firms and individuals can be effective in taking the lead. Race prejudice as such cannot, it is feared, be removed by government policy, legislation, or administrative measures—though these can go a long way to condition and direct the public. But racial discrimination can be removed, or at least minimized, by public action—by law and administrative regulations. Putting the two points differently, while governments may not make one race love another, government action can and should safeguard and guarantee the economic rights of the individual regardless of race, and help educate the public with respect to the disastrous economic consequences of racial discrimination.

(b) *Study on racial discrimination in the political, economic, social and cultural fields*

31. The Study on racial discrimination in the political, economic, social and cultural spheres was initiated by the Sub-Commission on Prevention of Discrimination and Protection of Minorities at its eighteenth session in 1966, when the Sub-Commission appointed one of its Members, Mr. Hernán Santa Cruz (Chile) as Special Rapporteur.

32. The Study, submitted to the Sub-Commission at its twenty-third session, in 1970, contains an analysis of many aspects of the problem of racial discrimination and a series of proposals for action. The Sub-Commission, after considering the Special Rapporteur's conclusions and recommendations, transmitted the Study to the Commission on Human Rights together with a series of proposals for action. These proposals were later considered by the Commission, the Economic and Social Council and the General Assembly.

33. In resolution 2784 (XXVI) of 6 December 1971, the General Assembly invited the Economic and Social Council "to request the Commission on Human Rights to continue its comprehensive studies of policies and practices of racial discrimination, taking into account in particular discrimination against peoples of African origin in all countries, and to submit a report to the General Assembly as soon as possible . . . together with recommendations for action to combat such policies and practices".

34. In resolution 2785 (XXVI), of the same date, the General Assembly urged "all States concerned to implement a programme of political, social, cultural and economic redress to improve the conditions of those suffering from the effects of past and present policies of racial discrimination" and, in particular, appealed "to Governments and all organizations in the United Nations system to devote their urgent attention to the problems involved in the education of youth, in a spirit of world peace, justice, mutual respect and understanding, as well as respect for the value and dignity of the human person and generally recognized principles of morality and international law concerning friendly relations and co-operation among States, in order to combat racial policies, and to promote equal rights and economic, social and cultural progress for all".

35. The General Assembly requested "every competent United Nations organ, specialized agency, regional intergovernmental organization and non-governmental organization in consultative status, acting in good faith without political motivation and in accordance with the Charter of the United Nations, to consider, as a matter of highest priority:

(a) The further action that it might itself take with a view to the speedy elimination of racial discrimination throughout the world;

(b) The action that it might suggest to its subsidiary organs, to States and to international and national bodies for this purpose;

(c) The follow-up measures required to ensure full and effective implementation of its decisions in this matter".

36. Further, the Assembly endorsed the invitation addressed by the Economic and Social Council, in resolution 1588 (L), to the International Labour Organisation and the United Nations Educational, Scientific and Cultural Organization "to provide the Commission on Human Rights with reports on the nature and effect of any racial discrimination of whose existence they have knowledge in their sphere of competence", and requested "that such reports should be submitted annually". The Assembly also endorsed the invitation addressed by the Council to the non-governmental organizations in consultative status "which have a special interest in the elimination of racism and racial discri-

mination, to communicate biennially to the Council, and for the information of any interested organ of the United Nations, their endeavours and progress in the struggle against racism, *apartheid* and racial discrimination in all its forms''.

37. In resolution 1697 (LII) of 2 June 1972, the Economic and Social Council requested the Sub-Commission on Prevention of Discrimination and Protection of Minorities ''to continue its studies on racial discrimination and, in particular, to update the study entitled *Racial Discrimination*, as appropriate, with special emphasis on discrimination based on colour''. On the recommendation of the Sub-Commission, the Council decided, on 18 May 1973, to request Mr. Hernán Santa Cruz to update the study which he had prepared.

38. The Sub-Commission examined the updated study[6] at its twenty-ninth session, in 1976. In resolution 4 (XXIX) of 31 August 1976, the Sub-Commission, after expressing its appreciation to the Special Rapporteur, approved the recommendations contained in the updated study and brought them to the attention of the Commission on Human Rights and the Economic and Social Council.

39. Other studies undertaken by United Nations bodies, aimed at eradicating discrimination, prejudice and intolerance in respect of the enjoyment of particular human rights and fundamental freedoms, are dealt with in chapters of the present publication relating to those rights and freedoms.

3. ACTIVITIES OF ILO AND UNESCO FOR THE ELIMINATION OF RACISM AND RACIAL DISCRIMINATION

40. Both the International Labour Organisation and the United Nations Educational, Scientific and Cultural Organization have adopted international instruments aimed at eliminating discrimination in various fields, such as employment, education and social security.

41. Among those prepared by the International Labour Conference are the Equal Remuneration Convention, 1951 (No. 100) and Recommendation (No. 90), adopted on 29 June 1951; the Discrimination (Employment and Occupation) Convention, 1958 (No. 111), and Recommendation (No. 111), adopted on 25 June 1958; the Equality of Treatment (Social Security) Convention, 1962 (No. 118), adopted on 28 June 1962; the Employment Policy Convention, 1964 (No. 122) and Recommendation (No. 122), adopted on 9 July 1964; the Migrant Workers (Supplementary Provisions) Convention, 1975 (No. 143) and Recommendation (No. 151), adopted on 24 June 1975; and the Vocational Rehabilitation and Employment (Disabled Persons) Convention, 1983 (No. 159), adopted on 22 June 1983.

42. Among those prepared by the General Conference of the United Nations Educational, Scientific and Cultural Organization are the Convention and the Recommendation against Discrimination in Education, adopted on 14 December 1960, and the Protocol Instituting a Conciliation and Good Offices Commission to be responsible for seeking a settlement of any disputes which may arise between States parties to the Convention against Discrimination in Education, adopted on 10 December 1962.

43. Within the framework of the International Labour Office's regular programme for the supervision of ILO Conventions and Recommendations, the Committee of Experts on the Application of Conventions and Recommendations, at its recent annual sessions, made a number of comments on the developments which have taken place in several of the countries that have ratified the Discrimination (Employment and Occupation) Convention, 1958 (No. 111) and other Conventions referred to above.

44. In accordance with article 19 of the Constitution of ILO, the Governing Body at its 224th Session (November 1983) requested Governments to report in 1985 on the position of their law and practice respecting equal pay for men and women workers, as laid down in the Equal Remuneration Convention (No. 100) and Recommendation (No. 90). The reports supplied by the Governments provided an opportunity for the Committee of Experts to make a general survey[7] of the situation as regards the implementation of the instruments, both in ratifying States and in countries which have not ratified the Convention.

45. UNESCO has continued its scientific study of racism based on its constitutional mandate and on the request of the Economic and Social Council, in 1948, that it ''consider the desirability of initiating and recommending the adoption of a programme of disseminating scientific facts designed to remove what is commonly known as racial prejudice''.

46. A major programme has been adopted by UNESCO's General Conference—one of the 14 major programmes in the Organization's Second Medium-Term Plan 1984-1989—including comprehensive and coordinated scientific research and action regarding racial discrimination and other forms of intolerance and prejudice. Activities undertaken within this programme are in direct line with the Programme of Action for the Second Decade to Combat Racism and Racial Discrimination, in which UNESCO is requested to continue various activities, notably ''its work (studies and research) on the factors of influence in the maintenance, transmission and alteration of prejudices and on the causes and effects of the various forms of racism and racial and ethnic discrimination . . .''.

47. An informal consultation of experts to select studies to be undertaken on the social, economic, cultural and political causes of racism and *apartheid* was held at Beijing, China, from 15 to 24 November 1984.

---

6 E/CN.4/Sub.2/370, Add.1-6 and Add.6/Corr.1; subsequently issued as a United Nations publication, Sales No. E.76.XIV.2.

7 International Labour Conference, 72nd Session, 1986: Equal Remuneration: *General Survey by the Committee of Experts on the Application of the Conventions and Recommendations.*

48. In 1986, in co-operation with the International Sociological Association Research Committee on Ethnic, Race and Minority Relations, UNESCO sponsored an international meeting on social science paradigms and empirical research at New Delhi, India. The paper prepared for the meeting indicated a number of areas in which further research was needed. Of crucial importance was the area of definition, particularly with regard to social race as against ethnic groups. Other issues discussed included research methods involved in deriving the data on which theory is based, epistemological assumptions from which theory flows; the specifics of the location of scholarship and processes of data generation, and the linkages between research and analysis.

4. United Nations Declaration on the Elimination of All Forms of Racial Discrimination

49. The United Nations Declaration on the Elimination of All Forms of Racial Discrimination, proclaimed by the General Assembly on 20 November 1963 in resolution 1904 (XVIII), is based on several important considerations, among them: (a) "that any doctine of racial differentiation of superiority is scientifically false, morally condemnable, socially unjust and dangerous, and that there is no justification for racial discrimination either in theory or in practice"; (b) "that all forms of racial discrimination and, still more so, governmental policies based on the prejudice of racial superiority or on racial hatred, besides constituting a violation of fundamental human rights, tend to jeopardize friendly relations among peoples, co-operation between nations and international peace and security"; (c) "that racial discrimination harms not only those who are its objects but also those who practise it"; and (d) "that the building of a world society free from all forms of racial segregation and discrimination, factors which create hatred and division among men, is one of the fundamental objectives of the United Nations".

50. In resolution 1904 (XVIII), adopting the Declaration, the General Assembly solemnly affirms "the necessity of speedily eliminating racial discrimination throughout the world, in all its forms and manifestations, and of securing understanding of and respect for the dignity of the human person", and points out "the necessity of adopting national and international measures to that end, including teaching, education and information, in order to secure the universal and effective recognition and observance" of the Declaration's principles.

51. Article 1 of the Declaration states that

Discrimination between human beings on the ground of race, colour or ethnic origin is an offence to human dignity and shall be condemned as a denial of the principles of the Charter of the United Nations, as a violation of the human rights and fundamental freedoms proclaimed in the Universal Declaration of Human Rights, as an obstacle to friendly and peaceful relations among nations and as a fact capable of disturbing peace and security among peoples.

52. In article 2 the basic provision is made that

No state, institution, group or individual shall make any discrimination whatsoever in matters of human rights and fundamental freedoms in the treatment of persons, groups of persons or institutions on the ground of race, colour or ethnic origin.

53. The articles which follow call upon States "to take effective measures to revise governmental and other public policies and to rescind laws and regulations which have the effect of creating and perpetuating racial discrimination", to pass laws "prohibiting such discrimination", and to take "appropriate measures to combat those prejudices which lead to racial discrimination". In particular, they provide that "effective steps shall be taken immediately in the fields of teaching, education and information, with a view to eliminating racial discrimination and prejudice and promoting understanding, tolerance and friendship among nations and racial groups"; and that "immediate and positive measures" shall be taken "to prosecute and/or outlaw organizations which promote or incite to racial discrimination, or incite to or use violence for purposes of discrimination based on race, colour or ethnic origin".

54. Article 10 of the Declaration provides that

The United Nations, the specialized agencies, States and non-governmental organizations shall do all in their power to promote energetic action which, by combining legal and other practical measures, will make possible the abolition of all forms of racial discrimination. They shall, in particular, study the causes of such discrimination with a view to recommending appropriate and effective measures to combat and eliminate it.

5. Committee on the Elimination of Racial Discrimination

55. The Committee on the Elimination of Racial Discrimination, established in accordance with article 8 of the International Convention on the Elimination of all Forms of Racial Discrimination,[8] consists of 18 experts of high moral standing and acknowledged impartiality, elected by States parties from among their nationals, consideration being given to equitable geographical distribution and to the representation of the different forms of civilization and of the principal legal systems. Members serve in their personal capacity as experts. They are elected at a meeting of States parties for a term of four years, and are eligible for re-election.

56. The Committee normally holds two regular sessions each year and submits an annual report, covering the work of those sessions, to the General Assembly. All meetings are held in public, and all elections are by secret ballot, unless the Commitee decides otherwise.

57. Articles 9 and 11 of the Convention read in part as follows:

Article 9

1. States Parties undertake to submit to the Secretary-General of the United Nations, for consideration by the Committee, a report on the legislative, judicial, administrative or other measures which they have adopted and which give effect to the provisions of this Convention: (a) within one year after the entry into force of the Convention

---

[8] For information concerning the Convention, see chapter II, section B.1.

for the State concerned; and (*b*) thereafter every two years and whenever the Committee so requests. The Committee may request further information from the States Parties.

2. The Committee shall report annually, through the Secretary-General, to the General Assembly of the United Nations on its activities and may make suggestions and general recommendations based on the examination of the reports and information received from the States Parties. Such suggestions and general recommendations shall be reported to the General Assembly together with comments, if any, from States Parties.

Article 11

1. If a State Party considers that another State Party is not giving effect to the provisions of this Convention, it may bring the matter to the attention of the Committee. The Committee shall then transmit the communication to the State Party concerned. Within three months, the receiving State shall submit to the Committee written explanations or statements clarifying the matter and the remedy, if any, that may have been taken by that State.

2. If the matter is not adjusted to the satisfaction of both parties, either by bilateral negotiations or by any other procedure open to them, within six months after the receipt by the receiving State of the initial communication, either State shall have the right to refer the matter again to the Committee by notifying the Committee and also the other State.

3. The Committee shall deal with a matter referred to it in accordance with paragraph 2 of this article after it has ascertained that all available domestic remedies have been invoked and exhausted in the case, in conformity with the generally recognized principles of international law. This shall not be the rule where the application of the remedies is unreasonably prolonged.

. . .

58. The rules relating to the functions of the Committee[9] provide that the Committee may, through the Secretary-General, inform the States parties of its wishes regarding the form and contents of the periodic reports required to be submitted to it under article 9 of the Convention, and notify the States parties of the opening date, duration and place of the session at which their respective reports will be examined. Representatives of the States parties may be present at the meetings of the Committee when their reports are examined. The Committee may also inform a State party from which it decides to seek further information that it may authorize its representative to be present at a specified meeting. Such a representative should be able to answer questions which may be put to him by the Committee and make statements on reports already submitted by his State, and may also submit additional information from his State.

59. When considering a report submitted by a State party under article 9 of the Convention, the Committee must first determine whether the report provides the information referred to in the relevant communications of the Committee. If a report, in the opinion of the Committee, does not contain sufficient information, the Committee may request that State to furnish additional information. Moreover if, on the basis of its examination of the reports and information supplied by the State party, the Committee determines that some of the obligations of that State under the Convention have not been discharged, it may make suggestions and general recommendations in accordance with article 9, paragraph 2, of the Convention. If the Committee decides to request an additional report or further information

from a State party, it may indicate the manner as well as the time within which the additional report or further information shall be supplied. In such a case its decision is transmitted through the Secretary-General for communication, within two weeks, to the State party concerned. In cases of non-receipt of reports or additional information, the Committee may transmit to the State party concerned, through the Secretary-General, a reminder concerning the submission of the report or additional information. If even after the reminder the State party does not submit the information required, the Committee shall include a reference to this effect in its annual report to the General Assembly.

60. Suggestions or general recommendations made by the Committee are communicated by the Committee, through the Secretary-General, to the States parties for their comments. The Committee may indicate a time limit within which comments from States parties are to be received. Suggestions and general recommendations of the Committee are reported to the General Assembly together with comments, if any, received from States parties.

61. With regard to communications received from States parties under article 11, paragraph 1, of the Convention, the Committee first examines the communication at a private meeting without considering its substance and then transmits it to the State party concerned. When it receives the explanations or statement of the receiving State, it transmits them to the State which submitted the communication.

62. As regards a dispute that has arisen under article 11, paragraph 2, of the Convention, the Committee first obtains and collates all the information it thinks necessary. The Chairman then notifies the States parties to the dispute and undertakes consultations with them concerning the composition of the *Ad Hoc* Conciliation Commission. Upon receiving the unanimous consent of the States parties to the dispute regarding the composition of the Commission, the Chairman proceeds with the appointment of the members of the Commission and informs the States parties to the dispute. If within three months those States fail to reach agreement on the composition of the Commission, the Chairman brings the situation to the attention of the Committee. In that event, the members of the Commission not agreed upon by the States parties to the dispute are elected by secret ballot by a two-thirds majority vote of the Committee from among its own members. The information obtained and collated by the Committee is made available to the members of the Commission. The Commission's report is communicated to each of the States parties to the dispute by the Chairman of the Committee, and those States have three months to inform him whether or not they accept the Commission's recommendations. The Chairman then communicates the report of the Commission and any declarations of States parties concerned to the other States parties to the Convention.

---

[9] CERD/C/35 (Part II).

82

63. In accordance with the Committee's decision 2 (VI) of 21 August 1972, representatives of ILO and UNESCO regularly attend its sessions.

(a) Activities of the Committee

64. The Committee held its first session at the Headquarters of the United Nations, New York, from 19 to 30 January 1970. Its normal pattern has since called for two sessions to be held each year ; however the thirty-fourth session, scheduled to be held from 4 to 22 August 1986, was postponed to 1987 because of the financial situation of the United Nations.

65. At each session the Committee considers reports, comments and information submitted by States parties under article 9 of the International Convention on the Elimination of All Forms of Racial Discrimination, on the measures they have adopted to implement the Convention. It also considers copies of petitions, copies of reports and other information relating to Trust and Non-Self-Governing Territories and to all other territories to which General Assembly resolution 1514 (XV) of 14 December 1960 applies, in conformity with article 15 of the Convention. Under article 11 of the Convention, the Committee may also take action with a view to settling disputes among States parties on the application of the Convention. Under article 14, a State party may at any time declare that it recognizes the competence of the Committee to receive and consider communications from individuals or groups of individuals within its jurisdiction claiming to be victims of a violation by that State party of any of the rights set forth in the Convention.

66. From its establishment until the closing date of its thirty-fifth session, the Committee received a total of 709 reports under article 9, paragraph 1, of the Convention (out of 842 due). In addition, it received 70 supplementary reports, containing additional information, submitted either on the initiative of the States parties concerned or at the Committee's request.

67. The Committee submitted its first annual report,[10] covering the work of its first and second sessions, to the General Assembly at its twenty-fifth session. In resolution 2648 (XXV) of 30 November 1970, the Assembly took note of the report with appreciation and stressed "the significance, for the fulfilment of the objectives of the United Nations in the field of human rights, of the coming into force of the International Convention on the Elimination of All Forms of Racial Discrimination and of the bringing into being of the Committee on the Elimination of Racial Discrimination, which was created by that Convention and which should play an effective role in the achievement of its purposes". The Assembly requested "all States parties to the Convention to give full co-operation to the Committee . . . in order that it may fulfil its mandate under the Convention".

68. In resolutions adopted at each regular session since 1970, and most recently in resolution 42/57 of 30 November 1987, the General Assembly has, *inter alia*, taken note of the Committee's annual report and commended the Committee for its contribution to the elimination of all forms of discrimination based on race, colour, descent, national or ethnic origin.

69. The Assembly has also commended the States parties to the Convention for measures taken to ensure within their jurisdiction the availability of appropriate recourse procedures for the victims of racial discrimination, and has called upon them to protect fully, by the adoption of relevant legislative and other measures, the rights of national or ethnic minorities, as well as the rights of indigenous populations. The Assembly has also called upon all Member States to adopt effective legislative, socio-economic and other necessary measures in order to ensure the elimination or prevention of discrimination based on race, colour, descent, national or ethnic origin.

70. The Committee has devoted much attention to the preparation, with the assistance of the United Nations Educational, Scientific and Cultural Organization, of guidelines for the implementation of article 7 of the Convention, in which States parties undertake to adopt immediate and effective measures, particularly in the fields of teaching, education, culture and information, with a view to combating prejudices which lead to racial discrimination and to promoting understanding, tolerance and friendship among nations and racial or ethnical groups. In 1977 the Committee set out general guidelines concerning the form and contents of reports relating to article 7, and in 1982 it drew the attention of States parties to some additional suggestions concerning these reports.

71. From time to time, the Committee has also considered its participation in, and contribution to, activities undertaken under the Programme for the Decade for Action to Combat Racism and Racial Discrimination, including the First and Second World Conferences to Combat Racism and Racial Discrimination.

72. On the occasion of the First World Conference, a study on the work of the Committee, and the progress made towards the achievement of the objectives of the International Convention on the Elimination of All Forms of Racial Discrimination, was prepared and published.[11] The publication sets out in detail the mandate of the Committee, its functions under the reporting system of the Convention, and its role with respect to Trust and Non-Self-Governing Territories. In addition, it presents the Committee's views as to its principal challenges, impediments and achievements, and its hopes for the future.

73. The Committee submitted two further studies to the Second World Conference—one on the implementation of article 4 and the other on the implementation of article 7 of the Convention.[12]

---

[10] *Official Records of the General Assembly, Twenty-fifth Session, Supplement No. 27* (A/8027).

[11] United Nations publication, Sales No. E.79.XIV.4.

[12] United Nations publications, Sales Nos. E.85.XIV.2 and E.85.XIV.3.

(b) *Problems faced by the Committee*

74.   One problem with which the Committee has been confronted stems from the fact that most of the reports have not been submitted on schedule and some have not been submitted at all. For example, of 82 reports received between the closing dates of the Committee's thirty-second and thirty-fifth sessions (28 August 1985 and 7 August 1987), only five met the target dates established by the Convention; the remainder were submitted after delays ranging from a few days to more than four years. As many as eight reminders had to be sent to some of the States parties before their reports were received.

75.   The problem was considered at the eleventh meeting of States parties to the Convention, held in New York on 29 April 1987. The meeting decided to recommend that, in order to facilitate the current work of the Committee, as a general practice, after submission of initial comprehensive reports to the Committee, States parties submit further comprehensive reports on every second occasion thereafter when reports were due, i.e., every four years, and brief updating reports at each intervening occasion when reports were due. The meeting invited the Committee to consider that matter at its next session as a matter of priority.

76.   At its thirty-fifth session, the Committee recognized the increasing burden that the co-existing reporting systems of United Nations conventions on human rights placed on Member States which were parties to those instruments, and decided that it would continue to be flexible in its procedure and practice concerning the content of periodic reports submitted in accordance with article 9 of the Convention. Some members of the Committee supported the recommendation of the eleventh meeting of States parties.

77.   A second problem with which the Committee has been confronted recently stems from the situation that arose in 1986 from the non-payment by a number of States parties of their assessed contributions as required under article 8, paragraph 6 of the Convention, which stipulates that "States Parties shall be responsible for the expenses of the members of the Committee while they are in performance of Committee duties". Until the end of 1985, a sizeable portion of the activities of the Committee had had to be financed from the United Nations General Fund, pending receipt of contributions from the States parties in arrears. In 1986, however, the financial crisis facing the Organization prevented it from continuing to advance funds as it had done in the past.

78.   Although some States parties responded favourably to repeated appeals made by the Secretary-General and the Chairman of the Committee, the total of outstanding assessments and arrears, as at 16 June 1986, was such that the Secretary-General had to defer the session scheduled to take place in Geneva from 4 to 22 August 1986. The Committee was thus unable to report to the General Assembly at its forty-first session on its 1986 activities, as required under article 9, paragraph 2, of the Convention.

79.   The General Assembly, in resolution 41/105 of 4 December 1986, appealed urgently to the States parties to fulfil their financial obligations under the Convention so as to enable the Committee to resume its work. In addition the Secretary-General, in response to the same Assembly resolution, explored all appropriate avenues to enable the Committee to meet in 1987 and advance the needed funds from the United Nations General Fund in order to cover the expenses of members of the Committee to attend the March 1987 session.

80.   At the eleventh (emergency) meeting of States parties, convened by the Secretary-General on 29 April 1987, the Controller of the United Nations indicated that the thirty-fifth session of the Committee, scheduled to meet in Geneva in August 1987, would have to be cancelled unless funds were made available by the States parties concerned. Although the amount of contributions received fell drastically short of the sum required to convene that session, the Secretary-General arranged for a one-week session of the Committee to be held in Geneva from 3 to 7 August 1987 to deal with a number of urgent matters and to adopt its 1986-1987 report to the General Assembly.

81.   At the thirty-fifth session, the Committee considered the financial situation affecting its future work and its inability fully to discharge its responsibility under the Convention. It noted that, in spite of numerous appeals made to States parties in arrears to pay their assessed contributions, the situation of the Committee continued to worsen. They observed that the insignificant amounts preventing the Committee from continuing to function might not be the real cause of the problem (the assessments outstanding as at 31 July 1987 ranged from a low of $75 in the case of one State party to a high of $7,606 in the case of another).

82.   Convinced that the General Assembly would not allow the most widely accepted instrument and mechanism against racism and racial discrimination to be impaired as a result of the cost of financing the expenses of its members to attend its two annual sessions, the Committee, in resolution 1 (XXXV) of 6 August 1987, recommended to the General Assembly that, pending a fully satisfactory solution to the present difficulties, it consider authorizing the Secretary-General to continue advancing the expenses of the members of the Committee, as was done in the past, to enable the Committee to continue its important work.

83.   The General Assembly, at its forty-second session, examined the report of the Committee covering its 1986 and 1987 sessions[13] and the report of the Secretary-General on the question of financing the expenses of the members of the Committee.[14] In resolution 42/47 of 30 November 1987, the Assembly commended the Committee for its work with regard to the implementation of the Convention and the Programme of Action for the Second Decade to Combat Racism and Racial Discri-

---

[13] *Official Records of the General Assembly, Forty-second Session, Supplement No. 18* (A/42/18).

[14] A/42/468 and Corr.1 and Add.1.

mination and took note of the Committee's report with appreciation.

84. In the same resolution the Assembly expressed its profound concern at the fact that a number of States parties to the Convention had not complied with their financial obligations under the Convention, which had led to the cancellation of the August 1986 session of the Committee and the curtailment by two weeks of the August 1987 session; expressed concern that such a situation prevented the Committee from submitting an annual report to the General Assembly at its forty-first session as required by the Convention and had led to further delay in discharging its substantive obligations under the Convention; and strongly appealed to all States parties to fulfil without delay their financial obligations under the Convention so as to enable the Committee to continue its work. It called upon States parties to explore, at a meeting scheduled for 15 January 1988, all appropriate measures, and to take a decision that would enable the Committee to meet regularly in the future; and invited the States parties to consider, pending a fully satisfactory solution of the existing financial difficulties, the possibility, as an exceptional measure, of the Committee holding one extended session per year.

6. INTERNATIONAL YEAR FOR ACTION TO COMBAT RACISM AND RACIAL DISCRIMINATION (1971)

85. The General Assembly, in resolution 2544 (XXIV) of 11 December 1969, designated the year 1971 as "International Year for Action to Combat Racism and Racial Discrimination", and expressed the view that the Year "should be observed in the name of the ever-growing struggle against racial discrimination in all its forms and manifestations and in the name of international solidarity with those struggling against racism". The Assembly approved the programme for the observance of the Year prepared by the Secretary-General[15] and urgently appealed to all States "to intensify and expand their efforts at the national and the international levels towards ensuring the rapid and total eradication of racial discrimination, including the policy of *apartheid*, nazism and all of its contemporary forms, as well as other manifestations of racism". The organs of the United Nations and the specialized agencies were invited "to co-operate and participate in the preparatory work and in the observance" of the Year.

86. A progress report submitted by the Secretary-General to the General Assembly at its twenty-sixth session[16] summarized information which he had received on measures and activities undertaken by Governments, the specialized agencies, regional inter-governmental organizations and international non-govermental organizations, in compliance with the resolution relating to

the International Year; it also contained a section dealing with the relevant activities of a number of United Nations bodies.

87. In resolution 2785 (XXVI) of 6 December 1971, the General Assembly, noting the measures taken and the progress achieved during the year-long observance, expressed its appreciation to the participating Governments, organs, agencies and organizations, and to the Secretary-General for the effective co-ordination of the observance. The Assembly recommended that "the measures and activities undertaken on the occasion of the International Year . . . be continued, developed and enlarged, and that the initiatives which have emerged from the observance of the . . . Year should serve as guide-lines for action-oriented programmes designed to ensure that the work accomplished in 1971 will be pursued".

88. In resolution 2784 (XXVI) of the same date, the Assembly invited the Commission on Human Rights to submit suggestions with a view to launching a "Decade for vigorous and continued mobilization against racism and racial discrimination in all its forms". The Commission enlisted the assistance of the Sub-Commission on Prevention of Discrimination and Protection of Minorities, and of the Secretary-General, in preparing a draft programme for a "Decade for Action to Combat Racism and Racial Discrimination".

7. UNESCO DECLARATION ON RACE AND RACIAL PREJUDICE

89. Adoption of the Declaration on Race and Racial Prejudice by the UNESCO General Conference at its twentieth session, in 1978, marked the culmination of a long period of research on the scientific facts of race.

90. In resolution 116 B (VI) of 1 March 1948, the Economic and Social Council advised UNESCO "of the interest of the United Nations in effective educational programmes in the fields of the prevention of discrimination and the protection of minorities"; suggested "collaboration between the United Nations and UNESCO in the formulation of such programmes"; and suggested, in particular, "that UNESCO consider the desirability of initiating and recommending the general adoption of a programme of disseminating scientific facts designed to remove what is commonly known as racial prejudice".

91. In response, the General Conference of UNESCO, in 1950, called upon the Director-General to sponsor research on the scientific facts of race, to diffuse these facts widely, and to prepare an educational programme based on them. Accordingly UNESCO has undertaken a number of studies designed to expose the unscientific foundations of racism and to show its close link to the social and economic context of the society in which it exists. Among the studies published are *The Race Question in Modern Science* (first published in 1956), *Race, Science and Society* (1975), and a series of booklets issued under the general title *Race Question and Mod-*

---

[15] *Ibid., Twenty-fourth Session, Annexes*, agenda item 55, document A/7649.

[16] A/8367 and Corr.1 and 2, and Add.1 and 2.

ern Thought examining the position of the major world religions on racism. UNESCO has also undertaken studies on the utilization of education and the media of communication to combat racism.

92. In 1950, UNESCO called upon a group of experts, acting in a personal capacity, to set out in clear and simple terms the findings of a scientific inquiry into the nature of racial differences, and to draw from them lessons which could be applied in social relations. The *Statement on Race* (1950), followed by the *Statement on the Nature of Race and Race Differences* (1951), which were based on the latest findings of scientific research at the time, rejected the idea that there were fundamental differences due to race in the human species and unequivocally condemned the theories based on the superiority of one or more races. These two statements, the personal work of eminent experts, were chiefly concerned with the biological and anthropological aspects of the problem and did not really take into account the economic and social situation of the various human communities, which are today recognized as being essential factors.

93. To take account of this new point of view, a further meeting of experts was convened by UNESCO in Moscow in August 1964. *The Propositions on the Biological Aspects of Race*, which resulted from it, incorporated the main arguments of the two previous statements, and added an interesting contribution in respect of the interaction of the genetic and cultural factors, the latter being understood as the whole body of knowledge and behaviour patterns acquired through contact with other human beings.

94. The Committee of Experts convened by UNESCO in September 1967 reflected the Organization's multidisciplinary concerns since it was composed of sociologists, jurists, a social psychologist, an ethnographer, an historian and two geneticists. The ethical and scientific interests of UNESCO underlie the *Statement on Race and Race Prejudice* of 1967 as they did the two preceding statements, and scientific analyses of universal significance provide the basis for the 1967 statement's contribution to the elucidation of the origins of racist theories and racial prejudices.

95. At its eighteenth session the UNESCO General Conference, referring to UNESCO participation in the Decade for Action to Combat Racism and Racial Discrimination, expressed the opinion that "one concrete measure in this respect should be the preparation of a draft universal declaration on race and racial prejudice . . . ". The Director-General subsequently communicated a preliminary draft of such a declaration to member States, and consulted a group of eminent human rights specialists who met at UNESCO headquarters in April 1977.

96. Adopted by acclamation by the General Conference on 27 November 1978, the Declaration on Race and Racial Prejudice lays down the fundamental principle of the equality of all human beings and hence of the unity of the human race. Condemning all those theories that postulate inequalities in the endowments or calling of different peoples, it affirms the right of men and groups to lay claim to their own identity, to consider themselves as different and to be regarded as such; but, at the same time, it provides that this right cannot be invoked by anyone seeking to justify a discriminatory practice on the basis of differences in ethnic origin, colour or religion for the purpose of establishing inequality among those displaying such differences. It consequently calls in question policies of forced assimilation that seek to destroy the specific character of a people as well as policies of segregation that are arbitrary because they are in conflict with the rights of nations and the rights of peoples. Linking the practices, attitudes and prejudices stemming from racism and the inequalities in power that, in varying degrees, facilitate their development, the Declaration seeks to refute racist ideas and to combat the socio-economic inequalities underlying and reinforcing them.

97. The Declaration contains a preamble and ten articles. In articles 1 and 2 it defines the concepts of race, racism and racial prejudice in the following terms:

Article 1

1. All human beings belong to a single species and are descended from a common stock. They are born equal in dignity and rights and all form an integral part of humanity.

2. All individuals and groups have the right to be different, to consider themselves as different and to be regarded as such. However, the diversity of life styles and the right to be different may not, in any circumstances, serve as a pretext for racial prejudice; they may not justify either in law or in fact any discriminatory practice whatsoever, nor provide a ground for the policy of *apartheid*, which is the extreme form of racism.

3. Identity of origin in no way affects the fact that human beings can and may live differently, nor does it preclude the existence of differences based on cultural, environmental and historical diversity nor the right to maintain cultural identity.

4. All peoples of the world possess equal faculties for attaining the highest level in intellectual, technical, social, economic, cultural and political development.

5. The differences between the achievements of the different peoples are entirely attributable to geographical, historical, political, economic, social and cultural factors. Such differences can in no case serve as a pretext for any rank-ordered classification of nations or peoples.

Article 2

1. Any theory which involves the claim that racial or ethnic groups are inherently superior of inferior, thus implying that some would be entitled to dominate or eliminate others, presumed to be inferior, or which bases value judgements on racial differentiation, has no scientific foundation and is contrary to the moral and ethical principles of humanity.

2. Racism includes racist ideologies, prejudiced attitudes, discriminatory behaviour, structural arrangements and institutionalized practices resulting in racial inequality as well as the fallacious notion that discriminatory relations between groups are morally and scientifically justifiable; it is reflected in discriminatory provisions in legislation or regulations and discriminatory practices as well as in anti-social beliefs and acts; it hinders the development of its victims, perverts those who practise it, divides nations internally, impedes international co-operation and gives rise to political tensions between peoples; it is contrary to the fundamental principles of international law and, consequently, seriously disturbs international peace and security.

3. Racial prejudice, historically linked with inequalities in power, reinforced by economic and social differences between individuals and

groups, and still seeking today to justify such inequalities, is totally without justification.

98. With regard to state and international responsibility for the elimination of racism and racial prejudice, the Declaration provides that:

Article 9

1. The principle of the equality in dignity and rights of all human beings and all peoples, irrespective of race, colour and origin, is a generally accepted and recognized principle of international law. Consequently any form of racial discrimination practised by a State constitutes a violation of international law giving rise to its international responsibility.

2. Special measures must be taken to ensure equality in dignity and rights for individuals and groups wherever necessary, while ensuring that they are not such as to appear racially discriminatory. In this respect, particular attention should be paid to racial or ethnic groups which are socially or economically disadvantaged, so as to afford them, on a completely equal footing and without discrimination or restriction, the protection of the laws and regulations and the advantages of the social measures in force, in particular in regard to housing, employment and health; to respect the authenticity of their culture and values; and to facilitate their social and occupational advancement, especially through education.

3. Population groups of foreign origin, particularly migrant workers and their families who contribute to the development of the host country, should benefit from appropriate measures designed to afford them security and respect for their dignity and cultural values and to facilitate their adaptation to the host environment and their professional advancement with a view to their subsequent reintegration in their country of origin and their contribution to its development; steps should be taken to make it possible for their children to be taught their mother tongue.

4. Existing disequilibria in international economic relations contribute to the exacerbation of racism and racial prejudice; all States should consequently endeavour to contribute to the restructuring of the international economy on a more equitable basis.

Article 10

International organizations, whether universal or regional, governmental or non-governmental, are called upon to co-operate and assist, so far as their respective fields of competence and means allow, in the full and complete implementation of the principles set out in this Declaration, thus contributing to the legitimate struggle of all men, born equal in dignity and rights, against the tyranny and oppression of racism, racial segregation, *apartheid* and genocide, so that all the peoples of the world may be forever delivered from these scourges.

99. At its fourth special session, in November 1982, the General Conference adopted the Medium-Term Plan for 1984-1989. The 15 Major Programmes approved by the General Conference include Major Programme XII on the elimination of prejudice, intolerance, racism and *apartheid*, which is composed of three programmes: studies and research on prejudice, intolerance and racism; action against prejudice, intolerance and racism in the fields of education, science, culture and communications; and the struggle against *apartheid*.

8. DECADE FOR ACTION TO COMBAT RACISM AND RACIAL DISCRIMINATION

100. In resolution 3057 (XXVIII) of 2 November 1972, the General Assembly designated "the ten-year period beginning on 10 December 1973 as the Decade for Action to Combat Racism and Racial Discrimination", approved the Programme for the Decade, and invited "Governments, United Nations organs, the spe-

cialized agencies and other intergovernmental organizations, and non-governmental organizations in consultative relationship concerned, to participate in the observance of the Decade . . .". As requested in that resolution, the Secretary-General transmitted the Programme to Governments, specialized agencies and other intergovernmental organizations, and took "the necessary measures for the implementation of those suggestions contained in the Programme which fall within the Secretary-General's area of responsibility or which require action by other organs of the United Nations".

101. The Programme for the Decade for Action to Combat Racism and Racial Discrimination, which appears as an annex to General Assembly resolution 3057 (XXVIII), stated that:

The ultimate goals of the Decade are to promote human rights and fundamental freedoms for all, without distinction of any kind on grounds of race, colour, descent or national or ethnic origin, especially by eradicating racial prejudice, racism and racial discrimination; to arrest any expansion of racist policies, to eliminate the persistence of racist policies and to counteract the emergence of alliances based on mutual espousal of racism and racial discrimination; to resist any policy and practices which lead to the strengthening of the racist régimes and contribute to the sustainment of racism and racial discrimination; to identify, isolate and dispel the fallacious and mythical beliefs, policies and practices that contribute to racism and racial discrimination; and to put an end to racist régimes.

102. To this end, the Programme proposed that appropriate measures should be taken to implement fully United Nations instruments and decisions concerning the elimination of racial discrimination, to ensure support for all peoples struggling for racial equality, to eradicate all forms of racial discrimination, and to pursue a vigorous world-wide campaign of information designed to dispel racial prejudice and to enlighten and involve world public opinion in the struggle against racism and racial discrimination, emphasizing, *inter alia*, the education of youth in the spirit of human rights and fundamental freedoms and in the dignity and worth of the human person and against theories of racism and racial discrimination, as well as the full involvement of women in the formulation and implementation of these measures".

103. The Programme suggested a number of measures to be taken during the Decade at the national, regional and international levels, and by organizations within the United Nations system.

(a) *World Conference to Combat Racism and Racial Discrimination*

104. The World Conference to Combat Racism and Racial Discrimination, provided for in paragraph 13 (a) of the Programme for the Decade, was held in Geneva from 14 to 25 August 1978. The Conference adopted a Declaration and Programme of Action, reproduced in chapter II of its report.[17] It also adopted a resolution condemning the *apartheid* régime of South Africa for

---

[17] United Nations publication, Sales No. E.79.XIV.2.

its act of aggression against Zambia, which had coincided with the Conference.

105. In the Declaration, the Conference affirmed that:

1. Any doctrine of racial superiority is scientifically false, morally condemnable, socially unjust and dangerous, and has no justification whatsoever;

2. All peoples and all human groups have contributed to the progress of civilization and cultures which constitute the common heritage of humanity;

3. All forms of discrimination and, in particular, governmental policies based on the theory of racial superiority, exclusiveness or hatred are a violation of fundamental human rigths and jeopardize friendly relations among peoples, co-operation between nations and international peace and security;

4. *Apartheid*, the extreme form of institutionalized racism, is a crime against humanity and an affront to the dignity of mankind and is a threat to peace and security in the world . . .''.

Further, the Conference declared that:

12. Bearing in mind that racism, racial discrimination and *apartheid* are gross violations of human rights with, *inter alia*, negative effects stemming from serious inequalities in the fields of education, health, nutrition, housing, job opportunities and cultural development, national, regional and international action to combat and eradicate the causes of such policies and practices and to ensure the full enjoyment of the above rights should include measures aimed at improving the living conditions of men and women of all nations at the political, economic, social and cultural levels.

106. The Programme of Action, designed to realize these principles and achieve these goals, called for action to be taken at the national, international and regional levels, and for support to be given to the victims of racism, racial discrimination and *apartheid* by Governments, specialized agencies, intergovernmental and non-governmental organizations.

107. The Conference recommended that another such conference should be held at the end of the Decade to review and evaluate the work undertaken during the Decade and to chart new measures where necessary.

108. The General Assembly, in resolution 33/99 of 16 December 1978, took note of the report of the Secretary-General on the Conference and approved the Declaration and Programme of Action. In doing so the Assembly reaffirmed that all forms of racism, racial discrimination and *apartheid* were abhorrent to the conscience and dignity of mankind and must be eradicated by effective international action; and further reaffirmed the special responsibility of the United Nations and the international community for the victims of racial discrimination as well as for peoples subjected to colonial or alien domination.

(b) *Second World Conference to Combat Racism and Racial Discrimination*

109. In resolution 35/33 of 14 November 1980, the General Assembly decided ''to hold in 1983, as an important event of the Decade, a Second World Conference to Combat Racism and Racial Discrimination, which, while reviewing and assessing the activities undertaken during the Decade, should have as its main purpose the formulation of ways and means and of specific measures aimed at ensuring the full and uni-

versal implementation of United Nations resolutions and decisions on racism, racial discrimination, and *apartheid*''. The Assembly invited the Economic and Social Council to begin the preparatory work for the Conference at its first regular session of 1981.

110. On 6 May 1981 the Council, by decision 1981/130, authorized its President, in consultation with the regional groups, to appoint a committee of twenty-three Member States which, acting as the Preparatory Sub-Committee of the Council, in consultation with the Secretary-General, should complete the preparations for the Second World Conference to Combat Racism and Racial Discrimination. The Preparatory Sub-Committee met at United Nations Headquarters, New York, from 15 to 26 March 1982 and from 21 to 25 March 1983.

111. On the recommendation of the Economic and Social Council, the General Assembly adopted resolution 37/41 of 3 December 1982, in which it approved organizational and procedural arrangements for the Conference, and called upon all States to contribute to the success of the Decade for Action to Combat Racism and Racial Discrimination, in particular by their active participation in the Conference.

112. The Second World Conference to Combat Racism and Racial Discrimination met at the Palais des Nations, Geneva, from 1 to 12 August 1983. The Governments of 128 States were represented. Also represented were the United Nations Council for Namibia, a number of United Nations bodies including the Committee on the Elimination of Racial Discrimination, the Commission on Human Rights and the Sub-Commission on Prevention of Discrimination and Protection of Minorities, six specialized agencies, four intergovernmental organizations, four liberation movements, and a number of non-governmental organizations in consultative status with the Economic and Social Council.

113. The Conference adopted a Declaration in which it solemnly reaffirmed and declared that:[18]

1. All human beings are born equal in dignity and rights. Any doctrine of racial superiority is, therefore, scientifically false, morally condemnable, socially unjust and dangerous, and has no justification whatsoever;

2. Racism and racial discrimination are continuing scourges which must be eradicated throughout the world;

3. Consequently, national, regional and international educational resources should be developed and used in ways which will promote mutual understanding between all human beings and demonstrate and teach the scientific basis of ethnic and racial equality and the value of cultural diversity with a view to destroying the basis of racist attitudes and practices;

4. All peoples and all human groups have contributed to the progress of civilization and cultures which constitute the common heritage of humanity;

5. All forms of discrimination are violations of fundamental human rights, and governmental policies which are based on the theory of racial superiority, exclusiveness or hatred also jeopardize friendly relations among peoples and co-operation between nations, and thereby jeopardize international peace and security;

[18] *Report of the Second World Conference to Combat Racism and Racial Discrimination, Geneva, 1-12 August 1983*, United Nations publication, Sales No. E.83.XIV.4, chap. II.

6. *Apartheid* as an institutionalized form of racism is a deliberate and totally abhorrent affront to the conscience and dignity of mankind, a crime against humanity and a threat to international peace and security;

7. In South Africa the most extreme form of racism has led to a form of exploitation and degradation which is in clear contradiction to the principle of human rights and fundamental freedoms for all without distinction as provided for in the Charter of the United Nations;

8. The creation of bantustans is an inhuman policy designed to dispossess the African people of their land, deprive them of their citizenship and consolidate the political and economic domination of the minority white population of South Africa; this policy has been condemned by the international community, and should continue to be rejected and condemned;

9. United Nations sanctions against the racist South African régime must be implemented strictly and faithfully by all States in order to isolate it further. Assistance and collaboration in the economic, military, nuclear and other fields constitutes an impediment to the struggle against *apartheid*. It is the obligation of all Governments to develop appropriate legislation and regulations that would prevent transnational corporations from following those practices which assist and support the racist régime in Pretoria or which exploit the natural resources and people of South Africa and Namibia;

10. All those who contribute to the maintenance of the system of *apartheid* are accomplices in the perpetuation of this crime;

11. The Conference commends the selfless efforts of the people of South Africa and Namibia under the leadership of their national liberation movements for national independence and the establishment of a non-racial democratic society. It also reaffirms the legitimacy of the struggles and calls upon the international community to increase its moral, political and material support to these peoples;

12. Support should be provided to national liberation movements recognized by their respective regional organizations as a concrete form of international solidarity with all oppressed peoples and with all victims of racism and racial discrimination, colonialism and *apartheid*;

13. The Conference condemns the frequent and unjustified acts of aggression, destruction and sabotage, which the racist South African régime, directly and through the use of mercenaries and armed bandits, continues to perpetrate against the front-line States and other independent African States in the subregion because of their opposition to *apartheid*, assistance to refugees and support for the liberation movements. It therefore calls on all States to offer such assistance as would enable the front-line States and the other independent African States in the subregion to strengthen their defence capacity and peacefully rebuild their countries;

14. The Conference expresses its deep concern that many neo-Nazi and Fascist organizations have stepped up their activities which have encouraged tendencies towards racism and racial discrimination. Accordingly, measures should be taken against all ideologies and practices, such as *apartheid*, nazism, fascism and neo-fascism based on racial or ethnic exclusiveness or intolerance, hatred, terror or systematic denials of human rights and fundamental freedoms;

15. The proscription of racism and racial discrimination by law should be accompanied by vigorous efforts to ensure equality in the economic, social and cultural fields; and in particular special programmes, such as affirmative action programmes, should be developed to address the problem of racism and racial discrimination inherent in the system and institutionalized;

16. Education and information should provide an efficient means of action to combat racism and racial discrimination; the Conference supports the efforts of the United Nations Educational, Scientific and Cultural Organization for a more efficient utilization of education and information to combat racism and racial prejudice; it is also the responsibility of all Governments and all leaders of opinion within each society to educate people, especially children and youth, by all available means, to promote an awareness of the evils of racism, racial discrimination and *apartheid* and to ensure respect for the dignity and worth of all human beings. Information media should be encouraged to disseminate information on United Nations activities and programmes related to the elimination of racial discrimination;

17. *Apartheid*, racism and systematic racial discrimination are gross violations of human rights emanating from and leading to serious inequalities in the political and economic fields as well as in the fields of education, health, nutrition, housing, job opportunities and cultural development, and consequently the action required to combat such policies and practices should include measures at the national, regional and international levels, to improve the political, economic, social and cultural living conditions of men and women of all nations. International co-operation for development has an important role to play in securing the resources required by the developing countries to overcome these obstacles;

18. Governments should make clear their condemnation of all propaganda and all organizations which are based on ideas and theories of the superiority of one race or group of persons of one colour or ethnic origin, which attempt to justify or promote racial hatred and discrimination in any form, and should adopt measures designed to eradicate all incitement to, or acts of, such discrimination in accordance with article 4 of the International Convention on the Elimination of All Forms of Racial Discrimination;

19. The Conference condemns any form of co-operation with South Africa, notably the existing and increasing relations between Israel and the racist régime of South Africa, in particular those in the economic and military fields, and deplores and warns against co-operation between them in the nuclear fields; it particularly deplores the expansion and intensification of those relations at the time when the international community is exerting all its efforts towards the objective of completely isolating the racist régime of South Africa; the Conference views this co-operation as an act of deliberate choice and a hostile act against the oppressed people of South Africa, as well as a defiance of the resolutions of the United Nations and the efforts of the society of nations to ensure freedom and peace in southern Africa; the Conference also notes with concern the insidious propaganda by Israel against the United Nations and against Governments which are firmly opposed to *apartheid*;

20. The Conference recalls with deep regret the practices of racial discrimination against the Palestinians as well as other inhabitants of the Arab occupied territories which have such an impact on all aspects of their daily existence that they prevent the enjoyment of their fundamental rights; the Conference expresses its deep concern about this situation and calls for the cessation of all the practices of racial discrimination to which the Palestinians and the other inhabitants of the Arab territories occupied by Israel are subjected;

21. Persons belonging to national, ethnic and other minorities can play a significant role in the promotion of international co-operation and understanding, and the national protection of the rights of persons belonging to minorities in accordance with the International Convention on the Elimination of All Forms of Racial Discrimination, and the International Covenant on Civil and Political Rights, including its article 27, is essential to enable them to fulfil this role; the Conference stresses that granting persons belonging to minority groups the opportunity to participate fully in the political, economic and social life of their country can contribute to the promotion of understanding, co-operation and harmonious relations between persons belonging to the different groups living in a country; the Conference also recognizes that in certain cases special protection of the rights of persons belonging to minority groups may be called for, in particular by the adoption of effective measures in favour of persons belonging to particularly disadvantaged minority groups; the Conference endorses the action taken so far by the competent United Nations bodies to protect persons belonging to minorities, especially the present action of the Commission on Human Rights to elaborate a draft declaration on the protection of the rights of persons belonging to minorities, and is confident that future action currently envisaged will appropriately enhance the international protection of the rights of persons belonging to minorities; in promoting and guaranteeing the rights of persons belonging to minorities, there should be strict respect for the sovereignty, territorial integrity and political independence of the countries where they live and for non-interference in their internal affairs;

22. The rights of indigenous populations to maintain their traditional economic, social and cultural structures, to pursue their own economic, social and cultural development and to use and further develop their own language, their special relationship to their land and

its natural resources should not be taken away from them; the need for consultation with indigenous populations as regards proposals which concern them should be fully observed; the Conference welcomes the establishment of the United Nations Group on Indigenous Populations;

23. Whenever there is racial discrimination, women are often doubly discriminated against; consequently, further special efforts are called for to eliminate the effects of racial discrimination on the status and situation of women, and to ensure conditions promoting women's equal participation in the political, economic, social and cultural life of their societies. In this context, the implementation of the International Convention on the Elimination of All Forms of Discrimination against Women is of particular importance;

24. Relevant national and international bodies should consider specifically the psychological and physical consequences for children who are victims of racial discrimination, and should take care that special measures to counteract these effects are included in their future programmes;

25. The general principle of non-discrimination, with particular regard to refugees fleeing from *apartheid*, racism and racial discrimination, should be applied scrupulously in regard to refugees, particularly in respect of their admission, treatment and *non-refoulement* in countries providing refuge, including refuge on a temporary basis, and of international solidarity in providing assistance and in promoting durable solutions;

26. The urgent need to protect the rights of immigrants, migrant workers, as well as the human rights of those who are undocumented, and their families all over the world requires that States should ensure that their legislation, administration and other practices fully conform with international standards protecting the rights of migrant workers and their families, to mitigate and eliminate the social, economic and other causes of discriminatory measures or attitudes still existing to the detriment of migrant workers and their families; the Conference urges States Members of the United Nations to speed up the present work within the United Nations to elaborate a draft Convention on the Protection of the Rights of Migrant Workers and Members of their Families;

27. States, international organizations, governmental and non-governmental organizations, local and private institutions, religious institutions and trade unions should ensure the total and effective realization of the goals and objectives of the Decade for Action to Combat Racism and Racial Discrimination;

28. A Second Decade to Combat Racism and Racial Discrimination should be launched by the General Assembly with a view to achieving the total elimination of racism, racial discrimination and *apartheid*.

114. The Conference also adopted a Programme of Action containing proposals for activities to be undertaken after the Conference[19] as a follow-up to the Programme of Activities which had been adopted for the second half of the Decade and the Programme of Action which had been adopted by the first World Conference to Combat Racism and Racial Discrimination.

115. In addition, it adopted a resolution[20] in which it took note with regret that, on 5 August 1983, Nelson Rolihlahla Mandela completed 21 years in prison in South Africa for his leadership in the struggle against *apartheid* and for a just and democratic society, recognized his outstanding contribution to the struggle against racism and racial discrimination, condemned the brutal repression by the racist régime of South Africa against opponents of *apartheid*, expressed its solidarity with Nelson Mandela and the National Liberation Movements of South Africa and Namibia and demanded the immediate and unconditional release of

Nelson Mandela and all other South African and Namibian political prisoners. The Conference called upon all Governments, national and international organizations and individuals to redouble their efforts in support of the campaign for the release of Nelson Mandela and all other South African political prisoners.

(c) *Study of achievements of the Decade and obstacles encountered*

116. On the recommendation of the Commission on Human Rights, the Economic and Social Council, in resolution 1984/24 of 24 May 1984, authorized the Sub-Commission on Prevention of Discrimination and Protection of Minorities to entrust Mr. Asbjørn Eide with carrying out a study on the achievements made and the obstacles encountered during the Decade for Action to Combat Racism and Racial Discrimination, with special emphasis on the progress made in this field, if any, between the first and second world conferences, taking into account also any resolutions adopted by the General Assembly on the report of the Second World Conference to Combat Racism and Racial Discrimination[21] and the first stage of the implementation of the Programme of Action for the Second Decade.[22] The Council recommended that the study should propose new or additional measures in this field which could be taken up for examination by the Sub-Commission, and asked that the study be presented to the Sub-Commission at its thirty-eighth session.

117. Mr. Eide submitted a preliminary report[23] to the Sub-Commission at its thirty-eighth session, in 1985. The report outlined the background to the Decade and summarized the goals and policy measures recommended. It reviewed the activities of the First Decade and pointed out some of the obstacles encountered during that Decade. He submitted a progress report[24] to the Sub-Commission at its thirty-ninth session, in 1987. In that report he presented an evaluation of the activities undertaken during the First Decade, a summary of the goals, objectives and policy measures adopted at the Second World Conference and for the Second Decade, and a review of the measures taken during the first part of the Second Decade. In addition, he presented an outline for the final study.

118. The Sub-Commission, in resolution 1987/6 of 31 August 1987, expressed its appreciation and thanks to Mr. Eide for his reports, for his constructive participation on the debates thereon, and for the suggestions he had made as regards the issues to be examined in the final study. It approved his outline and authorized him to proceed with the study.

---

19 *Ibid.*, chap. II.

20 *Ibid.*, chap. III, resolution 2 (II).

21 United Nations publication, Sales No. E.83.XIV.4 and corrigendum.

22 General Assembly resolution 38/14, annex.

23 E/CN.4/Sub.2/1985/7.

24 E/CN.4/Sub.2/1987/6.

9. SECOND DECADE FOR ACTION TO COMBAT RACISM AND RACIAL DISCRIMINATION

119. After reviewing the report of the Second World Conference to Combat Racism and Racial Discrimination the General Assembly, in resolution 42/47 of 30 November 1987, noted with concern that, despite the efforts of the international community, the principal objectives of the First Decade had not been attained, and that millions of human beings continued to be the victims of varied forms of racism, racial discrimination and *apartheid*.

120. Having considered the report of the Secretary-General outlining a proposed plan of activities to be implemented during the period 1990-1993,[25] prepared at the request of the Economic and Social Council, and a study relating to the implementation of the Programme of Action for the Second Decade,[26] and convinced of the need to take effective and sustained international measures for the elimination of all forms of racism and racial discrimination and the total eradication of *apartheid* in South Africa, the General Assembly:

Resolved once again that all forms of racism and racial discrimination, particularly in their institutionalized form, such as *apartheid*, or resulting from official doctrines of racial superiority or exclusivity, are among the most serious violations of human rights in the contemporary world and must be combated by all available means;

Decided that the international community, in general, and the United Nations in particular, should continue to give the highest priority to programmes for combating racism, racial discrimination and *apartheid*, and to intensify their efforts, during the Second Decade to Combat Racism and Racial Discrimination, to provide assistance and relief to the victims of racism and all forms of racial discrimination and *apartheid*, especially in South Africa and Namibia and in occupied territories and territories under alien domination;

Appealed to all Governments and to international and non-governmental organizations to increase and intensify their activities to combat racism, racial discrimination and *apartheid* and to provide relief and assistance to the victims of these evils;

Took note of the report submitted by the Secretary-General containing information on the activities of Governments, specialized agencies, regional intergovernmental organizations and non-governmental organizations, as well as United Nations organs, to give effect to the Programme of Action for the Second Decade to Combat Racism and Racial Discrimination;

Urgently requested the Secretary-General to ensure the effective and immediate implementation of those activities proposed for the first half of the Decade which had not been undertaken;

Took note of the report submitted by the Secretary-General concerning the study on the effects of racial discrimination in the field of education, training and employment as it affects the children of minorities, in particular those of migrant workers,[27] and requested that he continue that study by submitting, *inter alia*, specific recommendations for the implementation of measures to combat the effects of that discrimination;

Again requested the Secretary-General to transmit his study on the role of private group action to combat racism and racial discrimination[28] to Governments, specialized agencies, regional intergovernmental organizations and non-governmental organizations in consultative status with the Economic and Social Council in order to obtain their views and an indication from them of further relevant materials, and to submit to the General Assembly at its forty-third session a final report on this topic;

Requested the Secretary-General to prepare and issue as soon as possible a collection of model legislation for the guidance of Governments in the enactment of further legislation against racial discrimination;

Took note of the training course held in New York from 8 to 18 September 1987 that focused on the preparation of national legislation prohibiting racism and racial discrimination and requested the Secretary-General to submit a report on the subject to the Economic and Social Council at its first regular session of 1988;

Renewed its invitation to UNESCO to expedite the preparation of teaching materials and teaching aids to promote teaching, training and educational activities on human rights and against racism and racial discrimination, with particular emphasis on activities at the primary and secondary levels of education;

Again requested the Sub-Commission on Prevention of Discrimination and Protection of Minorities to consider the need for updating the *Study on Racial Discrimination*;[29]

Once again authorized the Secretary-General to organize in 1988 a global consultation on racial discrimination involving representatives of the United Nations system, regional intergovernmental organizations and interested non-governmental organizations in consultative status with the Economic and Social Council, to focus on the co-ordination of international activities to combat racism and racial discrimination, and requested him to disseminate widely the results of that consultation;

Again requested the Economic and Social Council to envisage the organization, within the framework of its plan of activities for 1985-1989, of a seminar of

[25] A/42/493.

[26] A/42/492.

[27] *Ibid.*

[28] A/41/550.

[29] United Nations publication, Sales No. E.76.XIV.2.

cultural dialogue between the countries of origin and the host countries of migrant workers;

Emphasized the importance of adequate recourse procedures for victims of racism and racial discrimination and therefore requested the Secretary-General, in the light of the results of the seminars held on this topic, to prepare and finalize, with the appropriate assistance of qualified experts, if possible, a handbook of recourse procedures;

Considered that all parts of the Programme of Action for the Second Decade to Combat Racism and Racial Discrimination should receive equal attention in order to attain the objectives of the Second Decade; and

Invited the Secretary-General to proceed with the implementation of the activities for the period 1990-1993 listed in the annex to the resolution.

121. The General Assembly, further, invited all Governments, United Nations bodies, specialized agencies and other intergovernmental organizations, as well as interested non-governmental organizations in consultative status with the Economic and Social Council, to participate fully in the implementation of the plan of activities for the periods 1985-1989 and 1990-1993 by intensifying and broadening their efforts to bring about the speedy elimination of *apartheid* and all forms of racism and racial discrimination. It appealed for contributions to the Trust Fund for the Programme for the Decade, and reiterated its request to the Economic and Social Council to submit annual reports, during the period of the Second Decade, to the General Assembly.

B. Intolerance and discrimination based on religion or belief

1. STUDIES

122. Three studies have been made on matters relating to intolerance and discrimination based on religion or belief.

123. The first, entitled *Study of Discrimination in the Matter of Religious Rights and Practices*,[30] prepared by Mr. Arcot Krishnaswami, Special Rapporteur of the Sub-Commission on Prevention of Discrimination and Protection of Minorities, was completed in 1960. On the basis of conclusions and recommendations put forward by the Special Rapporteur, the Sub-Commission and the Commission on Human Rights prepared a draft convention and a draft declaration on the elimination of all forms of religious intolerance. The draft convention was examined by the General Assembly at its twenty-second session, at which time the Third Committee adopted the preamble and article 1; however, further consideration of the draft convention was repeatedly postponed.

124. In resolution 3027 (XXVII) of 7 December 1962, the Assembly decided that priority should be accorded to completion of the Declaration. From 1974 to 1981 a working group of the Commission met annually to pre-

pare an appropriate text. The Commission forwarded the completed draft to the Assembly, which by resolution 36/55 of 25 November 1981 adopted the Declaration on the Elimination of All Forms of Intolerance and of Discrimination Based on Religion or Belief.

125. The second study on the subject, entitled *Study of the Current Dimensions of the Problems of Intolerance and of Discrimination on Grounds of Religion or Belief*,[31] was prepared by Mrs. Elizabeth Odio Benito, also a Special Rapporteur of the Sub-Commission on Prevention of Discrimination and Protection of Minorities. The study, completed in 1986 and examined by the Sub- Commission at its thirty-ninth session, in 1987, analyses existing constitutional and legal guarantees of freedom of thought, conscience, religion and belief on the basis of information furnished by Governments and non-governmental organizations, and describes some of the root causes of intolerance and discrimination based on religion or belief. It contains a number of recommendations, the first of which proposes that a new effort be made to elaborate an international convention for the elimination of all forms of intolerance and discrimination based on religion or belief.

126. The third study, entitled *Implementation of the Declaration on the Elimination of All Forms on Intolerance and of Discrimination Based of Religion or Belief*,[32] was prepared by Mr. Angelo Vidal d'Almeida Ribero, a Special Rapporteur appointed by the Commission on Human Rights. The study surveys the existing situation and shows the extent and seriousness of current manifestations of intolerance and discrimination based on religion or belief. After identifying factors that impede implementation of provisions of the Declaration and listing various infringements of its provisions, the Special Rapporteur formulates a number of recommendations, the first of which is the elaboration of an international convention on the subject.

2. DECLARATION ON THE ELIMINATION OF ALL FORMS OF INTOLERANCE AND OF DISCRIMINATION BASED ON RELIGION OR BELIEF

127. In resolution 36/55 of 25 November 1981, the General Assembly adopted and proclaimed the Declaration on the Elimination of All Forms of Intolerance and of Discrimination Based on Religion or Belief, and resolved to adopt all necessary measures for the speedy elimination of such intolerance in all its forms and manifestations and to prevent and combat discrimination on the grounds of religion or belief.

128. The Declaration defines the expression "intolerance and discrimination based on religion or belief" as meaning "any distinction, exclusion, restriction or preference based on religion or belief and having as its purpose or as its effect nullification or impairment of

---

[30] United Nations publication, Sales No. E.60.XIV.2.

[31] E/CN.4/Sub.2/1987/26.

[32] E/CN.4/1987/35.

the recognition, enjoyment or exercise of human rights and fundamental freedoms on an equal basis''.

129.   It states (article 3) that ''Discrimination between human beings on the grounds of religion or belief constitutes an affront to human dignity and a disavowal of the principles of the Charter of the United Nations, and shall be condemned as a violation of the human rights and fundamental freedoms proclaimed in the Universal Declaration of Human Rights and enunciated in detail in the International Covenants on Human Rights, and as an obstacle to friendly and peaceful relations between nations''.

130.   It provides (article 4) that ''All States shall take effective measures to prevent and eliminate discrimination on the grounds of religion or belief in the recognition, exercise and enjoyment of human rights and fundamental freedoms in all fields of civil, economic, political, social and cultural life''; and that ''All States shall make all efforts to enact or rescind legislation where necessary to prohibit such discrimination, and to take all appropriate measures to combat intolerance on the grounds of religion or other beliefs in this matter''.

131.   Article 5 deals with the right of parents or guardians to organize life within the family in accordance with their religion or belief, bearing in mind the moral education in which they believe their children should be brought up.

132.   Article 6 specifies a number of freedoms included in the concept of freedom of thought, conscience, religion or belief, as follows:

(a) To worship or assemble in connection with a religion or belief, and to establish and maintain places for these purposes;

(b) To establish and maintain appropriate charitable or humanitarian institutions;

(c) To make, acquire and use to an adequate extent the necessary articles and materials related to the rites or customs of a religion or belief;

(d) To write, issue and disseminate relevant publications in these areas;

(e) To teach a religion or belief in places suitable for these purposes;

(f) To solicit and receive voluntary financial and other contributions from individuals and institutions;

(g) To train, appoint, elect or designate by succession leaders called for by the requirements and standards of any religion or belief;

(h) To observe days of rest and to celebrate holidays and ceremonies in accordance with the precepts of one's religion or belief; and

(i) To establish and maintain communications with individuals and communities in matters of religion or belief at the national and international levels.

133.   Finally, article 7 provides that the rights and freedoms set forth in the Declaration ''shall be accorded in national legislations in such a manner that everyone shall be able to avail himself of such rights and freedoms in practice''.

3. IMPLEMENTATION OF THE DECLARATION

134.   The General Assembly, in resolution 37/187 of 18 December 1982, requested the Commission on Human Rights to consider what measures might be necessary to implement the Declaration and to encourage understanding, tolerance and respect in matters relating to freedom of religion or belief, and to report thereon.

135.   In response, the Commission in resolution 1983/40 of 9 March 1983 requested the Sub-Commission on Prevention of Discrimination and Protection of Minorities to undertake the study of the current dimensions of the problems of intolerance and of discrimination on grounds of religion or belief mentioned above, using the Declaration as terms of reference; and called upon the Secretary-General to hold, within the framework of the programme of advisory services in the field of human rights, a seminar on the encouragement of understanding, tolerance and respect in matters relating to freedom of religion or belief.

136.   Later, in resolution 1984/57 of 15 March 1984, the Commission proposed that the Economic and Social Council authorize the Sub-Commission to entrust Mrs. Odio Benito with the preparation of the study. In resolution 1985/51 of 14 March 1985 it noted with appreciation the report of the Seminar on the Encouragement of Understanding, Tolerance and Respect in matters relating to Freedom of Religion or Belief,[33] held in Geneva from 3 to 14 December 1984, and requested the Secretary-General to prepare a compendium of the national legislation and regulations of States on the question of freedom of religion or belief with particular regard to the measures taken to combat intolerance and discrimination in this field.

137.   At its forty-second session the Commission, in resolution 1986/19 of 10 March 1986, urged all States to take appropriate measures to combat intolerance and to encourage understanding, tolerance and respect in matters relating to freedom of religion or belief and, in this context, to examine where necessary the supervision and training of their civil servants, educators and other public officials to ensure that, in the course of their official duties, they respect different religions and beliefs and do not discriminate against persons professing other religions or beliefs.

138.   On the same day the Commission, in resolution 1986/20, expressed its deep concern about reports of incidents and governmental actions which are inconsistent with the provisions of the Declaration on the Elimination of All Forms of Intolerance and of Discrimination Based on Religion or Belief, and decided therefore to appoint a special rapporteur to examine such incidents and actions and to recommend remedial measures including, as appropriate, the promotion of a dialogue between communities of religion or belief and their Governments. The Commission's Special Rapporteur, Mr. Angelo Vidal d'Almeida Ribeiro, subsequently submitted the report mentioned above to the Commission. The Commission commended the report in resolution 1987/15 of 4 March 1987, and recognized the important contribution which a binding international instrument could make towards eliminating all forms of intolerance

---

[33] ST/HR/SER.A/16.

and of discrimination based on religion or belief. It decided to consider the question of the drafting of such an instrument at its forty-fourth (1988) session in the light of the study prepared by Mrs. Odio Benito, the observations of the Sub-Commission, and the report of the Secretary-General. At the same time it extended the mandate of its own Special Rapporteur for one year and invited him, in carrying out his functions, to bear in mind the need to be able to respond effectively to credible and reliable information that comes to his attention and to perform his work with discretion and independence.

139. The Sub-Commission, in resolution 1987/33 of 4 September 1987, welcomed the recommendations contained in the *Study of the Current Dimensions of the Problem of Intolerance and Discrimination on Grounds of Religion or Belief,*[34] in particular those relating to the need for further study of major aspects of the issue, the need for the elaboration of a binding international instrument, and the need for educational measures to promote tolerance, understanding and respect in matters relating to religion or belief. It requested its Chairman to entrust to one of the members the following tasks: (*a*) to consider which aspects of this issue should be studied in greater depth by the Sub-Commission; (*b*) to examine information, recommendations and other materials which may be submitted to the Sub-Commission by Governments, intergovernmental organizations, specialized agencies, non-governmental organizations in consultative status, academic institutions and religious bodies; (*c*) to examine, mindful of General Assembly resolution 41/120, the issues and factors which should be considered before any definitive drafting of a binding international instrument takes place; and (*d*) to report on the above issues to the Sub-Commission at its forty-first session.

140. The General Assembly, in resolution 42/97 of 7 December 1987, noted with satisfaction that the Sub-Commission had examined the study concluded by Mrs. Odio Benito, and had laid the foundation for future in-depth study of aspects of the issues raised in the study. It also welcomed the renewal of the mandate of the Special Rapporteur appointed by the Commission on Human Rights. It noted that the Commission intended to consider at its forty-fourth session the question of a binding international instrument relating to intolerance and discrimination based on religion or belief and emphasized the relevance of Assembly resolution 41/120 of 4 December 1986 entitled "Setting international standards in the field of human rights". It also requested the Commision to consider the study by Mrs. Odio Benito at its forty-fourth session in the light of the observations transmitted to it by the Sub-Commission; and to continue its consideration of measures to implement the Declaration.

141. In the resolution, the Assembly reaffirmed that freedom of thought, conscience, religion and belief is a right guaranteed to all without discrimination; urged States, therefore, in accordance with their respective constitutional systems and with the relevant international instruments, to provide, where they have not already done so, adequate constitutional and legal guarantees of freedom of thought, conscience, religion and belief, including the provision of effective remedies where there is intolerance or discrimination based on religion or belief; and stressed, in this connection, the value of the work in progress in the Commission on Human Rights on the preparation of a compendium of the national legislation and regulations of States on the question of freedom of religion or belief.

---

[34] E/CN.4/Sub.2/1987/26.

V. ELIMINATION OF *APARTHEID* AND ASSISTANCE TO ITS VICTIMS

Introduction

1. The racial policies of South Africa have been under discussion in the United Nations since 1946, when India complained that South Africa had enacted legislation against South Africans of Indian origin. At the seventh session of the General Assembly, in 1952, the wider question of *apartheid* was placed on its agenda under the title "The question of race conflict in South Africa resulting from the policies of *apartheid* of the Government of the Union of South Africa". The two related questions continued to be discussed as separate agenda items until the sixteenth session; at the seventeenth session, in 1962, they were combined under the title "The policies of *apartheid* of the Government of the Republic of South Africa".

2. By resolution 1761 (XVII) of 6 November 1962, the General Assembly established the Special Committee on the Policies of *Apartheid* of the Government of the Republic of South Africa to keep the racial policies of that Government under review when the Assembly was not in session, and to report, as appropriate, to the Assembly or to the Security Council, or to both, from time to time. Eight years later the Assembly shortened the title of the Committee to "Special Committee on *Apartheid*" and decided, in resolution 2671 A (XXV) of 8 December 1970, to expand its membership by not more than seven additional members and to widen its mandate so that it could constantly review all aspects of the policies of *apartheid* in South Africa and its international repercussions.

3. In resolution 3324 D (XXIX) of 16 December 1974 the General Assembly again changed the title of the Committee, this time to "Special Committee against *Apartheid*"; in that resolution, and later in resolution 34/93 R of 17 December 1979, the Assembly requested its President, in consultation with the regional groups, to expand the membership of the Special Committee, bearing in mind the principle of equitable geographical distribution. As at 31 December 1987, no additional members had been appointed. The Committee is composed of 18 Member States, and submits annual and special reports to the Assembly and to the Security Council.

4. In 1965 the Assembly set up the United Nations Trust Fund for South Africa to help the victims of *apartheid*. In 1966, it authorized the establishment of a special Unit on *Apartheid,* later called the Centre against *Apartheid.* In 1973 it adopted and opened for signature and ratification or accession the International Convention on the Suppression and Punishment of the Crime of *Apartheid,* and appealed to all States to sign and ratify it as soon as possible. In 1976 it initiated the preparation of the International Declaration against *Apartheid* in Sports, adopted and proclaimed in 1977, and the International Convention against *Apartheid* in Sports, adopted and opened for signature and ratification in 1985. In 1979, it adopted the Declaration on South Africa, affirming the legitimacy of the struggle of the people of South Africa for the elimination of *apartheid* and the establishment of a non-racial society.

5. In recent years the Assembly has repeatedly called upon the Security Council to take action under Chapter VII of the Charter of the United Nations with a view to applying comprehensive and mandatory sanctions against South Africa, but the Security Council has been unable to do so because of negative votes cast by one or more of its permanent Members. The Council did however initiate a mandatory arms embargo in 1984 and has endeavoured to secure an end to all military and nuclear co-operation with South Africa.

6. The Commission on Human Rights, which in 1967 completed a special study of *apartheid* and racial discrimination in southern Africa,[1] established on 6 March of that year its *Ad Hoc* Working Group of Experts to study the ill-treatment of prisoners, detainees and persons in police custody in South Africa, particularly the numerous opponents of *apartheid* imprisoned under arbitrary laws; it has since examined the reports of the Working Group of Experts annually and forwarded its conclusions and recommendations to the General Assembly and other organs concerned. The Working Group itself made a special study concerning the question of *apartheid* from the point of view of international penal law,[2] paving the way for preparation of the International Convention on the Suppression and Punishment of the Crime of *Apartheid*.

7. In addition, the Commission established the Group of Three to consider reports submitted periodically by States parties to the International Convention on the Suppression and Punishment of the Crime of *Apartheid,* and the Group has met annually since 1978 to perform that task. The Commission on the Status of Women examined in detail the situation of women and children under *apartheid,* while the Sub-Commission on Prevention of Discrimination and Protection of Minorities studied *apartheid* not only as an institutionalized system of racism and racial discrimination but also as a collective form of slavery. Nearly every agency and organization within the United Nations system eventually

---

[1] E/CN.4/949 and Corr.1 and Add.1 and Add.1/Corr.1 and Add.2-5.

[2] E/CN.4/1075 and Corr.1.

found itself involved in some aspect of the campaign against *apartheid,* the successful outcome of which is a major goal of the entire international community.

8. All of this extraordinary—but unavailing—campaign to wipe out once and for all the system of institutionalized racial segregation and discrimination prevailing in South Africa and known as *apartheid* had its beginnings in 1946, during the second part of the first session of the General Assembly, when the delegation of India asked the Assembly to consider the treatment of Indians in the Union of South Africa, charging that the Union Government had enacted discriminatory measures against Indians, in particular the Asiatic Land Tenure and Indian Representation Act of 1946, which restricted the rights of Indians in regard to trade and residence. These discriminatory measures, the Government of India charged, constituted a violation of certain international agreements (the so-called Capetown Agreements of 1927 and 1932) concluded between the Governments of India and South Africa, and of the principles of the Charter concerning human rights.

9. The South African Government denied the General Assembly's competence to deal with the complaint, considering that it concerned a matter "essentially within the domestic jurisdiction" of the Union as laid down in Article 2, paragraph 7, of the Charter, and proposed that the question be referred to the International Court of Justice.

10. On 8 December 1946, after a lengthy debate, the General Assembly adopted resolution 44 (I), in which it stated that, because of the treatment of Indians in the Union of South Africa, "friendly relations between the two Member States have been impaired and, unless a satisfactory solution is reached, these relations are likely to be further impaired". The Assembly therefore expressed the opinion that "the treatment of Indians in the Union should be in conformity with the international obligations under the agreements concluded between the two Governments and the relevant provisions of the Charter". The two Governments were requested to report to the General Assembly, at its next session, on the measures adopted to this effect.

11. In 1947, both Governments submitted reports to the second session of the Assembly. India reported that the Union Government had completely ignored the Assembly resolution and had impugned the judgement and impartiality of the United Nations. South Africa accused the Government of India of seeking to force a solution by the imposition of unilateral sanctions, and maintained that failure to record any progress towards a settlement of existing differences was due to India's insistence that the Union Government accept a condemnation said to be implied in the Assembly resolution. The question was debated in the First Committee, but neither of two draft resolutions submitted obtained the required two-thirds majority in the General Assembly. No further action was taken and it was left to the two disputants to reach agreement on their own initiative.

12. In 1948, the representative of India stated in a letter to the Secretary-General that the Government of the Union of South Africa had made no change whatever, either in its discriminatory laws or in the practice of discrimination on racial grounds against its nationals of Indian origin. In reply, the representative of South Africa reaffirmed the position of his Government which adjudged the matter to be one of purely domestic jurisdiction. He viewed any discussion of the question as a violation of Article 2, paragraph 7, of the Charter, and pointed out that the Government of India had enlarged the scope of its original objections so as to include all Asiatics and other non-whites in the Union; and suggested that deletion of the item from the Assembly's agenda would be a step towards restoring friendly relations between the two countries.

13. A draft resolution submitted to the First Committee by South Africa asked that the Assembly decide that the treatment of people of Indian origin in the Union of South Africa was a matter which was essentially within the domestic jurisdiction of the Union of South Africa and did not fall within the competence of the General Assembly. That draft resolution was rejected.

14. In resolution 265 (III), adopted on 14 May 1949, the Assembly invited the Governments of India, Pakistan and the Union of South Africa "to enter into discussion at a round-table conference, taking into consideration the purposes and principles of the Charter of the United Nations and the Declaration of Human Rights".

15. In 1950, at the fifth session of the General Assembly, the question was referred to the *Ad Hoc* Political Committee which, after deciding that it was competent to deal with the matter, recommended specific proposals for adoption by the General Assembly.

16. In resolution 395 (V) of 2 December 1950, the Assembly expressed the opinion that "a policy of 'racial segregation' (*apartheid*) is necessarily based on doctrines of racial discrimination" and again recommended a round-table conference. Such a conference has not materialized; indeed, in resolution 615 (VII) of 5 December 1952 the General Assembly noted that the Government of South Africa had expressed its inability to resume negotiations with the Governments of India and Pakistan. A United Nations Good Offices Commission established by that resolution "with a view to arranging and assisting in negotiations" reported to the Assembly in 1954 that it was unable to submit any proposal likely to lead to a peaceful settlement of the problem on account of the uncooperative attitude of the Government of the Union of South Africa.

17. On 12 September 1952 thirteen Member States requested that "The question of race conflict in South Africa resulting from the policies of *apartheid* of the Government of the Union of South Africa" be placed on the agenda for the seventh session of the General Assembly. An explanatory memorandum[3] stated that this race conflict was creating a dangerous and explosive situation, which constituted both a threat to inter-

---

[3] *Official Records of the General Assembly, Seventh Session, Annexes,* agenda item 66, document A/2183.

national peace and a flagrant violation of the basic principles of human rights and fundamental freedoms enshrined in the Charter. The memorandum pointed out that under the policy of *apartheid,* which implied a permanent white superiority over the 80 per cent of the population who were non-whites, the following measures were being taken: segregation of races under the notorious Group Areas Act; complete segregation in public services; suppression of democratic movements advocating racial equality under the Suppression of Communism Act; barring of non-whites from combat service; withholding of voting and other political rights from non-whites except in Cape Province; confinement of Africans to reserves and restriction of their movements; exclusion of non-whites from skilled work under the Mines Works Amendment Act; and provision of vastly inferior educational and housing conditions for non-whites. Unable to secure redress by constitutional methods, the non-whites of the Union had been compelled to launch a non-violent resistance movement against unjust and inhuman racial policies. It was therefore imperative, the memorandum concluded, that the General Assembly urgently consider the question so as to prevent further deterioriation and effect a settlement in accordance with the Charter.

18.   In the General Assembly's General Committee, the representative of the Union of South Africa protested formally against the inclusion of the item in the agenda. The Committee, however, recommended that the item be included. In the 381st plenary meeting, on 17 October 1952, the representative of South Africa moved that the item should be excluded from the agenda on the ground that the General Assembly was not competent to consider it. The Assembly, however, decided to accept the General Committee's recommendation to include the item on the agenda.

19.   After debate in the *Ad Hoc* Political Committee, the General Assembly, on 5 December 1952, adopted resolution 616 A and B (VII). By the first of these, the Assembly established "a Commission, consisting of three members, to study the racial situation in the Union of South Africa in the light of the Purposes and Principles of the Charter, with due regard to the provision of Article 2, paragraph 7, as well as the provisions of Article 1, paragraphs 2 and 3, Article 13, paragraph 1.b, Article 55 c and Article 56 of the Charter, and the resolutions of the United Nations on racial persecution and discrimination, and to report its conclusions to the General Assembly at its eighth session".

20.   The Commission submitted three reports to the General Assembly,[4] which were noted respectively in resolution 721 (VIII), 820 (IX) and 917 (X). In resolution 721 (VIII), adopted on 8 December 1953, the Assembly noted, in particular, the conclusion of the Commission that the continuance of the policy of *apartheid* "would make peaceful solutions increasingly difficult

[4] *Official Records of the General Assembly, Eighth Session, Supplement No. 16* (A/2505 and Add.1); *ibid., Ninth Session, Supplement No. 16* (A/2719); and *ibid., Tenth Session, Supplement No. 14* (A/2953).

and endanger friendly relations among nations". In resolution 820 (IX), adopted on 14 December 1954, the Assembly noted the Commission's conviction that "the policy of *apartheid* constitutes a grave threat to the peaceful relations between ethnic groups in the world". In resolution 917 (X), adopted on 6 December 1955, the Assembly recommended the Government of South Africa to take note of the Commission's third report.

21.   In the 30-year period between 1957 and 1987 a number of United Nations organs, *ad hoc* bodies and specialized agencies explored a wide variety of approaches in their endeavour to assist in the solution of the problem of race conflict resulting from *apartheid* in South Africa, but with little or no success. Indeed, during that period the institutionalized segregation and discrimination of *apartheid* has spread and is now imposed upon the people of Namibia by the illegal South African administration of that Territory.

A. General Assembly

1. PROGRAMME OF ACTION

22.   Thirty years after the United Nations was first seized of the problem of racism in South Africa, the General Assembly summed up, in its Programme of Action against *Apartheid* annexed to resolution 31/6 J of 9 November 1976, the efforts it had made to persuade the racist minority régimes to abandon the bitter legacy of the past and to work for a peaceful solution in accordance with the principles of human equality and international co-operation.

23.   In the Introduction to the Programme, the Assembly pointed out that the abolition of racist domination and exploitation in South Africa and assistance to the South African people to establish a non-racial society had become one of the primary concerns of the United Nations and the international community. *Apartheid,* it said, must be eradicated because it is a crime against humanity, because it is an affront to human dignity and a grave threat to international peace and security, and because the continent of Africa must be finally emancipated and enabled to play its rightful role in international affairs.

24.   The General Assembly, further, commended the courageous struggle of the oppressed people of South Africa, under the leadership of their national liberation movements recognized by the Organization of African Unity, to abolish racism. It reaffirmed that their struggle for the total eradiction of *apartheid* and the exercise of the right to self-determination by all the inhabitants of South Africa, is perfectly legitimate. It reiterated its solidarity with all South Africans struggling against *apartheid* and for the principles enshrined in the Charter of the United Nations and the Universal Declaration of Human Rights.

25.   In the Programme of Action, the General Assembly reiterated and renewed its many earlier calls, addressed to Governments, intergovernmental organiza-

tions and non-governmental organizations throughout the world, to take certain basic steps which would have a negative effect upon perpetrators of the crime of *apartheid* and which might eventually put an end to the commission of that crime. Among these basic steps was action to be taken in a number of fields of key importance, among them:

A. *Diplomatic, consular and other official relations*

(a) To terminate diplomatic, consular and other official relations with the racist régime of South Africa, or to refrain from establishing such relations;

B. *Military and nuclear collaboration*

(b) To implement fully the arms embargo against South Africa without any exceptions or reservations and, in this connexion:

(i) To refrain from the sale and shipment of arms, ammunition of all types and any vehicles or equipment for use of the armed forces and paramilitary organizations in South Africa;

(ii) To refrain from the sale and shipment of equipment and materials for the manufacture and maintenance of arms, ammunition and military vehicles and equipment in South Africa;

(iii) To refrain from the supply of spare parts for vehicles and equipment used by the armed forces and paramilitary organizations in South Africa;

(iv) To revoke any licences or patents granted to the racist régime of South Africa or to South African companies for the manufacture of arms, ammunition and military vehicles and equipment and to refrain from granting such licences and patents;

(v) To prohibit investment in, or technical assistance for, the manufacture of arms and ammunition, aircraft, naval craft and other military vehicles and equipment in South Africa;

(vi) To terminate any existing military arrangements with the racist régime of South Africa and to refrain from entering into any such arrangements;

(vii) To refrain from providing training for members of the South African armed forces;

(viii) To refrain from any joint military exercises with South Africa;

(ix) To prohibit warships or military aircraft from visiting South African ports and airports, and South African warships or military aircraft from visiting their territories;

(x) To prohibit visits of military personnel to South Africa and visits by South African military personnel to their countries;

(xi) To refrain from exchanges of military, naval or air attachés with South Africa;

(xii) To refrain from purchasing any military supplies manufactured by, or in collaboration with, South Africa;

(xiii) To refrain from any communications or contacts with the South African military establishment or installations;

(xiv) To refrain from any other form of military co-operation with South Africa;

(xv) To prohibit any violations of the arms embargo by corporations, institutions or individuals within their jurisdiction;

(xvi) To refrain from any collaboration with South Africa in the nuclear field;

(xvii) To prohibit any institutions, agencies or companies, within their national jurisdiction, from delivering to South Africa or placing at its disposal any equipment or fissionable material or technology that will enable the racist régime of South Africa to acquire nuclear-weapon technology;

C. *Economic collaboration*

(c) To terminate all economic collaboration with South Africa and, in particular:

(i) To refrain from supplying petroleum, petroleum products or other strategic materials to South Africa;

(ii) To refrain from extending loans, investments and technical assistance to the racist régime of South Africa and companies registered in South Africa;

(iii) To prohibit loans by banks or other financial institutions in their countries to the racist régime of South Africa or South African companies;

(iv) To prohibit economic and financial interests under their national jurisdiction from co-operating with the racist régime of South Africa and companies registered in South Africa;

(v) To deny tariff and other preferences to South African exports and any inducements or guarantees for investment in South Africa;

(vi) To take appropriate action in international agencies and organizations—such as the European Economic Community, the General Agreement on Tariffs and Trade, the International Monetary Fund and the International Bank for Reconstruction and Development—for denial by them of all assistance and commercial or other facilities to the South African régime;

(vii) To take appropriate action, separately or collectively, against transnational companies collaborating with South Africa;

D. *Airlines and shipping lines*

(d) To refuse landing and passage facilities to all aircraft belonging to the racist régime of South Africa and companies registered under the laws of South Africa;

(e) To close ports to all vessels flying the South African flag;

(f) To prohibit airlines and shipping lines registered in their countries from providing services to and from South Africa;

E. *Emigration*

(g) To prohibit or discourage the flow of immigrants, particularly skilled and technical personnel, to South Africa;

F. *Cultural, educational, sporting and other collaboration with South Africa*

(h) To suspend cultural, educational, sporting and other exchanges with the racist régime and with organizations or institutions in South Africa which practise *apartheid*;

(i) to implement United Nations resolutions on *apartheid* in sports and, in particular:

(i) To refrain from all contact with sports bodies established on the basis of *apartheid* or with racially selected sports teams from South Africa;

(ii) To withhold any support from sporting events which are organized in violation of the Olympic principle with the participation of racially selected teams from South Africa;

(iii) To encourage sports organizations to refrain from any exchanges with racially selected teams from South Africa;

G. *Assistance to the oppressed people of South Africa*

(j) To provide financial and material assistance, directly or through the Organization of African Unity, to the South African liberation movements recognized by that organization;

(k) To encourage public collections in the country for assistance to the South African liberation movements;

(l) To contribute generously and regularly to the United Nations Trust Fund for South Africa, the United Nations Educational and Training Programme for Southern Africa, the United Nations Trust Fund for Publicity against *Apartheid* and other intergovernmental and non-governmental funds for assistance to the oppressed people of South Africa and their liberation movements;

(m) To encourage judicial organizations, other appropriate bodies and the public in general to provide assistance to those persecuted by the racist régime of South Africa for their struggle against *apartheid*;

(n) To grant asylum and extend travel facilities and educational and employment opportunities to refugees from South Africa;

(*o*) To encourage the activities of anti-*apartheid* and solidarity movements and other organizations engaged in providing political and material assistance to the victims of *apartheid* and to the South African liberation movements;

H. *Dissemination of information on* apartheid

(*p*) To ensure, in co-operation with the United Nations and the South African liberation movements, the widest possible dissemination of information on *apartheid* and on the struggle for liberation in South Africa;

(*q*) To encourage the establishment of national organizations for the purpose of enlightening public opinion on the evils of *apartheid*;

(*r*) To encourage the information media to contribute effectively to the international campaign against *apartheid*;

(*s*) To provide broadcasting facilities to South African liberation movements;

(*t*) To take all necessary measures against the operations of propaganda organizations of the racist régime of South Africa and of private organizations which advocate *apartheid*;

I. *Other measures*

(*u*) To accede to the International Convention on the Suppression and Punishment of the Crime of *Apartheid*;

(*v*) To observe annually the International Day for the Elimination of Racial Discrimination, on 21 March, and the Day of Solidarity with South African Political Prisoners, on 11 October;

(*w*) To promote action by intergovernmental organizations in support of the struggle for liberation in South Africa;

(*x*) To provide, at their request, all necessary assistance to independent African States subjected to acts of aggression by the racist régime of South Africa in order to enable them to defend their sovereignty and territorial integrity.

26. In the Programme of Action, the General Assembly further called upon all specialized agencies and other intergovernmental organizations to contribute to the maximum to the international campaign against *apartheid,* and suggested in particular that they:

(*a*) Exclude the racist régime of South Africa from any participation in their organizations;

(*b*) Deny any assistance to the racist régime of South Africa;

(*c*) Invite representatives of the South African liberation movements recognized by the Organization of African Unity to attend, *inter alia,* their conferences and seminars and make financial provision for their participation;

(*d*) Provide appropriate assistance to the oppressed people of South Africa and to their liberation movements;

(*e*) Disseminate information against *apartheid* in co-operation with the United Nations;

(*f*) Provide employment within their secretariats and assistance for education and training to the oppressed people of South Africa.

27. The General Assembly, in the Programme of Action, also commended the activities of all public organizations in denouncing the racist régime of South Africa, in supporting United Nations resolutions against *apartheid,* and in assisting the oppressed people of South Africa in mobilizing public opinion against *apartheid*; and encouraged them to concert and redouble their efforts, in co-operation with the Special Committee against *Apartheid* and with the Centre against *Apartheid*:

(*a*) To exert their influence to persuade Governments which continue to collaborate with the racist régime of South Africa to desist from such collaboration;

(*b*) To press all Governments to implement United Nations resolutions against *apartheid*;

(*c*) To expand campaigns for the boycott of South African goods;

(*d*) To intensify campaigns against banks and other transnational companies which collaborate with South Africa;

(*e*) To establish solidarity funds and provide assistance to the South African liberation movements;

(*f*) To assist political refugees from South Africa;

(*g*) To publicize the struggle for liberation in South Africa;

(*h*) To observe annually the International Day for the Elimination of Racial Discrimination, on 21 March, and the Day of Solidarity with South African Political Prisoners, on 11 October.

The General Assembly called upon trade unions, in particular:

(*a*) To organize rallies and information campaigns among the workers to make them fully aware of the problem of *apartheid* and to secure their collaboration in industrial action against South Africa;

(*b*) To support internationally co-ordinated boycotts of South African goods;

(*c*) To organize international trade-union action to ban the handling of goods going to and from South Africa;

(*d*) To investigate the operations of companies with subsidiaries inside South Africa;

(*e*) To undertake, in the countries concerned, industrial action against transnational companies which refuse to recognize African trade unions in South Africa and fail to comply with internationally recognized labour standards;

(*f*) To give moral and financial support to the African and non-racial trade unions in South Africa, including legal assistance to imprisoned and restricted trade unionists;

(*g*) To intensify the campaigns against the emigration of workers to South Africa;

(*h*) To request workers not to handle any arms orders for South Africa and to give full support to those workers who on grounds of conscience, refuse to work on such orders.

The General Assembly appealed to churches and religious organizations, in particular:

(*a*) To exert all their influence and efforts to oppose any form of collaboration with the racist régime of South Africa;

(*b*) To expand campaigns against banks and transnational corporations collaborating with South Africa;

(*c*) To provide all forms of assistance to the oppressed people of South Africa and to their liberation movements;

(*d*) To disseminate information on the inhumanity of *apartheid* and on the righteous struggle of the oppressed people of South Africa.

The General Assembly appealed to sports bodies and sportsmen:

(*a*) To uphold the Olympic principle that no discrimination be allowed on the grounds of race, religion or political affiliation;

(b) To refrain from all contact with sports bodies established on the basis of *apartheid* or with racially selected sports teams from South Africa;

(*c*) To assist sportsmen and sports administrators persecuted in South Africa for their opposition to *apartheid* in sports;

(*d*) To take appropriate action to expel racist South African sports bodies from all international sports federations and competitions.

28. Finally, the General Assembly, in the Programme of Action, expanded the mandate of the Special Committee against *Apartheid* by requesting it to take all appropriate measures to encourage concerted action against *apartheid* by Governments and intergovernmental and non-governmental organizations and by inviting it to promote co-ordinated international campaigns:

(*a*) For assistance to the oppressed people of South Africa and their liberation movements;

(*b*) For an effective arms embargo against South Africa;

(*c*) Against all forms of nuclear co-operation with South Africa;

(*d*) Against all collaboration by Governments, banks and trans-national corporations with South Africa;

(*e*) Against propaganda by the racist régime of South Africa and its collaborators;

(*f*) For the unconditional release of South African political prisoners;

(*g*) For the boycott of racially selected South African sports teams.

29. The General Assembly has since continued to examine the policies of *apartheid* of the Government of South Africa at each regular session on the basis of the annual reports of its Special Committee against *Apartheid*. At its thirty-first session, in 1976, the Assembly for the first time discussed this item directly in plenary meeting and invited the South African liberation movements recognized by the OAU to participate in the discussion.

2. DECLARATION ON SOUTH AFRICA

30. In resolution 34/93 O of 12 December 1979, the General Assembly adopted the Declaration on South Africa, in which it set out the responsibilities of States for concerted action to eliminate *apartheid*. Article 1 of the Declaration provides that all States shall recognize the legitimacy of the struggle of the people of South Africa for the elimination of *apartheid* and the establishment of non-racial society guaranteeing the enjoyment of equal rights by all the people of South Africa, irrespective of race, colour or creed.

31. Under article 2, all States shall recognize the right of the oppressed people of South Africa to chose their means of struggle.

32. Under article 3, all States shall solemnly pledge to refrain from overt or covert military intervention in support or defence of the Pretoria régime in its effort to repress the legitimate aspirations and struggle of the African people of South Africa against it in the exercise of their right of self-determination, or in its threats or acts of aggression against the African States committed to the establishment of a democratic government of South Africa based on the will of the people as a whole, regardless of race, colour or creed, as the imperative guarantee to lasting peace and security in southern Africa.

33. Article 4 provides that all States shall take firm action to prevent the recruitment, financing, training or passage of mercenaries in support of the *apartheid* régime of South Africa or the bantustans created by it in South Africa.

34. Under article 5, all States shall take appropriate measures to discourage and counteract propaganda in favour of *apartheid*.

35. Under article 6, all States shall respect the desire of African States for the denuclearization of the continent of Africa and refrain from any co-operation with the South African régime in its plans to become a nuclear Power.

36. Under article 7, all States shall demonstrate international solidarity with the oppressed people of South Africa and with the independent African States subjected to threats or acts of aggression and subversion by the South African régime.

37. The Assembly has since repeatedly reaffirmed the legitimacy of the struggle of the oppressed people of South Africa and their national liberation movement, demanded that the *apartheid* régime treat captured freedom fighters as prisoners of war under the Geneva Conventions of 1949 and Additional Protocol I thereto, proclaimed its full support of the national liberation movement of South Africa as the authentic representative of the people of South Africa in their just struggle for liberation, and appealed to all States to provide all necessary humanitarian, educational, financial and other necessary assistance to the oppressed people of South Africa and their national liberation movement in their legitimate struggle.

38. It has also repeatedly urged the Security Council to take action without further delay to impose a mandatory embargo on the supply and shipping of oil and petroleum products to South Africa, as well as the supply of equipment and technology to its oil industry and coal liquefaction projects; and as requested all States concerned, pending a decision by the Council, to adopt measures and/or legislation for this purpose.

39. In resolution 42/23 G of 20 November 1987, the Assembly again strongly condemned the policy of *apartheid* which deprives the majority of the South African population of their citizenship, fundamental freedoms and human rights; and strongly condemned the South African authorities for the killings, arbitrary mass arrests and the detention of members of mass organizations as well as individuals, the overwhelming majority of whom belong to the majority population, for opposing the *apartheid* system and the state of emergency and for the use of violence against children. It demanded (para. 4) that the authorities of South Africa (*a*) release immediately and unconditionally Nelson Mandela and all other political prisoners, detainees and restrictees; (*b*) immediately lift the state of emergency; (*c*) abrogate discriminatory laws and lift bans on all organizations and individuals, as well as end restrictions on and censorship of the news media; (*d*) grant freedom of association and full trade union rights to all workers of South Africa; (*e*) initiate without pre-conditions a political dialogue with genuine leaders of the majority population with a view to eradicating *apartheid* without delay and establishing a representative government; (*f*) eradicate the bantustan structures; and (*g*) immediately withdraw all their troops from southern Angola and end the destabilization of front-line and other States.

40. At the same time, the Assembly appealed (para. 8) to all States, organizations and institutions recognizing the pressing need, existing and potential, of South Af-

rica's neighbouring States for economic assistance, to increase assistance to the front-line States and the Southern African Development Co-ordination Conference in order to increase their economic strength and independence from South Africa; and appealed to all Governments and organizations to take appropriate action for the cessation of all academic, cultural, scientific and sports relations that would support the *apartheid* régime of South Africa, as well as relations with individuals, institutions and other bodies endorsing or based on *apartheid*.

3. STUDIES ON *APARTHEID*

41.   Studies of various aspects of *apartheid* have been prepared from time to time on the initiative of the Commission on Human Rights and its Sub-Commission on Prevention of Discrimination and Protection of Minorities. Among these are:

Study of apartheid *and racial discrimination in southern Africa*[5] prepared by Mr. Manouchehr Ganji, Special Rapporteur appointed by the Commission on Human Rights in resolution 7 (XXIII) of 16 March 1967. The mandate of the Special Rapporteur was "to survey United Nations past action in its efforts to eliminate the policies and practices of *apartheid* in all its forms and manifestations, to study the legislation and practices in South Africa, South West Africa and Southern Rhodesia, instituted to establish and maintain *apartheid* and racial discrimination in all their forms and manifestations in the Republic of South Africa, South West Africa and Southern Rhodesia, including such matters as forced labour, inequality of opportunity in the economic, social and educational fields, arrest, detention and treatment of prisoners, right to counsel and fair trial, and to report and to make recommendations to the Commission. . .".

Study concerning the question of apartheid *from the point of view of international penal law*[6] prepared by the *Ad Hoc* Working Group of Experts of the Commission on Human Rights in accordance with a request made by the Commission in resolution 8 (XXVI) of 18 March 1970. The mandate of the *Ad Hoc* Working Group of Experts was "to study, from the point of view of international penal law, the question of *apartheid*, which has been declared a crime against humanity". The *Ad Hoc* Working Group entrusted the preparation of the draft of the study to one of its members, Mr. Felix Ermacora. After consideration of the draft, it drew up the study and submitted it to the Commission at its twenty-eighth session, in 1972.

Apartheid *as a collective form of slavery*[7] prepared by the Secretary-General in accordance with a request

contained in resolution 6 B (XXXI) of 13 September 1978 of the Sub-Commission on Prevention of Discrimination and Protection of Minorities. The mandate of the Secretary-General was "to carry out, as a matter of priority, a study of *apartheid* and colonialism as collective forms of slavery".

Adverse consequences for the enjoyment of human rights of political, military, economic and other forms of assistance given to the colonial and racist régimes in southern Africa[8] prepared by Mr. Ahmed Khalifa, Special Rapporteur appointed by the Sub-Commission on Prevention of Discrimination and Protection of Minorities. The study contains a list of banks, transnational corporations and other organizations giving assistance to the racist and colonial régime in South Africa, and is updated from time to time.

Ways and means of ensuring the implementation of international instruments such as the International Convention on the Suppression and Punishment of the Crime of Apartheid,[9] prepared by the *Ad Hoc* Working Group of Experts on Southern Africa in accordance with a request contained in resolution 12 (XXXVI) of 26 February 1980 of the Commission on Human Rights. The study begins with an inquiry into the significance of the term "implementation" in view of the nature of the International Convention on the Suppression and Punishment of the Crime of *Apartheid,* and concludes that in this context "implementation" signifies creation of an international criminal court. It proceeds to consider the state of international criminal law in terms of the theory and practicality of the operations of such a court, and with special attention to the particular nature of the crime of *apartheid*. It includes an assessment of the possible usefulness of such a court in combating the crime of *apartheid,* and provides a summary of issues requiring attention and means of addressing such issues.

42.   Part III of the study contains a draft convention on the establishment of an international penal tribunal for the suppression and punishment of the crime of *apartheid* and other international crimes; while part IV contains a draft additional protocol for the penal enforcement of the International Convention on the Suppression and Punishment of the Crime of *Apartheid*.

43.   The Commission on Human Rights, in resolution 6 (XXXVII) of 23 February 1981, requested the Secretary-General to obtain the comments and views of States parties to the Convention on the interim study prepared by the *Ad Hoc* Working Group of Experts.

---

[5] E/CN.4/979 and Add.1 and Add.1/Corr.1 and Add.2-8.

[6] E/CN.4/1075 and Corr.1.

[7] E/CN.4/Sub.2/449.

[8] The original report (E/CN.4/Sub.2/383/Rev.2) was issued as a United Nations publication, Sales No. E.79.XIV.3. An updated report was later issued as a United Nations publication, Sales No. E.85.XIV.4. In 1987 an updated report was considered by the Sub- Commission on Prevention of Discrimination and Protection of Minorities and other bodies (E/CN.4/Sub.2/1987/Rev.1 and Add.1), parts I and II.

[9] E/CN.4/1426.

Study on the effects of the policy of apartheid *on black women and children in South Africa,*[10] prepared by the *Ad Hoc* Working Group of Experts on Southern Africa in accordance with resolution 5 (XXXVII) of the Commission on Human Rights and resolution 1981/41 of the Economic and Social Council. The study examines the situation of black South African women in terms of their multiple roles—in the family, as workers, as political prisoners and as citizens—in the context of the race, class and sex oppression embodied in the operation of *apartheid*. It also examines the situation of children under *apartheid,* bearing in mind that the international community has defined the special rights of children as including the rights to: adequate nutrition and medical care; free education; full opportunity for play and recreation; a name and a nationality; special care, if handicapped; to be among the first to receive relief in times of disaster; to learn to be a useful citizen and to develop individual abilities; to be brought up in a spirit of peace and universal brotherhood; and to enjoy these rights regardless of race, colour, sex, religion, or national or social origin.

44. *List of those deemed responsible for the crime of* apartheid. The Commission on Human Rights, in resolution 7 (XXXIV) of 22 February 1978, called upon the competent United Nations organs to provide it with information relevant to the preparation of the list of individuals, organizations, institutions and representatives of States alleged to be responsible for crimes enumerated in article II of the International Convention on the Suppression and Punishment of the Crime of *Apartheid,* as well as those against whom legal proceedings had been undertaken by States parties to the Convention.

45. The General Assembly welcomed the efforts of the Commission to undertake the functions set out in article X of the Convention and, in resolution 33/103 of 16 December 1978, called upon the competent United Nations organs to provide the Commission with relevant information as well as with information concerning the obstacles which prevented the effective suppression and punishment of the crime of *apartheid*.

46. At its thirty-fifth session, in 1979, the Commission received a report drawn up by the Special Committee against *Apartheid*.[11] In resolution 12 (XXXV) of 6 March 1979 it requested its *Ad Hoc* Working Group of Experts to investigate the cases of torture and murder of detainees mentioned in that report and to submit a special report on the investigation to the Commission.

47. The Working Group, which had earlier included in its reports a list of persons deemed to be guilty of the crime of *apartheid* or of serious violations of human rights in Namibia in accordance with Commission resolutions 6 (XXXIII) of 4 March 1977 and 5 (XXXIV) of

22 February 1978,[12] prepared a special report on the application of the International Convention on the Suppression and Punishment of the Crime of *Apartheid,*[13] which it submitted to the Commission at its thirty-sixth session. The report examined 37 cases of murder, torture and deprivation of freedom and of fundamental rights, and concluded that:

. . . torture by the Security Police is common practice and, moreover, that the Government seems to acquiesce in it and to cover it up by all possible means. . . . The Group has been particularly struck by the concomitance of the acts of torture and murder committed by the South African police, especially since July 1976. It considers that these acts can constitute only a huge campaign of intimidation of African nationalists and that the attitude of the South African Government, which endeavours in almost every case to cover up the acts with which it is charged, can but lead to the conclusion that this is the true policy of South Africa.

Annex III of the report contains a list of the persons implicated in the cases examined. The Working Group recommended that the list of persons guilty of the crime of *apartheid* should be published in the greatest possible number of newspapers and brought to the knowledge of the public by all other information media.

48. The General Assembly, in resolution 35/39 of 25 November 1980, expressed its appreciation to the *Ad Hoc* Working Group of Experts for the compilation of the list, and called upon all States parties to give the list the widest possible dissemination. It welcomed the efforts of the Commission on Human Rights to undertake the functions set out in article X of the Convention and invited the Commission to intensify, in co-operation with the Special Committee against *Apartheid,* its efforts to compile such a list periodically. It requested the Commission, in preparing the list, to take into account General Assembly resolution 33/23 of 29 November 1978 and other documentation reaffirming that States giving assistance to the racist régime in South Africa became accomplices in the inhuman practices of racial discrimination and *apartheid*.

49. The Assembly, further, called upon the competent organs of the United Nations to continue to provide the Commission, through the Secretary-General, with information relevant to the periodic compilation of the list as well as with information concerning the obstacles which prevented the effective suppression and punishment of the crime of *apartheid;* and requested the Secretary-General to distribute the list among all States parties to the Convention and all States Members of the United Nations, and to bring such facts to the attention of the public by all means of mass communication.

50. In resolution 42/56 of 30 November 1987, the Assembly requested the Commission on Human Rights to intensify, in co-operation with the Special Committee against *Apartheid,* its efforts to compile periodically the progressive list of individuals, organizations, institutions and representatives of States deemed responsible for crimes enumerated in article II of the Convention, as well as those against whom or which legal proceed-

---

[10] E/CN.4/1497, submitted to the Commission at its thirty-eighth session, 1982. Additional information was submitted to the Commission at its thirty-ninth session, 1983, in a supplementary report, E/CN.4/1983/38.

[11] E/CN.4/1327/Add.2.

[12] E/CN.4/1270 and E/CN.4/1311.

[13] E/CN.4/1366.

ings have been undertaken; and requested the Secretary-General to circulate the above-mentioned list to all States parties to the Convention and all Member States, and to bring such facts to the attention of the public by all means of mass communication.

Study of the criminal effects of apartheid,[14] prepared by the *Ad Hoc* Working Group of Experts on Southern Africa in accordance with resolution 1983/9 of the Commission on Human Rights. In the study the Working Group attempted to identify the manifestations of *apartheid* and to examine the extent to which acts of *apartheid* might be likened to those which, under article II of the Convention on the Prevention and Punishment of the Crime of Genocide, are designated as acts of genocide. Further, it attempted to show whether the effects of *apartheid* may be related to the crime of genocide.

51. The Working Group's conclusion was that the practical implementation of *apartheid,* almost 40 years after its institutionalization, has resulted in certain criminal consequences which coincide with the acts prohibited under article II (*a*), (*b*) and (*d*) of the Convention on the Prevention and Punishment of the Crime of Genocide; and that the policy of *apartheid,* viewed as a whole and over the long term, will ultimately produce consequences which are identical with those of the acts of genocide prohibited under article II (*c*) of the Convention.

52. The Working Group recommended that "The way in which the South African régime implements the policy of *apartheid* should henceforth be considered as a kind of genocide", and suggested that consideration should be given to possible revision of the Genocide Convention since, through the practices described as "bordering on genocide", genocide had acquired new aspects, not only in South Africa but also in other countries.

4. THE GROUP OF THREE

53. In resolution 31/80 of 13 December 1976, the General Assembly welcomed the entry into force of the International Convention on the Suppression and Punishment of the Crime of *Apartheid*[15] and invited the Chairman of the thirty-third session of the Commission on Human Rights "to appoint a group consisting of three members of the Commission as provided for by article IX of the Convention". The Assembly further invited the Commission "to undertake the functions set out in article X . . . in particular to prepare a list of individuals, organizations, institutions and representatives of States . . . alleged to be responsible for the crimes enumerated in article II . . .".

54. In 1977 the Chairman of the Commission appointed for the first time three members of the Commission who were also representatives of States parties to the Convention, to consider the periodic reports submitted by the States parties on the legislative, judicial, administrative and other measures that had been adopted to give effect to the provisions of the Convention. The Commission decided that this Group of Three should meet for a period of five days immediately before the opening of its thirty-fourth session to examine the reports. Similar Groups of Three were appointed at the 1978 and each subsequent session.

55. In 1978, the Group of Three laid down general guidelines concerning the form and contents of the reports. In 1979, when it examined the first reports, it decided that each would be considered, if possible, in the presence of a representative of the reporting State—a practice which it has since followed. The Group of Three reports to the Commission on Human Rights, but its annual reports—and the conclusions and recommendations contained in them—are regularly considered by the General Assembly.

56. At its 1986 and 1987 sessions, the Group of Three, in accordance with a request of the Commission on Human Rights, also considered whether the actions of transnational corporations operating in South Africa and Namibia came under the definition of the crime of *apartheid* and whether or not some legal actions could be taken under the Convention; and examined the extent and nature of the responsibility of transnational corporations for the continued existence of the system of *apartheid* in South Africa.

57. In this context the Group pointed out, in its report to the Commission,[16] that in article 1, paragraph 2, of the Convention, the States parties declare criminal also organizations and institutions committing the crime of *apartheid*; its view was that, no doubt, the provision was applicable to transnational corporations. The Group concluded that by their complicity these transnational corporations, from the juridical point of view and in conformity with article III (*b*) of the International Convention, must be considered accomplices in the crime of *apartheid* and must be prosecuted for their responsibility in the continuation of this crime.

58. The Commission on Human Rights, in resolution 1987/11 of 26 February 1987, took note with appreciation of the report of the Group of Three,[16] and in particular of the conclusions and recommendations contained therein, drew the attention of all States to the opinion expressed by the Group of Three that transnational corporations operating in South Africa and Namibia must be considered accomplices in the crime of *apartheid,* in accordance with article III (*b*) of the Convention; and requested the Secretary-General once more to invite States parties to the Convention to express their views on the extent and nature of the responsibility of such corporations for the continued existence of the system of *apartheid* in South Africa. It requested

---

[14] E/CN.4/1985/14. The Group of Three of the Commission on Human Rights likewise reached the conclusion, at its 1985 session, that the crime of *apartheid* is a form of the crime of genocide. The Commission reflected the same view in resolution 1985/10 of 26 February 1985.

[15] For information concerning the Convention, see chapter II, section B, 2.

[16] E/CN.4/1987/28.

the Group of Three to continue, in the light of the views expressed by States parties to the Convention, the examination of the question, including legal action that may be taken under the Convention against transnational corporations whose operations in South Africa come under the crime of *apartheid,* and to report to the Commission at its forty-fourth session.

59. The General Assembly, in resolution 42/56 of 30 November 1987, also took note with appreciation of the report of the Group of Three, and drew the attention of all States to the opinion expressed in that report, that transnational corporations operating in South africa and Namibia must be considered accomplices in the crime of *apartheid,* in accordance with article III (*b*) of the Convention.

60. In the resolution, the Assembly reiterated the request made by the Commission on Human Rights to the Group of Three, that it continue to examine the question of the extent and nature of the responsibility of transnational corporations for the continued existence of the system of *apartheid* in South Africa. Further, it requested the Secretary-General to invite the States parties to the Convention, the specialized agencies and non-governmental organizations to provide the Commission on Human Rights with relevant information concerning the types of the crime of *apartheid,* as described in article II of the Convention, committed by transnational corporations operating in South Africa.

5. ACTION AGAINST *APARTHEID* IN SPORTS

61. The International Conference on Human Rights, in resolution XXVIII of 13 May 1968, strongly recommended that international sports federations and associations should exclude South Africa from their membership "until such time as the heinous policy of *apartheid* is brought to an end in that country". The General Assembly, in resolution 2775 D (XXVI) of 29 November 1971, (1) declared "its unqualified support of the Olympic principle that no discrimination be allowed on the grounds of race, religion or political affiliation"; (2) affirmed that "merit should be the sole criterion for participation in sports activities"; (3) called upon "all national and international sports organizations to uphold the Olympic principle of non-discrimination and to discourage and deny support to sporting events organized in violation of this principle"; (4) called upon individual sportsmen "to refuse to participate in any sports activity in a country in which there is an official policy of racial discrimination or *apartheid* in the field of sports"; (5) urged all States "to promote adherence to the Olympic principle of non-discrimination and to encourage their sports organizations to withhold support from sporting events organized in violation of this principle"; (6) requested national and international sports organizations and the public "to deny any form of recognition to any sports activity from which persons were debarred or . . . subjected to any discrimination on the basis of race, religion or

political affiliation"; (7) condemned "the actions of the Government of South Africa in enforcing racial discrimination and segregation in sports"; (8) noted with regret "that some national and international sports organizations have continued exchanges with teams from South Africa that have been selected for international competition on the basis of competition closed to otherwise qualified sportsmen solely on the basis of their race, colour, descent or national or ethnic origin"; (9) commended "those international and national sports organizations that have supported the international campaign against *apartheid* in sports"; (10) requested all States "to urge their national sports organizations to act in accordance with the present resolution"; and (11) requested the Secretary-General to bring the resolution to the attention of international sports organizations, to keep the Special Committee on *Apartheid* informed on the implementation of the resolution, and to submit a report on the matter to the Assembly at its twenty-seventh session.

62. In resolution 3411 E (XXX) of 28 November 1975, the General Assembly reaffirmed its "unqualified support" of the above-mentioned Olympic principle and commended all Governments, sports bodies and other organizations which had taken action "for the boycott of racially selected South African sports bodies or teams". The Assembly called upon all Governments, sports bodies and other organizations:

(*a*) To refrain from all contacts with sports bodies established on the basis of *apartheid* or racially selected sports teams from South Africa;

(*b*) To exert all their influence to secure the full implementation of the Olympic principle, especially by the national and international sports bodies which have continued co-operation with South African sports bodies established on the basis of *apartheid*.

63. In its annual report to the General Assembly, the Special Committee against *Apartheid* recommended in 1976 that the Assembly should consider the preparation of an international convention against *apartheid* in sports and that meanwhile the Assembly should adopt a declaration on the subject. The General Assembly, in resolution 31/6 F of 9 November 1976, welcomed "the proposal for an international convention against *apartheid* in sports to promote adherence to the Olympic principle of non-discrimination and to discourage and deny support to sporting events organized in violation of that principle". It established "an *Ad Hoc* Committee on the Drafting of an International Convention against *Apartheid* in Sports, composed of the existing members of the Special Committee against *Apartheid* and seven other Member States to be appointed by the President of the General Assembly". The *Ad Hoc* Committee was requested to prepare "a draft declaration on *apartheid* in sports, as an interim measure, and to submit it to the General Assembly at its thirty-second session". The Committee was further requested "to undertake preparatory steps towards the drafting of an international convention against *apartheid* in sports and to report thereon to the General Assembly at its thirty-second session".

64. The *Ad Hoc* Committee on the Drafting of an International Convention against *Apartheid* in Sports submitted a report to the General Assembly at its thirty-second session, in 1977, containing the draft of an international declaration against *apartheid* in sports.[17] After considering the report and the draft declaration the General Assembly, in resolution 32/105 M of 14 December 1977, adopted and proclaimed the International Declaration against *Apartheid* in Sports, annexed to that resolution.

(a) *International Declaration against* Apartheid *in Sports*

65. In the preamble to the International Declaration against *Apartheid* in Sports, reference is made to three United Nations human rights instruments: the Universal Declaration of Human Rights, which states that all human beings are born free and equal in dignity and right and that everyone is entitled to all the rights and freedoms set forth in the Declaration without distinction of any kind such as race, colour or national origin; the International Convention on the Elimination of All Forms of Racial Discrimination, by which States Parties undertake not to sponsor, defend or support racial discrimination; and the International Convention on the Suppression and Punishment of the Crime of *Apartheid,* which declares that *apartheid* is a crime violating the principles of international law and constituting a serious threat to international peace and security.

66. The preamble also contains a reaffirmation of the General Assembly's unqualified support for the Olympic principle that no discrimination be allowed on the grounds of race, religion or political affiliation and its belief that merit should be the sole criterion for participation in sports activities, and of its recognition "that participation in sports exchanges with teams selected on the basis of *apartheid* violates the fundamental human rights of the great majority of the people of South Africa and directly abets and encourages the commission of the crime of *apartheid* . . .".

67. The International Declaration calls upon States to take all appropriate action to bring about the total cessation of sporting contacts with any country practising *apartheid* and to refrain from official sponsorship, assistance or encouragement of such contacts; and to take all appropriate action towards the exclusion or expulsion of any country practising *apartheid* from international and regional sports bodies. States are enjoined, in particular and among other things:

Publicly to declare and express total opposition to *apartheid* in sports as well as full and active support for the total boycott of all teams and sportsmen from the racist *apartheid* sports bodies;

To pursue a vigorous programme of public education aimed at securing strict adherence to the Olympic principle of non-discrimination in sports;

[17] *Ibid., Thirty-second Session, Supplement No. 36* (A/32/36).

To refuse to provide financial or other assistance to enable sports bodies, teams or individuals to participate in sports activities in countries practising *apartheid* or with teams and individual sportsmen selected on the basis of *apartheid*;

To deny visas and/or entry to representatives of sports bodies, members of teams or individual sportsmen from any country practising *apartheid*;

To establish national regulations and guidelines against participation with *apartheid* in sports and to ensure that effective means exist for bringing about compliance with such guidelines; and

To co-operate with anti-*apartheid* movements and other organizations which are engaged in promoting the implementation of the principles of the Declaration.

International, regional and national sports bodies are also called upon, on the one hand, to cease all sports contact with the racist *apartheid* sports bodies and declare their opposition to *apartheid* in sports, and on the other hand, to encourage, assist and recognize genuine non-racial sports bodies in South Africa endorsed by the Special Committee against *Apartheid,* the Organization of African Unity and the South African liberation movements recognized by it.

(b) *International Convention against* Apartheid *in Sports*

68. The General Assembly, in resolution 40/64 of 10 December 1985, adopted and opened for signature and ratification the International Convention against *Apartheid* in Sports, and appealed to all States to sign and ratify the Convention as soon as possible.

69. In article 1, the expression *"apartheid"* is defined, for the purposes of the Convention, as meaning "a system of institutionalized racial segregation and discrimination for the purpose of establishing and maintaining domination by one racial group of persons over another racial group of persons and systematically oppressing them, such as that pursued by South Africa". "*Apartheid* in sports" is defined as meaning "the application of the policies and practices of such a system in sports activities, whether organized or on a professional or an amateur basis".

70. Article 2 provides that "States parties strongly condemn *apartheid* and undertake to pursue immediately by all appropriate means the policy of eliminating the practice of *apartheid* in all its forms from sports".

71. Articles 3 to 5 and 7 to 9 describe certain general measures to be taken with this end in view: not to permit sports contact with a country practising *apartheid* (article 3); to prevent sports contact with a country practising *apartheid* (article 4); to refuse to provide financial or other assistance to enable their sports bodies, teams and individual sportsmen to participate in sports activities in a country practising *apartheid* or with teams or individual sportsmen selected on the basis

of *apartheid* (article 5); to deny visas and/or entry permits to representatives of sports bodies, teams and individual sportsmen representing a country practising *apartheid* (article 7); to take all appropriate action to secure the expulsion of a country practising *apartheid* from international and regional sports bodies (article 8); and to take all appropriate measures to prevent international sports bodies from imposing financial or other penalties on affiliated bodies which refuse to participate in sports with a country practising *apartheid* (article 9).

72. Under article 6, States parties undertake to take appropriate action against their sports bodies, teams and individual sportsmen that participate in sports activities in a country practising *apartheid,* or with teams representing a country practising *apartheid,* including (*a*) refusal to provide financial or other assistance for any purpose to such sports bodies, teams and individual sportsmen; (*b*) restriction of access to national sports facilities to such sports bodies, teams and individual sportsmen; (*c*) non-enforceability of all sports contracts which involve sports activities in a country practising *apartheid* or with teams or individual sportsmen selected on the basis of *apartheid*; (*d*) denial and withdrawal of national honours or awards in sports to such teams and individual sportsmen; and (*e*) denial of official receptions in honour of such teams or sportsmen.

73. Article 10 sets out the measures which States parties undertake to apply in order to ensure universal compliance with the Olympic principle of non-discrimination and the provisions of the Convention. These include prohibition of entry of teams and individual sportsmen, and of their representatives, who represent a country practising *apartheid* or who have participated in sports competitions in South Africa; expulsion of South Africa from all sports federations, and if necessary the exclusion of the responsible national sports governing bodies, national sports federations or sportsmen of the countries concerned from international sports competition.

74. Article 11 authorizes the establishment of a Commission against *Apartheid* in Sports to monitor compliance with the provisions of the Convention. The Commission is to consist of 15 members of high moral character and experience in sports administration who are committed to the struggle against *apartheid*. They are to be selected by secret ballot from a list of persons nominated by the States parties, the initial election to be held six months after the Convention enters into force.

75. Under article 12 of the Convention, States parties undertake to submit to the Secretary-General of the United Nations, for consideration by the Commission, reports on the legislative, judicial, administrative or other measures which they have adopted to give effect to the provisions of the Convention. The Commission will report annually through the Secretary-General to the General Assembly on its activities, and may make suggestions and general recommendations based on the examination of those reports and of information received from the States parties. The suggestions and recommendations are to be reported to the General Assembly together with comments, if any, from the States parties concerned. The Commission is to examine, in particular, the implementation of the provisions of article 10 of the Convention. In cases of flagrant violation of the provisions of the Convention, a meeting of States parties is to be convened by the Secretary-General at the request of the Commission.

76. As at 31 December 1987, the Convention had not entered into force; accordingly, the Commission had not been established.

B. Security Council

77. The question of *apartheid* came before the Security Council for the first time in 1960. After having considered the complaint of 29 Member States concerning "the situation arising out of the large-scale killings of unarmed and peaceful demonstrators against racial discrimination and segregation in the Union of South Africa", the Council, in resolution 134 (1960), of 1 April 1960, recognized that the situation in that country was "one that has led to international friction and if continued might endanger international peace and security". It called upon the Government of the Union of South Africa "to abandon its policies of *apartheid* and racial discrimination" and requested the Secretary-General, in consultation with that Government, to make adequate arrangements to uphold the purposes and principles of the Charter. In January 1961 the Secretary-General visited South Africa at the invitation of the Government, but no mutually acceptable arrangement was reached in his discussions with the Prime Minister.

78. In resolution 181 (1963) of 7 August 1963, the Security Council strongly deprecated "the policies of South Africa in its perpetuation of racial discrimination" and called upon the South African Government "to liberate all persons imprisoned, interned or subject to other restrictions for having opposed the policy of *apartheid*". The Council also solemnly called upon all States "to cease forthwith the sale and shipment of arms, ammunition of all types and military vehicles to South Africa".

79. On 4 December 1963, in resolution 182 (1963), the Security Council unanimously reaffirmed resolution 181 (1963) and decided on the establishment, by the Secretary-General, of a group of recognized experts "to examine methods of resolving the present situation in South Africa through full, peaceful and orderly application of human rights and fundamental freedoms to all inhabitants of the territory as a whole, regardless of race, colour or creed, and to consider what part the United Nations might play in the achievement of that end". The Group of Experts established by the Secretary-General suggested in its report[18] that the Security Council should invite the South African Government

---

[18] *Official Records of the Security Council, Nineteenth Year, Supplement for April, May and June 1964,* document S/5658, annex.

to take part in discussions under the auspices of the United Nations on "the formation of a National Convention fully representative of all people of South Africa". The Group of Experts expressed the view that if no satisfactory reply was given by the South African Government, the Security Council "would be left with no effective peaceful means for assisting to resolve the situation, except to apply economic sanctions".

80. In June 1964, the Security Council adopted resolutions 190 and 191 (1964) on the question. In resolution 190 (1964), noting "with great concern" that the verdict to be delivered in the Rivonia trial "instituted against the leaders of the anti-*apartheid* movement" under arbitrary laws might have serious consequences, the Council urged the South African Government to renounce the execution of the persons sentenced to death, to end forthwith the trial in progress and to grant an amnesty to all persons subject to penal measures for having opposed the policy of *apartheid*. In resolution 191 (1964), the Council condemned the *apartheid* policies of the South African Government and "the legislation supporting these policies, such as the General Law Amendment Act, and in particular the ninety-day detention clause". The Council endorsed the main conclusion of the Group of Experts established by resolution 182 (1963), that "all the people of South Africa should be brought into consultation . . . to decide the future of their country at the national level". It invited the Government of South Africa to accept this conclusion, to co-operate with the Secretary-General and to submit its views to him. The South African Government, however, refused to respond to this invitation and claimed that the resolution represented intervention in matters falling within its domestic jurisdiction.

81. In resolution 282 (1970) of 23 July 1970, the Security Council stated that it was convinced of the "need to strengthen the arms embargo" called for in its earlier resolutions and that the situation in South Africa constituted "a potential threat to international peace and security". It reaffirmed its earlier resolutions, condemned the violations of the arms embargo called for in them, and called for additional measures to be taken by States.

82. In 1976 the Security Council considered a letter addressed to it by the representatives of Benin, the Libyan Arab Republic[19] and the United Republic of Tanzania, on behalf of the African Group at the United Nations, and a telegram sent to the Secretary-General by the president of the Democratic Republic of Madagascar, concerning "the measures of repression, including wanton killings, perpetrated by the *apartheid* régime in South Africa against the African people in Soweto and other areas" of the country, and stated that it was deeply shocked "over large-scale killings and wounding of Africans in South Africa, following the callous shooting of African people including schoolchildren and students demonstrating against racial discrimination on 16 June 1976". Convinced that the situation had been

brought about "by the continued imposition by the South African Government of *apartheid* and racial discrimination, in defiance of the resolutions of the Security Council and the General Assembly", the Council, in resolution 392 (1976) of 19 June 1976, strongly condemned the South African Government "for its resort to massive violence against and killings of the African people including schoolchildren and students and others opposing racial discrimination" and called upon that Government urgently "to end violence against the African people and to take urgent steps to eliminate *apartheid* and racial discrimination".

83. In resolution 417 (1977) of 31 October 1977, the Security Council expressed grave concern over "reports of torture of political prisoners and the deaths of a number of detainees, as well as the mounting wave of repression against individuals, organizations and the news media since 19 October 1977", and its conviction that "the violence and repression by the South African racist régime have greatly aggravated the situation in South Africa and will certainly lead to violent conflict and racial conflagration with serious international repercussions". The Council strongly condemned the South African racist régime "for its resort to massive violence and repression against the black people, who constitute the great majority of the country, as well as all other opponents of *apartheid*", and demanded that that régime:

(a) End violence and repression against the black people and other opponents of *apartheid*;

(b) Release all persons imprisoned under arbitrary security laws and all those detained for their opposition to *apartheid*;

(c) Cease forthwith its indiscriminate violence against peaceful demonstrators against *apartheid*, murders in detention and torture of political prisoners;

(d) Abrogate the bans on organizations and the news media opposed to *apartheid*;

(e) Abolish the "Bantu education" system and all other measures of *apartheid* and racial discrimination;

(f) Abolish the policy of bantustanization, abandon the policy of *apartheid* and ensure majority rule based on justice and equality.

84. In resolution 418 (1977) of 4 November 1977, the Security Council, acting under Chapter VII of the Charter of the United Nations, unanimously imposed a mandatory embargo on military and nuclear collaboration with the racist régime of South Africa. In resolution 421 (1977) of 9 December 1977, the Council established a committee consisting of all the members of the Council:

(a) To examine the report on the progress of the implementation of resolution 418 (1977) which will be submitted by the Secretary-General;

(b) To study ways and means by which the mandatory arms embargo could be made more effective against South Africa and to make recommendations to the Council;

(c) To seek from all States further information regarding the action taken by them concerning the effective implementation of the provisions laid down in resolution 418 (1977).

85. The General Assembly, in resolution 32/105 F of 14 December 1977, took note of Security Council resolution 418 (1977); expressed serious regret that three permanent members of the Council had "continued to

---

[19] Now the Libyan Arab Jamahiriya.

resist a comprehensive embargo on military and nuclear collaboration with the racist régime of South Africa''; and pointed out "the need for urgent measures to secure the full implementation of Security Council resolution 418 (1977) and to promote its extension to cover all co-operation with the racist régime of South Africa which, directly or indirectly, facilitates its military build-up and nuclear development, as well as all military and nuclear co-operation with it''. The Assembly called upon all States "to co-operate fully in effective international action, in accordance with Chapter VII of the Charter of the United Nations, to avert the grave menace to the peace resulting from the policies and actions of the racist régime of South Africa''; requested the Security Council to take a number of further steps, which it specified, under Chapter VII of the Charter; requested the Council to establish machinery for supervising the implementation of those measures; and invited all Governments and organizations "to take all appropriate action to promote the purposes" of the resolution.

86.   The Assembly repeated this request to the Council in resolution 33/183 H of 24 January 1979, after expressing its concern that the major Western and other trading partners of South Africa continued to collaborate with the racist régime and that their collaboration constituted the main obstacle to the liquidation of that régime and the elimination of the inhuman and criminal system of *apartheid*. On the same date, in resolution 33/183 E, the Assembly requested the Security Council to consider urgently a mandatory embargo on the supply of petroleum and petroleum products to South Africa under Chapter VII of the Charter of the United Nations, and requested all States to enact legislation to prohibit the sale or supply of such products to any person or body in South Africa.

87.   The Security Council took up the question of South Africa again in 1980 on the basis of a letter dated 29 May 1980 from the Permanent Mission of Morocco to the United Nations.[20]

88.   In resolution 473 (1980), adopted on 13 June 1980, the Council expressed its grave concern about "the aggravation of the situation in South Africa, in particular the repression and the killings of schoolchildren protesting against *apartheid,* as well as the repression directed against churchmen and workers''. It also expressed concern "that the racist régime has intensified further a series of arbitrary trials under its racist and repressive laws providing for death sentences" and stated that it was "convinced that this situation has been brought about by the continued imposition by the South African racist régime of *apartheid* in defiance of resolutions of the Security Council and the General Assembly''.

89.   The Council, further, called upon the Government of South Africa to end violence against the African people and to take urgent measures to eliminate *apartheid,* and to grant to all South African citizens equal rights, including equal political rights, and a full and free voice in the determination of their destiny. It expressed the hope that the inevitable change in the racial policies of South Africa could be attained through peaceful means, but declared that the violence and repression by the South African racist régime and its continuing denial of equal human and political rights to the great majority of the South African people gravely aggravated the situation in South Africa and would certainly lead to violent conflict and racial conflagration with serious international repercussions and the further isolation and estrangement of South Africa.

90.   In resolution 35/206 C of 16 December 1980 the General Assembly requested the Security Council to adopt comprehensive and mandatory sanctions against the racist régime of South Africa, and appealed to all States which had not yet done so to take unilateral legislative and other measures for sanctions against South Africa, pending action by the Security Council. In the resolution the Assembly once again condemned the continuing economic and other collaboration by certain Western and other States, and by transnational corporations and other institutions. In addition, in resolution 35/206 D of 16 December 1980, the Assembly again requested the Security Council to consider urgently a mandatory embargo on the supply of petroleum and petroleum products to South Africa.

91.   In a number of resolutions adopted since 1980, the General Assembly reaffirmed its conviction that comprehensive and mandatory sanctions by the Security Council under Chapter VII of the Charter of the United Nations, universally applied, were the most appropriate and effective means by which the international community could assist the legitimate struggle of the oppressed people of South Africa and discharge its responsibilities for the maintenance of international peace and security; deplored the attitude of those Western permanent members of the Security Council that had so far prevented the Council from adopting such sanctions; and once again requested the Council to consider action under Chapter VII of the Charter towards comprehensive and mandatory sanctions against South Africa.

92.   Although unable to adopt the comprehensive and mandatory sanctions called for by the General Assembly because of negative votes cast by one or more of its permanent Members, the Security Council, in resolution 558 (1984) of 13 December 1984, reaffirmed resolution 418 (1977), stressed the continuing need for the strict application of its provisions, and requested all States to refrain from importing arms, ammunition of all types and military vehicles produced in South Africa. The request was made in recognition of the fact that the effectiveness of the earlier mandatory arms embargo had been undermined by South Africa's intensified efforts to build up its capacity to manufacture armaments.

93.   In resolution 560 (1985) of 12 March 1985, the Council, deeply concerned by the preferment of "high treason" charges against officials of the United Democratic Front and other opponents of *apartheid* for their participation in the non-violent campaign for a united,

[20] See *Official Records of the Security Council, Thirty-fifth Year, Supplement for April, May and June 1980,* document S/13969.

non-racial and democratic South Africa, called upon the Pretoria régime to release all political prisoners unconditionally and immediately, including Nelson Mandela and all other black leaders with whom it must deal in any meaningful discussion of the future of the country.

94. In resolution 569 (1985) of 26 July 1985, the Council strongly condemned the *apartheid* system and all the policies and practices derived therefrom, the mass arrests and detentions carried out by the Pretoria Government and the murders which had been committed, as well as the establishment of a state of emergency in 36 districts. The Council demanded the immediate lifting of the state of emergency and again called upon the South African Government to set free immediately and unconditionally all political prisoners and detainees, first of all Mr. Nelson Mandela. In the resolution the Council reaffirmed its view that only the total elimination of *apartheid* and the establishment in South Africa of a free, united and democratic society on the basis of universal suffrage could lead to a solution of the country's problems. It repeated many of these demands later, in resolution 581 (1986) of 13 February 1986.

95. In resolution 591 (1986) of 28 November 1986, the Council urged all States to prohibit the export to South Africa of items that they have reason to believe are destined for the military and/or police forces of that country, have a military capacity, or are intended for military purposes. The Council proposed that thenceforth the term "arms and related *matériel*", referred to in resolution 418 (1977), should include, in addition to all nuclear, strategic and conventional weapons, all military, paramilitary, police vehicles and equipment, as well as weapons and ammunitions, spare parts and supplies for the aforementioned and the sale or transfer thereof. It again called upon all States to refrain from importing arms, ammunition of all types and military vehicles produced in South Africa and from participating in any activities in South Africa that they might have reason to believe might contribute to its military capability, called upon them to provide penalties to deter violations of the provisions of resolution 418 (1977), and requested them to adopt measures to investigate violations, prevent future circumventions and strengthen their machinery for the implementation of resolution 418 (1977) with a view to the effective monitoring and verification of transfers of arms and other equipment in violation of the arms embargo.

C. Specialized agencies

96. Several specialized agencies of the United Nations —notably the International Labour Organisation, the United Nations Educational, Scientific and Cultural Organization, the World Health Organization and the Food and Agriculture Organization of the United Nations—have been active in combating the effects of *apartheid*. Frequent consultations have taken place between the United Nations and these organizations on this matter. The Economic and Social Council, in resolution 1985/59 of 26 July 1985, requested the specialized agencies and other organizations within the United Nations system to intensify their support for the oppressed people of South Africa and to take such measures as will totally isolate the *apartheid* régime and mobilize world public opinion against *apartheid*.

1. INTERNATIONAL LABOUR ORGANISATION

97. On 8 July 1964, the International Labour Conference unanimously adopted the Declaration concerning the Policy of *Apartheid* of the Republic of South Africa, reaffirming its condemnation of "the degrading, criminal and inhuman racial policies of the Government of the Republic of South Africa, which policies are a violation of fundamental human rights and thus incompatible with the aims and purpose of the ILO".

98. The Declaration requested the Director-General of ILO "to follow the situation in South Africa in respect of labour matters and to submit every year for consideration by the [International Labour] Conference a special report concerning the application of the . . . Declaration including any necessary recommendations concerning any measures which should be adopted with a view to bringing to an end the policy of *apartheid* in the Republic of South Africa". In pursuance of this request and despite South Africa's withdrawal from the Organisation, the Director-General has submitted a report to the Conference every year, concentrating on one or more aspects of the labour situation in South Africa.

99. The International Labour Conference, at its sixty-seventh session (June 1981), adopted an updated Declaration concerning the Policy of *Apartheid* in South Africa. The updated Declaration vigorously condemns the degrading, criminal and inhuman racial policies of the Government of South Africa, and calls for an increase in ILO activities that would enable it to broaden the scope of its assistance in its fields of competence.

100. The Declaration establishes a permanent Conference Committee on *Apartheid* to monitor action against *apartheid,* or failure to take action, by Governments and employers' and workers' organizations of member States.

101. In accordance with paragraph 5 of the new Declaration, a report on the application of the Declaration is submitted each year to the International Labour Conference,[21] and is examined by the Conference Committee on *Apartheid*. The Committee regularly adopts a number of conclusions reaffirming ILO's full commitment to the updated Declaration, and requesting more detailed information to be included in future reports. The Committee has repeatedly stated that South Africa's illegal occupation of Namibia and the aggres-

---

21 ILO, *Special Reports of the Director-General on the Application of the Declaration concerning the Policy of* Apartheid *in South Africa,* International Labour Conference.

sion against the front-line States and other neighbouring countries, as well as the massive repression of workers and trade union leaders in South Africa, were to be condemned; and called for a vigorous campaign by the international community to eradicate *apartheid* totally. In 1987, the Committee requested in particular that the Declaration again be updated by the Conference.

102. For some time funds have been made available from ILO's regular technical co-operation budget for technical assistance to southern African national liberation movements. Thus, a number of fellowships have been provided for training in the elimination of discriminatory labour legislation. Following international tripartite meetings held in Livingstone, Zambia, in May 1981, and in Lusaka, Zambia, in May 1984, and consultations with those concerned, ILO technical co-operation and advisory services provided to the front-line States and other neighbouring States, the liberation movements, recognized by OAU and the black workers and their independent trade unions in South Africa, have increased. This assistance is provided in a number of fields, including vocational training and rehabilitation, employment planning and creation, workers' education, assistance to migrant workers and women refugees and equality of opportunity.

2. United Nations Educational, Scientific and Cultural Organization

103. UNESCO has for many years co-operated with the Secretary-General of the United Nations and the United Nations High Commissioner for Refugees, on assistance for the education of refugees from southern Africa. It has also given its co-operation to the United Nations Educational and Training Programme for Southern Africa.

104. Assistance made available to national liberation movements has been primarily in the field of education and has consisted of the granting of fellowships and schools stipends, the provision of school equipment, the payment of teachers' salaries, the printing of textbooks, the organization of training seminars and the provision of financial assistance for attendance at meetings in the various fields of competence of UNESCO. Along with many other organizations in the United Nations system, UNESCO has also contributed to the elaboration of the Nationhood Programme for Namibia.

105. In resolutions adopted in 1968 and 1970, the UNESCO General Conference drew the attention of the Executive Board and of the Director-General to the need to strengthen UNESCO's action regarding assistance to refugees from colonial countries and other peoples striving to liberate themselves from colonial domination and all forms of *apartheid*. In 1977 the General Conference again stressed the importance of UNESCO's continuing assistance to the liberation movements recognized by the Organization of African Unity and the peoples of the liberated areas, and called

for an increase in the resources to be made available for this purpose.

106. In recent years, UNESCO assistance to African national liberation movements has focused on South Africa and Namibia. The South African liberation movements, the African National Congress (ANC) and the Pan Africanist Congress of Azania (PAC), and the Namibian liberation movement, South West Africa People's Organization (SWAPO), received UNESCO assistance in the area of training (teachers' salaries, fellowships, and educational supplies and equipment) and in payment of expenses of representatives of those movements who attended conferences organized by UNESCO. In addition, action under UNESCO's youth programme included support of non-governmental youth organizations in arranging conferences of youth and students in solidarity with the struggle of the peoples, youth and students of South Africa, at the request of SWAPO and ANC and in co-operation with the Special Committee against *Apartheid*.

3. World Health Organization

107. Following consultations with the Organization of African Unity and various liberation movements on ways and means of implementing General Assembly resolutions on assistance by specialized agencies, the Director-General of the World Health Organization recommended to the Executive Board, as early as January 1972, that the Organization should provide support for the education and training of health workers on the basis of requests from Member States.

108. The Executive Board concurred in the recommendations of the Director-General that assistance to be provided in the health field should include: (*a*) arrangements for the training of health workers, particularly middle-level and auxiliary health personnel, including the strengthening of existing training institutions in host countries; (*b*) the provision of personnel for teaching and rehabilitation services; (*c*) the provision of fellowships; (*d*) teaching seminars; (*e*) the provision of such supplies as might be required for the implementation of the preceding proposals; and (*f*) the provision of supplies and equipment for the prevention of communicable diseases.

109. The Director-General has reported regularly to the WHO Executive Board and to the World Health Assembly on actions taken to support health programmes in the front-line States as well as in Lesotho and Swaziland. In its most recent action the Assembly, in resolution WHA40.23 (15 May 1987), resolved that the WHO should continue to take appropriate and timely measures to solve acute health problems in southern Africa and to provide countries, targets of destabilization by South Africa, with technical co-operation for the rehabilitation of their damaged health infrastructure and assistance to overcome problems arising from people being displaced within countries and across boundaries.

110. In 1981 the World Organization organized an International Conference on *Apartheid* and Health at its Regional Office for Africa, attended *inter alia* by representatives from national liberation movements recognized by the Organization of African Unity. The main background document was an analytical report dealing with the health implications of racial discrimination and social inequality. The report,[22] compiled on behalf of and published by the World Health Organization, includes chapters dealing with the nature of *apartheid*, the health care system in South Africa, living conditions, malnutrition, psychosocial development, occupational health and disease, and the politics of health care. The Conference adopted a plan of action for the struggle against *apartheid* and its deleterious effects in the African region on strategies for health for all by the year 2000.

111. To follow up, the WHO Regional Office for Africa held a Joint National Liberation Movements/World Health Organization Action Group Meeting in 1982. An emergency health programme for the post-*apartheid* period was discussed, along with the search for extrabudgetary sources of finance and the monitoring of the implementation of the relevant WHO and United Nations resolutions.[23]

112. The World Health Organization has continued to collect information regarding the impact of *apartheid* policies on the health status and psychosocial well-being of populations exposed to *apartheid*. A report on the health implications of racial discrimination is being prepared for publication; the report will update information contained in a 1983 report entitled Apartheid *and Health*. Special attention will be paid to the effects of the Second Emergency, declared by the South African Government on 12 June 1986, because investigations have brought to light the profound physical and psychological trauma suffered by an increasing number of victims, many of them young children. Medical care is grossly inadequate and its provision unsafe for some of those injured in the violence. Moreover, unnecessary death, disease, degradation and disability continue to be imposed by the racially structured inequalities and humiliations of the *apartheid* system.

113. On 27 January 1982, the Executive Board of the World Health Organization decided to discontinue official relations with the World Medical Association until it reversed its position regarding the admission of the Medical Association of the Transkei and the readmission of the Medical Association of South Africa. The Board acted after being informed by a representative of the Special Committee against *Apartheid* that the Medical Association of South Africa had shown a collusive and condoning attitude towards the murder of Steve Biko in detention, and that the conduct of the Association's members in cases of police torture and deaths in detention might fall within the scope of specific offences under article II of the International Convention on the Suppression and Punishment of the Crime of *Apartheid*.

4. FOOD AND AGRICULTURE ORGANIZATION OF THE UNITED NATIONS

114. The Food and Agriculture Organization of the United Nations has, in collaboration with the World Food Programme, given aid in the form of food to refugees from South Africa and Namibia, in response to requests from Governments. It has also assisted in projects that are helping refugees in settlements to develop technical and leadership capacities to meet future needs.

D. International conferences

115. Several major international conferences have considered the question of *apartheid* and have called for its speedy elimination.

116. The International Conference on Human Rights, meeting at Teheran, called upon the Security Council in resolution III of 11 May 1968 "to take appropriate action against the Republic of South Africa under Chapter VII, and in particular Article 41, of the Charter of the United Nations, including strong economic sanctions".[24] In resolution IV of the same date, the Conference expressed its concern that "those persons who oppose the racist minority régimes in South Africa, South West Africa, Southern Rhodesia and other parts of southern Africa are not, when captured, treated in accordance with the minimum standards of the Red Cross Geneva Conventions, and declared that such treatment constituted a flagrant violation of the Universal Declaration of Human Rights, a contemptuous disregard of the standards set forth in the International Covenants on Human Rights, and a flagrant defiance of universally-accepted international standards for the treatment of prisoners of war".

117. The International Trade Union Conference against *Apartheid*, held at Geneva in June 1973, and the Second International Trade Union Conference against *Apartheid*, held at Geneva on 10 and 11 June 1977, both adopted comprehensive resolutions on trade union action against *apartheid*, calling upon the international trade union organizations and the Organization of African Trade Union Unity, together with all other trade union centres throughout the world, to intensify world-wide action for the eradication of *apartheid*.

118. The World Conference for Action against *Apartheid*,[25] held at Lagos, Nigeria, from 22 to 26 August

---

[22] Apartheid *and Health*, WHO, Geneva, 1983.

[23] Final Report of the Joint NLM/WHO Action Group Meeting, WHO/AFRO document REP/02, 1982.

[24] See *Final Act of the International Conference on Human Rights* (United Nations publication, Sales No. E.68.XIV.2).

[25] *Report of the World Conference for Action against* Apartheid (United Nations publication, Sales No. E.77.XIV.2 and corrigendum).

1977, called on the Security Council to take the necessary measures, under Chapter VIII of the Charter of the United Nations, to ensure full implementation of the arms embargo against South Africa; and recommended that a watch-dog committee be established to follow up the observance of the embargo.

119. Both the International Conference on Women and Children under *Apartheid,* held at Arusha, United Republic of Tanzania, from 7 to 10 May 1985,[26] and the International Conference on Sports Boycott against South Africa, held in Paris from 16 to 18 May 1985,[27] adopted Declarations calling *inter alia* for comprehensive sanctions to be imposed upon South Africa by the Security Council.

120. The World Conference on Sanctions against Racist South Africa, held at Paris from 16 to 20 June 1986,[28] also adopted a Declaration calling for the imposition of comprehensive and mandatory sanctions by the Security Council. On recommendation of the Conference and the Special Committee against *Apartheid,* the General Assembly, in resolution 42/23 C of 20 November 1987, urgently requested the Security Council to take immediate action under Chapter VII of the Charter with a view to applying comprehensive and mandatory sanctions against the racist régime of South Africa, and urged the Governments of the United Kingdom of Great Britain and Northern Ireland, the United States of America and others that are opposed to the application of comprehensive and mandatory sanctions to reassess their policies and cease their opposition to the application of such sanctions by the Security Council. The Assembly further urged the Security Council, in the same resolution, to strengthen the mandatory arms embargo imposed by its resolutions 418 (1977) of 4 November 1977 and 558 (1984) of 13 December 1984 in order to bring to an end the continued violation of the arms embargo.

E. Assistance to victims of *apartheid*

121. A number of United Nations bodies, including the Commission on Human Rights, the Commission on the Status of Women and the Economic and Social Council, have collaborated closely with the General Assembly and the Security Council in seeking ways and means of putting an end to the oppression and repression of the black majority in South Africa and of achieving a peaceful, just and lasting solution of the problem in accordance with the principles of the Charter of the United Nations and the Universal Declaration of Human Rights.

---

[26] A/40/319-S/17197, annex.

[27] A/40/343-S/17224, annex.

[28] *Report of the World Conference on Sanctions against Racist South Africa, Paris, 16-20 June 1986* (United Nations publication, Sales No. E.86.I.23).

I. ILL-TREATMENT OF THOSE WHO OPPOSE *APARTHEID*

122. At its twenty-third session, in 1967, the Commission on Human Rights considered a note[29] drawn to its attention by the Secretary-General, in which the Acting Chairman of the General Assembly's Special Committee on the Policies of *Apartheid* of the Government of the Republic of South Africa referred to "the continuing ill-treatment of prisoners, detainees and persons in police custody in the republic of South Africa, particularly the numerous opponents of *apartheid* who have been imprisoned under arbitrary laws".

123. The note read in part as follows:

The Special Committee has always been gravely concerned over this matter and has reported on it to the General Assembly and the Security Council. A number of documents of the Special Committee, a list of which is attached, contain alarming evidence of ill-treatment of such persons in prisons and police stations.

In its reports of 30 November 1964, and 16 August 1965, the Special Committee suggested the establishment of an international commission composed of eminent jurists and prison officials to investigate the charges of torture and ill-treatment of prisoners in South Africa. The suggestion was not pressed in the General Assembly because it was hoped that the expression of international concern might persuade the South African Government to improve conditions so as to conform with civilized standards and the regulations in South Africa itself.

However, evidence of the continuing ill-treatment of prisoners, detainees and persons in police custody is still being received. Those being subjected to this treatment include not only the acknowledged leaders of the people and opponents of *apartheid* who have been persecuted under legislation which violates the fundamental principles of human rights, but also thousands who have been imprisoned for the infringement of *apartheid* laws. As the Special Committee observed in its report of 21 October 1966, the ruthless measures of the South African Government seem to be increasingly designed to wreak vengeance against the opponents of *apartheid*. In the view of the Special Committee, such measures contravene international standards of behaviour and the Universal Declaration of Human Rights.

The Special Committee therefore hopes that the Commission on Human Rights will consider the matter urgently and take steps to secure an international investigation with a view to ameliorating the conditions of these victims.

124. Having considered the note, the Commission, in resolution 2 (XXIII) of 6 March 1967, requested the Secretary-General to address a telegram immediately to the Government of the Republic of South Africa conveying "the deep distress and serious concern of the Commission at this situation and requesting that Government to take positive action so that its treatment of political prisoners shall conform with civilized standards of penal law and practice".

125. By the same resolution the Commission decided to establish, in accordance with resolution 9 (II) of the Economic and Social Council, an *Ad Hoc* Working Group of Experts composed of eminent jurists and prison officials to be appointed by the Chairman of the Commission, to:

(a) Investigate the charges of torture and ill-treatment of prisoners, detainees or persons in police custody in South Africa;

(b) Receive communications and hear witnesses and use such modalities of procedure as it may deem appropriate;

---

[29] E/CN.4/935.

(c) Recommend action to be taken in concrete cases;

(d) Report to the Commission on Human Rights at the earliest possible time.

2. INTERNATIONAL RELIEF AND ASSISTANCE

126. To provide relief and assistance to victims of *apartheid* and racial discrimination in southern Africa, the United Nations has established the United Nations Trust Fund for South Africa, the United Nations Fund for Namibia, and the United Nations Educational and Training Programme for Southern Africa.

127. In addition, mindful of the special responsibility of the United Nations and the international community towards the oppressed people of South Africa and their liberation movements and towards those imprisoned, restricted or exiled for their struggle against *apartheid,* the General Assembly proclaimed, in resolution 31/6 I of 9 November 1976, that the racist régime of South Africa was illegitimate and had no right to represent the people of South Africa, and reaffirmed that the national liberation movements recognized by the Organization of African Unity—the African National Congress of South Africa and the Pan Africanist Congress of Azania—were the authentic representatives of the overwhelming majority of the South African people. The Assembly later, in resolution 34/93 I of 12 December 1979, authorized adequate financial provision in the budget of the United Nations for the purpose of maintaining the offices in New York of the above-mentioned liberation movements, in order to ensure the due and proper representation of the people of South Africa through those movements.

128. In resolution 32/105 J of 14 December 1977, the General Assembly reaffirmed the legitimacy of the struggle of the oppressed people of South Africa and their national liberation movement—by all available and appropriate means, including armed struggle—for the seizure of power by the people and for the full exercise of their political rights, the elimination of the *apartheid* régime and the exercise of the right of self-determination by the people of South Africa as a whole; and declared that the international community should provide all necessary assistance to the national liberation movement in its legitimate struggle.

3. UNITED NATIONS TRUST FUND FOR SOUTH AFRICA

129. The United Nations Trust Fund for South Africa was established by the Secretary-General in pursuance of General Assembly resolution 2054 B (XX) of 15 December 1965. Its terms of reference, as revised and enlarged in 1968 and 1970, include: (a) legal assistance to persons persecuted under the repressive and discriminatory legislation of South Africa; (b) relief to such persons and their dependants; (c) education of such persons and their dependants; (d) relief for refugees

from South Africa; and (e) relief and assistance to persons persecuted under repressive and discriminatory legislation in Namibia and to their families.

130. The Fund is financed by voluntary contributions, and is used for grants to voluntary organizations and other appropriate bodies. A Committee of Trustees promotes contributions and decides on the uses of the Fund. The General Assembly, in a number of resolutions, has appealed to States, organizations and individuals for contributions to the Fund and for direct contributions to the voluntary organizations concerned.

131. At each regular session, the General Assembly receives the report of the Secretary-General on the United Nations Trust Fund for South Africa, to which is annexed the report of the Committee of Trustees of the Fund. In recent years the Assembly, after examining the Secretary-General's reports,[30] has endorsed them, expressed its appreciation to the Governments, organizations and individuals that have contributed to the Fund and to the voluntary agencies engaged in rendering humanitarian and legal assistance to the victims of *apartheid* and racial discrimination, and appealed for direct contributions to the Trust Fund and to the voluntary agencies engaged in rendering assistance to the victims of *apartheid* and racial discrimination in South Africa and Namibia.[31]

4. UNITED NATIONS EDUCATIONAL AND TRAINING PROGRAMME FOR SOUTHERN AFRICA

132. The United Nations Educational and Training Programme for Southern Africa was established by the General Assembly in resolution 2349 (XXII) of 19 December 1967 by itegrating earlier special programmes to assist persons from Namibia, South Africa, Southern Rhodesia and Territories under Portuguese administration in Africa. It is administered by the Secretary-General in consultation with the Advisory Committee in the United Nations Educational and Training Programme for Southern Africa which was established by General Assembly resolution 2431 (XXIII) of 18 December 1968, and is financed from the Trust Fund made up of voluntary contributions by States, organizations and individuals.

133. Since the twenty-fourth session of the General Assembly, the Secretary-General has submitted annual reports on the Programme and the Assembly has adopted resolutions on its continuation and strengthening. The Assembly, after examining the Secretary-General's reports,[32] has endorsed them and commended the Secretary-General and the Advisory Committee for their continued efforts to promote generous contributions to

---

[30] A/39/605, A/40/780, A/41/638 and A/42/659.

[31] Resolutions 39/72 F of 13 December 1984, 40/64 H of 10 December 1985, 41/35 G of 10 November 1986 and 42/23 H of 20 November 1987.

[32] A/39/351, A/40/781, A/41/678 and Corr.1, and A/42/628.

the Programme and to enhance co-operation with governmental, intergovernmental and non-governmental agencies involved in educational and technical assistance to southern Africa.[33]

5. UNITED NATIONS FUND FOR NAMIBIA

134. In resolution 283 (1970) of 29 July 1970, the Security Council requested that a United Nations fund be set up "to provide assistance to Namibians who have suffered from persecution and to finance a comprehensive educational and training programme for Namibians, with particular regard to their future administrative responsibilities in the Territory".

135. The General Assembly, by resolution 2679 (XXV) of 9 December 1970 and 2872 (XXVI) of 20 December 1971, established a United Nations Fund for Namibia. Its decision was based on the consideration that, having terminated South Africa's mandate to administer the Territory and having itself assumed direct responsibility for Namibia until independence, the United Nations had incurred a solemn obligation to assist and prepare the people of that Territory for self-determination and independence and that, to that end, the United Nations should provide them with comprehensive assistance.

136. The Fund became operative in 1972. Until 1973 the Council for Namibia acted only in an advisory capacity to the Secretary-General as regards the administration and supervision of the Fund. The General Assembly, by resolution 3112 (XXVIII) of 12 December 1973, appointed the Council as trustee of the Fund. Guidelines for the orientation, management and administration of the Fund were approved by the Assembly in resolution 31/151 of 20 December 1976.

137. Since the Fund became operative, its programmes of assistance have been continuously expanded by the General Assembly on the recommendations of the United Nations Council for Namibia and the Security Council. In 1975, the Fund became the vehicle for financing the United Nations Institute for Namibia. A special account was approved by the General Assembly, in resolution 33/182 C of 21 December 1978, for financing the Nationhood Programme for Namibia, which had been established pursuant to Assembly resolution 31/153 of 20 December 1976.

138. Voluntary contributions are the major source of financing of the Fund. The Assembly has repeatedly appealed to Governments and their respective national organizations and institutions for voluntary contributions to the Fund, and for special contributions earmarked for the Institute and the Nationhood Programme. Since the establishment of the Fund, each year the General Assembly has authorized as an interim measure an allocation from the regular budget of the United Nations to help implement the Fund's programme. Thus, by resolution 41/39 of 20 November

1986, the Assembly decided to allocate $US 1.5 million to the Fund from the regular budget for 1987.

6. UNITED NATIONS TRUST FUND FOR PUBLICITY AGAINST *APARTHEID*

139. The Special Committee against *Apartheid* and other United Nations organs have repeatedly emphasized the need for the widest possible dissemination of information on the inhumanity of *apartheid,* the repression against opponents of *apartheid* in South Africa, the struggle of the South African people, under the leadership of their liberation movements, for a nonracial society and the efforts of the United Nations and the international community to secure the eradication of *apartheid.*

140. A Unit on *Apartheid* was established in the United Nations Secretariat in January 1967 to promote publicity against *apartheid,* in consultation with the Special Committee against *Apartheid* and the Office of Public Information. In resolution 3151 C (XXVIII) of 14 December 1973, the General Assembly requested the Secretary-General to invite voluntary contributions to be used for the expansion of the activities of the Unit. The Trust Fund was accordingly established by the Secretary-General in January 1975. It is used primarily for the printing of publications in various languages for wider distribution, and grants to organizations for the reprinting and redistribution of United Nations material on *apartheid.*

F. Concerted international action for the elimination of *apartheid*

141. Thirty years after it began consideration of the item entitled "The question of race conflict in South Africa resulting from the policies of *apartheid* of the Government of the Union of South Africa", the United Nations was still, in the words of General Assembly resolution 37/69 B of 9 December 1982, "gravely concerned over the situation in South Africa, in particular the efforts of the racist régime of South Africa to perpetuate *apartheid,* its deportations of African people, its deprivation of the inalienable rights of the African people through the establishment of so-called 'independent' bantustans and its ruthless repression against all opponents of the criminal policy of *apartheid*".

142. In that resolution the General Assembly recalled the long struggle of the African and other people of South Africa for the elimination of racial discrimination and the establishment of a society in which all the people of the country as a whole—irrespective of race, colour or creed—could enjoy human rights and fundamental freedoms on the basis of equlity. Paying tribute to all those who had sacrificed their lives in the struggle for freedom and human dignity in South Africa, and expressing its solidarity with all those imprisoned, restricted or otherwise persecuted for participation in that

---

[33] Resolutions 39/44 of 5 December 1984, 40/54 of 2 December 1985, 41/27 of 31 October 1986 and 42/76 of 4 December 1987.

legitimate struggle, the Assembly appealed to all States and organizations to co-operate fully in effective international action to eliminate *apartheid* in South Africa, to promote the establishment of a democratic society in which all the people of that country would enjoy human and political rights, and to secure peace in the region; and renewed its appeal to all States and organizations to deny any assistance, direct or indirect, to the racist régime of South Africa and provide all necessary assistance to the oppressed people of South Africa and their national liberation movements in the current crucial period.

143. The Commission on Human Rights and the General Assembly have since received extensive reports prepared by the *Ad Hoc* Working Group of Experts on Southern Africa, and the Assembly has considered them together with reports of the Special Committee against *Apartheid,* the Special Committee on Decolonization, the Council for Namibia and the Group of Three. On the basis of the information thus brought to its attention, the Assembly has repeatedly demanded that the South African authorities (*a*) end repression against the black people and other opponents of *apartheid*; (*b*) cease all trials under arbitrary repressive laws; (*c*) refrain from the execution of persons sentenced under such repressive laws for acts arising from opposition to *apartheid*; (*d*) release all political prisoners in South Africa; and (*e*) abrogate bans imposed on organizations and the media for their opposition to *apartheid*.

144. In resolution 38/37 of 5 December 1983, the Assembly strongly condemned "the *apartheid* régime of South Africa for its brutal repression of all opponents of *apartheid,* its torture and killing of detainees, its execution of freedom fighters and its repeated acts of aggression, subversion and terrorism against independent African States". In resolution 39/72 A of 13 December 1984, it again condemned the South African régime "for its continued brutal oppression, repression and violence, including the recent use of armed forces against the black people, its illegal occupation of Namibia and its repeated acts of aggression, subversion and terrorism against independent African States".

145. In resolution 40/64 B of 10 December 1985 the Assembly expressed its grave concern at the continuing massacres, killings and other atrocities against defenceless opponents of *apartheid* perpetrated by the racist régime in Sharpeville, Soweto, Sebokeng and other black townships, and its alarm over the massive arrests and detentions of leaders and activists of liberation organizations inside the country as well as the increasing number of deaths resulting from police brutality and torture during detentions. In addition, it strongly condemned the régime for the killing of defenceless African people protesting against their forced removal from Crossroads and other places as well as the arbitrary arrests of members of the United Democratic Front, National Forum and other mass organizations opposed to *apartheid.*

146. In resolution 42/23 A of 20 November 1987, the General Assembly expressed its grave concern at the escalating repression of, and State terror against, opponents of *apartheid,* and the increasing intransigence of the racist régime of South Africa, as demonstrated by the extension of the state of emergency, the vast number of arbitrary detentions, trials, torture and killing, including those of women and children, the increased use of vigilante groups and the muzzling of the press. It reaffirmed its full support to the people of South Africa in their struggle, under the leadership of their liberation movements, to eradicate *apartheid* totally, so that they can exercise their right to self-determination in a free, democratic, unfragmented and non-racial South Africa; and reaffirmed also the legitimacy of the struggle of the people of South Africa and their right to choose the necessary means, including armed resistance, to attain the eradication of *apartheid*.

147. In resolution 42/23 C, the Assembly once again urgently requested the Security Council to take action under Chapter VII of the Charter with a view to applying comprehensive and mandatory sanctions against the racist régime of South Africa, and urged the Governments of Great Britain and Northern Ireland, the United States of America, and others that were opposed to such sanctions to reassess their policies and cease their opposition to them.

148. In resolution 42/23 G, the Assembly strongly condemned the policy of *apartheid* which deprives the majority of the South African population of their citizenship, fundamental freedoms and human rights; and strongly condemned the South African authorities for the killings, arbitrary mass arrests, and the detention of members of mass organizations as well as individuals, the overwhelming majority of whom belong to the majority population, for opposing the *apartheid* system and the state of emergency and for the detention of and use of violence against children by the South African authorities. The Assembly demanded that the authorities of South Africa (*a*) release immediately and unconditionally Nelson Mandela and all other political prisoners, detainees and restrictees; (*b*) imemdiately lift the state of emergency; (*c*) abrogate discriminatory laws and lift bans on all organizations and individuals, as well as end restrictions on and censorship of news media; (*d*) grant freedom of association and full trade union rights to all workers of South Africa; (*e*) initiate without pre-conditions a political dialogue with genuine leaders of the majority population with a view to eradicating *apartheid* without delay and establishing a representative government; (*f*) eradicate the bantustan structures; and (*g*) immediately withdraw all their troops from southern Angola and end the destabilization of front-line and other States.

VI. ADVANCEMENT OF WOMEN

Introduction

1. The Charter of the United Nations is the first international instrument to mention equal rights of men and women in specific terms. In its Preamble, the Charter proclaims the determination of the peoples of the United Nations "to reaffirm faith in fundamental human rights, in the dignity and worth of the human person, in the equal rights of men and women" and "to employ international machinery for the promotion of the economic and social advancement of all peoples". One of the purposes of the United Nations, as set out in Article 1, is "to achieve international co-operation in solving international problems of an economic, social, cultural, or humanitarian character, and in promoting and encouraging respect for human rights and fundamental freedoms for all without distinction as to race, sex, language or religion". Article 8 states that "The United Nations shall place no restrictions on the eligibility of men and women to participate in any capacity and under conditions of equality in its principal and subsidiary organs". Articles 13, 55 and 76 call for the realization of human rights and fundamental freedoms "for all without distinction as to race, sex, language or religion". Under Article 56, Member States have pledged themselves to take joint and separate action, in co-operation with the United Nations, to achieve such aims.

2. This basic principle is elaborated in the Universal Declaration of Human Rights, which proclaims that "all human beings are born free and equal in dignity and rights" (article 1), and that "everyone is entitled to all the rights and freedoms set forth [therein] without distinction of any kind", including distinction based on sex (article 2).

3. The principle of equality of men and women and the prohibition of discrimination against women are clearly set out in both International Covenants on Human Rights. They are also at the heart of many United Nations instruments which deal with particular rights of women, such as the Convention on the Political Rights of Women, the Convention on the Nationality of Married Women, the Convention and the Recommendation on Consent to Marriage, Minimum Age for Marriage and Registration of Marriages; and, in so far as they concern the status of women, the Supplementary Convention on the Abolition of Slavery, the Slave Trade, and Institutions and Practices Similar to Slavery and the Convention for the Suppression of the Traffic in Persons and of the Exploitation of the Prostitution of Others. In addition, these principles inspired a number of instruments adopted by the International Labour Conference, including the Underground Work (Women) Convention, 1935 (No. 45); the Night Work (Women) Convention (revised), 1949 (No. 89); the Equal Remuneration Convention for Men and Women Workers for Work of Equal Value of 1951 (No. 100); the Discrimination (Employment and Occupation) Convention of 1958 (No. 111); and the Workers with Family Responsibilities Convention, 1981 (No. 156); as well as the Convention against Discrimination in Education, adopted by the General Conference of the United Nations Educational, Scientific and Cultural Organization in 1960.

4. For more than forty years competent organs of the United Nations have worked energetically to improve the status of women in various fields and to eliminate discrimination against women. Within the established United Nations system, most of the measures designed to attain these goals originated in the Commission on the Status of Women, a functional commission of the Economic and Social Council. In recent years, the Committee on the Elimination of Discrimination against Women, a treaty-based body established in accordance with the Convention on the Elimination of All Forms of Discrimination against Women, has assumed the task of monitoring measures taken by Governments to put an end to discrimination on the basis of sex.[1]

5. In the early years of its existence, the Commission on the Status of Women concentrated on improving the status of women in law, particularly private law, and in broadening women's enjoyment of their rights to education, to employment and to health care. It submitted comments and made suggestions on matters of particular interest to women to the Commission on Human Rights and the Economic and Social Council relating to the Universal Declaration of Human Rights and both International Covenants on Human Rights as they were being drafted.

6. In addition, the Commission undertook studies and made recommendations on many other questions of interest to women, such as access to education at all levels, economic rights and opportunities for women, including equal pay for equal work, and various aspects of family law and property rights. It based its consideration of these questions on information contained in reports prepared by the Secretary-General of the United Nations and the Directors-General of the specialized agencies competent in the subject. The Commission's work resulted in the adoption of many resolutions addressing recommendations to Governments aimed at

---

[1] For information about the Committee, see chapter I, section C, 3.

116

improving the status of women and establishing the principle of equality of rights for men and women.

7. In 1949 the Commission decided to prepare an international convention as a further means of promoting equal political rights for men and women. On the basis of a draft prepared in the Commission, the Convention on the Political Rights of Women was adopted and opened for signature and ratification or accession by the General Assembly on 20 December 1952.

8. Three additional Conventions, one Declaration and one Recommendation have since been concluded under the auspices of the United Nations as a direct result of the work of the Commission. The first is the Convention on the Nationality of Married Women, adopted by the General Assembly in 1957. The second is the Convention on Consent to Marriage, Minimum Age for Marriage and Registration of Marriages, adopted by the General Assembly in 1962; this Convention was followed by a Recommendation on the same subject, adopted by the General Assembly in 1965.

9. The Declaration on the Elimination of Discrimination against Women, drafted by the Commission, was adopted and proclaimed by the General Assembly in 1967. It was followed by the Convention on the Elimination of all Forms of Discrimination against Women, adopted and opened for signature, ratification or accession by the General Assembly in 1979.

10. With the completion of the drafting of the Convention, which provided for the establishment of the Committee on the Elimination of Discrimination against Women, the Commission on the Status of Women assumed a new role: first it served as the preparatory body for two major international observances: of the International Women's Year (1975) and of the United Nations Decade for Women (1976-1985); then it served as the preparatory body for three world-wide conferences, held at Mexico City, Copenhagen and Nairobi respectively, in connection with the activities of the Decade.

11. The Commission's mandate was revised recently "to include the functions of promoting the objectives of equality, development and peace, monitoring the implementation of measures for the advancement of women, and reviewing and appraising the progress made at the national, sub-regional, regional, sectoral and global levels".

12. A brief overview of the broad historical background underlying action by the United Nations for the advancement of women, as seen by participants in the 1985 World Conference to Review and Appraise the Achievements of the United Nations Decade for Women: Equality, Development and Peace appears in the Introduction to the Forward-looking Strategies for the Advancement of Women which the Conference adopted by consensus; as follows:[2]

The founding of the United Nations after the victory in the Second World War and the emergence of independent States following decolonization were some of the important events in the political, economic and social liberation of women. The International Women's Year, the World Conferences held at Mexico City in 1975 and Copenhagen in 1980, and the United Nations Decade for Women: Equality, Development and Peace contributed greatly to the process of eliminating obstacles to the improvement of the status of women at the national, regional and international levels. In the early 1970s, efforts to end discrimination against women and to ensure their equal participation in society provided the impetus for most initiatives taken at all of those levels. Those efforts were also inspired by the awareness that women's reproductive and productive roles were closely linked to the political, economic, social, cultural, legal, educational and religious conditions that constrained the advancement of women and that factors intensifying the economic exploitation, marginalization and oppression of women stemmed from chronic inequalities, injustices and exploitative conditions at the family, community, national, subregional, regional and international levels.

In 1972, the General Assembly, in resolution 3010 (XXVII), proclaimed 1975 International Women's Year, to be devoted to intensified action to promote equality between men and women, to ensure the full integration of women in the total development effort and to increase women's contribution to the strengthening of world peace. The World Plan of Action for the Implementation of the Objectives of the International Women's Year,[3] adopted by the World Conference of the International Women's Year at Mexico City in 1975, was endorsed by the General Assembly in its resolution 3520 (XXX). The General Assembly, in that resolution, proclaimed 1976-1985 the United Nations Decade for Women: Equality, Development and Peace. In its resolution 33/185, the General Assembly decided upon the sub-theme "Employment, Health and Education" for the World Conference of the United Nations Decade for Women: Equality, Development and Peace, to be held at Copenhagen to review and evaluate the progress made in the first half of the Decade.

In 1980, at the mid-point of the Decade, the Copenhagen World Conference adopted the Programme of Action for the Second Half of the United Nations Decade for Women: Equality, Development and Peace[4] which further elaborated on the existing obstacles and on the existing international consensus on measures to be taken for the advancement of women. The Programme of Action was endorsed by the General Assembly that year in its resolution 35/136.

Also in 1980, the General Assembly, in resolution 35/36, adopted the International Development Strategy for the Third United Nations Development Decade and reaffirmed the recommendations of the Copenhagen World Conference (General Assembly resolution 35/56, annex, para. 51). In the Strategy, the importance of the participation of women in the development process, as both agents and beneficiaries, was stressed. Also, the Strategy called for appropriate measures to be taken in order to bring about profound social and economic changes and to eliminate the structural imbalances that compounded and perpetuated women's disadvantages in society.

The strategies contained in the World Plan of Action and in the Programme of Action were important contributions towards enlarging the perspective for the future of women. In most areas, however, further action is required. In this connection the General Assembly confirmed the goals and objectives of the Decade—equality, development and peace—stressed their validity for the future and indicated the need for concrete measures to overcome the obstacles to their achievement during the period 1986-2000.

13. Important international initiatives designed to further the advancement of women include the following:

[2] *Report of the World Conference to Review and Appraise the Achievements of the United Nations Decade for Women: Equality, Development and Peace, Nairobi, 15-26 July 1985* (United Nations publication, Sales No. E.85.IV.10), chap. I, sect. A, paras. 1-5.

[3] *Report of the World Conference of the International Women's Year, Mexico City, 19 June-2 July 1975* (United Nations publication, Sales No. E.76.IV.1), chap. I, sect. A.

[4] *Report of the World Conference of the United Nations Decade for Women: Equality, Development and Peace, Copenhagen, 24-30 July 1980* (United Nations publication, Sales No. E.80.IV.3), chap. I, sect. A.

Adoption of the Declaration on the Elimination of Discrimination against Women by the General Assembly of the United Nations (1967); adoption and opening for signature, ratification and accession of the Convention on the Elimination of All Forms of Discrimination against Women by the General Assembly (1979), and commencement of the work of the Committee on the Elimination of Discrimination against Women (1982);

Observance of International Women's Year (1975), convening of the World Conference of the International Women's Year, and adoption by the Conference of the Declaration of Mexico on the Equality of Women and their Contribution to Development and Peace;

Establishment of the United Nations Development Fund for Women (1974) and of the International Research and Training Institute for the Advancement of Women (1976);

Observance of the United Nations Decade for Women: Equality, Development and Peace (1976-1985), convening of the World Conference of the United Nations Decade for Women (1980), and adoption by the Conference of the Programme of Action for the second half of the United Nations Decade for Women;

Convening of the World Conference to Review and Appraise the Achievements of the United Nations Decade for Women (1985), and adoption by the Conference of the Nairobi Forward-Looking Strategies for the Advancement of Women.

14.   These major initiatives, and many of the activities which preceded or developed out of them, are described below.

A. Equality

1. THE MEANING OF EQUALITY AND OBSTACLES TO ITS ACHIEVEMENT

15.   As recognized in the Forward-looking Strategies,[5] equality is both a goal and a means whereby individuals are accorded equal treatment under the law and equal opportunities to enjoy their rights and to develop their potential talents and skills so that they can participate in national, political, economic, social and cultural development and can benefit from its results. For women in particular, equality means the realization of rights that they have been denied as a result of cultural, institutional, behavioural or attitudinal discrimination. Equality is important for development and peace because national and global inequities perpetuate themselves and increase tensions of all types.

16.   The Nairobi Conference examined many obstacles to the achievement of a major international objective: the full observance of the equal rights of women and

the elimination of *de jure* and *de facto* discrimination on the basis of sex. Its analysis of these obstacles included the following observations:[6]

One of the fundamental obstacles to women's equality is that *de facto* discrimination and inequality in the status of women and men derive from larger social, economic, political and cultural factors that have been justified on the basis of physiological differences. Although there is no physiological basis for regarding the household and family as essentially the domain of women, or the devaluation of domestic work and for regarding the capacities of women as inferior to those of men, the belief that such a basis exists perpetuates inequality and inhibits the structural and attitudinal changes necessary to eliminate such inequality.

Women, by virtue of their gender, experience discrimination in terms of denial of equal access to the power structure that controls society and determines development issues and peace initiatives. Additional differences, such as race, colour and ethnicity, may have even more serious implications in some countries, since such factors can be used as justification for compound discrimination.

Fundamental resistance creates obstacles, which have wide-ranging implications for the objectives of the Decade. Discrimination promotes an uneconomic use of women's talents and wastes the valuable human resources necessary for development and for the strengthening of peace. Ultimately, society is the loser if the talents of women are under-utilized as a result of discrimination.

The sharp contrasts between legislative changes and effective implementation of these changes are a major obstacle to the full participation of women in society. *De facto* and indirect discrimination, particularly by reference to marital or family status, often persists despite legislative action. The law as a recourse does not automatically benefit all women equally, owing to the socio-economic inequalities determining women's knowledge of and access to the law, as well as their ability to exercise their full legal rights without fear of recrimination or intimidation. The lack or inadequacy of the dissemination of information on women's rights and the available recourse to justice has hampered, in many instances, the achievement of expected results.

Some legislative changes are made without a thorough understanding of the relationship between existing legal systems. In practice, however, certain aspects of the law—for instance, customary provisions—may be in operation in societies with multiple and conflicting legal systems. Emerging and potential obstacles resulting from possible contradictions should be anticipated so that preventive measures can be taken. When passing new legislation, whatever its subject-matter, all possible care should be taken to ensure that it implies no direct or indirect discrimination so that women's right to equality is fully respected in law.

In some countries, discriminatory legislative provisions in the social, economic and political spheres still exist, including civil, penal and commercial codes and certain administrative rules and regulations. Civil codes in some instances have not yet been adequately studied to determine action for repealing those laws that still discriminate against women and for determining, on the basis of equality, the legal capacity and status of women, married women in particular, in terms of nationality, inheritance, ownership and control of property, freedom of movement and the custody and nationality of children. Above all, there is still a deeply rooted resistance on the part of conservative elements in society to the change in attitude necessary for a total ban on discriminatory practices against women at the family, local, national and international levels.

2. DECLARATION ON THE ELIMINATION OF DISCRIMINATION AGAINST WOMEN

17.   The Declaration on the Elimination of Discrimination against Women was adopted unanimously by the General Assembly in resolution 2263 (XXII) on 7 November 1967, after four years of debate and detailed

   [5] *Report of the World Conference to Review and Appraise the Achievements of the United Nations Decade for Women: Equality, Development and Peace, Nairobi, 15-26 July 1985* (United Nations publication, Sales No. E.85.IV.10), chap. I, sect. A, para. 11.

   [6] *Ibid.*, paras. 45-50.

drafting in the Commission on the Status of Women and in the Assembly. The need for this Declaration is stated in the preamble, which expresses concern that despite the Charter, the Universal Declaration of Human Rights, the International Covenants on Human Rights and other instruments, and despite the progress made, "there continues to exist considerable discrimination against women."

18. The Declaration represents a general pronouncement of United Nations policy in regard to equality of rights of men and women and the elimination of discrimination based on sex. It restates and consolidates a series of principles, many of which were embodied in earlier international instruments emanating from the Unites Nations and the specialized agencies. It also sets forth a series of important principles not contained in earlier treaties and recommendations.

19. The Declaration contains 11 articles. Those of a general nature are:

Article 1, which states that "discrimination against women, denying or limiting as it does their equality of rights with men, is fundamentally unjust and constitutes an offence against human dignity";

Article 2, which calls for the abolition of existing laws, customs, regulations and practices which are discriminatory against women, and the establishment of adequate legal protection for equal rights of men and women; and which also calls for the ratification of, or accession to, the international instruments of the United Nations and the specialized agencies relating to the elimination of discrimination against women, and their full implementation, as soon as possible;

Article 3, which, describes discrimination against women as "customary and all other practices which are based on the idea of the inferiority of women", and which contains the first reference, in an instrument of international law, to the need to educate public opinion and to direct national aspirations towards the eradication of prejudice and the abolition of discrimination against women. This article is of paramount importance because it touches upon a field in which the United Nations can make a substantial contribution for the advancement of women: the changing of attitudes towards the actual realization of the equal dignity and worth of all women and men and the different roles that women and men can play in society.

20. Other articles deal with specific rights or groups of rights: that is, political rights (article 4); the right to a nationality (article 5); rights under civil law (article 6); discriminatory provisions under penal law (article 7); traffic in women (article 8); educational rights (article 9); and economic and social rights (article 10).

21. By providing that all appropriate measures shall be taken to ensure to women, on equal terms with men and without any discrimination, the right to vote in all elections and be eligible for election to all publicly elected bodies, and the right to hold public office and to exercise all public functions, the Declaration restates the principal provisions of the 1952 Convention on the Political Rights of Women; however, it also includes a specific reference to the right to vote in all public referenda, which is not mentioned in the Convention.

22. In proclaiming the principle that women shall have the same rights as men to acquire, change or retain their nationality, and in providing that marriage to an alien shall not automatically affect the nationality of the wife, the Declaration restates the provisions of the Convention on the Nationality of Married Women of 1957, although in other provisions the Declaration is less far-reaching than the Convention.

23. In providing that "all appropriate measures, particularly legislative measures, shall be taken to ensure to women, married or unmarried, equal rights with men in the field of civil law", the Declaration lists a number of fields in which this equality shall apply. It thus consolidates a series of solemn statements by the General Assembly and the Economic and Social Council, adopted over the years on the initiative of the Commission on the Status of Women. Article 6 of the Declaration also restates provisions of earlier instruments such as the Convention on Consent to Marriage, Minimum Age for Marriage and Registration of Marriages of 1962 and its Recommendation of 1965. The Declaration also calls, in article 7, for the abolition of all provisions in penal codes which constitute discrimination against women.

24. In providing that "All appropriate measures shall be taken to ensure to girls and women . . . equal rights with men in education at all levels", the Declaration incorporates the principle on which the UNESCO Convention against Discrimination in Education of 1960 is based. In proclaiming that "All appropriate measures shall be taken to ensure to women . . . equal rights with men in the field of economic and social life", the Declaration incorporates principles set out in a number of International Labour Conventions, such as the Equal Remuneration Convention, 1951 (No. 100) and the Discrimination (Employment and Occupation) Convention, 1958 (No. 111).

25. The Declaration, in its categorical injunction that "all appropriate measures . . . shall be taken to combat all forms of traffic in women and exploitation of prostitution of women", reaffirms provisions of several earlier international instruments, including the Convention for the Suppression of the Traffic in Persons and of the Exploitation of the Prostitution of Others of 1949.

26. The Economic and Social Council, in resolution 1325 (XLIV) of 31 May 1968, adopted on the recommendation of the Commission on the Status of Women, initiated a reporting system on the implementation of the Declaration. Member States, the specialized agencies and the non-governmental organizations concerned were requested to inform the Secretary-General of publicity given to the Declaration, and of action taken by them in compliance with its principles. The Secretary-General was requested to submit reports on the information received for consideration by the Commission.

27. The Committee on the Elimination of Discrimination against Women has responsibility for monitoring implementation of provisions of the Convention on the Elimination of All Forms of Discrimination against Women on the basis of reports which States parties submit to the Committee at regular intervals.

28. All other issues relating to the advancement of women and the elimination of discrimination based on sex are monitored by the Commission on the Status of Women.

3. COMMITTEE ON THE ELIMINATION OF DISCRIMINATION AGAINST WOMEN

29. Members of the Committee on the Elimination of Discrimination against Women, established in accordance with the Convention on the Elimination of All Forms of Discrimination against Women,[7] were elected by representatives of States parties to the Convention at their first meeting, on 16 April 1982. The first session of the Committee was held at the United Nations Office at Vienna from 18 to 22 October 1982. The Committee elected a Chairman, three Vice-Chairmen and a Rapporteur, adopted its agenda, and considered a number of organizational questions. In accordance with article 17, paragraphs 5 and 6, of the Convention, the Chairman selected by lot the 11 experts of the Committee whose terms would expire in 1984. The Committee then examined and adopted its rules of procedure, and considered its programme of future work. In addition, it examined briefly the question of guidelines for reports by States parties to the Convention.

30. Up to the end of 1987 the Committee had held six sessions, had adopted its rules of procedure and had formulated general guidelines on the form and contents of reports received from States parties under article 18 of the Convention. It had also made a contribution to the World Conference at Nairobi, Kenya, in 1985 by submitting a report on the achievements of and obstacles encountered by States parties in the implementation of the Convention and decided on guidelines for the preparation of second periodic reports.

31. It had considered the initial reports of 34 States parties: Austria, Bangladesh, Bulgaria, Byelorussian Soviet Socialist Republic, Canada, China, Colombia, Cuba, Czechoslovakia, Denmark, Ecuador, Egypt, El Salvador, France, German Democratic Republic, Greece, Hungary, Mexico, Mongolia, Norway, Panama, Philippines, Poland, Portugal, Rwanda, Republic of Korea, Spain, Sri Lanka, Sweden, Ukrainian Soviet Socialist Republic, Union of Soviet Socialist Republics, Venezuela, Viet Nam and Yugoslavia.

32. It had also discussed at several sessions, ways and means of implementing article 21 of the Convention, which provides that the Committee may make suggestions and general recommendations based on the examination of reports. At the sixth session, the Committee repeated in general recommendation No. 2, a recommendation already adopted at its fifth session, namely that States parties, in preparing their reports, should follow the general guidelines, that initial reports should cover the situation up to the date of submission and, thereafter, reports should be submitted at least every four years after the due date of the first report and should cover obstacles encountered in the implementation of the Convention and measures adopted to overcome them. In general recommendation No. 3 the Committee urged all States parties effectively to adopt education and public information programmes, which should help eliminate prejudices and current practices that hindered the full operation of the principle of the social equality of women. By general recommendation No. 4 the Committee suggested to all States parties concerned to reconsider reservations made with a view to withdrawing them.

33. In resolution 42/60 of 30 November 1987, the General Assembly took note of the report of the Committee on the work of its sixth session,[8] and expressed concern about the Committee's account of the constraints under which it had operated with respect to the backlog of reports awaiting examination. It encouraged the Committee to intensify its discussion on ways and means of dealing with this problem, and welcomed its efforts to rationalize its procedures and to expedite the consideration of reports from States parties. It also requested the Secretary-General to provide, facilitate and encourage public information activities relating to the Committee and the Convention, giving priority to the dissemination of the Convention in the official languages of the United Nations.

4. INTERNATIONAL WOMEN'S YEAR (1975)

34. By resolution 3010 (XXVII) of 18 December 1972, the General Assembly proclaimed the year 1975 International Women's Year and decided to devote the year to intensified action.

(a) To promote equality between men and women;

(b) To ensure the full integration of women in the total development effort, especially by emphasizing women's responsibility and important role in economic, social and cultural development at the national, regional and international levels, particularly during the Second United Nations Development Decade;

(c) To recognize the importance of women's increasing contribution to the development of friendly relations and co-operation among States and to the strengthening of world peace.

The Assembly invited

all Member States and all interested organizations to take steps to ensure the full realization of the rights of women and their advancement on the basis of the Declaration on the Elimination of Discrimination against Women,

and requested the Secretary-General to prepare, in consultation with Member States, specialized agencies and

---

[7] For information concerning the Convention, see chapter II, section B, 3.

[8] *Officials Records of the General Assembly, Forty-second Session, Supplement No. 38* (A/42/38).

interested non-governmental organizations, a draft programme for the International Women's Year.

35. The Economic and Social Council, in resolution 1851 (LVI) of 16 May 1974, requested the Secretary-General to convene an international conference during the International Women's Year to examine to what extent the organizations of the United Nations system had implemented the recommendations for the elimination of discrimination against women made by the Commission on the Status of Women since its establishment, and to launch an international action programme including short-term and long-term measures aimed at achieving the integration of women as full and equal partners with men in the total development effort and eliminating discrimination on grounds of sex, and at achieving the widest involvement of women in strengthening international peace and eliminating racism and racial discrimination.

(a) World Conference of the International Women's Year

36. The focal point of the international celebration of the International Women's Year was the World Conference of the International Women's Year held in Mexico City from 19 June to 2 July 1975.[9] The Conference was attended by 133 States represented by more than 1,000 delegates, about 70 per cent of whom were women. Three Governments were represented by observers. Nine offices of the Secretariat, seven United Nations bodies, seven specialized agencies and IAEA were also represented. In accordance with General Assembly resolution 3276 (XXIX) of 10 December 1974, seven national liberation movements sent observers. The Commission on Human Rights and eight intergovernmental organizations were also represented by observers, as well as 114 non-governmental organizations in consultative status with the Economic and Social Council following Economic and Social Council decision 73 (LVIII) of 28 April 1975.

37. The Conference adopted the Declaration of Mexico on the Equality of Women and Their Contribution to Development and Peace, 1975; the World Plan of Action for the Implementation of the Objectives of the International Women's Year; regional plans of action; 35 resolutions; and a decision recommending the convening of a second world conference in 1980.

38. The Declaration promulgates 30 principles. These deal among other things with: equality between women and men; equal rights and responsibilities of women and men in the family and society; equal access to education and training; the right to work and to equal pay for work of equal value; the right of couples and individuals to determine the number and spacing of children; the right of every woman to decide freely whether to marry; the right to participate in and con-

tribute to the development effort; the full participation of women in the economic, social and cultural sectors; the role of women in the promotion of international co-operation and peace; the role of women in promoting human rights of all peoples; and the need to eliminate violations of human rights committed against women and girls.

39. The Declaration urges Governments, the United Nations system, regional and international intergovernmental organizations, and the international community to dedicate themselves to the creation of a just society where women, men and children can live in dignity, freedom, justice and prosperity.

40. The World Plan of Action for the Implementation of the Objectives of the International Women's Year was adopted to strengthen the implementation of the instruments and programmes which had been adopted concerning the status of women, and to broaden and place them in a more timely context. Its purpose was mainly to stimulate national and international action to solve the problems of underdevelopment and of the socio-economic structure which placed women in an inferior position, in order to achieve the goals of the International Women's Year. In order to promote equality between women and men, the Plan recommended that Governments ensure for both women and men equality before the law, the provision of facilities for equality of educational opportunities and training, equality in conditions of employment, including remuneration and adequate social security. The Plan drew attention to nine specific areas for national action and made several recommendations for international and regional action.

41. The General Assembly, at its thirtieth session, overwhelmingly endorsed the action proposals of the Conference by adopting ten resolutions and one decision outlining action for the future.[10]

(b) United Nations Development Fund for Women

42. The Economic and Social Council, in resolution 1850 (LVI) of 16 May 1974, welcomed voluntary contributions from Member States, intergovernmental and non-governmental organizations, private foundations and interested individuals, to supplement the resources available to implement the programme for the International Women's Year; and called upon the Secretary-General to accept such voluntary contributions.

43. At its 2441st plenary meeting, on 15 December 1975, the General Assembly decided that the voluntary fund for the International Women's Year should be extended to cover the period of the United Nations Decade for Women. At its thirty-first session, after con-

---

[9] For the report of the Conference, see United Nations publication, Sales No. E.76.IV.1.

[10] General Assembly resolutions 3416 (XXX) of 8 December 1975, 3490 (XXX) of 12 December 1975, 3505 (XXX), 3518 (XXX), 3519 (XXX), 3520 (XXX), 3521 (XXX), 3522 (XXX), 3523 (XXX) and 3524 (XXX) of 15 December 1975 and a decision taken at the 2441st plenary meeting on 15 December 1975.

sidering the report of the Secretary-General on the Voluntary Fund for the Decade,[11] the Assembly adopted, in resolution 31/133 of 16 December 1976, criteria for the management of the Voluntary Fund for the United Nations Decade for Women; requested the Secretary-General to report annually thereon; and requested the President of the General Assembly to select five Member States, each of which should appoint a representative to serve, for a three-year period, on the Consultative Committee to advise the Secretary-General on the application of the criteria to the use of the Fund.

44. In resolution 31/133 of 16 December 1976, the Assembly set out a series of criteria for the use of the Fund, requested the Secretary-General to report annually thereon, and requested its President to select five Member States, each of which should appoint a representative to serve, for a three-year period, on a Consultative Committee to advise the Secretary-General on the use of the Fund.

45. In resolution 31/137 of the same date, the General Assembly requested the Secretary-General to convene during its thirty-second session a pledging conference for contributions to be made to the Voluntary Fund for the United Nations Decade for Women and to the International Research and Training Institute for the Advancement of Women. The first Pledging Conference for the United Nations Decade for Women was accordingly held at United Nations Headquarters on 8 November 1977. Noting the results of that Conference with satisfaction, the General Assembly, in resolution 32/139 of 16 December 1977, called for a second pledging conference to be convened during its thirty-third session. Similar pledging conferences have been convened annually since then. At its thirty-fourth session the General Assembly, after considering the report of the Secretary-General on the Fund,[12] adopted resolution 34/156 of 17 December 1979 in which it noted with satisfaction the decisions of the Consultative Committee, expressed its desire to see the activities developed by the Fund continued beyond the United Nations Decade for Women, and requested the Secretary-General and the Committee to study that question.

46. The General Assembly continued its examination of various aspects of the operation of the Voluntary Fund on an annual basis up to 1985 (resolutions 32/141, 33/188, 34/156, 35/137, 36/129, 37/62, 38/106, 39/125 and 40/104); thereafter it considered the item biennially.

47. In resolution 39/125 of 14 December 1984, the Assembly decided that the activities of the Voluntary Fund should be continued through establishment of a separate and identifiable entity, in autonomous association with the United Nations Development Programme, which would play an innovative and catalytic role in relation to the United Nations system of development co-operation. Accordingly it endorsed arrangements for the future management of the Fund, annexed to the resolution, and requested the Consultative Committee to monitor their implementation.

48. The estabishment of the United Nations Development Fund for Women, in autonomous association with the UNDP, was effected on 1 July 1985; and the UNDP Administrator has since submitted to the General Assembly, through the Secretary-General, reports on its activities.[13]

49. The report submitted to the Assembly at the forty-second session[14] indicated that UNDP and the United Nations Development Fund for Women (UNIFEM) were preparing a set of guidelines to regulate their functional relationship and facilitate and deepen the close co-operation between the Fund and UNDP, and pointed out that the Governing Council of UNDP, in its decision 87/41 of 18 June 1987, commended the Fund's new operational directions, with special reference to its programming approach, urged the Fund to intensify its approaches to secure mainstream consideration of women, and noted the collaboration between the Fund and the UNDP Division for Women in Development.

50. In resolution 42/63 of 30 November 1987, the General Assembly took note of the note by the Secretary-General[14] containing the report of the Administrator of the United Nations Development Programme and the report of the Consultative Committee on the United Nations Development Fund for Women at its twenty-first session, and welcomed the constructive co-operation between the Programme and the Fund. It expressed its appreciation for the financial contributions to the Fund made by Governments, intergovernmental organizations, national committees and individuals; and invited States to continue and, where possible, to increase their contributions in order to enable the Fund to give greater support to deserving project requests received for technical assistance.

(c) *International Research and Training Institute for the Advancement of Women*

51. In resolution 26, the World Conference of the International Women's Year decided "to recommend the establishment, under the auspices of the United Nations, of an International Training and Research Institute for the Advancement of Women, financed through voluntary contributions, which in collaboration with appropriate national, regional and interregional economic and social research institutes and the specialized agencies", would

(a) Undertake research and the collection and dissemination of information as the basis for the formulation of programmes and policies for the effective participation of women;

(b) Assist in the design of research for the monitoring of changes in the situation of women and the impact on their lives of economic, social and technological changes;

---

[11] E/5773.

[12] A/34/612.

[13] A/41/600 and A/42/597/Rev. 1.

[14] A/42/597/Rev. 1.

(c) Develop, adapt and provide training programmes for women, in particular those of the developing countries, which would enable them to undertake national research, to assume leadership roles within their own societies and to increase their earning possibilities.

The Secretary-General was invited to appoint a group of experts to assist him in the establishment of this Institute and to draw up its terms of reference.

52. The General Assembly, in resolution 3520 (XXX) of 15 December 1975, decided in principle to establish such an Institute, and requested the Secretary-General to report to the Economic and Social Council on the basis of the recommendations of the Group of Experts.

53. The 11-member Group of Experts on the Establishment of an International Research and Training Institute for the Advancement of Women met at United Nations Headquarters from 17 to 23 February 1976. On the basis of its recommendations the Secretary-General submitted a report[15] to the Economic and Social Council at its sixtieth session in which he expressed agreement that the Institute should be established, subject to the availability of extrabudgetary funds that would be needed to ensure its operation for an initial period of at least three years, and to the Institute's scope and objectives, terms of reference and priorities.

54. The Council, in resolution 1998 (LX) of 12 May 1976, decided to establish the Institute not later than 1977, provided the necessary financial provisions were made, as an autonomous body under the auspices of the United Nations, funded by voluntary contributions. As guidelines, the Council decided that the Institute should work in close collaboration with all relevant organizations within the United Nations sytem, and national and regional centres and institutes which have similar objectives; that it should take the activities of those organizations fully into account and co-ordinate its work with theirs; that it should direct its activities with special attention to the needs of women in developing countries and their integration in the development process; and that it should maintain close contact with the Commission on the Status of Women.

55. Later the Council, in resolution 1979/11 of 9 May 1979, recommended that the Institute should be located in the Dominican Republic. The Assembly endorsed this decision in resolution 34/157 of 17 December 1979, and accepted with appreciation the offer of the Government of the Dominican Republic to act as host for the Institute. In resolution 1981/13 of 6 May 1981, the Council expressed its satisfaction at the conclusion of the agreement between the Government of the Dominican Republic and the United Nations concerning the installation of the Institute at Santo Domingo, welcomed the appointment of the Director of the Institute, and expressed the hope that the Institute would start functioning shortly.

56. At its thirty-fifth and thirty-sixth sessions, the General Assembly invited Governments to contribute to the United Nations Trust Fund for the Institute. At its thirty-seventh session it endorsed the network concept to be developed in stages with the organizations of the United Nations system, and regional and national organizations, as a mode of operation for the execution of its programme.

57. In 1983, the Assembly examined the report of the Institute on its programme activities.[16] In resolution 38/104 of 16 December 1983, it expressed its satisfaction at the official inauguration of the Institute at its permanent headquarters at Santo Domingo and requested it to continue activities that contribute to the full integration of women in the mainstream of development.

58. By decision 1984/124 of 24 May 1984, the Economic and Social Council approved the Statute of the Institute. Welcoming this development, the General Assembly in resolution 39/122 of 14 December 1984 took note with satisfaction of the Institute's programme, requested it to bear in mind trends in research and training relevant to women and development; and again invited contributions to the Institute's Trust Fund.

59. Further reports on the activities of the Institute were examined and noted with satisfaction by the General Assembly at its 1985 and 1987 sessions.[17] In resolution 42/65 of 30 November 1987, the Assembly expressed its satisfaction at the significance and scope of the activities of the Institute, particularly as they relate to statistics and indicators on women and training for the formulation of policy analysis, planning and programming relevant to an increased participation and the integration of women in development. The Institute was requested to continue and strengthen its research, training, information and communication activities, particularly the developing of innovative training methodologies on women and socio-economic issues related to development, networking as far as possible with other relevant research and training activities. It was also requested to promote general awareness and training on the pragmatic approach to the integration of women into policy designs, including the elaboration of special methodologies for monitoring and evaluation purposes, with particular reference to the implementation of the Nairobi Forward-looking Strategies for the Advancement of Women and the feedback of results into the operational system.

5. UNITED NATIONS DECADE FOR WOMEN: EQUALITY, DEVELOPMENT AND PEACE, 1976-1985

60. The General Assembly, in resolution 3520 (XXX) of 15 December 1975, after taking note of the report of the World Conference of the International Women's Year[18] and endorsing the action proposals emanating from that Conference, proclaimed the period from 1976 to 1985 United Nations Decade for Women: Equality,

---

[15] E/5772.

[16] A/38/406.

[17] A/40/707 and A/42/444, annex.

[18] United Nations publication, Sales No. E.76.IV.1.

Development and Peace, and called for it to be devoted to effective and sustained national, regional and international action to implement the resolutions of the Conference.

61. Also, pursuant to the decision of the Conference to recommend the convening of a second world conference in 1980, the Assembly, in the same resolution, decided to convene in 1980, at the mid-term of the Decade, a world conference to review and evaluate the progress made in implementing the objectives of the International Women's Year. The Assembly also called upon Governments, as a matter of urgency, to examine the recommendations of the Conference.

(a) World Conference of the United Nations Decade for Women: Equality, Development and Peace, 1980[19]

62. The World Conference of the United Nations Decade for Women: Equality, Development and Peace, was held at Copenhagen from 14 to 30 July 1980 in conformity with General Assembly resolution 33/191 of 29 January 1979.

63. The Conference was attended by 145 States represented by more than 2,000 delegates. Nine offices of the United Nations, 13 United Nations bodies and programmes and five specialized agencies were also represented. The United Nations Council for Namibia and the Special Committee Against *Apartheid* were represented, as well as 10 intergovernmental organizations attended as observers. A large number of non-governmental organizations in consultative status with the Economic and Social Council, or on the Roster, attended the Conference.

64. At the mid-point of the United Nations Decade for Women, the Conference formulated a Programme of Action for the Second Half of the Decade,[20] 1980-1985. The Programme was designed to promote the attainment of the three objectives of equality, development and peace, with special emphasis on the subthemes— namely, employment, health and education—as significant components of development, taking into account that human resources cannot achieve their full potential without integrated socio-economic development. It aimed at strengthening comprehensive and effective strategies to remove obstacles and constraints on women's full and equal participation in development, including actions to solve the problems of underdevelopment and of the socio-economic structure which places women in an inferior position and to increase their contribution to the strengthening of world peace.

65. In addition to preparing the Programme of Action for the Second Half of the Decade, the Conference reviewed and evaluated the progress made and obstacles encountered in attaining the objectives of the Decade at the national, regional and international levels from 1975

to 1980, and considered the effects of *apartheid* on women in southern Africa as well as the effects of Israeli occupation on Palestinian women inside and outside the occupied territories. It adopted 48 resolutions and suggested that, since all the objectives of the World Plan of Action could not be achieved within a short span of time, the possibility of a second Decade could be envisaged for the period 1985-1995.

66. The General Assembly took note with satisfaction of the report of the Conference in resolution 35/136 of 11 December 1980, and endorsed the Programme of Action for the Second Half of the Decade. It recognized that the Conference had made an important and constructive contribution by appraising the progress achieved and the obstacles encountered in the implementation of the objectives of the Decade and by preparing and adopting a programme for the coming five years, and affirmed that the implementation of the Programme of Action should result in the complete integration of women into the development process and the elimination of all forms of inequality between men and women and would guarantee broad participation by women in efforts to strengthen peace and security throughout the world. The Assembly, further, urged Governments to take appropriate measures to implement the Programme of Action and other relevant resolutions and decisions of the Conference at the national, regional and international levels; and urged all organizations of the United Nations system to take the necessary measures to ensure a concerted and sustained effort for the implementation of the Programme and of other relevant resolutions and decisions of the Conference in the course of the second half of the Decade.

(b) World Conference to Review and Appraise the Achievements of the United Nations Decade for Women, 1985

67. The General Assembly decided, in resolution 35/136 of 11 December 1980, to convene a World Conference to Review and Appraise the Achievements of the United Nations Decade for Women. In resolution 36/126 of 14 December 1981 it requested the Commission on the Status of Women to give priority to preparations for the Conference.

68. The Commission prepared its recommendations on the question at its twenty-ninth session, in 1982, on the basis of a report by the Secretary-General.[21] The Economic and Social Council considered these recommendations at its first regular session of 1982.

69. In resolution 1982/26 of 4 May 1982, the Council decided that the Commission should be the preparatory body for the World Conference, operating on the basis of consensus. The Council invited the widest possible participation of Member States in the deliberations of the preparatory body, and encouraged them to consider establishing national committees to assist, for example,

---

[19] For the report of the Conference, see United Nations publications, Sales No. E.80.IV.3.

[20] *Ibid.*, chap. I, sect. A.

[21] E/CN.6/1982/8.

in national-level preparations for the Conference. The Council also invited the regional commissions, the specialized agencies, and non-governmental organizations having consultative status with the Council, to contribute to the preparatory work. Further, the Council recommended that the Commission should meet at Vienna in extraordinary session in 1983 and again in 1985 with conference preparations as the sole item of the agenda, and that its thirtieth regular session, in 1984, should be extended to allow additional time for conference preparations. It proposed that the Advancement of Women Branch of the Centre for Social Development and Humanitarian Affairs should serve as the secretariat of the preparatory body as well as of the Conference. It also recommended that, with a view to the achievement of the goals of the Decade, a forward-looking draft perspective on the status of women to the year 2000 should be prepared by the preparatory body for consideration by the Conference.

70. The General Assembly, in resolution 37/60 of 3 December 1982, endorsed the Council's decisions, and noted that the first session of the Commission as the preparatory body of the Conference would be held at Vienna from 23 February to 4 March 1983. In the same resolution the Assembly took note with appreciation of the report of the Secretary-General on the progress made in the preparation of a world survey on the role of women in development,[22] and recommended that the survey should be submitted to the Conference.

71. The World Conference to Review and Appraise the Achievements of the United Nations Decade for Women: Equality, Development and Peace was held at Nairobi, Kenya, from 15 to 26 July 1985. The Conference was attended by 157 States. The United Nations Council for Namibia and the Special Committee against *Apartheid* were represented at the Conference. The Palestine Liberation Organization and the South West Africa People's Organization attended in the capacity of observers. Two national liberation movements, the African National Congress (South Africa) and the Pan Africanist Congress of Azania, were represented by observers. Five offices of the Secretariat, 18 United Nations bodies, eight specialized agencies, 17 intergovernmental organizations and 163 non-governmental organizations in consultative status with the Economic and Social Council were also represented. Miss Margaret Kenyatta, the head of the delegation of Kenya, was elected as President of the Conference.

72. The Conference considered two substantive agenda items: (1) Critical review and appraisal of progress achieved and obstacles encountered in attaining the goals and objectives of the United Nations Decade for Women: Equality, Development and Peace, and the sub-theme: Employment, Health and Education, bearing in mind the guidelines laid down at the World Conference of the International Women's Year held at Mexico City, and the World Conference of the United Nations Decade for Women: Equality, Develop-

ment and Peace, held at Copenhagen; and (2) Forward-looking Strategies of implementation for the advancement of women for the period up to the year 2000, and concrete measures to overcome obstacles to the achievement of the goals and objectives of the United Nations Decade for Women: Equality, Development and Peace, and the sub-theme: Employment, Health and Education, bearing in mind the International Development Strategy for the Third United Nations Development Decade and the establishment of a new international economic order.

73. Two main committees were established to consider a large number of draft resolutions and a draft Declaration. Owing to lack of time, the Conference was unable to take action on any of them; they were appended to the Conference report and it was understood that they would be brought to the attention of the General Assembly for consideration and action as appropriate.

74. Both main committees were however able to recommend to the Conference for adoption the text of paragraphs to be incorporated in the chapters of the Forward-looking Strategies, and the Conference considered these paragraphs, and others on which it had not been possible to reach agreement in the Committee concerned. At its twentieth plenary meeting, on 26 July 1985, the Conference adopted the text of the Forward-looking Strategies as a whole by consensus.[23]

(c) *Implementation of the Nairobi Forward-looking Strategies for the Advancement of Women*

75. The General Assembly considered the report of the World Conference to Review and Appraise the Achievements of the United Nations Decade for Women: Equality, Development and Peace, at its fortieth session. In resolution 40/108 of 13 December 1985, the Assembly took note of the report with satisfaction, endorsed the Nairobi Forward-looking Strategies for the Advancement of Women, and affirmed that the implementation of the Strategies should result in the elimination of all forms of inequality between women and men and in the complete integration of women into the development process—a development that would guarantee broad participation by women in efforts to strengthen peace and security in the world. The Assembly, further, called upon Governments to allocate adequate resources and to take effective appropriate measures to implement the Forward-looking Strategies as a matter of high priority, including the establishment or reinforcement, as appropriate, of national machineries to promote the advancement of women, and to monitor the implementation of these Strategies with a view to ensuring the full integration of women in the political, economic, social and cultural life of their countries.

---

[22] A/37/381.

[23] *Report of the World Conference to Review and Appraise the Achievements of the United Nations Decade for Women: Equality, Development and Peace,* Nairobi, 15-26 July 1985 (United Nations publication, Sales No. E.85.IV.10), chap. I, sect. A.

76. At its forty-first session, in resolution 41/111 of 4 December 1986, the General Assembly took note of two reports of the Secretary-General concerning the implementation of the Forward-looking Strategies;[24] reaffirmed the need to translate those Strategies immediately into concrete action by Governments, as determined by overall national priorities, as well as by the organizations of the United Nations system, the specialized agencies, and intergovernmental and non-governmental organizations; and called upon all Member States to establish specific targets at each level in order to increase the participation of women in professional and decision-making positions in their countries.

77. The Economic and Social Council, at its first regular session of 1987, considered the suggestions for monitoring and review and appraisal of the Nairobi Forward-looking Strategies set out in Chapter V, section C of the Strategies, together with the recommendations of the Commission on the Status of Women thereon and the recommendation in General Assembly resolution 40/108 of 13 December 1985 which called for the further development of the established integrated reporting system. In this connection the Council received and noted the report of the Secretary-General on the existing system which identified its problems and suggested remedial measures.[25]

78. In resolution 1987/18 of 26 May 1987, the Council set out a series of guidelines to be taken into account by the Secretary-General in further developing and implementing the reporting system. It invited the Secretary-General, the executive secretaries of the regional commissions, and the executive heads of the specialized agencies and other organizations of the United Nations system, to develop and implement, as an integral part of their programmes, a simple, concise and direct form of reporting to the Commission on the impact of their programmes and activities on women and the effectiveness of those programmes and activities in bringing the interests and needs of women into the mainstream of their organizations. Further, it authorized the Commission on the Status of Women, in consultation with the Statistical Commission, the Board of Trustees of the International Research and Training Institute for the Advancement of Women and other appropriate bodies, to establish formal arrangements for the collection and distribution of the information required for the Commission to carry out its monitoring and review and appraisal functions.

79. In other resolutions adopted at the same session on the recommendation of the Commission on the Status of Women, the Economic and Social Council:

Called for further improvement of the status of women in the United Nations, and in particular for the Secretary-General to take the necessary measures, as requested in General Assembly resolution 41/206 D of 11 December 1986, to increase the number of women in posts subject to geographical distribution with a view to achieving, to the extent possible, an overall participation rate of 30 per cent of the total by 1990, without prejudice to the principle of equitable geographical distribution (Economic and Social Council resolution 1987/19 of 26 May 1987);

Recommended that world conferences to review and appraise the progress achieved in the implementation of the Forward-looking Strategies be held during the decade of the 1990s, at a date to be determined by the General Assembly not later than 1990, and in 2000 (Economic and Social Council resolution 1987/20 of 26 May 1987);

Decided that, commencing with its thirty-second session, the Commission on the Status of Women shall meet annually until the year 2000, and recommended that the officers elected to the Commission's bureau should serve for a term of office of two years (Economic and Social Council resolution 1987/21 of 26 May 1987);

Decided to expand the terms of reference of the Commission on the Status of Women to include the functions of promoting the objectives of equality, development and peace, monitoring the implementation of measures for the advancement of women, and reviewing and appraising progress made at the national, subregional, regional, sectoral and global levels; and further decided to structure the agenda for the future sessions of the Commission around its functions, namely programming, co-ordination, monitoring and policy development (Economic and Social Council resolution 1987/22 of 26 May 1987);

Accepted in principle the need for an increase in the membership of the Commission, but referred the matter to the Commission with a request that it submit appropriate proposals (Economic and Social Council resolution 1987/23 of 26 May 1987);

Endorsed priority themes for the thirty-second to thirty-seventh sessions of the Commission on the Status of Women, and decided that the work of the Commission in relation to the priority themes should be closely related to the relevant provisions of the Forward-looking Strategies and of other policy documents, the programmes elaborated in the system-wide mid-term plan for women and development, and the relevant chapters of the World Survey on the Role of Womem in Development,[26] with a view to ensuring the effective implementation of the Forward-looking Strategies and lasting improvement in the situation of women (Economic and Social Council resolution 1986/24 of 26 May 1987);

Recommended observance of the tenth anniversary of the operational activities of the United Nations Development Fund for Women by the General Assembly and by non-governmental organizations, including national committees; and urged Member States to pledge contributions to the Fund (Economic and Social Council resolution 1987/26 of 26 May 1987).

---

[24] A/41/623 and A/41/672.

[25] E/CN.6/1986/2 and Add.1 and Add.1/Corr.1.

[26] United Nations publication, Sales No. E.86.IV.3.

80. Taking the relevant resolutions and decisions of the Commission on the Status of Women and of the Economic and Social Council into account, specifically endorsing Council resolutions 1987/21 and 1987/24, and taking note of the Secretary-General's 1987 reports concerning the implementation of the Nairobi Forward-looking Strategies, the General Assembly in resolution 42/62 of 30 November 1987 reaffirmed a number of decisions which it had taken at its 1985 and 1986 sessions, among them:

The need for the Forward-looking Strategies to be immediately translated into concrete action by Governments, as determined by overall national priorities, as well as by the organizations of the United Nations system, the specialized agencies and intergovernmental and non-governmental organizations;

The central role of the Commission on the Status of Women in matters related to the advancement of the status of women. In this connection the Assembly called upon the Commission to promote the implementation of the Forward-looking Strategies and urged all organizations of the United Nations system to co-operate with the Commission in this task;

The role of the Centre for Social Development and Humanitarian Affairs of the United Nations Office at Vienna, in particular the Branch for the Advancement of Women, in the implementation of the Forward-looking Strategies, as the substantive secretariat of the Commission on the Status of Women and as a focal point for matters relating to women;

The catalysing role of the United Nations Development Fund for Women and the role of the United Nations International Research and Training Institute for the Advancement of Women in the promotion of the role of women in the context of the participation of women in development;

The need for the United Nations to develop an integrated reporting system with the Commission on the Status of Women at its centre and, building upon existing information and resources, to monitor the review and appraisal of progress in the advancement of women, which are based on clear and relevant statistical and other measurable indicators and which will assist Member States in identifying problems and in developing remedial measures, at the national, regional and international levels.

81. The Assembly once again called upon the Secretary-General and the executive heads of the specialized agencies and other United Nations bodies to establish five-year targets at each level for the percentage of women in professional and decision-making positions, in accordance with the criteria established by the Assembly, in order that a definite upward trend in the application of Assembly resolution 41/206 D of 11 December 1986 be registered in the number of professional and decision-making positions held by women by 1990 and to set additional targets every five years. It requested the Secretary-General to extend the term of the women's Co-ordinator for a satisfactory period to ensure that the action programme—in which *inter alia* it is recommended that the situation of women in the United Nations Secretariat should be improved —will continue to be implemented. Further, it requested the Secretary-General to invite Governments, organizations of the United Nations system including the regional commissions and the specialized agencies, and intergovernmental and non-governmental organizations, to report periodically through the Commission on the Status of Women to the Economic and Social Council on the activities undertaken at all levels to implement the Forward-looking Strategies; and to report thereon to the General Assembly.

6. MEASURES TO ENSURE EQUALITY OF MEN AND WOMEN IN THE ENJOYMENT OF PARTICULAR RIGHTS AND FREEDOMS

82. Improvement of the legal status of women has been a concern of the Commission on the Status of Women since its first session, in 1947. On the recommendation of the Commission, the Economic and Social Council, in resolution 11 (II) of 21 June 1946, requested the Secretary-General "to make arrangements for a complete and detailed study of the legislation concerning the status of women and the practical application of such legislation".

83. Accordingly, the Secretary-General prepared a questionnaire on the legal status and treatment of women and circulated it to Governments. On the basis of the replies received, a number of reports were prepared and submitted to the Commission. Having examined these reports, the Commission made a series of recommendations to Governments through the Economic and Social Council.

(a) *Political rights and participation of women*

84. In one of its earliest decisions, resolution 56 (I) of 11 December 1946, the General Assembly, noting that certain Member States had not granted to women political rights equal to those of men, recommended that all Member States which had not done so should adopt the necessary measures to fulfil the aims of the Charter in that respect by granting women the same political rights as men. The Secretary-General was invited to communicate this recommendation to the Governments of all Member States.

85. The question of the political rights of women has since been dealt with, on the international level, in the Convention on the Political Rights of Women, adopted by the General Assembly on 20 December 1952, which entered into force on 7 July 1954; the Declaration on the Elimination of Discrimination against Women, proclaimed by the General Assembly on 7 November 1967; and the Convention on the Elimination of All Forms of Discrimination against Women, adopted by

the General Assembly on 18 December 1979, which entered into force on 3 September 1981.

86. The Convention on the Political Rights of Women contains the following provisions:

Article 1

Women shall be entitled to vote in all elections on equal terms with men, without any discrimination.

Article 2

Women shall be eligible for election to all publicly elected bodies, established by national law, on equal terms with men, without any discrimination.

Article 3

Women shall be entitled to hold public office and to exercise all public functions, established by national law, on equal terms with men, without any discrimination.

87. The Declaration on the Elimination of Discrimination against Women contains the following provision:

Article 4

All appropriate measures shall be taken to ensure to women on equal terms with men, without any discrimination:

(a) The right to vote in all elections and be eligible for election to all publicly elected bodies;

(b) The right to vote in all public referenda;

(c) The right to hold public office and to exercise all public functions.

Such rights shall be guaranteed by legislation.

88. The Convention on the Elimination of All Forms of Discrimination against Women contains the following provisions:

Article 7

States Parties shall take all appropriate measures to eliminate discrimination against women in the political and public life of the country and, in particular, shall ensure, on equal terms with men, the right:

(a) To vote in all elections and public referenda and to be eligible for election to all publicly elected bodies;

(b) To participate in the formulation of government policy and the implementation thereof and to hold public office and perform all public functions at all levels of government;

(c) To participate in non-governmental organizations and associations concerned with the public and political life of the country.

Article 8

States Parties shall take all appropriate measures to ensure to women, on equal terms with men, and without any discrimination, the opportunity to represent their Governments at the international level and to participate in the work of international organizations.

89. Implementation of the provisions of the Convention on the Elimination of All Forms of Discrimination against Women is monitored by the Committee on the Elimination of Discrimination against Women.

90. In addition to preparing drafts of each of these instruments for consideration by its parent bodies—the General Assembly and the Economic and Social Council—the Commission on the Status of Women, with the co-operation of the ILO, UNESCO, and other international organizations, carried on continuing programmes to encourage the civic and political education of women in public life, and encouraged Governments to do likewise. As early as 12 July 1963 the Economic and Social Council was able to note, in resolution 961 B (XXXVI), "that the great majority of States have

formally granted women the same political rights as men".

91. The Commission has also initiated measures to improve the status of women in the Secretariat of the United Nations in accordance with Article 8 of the Charter, which provides that the United Nations "shall place no restrictions on the eligibility of men and women to participate in any capacity and under conditions of equality in its principal and subsidiary organs". On its recommendation the General Assembly, in resolution 2715 (XXV) of 15 December 1970, expressed the hope that the United Nations, including its special bodies and all intergovernmental agencies in the United Nations system of organizations, would set an example with regard to opportunities for the employment of women at senior and other professional levels. It urged the United Nations and the other bodies concerned to take or continue to take appropriate measures to ensure equal opportunities for the employment of qualified women in senior and other professional positions. It requested the Secretary-General to include in his report on the composition of the Secretariat data relevant to this question.

92. Reports of the Secretary-General on the composition of the Secretariat presented ot the General Assembly at its twenty-sixth[27] and twenty-eighth[28] sessions included information on the employment of women in senior and other professional positions in the secretariats of organizations within the United Nations system. In resolution 3352 (XXIX) of 18 December 1974, the Assembly noted that these reports, and a report of the United Nations Training and Research Institute entitled *The Situation of Women in the United Nations,*[29] revealed an unsatisfactory situation which called for specific measures and programmes in order to achieve an equitable balance between the number of men and women, particularly in senior and policy-making positions, including those of Under-Secretary-General and Assistant Secretary-General.

93. More recent reports of the Secretary-General indicated that he had appointed a Steering Committee for the Improvement of the Status of Women in the Secretariat and had accepted a number of measures recommended by that Committee to overcome earlier constraints. In resolution 41/206 of 11 December 1986 the Assembly requested the Secretary-General to take the necessary measures to increase the number of women in posts subject to geographical distribution with a view to achieving, to the extent possible, an overall participation rate of 30 per cent of the total by 1990, without prejudice to the principle of equitable geographical distribution of posts.

94. At its forty-second session the General Assembly received and took note, in resolution 42/220 C of 21 December 1987, of a report by the Secretary-General on his continuing efforts to improve the status of

27 A/8483.

28 A/9120 and Corr.1 and 2.

29 UNITAR publication, RR No. 18 (1973).

women in the Secretariat,[30] and requested him to continue those efforts and to consider the introduction of additional measures, if necessary, in order to increase the number of women in posts subject to geographical distribution with a view to achieving, to the extent possible, an overall participation rate of 30 per cent of the total by 1990. In this connection it urged the Secretary-General to increase his efforts to ensure an equitable representation of women from developing countries in posts subject to geographical distribution, and particularly in posts at senior and policy-formulating levels; and reiterated its request to Member States to nominate more women candidates for such posts.

95. The Forward-looking Strategies for the Advancement of Women to the Year 2000,[31] adopted by the World Conference to Review and Appraise the Achievements of the United Nations Decade for Women: Equality, Development and Peace, held at Nairobi from 15 to 26 July 1985, include the following paragraphs relating to equality in political participation and decision-making:

Governments and political parties should intensify efforts to stimulate and ensure equality of participation by women in all national and local legislative bodies and to achieve equity in the appointment, election and promotion of women to high posts in executive, legislative and judiciary branches in these bodies. At the local level, strategies to ensure equality of women in political participation should be pragmatic, should bear a close relationship to issues of concern to women in the locality and should take into account the suitability of the proposed measures to local needs and values.

Governments and other employers should devote special attention to broader and more equitable access and inclusion of women in management in various forms of popular participation, which is a significant factor in the development and realization of all human rights.

Governments should effectively secure participation of women in the decision-making processes at national, state and local levels through legislative and administrative measures. It is desirable that governmental departments establish a special office in each of them, headed preferably by a women, to monitor periodically and accelerate the process of equitable representation of women. Special activities should be undertaken to increase the recruitment, nomination and promotion of women, especially to decision-making and policy-making positions, by publicizing posts more widely, increasing upward mobility and so on, until equitable representation of women is achieved. Reports should be compiled periodically on the numbers of women in public service and on their levels of responsibility in their areas of work.

With respect to the increase in the number of couples in which both partners are employed in the public service, especially the foreign service, Governments are urged to consider their special needs, in particular the couple's desire to be assigned to the same duty station, with a view to reconciling family and professional duties.

Awareness of women's political rights should be promoted through many channels, including formal and informal education, political education, non-governmental organizations, trade unions, the media and business organizations. Women should be encouraged and motivated and should help each other to exercise their right to vote and to be elected and to participate in the political process at all levels on equal terms with men.

Political parties and other organizations such as trade unions should make a deliberate effort to increase and improve women's participation within their ranks. They should institute measures to activate women's constitutional and legal guarantees of the right to be elected and appointed by selecting candidates. Equal access to the political machinery of the organizations and to resources and tools for developing skills in the art and tactics of practical politics, as well as effective leadership capabilities, should be given to women. Women in leadership positions also have a special responsibility to assist in this field.

Governments that have not already done so should establish institutional arrangements and procedures whereby individual women, as well as representatives of all types of women's interest groups, including those from the most vulnerable, least privileged and most oppressed groups, may participate actively in all aspects of the formulation, monitoring, review and appraisal of national and local policies, issues and activities.

96. With regard to participation in international affairs, the Strategies include the following paragraph:

Governments should take all appropriate measures to ensure to women, on equal terms with men and without discrimination, the opportunity to represent their Government at all levels on delegations to subregional, regional and international meetings. More women should be appointed as diplomats and to decision-making posts within the United Nations system, including posts in fields relating to peace and development activities. Support services, such as educational facilities and day care, for families of diplomats and other civil servants stationed abroad, of United Nations officials, as well as employment of spouses at the duty station, wherever possible, should be strongly encouraged.

(b) Nationality of married women

97. The problem of the nationality of married women has been the concern of the United Nations since the Commission on the Status of Women decided to study this question in 1948. At its second session, held in January of that year, the Commission noted the many and varied discriminations against women that resulted from conflicts in nationality laws, and recalled The Hague Convention on Certain Questions relating to the Conflict of Nationality Laws (1930), the Montevideo Convention on the Nationality of Women (1933), and the studies in the field which had been undertaken by the League of Nations. At its request the Economic and Social Council at its seventh session in 1948 requested the Secretary-General to prepare a report based on replies received to the Questionnaire on the Legal Status and Treatment of Women and a report on existing treaties and conventions in the field of nationality.

98. The Convention on the Nationality of Married Women was adopted by the General Assembly and opened for signature and ratification in resolution 1040 (XI) of 29 January 1957.

99. The Convention represented an important step in a development which had been foreshadowed in The Hague Convention on Certain Questions relating to the Conflict of Nationality Laws of 1930[32] and which tended to replace the traditional principle of the unity of the family with the principle of the independence of the nationality of the wife from that of her husband.

---

[30] A/C.5/42/24, and annex IV.

[31] Report of the World Conference to Review and Appraise the Achievements of the United Nations Decade for Women: Equality, Development and Peace, Nairobi, 15-26 July 1985 (A/CONF.116/28 and Corr.1-4), chap. I, C.3.

[32] League of Nations, Treaty Series, vol. CLXXIX, No. 4137, p. 89.

100. The Convention on the Nationality of Married Women contains the following provisions:

Article 1

Each Contracting State agrees that neither the celebration nor the dissolution of a marriage between one of its nationals and an alien, nor the change of nationality by the husband during marriage, shall automatically affect the nationality of the wife.

Article 2

Each Contracting State agrees that neither the voluntary acquisition of the nationality of another State nor the renunciation of its nationality by one of its nationals shall prevent the retention of its nationality by the wife of such national.

Article 3

1. Each Contracting State agrees that the alien wife of one of its nationals may, at her request, acquire the nationality of her husband through specially privileged naturalization procedures; the grant of such nationality may be subject to such limitations as may be imposed in the interests of national security or public policy.

2. Each Contracting State agrees that the present Convention shall not be construed as affecting any legislation or judicial practice by which the alien wife of one of its nationals may, at her request, acquire her husband's nationality as a matter of right.

101. The Declaration on the Elimination of Discrimination against Women contains the following provision:

Article 5

Women shall have the same rights as men to acquire, change or retain their nationality. Marriage to an alien shall not automatically affect the nationality of the wife either by rendering her stateless or by forcing upon her the nationality of her husband.

102. The Convention on the Elimination of All Forms of Discrimination against Women contains the following provision:

Article 9

1. States Parties shall grant women equal rights with men to acquire, change or retain their nationality. They shall ensure in particular that neither marriage to an alien nor change of nationality by the husband during marriage shall autmatically change the nationality of the wife, render her stateless or force upon her the nationality of the husband.

2. States Parties shall grant women equal rights with men with respect to the nationality of their children.

103. Implementation of the Convention is monitored by the Committee on the Elimination of Discrimination against Women.

(c) *Property rights of married women*

104. Property relations between husband and wife are, in most countries, governed by a special body of regulations, usually set forth by law, or by special contracts envisaged by the law. These sets of rules are often termed "matrimonial régimes"; they control ownership and administration of property and the division of property when the marriage is dissolved. In cases where marriage is ended by the husband's death, laws on inheritance also must be taken into consideration.

105. The most common types of matrimonial régimes are those of community property and separation of property. Under the former, the property of the spouses is usually owned jointly, administered by the husband and divided equally between the spouses on the dissolution of marriage. Under the latter each spouse retains ownership not only of property owned before marriage but also of gains, earnings and other assets acquired during marriage; there is no community property during marriage.

106. After studying the question of matrimonial régimes at its eighth session, in 1954, the Commission on the Status of Women prepared a draft resolution on the subject which the Economic and Social Council adopted as resolution 547 I (XVIII) of 12 July 1954. In that resolution the Council expressed the belief that statutory matrimonial régimes in many countries were incompatible with the principle of equality of rights of spouses during marriage and at its dissolution proclaimed in the Universal Declaration of Human Rights, some of them depriving the wife during marriage of her rights over community property and over her own property and others depriving her at the dissolution of marriage of her share in property in the acquisition of which she had participated either directly or indirectly. The Council recommended that Member States should take all necessary steps to eliminate such discriminatory provisions from their legislation. It also drew their attention to the desirability of a statutory matrimonial régime which would provide for the separation of the property belonging to the spouses at the time of marriage and either for the separation of property acquired during marriage or for common ownership of property acquired by both spouses during marriage, such community property to be administered jointly by the spouses; and in either case, on dissolution of marriage, property acquired during marriage would be divided equally between them or their heirs.

(d) *Right of married women to engage in independent work*

107. The Commission on the Status of Women also studied, at its eighth session in 1954, the right of a married woman to engage in a business, profession or other occupation, and noted that under some legal systems the husband had the power to prevent his wife from engaging in independent work and that under others he had control over her earnings. On its recommendation the Economic and Social Council, in resolution 547 J (XVIII) of 12 July 1954, recommended that Governments take all necessary measures to ensure the right of a married woman to undertake independent work, to carry it on and to administer and dispose of her earnings without the necessity of securing her husband's authorization.

(e) *Parental rights and duties, including guardianship*

108. In resolution 587 D (XX) of 3 August 1955 the Economic and Social Council, endorsing the recommendations of the Commission on the Status of

Women, noted that in some legal systems parental authority belonged exclusively or primarily to the father; that in some countries in the event of loss of such authority it did not automatically pass to the mother; and in some instances on dissolution of marriage the custody of the children was awarded to the father, regardless of the merits of the case. The Council was of the opinion that these limitations were incompatible with the principle of equality of rights of the spouses during marriage and at its dissolution and accordingly recommended that States Members of the United Nations take steps to ensure equality between parents in the exercise of rights and duties with respect to their children.

109. At its fifteenth session (1961), the Commission on the Status of Women decided to study this question further. It asked the Secretary-General to prepare a preliminary report on parental rights and duties, including guardianship, based on information available to him, including the documentation of the seminars on the status of women in family law.

110. A report on this subject was presented to the Commission at its twentieth session, in 1967. After considering this report the Commission recommended —and the Economic and Social Council adopted—resolution 1207 (XLII) of 29 May 1967, in which it welcomed the generally discernible trend in many legal systems towards a sharing of parental authority on a basis of equality. The Council recommended that Governments of Member States take all possible measures to ensure equality between men and women in the exercise of parental rights and duties. It further recommended the following principles for ensuring such equality, taking account of the special characteristics of legislation in different countries and bearing in mind that in all cases the interest of the children should be paramount:

(a) Women shall have equal rights and duties with men in respect to guardianship of their minor children and the exercise of parental authority over them, including care, custody, education and maintenance;

(b) Both spouses shall have equal rights and duties with regard to the administration of the property of their minor children, with the legal limitations necessary to ensure as far as possible that it is administered in the interest of the children;

(c) The interest of the children shall be the paramount consideration in proceedings regarding custody of children in the event of divorce, annulment of marriage or judicial separation;

(d) No discrimination shall be made between men and women with regard to decisions regarding custody of children and guardianship or other parental rights in the event of divorce, annulment of marriage or judicial separation.

(f) Domicile of married women

111. In resolution 587 D (XX) of 3 August 1955 the Economic and Social Council, accepting the proposals of the Commission relating to the domicile of married women, noted that in the legal systems of many countries the domicile of the wife follows that of her husband; in these countries the wife, upon marriage, loses her original domicile and acquires the domicile of her husband, which she retains until the dissolution of the marriage, even if residing separately. The Council expressed the belief that such legal systems are incompatible with the principle of equality of spouses during the marriage, proclaimed in the Universal Declaration of Human Rights, and noted that their application resulted in particular hardships for married women in countries where domicile determined the jurisdiction of courts in matrimonial matters and where the law in the place of domicile governs a person's status. The Council recommended that Governments take all necessary measures to ensure the right of a married woman to an independent domicile.

(g) Inheritance laws as they affect women

112. On the recommendation of the Commission on the Status of Women, the Economic and Social Council, in resolution 884 D (XXXIV) of 16 July 1962, recommended a number of measures designed to ensure equality of inheritance rights of men and women.

113. In the resolution, the Council noted that in the legal systems of many countries inheritance rights of women, in intestate as well as in testamentary succession, were not equal to those of men. In some systems, the law deprives women of all inheritance rights, while in other systems the share of a woman is a fraction of the share of a male heir in the same degree of relationship. In some systems, the male heir is always preferred to the female in the order of succession, and in some others, the interest of the widow in the estate is either smaller than that of the widower, or is affected by special restrictions. Moreover, in some countries the inheritance rights and the capacity of women to make a will, to accept or refuse an inheritance or to be administrators or executors of estates, are affected by marriage in a manner incompatible with the principle of equality of rights of the spouses.

114. The Council recommended that Governments take all possible measures to ensure equality of inheritance rights of men and women by providing that men and women, in the same degree of relationship to the deceased, shall be entitled to equal shares in the estate and shall have an equal rank in the order of succession; and by providing further that the inheritance rights and the capacity of women to make a will, to accept or refuse an inheritance or to be administrators or executors of estates shall not be affected by marriage, and that the interest of the widow in the estate shall be equal to that of the widower.

(h) Improvement of the status of the unmarried mother

115. In 1962, the Sub-Commission on Prevention of Discrimination and Protection of Minorities decided, in resolution 5 (XIV) of 2 February 1962, to undertake a study of discrimination against persons born out of wedlock, and appointed one of its members, Mr. Vieno

Voitto Saario, as Special Rapporteur. On the basis of the final report[33] examined in January 1967, the Sub-Commission adopted a set of draft general principles on equality and non-discrimination in respect of persons born out of wedlock and transmitted them to the Commission on Human Rights for further consideration.

116. The Commission on the Status of Women examined the study and the draft principles later in 1967, and requested the Secretary-General to prepare a report concerning law and practice with respect to unmarried mothers. The study[34] was presented to the Commission at its twenty-third session, in 1972. At that and the following sessions the Commission prepared a series of recommendations which were eventually adopted by the Economic and Social Council.

117. In resolution 1514 (XLVIII) of 28 May 1970, the Council noted that the number of unmarried mothers was still increasing in some countries, and that owing to her status and the inadequacy of measures of social protection in her favour, the unmarried mother and her child were still the subject of discrimination in many countries; urged Member States to take adequate measures of social assistance in favour of the unmarried mother and the child born out of wedlock; and invited Member States, the specialized agencies and non-governmental organizations concerned to study the problems posed by the integration of the unmarried mother and her child in all spheres of society.

118. In resolution 1679 (LII) of 2 June 1972, the Council recommended to Governments of Member States a set of general principles for securing the acceptance of the unmarried mother and her child on an equal footing with other members of society. Among the principles recommended by the Council were the following:

Maternal filiation shall be recognized in law, in all cases, automatically as a consequence of the fact of birth;

Whatever the legal system applying in the case of married parents, the unmarried mother, whether paternal filiation is established or not, shall enjoy in all cases, as a parent, the fullest set of rights and duties provided for by law. In particular:

If maternal filiation only is established, the surname of the mother should be transmitted to her child, if possible, in such a manner as not to reveal the fact of birth out of wedlock;

If maternal filiation only is established, the nationality of the unmarried mother shall be transmitted to her child as a consequence of birth;

The unmarried mother should be vested in law with full parental authority over her child, in all cases, as an automatic consequence of the fact of birth;

Maintenance rights and obligations as between the unmarried mother and her child should be the same as between a sole parent and a child born in wedlock;

There should be no discrimination against the offspring of unmarried mothers in all matters of inheritance;

The unmarried mother should enjoy all the measures of social assistance and social security devised for mothers in general and for single parents in particular; and

There should be no discrimination against the unmarried mother in matters of employment, education and training as well as in access to child care facilities.

119. Pursuant to Council resolution 1514 (XLVIII), mentioned above, the Secretary-General includes information on the problems of unmarried mothers and their children in his reports on implementation of the Declaration on the Elimination of Discrimination against Women.

(i) *Legal capacity of married women*

120. At its twenty-third session, in 1970, the Commission on the Status of Women initiated a programme of studies in the field of family law based on article 6 of the Declaration. The first study dealt with the legal capacity of married women and resulted in the adoption by the Economic and Social Council, on the recommendation of the Commission, of resolution 1853 (LVI) of 16 May 1974, in which the Council took note of several situations which failed to conform to the provisions of article 6 and recommended corrective measures. Among other things, the Council noted the fact that in a number of legal systems: (*a*) married women did not enjoy the right to engage freely in independent work, and (*b*) married women who worked independently did not possess the legal capacity to manage and dispose of their earnings and were subject to other limitations which did not apply to their husbands. The Council recommended that Member States take all the measures necessary to ensure that the legal capacity of married women was equal to that of men with respect to: (*a*) gainful employment outside the home; (*b*) capacity to administer their property and the revenue of their work; (*c*) administration of the joint property of spouses; (*d*) parental authority over their children and the interests of those children; and (*e*) dissolution of marriage and its legal effects. The Council called upon Member States to provide adequate remedies, judicial or otherwise, to both spouses to help them solve their disagreements with respect to the questions mentioned above. It placed particular emphasis, in the case of such disagreements, upon the necessity of mediation through competent authorities with the assistance of personnel trained in all aspects of family relations.

(j) *Discrimination against women in the administration of penal law*

121. In resolution 1980/40 of 2 May 1980, adopted on the recommendation of the Commission on the Status of Women, the Economic and Social Council expressed

---

[33] United Nations publication, Sales No. E.68.XIV.3.

[34] E/CN.6/540.

deep concern about the fact that close relatives, particularly the spouses, mothers and children, of persons accused of a penal offence are often, because of their relationship to those persons, the victims of persecution, harassment and other infringements of their rights. The Council reaffirmed the principles governing the fundamental guarantees of the individual, as set forth particularly in articles 3, 6, 7 and 10 of the Universal Declaration of Human Rights, and called upon Governments to ensure the strict application of those provisions, and particularly to ensure that no one could be prosecuted, persecuted or harassed simply because of a family or social relationship with an accused or convicted person. The Council recommended that the competent international bodies should find ways to put an end to such action and in particular to provide effective protection for women and children to safeguard them against any reprisals.

(k) *Consent to marriage, minimum age for marriage and registration of marriages*

122. After making a detailed study of marriage, with particular regard to free consent to marriage, minimum age for marriage and registration of marriages, the Commission on the Status of Women, in 1961, drafted an international convention and a recommendation on these subjects. The purpose of the proposed instruments was to eliminate such practices as child marriage, brideprice, inheritance of widows and other practices especially harmful to women.

123. The Convention on Consent to Marriage, Minimum Age for Marriage and Registration of Marriages was adopted by the General Assembly in 1962. The Recommendation on the subject, containing similar provisions but applicable to all States rather than only these States parties to the Convention, was adopted by the General Assembly in 1965.

124. The Convention contains the following provisions:

Article 1

1. No marriage shall be legally entered into without the full and free consent of both parties, such consent to be expressed by them in person after due publicity and in the presence of the authority competent to solemnize the marriage and of witnesses, as prescribed by law.

2. Notwithstanding anything in paragraph 1 above, it shall not be necessary for one of the parties to be present when the competent authority is satisfied that the circumstances are exceptional and that the party has, before a competent authority and in such manner as may be prescribed by law, expressed and not withdrawn consent.

Article 2

States Parties to the present Convention shall take legislative action to specify a minimum age for marriage. No marriage shall be legally entered into by any person under this age, except where a competent authority has granted a dispensation as to age, for serious reasons, in the interest of the intending spouses.

Article 3

All marriages shall be registered in an appropriate official register by the competent authority.

(l) *Modification or abolition of discriminatory laws, customs and practices*

125. The Declaration on the Elimination of Discrimination against Women contains the following provision:

Article 2

All appropriate measures shall be taken to abolish existing laws, customs, regulations and practices which are discriminatory against women, and to establish adequate legal protection for equal rights of men and women, in particular:

(*a*) The principle of equality of rights shall be embodied in the constitution or otherwise guaranteed by law;

(*b*) The international instruments of the United Nations and the specialized agencies relating to the elimination of discrimination against women shall be ratified or acceded to and fully implemented as soon as practicable.

126. The Convention on the Elimination of All Forms of Discrimination against Women contains the following provisions:

Article 2

States Parties condemn discrimination against women in all its forms, agree to pursue by all appropriate means and without delay a policy of eliminating discrimination against women and, to this end, undertake:

(*a*) To embody the principle of the equality of men and women in their national constitutions or other appropriate legislation if not yet incorporated therein and to ensure, through law and other appropriate means, the practical realization of this principle;

(*b*) To adopt appropriate legislative and other measures, including sanctions where appropriate, prohibiting all discrimination against women;

(*c*) To establish legal protection of the rights of women on an equal basis with men and to ensure through competent national tribunals and other public institutions the effective protection of women against any act of discrimination;

(*d*) To refrain from engaging in any act or practice of discrimination against women and to ensure that public authorities and institutions shall act in conformity with this obligation;

(*e*) To take all appropriate measures to eliminate discrimination against women by any person, organization or enterprise;

(*f*) To take all appropriate measures, including legislation, to modify or abolish existing laws, regulations, customs and practices which constitute discrimination against women;

(*g*) To repeal all national penal provisions which constitute discrimination against women.

Article 3

States Parties shall take in all fields, in particular in the political, social, economic and cultural fields, all appropriate measures, including legislation, to ensure the full development and advancement of women, for the purpose of guaranteeing them the exercise and enjoyment of human rights and fundamental freedoms on a basis of equality with men.

(m) *Forward-looking Strategies*

127. The Forward-looking Strategies for the Advancement of Women to the Year 2000,[35] adopted by the World Conference to Review and Appraise the Achieve-

---

[35] *Report of the World Conference to Review and Appraise the Achievements of the United Nations Decade for Women: Equality, Development and Peace,* Nairobi, 15-26 July 1985 (United Nations publication, Sales No. E.85.IV.10).

ments of the United Nations Decade for Women: Equality, Development and Peace, held at Nairobi from 15 to 26 July 1985,[36] include the following paragraphs concerning the relationship between the law and the role, status and material circumstances of women:

Governments that have not yet done so are urged to sign the Convention on the Elimination of All Forms of Discrimination against Women and to take all the necessary steps to ensure its ratification, or their accession to it. They should consider the possibility of establishing appropriate bodies charged with reviewing the national legislation concerned and with drawing up recommendations thereon to ensure that the provisions of the Convention and of the other international instruments to which they are parties that are relevant to the role, status and material circumstances of women are complied with.

Governments that have not yet done so should establish appropriate institutional procedures whereby the application of a revised set of laws and administrative measures may be effectively enforced from the village level up and may be adequately monitored so that individual women may, without obstruction or cost of themselves, seek to have discriminatory treatment redressed. Legislation that concerns women as a group should also be effectively enforced and monitored so that areas of systemic or *de facto* discrimination against women can be redressed. To this end, positive action policy should be developed.

Agrarian reform measures have not always ensured women's rights even in countries where women predominate in the agricultural labour force. Such reforms should guarantee women's constitutional and legal rights in terms of access to land and other means of production and should ensure that women will control the products of their labour and their income, as well as benefits from agricultural inputs, research, training, credits and other infrastructural facilities.

National research institutions, both governmental and private, are urged to undertake investigations of the problems associated with the relationship between the law and the role, status and material circumstances of women. These should be integrated into the curricula of relevant educational institutions in an attempt to promote general knowledge and awareness of the law.

In the past decade there have been significant advances in the development of statistical concepts and methods for measuring inequality between women and men. The capabilities of national institutions concerned with statistics and women's issues should be improved to implement these concepts and methods in the regular statistical programmes of countries and to make effective use of these statistics in the policy-planning process. Training for producers and users of statistics on women should play a key role in this process.

In-depth research should be undertaken to determine instances when customary law may be discriminatory or protective of women's rights and the extent to which the interfaces between customary and statutory law may retard progress in the implementation of new legislatives measures. Particular attention should be paid to double standards in every aspect of life, with a view to abolishing them.

Law-reform committees with equal representation of women and men from Governments and from non-governmental organizations should be set up to review all laws, not only as a monitoring device but also with a view to determining research-related activities, amendments and new legislative measures.

Employment legislation should ensure equity and provide benefits for women not only in the conventional and formal labour force but also in the informal sector, particularly with regard to migrant and service workers, by providing minimum wage standards, insurance benefits, safe working conditions and the right to organize. Opportunities for similar guarantees and benefits should also be extended to women making vital economic contributions in activities involving food production and processing, fisheries and food distribution through trade. These benefits should also pertain to women working in family enterprises and, if possible, to other self-employed women in an effort to give due recognition to the vital contribution of all these informal and invisible economic activities to the development of human resources.

Civil codes, particularly those pertaining to family law, should be revised to eliminate discriminatory practices where these exist and wherever women are considered minors. The legal capacity of married women should be reviewed in order to grant them equal rights and duties.

Such social and economic development should be encouraged as would secure the participation of women as equal partners with men in all fields of work, equal access to all positions of employment, equal pay for work of equal value and equal opportunities for education and vocational training, and would co-ordinate the legislation on the protection of women at work with the need for women to work and be highly productive producers and managers of all political, economic and social affairs and would develop branches of the social services to make domestic duties easier for women and men.[37]

Measures for the implementation of legislation relating to working conditions for women must be taken.

Legislative and/or other measures should be adopted and implemented to secure for men and women the same right to work and to unemployment benefits, as well as to prohibit, through, *inter alia,* the imposition of sanctions, dismissal on the grounds of pregnancy or of maternity leave and discrimination in dismissals on the grounds of marital status. Legislative and other measures should be adopted and implemented to facilitate the return to the labour market of women who have left it for family reasons and to guarantee the right of women to return to work after maternity leave.

Governments should continue to take special action to institute programmes that would inform women workers of their rights under legislation and other remedial measures. The importance of freedom of association and the protection of the right to organize should be emphasized, this being particularly relevant to the position of women in employment. Special measures should be taken to ratify and implement in national legislation the relevant conventions and recommendations of the International Labour Organisation concerning the rights of women as regards access to equal employment opportunities, equal pay for work of equal value, equal working conditions, job security and maternity protection.

Marriage agreements should be based on mutual understanding, respect and freedom of choice. Careful attention should be paid to the equal participation and valuation of both partners so that the value of housework is considered equivalent of financial contributions.

The right of all women, in particular married women, to own, administer, sell or buy property independently should be guaranteed as an aspect of their equality and freedom under the law. The right to divorce should be granted equally to both partners under the same conditions, and custody of children decided in a non-discriminatory manner with full awareness of the importance of the input from both parents in the maintenance, rearing and socialization of children. Women should not forfeit their right to custody of their children or to any other benefits and freedoms simply because they have initiated a divorce. Without prejudice to the religious and cultural traditions of countries, and taking into account the *de facto* situations, legal or other appropriate provisions should be made to eliminate discrimination against single mothers and their children.

Appropriate action is necessary to ensure that the judiciary and all paralegal personnel are fully aware of the importance of the achievement by women of rights set out in internationally agreed instruments, constitutions and the law. Appropriate forms of in-service training and retraining should be designed and carried out for this purpose, with special attention given to the recruitment and training of women.

Special attention should be given in criminology training to the particular situation of women as victims of violent crimes, including crimes that violate women's bodies and result in serious physical and psychological damage. Legislation should be passed and laws enforced in every country to end the degradation of women through sex-related crimes. Guidance should be given to law enforcement and other authorities on the need to deal sensibly and sensitively with the victims of such crimes.

---

[36] *Ibid.,* paras. 60-76.

[37] The United States reserved its position on paragraphs 69 and 72 specifically because it did not agree with the concept of "equal pay for work of equal value" and maintained the principle of "equal pay for equal work".

B. Development

1. IMPROVEMENT OF THE ROLE OF WOMEN IN DEVELOPMENT

128. Since their establishment the Commission on the Status of Women, the Economic and Social Council, the General Assembly and many other bodies within the United Nations system have sought to improve the role of women in development and in particular to achieve their effective mobilization and integration in development programmes.

129. In a number of resolutions and decisions these bodies have repeatedly affirmed that women and men should participate and contribute on a basis of equality in the social, economic and political processes of development, including desision-making, and should share in improved conditions of life; underlined the importance of the integration and participation of women in the process of industrial development; and pointed out that accelerated development required the real and effective participation of women and men in all aspects of the development process.

(a) Advancement of women in developing countries

130. In resolution 771 H (XXX) of 25 July 1960, the Economic and Social Council requested the Secretary-General to study, in collaboration with Governments, the need for and possibilities of further United Nations assistance specially directed towards the efforts of developing countries to advance the status of women.

131. The Secretary-General presented reports on the subject[38] to the Commission at its sixteenth session, in 1962. On the recommendation of the Commission the Economic and Social Council adopted resolution 884 E (XXXIV) of 16 July 1962, on United Nations assistance for the advancement of women in developing countries. In the resolution the Council recommended to Governments "that they make full use, for the purpose of promoting and advancing the status of women in developing countries, of the services available under the regular programme and the Expanded Programme of Technical Assistance, as well as of the advisory services programme in human rights and the advisory social welfare services, by requesting the advisory services of experts, by promoting the attendance at seminars and other meetings, and by taking advantage of the availability of fellowships and scholarships".

132. The International Labour Organisation, the United Nations Educational, Scientific and Cultural Organization, the Food and Agriculture Organization of the United Nations, the World Health Organization and the United Nations Children's Fund were invited to strengthen and expand their programmes designed to meet the needs of women in developing countries, and to seek new methods to achieve this purpose. Women's non-governmental organizations were urged to stimulate public opinion with regard to the programmes of the United Nations which contribute to the advancement of women and by supplementing the efforts of the United Nations on the international and national levels. The Secretary-General was requested to direct his attention, when planning the various United Nations programmes of assistance, to the needs of women in developing countries, to include in these programmes projects directed to meet such needs, and to continue to utilize the available resources of the United Nations to advance the condition of women in the developing countries.

(b) Participation of women in community development

133. In 1965 the Commission on the Status of Women called for a study on "the participation of women in community development and the possibility of increasing the scope and content of their contribution", noting at the same time "the great importance of community development in stimulating the advancement of women".

134. Community development has been defined as: "the processes by which the efforts of the people themselves are united with those of governmental authorities to improve the economic, social and cultural conditions of communities, to integrate these communities into the life of the nation, and to enable them to contribute fully to national progress. This complex of processes in then made up of two essential elements: the participation by the people themselves in efforts to improve their level of living with as much reliance as possible on their own initiative; and the provision of technical and other services in ways which encourage the initiative, self-help and mutual help, and make these more effective. It is expressed in programmes designed to achieve a wide variety of specific improvements".[39]

135. The goals of community development may be said, therefore, to be twofold: (a) the comprehensive improvement of conditions in communities; and (b) the integration of the development of communities with national development. The methods used emphasize: (a) the initiative and voluntary efforts of local people to raise their own levels of living; and (b) the provision, mainly by the Government, of the measures, services and facilities needed for local programmes and projects. Community development then is essentially a partnership between the local people and the Government.

136. The interest of the Commission on the Status of Women in community development is focused on three main points: (a) the examination of the extent to which women are participating at the present time in community development programmes, especially in rural areas; (b) the consideration of ways in which existing programmes have helped to advance the status of women; and (c) the making of recommendations that would

---

[38] E/3493 and E/3566 and Add.1.

[39] *Official Records of the Economic and Social Council, Twenty-fourth Session, Annexes,* agenda item 4, document E/2931, annex III, paras. 1-2.

both improve the status of women and benefit the programmes themselves.

137. In 1971 the Secretary-General completed a report on the participation of women in community development. The report was issued in printed form in 1972[40] at the request of the Commission in resolution 7 (XXII) of 10 February 1969.

138. The studies made for the Commission on the Status of Women on this subject have been based primarily on information furnished by Governments. It is apparent from the information received that women participate with enthusiasm and interest in community development programmes in many countries, and that their contribution is considered highly valuable. The community development programmes include activities connected with education and training, especially literacy and adult education, vocational training and civic and political education; activities in the economic and social fields aimed at raising levels of living, such as health, nutrition, social welfare, housing and home management, family planning, agriculture, small-scale industry and handicrafts and co-operatives; and activities which provide training for community development work.

(c) *Improvement of the situation of women in rural areas*

139. In resolution 21, on the condition of women in rural areas, the World Conference of the International Women's Year took up a subject which had already been the concern of the World Population Conference held at Bucharest in August 1974 and the World Food Conference held in Rome in November of that year: the question of the condition of women in rural areas.

140. Bearing in mind that rural women in the developing world accounted for a substantial share of food production, that women everywhere generally played the main role in procuring and preparing food for family consumption, and that severe problems of rural unemployment, underemployment and misallocation of human resources affected women as well as men, the Conference called upon Governments:

(*a*) To identify needs and to formulate and implement, with greater financial and policy support, rural development programmes, particularly those which benefit women living in situations of rural poverty and of disadvantage relative to men;

(*b*) To carry out the statistical and information work necessary to identify and evaluate the participation of women in productive life and to measure the results of programmes for the betterment of rural life;

(*c*) To ensure legal parity and economic rights of women in the peasant family as an essential part of any rural development programme.

The Conference suggested

that further research should be undertaken with regard to the most effective design of systems of rural non-formal education, needed to equip women in rural areas with the necessary and additional skills relevant to their social and economic roles.

141. The General Assembly, taking Conference resolution 21 into account, adopted resolution 3523 (XXX) of 15 December 1975, on women in rural areas, in which it urged Governments

to accord within their respective plans, higher priority for:

(*a*) Gathering relevant data on the status and role of women in rural and low-income areas;

(*b*) Achieving socio-economic conditions based on the realization of the full and equal partnership of men and women in the development of society, both in law and in fact;

(*c*) Promoting agricultural productivity, agro-based industries and integrated rural development programmes.

Governments were also urged

to develop extensive training programmes relevant to women and to make full use of all existing and proposed research institutes and centres, particularly the regional and international institutes and centres for the advancement of women in rural areas.

The Secretary-General was requested to prepare and submit "guidelines for non-formal educational programmes designed to enable rural women to use fully their capabilities and to contribute to the development of society".

142. The Secretary-General submitted a report on women in rural areas to the General Assembly at its thirty-second session,[41] in compliance with the Assembly's request for biennial reports on the progress achieved in efforts to enable rural women to use their capabilities fully and to contribute to their full integration in development. The report contained a brief account of activities undertaken by the United Nations on behalf of rural women, and clearly showed the concern of the United Nations for the improvement of the condition of those women, both as a response to national awareness and initiatives in this regard, and as a necessary component of national and international rural development strategies and programmes.

143. At its thirty-seventh session, the attention of the General Assembly was drawn to the Declaration of Principles and the Programme of Action adopted by the World Conference on Agrarian Reform and Rural Development, organized at Rome by FAO. The Declaration called for the improvement of the legal status of women, for increasing access of women to social and economic services, for strengthening women's organization and participation, and for improving women's opportunities in formal and informal education as well as on the labour market.

144. In resolution 37/59 of 3 December 1982, the Assembly called upon Member States to take additional appropriate measures for further improving the economic and social conditions of women in rural areas; requested the Economic and Social Council, the Commission on the Status of Women, the regional commissions and other bodies of the United Nations system—in particular the Food and Agriculture Organization of the United Nations—to devote greater atention to the problems of elevating the status of rural women; and requested the Secretary-General to prepare a comprehensive report containing the observations and com-

---

[40] *Participation of Women in Community Development* (United Nations publication, Sales No. E.72.IV.8).

[41] A/32/269.

ments received from Governments on national experience in improving the situation of women in rural areas, paying special attention to such aspects as social insurance, mother and child care, health facilities, training, education and employment opportunities.

145. The Convention on the Elimination of All Forms of Discrimination against Women, adopted and opened for signature and ratification by General Assembly resolution 34/180 of 18 December 1979, contains the following provisions relating to improvement of the situation of women in rural areas:

Article 14

1. States Parties shall take into account the particular problems faced by rural women and the significant roles which rural women play in the economic survival of their families, including their work in the non-monetized sectors of the economy, and shall take all appropriate measures to ensure the application of the provisions of the present Convention to women in rural areas.

2. States Parties shall take all appropriate measures to eliminate discrimination against women in rural areas in order to ensure, on a basis of equality of men and women, that they participate in and benefit from rural development and, in particular, shall ensure to such women the right:

(*a*) To participate in the elaboration and implementation of development planning at all levels;

(*b*) To have access to adequate health care facilities, including information, counselling and services in family planning;

(*c*) To benefit directly from social security programmes;

(*d*) To obtain all types of training and education, formal and non-formal, including that relating to functional literacy, as well as, *inter alia,* the benefit of all community and extension services, in order to increase their technical proficiency;

(*e*) To organize self-help groups and co-operatives in order to obtain equal access to economic opportunities through employment or self-employment;

(*f*) To participate in all community activities;

(*g*) To have access to agricultural credit and loans, marketing facilities, appropriate technology and equal treatment in land agrarian reform as well as in land resettlement schemes;

(*h*) To enjoy adequate living conditions, particularly in relation to housing, sanitation, electricity and water supply, transport and communications.

146. At its thirty-ninth session the General Assembly, in resolution 39/126 of 14 December 1984, reaffirmed the importance attached to the need to improve the status of women and to ensure their full participation in the development process as agents and beneficiaries of development, and noted with appreciation that an interregional seminar on national experience relating to the improvement of the status of women in rural areas had been held at Vienna from 17 to 28 September 1984. The Secretary-General was requested to submit the report of that seminar, together with comments and observations thereon, to the Assembly at its fortieth session.

147. Later the Assembly in resolution 40/106 of 13 December 1985, considered the report of the Secretary-General on the Interregional Seminar on National Experience Relating to the Improvement of the Situation of Women in Rural Areas, held at Vienna from 17 to 28 September 1984, as well as the compilation of observations and comments made by Member States.[42] In its resolution 40/106 of 13 December 1985, the Assembly called upon Governments to elaborate and implement, as a part of national development strategies, special comprehensive programmes for improving the situation of women in rural areas and to establish monitoring and evaluating mechanisms involving women themselves for these programmes; and requested the organizations and funds concerned of the United Nations system to pay greater attention to the needs of rural women and to assist Member States, especially the developing countries, in the implementation of their national policies and programmes aimed at the advancement of rural women. The Assembly, further, requested the Secretary-General to prepare, in consultation with the Member States, a comprehensive report on the present status and perspectives for the improvement of the situation of rural women, and to submit that report to the Assembly at its forty-fourth session through the Economic and Social Council.

(d) *Effective mobilization and integration of women in development*

148. The Declaration on Social Progress and Development, proclaimed by the General Assembly on 11 December 1969, provides that "Social progress and development shall aim at the continuous raising of the material and spiritual standards of living of all members of society, with respect for and in accordance with human rights and fundamental freedoms", through the attainment of certain goals. Among the goals set out in article 11 of the Declaration are: "The protection of the rights of the mother and child; . . . the provision of measures to safeguard the health and welfare of women and particularly of working mothers during pregnancy and the infancy of their children, as well as of mothers whose earnings are the sole source of livelihood for the family; the granting to women of pregnancy and maternity leave and allowances without loss of employment or wages . . .".

149. Since the proclamation of the Declaration, the effective mobilization and integration of women in development has been a major concern of the United Nations system of organizations. It was expressed in the International Development Strategy for the Second United Nations Development Decade set out in General Assembly resolution 2626 (XXV) of 24 October 1970, and reiterated in the Declaration and Programme of Action on the Establishment of a New International Economic Order, set out in Assembly resolutions 3201 and 3202 (S-VI) of 1 May 1974; the Charter of Economic Rights and Duties of States, set out in Assembly resolution 3281 (XXIX) of 12 December 1974; as well as in Assembly resolutions 3517 (XXX) of 15 December 1975, on the mid-term review and ap-

---

[42] See A/40/239 and Add.1.

praisal of progress in the implementation of the International Development Strategy for the Second United Nations Development Decade, and 3362 (S-VII) of 16 September 1975, on development and international economic co-operation.

150. At its thirty-first session the General Assembly, in resolution 31/175 of 21 December 1976, urged Member States to implement the recommendations it had made earlier, to facilitate the equal participation of women with men in all development efforts and, in particular, to ensure that women have equal access to political parties, trade unions, training, especially in agriculture, co-operatives, and credit and loan systems, as well as equal opportunities to participate in policy-making in the economic field, in commerce and trade and in the advanced efforts of industry. Later, in resolution 35/78 of 5 December 1980, it requested the Secretary-General to prepare a comprehensive and detailed outline for an interdisciplinary and multisectoral world survey on the role of women in overall development, taking into account the relevant recommendations of the World Conference of the United Nations Decade for Women as well as the results of the relevant United Nations conferences on development issues.

151. Pursuant to that resolution, the Secretary-General submitted the comprehensive outline of a world survey on the role of women in development, and in response to General Assembly resolution 37/60 of 3 December 1982, the survey[43] was submitted to the World Conference to Review and Appraise the Achievements of the United Nations Decade for Women: Equality, Development and Peace. The Conference considered the survey and took it into consideration in the formulation and adoption of the Nairobi Forward-looking Strategies for the Advancement of Women. It was further considered by the General Assembly at its fortieth session and in its resolution 40/204 of 17 December 1985, the Assembly invited the Commission on the Status of Women to make specific action-oriented recommendations based on the survey as a part of the overall implementation of, and follow-up to, the Nairobi Strategies; invited the Commission at its thirty-first session to make a recommendation on future updates of the survey after 1989, bearing in mind the need for effective co-ordination with the follow-up activities of the World Conference to Review and Appraise the Achievements of the United Nations Decade for Women: Equality, Development and Peace, and to suggest terms of reference for the first update of the survey which should contain improved data and information on the role of women in development, including, *inter alia*, their role in the informal sector of the economy. The first update should be prepared by the Secretary-General for submission to the Assembly at its forty-fourth session, in 1989.

(e) *Forward-looking Strategies*

152. The Forward-looking Strategies for the Advancement of Women to the Year 2000,[44] adopted by the World Conference to Review and Appraise the Achievements of the United Nations Decade for Women: Equality, Development and Peace, held at Nairobi from 15 to 26 July 1985 set out basic strategies for the effective participation of women in development, as contained in the following paragraphs:

107. The commitment to remove obstacles to the effective participation of all women in development as intellectuals, policy-makers and decision-makers, planners, contributors and beneficiaries should be strengthened according to the specific problems of women in different regions and countries and the needs of different categories of women in them. That commitment should guide the formulation and implementation of policies, plans, programmes and projects, with the awareness that development prospects will be improved and society advanced through the full and effective participation of women.

108. Different socio-economic and cultural conditions are to be taken into account when identifying the foremost obstacles to the advancement of women. The current economic situation and the imbalances within the world monetary and financial system need adjustment programmes to overcome the difficulties. These programmes should not adversely affect the most vulnerable segments of society among whom women are disproportionately represented.

109. Development, being conceived as a comprehensive process, must be characterized by the search for economic and social objectives and goals that guarantee the effective participation of the entire population, especially women, in the process of development. It is also necessary to work in favour of the structural changes needed for the fulfilment of these aspirations. In line with these concerns, one should endeavour to speed up social and economic development in developing countries; accelerate the development of the scientific and technological capabilities of those countries; promote an equitable distribution of national income; and eradicate absolute poverty, experienced disproportionately by women and children, with the shortest possible delay by applying an overall strategy that, on the one hand, eliminates hunger and malnutrition and, on the other, works towards the construction of more just societies, in which women may reach their full development.

110. As the primary objective of development is to bring about sustained improvement in the well-being of the individual and of society and to bestow benefits on all, development should be seen not only as a desirable goal in itself but also as an important means of furthering equality of the sexes and the maintenance of peace.

111. Women should be an integral part of the process of defining the objectives and modes of development, as well as of developing strategies and measures for their implementation. The need for women to participate fully in political processes and to have an equal share of power in guiding development efforts and in benefiting from them should be recognized. Organizational and other means of enabling women to bring their interests and preferences into the evaluation and choice of alternative development objectives and strategies should be identified and supported. This would include special measures designed to enhance women's autonomy, bringing women into the mainstream of the development process on an equal basis with men, or other measures designed to integrate women fully in the total development effort.

112. The actual and potential impact on women of macro-economic processes operating at the international and national levels, as well as of financial spatial and physical development policies, should be assessed and appropriate modifications made to ensure that women are not adversely affected. Initial emphasis should be placed on employment, health and education. Priority should be given to the

[43] *World Survey on the Role of Women in Development, Report of the Secretary-General,* A/CONF.116/4, 11 December 1984.

[44] *Report of the World Conference to Review and Appraise the Achievements of the United Nations Decade for Women: Equality, Development and Peace,* Nairobi, 15-26 July 1985 (A/CONF.116/28 and Corr.1-4), chap. I, sect. A.

development of human resources, bearing in mind the need to avoid further increases in the work-load of women, particularly when alternative policies are formulated to deal with the economic and debt crisis.

113. With due recognition of the difficulties involved, Governments, international and regional organizations, and non-governmental organizations should intensify their efforts to enhance the self-reliance of women in a viable and sustained fashion. Because economic independence is a necessary pre-condition for self-reliance, such efforts should above all be focused on increasing women's access to gainful activities. Grass-roots participatory processes and planning approaches using local talent, expertise and resources are vital and should be supported and encouraged.

114. The incorporation of women's issues in all areas and sectors and at the local, national, regional and international levels should be institutionalized. To this end, appropriate machinery should be established or strengthened, and further legislative action taken. Sectoral policies and plans should be developed, and the effective participation of women in development should be integrated both in those plans and in the formulation and implementation of mainstream programmes and projects and should not be confined solely to statements of intent within plans or to small-scale, transitory projects relating to women.

115. The gender bias evident in most development programmes should be eliminated and the prejudices hindering the solution of women's problems removed. Particular attention should be given to the restructuring of employment, health and education systems and to ensuring equal access to land, capital and other productive resources. Emphasis should be placed on strategies to assist women in generating and keeping income, including measures designed to improve women's access to credit. Such strategies must focus on the removal of legal, customary and other barriers and on strengthening women's capacity to use existing credit systems.

116. Governments should seek means to increase substantially the number of women who are decision-makers, policy-makers, managers, professionals and technicians in both traditional and non-traditional areas and sectors. Women should be provided with equal opportunities for access to resources, especially education and training, in order to facilitate their equal representation at higher managerial and professional levels.

117. The role of women as a factor of development is in many ways linked to their involvement in various forms and levels of decision-making and management in economic and social structures, such as worker participation in management, industrial democracy, worker self-management, trade unions and co-operatives. The development of these forms of participation, which have an impact on the development and promotion of working and living conditions, and the inclusion of women in these forms of participation on an equal footing with men is of crucial importance.

118. The relationships between development and the advancement of women under specific socio-cultural conditions should be studied locally to permit the effective formulation of policies, programmes and projects designed for stable and equitable growth. The findings should be used to develop social awareness of the need for effective participation of women in development and to create realistic images of women in society.

119. It is vital that the link between the advancement of women and socio-economic and political development be emphasized for the effective mobilization of resources for women.

120. The remunerated and, in particular, the unremunerated contributions of women to all aspects and sectors of development should be recognized, and appropriate efforts should be made to measure and reflect these contributions in national accounts and economic statistics and in the gross national product. Concrete steps should be taken to quantify the unremunerated contributions of women to agriculture, food production, reproduction and household activities.

121. Concerted action should be directed towards the establishment of a system of sharing parental responsibilities by women and men in the family and by society. To this end, priority should be given to the provision of a social infrastructure that will enable society to share these responsibilities with families and, simultaneously, to bring about changes in social attitudes so that new or modified gender roles will be accepted, promoted and become exercisable. Household tasks and parental responsibilities, including decision-making regarding family size and child spacing, should be re-examined with a view to a better sharing of responsibilities between men and women and therefore, be conducive to the attainment of women's and men's self-reliance and to the development of future human resources.

122. Monitoring and evaluation efforts should be strengthened and directed specifically towards women's issues and should be based on a thorough review and extensive development of improved statistics and indicators on the situation of women as compared with men, over time and in all fields.

123. Appropriate national machinery should be established and should be utilized to integrate women effectively in the development process. To be effective, this machinery should be provided with adequate resources, commitment and authority to encourage and enhance development efforts.

124. Regional and international co-operation, within the framework of technical co-operation among developing countries, should be strengthened and extended to promote the effective participation of women in development.

2. IMPROVEMENT OF THE ECONOMIC STATUS OF WOMEN

153. The Commission on the Status of Women, the Economic and Social Council and the General Assembly have on numerous occasions considered questions and adopted measures aimed at improving the economic status of women. They have been assisted by the extensive work of the International Labour Organisation in this field, and by the reports on ILO activities of special interest from the standpoint of the employment of women which are submitted to the Commission at each session.

154. In resolution 587 F III (XX) of 3 August 1955, adopted on the initiative of the Commission, the Council recommended that all States should adopt legislative and other measures "to provide women with suitable economic opportunities by granting them equal rights with men to employment, pay, education, rest and material security in case of old age, illness or loss of capacity to work," and "encourage such action as will secure for women, in the economic field, equal rights with men in all countries, including the Trust and Non-Self-Governing Territories." In the same resolution the Council urged non-governmental organizations to work for the eradication of all possible obstacles in the way of economic emancipation of women.

(a) *ILO instruments concerning the economic status of women*

155. Even before the establishment of the United Nations, the International Labour Organisation was actively engaged in activities aimed at improving the economic status of women. Between 1919 and 1935 the ILO General Conference adopted such international conventions as the Maternity Protection Convention 1919 (No. 3); the Night Work (Women) Convention, 1919 (No. 4); the White Lead (Painting) Convention,

1921 (No. 13); the Night Work (Women) Convention (Revised), 1934 (No. 41); and the Underground Work (Women) Convention, 1935 (No. 45).[45]

156.   Later, the General Conference adopted the Night Work (Women) Convention (Revised), 1948 (No. 89); the Equal Remuneration Convention, 1951 (No. 100); the Maternity Protection Convention (Revised), 1952 (No. 103); the Plantations Convention, 1958 (No. 110) (Part VII: Maternity Protection); the Discrimination (Employment and Occupation) Convention, 1958, (No. 111); the Equality of Treatment (Social Security) Convention, 1962 (No. 118) (articles 2 and 4, where they refer to maternity benefit); the Social Policy (Basic Aims and Standards) Convention, 1962 (No. 117) (Part V: Non-Discrimination on Grounds of . . . Sex . . .); the Maximum Weight Convention, 1967 (No. 127); and the Human Resources Development Convention, 1975 (No. 142) (article 1, paragraph 5, where it refers to non-discrimination).

157.   In 1975, the General Conference proclaimed the Declaration on Equality of Opportunity and Treatment for Women Workers. In 1981 it adopted the Workers with Family Responsibilities Convention (No. 156), providing that men and women with family responsibilities should be able to exercise their right to work without being discriminated against because of those responsibilities; and in 1982 it adopted the Maintenance of Social Security Rights Convention (No. 157), providing for the establishment of an international system for the maintenance of acquired social security rights.

(b) *Equal pay for work of equal value*

158.   The question of equal pay for work of equal values has been a concern of the Commission on the Status of Women, the Economic and Social Council and the International Labour Organisation for many years.

159.   The Council, in resolution 121 (VI) of 10 March 1948, adopted on the initiative of the Commission, reaffirmed the principle of equal rights of men and women laid down in the preamble of the Charter of the United Nations, approved the principle of equal remuneration for work of equal value for men and women workers, and called upon Member States to implement that principle in every way, irrespective of nationality, race, language and religion.

160.   The Council at the same time transmitted a memorandum of the World Federation of Trade Unions on the subject to the International Labour Organisation —inviting the latter to proceed as rapidly as possible with the further consideration of the subject—and to the Commission on the Status of Women for its consideration and any suggestions it might wish to make to the Council.

161.   The International Labour Conference, as a result of its consideration of the matter, adopted the above-mentioned Equal Remuneration Convention (No. 100) and a supplementary Recommendation (No. 90) in 1951. By the Convention, States parties undertake, "by means appropriate to the methods in operation for determining rates of remuneration, to promote and, in so far as is consistent with such methods, to ensure the application to all workers of the principle of equal remuneration for men and women workers for work of equal value" (article 2). This principle may be applied by means of national laws or regulations, legally established or recognized machinery for wage determination, collective agreements between employers and workers or a combination of these various measures. Differential rates between workers, which correspond, without regard to sex, to differences, as determined by objective appraisal, in the work to be performed, shall not be considered as being contrary to this principle. The Recommendation lays down more detailed rules concerning the measures and methods for implementing the equal remuneration principle, and also calls for action to facilitate the application of this principle through measures in regard to vocational guidance and training, vocational placement, the provision of social welfare services to meet the needs of women workers, particularly those with family responsibilities, and promotion of equality as regards access to employment and posts.

162.   On the initiative of the Commission on the Status of Women, the Economic and Social Council reviewed on many occasions the progress achieved towards implementation of the principle of equal remuneration for work of equal value. In a number of resolutions, the Council urged Member States to ratify the Equal Remuneration Convention or otherwise to implement its provisions, and to apply and promote consistently the principle of equal pay for equal work in accordance with the Convention. It also called upon ILO "to continue to follow the introduction of the principle of equal pay for equal work on a world scale, and to bear this principle in mind in considering working and social questions on an international level."

163.   The International Labour Conference in 1975, and again in 1986, reviewed a world-wide survey based on reports submitted by Governments under articles 19 and 22 of the ILO Constitution, on the position of their law and practice respecting the equal pay principle contained in the Equal Remuneration Convention, 1951 (No. 100). As mentioned above, the Conference adopted in 1975 a Declaration on Equality of Opportunity and Treatment for Women Workers and two resolutions, one concerning a plan of action with a view to promoting equality of opportunity and treatment for women workers and the other calling for a study of the need for new international instruments to supplement the provisions of the Equal Remuneration Convention, 1951 (No. 100), and the Discrimination (Employment and Occupation) Convention, 1958 (No. 111).

---

[45] For the texts of the Conventions, see *International Labour Conventions and Recommendations, 1919-1981,* International Labour Office, Geneva, Switzerland, 1985.

(c) Workers with family responsibilities

164. A significant early development in this field was the unanimous adoption by the International Labour Conference in 1965 of the Employment (Women with Family Responsibilities) Recommendation (No. 123), providing that the competent national authorities should, in co-operation with the public and private organizations concerned, in particular employers' and workers' organizations and in accordance with national and local needs and possibilities, (a) pursue an appropriate policy with a view to enabling women with family responsibilities who work outside their home to exercise their right to do so without being subject to discrimination and in accordance with the principles laid down in the Discrimination (Employment and Occupation) Convention, 1958, as well as in other standards adopted by the International Labour Conference relating to women; and (b) encourage, facilitate or themselves undertake the development of services to enable women to fulfil their various responsibilities at home and at work harmoniously. Other provisions are intended to facilitate women's entry into employment, or re-entry after a comparatively long absence, so that they may enjoy equality of opportunity and training to enable them to become integrated into the labour force on a footing of equality.

165. A second significant development occurred in 1981 with the adoption of the Workers with Family Responsibilities Convention (No. 156) and Recommendation (No. 165). These instruments apply to both men and women workers who have responsibilities in relation to their dependent children and other members of their immediate family who clearly need their care and support. The Convention includes the following substantive provisions:

Article 1

1. This Convention applies to men and women workers with responsibilities in relation to their dependent children, where such regulations-sponsibilities restrict their possibilities of preparing for, entering, participating in or advancing in economic activity.

2. The provisions of this Convention shall also be applied to men and women workers with responsibilities in relation to other members of their immediate family who clearly need their care or support, where such responsibilities restrict their possibilities of preparing for, entering, participating in or advancing in economic activity.

3. For the purposes of this Convention, the terms "dependent child" and "other member of the immediate family who clearly needs care or support" mean persons defined as such in each country by one of the means referred to in article 9 of this Convention.

4. The workers covered by virtue of paragraphs 1 and 2 of this article are hereinafter referred to as "workers with family responsibilities".

Article 2

This Convention applies to all branches of economic activity and all categories of workers.

Article 3

1. With a view to creating effective equality of opportunity and treatment for men and women workers, each Member shall make it an aim of national policy to enable persons with family responsibilities who are engaged or wish to engage in employment to exercise their right to do so without being subject to discrimination and, to the extent possible, without conflict between their employment and family responsibilities.

2. For the purposes of paragraph 1 of this article, the term "discrimination" means discrimination in employment and occupation as defined by articles 1 and 5 of the Discrimination (Employment and Occupation) Convention, 1958.

Article 4

With a view to creating effective equality of opportunity and treatment for men and women workers, all measures compatible with national conditions and possibilities shall be taken—

(a) to enable workers with family responsibilities to exercise their right to free choice of employment; and

(b) to take account of their needs in terms and conditions of employment and in social security.

Article 5

All measures compatible with national conditions and possibilities shall further be taken—

(a) to take account of the needs of workers with family responsibilities in community planning; and

(b) to develop or promote comunity services, public or private, such as child-care and family services and facilities.

Article 6

The competent authorities and bodies in each country shall take appropriate measures to promote information and education which engender broader public understanding of the principle of equality of opportunity and treatment for men and women workers and of the problems of workers with family responsibilities, as well as a climate of opinion conducive to overcoming these problems.

Article 7

All measures compatible with national conditions and possibilities, including measures in the field of vocational guidance and training, shall be taken to enable workers with family responsibilities to become and remain integrated in the labour force, as well as to re-enter the labour force after an absence due to those responsibilities.

Article 8

Family responsibilities shall not, as such, constitute a valid reason for termination of employment.

Article 9

The provisions of this Convention may be applied by laws or regulations, collective agreements, works rules, arbitration awards, court decisions or a combination of these methods, or in any other manner consistent with national practice which may be appropriate, account being taken of national conditions.

Article 10

1. The provisions of this Convention may be applied by stages if necessary, account being taken of national conditions: Provided that such measures of implementation as are taken shall apply in any case to all the workers covered by article 1, paragraph 1.

. . .

(d) Age of retirement and social security benefits

166. Two subjects studied by the Commission on the Status of Women at several sessions between the years 1958-1963 were the age of retirement and pension rights, which in many countries are not the same for men and women workers. After preliminary consideration of the question on the basis of information furnished by the United Nations Secretariat and by ILO, the Commission recognized that the question was one of

some complexity on which differences of opinion existed; and it decided in 1960 to recommend that the Economic and Social Council invite ILO to make a complete study of the subject. The Council endorsed this recommendation in resolution 771 F (XXX) of 25 July 1960. ILO submitted a comprehensive report to the Commission, which was first discussed in 1963.[46] The Commission noted, in resolution 9 (XVII) of 25 March 1963, that although there was a trend towards equal provisions in retirement for men and women, a divergence of views existed among Governments and women's organizations in various countries about the pensionable ages for men and women. It recommended that the provisions on age of retirement and right to a pension "should be sufficiently flexible to meet varied and changing circumstances, individual needs and reasonable individual preferences as regards effective retirement, bearing in mind the encouraging trend towards equal economic conditions for the work of men and women, including equal provisions in the matter of the age of retirement and the right to pension".

167. The Declaration on Equality of Opportunity and Treatment for Women Workers, adopted by the ILO General Conference in 1975, specified that there should be no discrimination against women in respect of social security and provisions concerning retirement and pensions, and that differences in the treatment of men and women under such schemes should be reviewed and revised. The Declaration also called for special measures to be taken, as necessary and appropriate, to ensure equality of treatment for workers employed regularly on a part-time basis, the majority of whom were women, with respect to *pro rata* fringe benefits.

168. With regard to maternity benefits and protection, part VII (Maternity Benefit) of the ILO Social Security (Minimum Standards) Convention, 1952 (No. 102) requires women in prescribed classes of employees or of the economically active population to be protected against contingencies including pregnancy and confinement and their consequences and suspension of earnings. More generally, under ILO Conventions Nos. 3, 103 and 110 (part VII) and the supplementary Recommendations, appropriate arrangements affecting the economic status of women workers in case of maternity include the provision of medical care, the granting of leave before and after childbirth, the provision of cash benefits during such leave, the right to be given other suitable work in case of otherwise harmful employment, safeguarding of remuneration or means of subsistence where they are unable to perform their normal work during pregnancy or after confinement, protection against termination of employment or diminution of connected rights, and adaptation of working hours for working mothers.

(e) *Repercussions of scientific and technical progress*

169. In resolution 1136 (XLI) of 26 July 1966, the Economic and Social Council invited the International Labour Organisation "to study the repercussions of scientific and technical progress on the position of women in the matter of labour and employment", and to submit a report to the Commission on the Status of Women, covering the results of its study and the measures taken by ILO with regard to such repercussions. The reports prepared by ILO[47] were considered by the Commission and the Council. The Council, in resolution 1513 (XLVIII) of 28 May 1970, noted that certain unfavourable consequences of scientific and technical progress weighed more heavily upon the status of women workers, due in part to the low degree of skill of most women workers and the difficulty in changing occupations resulting therefrom, and also to women's limited geographical mobility, resulting usually from their family responsibilities.

170. The Council requested Member States:

(a) To make provision in school programmes for appropriate general education that prepares the ground for a flexible vocational training which can be adjusted at all times to the structure of employment, and to which girls and boys have equal access under the same conditions;

(b) To ensure that lifelong adult education, accelerated vocational training and vocational and other retraining are available to men and women under the same conditions;

(c) To see to it that new opportunities for employment are accorded on the basis of individual ability and aptitudes, irrespective of sex and without division of work into men's and women's work;

(d) To see to it that no reduction is permitted in the employment of women, in particular in skilled work;

(e) To pay special attention to the problems of environment, social installations, hygiene and occupational safety associated with scientific and technological progress.

171. The Council requested the Secretary-General and the specialized agencies concerned, in particular ILO, as well as Member States, to continue to study the question and to submit reports to the Commission on the Status of Women. ILO was also requested to continue its review of international conventions from the point of view of changes that occurred as a result of scientific and technical progress.

(f) *Access of women to financial assistance*

172. Recognizing the difficulties encountered by women in many countries of the world in securing credit and loans for activities which enhanced their productive capacities and thus the contribution of their full share to the development of their families and communities and to their consequent full integration into development, the World Conference of the International Women's Year adopted resolution 10, on access of women to financial assistance, in which it recommended that Governments in the countries concerned:

[46] E/CN.6/394 and Corr.1; E/CN.6/410.

[47] E/CN.6/499, E/CN.6/500 and E/CN.6/539 and Add.1.

(a) Establish mechanisms to facilitate the extension of credit to meet the special needs of women of low-income groups in rural and urban areas;

(b) Facilitate also the access of women in low-income groups to existing financial institutions;

(c) Encourage and commend the initiatives taken by non-governmental and voluntary women's organizations to establish their own financial institutions and banks.

173. Reaffirming the above-mentioned resolution, the General Assembly in resolution 3522 (XXX) of 15 December 1975 urged "Governments and governmental and non-governmental organizations to support more vigorously official and private efforts to extend to women the facilities now being offered only to men by financial and lending institutions"; and requested "Governments to encourage all efforts by women's organizations, co-operatives and lending institutions which will enable women at the lowest level in rural and urban areas to obtain credit and loans to improve their economic activities and integration in national development". The Assembly further urged "Governments and the organizations of the United Nations development system, including specialized agencies and non-governmental organizations, to incorporate, in their training programmes, workshops and seminars, courses designed to improve the efficiency of women in business and financial management".

(g) *Participation of women in rural development*

174. The Declaration of Principles and Programme of Action adopted in July 1979 by the World Conference on Agrarian Reform and Rural Development, meeting at Rome, stresses the basic principle that "Women should participate and contribute on an equal basis with men in the social, economic and political process of rural development and share fully in improved conditions of life in rural areas". The Declaration further states that "Recognition of the vital role of women in socio-economic life, in both agricultural and non-agricultural activities, . . . is a prerequisite for successful rural development planning and implementation. Rural development based on growth with equity will require full integration of women . . .".

(h) *Provisions of international instruments*

175. The question of discrimination against women in employment and in other areas of economic and social life has been dealt with in a number of international instruments, mentioned in section (a) above, including the ILO Discrimination (Employment and Occupation) Convention, 1958 (No. 111), adopted by the International Labour Conference on 25 June 1958; the Declaration on the Elimination of Discrimination against Women, proclaimed by General Assembly resolution 2263 (XXII) of 7 November 1967; and the Convention on the Elimination of All Forms of Discrimination against Women, adopted by General Assembly resolution 34/180 of 18 December 1979.

176. The Discrimination (Employment and Occupation) Convention contains the following provisions:

Article 1

1. For the purpose of this Convention the term "discrimination" includes—

(a) any distinction, exclusion or preference made on the basis of race, colour, sex, religion, political opinion, national extraction or social origin, which has the effect of nullifying or impairing equality of opportunity or treatment in employment or occupation;

(b) such other distinction, exclusion or preference which has the effect of nullifying or impairing equality of opportunity or treatment in employment or occupation as may be determined by the Member concerned after consultation with representative employers' and workers' organisations, where such exist, and with other appropriate bodies.

2. Any distinction, exclusion or preference in respect of a particular job based on the inherent requirements thereof shall not be deemed to be discrimination.

3. For the purpose of this Convention the terms employment and occupation include access to vocational training, access to employment and to particular occupations, and terms and conditions of employment.

Article 2

Each Member for which this Convention is in force undertakes to declare and pursue a national policy designed to promote, by methods appropriate to national conditions and practice, equality of opportunity and treatment in respect of employment and occupation, with a view to eliminating any discrimination in respect thereof.

Article 3

Each Member for which this Convention is in force undertakes, by methods appropriate to national conditions and practice—

(a) to seek the co-operation of employers' and workers' organisations and other appropriate bodies in promoting the acceptance and observance of this policy;

(b) to enact such legislation and to promote such educational programmes as may be calculated to secure the acceptance and observance of the policy;

(c) to repeal any statutory provisions and modify any administrative instructions or practices which are inconsistent with the policy;

(d) to pursue the policy in respect of employment under the direct control of a national authority;

(e) to ensure observance of the policy in the activities of vocational guidance, vocational training and placement services under the direction of a national authority;

(f) to indicate in its annual reports on the application of the Convention the action taken in pursuance of the policy and the results secured by such action.

Article 4

Any measures affecting an individual who is justifiably suspected of, or engaged in, activities prejudicial to the security of the State shall not be deemed to be discrimination, provided that the individual concerned shall have the right to appeal to a competent body established in accordance with national practice.

Article 5

1. Special measures of protection or assistance provided for in other Conventions or Recommendations adopted by the International Labour Conference shall not be deemed to be discrimination.

2. Any Member may, after consultation with representative employers' and workers' organisations, where such exist, determine that other special measures designed to meet the particular requirements of persons who, for reasons such as sex, age, disablement, family responsibilities or social or cultural status, are generally recognised to require special protection or assistance, shall not be deemed to be discrimination.

177. The Declaration on the Elimination of Discrimination against Women contains the following provision:

Article 10

1. All appropriate measures shall be taken to ensure to women, married or unmarried, equal rights with men in the field of economic and social life, and in particular:

(a) The right, without discrimination on grounds of marital status or any other grounds, to receive vocational training, to work, to free choice of profession and employment, and to professional and vocational advancement;

(b) The right to equal remuneration with men and to equality of treatment in respect of work of equal value;

(c) The right to leave with pay, retirement privileges and provision for security in respect of unemployment, sickness, old age or other incapacity to work;

(d) The right to receive family allowances on equal terms with men.

2. In order to prevent discrimination against women on account of marriage or maternity and to ensure their effective right to work, measures shall be taken to prevent their dismissal in the event of marriage or maternity and to provide paid maternity leave, with the guarantee of returning to former employment, and to provide the necessary social services, including child-care facilities.

3. Measures taken to protect women in certain types of work, for reasons inherent in their physical nature, shall not be regarded as discriminatory.

178. The Convention on the Elimination of All Forms of Discrimination against Women contains the following provisions:

Article 11

1. States Parties shall take all appropriate measures to eliminate discrimination against women in the field of employment in order to ensure, on a basis of equality of men and women, the same rights, in particular:

(a) The right to work as an inalienable right of all human beings;

(b) The right to the same employment opportunities, including the application of the same criteria for selection in matters of employment;

(c) The right to free choice of profession and employment, the right to promotion, job security and all benefits and conditions of service and the right to receive vocational training and retraining, including apprenticeships, advanced vocational training and recurrent training;

(d) The right to equal remuneration, including benefits, and to equal treatment in respect of work of equal value, as well as equality of treatment in the evaluation of the quality of work;

(e) The right to social security, particularly in cases of retirement, unemployment, sickness, invalidity and old age and other incapacity to work, as well as the right to paid leave;

(f) The right to protection of health and to safety in working conditions, including the safeguarding of the function of reproduction.

2. In order to prevent discrimination against women on the grounds of marriage or maternity and to ensure their effective right to work, States Parties shall take appropriate measures:

(a) To prohibit, subject to the imposition of sanctions, dismissal on the grounds of pregnancy or of maternity leave and discrimination in dismissals on the basis of marital status;

(b) To introduce maternity leave with pay or with comparable social benefits without loss of former employment, seniority or social allowances;

(c) To encourage the provision of the necessary supporting social services to enable parents to combine family obligations with work responsibilities and participation in public life, in particular through promoting the establishment and development of a network of child-care facilities;

(d) To provide special protection to women during pregnancy in types of work proved to be harmful to them.

3. Protective legislation relating to matters covered in this article shall be reviewed periodically in the light of scientific and technological knowledge and shall be revised, repealed or extended as necessary.

Article 13

States Parties shall take all appropriate measures to eliminate discrimination against women in other areas of economic and social life in order to ensure, on a basis of equality of men and women, the same rights, in particular:

(a) The right to family benefits;

(b) The right to bank loans, mortgages and other forms of financial credit;

(c) The right to participate in recreational activities, sports and all aspects of cultural life.

(i) Forward-looking Strategies

179. The Forward-looking Strategies for the Advancement of Women to the Year 2000,[48] adopted by the World Conference to Review and Appraise the Achievements of the United Nations Decade for Women: Equality, Development and Peace, held at Nairobi from 15 to 26 July 1985, include measures for specific action in the area of employment, as contained in the following paragraphs:

132. Special measures aimed at the advancement of women in all types of employment should be consistent with the economic and social policies promoting full productive and freely chosen employment.

133. Policies should provide the means to mobilize public awareness, political support, and institutional and financial resources to enable women to obtain jobs involving more skills and responsibility, including those at the managerial level, in all sectors of the economy. These measures should include the promotion of women's occupational mobility, especially in the middle and lower levels of the workforce, where the majority of women work.

134. Governments that have not yet done so should ratify and implement the Convention on the Elimination of All Forms of Discrimination against Women and other international instruments relating to the improvement of the conditions of women workers.

135. Measures based on legislation and trade union action should be taken to ensure equity in all jobs and avoid exploitative trends in part-time work, as well as the tendency towards the feminization of part-time, temporary and seasonal work.

136. Flexible working hours for all are strongly recommended as a measure for encouraging the sharing of parental and domestic responsibilities by women and men, provided that such measures are not used against the interests of employees. Re-entry programmes, complete with training and stipends, should be provided for women who have been out of the labour force for some time. Tax structures should be revised so that the tax liability on the combined earnings of married couples does not constitute a disincentive to women's employment.

137. Eliminating all forms of employment discrimination, *inter alia* through legislative measures, especially wage differentials between women and men carrying out work of equal value, is strongly recommended to all parties concerned. Additional programmes should help

---

[48] *Report of the World Conference to Review and Appraise the Achievements of the United Nations Decade for Women: Equality, Development and Peace,* Nairobi, 15-26 July 1985 (United Nations publication, Sales No. E.85.IV.10), chap. II, C. 2.

to overcome still existing disparities in wages between women and men. Differences in the legal conditions of work of women and men should also be eliminated, where there are disadvantages to women, and privileges should be accorded to male and female parents. Occupational desegregration of women and men should be promoted.

138. The public and private sectors should make concerted efforts to diversify and create new employment opportunities for women in the traditional, non-traditional and high productivity areas and sectors in both rural and urban areas through the design and implementation of incentive schemes for both employers and women employees and through widespread dissemination of information. Gender stereotyping in all areas should be avoided and the occupational prospects of women should be enhanced.

139. The working conditions of women should be improved in all formal and informal areas by the public and private sectors. Occupational health and safety and job security should be enhanced and protective measures against work-related health hazards effectively implemented for women and men. Appropriate measures should be taken to prevent sexual harassment on the job or sexual exploitation in specific jobs, such as domestic service. Appropriate measures for redress should be provided by Governments and legislative measures guaranteeing these rights should be enforced. In addition, Governments and the private sector should put in place mechanisms to identify and correct harmful working conditions.

140. National planning should give urgent consideration to the development and strengthening of social security and health schemes and maternity protection schemes in keeping with the principles laid down in the ILO maternity protection convention and maternity protection recommendation and other relevant ILO conventions and recommendations as a prerequisite to the hastening of women's effective participation in production, and all business and trade unions should seek to promote the rights and compensations of working women and to ensure that appropriate infrastructures are provided. Parental leave following the birth of a child should be available to both women and men and preferably shared between them. Provision should be made for accessible child-care facilities for working parents.

141. Governments and non-governmental organizations should recognize the contribution of older women and the importance of their input in those areas that directly affect their well-being. Urgent attention should be paid to the education and training of young women in all fields. Special retraining programmes including technical training should also be developed for young women in both urban and rural sectors, who lack qualifications and are ill-equipped to enter productive employment. Steps should be taken to eliminate exploitative treatment of young women at work, in line with ILO Convention No. 111 concerning discrimination in respect of employment and occupation, 1958 and ILO Convention No. 122 concerning employment policy, 1964.

142. National planning, programmes and projects should launch a twofold attack on poverty and unemployment. To enable women to gain access to equal economic opportunities, Governments should seek to involve and integrate women in all phases of the planning, delivery and evaluation of multisectoral programmes that eliminate discrimination against women, provide required supportive services and emphasize income generation. An increased number of women should be hired in national planning mechanisms. Particular attention should be devoted to the informal sector since it will be the major employment outlet of a considerable number of underprivileged urban and rural women. The co-operative movement could play an indispensable role in this area.

143. Recognition and application should be given to the fact that women and men have equal rights to work and, on the same footing, to acquire a personal income on equal terms and conditions, regardless of the economic situation. They should be given opportunities in accordance with the protective legislation of each country and especially in the labour market, in the context of measures to stimulate economic development and to promote employment growth.

144. In view of the persistence of high unemployment levels in many countries, Governments should endeavour to strengthen the efforts to cope with this issue and provide more job opportunities for women. Given that in many cases women account for a disproportionate share of total unemployment, that their unemployment rates

are higher than those of men and that, owing to lower qualifications, geographical mobility and other barriers, women's prospects for alternative jobs are mostly limited, more attention should be given to unemployment as it affects women. Measures should be taken to alleviate the consequences of unemployment for women in declining sectors and occupations. In particular, training measures must be instituted to facilitate the transition.

145. Although general policies designed to reduce unemployment or to create jobs may benefit both men and women, by their nature they are often of greater assistance to men than to women. For this reason, specific measures should be taken to permit women to benefit equally with men from national policies to create jobs.

146. As high unemployment among youth wherever it exists, is a matter of serious concern, policies designed to deal with this problem should take into account that unemployment rates for young women are often much higher than those for young men. Moreover, measures aimed at mitigating unemployment among youth should not negatively affect the employment of women in other age groups—for example, by lowering minimum wages. Women should not face any impediment to employment opportunities and benefits in cases where their husbands are employed.

147. Governments should also give special attention to women in the peripheral or marginal labour market, such as those in unstable temporary work or unregulated part-time work, as well as to the increasing number of women working in the informal economy.

180. The Forward-looking Strategies also outline measures for action to enhance the role of women in science and technology for development and to deal with repercussions of scientific and technical progress, as contained in the following paragraphs:

200. The full and effective participation of women in the decision-making and implementation process related to science and technology, including planning and setting priorities for research and development, and the choice, acquisition, adaptation, innovation and application of science and technology for development should be enhanced. Governments should reassess their technological capabilities and monitor current processes of change so as to anticipate and ameliorate any adverse impact on women, particularly adverse effects upon the quality of job.

201. The involvement of women in all of the peaceful uses of outer space should be enhanced, and effective measures should be undertaken to integrate women into all levels of decision-making and the implementation of such activities. In all countries special efforts should be made by Governments and non-governmental organizations to provide women and women's organizations with information on the peaceful uses of outer space. Special incentives should be provided to enable women to obtain advanced education and training in areas related to outer space in order to expand their participation in the application of outer space technology for peaceful uses, especially in the high-priority development areas of water, health, energy, food production and nutrition. To achieve these goals, increased opportunities and encouragement should be given to women to study science, mathematics and engineering at the university levels and to girls to study mathematics and science at the pre-university level.

202. Women with appropriate skills should be employed at managerial and professional levels and not restricted to service-level jobs. Special measures should be taken to improve working conditions for women in the science and technology fields, to eliminate discriminatory classification of jobs and to protect the right of women to promotion. Efforts should be made to ensure that women obtain their fair share of jobs at all levels in new technology industries.

203. Major efforts should be undertaken and effective incentives created to increase the access of women to both scientific and technological education and training. To achieve these goals, efforts should be made by Governments and women themselves to enhance, where necessary, the change of attitudes towards women's performance in scientific fields.

204. The potential and actual impact of science and technology on the developments that affect women's integration into the various sectors of the economy, as well as on their health, income and status, should be assessed. Relevant findings should be integrated in policy

formulation to ensure that women benefit fully from available technologies and that any adverse effects are minimized.

205. Efforts in the design and delivery of appropriate technology to women should be intensified, and attention should be given to the achievement of the best possible standard in such technologies. In particular, the implications of advances in medical technology for women should be carefully examined.

3. IMPROVEMENT OF THE STATUS AND ROLE OF WOMEN IN EDUCATION, SCIENCE AND CULTURE

181. Improvement of the status and role of women in education, science and culture, and the elimination of discrimination against women in the field of education, are questions which have been considered on many occasions by the Commission on the Status of Women, the Economic and Social Council and the General Assembly.

182. The Council, on the recommendation of the Commission, requested Members of the United Nations "to grant women equal educational rights with men and to ensure that they are afforded genuine educational opportunities, irrespective of nationality, race or religion", in resolution 154 F (VII) of 23 August 1948. In the same resolution, the Council suggested that UNESCO include in its reports information on progress achieved and plans for improving educational opportunities for women.

183. A few years later, in resolution 547 K (XVIII) of 12 July 1954, the Council recommended that States should:

(a) Take the necessary steps to ensure that women have equal access with men to all types of education, without any of the distinctions mentioned in article 2 of the Universal Declaration of Human Rights;

(b) Enact the necessary laws and regulations to eliminate all forms of discrimination against women in education and to ensure access for women to all types of education, including vocational and technical education, and equal opportunities to obtain State scholarships for education in any field and in preparation for all careers;

(c) Take the necessary measures to institute free, compulsory primary education and take full advantage of the facilities and resources of UNESCO in developing additional educational opportunities for girls and women, as needed.

184. In the following years, the Commission on the Status of Women and the Economic and Social Council have examined at regular intervals reports prepared by UNESCO on particular aspects of the education of girls and women, and adopted recommendations to Member States on such subjects as the access of girls and women to primary, secondary and higher education; to technical and vocational education; and to the teaching profession.

(a) *Programme for the advancement of women through access to education, science and culture*

185. A development of considerable importance in UNESCO's activities to improve the access of girls and women to education is its elaboration of a long-term programme for the advancement of women through access to education, science and culture. The programme was approved by the General Conference of UNESCO at its fourteenth session in 1966.

186. The Director-General of UNESCO was authorized by the General Conference,

in co-operation with the United Nations and the appropriate specialized agencies, to intensify long-term action to achieve full equality for women and, consequently, to hasten the advancement of women and their full participation in the economic and social development of their countries through access to education, science and culture, and to assist Member States at their request in their efforts to elaborate and apply a general policy directed to this end, in particular:

(a) to implement a study, research and training programme carried out in co-operation with Member States in the field of education, the social and natural sciences and communication;

(b) to aid government projects within UNESCO's sphere of activity which are designed to meet the need for the advancement of women and girls in various regions both rural and urban and to participate, in co-operation with a Member State, in the implementation of an experimental project, and to this end to participate in the activities of Member States;

(c) to give technical and financial support to activities planned and carried out by international non-governmental organizations working within the field of UNESCO's activities to facilitate the full participation of women and girls in the economic and social development of their countries.[49]

187. United Nations organs welcomed the initiative taken by UNESCO and expressed their support for the programme. Since 1969, UNESCO has submitted a report on its activities of special interest to women to the Commission on the Status of Women at each session. Members of the Commission have commented upon UNESCO's programme and activities and have pointed out areas where, in their view, either too much or too little emphasis was being given.

188. In recent years UNESCO's action—while still comprising an important educational element—has increasingly broadened to include other concerns, notably the promotion of the role of women in decision-making processes and in the promotion of peace, the teaching of women's studies as an integral part of human rights teaching, the improvement of the access of women to science and technology, and the study of the structure of the mass media in society and their relationship to the status of women.

(b) *Provisions of international instruments*

189. The question of discrimination against women in education has been dealt with, on the international level, in the Convention and Recommendation against Discrimination in Education, adopted by the General Conference of UNESCO on 14 December 1960; the Declaration on the Elimination of Discrimination against Women, proclaimed by the General Assembly in resolution 2263 (XXII) of 7 November 1967; and the Convention on the Elimination of All Forms of Discri-

---

49 United Nations Educational, Scientific and Cultural Organization, *Records of the General Conference, Fourteenth Session, Resolutions,* resolution 1.1322.

mination against Women, adopted by General Assembly resolution 34/180 of 18 December 1979.

190. The UNESCO Convention against Discrimination in Education contains the following provisions:

Article 1

1. For the purpose of this Convention, the term "discrimination" includes any distinction, exclusion, limitation or preference which, being based on race, colour, sex, language, religion, political or other opinion, national or social origin, economic condition or birth, has the purpose or effect of nullifying or impairing equality of treatment in education and in particular:

(*a*) Of depriving any person or group of persons of access to education of any type or at any level;

(*b*) Of limiting any person or group of persons to education of an inferior standard;

(*c*) Subject to the provisions of article 2 of this Convention, of establishing or maintaining separate educational systems or institutions for persons or groups of persons; or

(*d*) Of inflicting on any person or group of persons conditions which are incompatible with the dignity of man.

2. For the purposes of this Convention, the term "education" refers to all types and levels of education, and includes access to education, the standard and quality of education, and the conditions under which it is given.

Article 2

When permitted in a State, the following situations shall not be deemed to constitute discrimination, within the meaning of article 1 of this Convention.

(*a*) The establishment or maintenance of separate educational systems or institutions for pupils of the two sexes, if these systems or institutions offer equivalent access to education, provide a teaching staff with qualifications of the same standard as well as school premises and equipment of the same quality, and afford the opportunity to take the same or equivalent courses of study;

. . .

191. The Convention entered into force on 22 May 1962. The Recommendation contains similar substantive provisions. Implementation of the Convention is monitored by the Conciliation and Good Offices Commission established in accordance with the Protocol Instituting a Conciliation and Good Offices Commission to be responsible for seeking a settlement of any disputes which may arise between States parties to the Convention, adopted by the General Conference of UNESCO on 10 December 1962. The Protocol entered into force on 24 October 1968.

192. The Declaration on the Elimination of Discrimination against Women contains the following provision:

Article 9

All appropriate measures shall be taken to ensure to girls and women, married or unmarried, equal rights with men in education at all levels, and in particular:

(*a*) Equal conditions of access to, and study in, educational institutions of all types, including universities and vocational, technical and professional schools;

(*b*) The same choice of curricula, the same examinations, teaching staff with qualifications of the same standard, and school premises and equipment of the same quality, whether the institutions are coeducational or not;

(*c*) Equal opportunities to benefit from scholarships and other study grants;

(*d*) Equal opportunities for access to programmes of continuing education, including adult literacy programmes;

(*e*) Access to educational information to help in ensuring the health and well-being of families.

193. The Convention on the Elimination of All Forms of Discrimination against Women contains the following provision:

Article 10

States Parties shall take all appropriate measures to eliminate discrimination against women in order to ensure to them equal rights with men in the field of education and in particular to ensure, on a basis of equality of men and women:

(*a*) The same conditions for career and vocational guidance, for access to studies and for the achievement of diplomas in educational establishments of all categories in rural as well as in urban areas; this equality shall be ensured in pre-school, general, technical, professional and higher technical education, as well as in all types of vocational training;

(*b*) Access to the same curricula, the same examinations, teaching staff with qualifications of the same standard and school premises and equipment of the same quality;

(*c*) The elimination of any stereotyped concept of the roles of men and women at all levels and in all forms of education by encouraging coeducation and other types of education which will help to achieve this aim and, in particular, by the revision of textbooks and school programmes and the adaptation of teaching methods;

(*d*) The same opportunities to benefit from scholarships and other study grants;

(*e*) The same opportunities for access to programmes of continuing education, including adult and functional literacy programmes, particularly those aimed at reducing, at the earliest possible time, any gap in education existing between men and women;

(*f*) The reduction of female student drop-out rates and the organization of programmes for girls and women who have left school prematurely;

(*g*) The same opportunities to participate actively in sports and physical education;

(*h*) Access to specific educational information to help to ensure the health and well-being of families, including information and advice on family planning.

194. Implementation of the provisions of the Convention is monitored by the Committee on the Elimination of Discrimination against Women.

(c) *Forward-looking Strategies*

195. The Forward-looking Strategies for the Advancement of Women to the Year 2000,[50] adopted by the World Conference to Review and Appraise the Achievements of the United Nations Decade for Women: Equality, Development and Peace, held at Nairobi from 15 to 26 July 1985, outline measures for action relating to education as the basis for the improvement of the status of women, as contained in the following paragraphs:

163. Education is the basis for the full promotion and improvement of the status of women. It is the basic tool that should be given to women in order to fulfil their role as full members of society. Governments should strengthen the participation of women at all levels of national educational policy and in formulating and implementing plans, programmes and projects. Special measures should

---

[50] *Report of the World Conference to Review and Appraise the Achievements of the United Nations Decade for Women: Equality, Development and Peace,* Nairobi, 15-26 July 1985 (United Nations publication, Sales. No. E.85.IV.10), chap. II, C. 2.

be adopted to revise and adapt women's education to the realities of the developing world. Existing and new services should be directed to women as intellectuals, policy-makers, decision-makers, planners, contributors and beneficiaries, with particular attention to the UNESCO Convention against Discrimination in Education (1960). Special measures should also be adopted to increase equal access to scientific, technical and vocational education, particularly for young women, and evaluate progress made by the poorest women in urban and rural areas.

164. Special measures should be taken by Governments and the international organizations, especially UNESCO, to eliminate the high rate of illiteracy by the year 2000, with the support of the international community. Governments should establish targets and adopt appropriate measures for this purpose. While the elimination of illiteracy is important to all, priority programmes are still required to overcome the special obstacles that have generally led to higher illiteracy rates among women than among men. Efforts should be made to promote functional literacy, with special emphasis on health, nutrition and viable economic skills and opportunities, in order to eradicate illiteracy among women and to produce additional material for the eradication of illiteracy. Programmes for legal literacy in low-income urban and rural areas should be initiated and intensified. Raising the level of education among women is important for the general welfare of society and because of its close link to child survival and child spacing.

165. The causes of high absenteeism and drop-out rates of girls in the educational system must be addressed. Measures must be developed, strengthened and implemented that will, *inter alia,* create the appropriate incentives to ensure that women have an equal opportunity to acquire education at all levels, as well as to apply their education in a work or career context. Such measures should include the strengthening of communication and information systems, the implementation of appropriate legislation and the reorientation of educational personnel. Moreover, Governments should encourage and finance adult education programmes for those women who have never completed their studies or were forced to interrupt their studies, owing to family responsibilities, lack of financial resources or early pregnancies.

166. Efforts should be made to ensure that available scholarships and other forms of support from governmental, non-governmental and private sources are expanded and equitably distributed to girls and boys and that boarding and lodging facilities are equally accessible to them.

167. The curricula of public and private schools should be examined, textbooks and other educational materials reviewed and educational personnel retrained in order to eliminate all discriminatory gender stereotyping in education. Educational institutions should be encouraged to expand their curricula to include studies on women's contribution to all aspects of development.

168. The Decade has witnessed the rise of centres and programmes of women's studies in response to social forces and to the need for developing a new scholarship and a body of knowledge on women's studies from the perspective of women. Women's studies should be developed to reformulate the current models influencing the constitution of knowledge and sustaining a value system that reinforces inequality. The promotion and application of women's studies inside and outside conventional institutions of learning will help to create a just and equitable society in which men and women enjoy equal partnership.

169. Encouragement and incentives, as well as counselling services, should be provided for girls to study scientific, technical and managerial subjects at all levels, in order to develop and enhance the aptitudes of women for decision-making, management and leadership in these fields.

170. All educational and occupational training should be flexible and accessible to both women and men. It should aim to improve employment possibilities and promotion prospects for women including those areas where technologies are improving rapidly, and vocational training programmes, as well as workers' educational schemes dealing with co-operatives, trade unions and work associations, should stress the importance of equal opportunity for women at all levels of work and work-related activities.

171. Extensive measures should be taken to diversify women's vocational education and training in order to extend their opportunities for employment in occupations that are non-traditional or are new to women and that are important to development. The present educational system, which in many countries is sharply divided by sex, with girls receiving instruction in home economics and boys in technical subjects, should be altered. Existing vocational training centres should be opened to girls and women instead of continuing a segregated training system.

172. A fully integrated system of training, having direct linkages with employment needs, pertinent to future employment and development trends should be created and implemented in order to avoid wastage of human resources.

173. Educational programmes to enable men to assume as much responsibility as women in the upbringing of children and the maintenance of the household should be introduced at all levels of the educational system.

4. IMPROVEMENT OF THE STATUS AND ROLE OF WOMEN IN THE FIELD OF HEALTH CARE

196. Because women are the main providers of primary health care in their capacity as wives, mothers and community health workers, the Commission on the Status of Women, in close co-operation with the World Health Organization and the United Nations Children's Fund, has given special attention to the health needs of women, the utilization of health services by women, and women's role in the promotion of health. In recent years the Commission has placed increased emphasis upon the occupational health and safety of women, the ability of women to control their own fertility and to take decisions about their desired number of children, and the access of women to adequate nutrition and health care for themselves and their children. Meanwhile the Sub-Commission on Prevention of Discrimination and Protection of Minorities has completed a study of traditional practices affecting the health of women and children.

(a) *Traditional practices affecting the health of women and children*

197. The question of traditional practices affecting the health of women and children was first discussed by the Commission on Human Rights in 1952, in connection with its study of human rights in Trust and Non-Self-Governing Territories. At that time the Commission expressed the view that certain practices are not only dangerous to health but also seriously impair the human dignity of women; and noted that some of the Governments concerned were working towards the elimination of these practices. On the initiative of the Commission the Economic and Social Council, in resolution 680 B II (XXVI) of 10 July 1958, invited the World Health Organization to undertake a study "of the persistence of customs which subject girls to ritual operations" and of the measures adopted or planned to put an end to these practices.

198. The question was also discussed at the United Nations Seminar on the Participation of Women in

Public Life, held at Addis Ababa in 1960 for African participants. In resolution 821 II (XXXII) of 19 July 1961 the Council drew the attention of the World Health Organization to this report and asked the agency whether it would undertake a study of the medical aspects of operations based on customs to which many women were still being subjected. Noting this request, the WHO Executive Board stated, in resolution EB 29.R.50 of 25 January 1962, that "a study of the medical aspects of this subject could not be undertaken in isolation but must be related to the cultural and socio-economic background of the countries concerned". The Board authorized the Director-General, "in the event that the wide socio-economic study indicated is undertaken, . . . to provide any information of a medical character he may have available which is related to the question in its socio-economic context".[51]

199. The 1975 World Health Assembly gave particular attention to traditional practices and their effects on the health of women and children. A seminar on the subject, organized by the WHO Regional Office for the Eastern Mediterranean, was held at Khartoum, Sudan, from 10 to 15 February 1979.[52]

200. The World Conference of the United Nations Decade for Women, held at Copenhagen in July 1980, appealed to African Governments and women's organizations to search for a solution to the problem of female circumcision and infibulation.[53] The question was also raised during a meeting of the Association of African Women for Research and Development, held at Addis Ababa in 1981 under the aegis of the Economic Commission for Africa.[54]

201. The Working Group on Slavery of the Sub-Commission on Prevention of Discrimination and Protection of Minorities considered information on traditional practices affecting the health of women and children at its session in 1981, and recommended that this information be drawn to the attention of the competent intergovernmental organizations. In 1982 the Working Group recommended that a study on female circumcision should be undertaken with a view to examining all aspects of the problem.

202. The Sub-Commission, in resolution 1982/15 of 7 September 1982, requested two of its members, Mr. Mudawi and Mrs. Warzazi, to carry out such a study. Later, the Commission on Human Rights, in resolution 1984/48 of 13 March 1984, recommended that the Economic and Social Council should request the Secretary-General "to entrust a working group composed of experts designated by the Sub-Commission on Prevention of Discrimination and Protection of Minorities, the United Nations Children's Fund and the United Nations Educational, Scientific and Cultural Organization with the task of conducting a comprehensive study on the phenomenon of traditional practices affecting the health of women and children". The Council endorsed the recommendation by resolution 1984/34.

203. A Seminar on Traditional Practices Affecting the Health of Women and Children in Africa was held at Dakar, Senegal, in February 1984 under the sponsorship of the Working Group on Traditional Practices, WHO, UNICEF, UNFPA and the Government of Senegal. The Seminar created the Inter-African Committee on Traditional Practices to follow up the implementation of its recommendations. The Inter-African Committee, which has a co-ordinating office at Addis Ababa and a liaison office at Geneva, has set up national committees to deal with the problem in a number of countries, including Djibouti, Egypt, Ethiopia, Gambia, Ghana, Liberia, Mali, Nigeria, Senegal, Sudan and Togo.

204. The problem was further considered at the Khartoum Workshop, "African Women Speak on Female Circumcision," organized by the Babiker Badri Scientific Association for Women's Studies in October 1984, and at the Afro-Arab International Conference on the Condition of Women, organized by the Arab Lawyers Union at Cairo in February 1985. The World Health Assembly, meeting at Geneva in May 1985, adopted a resolution (38/27) recognizing the problem of harmful traditional practices and calling for concrete action to eradicate them.

205. The report of the Working Group on Traditional Practices Affecting the Health of Women and Children,[55] on which Mrs. Halima Embarek Warzazi and Mr. Murlidhar C. Bhandare served as experts designated by the Sub-Commission on Prevention of Discrimination and Protection of Minorities, was examined and noted by the Commission on Human Rights in resolution 1986/28 of 11 March 1986.

206. In the study, the Working Group gave priority consideration to three traditional practices adversely affecting the health of women and children: (a) female circumcision, (b) traditional birth practices, and (c) preferential treatment for male children. Other adverse practices studied included forced feeding, early marriage and adolescent childbearing, other taboos or practices which prevent women from controlling their own fertility, such as nutritional taboos and differential feeding patterns (for example, withholding certain nutritious foods from women and children); traditional birth practices, including the work of untrained traditional birth attendants; and the application of contaminated substances or the use of dangerous medicaments during childbirth. At the same time, it also studied certain beneficial practices, such as breastfeeding and the use of traditional methods of birth-spacing.

207. After examining the report, the Commission on Human Rights requested the Secretary-General to transmit it to Governments, the competent organizations and the specialized agencies, drawing their attention to the recommendations which it contained; and called upon the specialized agencies and the interested

---

[51] See E/3592.

[52] See Final Report of the Seminar: EM/SEM.T.PR.AFR.HTH.WM/44.

[53] A/CONF. 94, para. 45.

[54] ST/ECA/ATRCW/81/02.

[55] E/CN.4/1986/42.

non-governmental organizations, in their respective fields of competence, to provide the necessary assistance to the Governments which request it to help them combat such practices.

(b) Provisions of an international instrument

208. The question of discrimination against women in the field of health care is dealt with in the Convention on the Elimination of All Forms of Discrimination against Women, which contains the following provision:

Article 12

1. States Parties shall take all appropriate measures to eliminate discrimination against women in the field of health care in order to ensure, on a basis of equality of men and women, access to health care services, including those related to family planning.

2. Notwithstanding the provisions of paragraph 1 of this article, States Parties shall ensure to women appropriate services in connexion with pregnancy, confinement and the post-natal period, granting free services where necessary, as well as adequate nutrition during pregnancy and lactation.

(c) Forward-looking Strategies

209. The Forward-looking Strategies for the Advancement of Women to the Year 2000,[56] adopted by the World Conference to Review and Appraise the Achievements of the United Nations Decade for Women: Equality, Development and Peace, held at Nairobi from 15 to 26 July 1985 outline measures for action relating to the improvement of the status and role of women in health, as contained in the following paragraphs:

148. The vital role of women as providers of health care both inside and outside the home should be recognized, taking into account the following: the creation and strengthening of basic services for the delivery of health care, with due regard to levels of fertility and infant and maternal mortality and the needs of the most vulnerable groups and the need to control locally prevalent endemic and epidemic diseases. Governments that have not already done so should undertake, in co-operation with the World Health Organization, the United Nations Children's Fund and the United Nations Fund for Population Activities, plans of action relating to women in health and development in order to identify and reduce risks to women's health and to promote the positive health of women at all stages of life, bearing in mind the productive role of women in society and their responsibilities for bearing and rearing children. Women's participation in the achievement of Health for All by the Year 2000 should be recognized, since their health knowledge is crucial in their multiple roles as health providers and health brokers for the family and community, and as informed consumers of adequate and appropriate health care.

149. The participation of women in higher professional and managerial positions in health institutions should be increased through appropriate legislation; training and supportive action should be taken to increase women's enrolment at higher levels of medical training and training in health-related fields. For effective community involvement to ensure the attainment of the World Health Organization's goal of Health for All by the Year 2000 and responsiveness to women's health needs, women should be represented in national and

local health councils and committees. The employment and working conditions of women health personnel and health workers should be expanded and improved at all levels. Female traditional healers and birth attendants should be more fully and constructively integrated in national health planning.

150. Health education should be geared towards changing those attitudes and values and actions that are discriminatory and detrimental to women's and girls' health. Steps should be taken to change the attitudes and health knowledge and composition of health personnel so that there can be an appropriate understanding of women's health needs. A greater sharing by men and women of family and health-care responsibilities should be encouraged. Women must be involved in the formulation and planning of their health education needs. Health education should be available to the entire family not only through the health care system, but also through all appropriate channels and in particular the educational system. To this end, Governments should ensure that information meant to be received by women is relevant to women's health priorities and is suitably presented.

151. Promotive, preventive and curative health measures should be strengthened through combined measures and a supportive health infrastructure which, in accordance with the International Code of Marketing of Breast Milk Substitutes, should be free of commercial pressure. To provide immediate access to water and sanitary facilities for women, Governments should ensure that women are consulted and involved in the planning and implementation of water and sanitation projects, trained in the maintenance of water-supply systems, and consulted with regard to technologies used in water and sanitation projects. In this regard, recommendations arising from the activities generated by the International Drinking Water Supply and Sanitation Decade and other public health programmes should be taken into account.

152. Governments should take measures to vaccinate children and pregnant women against certain endemic local diseases as well as other diseases as recommended by the vaccination schedule of the World Health Organization and to eliminate any differences in coverage between boys and girls (cf. WHO report EB 75/22). In regions where rubella is prevalent, vaccinations should preferably be given to girls before puberty. Governments should ensure that adequate arrangements are made to preserve the quality of vaccines. Governments should ensure the quality of vaccines. Governments should also ensure the full and informed participation of women in programmes to control chronic and communicable diseases.

153. The international community should intensify efforts to eradicate the trafficking, marketing and distribution of unsafe and ineffective drugs and to disseminate information on their ill effects. Those efforts should include educational programmes to promote the proper prescription and informed use of drugs. Efforts should also be strengthened to eliminate all practices detrimental to the health of women and children. Efforts should be made to ensure that all women have access to essential drugs appropriate to their specific needs and as recommended in the WHO List of Essential Drugs as applied in 1978. It is imperative that information on the appropriate use of such drugs is made widely available to all women. When drugs are imported or exported Governments should use the WHO Certification Scheme on the Quality of Pharmaceutical Products Moving in International Commerce.

154. Women should have access to and control over income to provide adequate nutrition for themselves and their children. Also, Governments should foster activities that will increase awareness of the special nutritional needs of women; provide support to ensure sufficient rest in the last trimester of pregnancy and while breast-feeding; and promote interventions to reduce the prevalence of nutritional diseases such as anaemia in women of all ages, particularly young women, and promote the development and use of locally produced weaning food.

155. Appropriate health facilities should be planned, designed, constructed and equipped to be readily accessible and acceptable. Services should be in harmony with the timing and patterns of women's work, as well as with women's needs and perspectives. Maternal and child-care facilities, including family planning services, should be within easy reach of all women. Governments should also ensure that women have the same access as men to affordable cura-

[56] Report of the World Conference to Review and Appraise the Achievements of the United Nations Decade for Women: Equality, Development and Peace, Nairobi, 15-26 July 1985 (United Nations publication, Sales No. E.85.IV.10).

tive, preventive and rehabilitative treatment. Wherever possible, measures should be taken to conduct general screening and treatment of women's common diseases and cancer. In view of the unacceptably high levels of maternal mortality in many developing countries, the reduction of maternal mortality from now to the year 2000 to a minimum level should be a key target for Governments and non-governmental organizations, including professional organizations.

156. The ability of women to control their own fertility forms an important basis for the enjoyment of other rights. As recognized in the World Population Plan of Action and reaffirmed at the International Conference on Population, 1984, all couples and individuals have the basic human right to decide freely and informedly the number and spacing of their children; maternal and child health and family-planning components of primary health care should be strengthened; and family-planning information should be produced and services created. Access to such services should be encouraged by Governments irrespective of their population policies and should be carried out with the participation of women's organizations to ensure their success.[57]

157. Governments should make available, as a matter of urgency, information, education and the means to assist women and men to take decisions about their desired number of children. To ensure a voluntary and free choice, family-planning information, education and means should include all medically approved and appropriate methods of family planning. Education for responsible parenthood and family-life education should be widely available and should be directed towards both men and women. Non-governmental organizations, particularly women's organizations, should be involved in such programmes because they can be the most effective media for motivating people at that level.

158. Recognizing that pregnancy occurring in adolescent girls, whether married or unmarried, has adverse effects on the morbidity and mortality of both mother and child, Governments are urged to develop policies to encourage delay in the commencement of childbearing. Governments should make efforts to raise the age of entry into marriage in countries in which this age is still quite low. Attention should also be given to ensuring that adolescents, both girls and boys, receive adequate information and education.

159. All Governments should ensure that fertility-control methods and drugs conform to adequate standards of quality, efficiency and safety. This should also apply to organizations responsible for distributing and administering these methods. Information on contraceptives should be made available to women. Programmes of incentives and disincentives should be neither coercive nor discriminatory and should be consistent with internationally recognized human rights, as well as with changing individual and cultural values.

160. Governments should encourage local women's organizations to participate in primary health-care activities including traditional medicine, and should devise ways to support women, especially underprivileged women, in taking responsibility for self-care and in promoting community care, particularly in rural areas. More emphasis should be placed on preventive rather than curative measures.

161. The appropriate gender-specific indicators for monitoring women's health that have been or are being developed by the World Health Organization should be widely applied and utilized by Governments and other interested organizations in order to develop and sustain measures for treating low-grade ill health and for reducing high morbidity rates among women, particularly when illnesses are psychosomatic or social and cultural in nature. Governments that have not yet done so should establish focal points to carry out such monitoring.

162. Occupational health and safety should be enhanced by the public and private sectors. Concern with the occupational health risks should cover female as well as male workers and focus among other things on risks endangering their reproductive capabilities and unborn children. Efforts should equally be directed at the health of pregnant and lactating women, the health impact of new technologies and the harmonization of work and family responsibilities.

---

[57] The Holy See delegation reserved its position with respect to paragraphs 156 to 159 because it did not agree with the substance of those paragraphs.

5. IMPROVEMENT OF THE STATUS AND ROLE OF WOMEN IN SOCIETY

210. The Commission on the Status of Women examined a preliminary report of the Secretary-General on the influence of mass communication media on the formation of new attitudes towards the roles of women in present-day society[58] at its twenty-fourth session, in 1972, and expressed concern that in several countries those media perpetuated the traditional deep-rooted attitudes held by women and men about their respective roles in present-day society, and that the influence of those media in the determination of cultural patterns hindered efforts to promote equal rights of women and men and the integration of women in the development effort. On the recommendation of the Commission the Economic and Social Council, in resolution 1862 (LVI) of 16 May 1974, noted that the report substantiated the Commission's concern and invited all organizations of the United Nations system, and particularly UNESCO, to make a special effort to increase their audiovisual material and to develop their programmes in such a way as to promote the integration of women in development; and invited Governments to urge the mass media, with due regard to freedom of expression, to adapt their programmes in order to provide for men as well as women a continuing education as to their economic and professional prospects and opportunities for leisure, family life and broadening horizons.

211. The World Conference of the International Women's Year, held in Mexico City from 19 June to 2 July 1975, condemned, in resolution 19, "the degrading exploitation of women as a sex symbol and instrument of economic interests by certain media of social communication", and requested "Governments and responsible organizations, as appropriate, to promote and encourage, in the mass communication media of their countries, the projection of a dignified and positive image of women, divesting them of their role as vehicles for publicity and as targets for the sale of consumer goods, with a view to bringing about changes in the attitudes and ways of thinking of both men and women that will be conducive to securing the equality and integrity of women and their full participation in society". The Conference likewise requested "those in charge of the mass communication media to cease projecting and gradually eliminate commercialized, tasteless and stereotyped images of women, particularly in pornographic publications, the use of such images in depicting sexual crimes and crimes of violence, and the dissemination of any material tending to create prejudices and negative attitudes with regard to the changes necessary for the revaluation of the role of women and to transmit an image of men's and women's roles that is as varied as possible". The Conference called for "the critical and creative participation of women in all systems of mass communication, at the programming, production, distribution, reception and consumer levels".

---

[58] E/CN.6/581.

(a) *Media perpetuation of traditional attitudes held by women and men about their respectives roles in society*

212. The Secretary-General submitted a progress report[59] on the subject of the influence of the mass communication media on attitudes towards the roles of women and men in present-day society to the Commission on the Status of Women at its twenty-sixth session, in 1976. The report indicated that little information was available on the images of women projected by the more traditional types of mass communication media or on their influence on the perpetuation of sex-role stereotypes, and that there was a need for research in this area.

213. On the recommendation of the Commission the Economic and Social Council, in resolution 2063 (LXII) of 12 May 1977, decided to appoint a special rapporteur to prepare a study on the impact of the mass communication media on the changing roles of men and women, including action taken by the public and private sectors at national, regional and international levels to remove prejudices and sex-role stereotyping, to accelerate the acceptance of women's new and expanded roles in society and to promote their integration into the development process as equal partners with men.

214. The Special Rapporteur, Mrs. Esmeralda Arboleda Cuevas, submitted her report on the influence of the mass communication media on attitudes towards the roles of women and men in present-day society[60] to the Commission on the Status of Women at its twenty-eighth session, in 1980. The report included a brief history of relevant United Nations efforts, a chapter dealing with the pervasive social obstacles which maintained image-stereotyping, summaries of measures taken in the field by Governments and non-governmental organizations, and a series of recommendations.

215. On the recommendation of the Commission, the Council in resolution 1980/5 of 17 April 1980, took note of the report and of the importance of the problems which it raised. Regretting a tendency in mass communication media to present women in stereotyped roles and pointing to the need to correct that tendency, the Council called upon those responsible for the content and presentation of material by mass communication media to make additional efforts to present in a more comprehensive and balanced way the right of women to enjoy equal rights and equal opportunities with men, and encouraged all relevant organizations, institutions and other associations to exercise their influence on those responsible in order to achieve that goal.

216. As suggested by the Commission and the Council, the report served as a background document for the World Conference of the United Nations Decade for Women.

(b) *Forward-looking Strategies*

217. The Nairobi Forward-looking Strategies for the Advancement of Women to the Year 2000,[61] adopted by the World Conference to Review and Appraise the Achievements of the United Nation Decade for Women: Equality, Development and Peace, held at Nairobi from 15 to 26 July 1985, outline measures for action to enhance the role of mass communications in promoting the advancement of women and the role of women in this sector, including decision-making relating to communications, as contained in the following paragraphs:

206. In view of the critical role of this sector in eliminating stereotyped images of women and providing women with easier access to information, the participation of women at all levels of communications policy and decision-making and in programme design, implementation and monitoring should be given high priority. The media's portrayal of stereotyped images of women and also that of the advertising industry can have a profoundly adverse effect on attitudes towards and among women. Women should be made an integral part of the decision-making concerning the choice and development of alternative forms of communication and should have an equal say in the determination of the content of all public information efforts. The cultural media, involving ritual, drama, dialogue, oral literature and music, should be integrated in all development efforts to enhance communication. Women's own cultural projects aimed at changing the traditional images of women and men should be promoted and women should have equal access to financial support. In the field of communication, there is ample scope for international co-operation regarding information related to the sharing of experience by women and to projecting activities concerning the role of women in development and peace in order to enhance the awareness of both accomplishments and the tasks that remain to be fulfilled.

207. The enrolment of women in publicly operated mass communication networks and in education and training should be increased. The employment of women within the sector should be promoted and directed towards professional, advisory and decision-making positions.

208. Organizations aimed at promoting the role of women in development as contributors and beneficiaries should be assisted in their efforts to establish effective communications and information networks.

(c) *Integration of women in society*

218. In resolution 42/64 of 30 November 1987, the General Assembly expressed its awareness of the fact that efforts to promote the status of women in all its aspects and their complete integration in society go beyond the problem of legal equality and that deeper structural transformations of society and changes in present-day economic relations, as well as elimination of traditional prejudices through education and dissemination of information, are required to create conditions for women to develop fully their intellectual and physical capacities and to participate actively in the decision-making process in political, economic, social and cultural development.

219. Mindful of the necessity to enlarge the possibilities for both men and women to combine parental du-

---

[59] E/CN.6/601 and Corr.1.
[60] E/CN.6/627.

---

[61] *Report of the World Conference to Review and Appraise the Achievements of the United Nations Decade for Women: Equality, Development and Peace,* Nairobi, 15-26 July 1985 (United Nations publication, Sales No. E.85.IV.10).

ties and household work with paid employment and social activities and to ensure that the role of women in childbearing should not be the cause of inequality and discrimination and that childrearing demands shared responsibilities among women, men and society as a whole, the Assembly appealed to all Governments, international organizations and intergovernmental and non-governmental organizations to pay due attention in their activities to the importance of the role of women in society in all its interrelated aspects—as mothers, as participants in political, economic, social and cultural development and as participants in public life.

220. The Assembly invited all Governments to encourage such social and economic development as will ensure the equal participation of women in all spheres of work, equal pay for work of equal value and equal opportunities for education and vocational training, taking into consideration the necessity of combining all aspects of the role of women in society as well as the challenges faced by women in all countries when seeking to combine parental duties and family responsibilities with their full involvement in political, social, economic and cultural development. It appealed to them to promote conditions that will enable women to participate as equal partners with men in public and political life, in the decision-making process at all levels and in the management of different spheres of life in society.

221. Further, the Assembly urged all Governments to recognize the special status and social importance of childbearing and childrearing and to take all necessary measures to encourage the support of parenthood, including paid maternity and parental and child-care leave, and to provide women with security for their jobs as long as necessary with a view to allowing them, if they so wish, to fulfil their role as mothers without prejudice to their professional and public activities; and appealed to them to promote the establishment of appropriate facilities for the care and education of children as a means of combining parenthood with economic, political, social, cultural and other activities, and thus to assist women towards full integration in society.

222. Finally, it called upon Member States to adopt the necessary effective measures with a view to implementing the Nairobi Forward-looking Strategies as a matter of priority, including the establishment or strengthening of appropriate mechanisms for the advancement of women in order to ensure the full participation of women in all spheres of life in their countries; requested the Secretary-General to pay due attention to all the interrelated aspects of the role of women in society when preparing surveys on the role of women in development as well as reports on the world social situation and other relevant surveys; and invited the Commission on the Status of Women to pay due attention to the provisions of the present resolution during the consideration at its next sessions of the priority themes under the heading "Equality", with a view to formulating recommendations for appropriate action by concerned United Nations organs and bodies.

6. PROTECTION OF WOMEN AND CHILDREN IN EMERGENCY AND ARMED CONFLICT

223. At its twenty-fourth session, in 1972, the Commission on the Status of Women considered a report on the protection of women in emergency situations[62] prepared by the Secretary-General in accordance with its resolution 4 (XXII) of 3 February 1969. On the recommendation of the Commission, the Economic and Social Council adopted resolution 1515 (XLVIII) of 28 May 1970, in which it requested the Secretary-General to submit to the Commission a report on the conditions of women and children in emergency and armed conflicts in the struggle for peace, self-determination, national liberation and independence. The Council also requested the General Assembly to consider the possibility of drafting a declaration on the protection of women and children in emergency or wartime.

224. At its twenty-fifth session, in 1974, the Commission proposed for adoption by the General Assembly a draft declaration on the protection of women and children in emergency and armed conflict in the struggle for peace, self-determination, national liberation and independence. The Economic and Social Council endorsed this decision in resolution 1861 (LVI) of 16 May 1974. The General Assembly, in resolution 3318 (XXIX) of 14 December 1974, adopted and proclaimed the Declaration on the Protection of Women and Children in Emergency and Armed Conflict, and called for its strict observance by all Member States.

225. The Declaration states, in article 1, that attacks and bombings on the civilian population shall be prohibited and such acts condemned, since they inflict incalculable suffering, especially on women and children, who are the most vulnerable members of the population. It also condemns the use of chemical and bacteriological weapons in the course of military operations as constituting one of the most flagrant violations of the Geneva Protocol of 1925,[63] the Geneva Conventions of 1949[64] and the principles of international humanitarian law.

226. The Declaration provides that "all efforts shall be made by States involved in armed conflicts . . . to spare women and children from the ravages of war"; and that "all the necessary steps shall be taken to ensure the prohibition of measures such as persecution, torture, punitive measures, degrading treatment and violence, particularly against that part of the civilian population that consists of women and children". It specifies that "all forms of repression and cruel and inhuman treatment of women and children, including imprisonment, torture, shooting, mass arrests, collective punishment, destruction of dwellings and forcible eviction, committed by belligerents in the course of military operations or in occupied territories shall be considered criminal". Finally, it provides that "women and

---

62 E/CN.6/561 and Add.1 and 2.

63 League of Nations, *Treaty Series*, vol. XCIV, No. 2138, p. 65.

64 United Nations, *Treaty Series,* vol. 75, Nos. 970-973.

children belonging to the civilian population and finding themselves in circumstances of emergency and armed conflict in the struggle for peace, self-determination, national liberation and independence, or who live in occupied territories, shall not be deprived of shelter, food, medical aid or other inalienable rights, in accordance with the provisions of the Universal Declaration of Human Rights, the International Covenant on Economic, Social and Cultural Rights, the Declaration of the Rights of the Child or other instruments of international law''.

227. At its twenty-seventh session, in 1978, the Commission was informed by the Secretary-General[65] that two Protocols additional to the Geneva Conventions of 1949,[66] dealing with the protection of victims of international armed conflicts and non-international armed conflicts respectively, had been adopted at the fourth session of the Diplomatic Conference on the Reaffirmation and Development of International Humanitarian Law Applicable in Armed Conflicts, in 1977. These Protocols contain provisions with respect to the protection of women and children, which strengthen those of the Geneva Conventions and include provisions for the evacuation of children and the protection of women and children against rape, enforced prostitution and any form of indecent assault.

228. In resolution 7 (XXVII) of 31 March 1978, the Commission called upon all States and all parties to armed conflicts, in emergency situations in the struggle for peace, self-determination, national liberation and independence, to accord special protection to women and children in accordance with the relevant international provisions applicable in armed conflicts and to give every possible support to the work of international humanitarian organizations to alleviate the suffering of the civilian population, especially women and children, in these conflicts; called upon relevant international humanitarian organizations such as the International Committee of the Red Cross to continue to do their utmost for the protection of the civilian population, especially women and children, in emergency and armed conflicts, including those in the struggle for peace, self-determination, national liberation and independence; and requested international humanitarian organizations helping the civilian population in armed conflicts to give special care to pregnant women and mothers with small children and to orphans.

229. The Nairobi Forward-looking Strategies for the Advancement of Women to the Year 2000,[67] adopted by the World Conference to Review and Appraise the Achievements of the United Nations Decade for Women: Equality, Development and Peace, held at

Nairobi from 15 to 26 July 1985, reiterated the need to implement measures proposed in the 1974 Declaration on the Protection of Women and Children in Emergency and Armed Conflict for the protection of women and children in emergency and armed conflict, as contained in the following paragraphs:

261. Armed conflicts and emergency situations impose a serious threat to the lives of women and children, causing constant fear, danger of displacement, destruction, devastation, physical abuse, social and family disruption, and abandonment. Sometimes these result in complete denial of access to adequate health and educational services, loss of job opportunities and overall worsening of material conditions.

262. International instruments, ongoing negotiations and international discussions aimed at the limitation of armed conflicts, such as the Fourth Geneva Convention of 1949 and the First Additional Protocol to the Geneva Conventions of 1949, adopted in 1977, provide a general framework for the protection of civilians in times of hostilities and the basis of provisions of humanitarian assistance and protection to women and children. Measures proposed in the 1974 Declaration on the Protection of Women and Children in Emergency and Armed Conflict (General Assembly resolution 3318 (XXIX)) should be taken into account by Governments.

7. Additional areas of special concern

230. The Nairobi Forward-looking Strategies for the Advancement of Women to the Year 2000[68] refer to an increasing number of categories of women who, because of their special characteristics, are experiencing not only the common problems dealt with above but also specific difficulties due to their socio-economic and health condition, age, minority status or a combination of these factors. These special groups of women are extremely diverse, and their problems vary tremendously from one country to another; accordingly no single strategy or group of measures can apply adequately to all cases. The basic strategy must remain one of fundamentally changing the economic conditions that produce such deprivation and of upgrading women's low status in society, which accounts for their extreme vulnerability to such conditions, especially to poverty. It is suggested in the Strategies that:[69]

280. The economic, social, cultural and political conditions of those groups of women should be improved basically by the implementation of the measures proposed for the attainment of equality, development and peace for women in general. Additional efforts should be directed towards ensuring the gainful and productive inclusion of these women in mainstream development and in political activities. Priority emphasis should be placed upon income-generating opportunities and for the independent and sustained improvement of their condition and by the full integration and active participation of women as agents and beneficiaries of development.

231. The categories of women concerned, and the Strategies recommended for the improvement of their condition, are as follow:[70]

[65] E/CN.6/612 and Corr.1.

[66] International Committee of the Red Cross, *Protocols additional to the Geneva Conventions of 12 August 1949,* Geneva, 1977.

[67] *Report of the World Conference to Review and Appraise the Achievements of the United Nations Decade for Women: Equality, Development and Peace,* Nairobi, 15-26 July 1985 (United Nations publication, Sales No. E.85.IV.10).

[68] *Ibid.,* chap. I, sect. A.

[69] *Ibid.,* para. 280.

[70] *Ibid.,* paras. 283-304.

(a) Women in areas affected by drought

283. During the Decade, the phenomenon of drought and desertification grew and developed incessantly, no longer affecting merely some localities in a single country but several entire countries. The scale and persistence of drought constitutes a grave threat, particularly for the countries of the Sahel, in which famine and a far-reaching deterioration of the environment set in as a result of the desertification process. Hence, despite the considerable efforts of the international community, the living conditions of the peoples, particularly those of women and children, which were already precarious, have become particularly miserable.

In view of that situation steps should be taken to promote concerted programmes between the countries concerned for combating drought and desertification. Efforts should be intensified for the formulation and implementation of programmes aimed at food security and self-sufficiency, in particular by the optimum control and exploitation of hydro-geological resources.

A distinction should be made between emergency aid and productive activities. Emergency aid should be intensified when necessary and as far as ever possible directed towards development aid.

Measures should be adopted to take into account women's contribution to production, involve them more closely in the design, implementation and evaluation of the programmes envisaged and ensure ample access for them to the means of production and processing and preservation techniques.

(b) Urban poor women

284. Urbanization has been one of the major socio-economic trends over the past few decades and is expected to continue at an accelerating rate. Although the situation varies considerably from one region to another, it can generally be expected that by the year 2000 close to half the number of women in the world will be living in urban areas. In developing countries, the number of urban women could nearly double by the year 2000, and it is envisaged that there could be a considerable increase in the number of poor women among them.

285. To deal effectively with the issue, Governments should organize multi-sectoral programmes with emphasis on economic activities, elimination of discrimination and the provision of supportive services and, *inter alia*, adequate child-care facilities and, where necessary, workplace canteens to enable women to gain access to economic, social and educational opportunities on an equal basis with men. Particular attention should be devoted to the informal sector, which constitutes a major outlet for employment of a considerable number of urban poor women.

(c) Elderly women

286. The International Plan of Action on Aging adopted by the World Assembly on Aging in 1982 emphasized both the humanitarian and developmental aspects of aging. The recommendations of the Plan of Action are applicable to women and men with a view to providing them with protection and care, and ensuring their involvement and participation in social life and development. However, the Plan of Action recognizes a number of specific areas of concern for elderly women since their longer life expectancy frequently means an old age aggravated by economic need and isolation for both unmarried women and widows, possibly with little or no prospect of paid employment. This applies particularly to those women whose lifetimes were spent in unpaid and unrecognized work in the home with little or no access to a pension. If women have an income, it is generally lower than men's, partly because their former employment status has in the majority of cases been broken by maternity and family responsibilities. For this reason, the Plan of Action also noted the need for long-term policies directed towards providing social insurance for women in their own right. Governments and non-governmental organizations should, in addition to the measures recommended, explore the possibilities of employing elderly women in productive and creative ways and encouraging their participation in social and recreational activities.

It is also recommended that the care of elderly persons, including women, should go beyond disease orientation and should include their total well-being. Further efforts, in particular primary health care, health services and suitable accommodation and housing as strategies should be directed at enabling elderly women to lead a meaningful life as long as possible, in their own home and family and in the community.

Women should be prepared early in life, both psychologically and socially, to face the consequences of longer life expectancy. Although, while getting older, professional and family roles of women are undergoing fundamental changes, aging, as a stage of development, is a challenge for women. In this period of life, women should be enabled to cope in a creative way with new opportunities. The social consequences arising from the stereotyping of elderly women should be recognized and eliminated. The media should assist by presenting positive images of women, particularly emphasizing the need for respect because of their past and continuing contributions to society.

Attention should be given to studying and treating the health problems of aging, particularly in women. Research should also be directed towards the investigation and slowing down of the process of premature aging due to a lifetime of stress, excessive work-load, malnutrition and repeated pregnancy.

(d) Young women

287. Initiatives begun for the 1985 International Youth Year should be extended and expanded so that young women are protected from abuse and exploitation and assisted to develop their full potential. Girls and boys must be provided with equal access to health, education and employment to equip them for adult life. Both girls and boys should be educated to accept equal responsibilities for parenthood.

Urgent attention should be paid to the educational and vocational training of young women in all fields of occupation, giving particular emphasis to those who are socially and economically disadvantaged. Self-employed young women and girls should be assisted to organize co-operatives and ongoing training programmes to improve their skills in production, marketing and management techniques. Special retraining programmes should also be developed for teenage mothers and girls who have dropped out of school and are ill equipped to enter productive employment.

Steps should be taken to eliminate exploitative treatment of young women at work in line with ILO Convention No. 111 concerning discrimination in respect of employment and occupation, 1958 and ILO Convention No. 122 concerning employment policy, 1964. Legislative measures guaranteeing young women their rights should be enforced.

Governments should recognize and enforce the rights of young women to be free from sexual violence, sexual harassment and sexual exploitation. In particular, Governments should recognize that many young women are victims of incest and sexual abuse in the family, and should take steps to assist the victims and to prevent such abuse by education, by improving the status of women and by appropriate action against offenders. Young women should be educated to assert their rights. Particular attention should also be given to sexual harassment and exploitation in employment, especially those areas of employment such as domestic service, where sexual harassment and exploitation are most prevalent.

Governments must also recognize their obligation to provide housing for young women who, because of unemployment and low incomes, suffer special problems in obtaining housing. Homeless young women are particularly vulnerable to sexual exploitation.

In the year 2000, women aged 15-24 will constitute over 8 per cent of both rural and urban populations in developing countries. The great majority of these women will be out of school and in search of jobs. For those employed, frequent exploitation, long working hours and stress have serious implications for their health. Low nutritional levels and unplanned and repeated pregnancies are also aggravating factors.

(e) Abused women

288. Gender-specific violence is increasing and Governments must affirm the dignity of women, as a priority action.

Governments should therefore intensify efforts to establish or strengthen forms of assistance to victims of such violence through the provision of shelter, support, legal and other services.

In addition to immediate assistance to victims of violence against women in the family and in society, Governments should undertake to increase public awareness of violence against women as a societal problem, establish policies and legislative measures to ascertain its causes and prevent and eliminate such violence, in particular by suppressing degrading images and representations of women in society, and finally encourage the development of educational and re-educational measures for offenders.

(f) Destitute women

289. Destitution is an extreme form of poverty. It is estimated that its effects on large segments of the population in developing and developed countries are on the increase. Forward-looking Strategies to promote the objectives of the United Nations Decade for Women: Equality, Development and Peace at the national and international levels are the basis for dealing with this problem. In addition strategies already specified for the implementation of the International Development Strategy for the Third United Nations Development Decade and the new international economic order are suggested in these recommendations. Governments should therefore ensure that the special needs and concerns of destitute women are given priority in the above-mentioned strategies. Moreover, efforts being undertaken for the International Year of Shelter for the Homeless (1987) should focus attention on the particular situation of women commensurate with their relative needs.

(g) Women victims of trafficking and involuntary prostitution

290. Forced prostitution is a form of slavery imposed on women by procurers. It is, *inter alia,* a result of economic degradation that alienates women's labour through processes of rapid urbanization and migration resulting in underemployment and unemployment. It also stems from women's dependence on men. Social and political pressures produce refugees and missing persons. Often these include vulnerable groups of women who are victimized by procurers. Sex tourism, forced prostitution and pornography reduce women to mere sex objects and marketable commodities.

291. States parties to the United Nations Convention for the Suppression of the Traffic in Persons and of the Exploitation of the Prostitution of Others should implement the provisions dealing with the exploitation of women as prostitutes. Urgent consideration should also be given to the improvement of international measures to combat trafficking in women for the purposes of prostitution. Resources for the prevention of prostitution and assistance in the professional, personal and social reintegration of prostitutes should be directed towards providing economic opportunities, including training, employment, self-employment and health facilities for women and children. Governments should also endeavour to co-operate with non-governmental organizations to create wider employment possibilities for women. Strict enforcement provisions must also be taken at all levels to stem the rising tide of violence, drug abuse and crime related to prostitution. The complex and serious problems of the exploitation of and violence against women associated with prostitution call for increased and co-ordinated efforts by police agencies internationally.

(h) Women deprived of their traditional means of livelihood

292. The excessive and inappropriate exploitation of land by any party for any purpose, *inter alia,* by transnational corporations, as well as natural and man-made disasters are among the predominant causes of deprivation of traditional means of livelihood. Droughts, floods, hurricanes and other forms of environmental hazards, such as erosion, desertification and deforestation, have already pushed poor women into marginal environments. At present the pressures are greatest in drought-afflicted arid and semi-arid areas. Urban slums and squatter settlements are also seriously affected. Critically low levels of water supplies, shortage of fuel, over-utilization of grazing and arable lands, and population density are all factors that deprive women of their livelihood.

293. National and international emphasis on ecosystem management should be strengthened, environmental degradation should be controlled and options provided for alternative means of livelihood.

Measures should be established to draw up national conservation strategies aimed at incorporating women's development programmes, among which are irrigation and tree planting and also orientation in the area of agriculture, with women constituting a substantial part of the wage-earning labour force for those programmes.

(i) Women who are the sole supporters of families

294. Recent studies have shown that the number of families in which women are the sole supporters is on the increase. Owing to the particular difficulties (social, economic and legal) which they face, many such women are among the poorest people concentrated in urban informal labour markets and they constitute large numbers of the rural unemployed and marginally employed. Those with very little economic, social and moral support face serious difficulties in supporting themselves as well as in bringing up their children alone. This has serious repercussions for society in terms of the quality, character, productivity and human resource capabilities of its present and future citizenry.

295. The assumptions that underlie a large part of the relevant legislation, regulations and household surveys that confine the role of supporter and head of household to men hinder women's access to credit, loans and material and non-material resources. Changes are needed in these areas to secure for women equal access to resources. There is a need to eliminate terms such as "head of household" and introduce others that are comprehensive enough to reflect women's role appropriately in legal documents and household surveys to guarantee the rights of these women. In the provision of social services, special attention has to be given to the needs of these women. Governments are urged to ensure that women with sole responsibility for their families receive a level of income and social support sufficient to enable them to attain or maintain economic independence and to participate effectively in society. To this end, the assumptions that underlie policies, including research used in policy development, and legislation that confines the role of supporter or head of household to men should be identified and eliminated. Special attention, such as accessible, quality child care, should be given to assisting those women in discharging their domestic responsibilities and to enabling them to participate in and benefit from education, training programmes and employment. The putative father should be made to assist in the maintenance and education of those children born out of wedlock.

(j) Women with physical and mental disabilities

296. It is generally accepted that women constitute a significant number of the estimated 500 million people who are disabled as a consequence of mental, physical or sensory impairment. Many factors contribute to the rising numbers of disabled persons, including war and other forms of violence, poverty, hunger, nutritional deficiencies, epidemics and work-related accidents. The recognition of their human dignity and human rights and the full participation by disabled persons in society is still limited, and this presents additional problems for women who may have domestic and other responsibilities. It is recommended that Governments should adopt the Declaration on the Rights of Disabled Persons (1975) and the World Programme of Action concerning Disabled Persons (1982) which provide an overall framework for action and also refer to problems specific to women that have not been fully appreciated by society because they are still not well known or understood. Community-based occupational and social rehabilitation measures, support services to help them with their domestic responsibilities, as well as opportunities for the participation of such women in all aspects of life should be provided. The rights of intellectually disabled women to obtain health information and advice and to consent to or refuse medical treatment should be respected; similarly, the rights of intellectually disabled minors should be repected.

(k) Women in detention and subject to penal law

297. One of the major areas of current concern in the field of crime prevention and criminal justice is the need for equal treatment of women by the criminal justice system. In the context of changing socio-economic and cultural conditions some improvements have taken place but more need to be made. The number of women in detention has increased over the Decade and this trend is expected to

continue. Women deprived of freedom are exposed to various forms of physical violence, sexual and moral harassment. The conditions of their detention are often below acceptable hygienic standards and their children are deprived of maternal care. The recommendations of the Sixth United Nations Congress on the Prevention of Crime and the Treatment of Offenders, held at Caracas, in 1980, and the principles of the Caracas Declaration with special reference to the "fair and equal treatment of women", should be taken into account in designing and implementing concrete measures at the national and international levels. The proportions of indigenous women imprisoned in some countries is a matter of concern.

(l) *Refugee and displaced women and children*

298. The international community recognizes a humanitarian responsibility to protect and assist refugees and displaced persons. In many cases refugee and displaced women are exposed to a variety of difficult situations affecting their physical and legal protection as well as their psychological and material well-being. Problems of physical debility, physical safety, emotional stress and socio-psychological effects of separation or death in the family, as well as changes in women's roles, together with limitations often found in the new environment including lack of adequate food, shelter, health care and social services call for specialized and enlarged assistance. Special attention has to be offered to women with special needs. Furthermore, the potential and capacities of refugee and displaced women should be recognized and enhanced.

299. It is recognized that a lasting solution to the problems of refugees and displaced women and children should be sought in the elimination of the root causes of the flow of refugees and durable solutions should be found leading to their voluntary return to their homes in conditions of safety and honour and their full integration in the economic, social and cultural life of their country of origin in the immediate future. Until such solutions are achieved, the international community, in an expression of international solidarity and burden-sharing, should continue providing relief assistance and also launching special relief programmes taking into account the specific needs of refugee women and children in countries of first asylum. Similarly, relief assistance and special relief programmes should also continue to be provided to returnees and displaced women and children. Legal, educational, social, humanitarian and moral assistance should be offered as well as opportunities for their voluntary repatriation, return or resettlement. Steps should also be taken to promote accession by Governments to the 1951 Convention relating to the Status of Refugees and to implement, on a basis of equity for all refugees, provisions contained in this Convention and its 1987 Protocol.

(m) *Migrant women*

300. The Decade has witnessed the increasing involvement of women in all forms of migration, including rural-rural, rural-urban and international movements of a temporary, seasonal or permanent nature. In addition to their lack of adequate education, skills and resources, migrant women may also face severe adjustment problems due to differences in religion, language, nationality, and socialization as well as separation from their original families. Such problems are often accentuated for international migrants as a result of the openly expressed prejudices and hostilities, including violation of human rights in host countries. Thus recommendations of the World Population Plan of Action and the Programme of Action for the Second Half of the United Nations Decade for Women pertaining to migrant women should be implemented and expanded in view of the anticipated increase in the scope of the problem. It is also urgent to conclude the elaboration of the draft International Convention on the Protection of the Rights of All Migrant Workers and their Families, as agreed by the General Assembly in the relevant resolutions.

301. The situation of migrant women, who are subject to double discrimination as women and as migrants, should be given special attention by the Governments of host countries, particularly with respect to protection and maintenance of family unity, employment opportunities and equal pay, equal conditions of work, health care, benefits to be provided in accordance with the existing social security rights in the host country, and racial and other forms of discrimination. Particular attention should also be given to the second genera-

tion of migrant women, especially with regard to education and professional training, to allow them to integrate themselves in their countries of adoption and to work according to their education and skills. In this process, loss of cultural values of their countries of origin should be avoided.

(n) *Minority and "indigenous" women*

302. Some women are oppressed as a result of belonging to minority groups or populations which have historically been subjected to domination and suffered dispossession and dispersal. These women suffer the full burden of discrimination based on race, colour, descent, ethnic and national origin and the majority experience serious economic deprivation. As women, they are therefore doubly disadvantaged. Measures should be taken by Governments in countries in which there are minority and indigenous populations to respect, preserve and promote all of their human rights, their dignity, ethnic, religious, cultural and linguistic identity and their full participation in societal change.

303. Governments should ensure that the fundamental human rights and freedoms as enshrined in relevant international instruments are fully guaranteed also to women belonging to minority groups and indigenous populations. Governments in countries in which there are indigenous and minority populations should ensure respect for the economic, social and cultural rights of these women and assist them in the fulfilment of their family and parental responsibilities. Specific measures should address dietary deficiencies, high levels of infant and maternal mortality and other health problems, lack of education, housing and child care. Vocational, technical, professional and other training should be provided to enable these women to secure employment or to participate in income-generating activities and projects, and to secure adequate wages, occupational health and safety and their other rights as workers. As far as possible, Governments should ensure that these women have access to all services in their own languages.

304. Women belonging to minority groups or indigenous populations should be fully consulted and should participate in the development and implementation of programmes affecting them. The Governments of countries where minorities and indigenous populations exist should take proper account of the work of bodies such as the Committee on the Elimination of Racial Discrimination and the Sub-Commission on Prevention of Discrimination and Protection of Minorities, in particular its Working Group which is developing a set of international standards to protect the rights of indigenous populations. The General Assembly should consider the advisability of designating an international year of indigenous and traditional cultures in order to promote international understanding and to emphasize the distinctive role of women in sustaining the identity of their people.

C. Peace

1. INVOLVEMENT OF WOMEN IN STRENGTHENING INTERNATIONAL PEACE AND CO-OPERATION

232. The World Conference of the International Women's Year, held at Mexico City in 1975, examined a report on the involvement of women in strengthening international peace and eliminating racism and racial discrimination.[71]

233. In resolution 29, on women's participation in the strengthening of international peace and security and in the struggle against colonialism, racism, racial discrimination and foreign domination, the Conference called upon "all Governments, intergovernmental and non-governmental organizations, women's organizations

---

[71] E/CONF.66/3/Add.2.

157

and women's groups to intensify their forces in order to strengthen peace, to expand and deepen the process of détente and to implement its irreversible character, to eliminate completely and definitely all forms of colonialism, to put an end to the policy and practice of *apartheid* and racism, and to foreign domination and aggression". Further, it urged all Governments "to take effective measures towards bringing about general and complete disarmament".

234. In the Declaration of Mexico on the Equality of Women and Their Contribution to Development and Peace, the Conference pointed out that "Women have a vital role to play in the promotion of peace in all spheres of life: in the family, the community, the nation and the world. Women must participate equally with men in the decision-making processes which help to promote peace at all levels." It further stated that "Peace requires that women as well as men should reject any type of intervention in the domestic affairs of States, whether it be openly or covertly carried on by other States or by transnational corporations. Peace also requires that women as well as men should also promote respect for the sovereign right of a State to establish its own economic, social and political system without undergoing political and economic pressures or coercion of any type."

235. After considering the report of the Conference the General Assembly, in resolution 3519 (XXX) of 15 December 1975, called upon "all Governments, intergovernmental and non-governmental organizations and women's groups, to intensify their efforts to strengthen peace, to expand and deepen the process of international détente and make it irreversible, to eliminate completely and definitely all forms of colonialism and to put an end to the policy and practice of *apartheid,* all forms of racism, racial discrimination, aggression, occupation and foreign domination".

2. DECLARATION ON THE PARTICIPATION OF WOMEN IN PROMOTING INTERNATIONAL PEACE AND CO-OPERATION

236. Two years later, in resolution 32/142 of 16 December 1977, the General Assembly requested the Commission on the Status of Women to consider the elaboration of a draft declaration on the participation of women in the struggle for the strengthening of international peace and security and against colonialism, racism, racial discrimination, foreign aggression and occupation and all forms of foreign domination. The Economic and Social Council expressed the hope, in resolution 1978/29 of 5 May 1978, that the Commission would make every effort to elaborate such a draft, and invited all Governments, specialized agencies and organizations to transmit their views and/or proposals concerning the nature and content of the draft, to the Secretary-General.

237. The Economic and Social Council, at it first regular session in 1978, expressed the hope, in resolution 1978/29 of 5 May 1978, that the Commission on the Status of Women would make every effort to consider elaborating the draft declaration on the participation of women in the struggle for the strengthening of international peace and security and against colonialism, racism, racial discrimination, foreign aggression and occupation and all forms of foreign domination requested by the Assembly in resolution 32/142; and invited all Governments, the specialized agencies and other intergovernmental organizations, as well as concerned non-governmental organizations in consultative status, to transmit to the Secretary-General their views and/or proposals concerning the nature and content of the proposed declaration.

238. The Secretary-General's report to the Commission[72] contained the text of a draft declaration submitted by the German Democratic Republic, as well as excerpts from replies received from 19 Governments and a brief summary of replies received from specialized agencies and non-governmental organizations.

239. The Commission set up a Working Group at its twenty-eighth session to consider the elaboration of the draft declaration. When it became apparent that the work could not be completed rapidly, the Commission recommended, and the Economic and Social Council agreed, in resolution 1980/36 of 2 May 1980, that the question should be referred to the General Assembly.

240. At its thirty-fifth session, the General Assembly considered a proposal submitted to its Third Committee[73] entitled "Draft Declaration on the Participation of Women in the Struggle for the Strengthening of International Peace and Security and against Colonialism, Racism, Racial Discrimination, Foreign Aggression, Occupation and All Forms of Foreign Domination". After extensive discussion in the Committee, the Assembly, by decision 35/429 of 11 December 1980, requested the Secretary-General to seek, and report on, the views of Governments.

241. The draft declaration was again discussed extensively in the Third Committee at the thirty-sixth session of the Assembly, but again the Committee was unable to conclude the discussions or even to examine fully the various proposals before it. The Assembly accordingly requested the Secretary-General, by decision 36/428 of 14 December 1981, to seek and to report further comments from Member States.

242. At the thirty-seventh session of the General Assembly, the Third Committee received and considered a draft resolution sponsored by 20 Member States[74] and adopted it as orally revised. On the recommendation of the Committee the General Assembly proclaimed, in

---

72 E/CN.6/626 and Add.1.

73 See *Official Records of the General Assembly, Thirty-fifth Session, Annexes,* agenda item 80, document A/35/639, paras. 6 and 7.

74 A/C.3/37/L.38.

resolution 37/63 of 3 December 1982, the Declaration on the Participation of Women in Promoting International Peace and Co-operation.

243. The Declaration contains a preamble and 14 articles. The preamble recalls that the Convention on the Elimination of All Forms of Discrimination against Women affirms that the strengthening of international peace and security, the relaxation of international tension, mutual co-operation among all States irrespective of their social and economic systems, general and complete disarmament and in particular, nuclear disarmament under strict and effective international control, the affirmation of the principles of justice, equality and mutual benefit in relations among countries and the realization of the right of peoples under alien and colonial domination and foreign occupation to self-determination and independence, as well as respect for national sovereignty and territorial integrity, will promote social progress and development, and as a consequence, will contribute to the attainment of full equality between men and women.

244. The articles of a general nature, contained in part I of the Declaration, include:

Article 1, which states that women and men have an equal and vital interest in contributing to international peace and co-operation, and that, to this end, women must be enabled to exercise their right to participate in the economic, social, cultural, civil and political affairs of society on an equal footing with men;

Article 2, which points out that the full participation of women in the econimic, social, cultural, civil and political affairs of society and in the endeavour to promote international peace and co-operation is dependent on a balanced and equitable distribution of roles between men and women in the family and in society as a whole;

Article 3, which states that the increasing participation of women in the economic, social, cultural, civil and political affairs of society will contribute to international peace and co-operation;

Article 4, which concludes that the full enjoyment of the rights of women and men and the full participation of women in promoting international peace and co-operation will contribute to the eradication of *apartheid*, of all forms of racism, racial discrimination, colonialism, neo-colonialism, aggression, foreign occupation and domination and interference in the internal affairs of States; and

Article 5, which indicates that special national and international measures are necessary to increase the level of women's participation in the sphere of international relations so that women can contribute, on an equal basis with men, to national and international efforts to secure world peace and economic and social progress and to promote international co-operation.

245. Articles 6 to 13, in part II of the Declaration, enumerate measures to be taken to improve the participation of women in promoting international peace and co-operation, including measures to ensure the equal participation of women in the economic, social, cultural, civil and political affairs of society through a balanced and equitable distribution of roles between men and women in the domestic sphere and in society as a whole, to promote the exchange of experience at the national and international levels for the purpose of furthering the involvement of women in promoting international peace and co-operation and in solving other vital national and international problems, to encourage women to participate in non-governmental and intergovernmental organizations aimed as the strengthening of

international peace and security, and to establish adequate legal protection of the rights of women on an equal basis with men in order to ensure effective participation of women in the activities referred to above.

246. Article 14, which concludes the Declaration, urges Governments, non-govermental and international organizations, including the United Nations and the specialized agencies, and individuals, to do all in their power to promote the implementation of the principles contained in the Declaration.

3. FORWARD-LOOKING STRATEGIES

247. The Nairobi Forward-looking Strategies for the Advancement of Women to the Year 2000,[75] adopted by the World Conference to Review and Appraise the Achievements of the United Nations Decade for Women: Equality, Development and Peace, held at Nairobi from 15 to 26 July 1985, outlined basic strategies for the participation of women in promoting international peace and co-operation, as contained in the following paragraphs:

239. The main principles and directions for women's activities aimed at strengthening peace and formulated in the Declaration on the Participation of Women in Promoting International Peace and Co-operation should be put into practice. The Declaration calls for Governments, the United Nations system, non-governmental organizations, relevant institutions and individuals to strengthen women's participation in this sphere and it provides the overall framework for such activities.

240. Women and men have an equal right and the same vital interest in contributing to international peace and co-operation. Women should participate fully in all efforts to strengthen and maintain international peace and security and to promote international co-operation, diplomacy, the process of détente, disarmament in the nuclear field in particular, and respect for the principles of the Charter of the United Nations, including respect for the sovereign rights of States, guarantees of fundamental freedoms and human rights, such as recognition of the dignity of the individual and self-determination, and freedom of thought, conscience, expression, association, assembly, communication and movement without distinction as to race, sex, political and religious beliefs, language or ethnic origin. The commitment to remove the obstacles to women's participation in the promotion of peace should be strengthened.

241. In view of the fact that women are still very inadequately represented in national and international political processes dealing with peace and conflict settlement, it is essential that women support and encourage each other in their initiatives and action relating either to universal issues, such as disarmament and the development of confidence-building measures between nations and people, or to specific conflict situations between or within States.

242. There exist situations in several regions of the world where the violation of principles of non-use of force, non-intervention, non-interference, non-aggression and the right to self-determination endangers international peace and security and creates massive humanitarian problems which constitute an impediment to the advancement of women and hence to the full implementation of the Forward-looking Strategies. In regard to these situations strict adherence to and respect for the cardinal principles enshrined in the Charter of the United Nations and implementation of relevant resolutions consistent

[75] *Report of the World Conference to Review and Appraise the Achievements of the United Nations Decade for Women: Equality, Development and Peace,* Nairobi, 15-26 July 1985 (United Nations publication, Sales No. E.85.IV.10).

with the principles of the Charter are an imperative requirement with a view to seeking solutions to such problems; thereby ensuring a secure and better future for the people affected, most of whom are invariably women and children.

243. Since women are one of the most vulnerable groups in the regions affected by armed conflicts, special attention has to be drawn to the need to eliminate obstacles to the fulfilment of the objectives of equality, development and peace and the principles of the Charter of the United Nations.

244. One of the important obstacles to achieving international peace is the persistent violation of the principles and objectives of the Charter of the United Nations and the lack of political will of Governments of some countries to promote constructive negotiations aimed at decreasing international tension on the issues that seriously threaten the maintenance of international peace and security. For this reason, the strategies in this field should include the mobilization of women in favour of all acts and actions that tend to promote peace, in particular, the elimination of wars and danger of nuclear war.

245. Immediate and special priority should be given to the promotion and the effective enjoyment of human rights and fundamental freedoms for all without distinction as to sex, the full application of the rights of peoples to self-determination and the elimination of colonialism, neo-colonialism, *apartheid,* of all forms of racism and racial discrimination, oppression and aggression, foreign occupation, as well as domestic violence and violence against women.

246. In South-West Asia women and children have endured serious suffering owing to the violation of the Charter of the United Nations, leading, among other things, to the vast problem of refugees in neighbouring countries.

247. The situation of violence and destabilization that exists in Central America constitutes the most serious obstacle to the achievement of peace in the region and thus hinders the fulfilment of the Forward-looking Strategies vital to the advancement of women. In this regard and to promote conditions favourable to the objectives of the Strategies, it is important to reiterate the principles of non-intervention and self-determination, as well as the non-use of force or rejection of the threat of use of force in the solution of conflicts in the region. Therefore, the validity of the United Nations resolutions that establish the right of all sovereign States in the area to live in peace, free from all interference in their internal affairs, should be reaffirmed. It is necessary to support the negotiated political solutions and the peace proposals that the Central American States adopt under the auspices of the Contadora Group, as the most viable alternative for the solution of the crisis in Central America for the benefit of their people. In this sense it is important that the five Central American Governments speed up their consultations with the Contadora Group with the aim of bringing to a conclusion the negotiation process with the early signing of the Contadora Act on Peace and Co-operation in Central America (see A/39/562-S/16775, annex).

248. Women have played and continue to play an important role in the self-determination of peoples, including through national liberation, in accordance with the United Nations Charter. Their efforts should be recognized and commended and used as one basis for their full participation in the construction of their countries, and in the creation of humane and just social and political systems. Women's contribution in this area should be ensured by their equal access to political power and their full participation in the decision-making process.

249. Strategies at the national, regional and the global levels should be based on a clear recognition that peace and security, self-determination and national independence are fundamental for the attainment of the three objectives of the Decade: equality, development and peace.

250. Safeguarding world peace and averting a nuclear catastrophe is one of the most important tasks today in which women have an essential role to play, especially by supporting actively the halting of the arms race followed by arms reduction and the attainment of a general and complete disarmament under effective international control, and thus contributing to the improvement of their economic position. Irrespective of their socio-economic system, the States should strive to avoid confrontation and to build friendly relations instead, which should be also supported by women.

251. Peace requires the participation of all members of society, women and men alike, in rejecting any type of intervention in the domestic affairs of States, whether it is openly or covertly carried out by other States or by transnational corporations. Peace also requires that women and men alike should promote respect for the sovereign right of a State to establish its own economic, social and political system without undergoing political and economic pressures or coercion of any type.

252. There exists a relationship between the world economic situation, development and the strengthening of international peace and security, disarmament and the relaxation of international tension. All efforts should be made to reduce global expenditures on armaments and to reach an agreement on the internationally agreed disarmament goals in order to prevent the waste of immense material and human resources, some part of which might otherwise be used for development, especially of the developing countries, as well as for the improvement of standards of living and well-being of people in each country. In this context, particular attention should be given to the advancement of women, including to the participation of women in the promotion of international peace and co-operation and the protection of mothers and children who represent a disproportionate share of the most vulnerable group, the poorest of the poor.

253. Women's equal role in decision-making with respect to peace and related issues should be seen as one of their basic human rights and as such should be enhanced and encouraged at the national, regional and international levels. In accordance with the Convention on the Elimination of All Forms of Discrimination against Women, all existing impediments to the achievement by women of equality with men should be removed. To this end, efforts should be intensified at all levels to overcome prejudices, stereotyped thinking, denial to women of career prospects and appropriate educational possibilities, and resistance by decison-makers to the changes that are necessary to enable equal participation of women with men in the international and diplomatic service.

254. Mankind is confronted with a choice: to halt the arms race and proceed to disarmament or face annihilation. The growing opposition of women to the danger of war, especially a nuclear war, which will lead to a nuclear holocaust, and their support for disarmament must be respected. States should be encouraged to ensure unhindered flow and access to information, including to women, with regard to various aspects of disarmament to avoid dissemination of false and tendentious information concerning armaments and to concentrate on the danger of the escalation of the arms race and on the need for general and complete disarmament under effective international control. The resources released as a result of disarmament measures should be used to help promote the well-being of all peoples and improve the economic and social conditions of the developing countries. Under such conditions, States should pay increased attention to the urgent need to improve the situation of women.

255. Peace education should be established for all members of society, particularly children and young people. Values, such as tolerance, racial and sexual equality, respect for and understanding of others, and good-neighbourliness should be developed, promoted and strengthened.

256. Women of the world, together with men, should, as informal educators and socialization agents, play a special role in the process of bringing up younger generations in an atmosphere of compassion, tolerance, mutual concern and trust, with an awareness that all people belong to the same world community. Such education should be part of all formal and informal educational processes as well as of communications, information and mass-media systems.

257. Further action should be taken at family and neighbourhood levels, as well as at national and international levels, to achieve a peaceful social environment compatible with human dignity. The questions of women and peace and the meaning of peace for women cannot be separated from the broader question of relationships between women and men in all spheres of life and in the family. Discriminatory practices and negative attitudes towards women should be eliminated and traditional gender norms changed to enhance women's participation in peace.

258. Violence against women exists in various forms in everyday life in all societies. Women are beaten, mutilated, burned, sexually

abused and raped. Such violence is a major obstacle to the achievement of peace and the other objectives of the Decade and should be given special attention. Women victims of violence should be given particular attention and comprehensive assistance. To this end, legal measures should be formulated to prevent violence and to assist women victims. National machinery should be established in order to deal with the question of violence against women within the family and society. Preventive policies should be elaborated, and institutionalized forms of assistance to women victims provided.

D. Long-term programme of work for the advancement of women

1. SYSTEM-WIDE, MEDIUM-TERM PLAN FOR WOMEN AND DEVELOPMENT, 1990-1995

248. In resolution 1985/46 of 31 May 1985, the Economic and Social Council urged all United Nations bodies, including the regional commissions, and the specialized agencies which had not then done so, to develop and implement comprehensive policies for women and development and to incorporate them into their medium-term plans, statements of objectives, programmes and other major policy statements. The Council, further, requested the Secretary-General, in his capacity as Chairman of the Administrative Committee on Co-ordination, to take the initiative in formulating a system-wide, medium-term plan for women and development. The World Conference to Review and Appraise the Achievements of the United Nations Decade for Women also called for a system-wide, medium-term plan in order to achieve greater coherence and efficiency of the policies and programmes of the United Nations system related to women and development.

249. A report on the proposed framework of the plan (E/1986/8) was submitted to the Economic and Social Council at its second regular session of 1986 through the Commission on the Status of Women and the Committee for Programme and Co-ordination. The Council, in resolution 1986/71 of 23 July 1986, took note of the proposed framework and arranged for it to be analysed and reviewed by the Committee for Programme and Co-ordination and the Commission on the Status of Women.

250. A draft of the system-wide, medium-term plan for women and development (E/CN.6/1987/2) was submitted by the Secretary-General to the Commission on the Status of Women at its session held from 12 to 16 January 1987. The draft was revised, taking into account the recommendations of the Commission, and submitted by the Administrative Committee on Co-ordination to the Council (E/1987/52).

251. When the Council considered the plan, it recommended, in paragraph 5 of its resolution 1987/86 of 8 July 1987, that the Administrative Committee on Co-ordination should report to it, through the Commission on the Status of Women, on arrangements to implement the system-wide plan.

2. LONG-TERM PROGRAMME OF WORK OF THE COMMISSION ON THE STATUS OF WOMEN

252. The Commission on the Status of Women at its 1987 session made significant progress and self-reform. It restructured its agenda along functional lines, developed a systematic long-term programme of work and urged improvements in the system of reporting, monitoring and appraising the implementation of the Forward-looking Strategies; it strengthened and rationalized its role and functions in the mobilization of the resources of the United Nations system as a whole towards the advancement of women, by integrating this objective in the programme planning and budgeting processes of the Organization; it agreed to hold annual sessions until the year 2000.

253. In resolution 1987/24 of 26 May 1987, the Economic and Social Council endorsed the long-term programme of work of the Commission, including an annual consideration of three themes, one under each of the three objectives—equality, development and peace —beginning with its thirty-second session in 1988, in the order listed below:

(a) *Equality*

1. National machinery for monitoring and improving the status of women;
2. Equality in economic and social participation;
3. Equality in political participation and decision-making;
4. Vulnerable women, including migrant women;
5. Elimination of *de jure* and *de facto* discrimination against women.

(b) *Development*

1. Problems of rural women, including food, water resources, agricultural technology, rural employment, transportation and environment;
2. Women and education, eradication of illiteracy, employment, health and social services, including population issues and child care;
3. Negative effects of the international economic situation on the improvement of the status of women;
4. National, regional and international machinery for the effective integration of women in the development process, including non-governmental organizations;
5. Integration of women in the process of development.

(c) *Peace*

1. Access to information, education for peace, and efforts to eradicate violence against women within the family and society;
2. Full participation of women in the construction of their countries and in the creation of just social and political systems;
3. Women in areas affected by armed conflicts, foreign intervention, alien and colonial domination, foreign occupation and threats to peace;

4. Refugee and displaced women and children;

5. Equal participation in all efforts to promote international co-operation, peace and disarmament.

254. The Council further decided that the work of the Commission in relation to the priority themes should be closely related to the relevant provisions of the Forward-looking Strategies and other policy documents, the programmes elaborated in the system-wide, medium-term plan for women and development and the relevant chapters of the *World Survey on the Role of Women in Development*,[76] with a view to ensuring the effective implementation of the Forward-looking Strategies and lasting improvement in the situation of women.

---

[76] United Nations publication, Sales No. E.86.IV.3.

VII. REALIZATION OF ECONOMIC, SOCIAL AND CULTURAL RIGHTS

Introduction

1. A number of United Nations organs are engaged in activities aimed at ensuring the realization of economic, social and cultural rights under the general obligations undertaken by all Member States in accordance with the Charter; these include the General Assembly, the Economic and Social Council, the Commission on Human Rights, the Sub-Commission on Prevention of Discrimination and Protection of Minorities and the Commission on the Status of Women. In addition, several specialized agencies are engaged in such activities under the provisions of their respective Constitutions; these include the International Labour Organisation, the United Nations Educational, Scientific and Cultural Organization, the Food and Agriculture Organization and the World Health Organization. Recently, a new United Nations organ was especially created to monitor the realization of economic, social and cultural rights: the Committee on Economic, Social and Cultural Rights.

2. The International Covenant on Economic, Social and Cultural Rights, adopted by the General Assembly on 16 December 1966, entered into force on 3 January 1976, and for some time the Economic and Social Council endeavoured to establish effective machinery to supervise the application of its provisions. The Commission on Human Rights, in resolution 1985/42 of 14 March 1985, recalled that the International Conference on Human Rights had pointed out in the Proclamation of Teheran[1] that the full realization of civil and political rights without the enjoyment of economic, social and cultural rights was impossible, and expressed its own concern with regard to the implementation of economic, social and cultural rights in many countries of the world. Feeling that the promotion and implementation of economic, social and cultural rights and the obstacles to their realization had not received sufficient attention within the framework of the United Nations system, the Commission appealed to all States to pursue a policy directed towards the implementation of those rights. In this connection it requested the Sub-Commission to examine and update the conclusions and recommendations contained in the report entitled *The Realization of Economic, Social and Cultural Rights: Problems, Policies, Progress,*[2] taking account of the latest develop-

ments in the field; and to pursue its study on the right to food as a matter of priority.

3. At its forty-second session, the Commission received reports of the ILO, UNESCO, FAO and WHO on the state of implementation of the rights to food, health, education and work.[3] In resolution 1986/15 of 10 March 1986, it repeated its request to the Sub-Commission and called upon the Secretary-General to prepare for the Commission a report containing the comments made by Governments, United Nations organs, specialized agencies and non-governmental organizations on the realization of economic, social and cultural rights.

4. The following year, in resolution 1987/20 of 10 March 1987, the Commission, after noting the studies of the Sub-Commission in the field of economic, social and cultural rights, found that despite progress achieved by the international community with respect to the setting of standards for the realization of those rights, much remained to be done with regard to their implementation. It pointed out that full respect for the rights contained in the International Covenant on Economic, Social and Cultural Rights is inextricably linked with the process of development, the central purpose of which is the realization of the potentialities of the human person in harmony with the community, and that full and sustained implementation of the Covenant requires the effective participation of all members of society in relevant decision-making processes as agents and beneficiaries of development, as well as fair distribution of the benefits of development.

5. The Commission, further, emphasized the direct relevance of the work of the Committee on Economic, Social and Cultural Rights to activities being undertaken throughout the United Nations system in the field of economic, social and cultural development and the need to improve co-ordination of these activities; and urged the Economic and Social Council to bear in mind its central responsibility in relation to the implementation of the International Covenant on Economic, Social and Cultural Rights. At the same time it requested the Sub-Commission on Prevention of Discrimination and Protection of Minorities to make further recommendations on how to promote more effectively the implementation of the provisions of the Covenant on Economic, Social and Cultural Rights through United Nations development programmes and other activities.

6. Under agreements between the United Nations and the specialized agencies, the Economic and Social Council co-ordinates the activities of those agencies

---

[1] *Final Act of the International Conference on Human Rights, Teheran, 22 April-13 May 1968* (United Nations publication, Sales No. E.68.XIV.2), chap. II.

[2] United Nations publication, Sales No. E.75.XIV.2, part six, chaps. II and III.

[3] E/CN.4/1986/38 and Corr.1 and Add.1-3.

through recommendations to the General Assembly and to Member States. Under Article 64 of the Charter of the United Nations, the Council has taken steps to obtain regular reports from the specialized agencies, including reports on the measures taken by them to give effect to the Council's own recommendations and to recommendations on matters falling within its competence made by the General Assembly. Under Article 70 of the Charter, the Council has made arrangements for representatives of the specialized agencies to participate, without vote, in its deliberations and in those of the commissions established by it. The agreements also provide for the right of each of the two organizations, after prior consultation, to include questions in the agenda of certain bodies of the other organization, for the fullest and most speedy exchange of information and documents, and for administrative and financial arrangements designed to prevent, as far as possible, the establishment of competing or overlapping departments within the United Nations and the specialized agencies.

A. The right to work

7. The enjoyment of the right to work is ensured not only by international instruments prepared by United Nations bodies, such as the Universal Declaration of Human Rights, the International Covenant on Economic, Social and Cultural Rights, the International Convention on the Elimination of All Forms of Racial Discrimination, the Declaration on the Elimination of Discrimination against Women and the Convention on the Elimination of All Forms of Discrimination against Women, but also by international instruments prepared under the auspices of ILO, including the Discrimination (Employment and Occupation) Convention and Recommendation, 1958 (No. 111), the Employment Policy Convention, 1964 (No. 122), the Recommendations of 1964 and 1984 on the same subject, and the instruments on equality of opportunity and treatment.

1. PROVISIONS OF UNITED NATIONS INSTRUMENTS

8. Article 23 of the Universal Declaration of Human Rights provides that:

1. Everyone has the right to work, to free choice of employment, to just and favourable conditions of work and to protection against unemployment.

2. Everyone, without any discrimination, has the right to equal pay for equal work.

3. Everyone who works has the right to just and favourable remuneration ensuring for himself and his family an existence worthy of human dignity, and supplemented, if necessary, by other means of social protection.

4. Everyone has the right to form and to join trade unions for the protection of his interests.

9. Articles 6 and 7 of the International Covenant on Economic, Social and Cultural Rights read as follows:

Article 6

1. The States Parties to the present Covenant recognize the right to work, which includes the right of everyone to the opportunity to gain his living by work which he freely chooses or accepts, and will take appropriate steps to safeguard this right.

2. The steps to be taken by a State Party to the present Covenant to achieve the full realization of this right shall include technical and vocational guidance and training programmes, policies and techniques to achieve steady economic, social and cultural development and full and productive employment under conditions safeguarding fundamental political and economic freedoms to the individual.

Article 7

The States Parties to the present Covenant recognize the right of everyone to the enjoyment of just and favourable conditions of work which ensure, in particular:

(a) Remuneration which provides all workers, as a minimum, with:

(i) Fair wages and equal remuneration for work of equal value without distinction of any kind, in particular women being guaranteed conditions of work not inferior to those enjoyed by men, with equal pay for equal work;

(ii) A decent living for themselves and their families in accordance with the provisions of the present Covenant;

(b) Safe and healthy working conditions;

(c) Equal opportunity for everyone to be promoted in his employment to an appropriate higher level, subject to no considerations other than those of seniority and competence;

(d) Rest, leisure and reasonable limitation of working hours and periodic holidays with pay, as well as remuneration for public holidays.

10. Under article 5 of the International Convention on the Elimination of All Forms of Racial Discrimination, adopted and opened for signature and ratification by the General Assembly in resolution 2106 A (XX) of 21 December 1965, "States Parties undertake to prohibit and eliminate racial discrimination in all its forms and to guarantee the right of everyone, without distinction as to race, colour, or national or ethnic origin, to equality before the law", notably in the enjoyment of certain economic, social and cultural rights, including the right to work, to free choice of employment, to just and favourable conditions of work, to protection against unemployment, to equal pay for equal work, and to just and favourable remuneration.

11. Article 10 of the Declaration on the Elimination of Discrimination against Women, proclaimed by the General Assembly on 7 November 1967 in resolution 2263 (XXII), provides that:

1. All appropriate measures shall be taken to ensure to women, married or unmarried, equal rights with men in the field of economic and social life, and in particular:

(a) The right, without discrimination on grounds of marital status or any other grounds, to receive vocational training, to work, to free choice of profession and employment, and to professional and vocational advancement;

(b) The right to equal remuneration with men and to equality of treatment in respect of work of equal value;

(c) The right to leave with pay, retirement privileges and provision for security in respect of unemployment, sickness, old age or other incapacity to work;

(d) The right to receive family allowances on equal terms with men.

2. In order to prevent discrimination against women on account of marriage or maternity and to ensure their effective right to work, measures shall be taken to prevent their dismissal in the event of marriage or maternity and to provide paid maternity leave, with the guarantee of returning to former employment, and to provide the necessary social services, including child-care facilities.

3. Measures taken to protect women in certain types of work, for reasons inherent in their physical nature, shall not be regarded as discriminatory.

12. Article 11 of the Convention on the Elimination of All Forms of Discrimination against Women, adopted and opened for signature, ratification and accession by the General Assembly in resolution 34/180 of 18 December 1979, reads as follows:

1. States Parties shall take all appropriate measures to eliminate discrimination against women in the field of employment in order to ensure, on a basis of equality of men and women, the same rights, in particular:

(a) The right to work as an inalienable right of all human beings;

(b) The right to the same employment opportunities, including the application of the same criteria for selection in matters of employment;

(c) The right to free choice of profession and employment, the right to promotion, job security and all benefits and conditions of service and the right to receive vocational training and retraining, including apprenticeships, advanced vocational training and recurrent training;

(d) The right to equal remuneration, including benefits, and to equal treatment in respect of work of equal value, as well as equality of treatment in the evaluation of the quality of work;

(e) The right to social security, particularly in cases of retirement, unemployment, sickness, invalidity and old age and other incapacity to work, as well as the right to paid leave;

(f) The right to protection of health and to safety in working conditions, including the safeguarding of the function of reproduction.

2. In order to prevent discrimination against women on the grounds of marriage or maternity and to ensure their effective right to work, States Parties shall take appropriate measures:

(a) To prohibit, subject to the imposition of sanctions, dismissal on the grounds of pregnancy or of maternity leave and discrimination in dismissals on the basis of marital status;

(b) To introduce maternity leave with pay or with comparable social benefits without loss of former employment, seniority or social allowances;

(c) To encourage the provision of the necessary supporting social services to enable parents to combine family obligations with work responsibilities and participation in public life, in particular through promoting the establishment and development of a network of childcare facilities;

(d) To provide special protection to women during pregnancy in types of work proved to be harmful to them.

3. Protective legislation relating to matters covered in this article shall be reviewed periodically in the light of scientific and technological knowledge and shall be revised, repealed or extended as necessary.

2. PROVISIONS OF ILO INSTRUMENTS

13. Article 1 of the Employment Policy Convention, 1964 (No. 122), reads as follows:

1. With a view to stimulating economic growth and development, raising levels of living, meeting manpower requirements and overcoming unemployment and underemployment, each Member shall declare and pursue, as a major goal, an active policy designed to promote full, productive and freely chosen employment.

2. The said policy shall aim at ensuring that:

(a) There is work for all who are available for and seeking work;

(b) Such work is as productive as possible;

(c) There is freedom of choice of employment and the fullest possible opportunity for each worker to qualify for, and to use his skills and endowments in, a job for which he is well suited, irrespective of race, colour, sex, religion, political opinion, national extraction or social origin.

3. The said policy shall take due account of the stage and level of economic development and the mutual relationships between employment objectives and other economic and social objectives, and shall be pursued by methods that are appropriate to national conditions and practices.

14. The Employment Policy Recommendation, 1964 (No. 122), provides further guidelines on measures and methods of implementation. The Employment Policy (Supplementary Provisions) Recommendation, 1984 (No. 169), places the issues within the wider framework of the principles and programmes of action set in 1976 by the Tripartite World Conference on Employment.

15. The subject of discrimination in employment and occupation was included in the agenda of the International Labour Conference in 1957, at the invitation of the Sub-Commission on Prevention of Discrimination and Protection of Minorities and the Commission on Human Rights. Their views on the draft texts of the proposed ILO instruments were communicated to the International Labour Conference at its 1958 session, at which the Discrimination (Employment and Occupation) Convention, 1958 (No. 111), and Recommendation, 1958 (No. 111), were adopted.

3. MEASURES TO ELIMINATE DISCRIMINATION IN EMPLOYMENT AND OCCUPATION[4]

16. Under article 2 of the Discrimination (Employment and Occupation) Convention, 1958 (No. 111), ratifying States undertake to declare and pursue a national policy designed to promote equality of opportunity and treatment with a view to eliminating discrimination in employment and occupation. Legislative and administrative action, and educational programmes, are envisaged by article 3, which also calls for the co-operation of employers' and workers' organizations and other appropriate bodies. "Discrimination", as defined in article 1, includes "any distinction, exclusion or preference made on basis of race, colour, sex, religion, political opinions, national extraction or social origin which has the effect of nullifying of impairing equality of opportunity or treatment". Distinctions, exclusions or preferences in respect of particular jobs, based on the inherent requirements thereof, shall not be deemed to be discrimination; nor shall be so deemed any measures affecting an individual for activities prejudicial to the security of the State as stipulated in article 4, and special measures or protection or assistance referred to in article 5.

17. The Discrimination (Employment and Occupation) Recommendation, 1958 (No. 111), provides scientific guidelines for the formulation and implementation of the relevant national policy.

---

[4] For information on ILO procedures for the implementation of Conventions and Recommendations, see chap. XIV, sect. D, 1.

18. In addition, the Workers with Family Responsibilities Convention, 1981 (No. 156), and Recommendation, 1981 (No. 165), aim at creating effective equality of opportunity and treatment with respect to economic activity, for men and women workers having such responsibilities.

B. The right to education

19. The United Nations and the United Nations Educational, Scientific and Cultural Organization have co-operated closely in matters relating to the right to education, including the eradication of illiteracy, the education of youth in respect for human rights and fundamental freedoms, and the eradication of discrimination in education. There has also been co-operation in such matters as the observance of 1970 as International Education Year and in the establishment of the United Nations University.

20. The enjoyment by everyone of the right to education is ensured not only by the International Covenant on Economic, Social and Cultural Rights, the International Convention on the Elimination of All Forms of Racial Discrimination and the Convention on the Elimination of All Forms of Discrimination against Women, prepared by the United Nations, but also by the Convention and Recommendation against Discrimination in Education, the Protocol to the Convention, and other instruments prepared under the auspices of UNESCO.

1. PROVISIONS OF UNITED NATIONS INSTRUMENTS

21. Article 26 of the Universal Declaration of Human Rights provides that:

1. Everyone has the right to education. Education shall be free, at least in the elementary and fundamental stages. Elementary education shall be compulsory. Technical and professional education shall be made generally available and higher education shall be equally accessible to all on the basis of merit.

2. Education shall be directed to the full development of the human personality and to the strengthening of respect for human rights and fundamental freedoms. It shall promote understanding, tolerance and friendship among all nations, racial or religious groups, and shall further the activities of the United Nations for the maintenance of peace.

3. Parents have a prior right to chose the kind of education that shall be given to their children.

22. Articles 13 and 14 of the International Covenant on Economic, Social and Cultural Rights deal with the right to education in the following provisions:

Article 13

1. The States Parties to the present Covenant recognize the right of everyone to education. They agree that education shall be directed to the full development of the human personality and the sense of its dignity, and shall strengthen the respect of human rights and fundamental freedoms. They further agree that education shall enable all persons to participate effectively in a free society, promote understanding, tolerance and friendship among all nations and all racial, ethnic or religious groups, and further the activities of the United Nations for the maintenance of peace.

2. The States Parties to the present Covenant recognize that, with a view to achieving the full realization of this right:

(*a*) Primary education shall be compulsory and available free to all;

(*b*) Secondary education in its different forms, including technical and vocational secondary education, shall be made generally available and accessible to all by every appropriate means, and in particular by the progressive introduction of free education;

(*c*) Higher education shall be made equally accessible to all, on the basis of capacity, by every appropriate means, and in particular by the progressive introduction of free education;

(*d*) Fundamental education shall be encouraged or intensified as far as possible for those persons who have not received or completed the whole period of their primary education;

(*e*) The development of a system of schools at all levels shall be actively pursued, an adequate fellowship system shall be established, and the material conditions of teaching staff shall be continuously improved.

3. The States Parties to the present Covenant undertake to have respect for the liberty of parents and, when applicable, legal guardians to choose for their children schools, other than those established by the public authorities, which conform to such minimum educational standards as may be laid down or approved by the State and to ensure the religious and moral education of their children in conformity with their own convictions.

4. No part of this article shall be construed so as to interfere with the liberty of individuals and bodies to establish and direct educational institutions, subject always to the observance of the principles set forth in paragraph 1 of this article and to the requirement that the education given in such institutions shall conform to such minimum standards as may be laid down by the State.

Article 14

Each State Party to the present Covenant which, at the time of becoming a Party, has not been able to secure in its metropolitan territory or other territories under its jurisdiction compulsory primary education, free of charge, undertakes, within two years, to work out and adopt a detailed plan of action for the progressive implementation, within a reasonable number of years, to be fixed in the plan, of the principle of compulsory education free of charge for all.

23. Under article 5 of the International Convention on the Elimination of All Forms of Racial Discrimination, adopted and opened for signature and ratification by General Assembly resolution 2106 A (XX) of 21 December 1965, States parties undertake to prohibit and eliminate racial discrimination in all its forms and to guarantee the right of everyone, without distinction as to race, colour, or national or ethnic origin, to equality before the law, notably in the enjoyment of certain economic, social and cultural rights, including the right to education and training.

24. Paragraph 14 of the Proclamation of Teheran, adopted at the twenty-seventh plenary meeting of the International Conference on Human Rights on 13 May 1968, points out that "the existence of over seven hundred million illiterates throughout the world is an enormous obstacle to all efforts at realizing the aims and purposes of the Charter of the United Nations and the provisions of the Universal Declaration of Human Rights. International action aimed at eradicating illiteracy from the face of the earth and promoting education at all levels requires urgent attention."

25. Article 10 of the Convention on the Elimination of All Forms of Discrimination against Women, adopted and opened for signature, ratification and accession by the General Assembly in resolution 34/180 of 18 December 1979, reads as follows:

States Parties shall take all appropriate measures to eliminate discrimination against women in order to ensure to them equal rights with men in the field of education and in particular to ensure, on a basis of equality of men and women:

(a) The same conditions for career and vocational guidance, for access to studies and for the achievement of diplomas in educational establishments of all categories in rural as well as in urban areas; this equality shall be ensured in pre-school, general, technical, professional and higher technical education, as well as in all types of vocational training;

(b) Access to the same curricula, the same examinations, teaching staff with qualifications of the same standard and school premises and equipment of the same quality;

(c) The elimination of any stereotyped concept of the roles of men and women at all levels and in all forms of education by encouraging coeducation and other types of education which will help to achieve this aim and, in particular, by the revision of textbooks and school programmes and the adaptation of teaching methods;

(d) The same opportunities to benefit from scholarships and other study grants;

(e) The same opportunities for access to programmes of continuing education, including adult and functional literacy programmes, particularly those aimed at reducing, at the earliest possible time, any gap in education existing between men and women;

(f) The reduction of female student drop-out rates and the organization of programmes for girls and women who have left school prematurely;

(g) The same opportunities to participate actively in sports and physical education;

(h) Access to specific educational information to help to ensure the health and well-being of families, including information and advice on family planning.

2. PROVISIONS OF UNESCO INSTRUMENTS

26. The *Study of Discrimination in Education*[5] was the first of a series of studies of discrimination in various fields prepared by the Sub-Commission on Prevention of Discrimination and Protection of Minorities under the authorization of the Commission on Human Rights and the Economic and Social Council.

27. At its sixth session, in 1954, the Sub-Commission decided to undertake the study and appointed one of its members, Mr. Charles D. Ammoun, as its Special Rapporteur. The Sub-Commission prepared directives to govern the Special Rapporteur's work which were later approved, with slight amendments, by the Commission and the Council. These directives later were applied in the case of all studies of discrimination undertaken by the Sub-Commission. The study was completed and published in 1957.

28. At its eleventh session, in 1959, the Sub-Commission was advised of action which had been taken by the General Conference of UNESCO at its tenth session in 1958. The General Conference had decided that UNESCO should assume responsibility for drafting recommendations to member States and an international convention on various aspects of discrimination in education, and had authorized the Director-General "to prepare a preliminary report, draft recommendations, and a draft Convention to be circulated to Member States for comments, and to convene in 1960 a com-

mittee of technical and legal experts appointed by Member States with a view to submitting revised drafts of such recommendations and of a Convention to the eleventh session of the General Conference".

29. At its thirteenth session, in 1961, the Director-General informed the Sub-Commission that the General Conference had adopted the Convention and the Recommendation against Discrimination in Education on 14 December 1960. The Director-General indicated that the General Conference had also adopted a resolution requesting him to prepare and submit to an *Ad Hoc* Committee of the Conference, consisting of government experts, a draft protocol instituting a conciliation and good offices committee competent to seek a settlement of any disputes which might arise between States parties concerning the application or interpretation of the Convention.

3. MEASURES TO ELIMINATE DISCRIMINATION IN EDUCATION[6]

30. States parties to the UNESCO Convention against Discrimination in Education undertake:

(a) To abrogate any statutory provisions and any administrative instructions and to discontinue any administrative practices which involve discrimination in education;

(b) To ensure, by legislation where necessary, that there is no discrimination in the admission of pupils to educational institutions;

(c) Not to allow any differences of treatment by the public authorities between nationals, except on the basis of merit or need, in the matter of school fees and the grant of scholarships or other forms of assistance to pupils and necessary permits and facilities for the pursuit of studies in foreign countries;

(d) Not to allow, in any form of assistance granted by the public authorities to educational institutions, any restrictions or preference based solely on the ground that pupils belong to a particular group;

(e) To give foreign nationals resident within their territory the same access to education as that given to their own nationals.

31. The Convention further provides that the States parties undertake to "develop and apply a national policy which, by methods appropriate to the circumstances and to national usage, will tend to promote equality of opportunity and of treatment in the matter of education . . .".

32. The adoption by the General Conference of a Recommendation, simultaneously with the Convention, was a response to the desire to take account of the difficulties which certain States might, for various reasons —and particularly because of their federal structure—experience in ratifying the Convention. Subject to the differences of wording and of statutory scope inherent in the nature of these two categories of instruments, the content of the Recommendation is identical to that of the Convention.

33. In resolution 821 V B (XXXII) of 19 July 1961, the Economic and Social Council noted with appreciation the Convention and Recommendation against Discrimination in Education and invited the Governments

---

[5] United Nations publication, Sales No. E.57.XIV.3.

[6] For information on UNESCO procedures for the implementation of Conventions and Recommendations, see chap. XIV, sect. D, 2.

of Member States to apply the provisions of those instruments as fully as possible and to provide full opportunities for young persons of both sexes to take the same or equivalent courses of study.

34. On 10 December 1962 the General Conference of UNESCO adopted the Protocol Instituting a Conciliation and Good Offices Commission to be responsible for seeking a settlement of any disputes which may arise between States Parties to the Convention against Discrimination in Education. The Protocol entered into force on 24 October 1968.

35. In addition to the Convention, Recommendation and Protocol, UNESCO has adopted several instruments on the realization of the right to education. One of these was the Recommendation concerning Education for International Understanding, Co-operation and Peace and Education relating to Human Rights and Fundamental Freedoms, adopted by the General Conference of UNESCO on 19 November 1974 and directed at the implementation of article 26, paragraph 2, of the Universal Declaration of Human Rights and article 13, paragraph 1, of the International Covenant on Economic, Social and Cultural Rights. Among the principles set out in the Recommendation are that education should be so conceived as to promote: "an international dimension and a global perspective in education at all levels and in all its forms"; "understanding and respect for all peoples, their cultures, civilizations, values and ways of life, including domestic ethnic cultures and cultures of other nations"; "awareness of the increasing global interdependence between peoples and nations"; and understanding of "the inadmissibility of recourse to war for purposes of expansion, aggression or domination, or to the use of force and violence for purposes of repression . . .". Member States are urged to "take steps to ensure that the principles of the Universal Declaration of Human Rights and of the International Convention on the Elimination of All Forms of Racial Discrimination become an integral part of the developing personality of each child, adolescent, young person and adult by applying these principles in the daily conduct of education at each level and in all its forms . . .".

36. Other UNESCO instruments having a bearing on the right to education include the Declaration of the Principles of International Cultural Co-operation of 4 November 1966; the Declaration of Guiding Principles on the Use of Satellite Broadcasting for the Free Flow of Information, the Spread of Education and Greater Cultural Exchange of 15 November 1972; the Declaration on Race and Racial Prejudice of 27 November 1978; the Declaration on Fundamental Principles concerning the Contribution of the Mass Media to Strengthening Peace and International Understanding, to the Promotion of Human Rights and to Countering Racialism, *Apartheid* and Incitement to War of 28 November 1978; and the Convention concerning the Protection of the World Cultural and Natural Heritage of 16 November 1972.

37. In addition to the Recommendation against Discrimination in Education, mentioned above, UNESCO has adopted a number of recommendations having a bearing on the right to education, including the Recommendation concerning the Status of Teachers of 5 October 1966; the Recommendation concerning Education for International Understanding, Co-operation and Peace and Education relating to Human Rights and Fundamental Freedoms of 19 November 1974; the Recommendation on the Development of Adult Education of 26 November 1976; the Recommendation on Participation by the People at Large in Cultural Life and Their Contribution to It of 16 November 1976; and the Recommendation concerning the International Exchange of Cultural Property of 26 November 1976. As regards the Recommendation on the Development of Adult Education, the Director-General presented to the General Conference at its 24th session (October-November 1987) his proposals on the procedure and periodicity for the presentation and examination of the reports from Member States relating to its application.

38. In a report submitted to the General Assembly in 1980,[7] in accordance with paragraph 3 of Assembly resolution 34/170, the Director-General of UNESCO stated that:

The adoption of the 1960 Convention and Recommendation coincided with the beginning of a series of regional conferences on educational planning at ministerial level. These meetings have, ever since, encouraged the elaboration and implementation of educational policies and plans with a view to ensuring equality of opportunity and treatment in education and relating education to economic and social development. These conferences have brought together the ministers of education of Africa in 1961, 1964, 1968 and 1976; of Asia in 1962, 1965, 1971 and 1978; of Latin America and the Caribbean in 1962, 1966, 1971 and 1979; of the Arab States in 1966, 1970 and 1977; and of Europe in 1967, 1973 and 1980 in order to reaffirm both the right of everyone to education and the objective of democratization, to assess achievements and difficulties and to study trends, problems, solutions and prospects for the development of education. Ministers or senior officials responsible for economic development also participated in these meetings, and the meetings provided an opportunity to discuss quantitative and qualitative objectives for the training of the qualified senior staff needed, particularly in recent years, for the development of developing countries, in the perspective of the establishment of the new international economic order.

At the last of the meetings held in the Latin-American and Caribbean region (Mexico, December 1979), a statement was issued stressing the decisive role which should be assigned to education within a new style of development and the relationship between the final aims of education and the desire to achieve international equity and respect for human dignity. All recent regional conferences particularly emphasized the need to ensure to all, without any discrimination whatsoever, the enjoyment of the right to education, stressed the importance of the democratization of education, and they adopted various recommendations accordingly.

4. EDUCATION OF YOUTH IN THE RESPECT FOR HUMAN RIGHTS AND FUNDAMENTAL FREEDOMS

39. The International Conference on Human Rights at its twenty-fifth plenary meeting on 12 May 1968 adopted resolution XX, entitled "Education of youth in the respect for human rights and fundamental

---

[7] A/35/148, paras. 9 and 10.

freedoms".[8] In adopting the resolution the Conference recalled the principles embodied in the United Nations Declaration on the Promotion among Youth of the Ideals of Peace, Mutual Respect and Understanding between Peoples and noted with satisfaction that UNESCO and other specialized agencies had been engaged in joint efforts to implement the Declaration. It took into consideration several factors, among them: (a) that "it is the hope of humanity that there should be in the future a world in which there does not exist any transgression of human rights and fundamental freedoms and that to that end it is imperative to implant in the consciousness of youth lofty ideals of human dignity and of equal rights for all persons without any discrimination"; (b) that "youth is particularly sensitive to any infringement of human rights . . ."; and (c) that "within the process of social, economic and spiritual renewal in which humanity is engaged, the enthusiasm and the creative spirit of youth must be dedicated to eliminating any kind of violation of human rights".

40. In the resolution, the Conference called upon all States: (a) "to ensure that all means of education should be employed so that youth grows up and develops in a spirit of respect for human dignity and for equal rights of all men and all peoples without discrimination as to race, colour, language, sex or faith"; (b) "to take all appropriate measures to prepare youth for social life, to stimulate its interests in the problems of the changing world and to secure for it an ever-growing and active share in the life and in the development of society"; (c) "to engage in directing wherever possible and encouraging information media, in order that youth may learn of the aspirations of the world of today and learn to appreciate human values and to understand other peoples and in order to strengthen its resolve to fight for the promotion of moral and spiritual health of society"; and (d) "to promote among youth a broad dissemination of ideas and knowledge, based on objective information and free discussion, as an essential prerequisite for enhancing respect for the dignity of man and the variety of human culture".

41. The Conference recommended "the fulfilment of initiatives designed to promote amongst youth the most noble ideals of humanity by means of practical programmes instituted by States, the United Nations, its specialized agencies and especially UNESCO, and by youth organizations". UNESCO was invited "to develop its programmes aimed at making children aware, from the time they start school, of respect for the dignity and rights of man and at making the principles of the Universal Declaration [of Human Rights] prevail at all levels of education, particularly in institutions of higher learning where the future cadres are trained". Functional organs of the United Nations and of the specialized agencies concerned were recommended to "start a detailed examination and study of the question of the

education of youth all over the world for the development of its personality and strengthening of its respect" for human rights everywhere.

5. INTERNATIONAL EDUCATION YEAR (1970)

42. At its twenty-third session, in resolution 2412 (XXIII) of 17 December 1968, the General Assembly decided to designate 1970 as International Education Year, endorsed the programme of action for the International Education Year set out in resolution 4.2.2 adopted by the General Conference of UNESCO, and recommended that States take stock of the situation with respect to education and training in their countries and plan and initiate or stimulate action and studies linked to the objectives and themes of the International Education Year in the context of their preparation for the Second United Nations Development Decade. The implementation of the idea was pursued by the Economic and Social Council and the Secretary-General, in co-operation with UNESCO, submitted a report[9] on the project. In resolution 1436 (XLVII) of 31 July 1969, the Economic and Social Council requested "UNESCO and the organizations of the United Nations system concerned to intensify their co-ordinated efforts to pursue the objectives of International Education Year".

43. The General Assembly, by resolution 2572 (XXIV) of 13 December 1969, took note of the Secretary-General's report and endorsed Council resolution 1436 (XLVII).

6. INTERNATIONAL LITERACY YEAR (1990)

44. At its twenty-third session, held in 1986, the General Conference of the United Nations Educational, Scientific and Cultural Organization expressed deep concern about the problem of illiteracy, said to affect an estimated 889 million adults, and appealed to the United Nations to proclaim and observe an International Literacy Year as a means of stimulating public understanding of the problem and of provoking greater efforts to spread literacy and education.

45. Approving the UNESCO appeal in resolution 41/118 of 4 December 1986, the General Assembly invited the Economic and Social Council to consider the question further and asked the Director-General of UNESCO to draw up suggestions for the observance. Further, the Assembly encouraged UNESCO to elaborate a plan of action designed to assist all States in eradicating illiteracy by the year 2000.

46. The Executive Board of UNESCO suggested, on 18 June 1987, that the year 1990 should be proclaimed the International Literacy Year. This suggestion was endorsed by the Economic and Social Council in resolution 1987/80 of 8 July 1987. The Council also took note

[8] See *Final Act of the International Conference on Human Rights* (United Nations publication, Sales No. E.68.XIV.2).

[9] E/4707 and Corr.1 and 2 and Add.1 and 2.

of the proposals prepared by the Director-General of UNESCO for the observance of the Year.[10]

47. The General Assembly proclaimed 1990 as International Literacy Year on 7 December 1987. In resolution 42/104 of that date, it invited UNESCO to assume the role of lead organization for the observance of the Year. Recognizing that the elimination of illiteracy constitutes a prerequisite for ensuring the right to education, and considering that the complete elimination of illiteracy should be recognized as a priority.

C. The right to health

48. The Constitution of the World Health Organization, adopted two years before the Universal Declaration of Human Rights was proclaimed, explicitly states that "the enjoyment of the highest attainable standard of health is one of the fundamental rights of every human being without distinction of race, religion, political belief, economic or social condition".

49. Since their establishment the United Nations and the World Health Organization have co-operated closely on matters relating to the right to health, and in 1981 the General Assembly of the United Nations endorsed the Global Strategy for Health for All by the Year 2000 which had been adopted earlier by the World Health Assembly. In 1982, the General Assembly adopted the Principles of Medical Ethics relevant to the role of health personnel, particularly physicians, in the protection of prisoners and detainees against torture and other cruel, inhuman or degrading treatment or punishment, which it had invited the World Health Organization to prepare.

50. In 1981 the World Health Assembly, in resolution WHA34.38, decided to establish a committee of scientists and experts, selected by the Director-General, to study and report on the contribution WHO could make to the implementation of United Nations resolutions on strengthening peace, détente and disarmament and preventing nuclear conflict. The Committee submitted a report entitled "Effects of nuclear war on health and health services", which was published by WHO in 1984. The experts' main conclusion, later endorsed by the World Health Assembly, was that it was impossible to prepare health services to deal in any systematic way with a catastrophe resulting from nuclear warfare.

51. In resolution WHA36.28 (1983) the World Health Assembly decided that a management group, selected by the Director-General and known as "WHOPAX", should continue the collection and analysis of data in this sphere. That group's report, issued in May 1987, updates the 1984 publication and incorporates the results of new studies on radiation mortality in nuclear war, the immunological consequences, the possible climatic and environmental effects and the psychosocial effects of the nuclear threat. The experts concluded once more that no health services anywhere in the world

would be able to deal significantly with the health consequences of nuclear war, especially since they themselves would be largely destroyed or incapacitated. They therefore emphasized the importance of preventing a nuclear conflict. The report, entitled "Effect of Nuclear War on Health and Health Services, Second Edition", was published by WHO in 1987.

1. PROVISIONS OF UNITED NATIONS INSTRUMENTS

52. Article 25 of the Universal Declaration of Human Rights provides, in paragraph 1, that:

Everyone has the right to a standard of living adequate for the health and well-being of himself and of his family, including food, clothing, housing and medical care and necessary social services, and the right to security in the event of unemployment, sickness, disability, widowhood, old age or other lack of livelihood in circumstances beyond his control . . .

53. Article 12 of the International Covenant on Economic, Social and Cultural Rights reads as follows:

1. The States Parties to the present Covenant recognize the right of everyone to the enjoyment of the highest attainable standard of physical and mental health.

2. The steps to be taken by the States Parties to the present Covenant to achieve the full realization of this right shall include those necessary for:

(a) The provision for the reduction of the stillbirth-rate and of infant mortality and for the healthy development of the child;

(b) The improvement of all aspects of environmental and industrial hygiene;

(c) The prevention, treatment and control of epidemic, endemic, occupational and other diseases;

(d) The creation of conditions which would assure to all medical service and medical attention in the event of sickness.

54. Article 12 of the Convention on the Elimination of All Forms of Discrimination against Women reads as follows:

1. States Parties shall take all appropriate measures to eliminate discrimination against women in the field of health care in order to ensure, on a basis of equality of men and women, access to health care services, including those related to family planning.

2. Notwithstanding the provisions of paragraph 1 of this article, States Parties shall ensure to women appropriate services in connexion with pregnancy, confinement and the post-natal period, granting free services where necessary, as well as adequate nutrition during pregnancy and lactation.

55. Article 19 of the Declaration on Social Progress and Development calls for:

(a) The provision of free health services to the whole population and of adequate preventive and curative facilities and welfare medical services accessible to all . . .

56. Paragraph 2 of the Declaration on the Rights of Mentally Retarded Persons, proclaimed by the General Assembly in resolution 2856 (XXVI) of 20 December 1971, provides that:

The mentally retarded person has a right to proper medical care and physical therapy and to such education, training, rehabilitation and guidance as will enable him to develop his ability and maximum potential.

57. Paragraph 6 of the Declaration on the Rights of Disabled Persons, proclaimed by the General Assembly in resolution 3447 (XXX) of 9 December 1975, reads as follows:

---

[10] E/1987/113.

Disabled persons have the right to medical, psychological and functional treatment, including prosthetic and orthetic appliances, to medical and social rehabilitation, education, vocational training and rehabilitation, aid, counselling, placement services and other services which will enable them to develop their capabilities and skills to the maximum and will hasten the process of their social integration or reintegration.

58.   Principles 1, 2 and 3 of the Principles of Medical Ethics relevant to the role of health personnel, particularly physicians, in the protection of prisoners and detainees against torture and other cruel, inhuman or degrading treatment or punishment, adopted by the General Assembly in resolution 37/194 of 18 December 1982, are as follows:[11]

Principle 1: Health personnel, particularly physicians, charged with the medical care of prisoners and detainees, have a duty to provide them with protection of their physical and mental health and treatment of disease of the same quality and standard as is afforded to those who are not imprisoned or detained.

Principle 2: It is a gross contravention of medical ethics, as well as an offence under applicable international instruments, for health personnel, particularly physicians, to engage, actively or passively, in acts which constitute participation in, complicity in, incitement to or attempts to commit torture or other cruel, inhuman or degrading treatment or punishment.

Principle 3: It is a contravention of medical ethics for health personnel, particularly physicians, to be involved in any professional relationship with prisoners or detainees the purpose of which is not solely to evaluate, protect or improve their physical and mental health.

2. GLOBAL STRATEGY FOR HEALTH FOR ALL BY THE YEAR 2000

59.   In resolution 34/58 of 29 November 1979 the General Assembly noted that a substantial portion of the population in many countries, developing as well as developed, lacked access to basic health services, and that people lacking adequate health could not fully participate in or contribute to the economic and social development of their nation. The Assembly endorsed the Declaration of Alma Ata, adopted by the International Conference on Primary Health Care, jointly sponsored by the World Health Organization and the United Nations Children's Fund, held at Alma Ata, Union of Soviet Socialist Republics, from 6 to 12 September 1978, and noted with approval the subsequent decision of the World Health Assembly that the development of the programmes of the World Health Organization and the allocation of its resources should reflect the commitment of that organization to the priority of the achievement of health for all by the year 2000. The Assembly, further, called upon the relevant bodies of the United Nations system to co-ordinate with and support the efforts of WHO, and appealed to Member States to carry out the actions called for in the Declaration of Alma Ata.

60.   The World Health Assembly, by resolution WHA34.36 of 22 May 1981, unanimously adopted the Global Strategy for Health for All by the Year 2000.

This action was noted with approval by the General Assembly in resolution 36/43 of 19 November 1981. In that resolution the Assembly endorsed the Global Strategy, urged all Member States to ensure its implementation, and requested all appropriate organizations and bodies of the United Nations system to collaborate fully with the World Health Organization in carrying it out.

61.   The Organization has developed procedures and tools whereby Member States themselves can monitor and evaluate the progress achieved in implementing the Global Strategy for Health for All by the Year 2000. In 1984 a report on monitoring the Strategy was submitted to the World Health Assembly. The report comprised assessments made by about three quarters of WHO member States of the relevance of their national policies and the progress made in implementing the Strategy. The synthesis of national experiences indicated, *inter alia,* that the political will to achieve the goal of health for all existed in a large majority of the countries reporting; nevertheless only a few had well-defined plans of action for implementing their strategies.

62.   In resolution WHA37.17 (May 1984) the Health Assembly urged Member States and their regional committees to accord priority to continued monitoring, both individually and collectively, and requested the Director-General to continue to provide appropriate and targeted support to member States. By 1986, almost ninety per cent of WHO member States (146 out of 166) had carried out an evaluation of their strategies for health for all and reported the results to WHO. This gigantic task revealed that in a number of countries impressive progress had been made in strengthening the health infrastructure, but that, on the other hand, many countries faced formidable managerial and financial problems in trying to ensure the essential elements of primary health care. The Health Assembly, in resolution WHA39.7 (May 1986) congratulated Member States on their efforts and forthrightness, and urged them to maintain a high level of political commitment to social equality and leadership for the further implementation of national strategies, including the reduction of socioeconomic and related health disparities among people. The Director-General was requested to intensify support to the least-developed countries and to support the monitoring and evaluation efforts of all member States.

3. PROTECTION AGAINST PRODUCTS HARMFUL TO HEALTH AND THE ENVIRONMENT

63.   In resolution 34/173 of 17 December 1979 the General Assembly pointed out that the exportation of banned hazardous chemicals and unsafe pharmaceutical products could have serious and adverse effects on the health of peoples in the importing countries, and urged Member States to exchange information on such products and to discourage their exportation to other countries.

---

[11] For further information about the Principles of Medical Ethics, see chap. VIII, sect. D, 2 (*e*).

64. Later, in resolution 37/137 of 17 December 1982, the Assembly dealt in particular with the problem of the damage to health and the environment which the continued production and export of products that had been banned and/or permanently withdrawn on grounds of human health and safety from domestic markets was causing in the importing countries. It agreed that products that had been banned from domestic consumption and/or sale because they had been judged to endanger health and the environment should be sold abroad only under severe restrictions, and that all countries that had adopted such restrictions or had not approved the domestic consumption and/or sale of specific products, in particular pharmaceuticals and pesticides, should make available full information on those products with a view to safeguarding the health and environment of the importing country. The Secretary-General was requested to prepare and regularly update a consolidated list of products whose consumption and/or sale had been banned, withdrawn, severely restricted, or, in the case of pharmaceuticals, not approved by Governments, and to make that list available not later than December 1983.

65. The General Assembly, in resolution 38/149 of 19 December 1983, urged the relevant organs, organizations and bodies of the United Nations system, and other intergovernmental organizations, to continue to co-operate fully in providing information for the consolidated list and for its updated versions, and requested the competent United Nations bodies to continue to provide, within available resources, the necessary technical assistance to the developing countries, at their request, for the establishment or strengthening of national systems for better use by those countries of the information provided with regard to banned hazardous chemicals and unsafe products, as well as for an adequate monitoring of the importation of those products.

66. At its thirty-ninth session the Assembly received the report of the Secretary-General on products harmful to health and the environment,[12] and the first issue of the consolidated list of products whose consumption and/or sale have been banned, withdrawn, severely restricted or, in the case of pharmaceuticals, not approved by Governments. After expressing its appreciation to all who participated in the preparation of the list, the Assembly decided, in resolution 39/229 of 18 December 1984, that an updated consolidated list should be issued annually and that the date should be made available to Governments and other users in such a form as to permit direct computer access to it. It urged importing countries, bearing in mind the extensive legal, public health and safety information already available from a number of United Nations organizations, to avail themselves of the information provision facilities of those organizations and thus to supplement the data in the consolidated list.

67. In 1986 the Economic and Social Council reviewed a later report by the Secretary-General on products harmful to health and the environment,[13] describing work undertaken in preparing the consolidated list and in advancing work towards improvement of the list in future editions. In resolution 1986/72 of 23 July 1986 the Council commended the Secretary-General for initiating the memoranda of understanding between the United Nations and the World Health Organization and between the United Nations and the United Nations Environment Programme/International Register of Potentially Toxic Chemicals, and for developing constructive and appropriate delegation of responsibility for the preparation of the consolidated list. It decided that the consolidated list of products which have been banned, withdrawn, severely restricted or not approved by Governments should continue to be published as one document, including generic/chemical and brand names and the names of all manufacturers of such products. The General Assembly, in decision 41/450 of 8 December 1986, endorsed the Council resolution.

68. Under the memoranda of understanding, a smooth working relationship has developed for the production of the consolidated list, with WHO and UNEP sharing responsibility for collecting, processing and screening the information and the United Nations assuming responsibility for editing, translating and publishing it.

D. The right to adequate food

69. The right of everyone to a standard of living adequate for the health and well-being of himself and of his family includes, in the words of article 25 of the Universal Declaration of Human Rights, "food, clothing, housing and medical care and necessary social services, and the right to security in the event of unemployment, sickness, disability, widowhood, old age or other lack of livelihood in circumstances beyond his control . . .". United Nations bodies have sought to implement this principle in a variety of ways, including joint endeavours to solve the world food problem, to eradicate hunger and malnutrition, to preserve and enhance the human environment, to provide shelter for the homeless and to establish a new international economic order.

70. Article 11, paragraph 2, of the International Covenant on Economic, Social and Cultural Rights reads as follows:

The States Parties to the present Covenant, recognizing the fundamental right of everyone to be free from hunger, shall take, individually and through international co-operation, the measures, including specific programmes, which are needed:

(a) To improve methods of production, conservation and distribution of food by making full use of technical and scientific knowledge, by disseminating knowledge of the principles of nutrition and by developing or reforming agrarian systems in such a way as to achieve the most efficient development and utilization of natural resources;

---

[12] A/39/452.

[13] A/41/329-E/1986/83.

(b) Taking into account the problems of both food-importing and food-exporting countries, to ensure an equitable distribution of world food supplies in relation to need.

1. WORLD FOOD CONFERENCE

71. The General Assembly, in resolution 3180 (XXVIII) of 17 December 1973, decided to convene a World Food Conference. The Conference, held at Rome from 5 to 6 November 1974, adopted 22 resolutions and the Universal Declaration on the Eradication of Hunger and Malnutrition.[14]

72. In the preamble of the Declaration, the Conference recognized that:

(a) The grave food crisis that is afflicting the peoples of the developing countries where most of the world's hungry and ill-nourished live and where more than two thirds of the world's population produce about one third of the world's food—an imbalance which threatens to increase in the next ten years—is not only fraught with grave economic and social implications, but also acutely jeopardizes the most fundamental principles and values associated with the right to life and human dignity as enshrined in the Universal Declaration of Human Rights;

(b) The elimination of hunger and malnutrition, included as one of the objectives in the United Nations Declaration on Social Progress and Development, and the elimination of the causes that determine this situation are the common objectives of all nations;

(c) The situation of the peoples afflicted by hunger and malnutrition arises from their historical circumstances, especially social inequalities, including in many cases alien and colonial domination, foreign occupation, racial discrimination, *apartheid* and neo-colonialism in all its forms, which continue to be among the greatest obstacles to the full emancipation and progress of the developing countries and all the peoples involved . . .

73. In the first operative paragraph of the Declaration, the Conference proclaimed the principle that:

Every man, woman and child has the inalienable right to be free from hunger and malnutrition in order to develop fully and maintain their physical and mental faculties. Society today already possesses sufficient resources, organizational ability and technology and hence the competence to achieve this objective. Accordingly, the eradication of hunger is a common objective of all the countries of the international community, especially of the developed countries and others in a position to help.

74. The Conference affirmed the determination of the participating States to make full use of the United Nations system in the implementation of the Declaration and other decisions which it had adopted, and called upon all peoples expressing their will as individuals, and through their Governments and non-governmental organizations, to work together to bring about the end of the age-old scourge of hunger.

75. The General Assembly, in resolution 3348 (XXIX) of 17 December 1974, endorsed the Universal Declaration on the Eradication of Hunger and Malnutrition and the resolutions adopted at the World Food Conference, and called upon Governments to take urgent action to implement the decisions of the Conference.

76. The goal of eliminating hunger and malnutrition is also reflected in the FAO Constitution as well as in numerous resolutions of FAO bodies. Among the

important milestones are: (a) the International Undertaking on World Food Security (resolution 164 of the 64th session of the FAO Council (1974)), endorsed in resolution 17 of the World Food Conference (1974); (b) the Plan of Action on World Food Security (resolution 1/75 of the 75th session of the FAO Council (1979)); (c) the Agenda for Consultations and Possible Action to deal with Acute and Large-scale Food Shortages (adopted at the sixth session of the FAO Committee on World Food Security (1981)); and (d) the World Food Security Compact (adopted by the 23rd session of the FAO Conference (1985)). These represent the international understandings reached on concrete proposals towards progress to world food security.

77. The World Food Security Compact emphasizes that "no one can remain indifferent to the fate of those whose daily food is insecure". It stresses that world food security is a common responsibility of mankind. In a more practical sense, the Compact points to the necessity of not only expanding production, but also of increasing stability in the flow of supplies and of ensuring access to food by all, including the poor.

2. WORLD FOOD DAY

78. The Conference of the Food and Agriculture Organization of the United Nations unanimously decided, in resolution 1/79 of 28 November 1979, that World Food Day should be observed for the first time on 16 October 1981 and annually thereafter. The objectives are to heighten public awareness of the nature and dimensions of the world food problem and to mobilize support for the long-term effort to overcome widespread malnutrition.

79. The General Assembly, in resolution 35/70 of 5 December 1980, welcomed the observance of World Food Day and urged Governments and international, regional and national organizations to contribute to the commemoration. The FAO Conference, in resolution 7/81 of 25 November 1981, urged that Governments and non-governmental organizations should intensify their efforts in future years, in the framework of World Food Day, so as to strengthen co-operative action in the struggle against hunger, malnutrition and poverty. These views were reiterated by the Conference in resolution 5/83 of 22 November 1983.

3. WORLD FOOD PROGRAMME

80. The entire programme of the Food and Agriculture Organization of the United Nations is designed to serve this principle. Measures taken include the elaboration of standards, the promotion of policies, and the planning and execution of activities in various technical fields pertaining to food production, conservation, distribution and nutrition.

81. Measures to implement this principle are also taken by the World Food Programme, a subsidiary organ of the United Nations. After operating for three

---

[14] *Report of the World Food Conference* (United Nations publication, Sales No. E.75.II.A).

years on an experimental basis, the Programme was extended by General Assembly resolution 2095 (XX) of 20 December 1965 and FAO Conference resolution 4/65 of 6 December 1965, on a continuing basis, for as long as multilateral food aid remained feasible and desirable. The Programme provides food aid in support of development projects and to meet emergency needs.

82. The Economic and Social Council and the General Assembly review the operation of the World Food Programme each year. The Assembly, in resolution 34/110 of 14 December 1979, endorsed the World Food Council's call for greater equity in food distribution through more direct action by Governments, and called upon Governments, organizations and bodies of the United Nations system, other organizations and the international community as a whole to give very high priority to their policies, programmes and actions aimed at the eradication of hunger and malnutrition everywhere in the world. In a number of resolutions, and most recently in resolution 41/191 of 8 December 1986, the General Assembly has reaffirmed that the right to food is a universal human right which should be guaranteed to all people and has expressed its belief in the general principle that food should not be used as an instrument of political pressure, either at the national or at the international level.

4. STUDY OF THE RIGHT TO ADEQUATE FOOD

83. On recommendation of the Sub-Commission on Prevention of Discrimination and Protection of Minorities and the Commission on Human Rights, the Economic and Social Council in decision 1983/140 of 27 May 1983 authorized the Sub-Commission to entrust one of its members, Mr. Asbjørn Eide, with the preparation of a study on the right to adequate food as a human right, taking into account all the relevant work under way within the United Nations system. The Council asked the Special Rapporteur to give special attention to the normative content of the right to food and its significance in relation to the establishment of the new international economic order.

84. The Special Rapporteur presented a preliminary report on the subject[15] to the Sub-Commission at its thirty-sixth session and a progress report[16] at its thirty-seventh session. His final report[17] was considered by the Sub-Commission at its thirty-ninth session, held in 1987.

85. In the report the Special Rapporteur deals with such questions as the nature of economic, social and cultural rights, the recognition of the right to food in international law, the national and international obligations undertaken by States as regards the right to food, and the question of national and international monitoring systems to determine the extent to which that right is enjoyed.

86. The Special Rapporteur reaches the conclusion that although the right to food is already widely recognized in international law, international monitoring is necessary in order to determine to what extent the right is realized in practice. Systematic monitoring, he points out, would be helpful in encouraging and promoting national food security efforts and might also create an awareness of situations where actions by other States are detrimental to the progressive realization of the right to food within a State. He suggests that the logical monitoring body within the human rights field would be the Committee on Economic, Social and Cultural Rights.

87. After examining the report the Sub-Commission, in resolution 1987/27 of 3 September 1987, expressed its appreciation to the Special Rapporteur and submitted the study to the Commission on Human Rights with a recommendation that it be published and given the widest possible distribution and that the Committee on Economic, Social and Cultural Rights should be asked to examine and to comment on the Special Rapporteur's recommendations.

88. The Sub-Commission requested the Secretary-General to obtain from all States a description of any laws they have pertaining to the right to food, and to ask the Food and Agriculture Organization of the United Nations to provide all such information at its disposal; and decided to return to a debate on the normative content of the right to food at a subsequent session.

5. BEIJING DECLARATION OF THE WORLD FOOD COUNCIL

89. At the thirteenth session of the World Food Council, held at Beijing from 8 to 11 June 1987, the Council adopted the Beijing Declaration, proclaiming the intention of its members "to join together and, in our united strength and interest, to eliminate the scourge of hunger for ever". The Declaration was endorsed by the Economic and Social Council in resolution 1987/90 of 9 July 1987 as a reaffirmation of the commitment of the world community to the eradication of hunger and malnutrition and as a framework to accelerate action to attain that objective.

E. The right to adequate shelter and services

90. The Vancouver Declaration on Human Settlements, adopted and proclaimed by the United Nations Conference on Human Settlements in 1976,[18] affirmed that adequate shelter and services are a basic human right and that, in striving to uphold that right, priority must be given to the needs of the poor, the homeless and the most vulnerable groups of society.

---

[15] E/CN.4/Sub.2/1983/25.

[16] E/CN.4/Sub.2/1984/22.

[17] E/CN.4/Sub.2/1987/23.

[18] *Report of Habitat: United Nations Conference on Human Settlements, Vancouver, 31 May-11 June 1976* (United Nations publication, Sales No. E.76.IV.7 and Corrigendum), chap. I.

91. In later resolutions the General Assembly reaffirmed this view and noted with concern that in the years since 1976 conditions in human settlements in developing countries had, by and large, worsened, particularly in the urban areas where the growth of slums and squatter settlements had continued unabated in the midst of poverty, squalor, overcrowding and human degradation.

92. In 1980 the General Assembly expressed the view that an international year devoted to the problems of homeless people in urban and rural areas could be an appropriate occasion to focus the attention of the international community on those problems. In resolution 37/221 of 20 December 1982, it proclaimed the year 1987 International Year of Shelter for the Homeless, and decided that the objective of activities before and during the Year would be to improve the shelter and neighbourhoods of some of the poor and disadvantaged and to demonstrate how this could be done by the year 2000. The Commission on Human Settlements was designated as the United Nations intergovernmental body responsible for organizing the activities of the Year.

93. The General Assembly, in resolution 40/201 of 17 December 1985, took note with concern of the report of the Secretary-general on the living conditions of the Palestinian people in the occupied Palestinian territories,[19] expressed its alarm at the deterioration in the living conditions of those people as a result of the Israeli occupation, and affirmed that the occupation is contrary to the basic requirements for their social and economic development.

94. In resolution 41/190 of 8 December 1986, the Assembly urged Governments to demonstrate renewed political commitment to the shelter needs of the poor and disadvantaged by taking significant measures before 1987, including providing access to land and ensuring security of tenure in squatter settlements, adapting codes and regulations to the needs of the people, facilitating community participation, improving access to credit and loans and promoting local and affordable building materials.

95. A commemorative session of the Commission on Human Settlements was held during 1987, the International Year of Shelter for the Homeless, with the participation of all Members of the United Nations.[20] Taking note of the comments made by Governments at that session, and of the reports of the Executive Director of the United Nations Centre for Human Settlements on "Shelter and services for the poor—a call to action",[21] and "A new agenda for human settlements",[22] the General Assembly in resolution 42/191 of 11 December 1987 expressed its deep concern about the alarming situation in which, despite the efforts of Governments at the national and local levels and of international organizations, more than one billion people find themselves either completely without shelter or living in homes unfit for human habitation; and that, owing to prevailing demographic trends, the already formidable problems will escalate in the coming years unless concerted and determined measures are taken immediately.

96. The Assembly, further, recognized that a squalid residential environment is a constant threat to health and to life itself and thereby constitutes a drain on human resources, a nation's most valuable asset; and noted that this lamentable situation can adversely affect the social and political stability of countries. Convinced that the alarming trands can be reversed, the Assembly decided that there shall be a Global Strategy for Shelter to the Year 2000, including a plan for its implementation, monitoring and evaluation, and requested the Commission on Human Settlements to formulate such a Strategy. The objective of the Strategy will be to stimulate measures that will facilitate adequate shelter for all by the year 2000.

F. The right to culture

97. The United Nations and the United Nations Educational, Scientific and Cultural Organization have worked together for many years on matters relating to the right to culture, particularly with respect to the preservation and further development of cultural values and the protection of the rights of creators and transmitters of culture.

1. PROVISIONS OF UNITED NATIONS INSTRUMENTS

98. Article 27 of the Universal Declaration of Human Rights provides that:

1. Everyone has the right freely to participate in the cultural life of the community, to enjoy the arts and to share in scientific advancement and its benefits.

2. Everyone has the right to the protection of the moral and material interests resulting from any scientific, literary or artistic production of which he is the author.

99. Article 15 of the International Covenant on Economic, Social and Cultural Rights read as follows:

1. The States Parties to the present Covenant recognize the right of everyone:

(*a*) To take part in cultural life;

(*b*) To enjoy the benefits of scientific progress and its applications;

(*c*) To benefit from the protection of the moral and material interests resulting from any scientific, literary or artistic production of which he is the author.

2. The steps to be taken by the States Parties to the present Covenant to achieve the full realization of this right shall include those necessary for the conservation, the development and the diffusion of science and culture.

3. The States Parties to the present Covenant undertake to respect the freedom indispensable for scientific research and creative activity.

4. The States Parties to the present Covenant recognize the benefits to be derived from the encouragement and development of international contacts and co-operation in the scientific and cultural fields.

[19] A/40/373-E/1985/99.

[20] See *Official Records of the General Assembly, Forty-second Session, Supplement No. 8* (A/42/8).

[21] HS/C/10/3.

[22] HS/C/10/2 and Corr.1 and 4.

100. Under article 5 of the International Convention on the Elimination of All Forms of Racial Discrimination, States parties undertake to prohibit and eliminate racial discrimination in all its forms and to guarantee the right of everyone, without distinction as to race, colour, or national or ethnic origin, to equality before the law, notably in the enjoyment of the right to equal participation in cultural activities.

2. DECLARATION OF THE PRINCIPLES OF INTERNATIONAL CULTURAL CO-OPERATION

101. The Declaration, proclaimed by the General Conference of UNESCO at its fourteenth session, on 4 November 1966, sets out a series of principles in this field "to the end that governments, authorities, organizations, associations and institutions responsible for cultural activities may constantly be guided by these principles; and for the purpose, as set out in the Constitution of the Organization, of advancing, through the educational, scientific and cultural relations of the peoples of the world, the objectives of peace and welfare that are defined in the Charter of the United Nations".

102. Among the principles contained in the Declaration are the following:

Article I

1. Each culture has a dignity and value which must be respected and preserved.

2. Every people has the right and the duty to develop its culture.

3. In their rich variety and diversity, and in the reciprocal influences they exert on one another, all cultures form part of the common heritage belonging to all mankind.

Article II

Nations shall endeavour to develop the various branches of culture side by side and, as far as possible, simultaneously, so as to establish a harmonious balance between technical progress and the intellectual and moral advancement of mankind.

Article III

International cultural co-operation shall cover all aspects of intellectual and creative activities relating to education, science and culture.

Article IV

The aims of international cultural co-operation in its various forms, bilateral or multilateral, regional or universal, shall be:

1. To spread knowledge, to stimulate talent and to enrich cultures;

2. To develop peaceful relations and friendship among the peoples and bring about a better understanding of each other's way of life;

3. To contribute to the application of the principles set out in the United Nations Declarations that are recalled in the Preamble to this Declaration;

4. To enable everyone to have access to knowledge, to enjoy the arts and literature of all peoples, to share in advances made in science in all parts of the world and in the resulting benefits, and to contribute to the enrichment of cultural life;

5. To raise the level of the spiritual and material life of man in all parts of the world.

Article V

Cultural co-operation is a right and a duty for all peoples and all nations, which should share with one another their knowledge and skills.

3. PROMOTION OF THE RIGHT TO CULTURE

103. UNESCO has worked for many years to give concrete meaning to the idea of cultural rights as human rights. Its activities have been directed mainly to encouraging everyone to participate freely in the cultural life of the community, to finding the means of preserving cultural identity and values, and to arranging copyright protection for literary, scientific and artistic works.

(a) Participation in cultural life

104. A series of conferences on cultural policies assisted UNESCO in clarifying the right of everyone to full participation in cultural life. A conference of experts, convened by the Director-General in 1968, considered the question "Cultural rights as human rights" and discussed the evolution of the concept of the right to culture, factors which affect the recognition of that right, and measures to ensure its realization. The Intergovernmental Conference on the Institutional, Administrative and Financial Aspects of Cultural Policies, convened by UNESCO in 1970, concluded that the provision of article 27 of the Universal Declaration of Human Rights which reads: "everyone has the right freely to participate in the cultural life of the community . . ." implies that it is the duty of those responsible for communities to provide everyone in them with the effective means of participating in cultural life, and not merely to respect their right to participate, thus placing the responsibility for implementation of the right to culture upon Governments. Regional conferences of ministers on cultural policies were later organized in Europe (Helsinki, 1972), Asia (Jogjakarta, 1973), Africa (Accra, 1975) and Latin America and the Caribbean (Bogotá, 1978). The recommendations of the European, Asian and African conferences were taken into consideration in the elaboration of the Recommendation on Participation by the People at Large in Cultural Life and Their Contribution to It, approved by the UNESCO General Conference on 26 November 1976. The Recommendation provides that States should guarantee cultural rights as human rights, should guarantee equality of cultures, should provide access to the treasures of national and world culture without discrimination, and should protect and develop authentic forms of expression.

105. These principles have recently been reaffirmed and developed further at the World Conference on Cultural Policies, held at Mexico City in 1982, which took stock of the experience acquired in policies and practices in the field of culture and gave new impetus to the world-wide action carried out under the aegis of UNESCO since the end of the 1960s with a view to promoting international reflection on the problems of culture in the contemporary world. It confirmed, at the highest international levels, the clear understanding of culture as a fundamental dimension and objective of

global economic and social development. It recognized that "democratization" must become "cultural democracy", which might be considered the ultimate aim of cultural policy. It emphasized that the founding of a real cultural democracy took place through a combination of activities designed to guarantee the effective exercise of cultural rights.

106. The Conference adopted the Mexico City Declaration on Cultural Policies proclaiming the guiding principles for promoting culture and strengthening the cultural dimension of development. As to cultural rights, the Declaration reaffirms that States must take the necessary steps to attain the objective fixed in this respect by article 27 of the Universal Declartion of Human Rights.

107. Apart from the Declaration, the Mexico Conference adopted recommendations 28 to 34 related to various aspects of cultural rights and culture and democracy. Recommendation 28 on cultural rights and cultural democracy stipulates in paragraph 1 (*a*) that member States should "take appropriate measures to strengthen the democratization of culture by means of policies that ensure the right to culture and guarantee the participation of society in its benefits without restriction".

108. In the period 1985-1986 UNESCO carried out an evaluation of the impact of the Recommendation on Participation of the People at Large in Cultural Life and Their Contribution to It. A questionnaire was sent to national UNESCO commissions with a view to evaluating the implementation of the measures mentioned in the Recommendation. The replies indicated that the Recommendation had lost none of its relevance 10 years after its adoption by the General Conference, but that the costs of its realization were a factor emphasized in all of the replies.

109. UNESCO has also participated in research projects, pilot projects and meetings of experts on matters relating to the status of women and their participation in cultural development.

(b) *Preservation of cultural identity and values*

110. In addition to proclaiming the Declaration of the Principles of International Cultural Co-operation and adopting the Recommendation on Participation by the People at Large in Cultural Life and Their Contribution to It, mentioned above, UNESCO has adopted a number of international instruments for the protection of cultural property, including the Hague Convention for the Protection of Cultural Property in the Event of Armed Conflict, with Regulations for the Execution of the Convention (1954); the Recommendation and Convention on the Means of Prohibiting and Preventing the Illicit Import, Export and Transfer of Ownership of Cultural Property (adopted in 1964 and 1970 respectively), the Convention concerning the Protection of the World Cultural and Natural Heritage (1972), and the Recommendation concerning the International Ex-

change of Cultural Property (1976). It has also undertaken extensive international campaigns to safeguard endangered sites and monuments, to protect the cultural property of developing countries, and to encourage studies of the cultures of various regions.

111. The General Assembly has requested UNESCO to present its views on the preservation and further development of cultural values, and since 1973, has examined reports on this subject communicated to the United Nations by the Director-General of UNESCO.

(b) *Return or restoration of cultural property to the countries of origin*

112. At its twenty-eighth session, in 1973, the General Assembly included in its agenda the item, "Restitution of works of art to countries victims of expropriation", and in resolution 3187 (XXVIII) of 18 December 1973 affirmed that the prompt restitution to a country of its *objets d'art*, monuments, museum pieces, manuscripts and documents by another country, without charge, is calculated to strengthen international co-operation inasmuch as it constitutes just reparation for damage done. It recognized the special obligations in that connection of those countries that had had access to such valuable objects only as a result of colonial or foreign occupation, and called upon all the States concerned to prohibit the expropriation of works of art from Territories under colonial or alien domination.

113. At its thirty-fourth session the General Assembly, in resolution 34/64 of 29 November 1979, welcomed the establishment by the General Conference of UNESCO of the Intergovernmental Committee for Promoting the Return of Cultural Property to its Countries of Origin or its Restitution in Case of Illicit Appropriation, and invited all Governments to accede to the Convention on the Means of Prohibiting and Preventing the Illicit Import, Export and Transfer of Ownership of Cultural Property which had been adopted by the General Conference of UNESCO in 1970. It requested the Secretary-General to take the necessary steps to associate the United Nations with the activities of UNESCO directed towards the restitution of cultural property to the countries of origin.

114. At its thirty-eighth session the Assembly, in resolution 38/34 of 25 November 1983, commended UNESCO and its Intergovernmental Committee on the work they had accomplished; took note of the importance accorded to the question of the return or restitution of cultural properties by the World Conference on Cultural Properties, held at Mexico City in 1982; and again called upon Member States that had not yet done so to sign and ratify the Convention on the subject.

115. At its fortieth and forty-second sessions, in resolutions 40/19 of 21 November 1985 and 42/7 of 22 October 1987 respectively, the General Assembly took note of reports of the Secretary-General submitted in

co-operation with the Director-General of UNESCO,[23] and again commended UNESCO and the Intergovernmental Committee on the work they had accomplished. It recommended that Member States adopt or strengthen the necessary protective legislation with regard to their own heritage and that of other peoples; invited Member States to continue drawing up, in co-operation with UNESCO, systematic inventories of cultural property existing in their territory and of their cultural property abroad; and also invited Member States engaged in seeking the recovery of cultural and artistic treasures from the sea-bed, in accordance with international law, to facilitate by mutually acceptable conditions the participation of States having a historical and cultural link with those treasures.

(d) *Recommendation concerning the status of the artist*

116. The Recommendation, adopted by the General Conference of UNESCO at its twenty-first session (1980), sets out the guiding principles to be adopted by member States with reference to the status of artists:

They should ensure that the population as a whole has access to art, and should encourage all activities designed to highlight the action of artists for cultural development;

They have a duty to protect, defend and assist artists and their freedom of creation, and ensure their right to establish trade unions and professional organizations of their choosing;

They should make it possible for organizations representing artists to participate in the formulation of cultural policies and employment policies;

They should define a policy of providing assistance and material and moral support for artists;

They should see to it that artists are accorded the protection provided for in respect of freedom of expression and communication by international legislation concerning human rights; and

They should ensure that all individuals have the same opportunities to acquire and develop the skills necessary for the complete development and exercise of their artistic talents, to obtain employment and to exercise their profession without discrimination.

117. In the Recommendation, member States are invited to take appropriate measures to encourage the vocation and training of artists, to promote and protect their social status, to improve their employment, working and living conditions, and to associate artists closely with decisions relating to cultural policies and their implementation.

118. In order to ascertain the progress made in implementing the Recommendation, UNESCO in December 1986 sent a questionnaire to member States and to the national committees of the non-governmental organizations concerned. The replies received up to August 1987 indicated that a number of legislative and/or administrative measures had been adopted to improve the status of artists, but that considerable progress is necessary if all the provisions of the Recommendation are to be given effect. UNESCO proposes, during the 1988-1989 biennium, to draw up a 10-year plan for the systematic implementation of the Recommendation, in consultation with governmental authorities and artists in various fields.

(e) *World Decade for Cultural Development*

119. The General Assembly, in resolution 41/187 of 8 December 1986, proclaimed the period 1988-1997 the World Decade for Cultural Development, to be observed under the auspices of the United Nations and UNESCO. The four main objectives of the Decade will be: acknowledging the cultural dimension of development; affirming and enriching cultural identities; broadening participation in culture; and promoting international cultural co-operation.

120. The idea for the Decade was first put foward by the World Conference on Cultural Policies, convened by UNESCO at Mexico City in 1982, in resolution No. 27. A draft plan of action, prepared by the Director-General of UNESCO, was noted by the Assembly in resolution 41/187. Voluntary efforts at the national level by interested individuals and non-governmental and governmental organizations are the principle vehicles for advancing the objectives of the Decade.

G. The right to a clean environment

121. The Declaration of the United Nations Conference on the Human Environment, adopted by the Conference on 16 June 1972, is designed to "inspire and guide the peoples of the world in the preservation and enhancement of the human environment".

122. The first paragraph of the preamble reads as follows:

Man is both creature and moulder of his environment, which gives him physical sustenance and affords him the opportunity for intellectual, moral, social and spiritual growth. In the long and tortuous evolution of the human race on this planet a stage has been reached when, through the rapid acceleration of science and technology, man has acquired the power to transform his environment in countless ways and on an unprecedented scale. Both aspects of man's environment, the natural and the man-made, are essential to his well-being and to the enjoyment of basic human rights—even the right of life itself.

123. Principle 1 reads as follows:

Man has the fundamental right to freedom, equality and adequate conditions of life, in an environment of a quality that permits a life of dignity and well-being, and he bears a solemn responsibility to protect and improve the environment for present and future generations. In this respect, policies promoting or perpetuating *apartheid*, racial segregation, discrimination, colonial and other forms of oppression and foreign domination stand condemned and must be eliminated.

124. After taking note of the report of the Conference[24] held at Stockholm from 5 to 16 June 1972, and the report of the Secretary-General thereon,[25] the General Assembly, by resolution 2997 (XXVII) of 15 December 1972, set up the United Nations Environ-

---

[23] A/40/344 and A/42/533.

[24] United Nations publication, Sales No. E.73.II.A.14.

[25] A/8783 and Add. 1, Add.1/Corr.1 and Add.2.

ment Programme (UNEP). The Governing Council of the Programme reports annually to the Assembly through the Economic and Social Council.

1. MATERIAL REMNANTS OF WAR

125. In resolution 35/71 of 5 December 1980, the General Assembly, recalling a number of earlier resolutions and decisions concerning the problem of material remnants of war, particularly mines, and their effect upon the environment, regretted that no real action had been taken to solve the problem. The Assembly recognized that most developing countries had been subjected to foreign occupation and exposed to wars waged by certain colonial Powers, thus incurring tremendous loss of life and property; and that the presence of material remnants of war in those countries seriously impeded their development efforts and entailed loss of life and property. It expressed the view that the removal of those remnants of war should be the responsibility of the countries that had implanted them and should be carried out at their expense.

126. In resolution 40/197 of 17 December 1985, the Assembly took note of the Secretary-General's 1985 report on the problems of remnants of war,[26] which indicated that the situation had not changed appreciably. Noting that the presence of material remnants of war, including mines, in the territories of developing countries seriously impedes their development efforts and causes loss of life and property, the Assembly requested the Secretary-General, in co-operation with the Executive Director of the United Nations Environment Programme, to continue his efforts with the countries planting mines and the affected developing countries in order to ensure the removal of all material remnants of war.

2. THE ENVIRONMENTAL PERSPECTIVE TO THE YEAR 2000 AND BEYOND

127. The General Assembly, in resolution 42/186 of 11 December 1987, adopted the Environmental Perspective to the Year 2000 and Beyond which had been prepared by the Governing Council of the United Nations Environment Programme and its Intergovernmental Inter-sessional Preparatory Committee.[27]

128. In adopting the Environmental Perspective, the Assembly welcomed as the overall aspirational goal for the world community the achievement of sustainable development on the basis of prudent management of available global resources and environmental capacities and the rehabilitation of the environment previously subjected to degradation and misuse. It also welcomed the aspirational goals set out in the Environmental Perspective, namely:

(*a*) Achievement over time of such a balance between population and environmental capacities as would make possible sustainable development, keeping in view the links among population levels, consumption patterns, poverty and the natural resource base;

(*b*) Achievement of food security without resource depletion or environmental degradation and restoration of the resource base where environmental damage has been occurring;

(*c*) Provision of sufficient energy at reasonable cost, notably by increasing access to energy substantially in the developing countries, to meet current and expanding needs in ways which minimize environmental degradation and risks, conserve non-renewable sources of energy and realize the full potential of renewable sources of energy;

(*d*) Sustained improvements in levels of living in all countries, especially the developing countries, through indusrial development that prevents or minimizes environmental damage and risks;

(*e*) Provision of improved shelter with access to essential amenities in a clean and secure setting conductive to health and to the prevention of environment-related diseases, while alleviating serious environmental degradation; and

(*f*) Establishment of an equitable system of international economic relations aimed at achieving continuing economic advancement for all States based on principles recognized by the international community in order to stimulate and sustain environmentally sound development, especially in developing countries.

H. The right to development

129. In resolution 4 (XXXIII) of 21 February 1977, the Commission on Human Rights decided to pay special attention to the consideration of the obstacles hindering the full realization of economic, social and cultural rights, particularly in the developing countries, as well as of the actions taken on the national and international levels to secure the enjoyment of those rights. It recommended to the Economic and Social Council that it should invite the Secretary-General, in co-operation with UNESCO and other competent specialized agencies, "to undertake a study on the subject 'The international dimensions of the right to development as a human right in relation with other human rights based on international co-operation, including the right to peace, taking into account the requirements of the New International Economic Order and the fundamental human needs', and to make this study available" to the Commission at its thirty-fifth session. The Council endorsed this recommendation in decision 229 (LXII) of 13 May 1977.

130. The report of the Secretary-General[28] and the report of UNESCO[29] were considered by the Commission on Human Rights at its thirty-fifth session, in 1979. Separate analyses of the right to development, written by Mr. Keba M'Baye and Mr. Héctor Gros Espiell, were annexed to the UNESCO report. After noting both reports with satisfaction, the Commission, in resolution 4 (XXXV) of 2 March 1979, requested the Secretary-General to transmit them to all Governments, specialized agencies, regional intergovernmental organizations, non-governmental organizations and other appropriate international organizations, inviting their comments. The Commission invited the competent

---

[26] A/40/650.

[27] General Assembly resolution 42/186, annex.

[28] E/CN.4/1334.

[29] E/CN.4/1340.

economic and social organs of the United Nations to take account of the Secretary-General's study in their respective activities and fields and, in particular, invited the Preparatory Committee for the New International Development Strategy to pay due attention to the integration of human rights in the development process. The Commission recommended that the Secretary-General should be invited, in co-operation with UNESCO and other competent specialized agencies, to follow up the study with a further study of the regional and national dimensions of the right to development as a human right, paying particular attention to the obstacles encountered by developing countries in their efforts to secure the enjoyment of this right. The Economic and Social Council endorsed this recommendation in resolution 1979/29 of 10 May 1979.

131.   At its thirty-seventh session the Commission received and took note of the first part of the Secretary-General's study on the regional and national dimensions of the right to development as a human right,[30] and also of the conclusions and recommendations of the Seminar on the Effects of the Existing Unjust International Economic Order on the Economies of the Developing Countries and the Obstacles that this Represents for the Implementation of Human Rights and Fundamental Freedoms, held at Geneva from 30 June to 11 July 1980.[31] In resolution 36 (XXXVII) of 11 March 1981, it decided to establish a working group of 15 governmental representatives appointed by the Chairman of the Commission taking into account the need for equitable geographic distribution, to study the scope and contents of the right to development and the most effective means to ensure the realization, in all countries, of the economic, social and cultural rights enshrined in various international instruments, paying particular attention to the obstacles encountered by developing countries in their efforts to secure the enjoyment of human rights. The Working Group was requested to take into account especially the observations of Governments and specialized agencies on this subject, the report and study prepared by the Secretary-General, the conclusions and recommendations of relevant seminars, and the conclusions and recommendations of the Special Rapporteur on the The New International Economic Order and the Promotion of Human Rights.

132.   Between 1981 and 1984, the Working Group held nine sessions. At the eighth and ninth sessions, held in 1984, it adopted a report[32] which the Commission transmitted to the General Assembly through the Economic and Social Council, enabling the Assembly to adopt the Declaration on the Right to Development in resolution 41/128 of 4 December 1986.

133.   The Declaration proclaims, in article 1, that "The right to development is an inalienable human right by virtue of which every human person and all peoples are entitled to participate in, contribute to and enjoy economic, social, cultural and political development, in which all human rights and fundamental freedoms can be fully realized. It states, in article 2, that "The human person is the central subject of development and should be the active participant and beneficiary of the right to development", and adds that "All human beings have a responsibility for development, individually and collectively, taking into account the need for full respect of their human rights and fundamental freedoms as well as their duties to the community, which alone can ensure the free and complete fulfilment of the human being, and they should therefore promote and protect an appropriate political, social and economic order for development." The right and duty to formulate appropriate national development policies that aim at the constant improvement of the well-being of the entire population and of all individuals, on the basis of their active, free and meaningful participation in development and in the fair distribution of the benefits resulting therefrom, is placed upon the State.

134.   The Working Group held its tenth session from 5 to 20 January 1987 to prepare a report and proposals concerning concrete measures to promote the right to development, as requested in Commission on Human Rights resolution 1986/16. In the report of that session,[33] it included a set of proposals on which the experts had agreed by a large majority, including widespread dissemination of the text of the Declaration and of general information on the nature and content of the right to development, the organization of a series of seminars and workshops on the subject, and the preparation of a study on the implementation of the Declaration.

135.   The Commission on Human Rights, in resolution 1987/23 of 10 March 1987, requested the Secretary-General to circulate the Declaration on the Right to Development and the report of the Working Group to all Governments, specialized agencies and governmental and non-governmental organizations, inviting them as a matter of urgency and high priority to offer their comments and views on the subject of the implementation of the Declaration. It directed the Working Group to study the materials received and to submit to the Commission its recommendations as to which proposals would best contribute to the further enhancement and implementation of the Declaration. It further decided to consider later the question of the further activities and the possible enlargement of the Working Group, taking into account the interest of States in this subject. The General Assembly endorsed these decisions in resolution 42/117 oe 7 December 1987, and invited the Commission to report to it at its 1988 session on the organizational and substantial measures to implement the Declaration at all levels.

---

[30] E/CN.4/1421.

[31] ST/HR/SER.A/8.

[32] E/CN.4/1985/11.

[33] E/CN.4/1987/10.

I. Improvement of social life

136. Bearing in mind that the Member States of the United Nations have undertaken in the Charter to promote social progress and better standards of life in larger freedom, the General Assembly, in resolution 41/152 of 4 December 1986, acknowledged that the progress achieved in this area was still inadequate and that greater progress was necessary, and that efforts to this end should be continued.

137. The Assembly confirmed the need to ensure the well-being of all persons and the enjoyment of all the other basic human rights, particularly freedom of expression, worship and association, and the ensuring of equality of rights and opportunities on an equal footing for all the people in respect of employment, health, education, culture, rest and social security. It reiterated the right of every person to the enjoyment of the greatest possible degree of physical and mental health and emphasized that participation in cultural, sports and recreational activities and the use of free time without discrimination of any kind promotes the improvement of social life. Any such improvement, it pointed out, must be based on respect for and the promotion of all human rights and on the elimination of all forms of discrimination.

138. One years later, in resolution 42/145 of 7 December 1987, the Assembly reiterated these views and called upon Member States to make all efforts to promote the accelerated and complete elimination of such fundamental elements hindering economic and social progress and development as colonialism, neo-colonialism, racism and all forms of racial discrimination, *apartheid*, aggression, foreign occupation, alien domination and all forms of inequality and exploitation of peoples, and also to undertake effective measures to lessen international tensions.

J. Human rights and the new international economic order

139. One of the concepts set out by the General Assembly in resolution 32/130 of 16 December 1977 to guide future work within the United Nations system with respect to human rights questions was that: "The realization of the new international economic order is an essential element for the effective promotion of human rights and fundamental freedoms and should . . . be accorded priority."

140. The Commission on Human Rights, in resolution 5 (XXXV) of 2 March 1979, recognized "that it is indispensable to establish a more equitable and just international economic order which will permit the achievement of balanced development levels in all countries, thus turning into reality the principle contained in the Universal Declaration of Human Rights which recognizes the equal right of all human beings to enjoy an adequate standard of living". The Commission recommended that a seminar be held in 1980,

within the framework of the advisory services programme, on the effects of the existing unjust international economic order on the economies of the developing countries, and the obstacle that it represented for the implementation of human rights and fundamental freedoms, particularly the right to enjoy adequate standards of living as proclaimed in article 25 of the Universal Declaration of Human Rights.

141. The Seminar was held at Geneva from 30 June to 11 July 1980. The Commission on Human Rights took note of its conclusions and recommendations in resolution 36 (XXXVII) of 11 March 1981, and expressed its deep concern with the situation then existing in the attainment of the aims and objectives of the Declaration and Programme of Action for the Establishment of a New International Economic Order and the consequent adverse effects on the full achievement of human rights, including the right to development.

142. The Sub-Commission on Prevention of Discrimination and Protection of Minorities, in resolution 8 (XXXII) of 5 September 1979, requested the authorization of its parent bodies to appoint one of its members, Mr. Raúl Ferrero, as Special Rapporteur to prepare a study on "The New International Economic Order and the Promotion of Human Rights". The Sub-Commission indicated that in preparing the study the Special Rapporteur should take into account the conclusions of the Seminar, scheduled to be held in 1980, on the effects of the existing unjust international economic order on the economies of the developing countries and the obstacle that this represents for the implementation of human rights and fundamental freedoms, particularly the right to enjoy adequate standards of living as proclaimed in article 25 of the Universal Declaration of Human Rights. He was further to examine the effect, if any, that the new international economic order would have on the implementation of some human rights and fundamental freedoms; and to collect and analyse from a human rights perspective recommendations and guidelines contained in resolutions and reports adopted by organs of the United Nations system.

143. The Sub-Commission's proposal was approved by the Commission on Human Rights and by the Economic and Social Council, and the Special Rapporteur presented an oral report on the Seminar[34] to the Sub-Commission at its thirty-third session, in 1980. He submitted a progress report[35] to the Sub-Commission at its thirty-fourth session, the first part of the final report[36] at its thirty-fifth session, and the completed final report[37] at its thirty-sixth session.

144. The major objective of the Study was to demonstrate the fundamental links which exist between the achievement of full respect for human rights and the establishment of an equitable international economic order. The Study was also designed to lay the basic

---

[34] E/CN.4/Sub.2/SR.861.

[35] E/CN.4/Sub.2/477.

[36] E/CN.4/Sub.2/1982/19/Rev.1 and Add.1.

[37] E/CN.4/Sub.2/1983/24 and Add.1 and 2.

groundwork for the future examination of specific issues, such as the study on the right to food as a human right.

145. One of the broad conclusions that emerged from the Study was that progress towards the adoption of specific elements of the New International Economic Order has been painfully slow and in some respects non-existent; and that the continued deferral of the proposed global negotiations on international economic co-operation for development can only have an adverse impact on the prospects for the full realization of human rights, particularly in developing countries.

146. With respect to more specific issues, one of the most important recommendations which emerged from the Study concerned the impact on human rights of the policies and practices of the major international financial institutions, most notably the World Bank and the International Monetary Fund. The Study emphasized the need to ensure the continuing, and indeed increased, availability of financial resources to facilitate the development efforts of all the developing countries and particularly the least developed. At the same time, it made it clear that the assistance provided by such institutions must be of such a nature that its impact on the enjoyment of human rights is positive.

147. After examining the Study, the Sub-Commission in resolution 1983/35 of 6 September 1983 expressed its appreciation to the Special Rapporteur, transmitted the Study to the Commission on Human Rights with the recommendation that it should be published and given the widest possible distribution, and expressed the view that it would be advisable to undertake in the near future a study on the impact on human rights of the policies and practices of the major international financial institutions, most notably the International Monetary Fund and the World Bank.

K. Committee on Economic, Social and Cultural Rights

148. Articles 16 to 22 of the International Covenant on Economic, Social and Cultural Rights provide that:

Article 16

1. The States Parties to the present Covenant undertake to submit in conformity with this part of the Covenant reports on the measures which they have adopted and the progress made in achieving the observance of the rights recognized herein.

2. (*a*) All reports shall be submitted to the Secretary-General of the United Nations, who shall transmit copies to the Economic and Social Council for consideration in accordance with the provisions of the present Covenant.

(*b*) The Secretary-General of the United Nations shall transmit to the specialized agencies copies of the reports, or any relevant parts therefrom, from States Parties to the present Covenant which are also members of these specialized agencies in so far as these reports, or parts therefrom, relate to any matters which fall within the responsibilities of the said agencies in accordance with their constitutional instruments.

Article 17

1. The States Parties to the present Covenant shall furnish their reports in stages, in accordance with a programme to be established by the Economic and Social Council within one year of the entry into force of the present Covenant after consultation with the States Parties and the specialized agencies concerned.

2. Reports may indicate factors and difficulties affecting the degree of fulfilment of obligations under the present Covenant.

3. Where relevant information has previously been furnished to the United Nations or to any specialized agency by any State Party to the present Covenant, it will not be necessary to reproduce that information, but a precise reference to the information so furnished will suffice.

Article 18

Pursuant to its responsibilities under the Charter of the United Nations in the field of human rights and fundamental freedoms, the Economic and Social Council may make arrangements with the specialized agencies in respect of their reporting to it on the progress made in achieving the observance of the provisions of the present Covenant falling within the scope of their activities. These reports may include particulars of decisions and recommendations on such implementation adopted by their competent organs.

Article 19

The Economic and Social Council may transmit to the Commission on Human Rights for study and general recommendation or, as appropriate, for information the reports concerning human rights submitted by States in accordance with articles 16 and 17, and those concerning human rights submitted by the specialized agencies in accordance with article 18.

Article 20

The States Parties to the preset Covenant and the specialized agencies concerned may submit comments to the Eonomic and Social Council on any general recommendation under article 19 or reference to such general recommendation in any report of the Commission on Human Rights or any documentation referred to therein.

Article 21

The Economic and Social Council may submit from time to time to the General Assembly reports with recommendations of a general nature and a summary of the information received from the States Parties to the present Covenant and the specialized agencies on the measures taken and the progress made in achieving general observance of the rights recognized in the present Covenant.

Article 22

The Economic and Social Council may bring to the attention of other organs of the United Nations, their subsidiary organs and specialized agencies concerned with furnishing technical assistance any matters arising out of the reports referred to in this part of the present Covenant which may assist such bodies in deciding, each within its field of competence, on the advisability of international measures likely to contribute to the effective progressive implementation of the present Covenant.

149. With a view to fulfilling these responsibilities, the Council by decision 1978/10 of 3 May 1978 decided to establish a Sessional Working Group on the Implementation of the International Covenant on Economic, Social and Cultural Rights.[38] The Working Group encountered some difficulty in establishing its methods of work, and in 1981 and 1982 its composition, organization and administrative arrangements were modified by the Council. Later the Council, in resolution 1985/17 of 28 May 1985, renamed the Working Group "Com-

---

[38] For information concerning the establishment of the Committee, see chap. I, sect. C, 5.

mittee on Economic, Social and Cultural Rights", and decided that the Committee should be composed of 18 experts with recognized competence in the field of human rights, serving in their personal capacity. Members of the Committee are elected for a term of four years by the Council by secret ballot from a list of persons nominated by States parties to the International Covenant on Economic, Social and Cultural Rights.

1. METHODS OF WORK OF THE COMMITTEE

150.   In accordance with article 16 of the Covenant, reproduced above, States parties submit to the Secretary-General periodically reports on the measures they have adopted and the progress made in achieving the observance of the rights recognized in that instrument. The Secretary-General transmits copies of the reports to the Council and to the competent specialized agencies for consideration.

151.   In accordance with article 17, the reports are furnished in three stages: first stage: the rights covered by articles 6 to 9; second stage: the rights covered by articles 10 to 12; and third stage: the rights covered by articles 13 to 15. By decision 1985/132, the Council established a two-year periodicity for first-stage reports and a three-year periodicity for second- and third-stage reports.

152.   Under Council resolution 1979/43 and subsequent decisions and resolutions, the Committee considers the reports in the order in which they were received by the Secretary-General. Representatives of the reporting States are entitled to be present at the meetings of the Committee when their reports are examined, to make statements on the reports submitted by their States and to answer questions which may be put to them by the members of the Committee. The Committee submits to the Council a report on its activities, including a summary of its consideration of the reports submitted by States and those submitted by the specialized agencies concerned, with a view to assisting the Council to fulfil its responsibilities under articles 21 and 22 of the Covenant.

2. ACTIVITIES OF THE COMMITTEE

153.   The first session of the Committee on Economic, Social and Cultural Rights was held at the United Nations Office at Geneva from 9 to 27 March 1987.

154.   Eleven reports, submitted by eight States parties to the Covenant, were examined by the Committee at its first session. Representatives of all the reporting States participated in the meetings of the Committee when their reports were considered. For each report, the Committee heard introductory statements by a representative of the State party whose report was being considered. Comments were then made by the members of the Committee on the report and the introductory statements, and questions were asked of the representative of the reporting State, who then replied to those questions.

155.   The Committee included in its report to the Economic and Social Council[39] a summary of its consideration of the reports submitted by States parties to the Covenant. In addition, it drew the attention of the Council to a number of suggestions and recommendations of a general nature with regard to (a) the submission of reports, (b) the content of reports, (c) the availability of information to the Committee, (d) the role of the specialized agencies, (e) the role of non-governmental organizations, and (f) future sessions of the Committee.

156.   The Council, in resolution 1987/5 of 26 May 1987, noted with appreciation the report, suggestions and recommendations of the Committee, and invited States parties to the Covenant to take them into account. It urged the specialized agencies, regional commissions and other relevant United Nations bodies to extend their full co-operation and support to the Committee, and invited non-governmental organizations in consultative status to submit written statements to the Committee. In addition, the Council invited the Secretary-General to bring the Committee's report to the attention of the United Nations bodies and specialized agencies concerned, to publicize the work of the Committee, and to continue his efforts under the programme of advisory services in the field of human rights to assist States parties in discharging their reporting obligations under the Covenant, including holding training courses on the preparation of reports.

157.   The General Assembly, in resolution 42/103 of 7 December 1987, also noted the Committee's report, suggestions and recommendations; commended the States parties that had submitted their reports under article 16 of the Covenant, and urged States parties that had not done so to submit their reports as soon as possible.

---

[39] *Official Records of the Economic and Social Council, 1987, Supplement No. 17* (E/1987/28; E/C.12/1987.5).

VIII. REALIZATION OF CIVIL AND POLITICAL RIGHTS

Introduction

1. As in the case of economic, social and cultural rights, a number of United Nations organs are engaged in activities aimed at ensuring the realization of civil and political rights under the general obligations undertaken by all Member States in accordance with the Charter; these include the General Assembly, the Economic and Social Council, the Commission on Human Rights, the Sub-Commission on Prevention of Discrimination and Protection of Minorities and the Commission on the Status of Women.

2. In addition, the Human Rights Committee has now for more than a decade monitored the realization of the rights set out in the International Covenant on Civil and Political Rights, while the Committee against Torture was established recently to monitor the realization of the provisions of the Convention against Torture and Other Cruel, Inhuman or Degrading Treatment or Punishment.

3. Several specialized agencies also play a part in ensuring the realization of civil and political rights, including the International Labour Organisation, the United Nations Educational, Scientific and Cultural Organization, the Food and Agriculture Organization of the United Nations and the World Health Organization.

4. Supervisory activities of these organs and agencies, as well as monitoring activities of the Human Rights Committee and the Committee against Torture, are summarized below.

A. The right to life, liberty and security of person

1. PROVISIONS OF UNITED NATIONS INSTRUMENTS

5. Article 3 of the Universal Declaration of Human Rights proclaims that:

Everyone has the right to life, liberty and security of person.

6. Article II of the Convention on the Prevention and Punishment of the Crime of Genocide, approved and proposed for signature and ratification or accession by General Assembly resolution 260 A (III) of 9 December 1948, defines genocide as meaning:

. . . any of the following acts committed with intent to destroy, in whole or in part, a national, ethnical, racial or religious group, as such:

(*a*) Killing members of the group;

(*b*) Causing serious bodily or mental harm to members of the group;

(*c*) Deliberately inflicting on the group conditions of life calculated to bring about its physical destruction in whole or in part;

(*d*) Imposing measures intended to prevent births within the group;

(*e*) Forcibly transferring children of the group to another group.

7. Article II of the International Convention on the Suppression and Punishment of the Crime of *Apartheid,* adopted and opened for signature and ratification by General Assembly resolution 3068 (XXVIII) of 30 November 1973, defines the term "the crime of *apartheid*" as applying "to the following inhuman acts committed for the purpose of establishing and maintaining domination by one racial group of persons over any other racial group of persons and systematically oppressing them:

(*a*) Denial to a member or members of a racial group or groups of the right to life and liberty of person:

(i) By murder of members of a racial group or groups;

(ii) By the infliction upon the members of a racial group or groups of serious bodily or mental harm, by the infringement of their freedom or dignity, or by subjecting them to torture or to cruel, inhuman or degrading treatment or punishment;

(iii) By arbitrary arrest and illegal imprisonment of the members of a racial group or groups;

(*b*) Deliberate imposition on a racial group or groups of living conditions calculated to cause its or their physical destruction in whole or in part.

8. Article 6 of the International Covenant on Civil and Political Rights, adopted and opened for signature, ratification and accession by General Assembly resolution 2200 A (XXI) of 16 December 1966, reads as follows:

1. Every human being has the inherent right to life. This right shall be protected by law. No one shall be arbitrarily deprived of his life.

2. In countries which have not abolished the death penalty, sentence of death may be imposed only for the most serious crimes in accordance with the law in force at the time of the commission of the crime and not contrary to the provisions of the present Covenant and to the Convention on the Prevention and Punishment of the Crime of Genocide. This penalty can only be carried out pursuant to a final judgement rendered by a competent court.

3. When deprivation of life constitutes the crime of genocide, it is understood that nothing in this article shall authorize any State Party to the present Covenant to derogate in any way from any obligation assumed under the provisions of the Convention on the Prevention and Punishment of the Crime of Genocide.

4. Anyone sentenced to death shall have the right to seek pardon or commutation of the sentence. Amnesty, pardon or commutation of the sentence of death may be granted in all cases.

5. Sentence of death shall not be imposed for crimes committed by persons below eighteen years of age and shall not be carried out on pregnant women.

6. Nothing in this article shall be invoked to delay or to prevent the abolition of capital punishment by any State Party to the present Covenant.

2. MEASURES TAKEN BY UNITED NATIONS BODIES

(a) *Capital punishment*

9. The question of capital punishment, with which article 6 of the International Covenant on Civil and Political Rights is largely concerned, has been considered in United Nations bodies since 1959. Although some slight movement towards the eventual world-wide abolition of the death penalty has been recorded from time to time, it is not at all certain that there is a uniform progression in this direction. Indeed, in areas such as southern Africa, the threat or use of capital punishment as a means of suppressing the natural aspirations of peoples for social and economic justice, civil rights, and political freedoms has notably increased in recent years.

10. On 20 November 1959, during its fourteenth session, the General Assembly adopted resolution 1396 (XIV), by which it invited the Economic and Social Council "to initiate a study of the question of capital punishment, of the laws and practices relating thereto, and of the effects of capital punishment, and the abolition thereof, on the rate of criminality".

11. The Council, in resolution 747 (XXIX) of 6 April 1960, indicated that it needed as a basis for further consideration of the matter a factual review of the various aspects of the question of capital punishment, and requested the Secretary-General to prepare such a review, consulting as appropriate the *Ad Hoc* Advisory Committee of Experts on the Prevention of Crime and the Treatment of Offenders which the General Assembly had established in resolution 415 (V) of 1 December 1950.

12. The Secretary-General accordingly submitted to the Council at its thirty-fifth session a study on capital punishment[1] prepared by a consultant, Mr. Marc Ancel (France), on the basis of a Secretariat questionnaire circulated to Governments concerning laws, regulations and practices relating to capital punishment in their countries, and of a second questionnaire addressed to national social defence correspondents and certain non-governmental organizations requesting information on the deterrent effect of the death penalty and the consequences of its abolition. The study was discussed by the *Ad Hoc* Advisory Committee at its seventh session, in 1963, and the report together with the comments of that body were considered by the Council at its thirty-fifth session.

13. After considering the study and the comments of the *Ad Hoc* Advisory Committee the Council, in resolution 934 (XXXV) of 9 April 1963, addressed certain recommendations to Member Governments. At the same time it requested the Secretary-General to prepare a report based on information received from Governments on any new developments with respect to the law and practice in their countries concerning the death penalty and on information concerning legislation and military penal jurisdiction, especially in connection with any differences which existed as compared with their ordinary penal legislation regarding the application of capital punishment; and to submit the report to the United Nations Consultative Group on the Prevention of Crime and the Treatment of Offenders established by General Assembly resolution 415 (V).

14. At the eighteenth session of the General Assembly, held later in 1963, the Third Committee expressed the view that the subject of capital punishment, which up to that time had been considered by the Social Commission, should be considered from the standpoint of human rights by the Commission on Human Rights. Accordingly the Assembly, in resolution 1918 (XVIII) of 5 December 1963, endorsed the action taken by the Council, requested it to invite the Commission on Human Rights to study the report on capital punishment and the *Ad Hoc* Advisory Committee's comments thereon, and to make such recommendations on the matter as it deemed appropriate.

15. The Commission on Human Rights was unable, owing to lack of time, to consider the question until its twenty-fourth session, in 1968. At that time it had before it, in addition to the documentation referred to above, a study entitled *Capital Punishment: Developments 1961-1965,*[2] prepared by a consultant, Professor Norval Morris (Australia), a member of the Advisory Committee of Experts on the Prevention of Crime and the Treatment of Offenders.

16. The General Assembly, after considering the reports on capital punishment and other relevant documentation, adopted resolution 2993 (XXIII) of 26 November 1968. In that resolution the Assembly took note of the conclusion drawn by the Advisory Committee from part I of the report, namely that "if one looked at the whole problem of capital punishment in a historical perspective, it became clear that there was a world-wide tendency towards a considerable reduction in the number and categories of offences for which capital punishment might be imposed". It also took note of the view expressed in part II of the report, namely that there was "an overall tendency in the world towards fewer executions". In addition, it noted the report of the consultative Group on the Prevention of Crime and the Treatment of Offenders on the meeting which it held in 1968, in so far as the report related to capital punishment.[3]

17. The General Assembly invited the Governments of Member States:

(*a*) To ensure the most careful legal procedures and the greatest possible safeguards for the accused in capital cases in countries where the death penalty obtains, *inter alia,* by providing that:

---

[1] United Nations publication, Sales No. E.62.IV.2; reprinted as part I of Sales No. E.67.IV.15.

[2] United Nations publication, Sales No. E.67.IV.15, part II.

[3] *Official Records of the General Assembly, Twenty-third Session, Annexes,* agenda item 59, document A/7243, annex.

(i) A person condemned to death shall not be deprived of the right to appeal to a higher judicial authority or, as the case may be, to petition for pardon or reprieve;

(ii) A death sentence shall not be carried out until the procedures of appeal or, as the case may be, of petition for pardon or reprieve have been terminated;

(iii) Special attention be given in the case of indigent persons by the provision of adequate legal assistance at all stages of the proceedings;

(b) To consider whether the careful legal procedures and safeguards referred to in sub-paragraph (a) above may not be further strengthened by the fixing of a time-limit or time-limits before the expiry of which no death sentence shall be carried out, as has already been recognized in certain international conventions dealing with specific situations; . . .

In the same resolution, the General Assembly called upon Governments to supply information on their attitude towards possible further restriction of the use of the death penalty or its total abolition.

18. In resolution 2857 (XXVI) of 20 December 1971 and 32/61 of 8 December 1977, the General Assembly confirmed the continuing interest of the United Nations in the study of the question of capital punishment with a view to promoting full respect for everyone's right to life, and reaffirmed that the main objective to be pursued was the progressive restriction of the number of offences for which the death penalty might be imposed with a view to the desirability of abolishing that punishment.

19. At its thirty-fifth session, in 1980, the Assembly, by decision 35/437, took note of a draft resolution which had been submitted to its Third Committee entitled "Measures aiming at the ultimate abolition of capital punishment (Draft Second Optional Protocol to the International Covenant on Civil and Political Rights)";[4] decided to consider this idea at its thirty-sixth session; and requested the Secretary-General to transmit the text of the draft resolution to Governments for their comments and observations.

20. The General Assembly postponed further consideration of the item at its thirty-sixth session; however, in resolution 36/59 of 25 November 1981 it took note of the Secretary-General's report.[5] The following year, in resolution 37/192 of 18 December 1982, it requested the Commission on Human Rights to consider the idea of elaborating the proposed second draft protocol.

21. The Commission, in March 1984, transmitted the draft protocol to the Sub-Commission on Prevention of Discrimination and Protection of Minorities, which authorized Mr. Marc Bossuyt to prepare an analysis of the proposal, taking into account all of the available documentation.

22. In 1985 the Secretary-General submitted to the Economic and Social Council a periodic report on the situation, trends and safeguards concerning capital punishment,[6] updating earlier reports which had been prepared in accordance with Council resolution 1745 (LIV)

of 16 May 1973.[7] The report indicated that: (a) the laws of 29 countries did not provide for the death penalty; (b) in 12 countries the death penalty was imposed only in the case of exceptional crimes; (c) in two countries no one had been executed for at least 40 years; (d) in nine countries no one had been executed for at least 10 years; and (e) in the remaining countries capital punishment had been retained.

23. One of the reasons, cited by several Governments, for the decision to abolish capital punishment was that such punishment could not be reconciled with observance of the fundamental right to life; in their view it was the duty of government to ensure the full protection of life by not taking it even in the name of the law. Another was that no evidence had been found to prove that capital punishment had any perceptible effect on the overall crime rate or on rates of specific types of crime.

24. Mr. Bossuyt presented his report[8] to the Sub-Commission at its thirty-ninth session. In it, he reviewed international law provisions relating to the death penalty and summarized the views expressed by Governments on the question of the proposed second optional protocol. The Sub-Commission was unable to examine the report in detail at that session.

(b) Summary or arbitrary executions

25. The General Assembly, in resolution 2393 (XXIII) of 26 November 1968, invited the Governments of Member States to ensure the most careful legal procedures and the greatest possible safeguards for the accused in capital cases in countries where the death penalty obtains. Twelve years later the Assembly, alarmed at the incidence of summary executions, as well as of arbitrary executions, in many parts of the world, urged Member States in resolution 35/172 of 15 December 1980 (a) to respect as a minimum standard the content of the provisions of articles 6, 14 and 15 of the International Covenant on Civil and Political Rights and, where necessary, to review their legal rules and practices so as to guarantee the most careful legal procedures and the greatest possible safeguards for the accused in capital cases; (b) to examine the possibility of making automatic the appeal procedure, where it existed, in cases of death sentences, as well as the consideration of an amnesty, pardon or commutation in those cases; and (c) to provide that no death sentence should be carried out until the procedures of appeal and pardon had been terminated and, in any case, not until a reasonable time after the passing of the sentence in the court of first instance. The Assembly further requested the Secretary-General to use his best endeavours in cases where the minimum standard of legal safeguards mentioned above appeared not to be respected.

---

[4] A/35/742, para. 20.

[5] A/36/441 and Add.1 and 2.

[6] E/1985/43/Add.1.

[7] E/5616 and Add.1 and Corr.1 and 2, E/1980/9 and Corr.1 and 2 and Add.1-3, and E/1985/43.

[8] E/CN.4/Sub.2/1987/20.

26. The General Assembly repeated these views in resolution 36/22 of 9 November 1981, in which it strongly deplored "the increasing number of summary executions as well as the continued incidence of arbitrary executions in different parts of the world".

27. The Sixth United Nations Congress on the Prevention of Crime and Treatment of Offenders adopted a resolution (resolution 5) condemning extra-legal executions,[9] and thereby convinced the Commission on Human Rights and the Economic and Social Council of the need to deal with that question urgently. In resolution 1982/35 of 7 May 1982, adopted on the recommendation of the Commission, the Council decided to appoint for one year a special rapporteur to examine questions related to summary or arbitrary executions, and requested the Special Rapporteur to submit a comprehensive report on the subject to the Commission on Human Rights.

28. On the basis of recommendations prepared by the Committee on Crime Prevention and Control the Economic and Social Council, in resolution 1984/50 of 25 May 1984, approved a series of safeguards guaranteeing protection of the rights of those facing the death penalty and invited the Seventh United Nations Congress on the Prevention of Crime and Treatment of Offenders to consider them with a view to establishing an implementation mechanism. The safeguards are as follows:

1. In countries which have not abolished the death penalty, capital punishment may be imposed only for the most serious crimes, it being understood that their scope should not go beyond intentional crimes with lethal or other extremely grave consequences.

2. Capital punishment may be imposed only for a crime for which the death penalty is prescribed by law at the time of its commission, it being understood that if, subsequent to the commission of the crime, provision is made by law for the imposition of a lighter penalty, the offender shall benefit thereby.

3. Persons below 18 years of age at the time of the commission of the crime shall not be sentenced to death, nor shall the death sentence be carried out on pregnant women, or on new mothers, or on persons who have become insane.

4. Capital punishment may be imposed only when the guilt of the person charged is based upon clear and convincing evidence leaving no room for an alternative explanation of the facts.

5. Capital punishment may only be carried out pursuant to a final judgement rendered by a competent court after legal process which gives all possible safeguards to ensure a fair trial, at least equal to those contained in article 14 of the International Covenant on Civil and Political Rights, including the right of anyone suspected of or charged with a crime for which capital punishment may be imposed to adequate legal assistance at all stages of the proceedings.

6. Anyone sentenced to death shall have the right to appeal to a court of higher jurisdiction, and steps should be taken to ensure that such appeals shall become mandatory.

7. Anyone sentenced to death shall have the right to seek pardon, or commutation of sentence; pardon or commutation of sentence may be granted in all cases of capital punishment.

8. Capital punishment shall not be carried out pending any appeal or other recourse procedure or other proceeding relating to pardon or commutation of the sentence.

9. Where capital punishment occurs, it shall be carried out so as to inflict the minimum possible suffering.

29. The Special Rapporteur, Mr. S. Amos Wako, submitted five reports to the Commission on Human Rights between 1983 and 1987.[10] Their basic finding was that the phenomenon of summary or arbitrary executions persists in all regions of the world and that although the causes identified have been several, the situation of armed conflict in a number of territories caused the largest loss of life of persons not directly involved in such conflicts. The Special Rapporteur's conclusion was that "In spite of existing international norms designed to control the conduct of armed conflicts, and the repeated calls by international and regional bodies to parties to conflicts to respect the right to life of innocent civilians, the loss of human life continues to be considerable". In the opinion of the Special Rapporteur "this is due to a fundamental absence of understanding and respect for the right to life among those responsible for the direction of military operations in such conflicts".

30. A second principal cause of loss of life, according to the Special Rapporteur, is attributable to indiscriminate violence, such as that characterized by so-called "terrorism", the victims of which are very often innocent civilians; a third principal cause of non-respect for the right to life is that resulting from executions without trial or after a trial which does not afford adequate safeguards to protect the accused. Still another principal cause, in his view, is the inability of the authorities to control the group concerned and to enforce order and respect for the right to life.

31. In the report submitted to the forty-third session of the Commission, in 1987, the Special Rapporteur presented a series of recommendations, as follows:[11]

(a) That Governments:

(i) Ratify international human rights instruments, such as the International Covenant on Civil and Political Rights, including the Optional Protocol thereto, and the Convention against Torture and Other Cruel, Inhuman or Degrading Treatment or Punishment;

(ii) Review national laws and regulations with a view to strengthening the preventive measures against death caused by illegal or excessive use of force by security, law enforcement or other government officials;

(iii) Review the machinery for investigation of deaths under suspicious circumstances in order to secure an impartial, independent investigation on such deaths, including an adequate autopsy;

(iv) Review the trial procedures of tribunals, including those of special tribunals, in order to ensure that they embody adequate safeguards to protect the rights of the accused in the trial proceedings, as stipulated in the relevant international instruments;

(v) Emphasize the importance of the right to life in the training of all law enforcement personnel and inculcate in them respect for life;

(b) That international organizations:

(i) Strengthen their co-ordination in dealing with the immediate problems and the root causes of summary or arbitrary executions, in particular by sharing information, publications, studies, expertise, etc.;

---

[9] See *Sixth United Nations Congress on the Prevention of Crime and the Treatment of Offenders: Report prepared by the Secretariat* (United Nations publication, Sales No. E.81.IV.4), chap. I, sect. B.

[10] E/CN.4/1983/16 and Add.1, E/CN.4/1984/29, E/CN.4/1985/17, E/CN.4/1986/21 and E/CN.4/1987/20.

[11] E/CN.4/1987/20, paras. 246-248.

(ii) Make a concerted effort to draft international standards designed to ensure proper investigation by appropriate authorities into all cases of suspicious death, including provisions for adequate autopsy.

In addition, Governments, individually and through the international community, should support and encourage peace initiatives and political solutions to situations of armed conflict. Also Governments should be encouraged to take appropriate and effective measures, on national, regional and international levels, to combat terrorism and/or terrorist acts.

Furthermore Governments should be encouraged to enter into bilateral or regional agreements with a view to extending mutual assistance and co-operation to enhance the capacity of their authorities to safeguard the individual's right to life. At the international level, organs within the United Nations system should undertake action with a view to assisting Governments to reconstruct the infrastructure that will enable the authorities concerned effectively to carry out their basic obligation to protect the right to life of individuals in their societies.

32.   The Commission on Human Rights, the Economic and Social Council and the General Assembly all welcomed the recommendations prepared by the Committee on Crime Prevention and Control and by the Special Rapporteur. The Special Rapporteur's recommendation on the need to develop international standards designed to ensure effective legislation and other domestic measures so that proper investigations are conducted by appropriate authorities into all cases of suspicious death, including provisions for adequate autopsy, were singled out for endorsement.

33.   The General Assembly, in resolution 42/141 of 7 December 1987, solemnly condemned once again the large number of summary or arbitrary executions, including extra-legal executions, that continue to take place in various parts of the world, and demanded that the practice of summary or arbitrary executions be brought to an end. It invited the Special Rapporteur to continue to receive information from appropriate United Nations bodies and other international organizations and to respond effectively to information that comes before him, in particular when a summary or arbitrary execution is imminent or threatened, or when such an execution has recently occurred. The Assembly, further, requested the Secretary-General to continue to use his best endeavours in cases where the minimum standard of legal safeguards provided for in articles 6, 14 and 15 of the International Covenant on Civil and Political Rights appears not to be respected.

(c) *Hostage-taking*

34.   The International Convention against the Taking of Hostages, adopted and opened for signature and ratification, or for accession, by General Assembly resolution 34/146 of 17 December 1979, recognizes in particular, in its second preambular paragraph, "that everyone has the right to life, liberty and security of person, as set out in the Universal Declaration of Human Rights and the International Covenant on Civil and Political Rights". In its third preambular paragraph, the Convention reaffirms the principle of equal rights and self-determination of peoples.

35.   The Convention establishes the taking of hostages as "an offence of grave concern to the international community", provides that" any person committing an act of hostage-taking shall be either prosecuted or extradited", and established the need for international co-operation between States in devising and adopting effective measures for the prevention, prosecution and punishment of all acts of taking of hostages as manifestations of international terrorism.

36.   Taking this Convention into account, the Commission on Human Rights, in resolution 27 (XXXVII) of 11 March 1981, expressed its concern about the increasing number of hostage-takings, including those involving diplomatic personnel, and affirmed that the taking of hostages "constitutes a grave violation of human rights exposing the hostages to privation, hardship, anguish and danger to life and health". The Commission called on all States to observe fully and unconditionally their international obligations to protect diplomatic and consular personnel and premises and to prevent the taking of hostages; and resolved that it would accord due consideration to violations of human rights occasioned by hostage-taking.

37.   In 1986 and 1987 the Commission on Human Rights returned to the subject of hostage-taking, bearing in mind the provisions of the Convention against Torture and Other Cruel, Inhuman or Degrading Treatment or Punishment that had been adopted by the General Assembly on 10 December 1984 and Security Council resolution 579 (1985) of 18 December 1985, as well as the statement made by the President of the Security Council on 28 January 1987,[12] all condemning hostage-taking.

38.   In resolution 1987/28 of 10 March 1987, the Commission strongly condemned the taking of any person hostage, whoever those responsible and whatever the circumstances, and whether or not he is chosen at random, and whatever is his nationality. The Commission censured the actions of all persons responsible for taking hostages, whatever their motives, and demanded that they should immediately release those they are holding. It called upon all States to take any measures necessary to prevent and punish the taking of hostages and to put an immediate end to cases of abduction and unlawful restraint on their territory. It further requested the Secretary-General, whenever so requested by a State, to employ all means at his disposal in order to secure the immediate release of persons held hostage.

39.   In the resolution, the Commission expressed the view that hostage-taking is a serious violation of fundamental rights and of the dignity of the human being, and that arbitrary detention of persons is an unquestionable violation of human rights.

(d) *International terrorism*

40.   An item entitled "Measures to prevent international terrorism which endangers or takes innocent hu-

---

[12] S/18641.

man lives or jeopardizes fundamental freedoms, and study of the underlying causes of those forms of terrorism and acts of violence which lie in misery, frustration, grievance and despair and which cause some people to sacrifice human lives, including their own, in an attempt to effect radical changes", was included in the agenda of the twenty-seventh session of the General Assembly on the initiative of the Secretary-General.[13] At that session the Assembly established the 35-member *Ad Hoc* Committee on International Terrorism, which met at United Nations Headquarters, New York, in 1973, 1977 and 1979.

41.   The General Assembly examined the report of the *Ad Hoc* Committee[14] at its thirty-fourth session, in 1979, and adopted a number of recommendations relating to practical measures of co-operation for the speedy elimination of the problem of international terrorism which the Committee had prepared. In resolution 34/145 of 17 December 1979 the Assembly also took note of the study of the underlying causes of international terrorism contained in the *Ad Hoc* Committee's report, and urged all States, unilaterally and in co-operation with other States, as well as relevant United Nations organs, to contribute to the progressive elimination of the causes underlying international terrorism. Deeply concerned about continuing acts of international terrorism which take a toll of innocent human lives, the Assembly unequivocally condemned all acts of international terrorism which endanger or take human lives or jeopardize fundamental freedoms, and condemned the continuation of repressive and terrorist acts by colonial, racist and alien régimes in denying peoples their legitimate right to self-determination and independence and other human rights and fundamental freedoms.

42.   The Assembly has since reviewed the situation periodically on the basis of reports by the Secretary-General on the implementation of the recommendations of the *Ad Hoc* Committee. In resolutions 36/109 of 10 December 1981, 38/130 of 19 December 1983, 40/61 of 9 December 1985 and 42/159 of 7 December 1987 it has repeatedly condemned as criminal all acts, methods and practices of terrorism, wherever and by whomever committed, including those which jeopardize friendly relations among States and their security; has deeply deplored the loss of human lives which results from such acts of terrorism; and has called upon all States to fulfil their obligations under international law to refrain from organizing, instigating, assisting or participating in terrorist acts in other States, or acquiescing in activities within their territory directed towards the commission of such acts. Further, it has urged all States, unilaterally and in co-operation with other States, as well as relevant United Nations organs, to contribute to the progressive elimination of the causes underlying international terrorism and to pay special attention to all situations, including colonialism, racism, and situations in-

volving mass and flagrant violations of human rights and fundamental freedoms and those involving alien domination and occupation, that may give rise to international terrorism and may endanger international peace and security.

(e)   *The nuclear arms race*

43.   The General Assembly, in resolution 38/75 of 15 December 1983, resolutely, unconditionally and for all time condemned nuclear war as being contrary to human conscience and reason, as the most monstrous crime against peoples, and as a violation of the foremost human right, the right to life. It called upon all States to unite and redouble their efforts aimed at removing the threat of nuclear war, halting the nuclear arms race and reducing nuclear weapons until they are completely eliminated.

44.   The Commission on Human Rights and the Sub-Commission on Prevention of Discrimination and Protection of Minorities have since studied in detail the relationship that exists between disarmament, peace and development. The Commission affirmed, in resolution 1984/28 of 12 March 1984, that resources released as a result of disarmament were of particular importance in securing economic and social development and, consequently, the inherent right of all peoples to life. The Sub-Commission, in resolution 1984/30 of 30 August 1984, also stressed—as it had on earlier occasions—the threat that the arms race, particularly the nuclear arms race, posed for the achievement of social and economic progress and for the universal realization of all human rights.

45.   Having reviewed these studies the General Assembly, in resolution 42/99 of 7 December 1987, agreed that all the rights and freedoms, as well as all the material goods and spiritual wealth that both man and nations possess, have a common foundation: the right to life, freedom, peace and aspiration for happiness. It reaffirmed that all peoples and all individuals have an inherent right to life and that the safeguarding of this cardinal right is an essential condition for the enjoyment of the entire range of economic, social and cultural, as well as civil and political, rights.

46.   The Assembly stressed the urgent need for the international community to make every effort to strengthen peace, remove the growing threat of war, particularly nuclear war, halt the arms race and achieve general and complete disarmament under effective international control and prevent violations of the principles of the Charter of the United Nations regarding the sovereignty and territorial integrity of States and the self-determination of peoples, thus contributing to ensuring the right to life. It called upon all States, appropriate United Nations organs, specialized agencies and intergovernmental and non-governmental organizations concerned to take the necessary measures to ensure that the results of scientific and technological progress, the material and intellectual potential of mankind, are used

---

[13] A/8791 and Add.1 and Add.1/Corr.1.

[14] A/34/37.

189

to solve global problems exclusively in the interests of international peace, for the benefit of mankind and for promoting and encouraging universal respect for human rights and fundamental freedoms.

B. Abolition of slavery and slavery-like practices

1. PROVISIONS OF UNITED NATIONS INSTRUMENTS

47. A number of international instruments prepared for the purpose of abolishing slavery and slavery-like practices are in effect, some of them having originated in conventions prepared under the auspices of the League of Nations.

(a) *Slavery Convention of 1926*

48. In 1922, the League of Nations took steps to examine the question of slavery and established a Temporary Slavery Commission to ascertain the facts regarding slavery and to make proposals for dealing with the problem. The Commission recommended that some of its proposals should be embodied in an international convention. A draft Convention on Slavery was considered by the Assembly of the League in 1925 and 1926; a Convention was approved by the Assembly on 25 September 1926.

49. Article 1 of the Slavery Convention signed at Geneva on 25 September 1926 defines slavery as "the status or condition of a person over whom any or all of the powers attaching to the right of ownership are exercised", while the slave trade is defined as including "all acts involved in the capture, acquisition or disposal of a person with intent to reduce him to slavery; all acts involved in the acquisition of a slave with a view to selling or exchanging him; all acts of disposal by sale or exchange of a slave acquired with a view to being sold or exchanged, and, in general, every act of trade of transport in slaves".

50. Parties to the Convention undertake, in article 2, "to prevent and suppress the slave trade" and "to bring about, progressively and as soon as possible, the complete abolition of slavery in all its forms". Parties undertake further, in article 3, "to adopt all appropriate measures with a view to preventing and suppressing the embarkation, disembarkation and transport of slaves in their territorial waters and upon all vessels flying their respective flags"; and, in article 4, to "give to one another every assistance with the object of securing the abolition of slavery and the slave trade". As regards implementation, parties undertake (article 7) "to communicate to each other and to the Secretary-General of the League of Nations any laws and regulations which they may enact with a view to the application of the provisions of the . . . Convention".

(b) *Protocol amending the Slavery Convention of 1926*

51. In resolution 475 (XV) of 27 April 1953, the Economic and Social Council recommended that the General Assembly invite the State parties, or States which might become parties, to the Slavery Convention signed at Geneva on 25 September 1926 to agree to the transfer to the United Nations of the functions undertaken by the League of Nations under that Convention, and requested the Secretary-General to prepare a draft Protocol to that end. The Secretary-General submitted the draft Protocol to the eighth session of the General Assembly, in 1953. In resolution 794 (VIII) of 23 October 1953 the Assembly approved an amended version of the draft Protocol, urged all States parties to the Slavery Convention of 1926 to sign and accept the Protocol, and recommended that all other States accede to the Convention as amended by the Protocol at their earliest opportunity.

(c) *Universal Declaration of Human Rights*

52. Article 4 of the Universal Declaration of Human Rights proclaims that:

No one shall be held in slavery or servitude; slavery and the slave trade shall be prohibited in all their forms.

Article 6 of the Declaration provides that:

Everyone has the right to recognition everywhere as a person before the law.

53. In this connection it may be noted that the term "slavery" implies the destruction of the juridical personality and is a relatively limited and technical notion, whereas "servitude" is a more general idea covering all possible forms of man's domination of man. While slavery is the best-known and worst form of bondage, other slavery-like practices exist in modern society which tend to reduce the dignity of man; these are referred to in the Supplementary Convention on the Abolition of Slavery of 1956 as "institutions and practices similar to slavery".

(d) *Convention for the Suppression of the Traffic in Persons and of the Exploitation of the Prostitution of Others*

54. By resolution 317 (IV) of 2 December 1949, the General Assembly approved the Convention for the Suppression of the Traffic in Persons and of the Exploitation of the Prostitution of Others, which consolidated four international instruments on the subject prepared earlier under the auspices of the League of Nations. Under the Convention, the parties agree to punish any person who "procures, entices or leads away, for purposes of prostitution, another person, even with the consent of that person"; "exploits the prostitution of another person, even with the consent of that person"; "keeps or manages, or knowingly finances or takes part in the financing of a brothel"; or "knowingly lets or

rents a building or other place or any part thereof for the purpose of the prostitution of others''. The parties agree further (article 21) to communicate to the Secretary-General "such laws and regulations as have already been promulgated in their States, and thereafter annually such laws and regulations as may be promulgated, relating to the subjects of the . . . Convention, as well as all measures taken by them concerning the application of the Convention''.

(e) *Supplementary Convention on the Abolition of Slavery, the Slave Trade, and Institutions and Practices Similar to Slavery*

55. In resolution 564 (XIX) of 7 April 1955 the Economic and Social Council expressed the view that it was desirable to prepare a draft supplementary convention which would deal with practices resembling slavery not covered by the Slavery Convention signed at Geneva on 25 September 1926, and appointed a Committee to prepare such a draft. The Committee met early in 1956 and adopted a draft Supplementary Convention on the Abolition of Slavery, the Slave Trade and Institutions and Practices Similar to Slavery. In resolution 608 (XXI) of 30 April 1956 the Council decided that a conference of plenipotentiaries should be convened in order to complete the drafting of the Supplementary Convention. The Conference adopted the Supplementary Convention on the Abolition of Slavery, the Slave Trade and Institutions and Practices Similar to Slavery on 7 September 1956.

56. The Supplementary Convention provides that each State party shall take all practicable and necessary legislative and other measures to bring about progressively and as soon as possible the complete abolition or abandonment of certain institutions and practices, where they still exist and whether or not they are covered by the definition of slavery contained in article 1 of the Slavery Convention signed at Geneva on 25 September 1926. The practices referred to are the following:

(*a*) Debt bondage, that is to say, the status or condition arising from a pledge by a debtor of his personal services or of those of a person under his control as security for a debt, if the value of those services as reasonably assessed is not applied towards the liquidation of the debt or the length and nature of those services are not respectively limited and defined;

(*b*) Serfdom, that is to say, the condition or status of a tenant who is by law, custom or agreement bound to live and labour on land belonging to another person and to render some determinate service to such other person, whether for reward or not, and is not free to change his status;

(*c*) Any institution or practice whereby:

(i) A woman, without the right to refuse, is promised or given in marriage on payment of a consideration in money or in kind to her parents, guardian, family or any other person or group; or

(ii) The husband of a woman, his family, or his clan, has the right to transfer her to another person for value received or otherwise; or

(iii) A woman on the death of her husband is liable to be inherited by another person;

(*d*) Any institution or practice whereby a child or young person under the age of 18 years is delivered by either or both of his natural parents or by his guardian to another person, whether for reward or not, with a view to the exploitation of the child or young person or of his labour.

57. The Supplementary Convention also provides, in article 8, for co-operation between States parties to give effect to its provisions. In particular "The Parties undertake to communicate to the Secretary-General . . . copies of any laws, regulations and administrative measures enacted or put into effect to implement the provisions'' of the Convention; and the Secretary-General communicates the information received "to the other Parties and to the Economic and Social Council as part of the documentation for any discussion which the Council might undertake with a view to making further recommendations for the abolition of slavery, the slave trade'', and institutions and practices similar to slavery.

(f) *Convention on the High Seas*

58. In resolution 1105 (XI) of 21 February 1957, the General Assembly decided to convene an international conference of plenipotentiaries to examine the law of the sea, taking account not only of the legal but also of the technical, biological, economic and political aspects of the problem, and to embody the results of its work in one or more international conventions or such other instruments as it might deem appropriate.

59. Among the Conventions adopted by the Conference was the Convention on the High Seas, laying down conditions for the exercise of freedom of the high seas. Under article 22 of the Convention, a warship may board a foreign merchant ship on the high seas if there is reasonable ground for suspecting that the ship is engaged in the slave trade.

(g) *International Covenant on Civil and Political Rights*

60. Article 8 of the International Covenant on Civil and Political Rights, adopted by the General Assembly in resolution 2200 A (XXI) of 16 December 1966, reads as follows:

1. No one shall be held in slavery; slavery and the slave-trade in all their forms shall be prohibited.

2. No one shall be held in servitude . . .

(h) *Convention on the Elimination of All Forms of Discrimination against Women*

61. Article 6 of the Convention, adopted by the General Assembly in resolution 34/180 of 18 December 1979, reads as follows:

States Parties shall take all appropriate measures, including legislation, to suppress all forms of traffic in women and exploitation of prostitution of women.

2. MEASURES TAKEN BY UNITED NATIONS BODIES

62. In resolution 278 (III) of 13 May 1949, the General Assembly requested the Economic and Social Council to study the problem of slavery. Since that time a number of studies, surveys and reports on the subject have been prepared and examined by the General Assembly, the Council, the Commission on Human Rights and the Sub-Commission on Prevention of Discrimination and Protection of Minorities.

63. The Sub-Commission has undertaken regular consideration of the question of the abolition of slavery in all its forms, and has set up permanent machinery to assist it in this endeavour in the form of a Working Group on Slavery which meets briefly before each Sub-Commission session and prepares a report and recommendations based upon the information made available to it.

64. To a certain extent the emphasis in this field has shifted in recent years from the prevention and suppression of the slave trade, which appears to have been eradicated through international co-operation, to the abolition of slavery and various institutions and practices similar to slavery, including the slavery-like practices of *apartheid* and colonialism.

(a) Surveys and reports, and action taken thereon

65. The first survey of slavery, the slave trade, and institutions or customs resembling slavery[15] was prepared by the *Ad Hoc* Committee on Slavery appointed by the Secretary-General in accordance with Economic and Social Council resolution 238 (IX) of 20 July 1949. The *Ad Hoc* Committee consisted of four members, serving in their individual capacity. The Committee met in February/March 1950 and in April 1951, and at the end of the latter session submitted its report to the Council.

66. The *Ad Hoc* Committee informed the Council that, after considering the information available, it had reached the unanimous conclusion that slavery in its crudest form was still present in the world and should continue to be of concern to the international community. It proposed that the definition contained in article 1 of the Slavery Convention signed at Geneva on 25 September 1926 should continue to be accepted as an accurate and adequate international definition of slavery and the slave trade, and drafted the Protocol under which the United Nations later assumed the functions and powers formerly exercised by the League of Nations under that Convention. It recommended the preparation of the Supplementary Convention which the United Nations subsequently adopted in 1956.

67. After considering the *Ad Hoc* Committee's report the Economic and Social Council, in resolution 388 (XIII) of 10 September 1951, noted that the material was not in such form as to allow the Council to act upon it at that session and requested the Secretary-General to obtain further information and report on "what action the United Nations and specialized agencies could most appropriately take in order to achieve the elimination of slavery, the slave trade, and forms of servitude resembling slavery in their effects".

68. A survey completing the information contained in the report submitted by the *Ad Hoc* Committee was prepared by the Secretary-General and submitted to the Council at its seventeenth session, in 1954.[16] The Council, in resolution 525 (XVII) of 29 April 1954, expressed the view that the information was still not in such a form as to give a clear and concise statement as to the extent to which slavery, and practices resembling slavery, existed, and appointed Mr. Hans Engen as Rapporteur to prepare a summary of all the available information on the subject.

69. Mr. Engen's survey[17] was submitted to the Council at its nineteenth session, in 1955. At that session the Council, in resolution 564 (XIX) of 7 April 1955, expressed the view that, in the light of the situation as revealed in that survey and in earlier reports on the subject, it was desirable to prepare a draft supplementary convention which would deal with those practices resembling slavery but not covered by the Slavery Convention signed at Geneva on 25 September 1926. The Council appointed an *Ad Hoc* Committee consisting of the representatives of ten Member States to prepare the draft supplementary convention. At its twenty-first session, in 1956, the Council, having examined the report of the drafting committee, decided in resolution 608 (XXI) of 30 April 1956, that a conference of plenipotentiaries should be convened in order to complete the drafting of the supplementary convention.

70. The Conference of Plenipotentiaries was held at Geneva from 13 August to 4 September 1956 and used as the basis of its discussions the draft supplementary convention on the abolition of slavery, the slave trade, and institutions and practices similar to slavery, which had been prepared by the *Ad Hoc* Committee. On 7 September 1956 the Conference adopted the Supplementary Convention on the Abolition of Slavery, the Slave Trade, and Institutions and Practices Similar to Slavery by 40 votes in favour, none against, with three abstentions, and opened it for signature.

71. In 1960, 1961 and 1962 the Council urged those Governments of States Members of the United Nations and members of the specialized agencies which had not already done so to adhere to the Conventions. The General Assembly, in resolution 1841 (XVII) of 19 December 1962, made a similar appeal and, at the same time, urged all States parties to the conventions on slavery to co-operate fully in carrying out their terms, in particular, by furnishing the Secretary-General, if they had not already done so, with the information called for under article 8 of the Supplementary Convention.

---

[15] E/1988.

[16] E/2540.

[17] E/2673.

72. In 1963, the Council, feeling a need for acurate, comprehensive and up-to-date information on the extent to which slavery, the slave trade, and institutions and practices similar to slavery persisted, requested the Secretary-General, in resolution 960 (XXXVI) of 12 July 1963, to appoint a special rapporteur on slavery to bring the Engen report up to date. The Secretary-General accordingly appointed Mr. Mohamed Awad as Special Rapporteur.

73. After considering and noting the Special Rapporteur's report[18] which was based on replies received to a questionnaire formulated by the Secretary-General in consultation with the Special Rapporteur, the Council, in resolution 1126 (XLI) of 26 July 1966, referred the question of slavery and the slave trade in all their practices and manifestations, including the slavery-like practices of *apartheid* and colonialism, to the Commission on Human Rights and requested the Commission to submit to it a report "containing specific proposals for effective and immediate measures which the United Nations could adopt to put an end to slavery in all its practices and manifestations". At the same time the Council called again upon all Member States which were not parties to become parties as soon as possible to the Slavery Convention of 1926 and to the Supplementary Convention of 1956. The Council also invited UNESCO to continue its programme of education designed to correct a social outlook that tolerated the existence of slavery or forms of servitude similar to slavery.

74. Pursuant to Economic and Social Council resolution 1126 (XLI) the Commission on Human Rights (in the report on its twenty-third session[19] (1967)) recommended to the Economic and Social Council a series of measures for combating slavery. On the recommendation of the Commission, the Economic and Social Council adopted resolution 1232 (XLII) of 6 June 1967 on the subject, in which it expressed the view that "both the International Slavery Convention of 1926 and the Supplementary Convention of 1956 on the Abolition of Slavery, the Slave Trade, and Institutions and Practices Similar to Slavery should be reconsidered in order to embrace the contemporary manifestations of slavery exemplified by *apartheid* and colonialism".

75. The Council also requested the Commission on the Status of Women, the Commission for Social Development, ILO, UNESCO and WHO to give attention to the problem of slavery and the slave trade in their work.

76. At its twenty-third session the Commission on Human Rights, in resolution 13 (XXIII) of 21 March 1967, also requested the Sub-Commission on Prevention of Discrimination and Protection of Minorities to undertake regular considerations of the question of slavery in all its forms, including the slavery-like practices of *apartheid* and colonialism, taking into account the study and recommendations prepared by the Council's Special Rapporteur and such other material as it believed pertinent, and to consider information submitted by the States parties to the Supplementary Convention of 1956 in accordance with article 8 of that Convention.

77. At its forty-fourth session, in 1968, the Economic and Social Council, on the recommendation of the Commission on Human Rights, adopted resolution 1330 (XLIV) of 31 May 1968, by which it authorized the Sub-Commission to undertake a study of the measures that might be taken to implement the Slavery Convention of 1926, the Supplementary Convention of 1956 and the various recommendations included in the resolutions of the General Assembly, the Economic and Social Council and the Commission on Human Rights relating to the slavery-like practices of *apartheid* and colonialism. The Council further authorized the Sub-Commission "to initiate a study of the possiblities of international police co-operation to interrupt and punish the transportation of persons in danger of being enslaved". The Council requested the Secretary-General to establish a list of experts in economic, sociological, legal and other relevant disciplines, whose advice would be available to States concerned with the liquidation of slavery and the slave trade in all their practices and manifestations, including the slavery-like practices of *apartheid* and colonialism. It also reminded Governments of the facilities available under the technical assistance programmes for assisting Governments in eliminating slavery and slavery-like practices and in helping them to solve resulting economic and social problems. The Council requested all Governments to exert their full influence and resources to assist in the total eradication of the slavery-like practices of *apartheid* and colonialism. It affirmed that the master-and-servant laws enforced in Southern Rhodesia, South West Africa and South Africa constituted clear manifestations of slavery and the slave trade.

78. In resolution 1331 (XLIV) of the same date, which had been recommended to the Council by the Commission on the Status of Women, the Council expressed its concern that the *Report on Slavery* prepared by the Special Rapporteur[20] indicated that slavery, the slave trade and similar institutions and practices still existed in many parts of the world and that women especially were among the victims of such institutions and practices. The Council condemned slavery, including the slavery-like practices of *apartheid* and colonialism, the slave trade and similar institutions and practices such as marriages without consent, traffic in persons for purposes of prostitution, transference and inheritance of women and other similar degrading practices.

79. At its forty-sixth session the Economic and Social Council, in resolution 1419 (XLVI) of 6 June 1969, adopted on the recommendation of the Commission on Human Rights, confirmed the decision of the Sub-Commission to designate a Special Rapporteur to carry out a study within the terms of Council resolution 1330 (XLIV).

---

[18] E/4168 and Add.1-5.

[19] *Official Records of the Economic and Social Council, Forty-second Session, Supplement No. 6* (E/4322 and Corr.1).

[20] United Nations publication, Sales No. E.67.XIV.2.

80. At its twenty-fourth session, in 1971, the Sub-Commission received the final report of its Special Rapporteur.[21] In resolution 3 (XXIV) of 17 August 1971, the Sub-Commission expressed its deep appreciation to the Special Rapporteur, transmitted his report to the Commission on Human Rights and to the Economic and Social Council, and requested the Council to adopt a comprehensive draft resolution on slavery.

81. Accordingly the Council, in resolution 1695 (LII) of 2 June 1972, called upon all eligible States which were not parties to the Slavery Convention of 1926 and the Supplementary Convention of 1956 to become parties as soon as possible; drew attention "to the close relationship between the effects of slavery, *apartheid* and colonialism and to the need to take concrete measures to ensure the effective implementation of the relevant international conventions and decisions of the United Nations with a view to bringing about the complete elimination of these shameful phenomena"; and called upon all States "to enact any legislation necessary to prohibit slavery and the slave trade in all their practices and manifestations and to provide effective penal sanctions for persons committing, or ordering to be committed, any of the following acts: (*a*) abduction, or planning the abduction, or giving instructions for the abduction, of any persons by force, treachery, gifts, abuse of authority or power, or intimidation, which results in that person being placed in a status of slavery or servitude as defined in the . . . Slavery Convention of 1926 and the Supplementary Convention of 1956". The Council also called upon all States "to search for persons alleged to have committed, or to have ordered to be committed, any such acts, and to bring such persons, regardless of their nationality, before its own courts, or to hand such persons over for trial to another State concerned".

82. The Council invited the International Criminal Police Organization (INTERPOL) to co-operate within the limits established by its constitution and in accordance with the special arrangement between the United Nations and INTERPOL approved by the Council under resolution 1579 (L) of 20 May 1971, with the United Nations in its efforts to eliminate slavery, the slave trade, and institutions and practices similar to slavery, and in particular to forward to the Secretary-General annually any information at its disposal with regard to the international traffic in persons, including reports on the subject received from its national central bureaux.

83. The Council called upon all States where the total emancipation of slaves and other persons of servile status had not taken place to make every effort to absorb such persons into the general labour force and to give them access to vocational guidance and training facilities, and recommended to all specialized agencies, intergovernmental organizations and non-governmental organizations concerned that they continue and expand their assistance to such persons, including vocational guidance and training in particular. It recommended to Governments of countries of refuge that refugee facilities and travel documents should be made easily available to the victims of racial discrimination who had to leave their countries to escape the slavery-like practices of *apartheid,* enabling them in particular to return to their country of refuge; and further recommended that Governments made use of the list of experts on slavery prepared by the Secretary-General in accordance with Council resolution 1330 (XLIV) of 31 May 1968, when seeking advice on matters relating to the elimination of slavery and the slave trade.

84. In resolution 15 (XXXVI) of 29 February 1980, the Commission on Human Rights recommended to the Economic and Social Council that it authorize the Sub-Commission on Prevention of Discrimination and Protection of Minorities to entrust Mr. Benjamin Whitaker, a member of the Sub-Commission, with the further extension and updating of the *Report on Slavery*. The Council concurred in decision 1980/123 of 2 May 1980, and requested the Secretary-General to give the Special Rapporteur assistance, including all relevant information from reliable sources.

85. The Special Rapporteur prepared a preliminary report[22] for the thirty-fourth session of the Sub-Commission, in 1981; and a final report[23] for the thirty-fifth session, in 1982.

(b) *Updated* Report on Slavery

86. In the updated *Report on Slavery* the Special Rapporteur first presented some general observations on the scope of the problem, then summarized the action taken to abolish slavery and the slave trade at the national and international levels.

87. In his conclusions, the Special Rapporteur pointed out that:

The phenomenon of slavery manifests several of the gravest forms of the violation of human rights; often it combines coercion, severe discrimination and the most extreme form of economic exploitation. It is the ultimate structural abuse of human power; that any vestiges should remain in the 1980s is a disgrace to professed international standards.

The cumulative evidence contained in this report substantiates *prima facie* that, although chattel-slavery in the former traditional sense no longer persists in any significant degree, the prevalence of several forms of slavery-like practice continues unabated. Indeed, instances of new forms of servitude and gross exploitation have come to light in recent years, as violators seek to circumvent laws or to take advantage of changing economic and social conditions. Some of the individual cases, although they may appear isolated, highlight wider and deeper problems that deserve attention. Hence the necessity to re-examine continuously both the nature of the problem and what response the international community should best make.

88. In his recommendations, the Special Rapporteur proposed:

Appealing to Member States to sign or ratify the relevant Conventions as soon as possible, or to explain in writing why they felt unable to do so;

---

[21] E/CN.4/Sub.2/322.

[22] E/CN.4/Sub.2/478.

[23] E/CN.4/Sub.2/1982/20 and Add.1.

Asking all States to report regularly upon compliance with and enforcement of the provisions of the Conventions;

Arranging for the United Nations Development Programme to provide help to rehabilitate freed slaves;

Arranging optimum co-ordination of all United Nations bodies in the campaign to eliminate slavery-type practices; and

Strengthening the Working Group on Slavery and the Centre for Human Rights.

89. At the same time, he pointed out that:

It is self-evident from the situation prevailing several decades after the coming into effect of the Conventions, that international instruments and even national legislation—while essential—are not enough. Legal abolition does not *ipso facto* result in effective abolition. Besides the proper enforcement of laws, if their principles are to become a reality, concrete practical prescriptions are necessary, which should include preventive reformative measures as well as restrictive ones. The roots of slavery-type exploitation are often deep and complex. Condemnation, while morally satisfying, is relatively easy; we should also undertake the harder but more constructive work of diagnosing—as a good doctor would—the roots of the problem (whether economic, social, traditional, psychological or historical) in order to prescribe the correct remedies. It is crucial to deal with the causes —including the structural economic foundations—and not just the symptoms. Budgetary considerations are sometimes invoked as an excuse for resisting more effective action: but those who shelter behind such a philosophy should be asked to say what price is too high to pay for the release of even one victim of slavery. The outlay required is miniscule when weighed in the scale of human rights and the concepts underlying the United Nations.

(c) *Establishment of permanent machinery to deal with slavery and slavery-like practices*

90. After considering the Council's request that it examine the possibility of the establishment of some form of permanent machinery to give advice on the elimination of slavery and on the suppression of the traffic in persons and exploitation of the prostitution of others, the Sub-Commission on Prevention of Discrimination and Protection of Minorities, in resolution 7 (XXVI) of 19 September 1973, recommended that it should be authorized to appoint a group of five from among its membership to meet for not more than three working days, prior to each session of the Sub-Commission, to review developments in the field of slavery and the slave trade in all their practices and manifestations, and to consider and examine any information from credible sources on the subject with a view to recommending remedial action. The Commission on Human Rights endorsed this recommendation and the Economic and Social Council, in decision 16 (LVI) of 17 May 1974, authorized the Sub-Commission to appoint the group of five.

91. At its twenty-seventh session, in 1974, the Sub-Commission, in resolution 11 (XXVII) of 21 August 1974, established the Working Group on Slavery which the Council had authorized, and requested it to prepare a report for consideration at the Sub-Commission's twenty-eighth session including proposals for the future method of work of the Working Group and of the Sub-Commission in their examination of this question.

92. The Working Group has since held 12 sessions. Its mandate has been progressively interpreted in such a way as to cover a growing number of additional relevant issues such as the sale of children, the exploitation of child labour, the sexual mutilation of female children, abuses against workers and indigenous populations, debt bondage, and the exploitation of the prostitution of others. This evolution reflects the opinion of the Working Group that there is evidence not only that slavery and the slave trade in all their practices and manifestations continue to exist, but also that new forms of practices analogous to slavery are being discovered or devised and permitted to continue unchecked. In order to enable the Group to deal with this wide range of issues, its members have emphasized that ways must be found to improve the sources of information available to it.

93. In its resolution 1987/32 of 4 September 1987, the Sub-Commission recommended to the Commission that the name of the working group be changed to Working Group on Contemporary Forms of Slavery.

(d) *Studies and inquiries*

94. As a result of initiatives taken by the Working Group on Slavery, a number of studies concerning various aspects of slavery and slavery-like practices have been undertaken or are under consideration.

95. For example, on the recommendation of the Working Group the Sub-Commission on Prevention of Discrimination and Protection of Minorities, in paragraph 16 of resolution 6 B (XXXI) of 13 September 1978, requested the Secretary-General "to carry out, as a matter of priority, a study of *apartheid* and colonialism as collective forms of slavery". The Secretary-General's report was presented to the Sub-Commission at its thirty-third session, in 1980.

96. In the report, the Secretary-General noted "that the international community has recognized that the *apartheid* system in South Africa is not simply a racial discrimination problem to be solved through education and political and social reforms. Rather, it has been increasingly understood that the essence of *apartheid* lies in the dispossession of the black population through the imposition of quasi-colonial rule, and in the harnessing of the labour of the vanquished indigenous people through a variety of coercive measures for the profit of white investors, both South African and foreign. The international community has therefore described the *apartheid* system as a slavery-like practice imposed on an entire collectivity, which can be eradicated only through a complete restructuring of the existing political and economic relationships".

97. After examining and taking note of the report, the Sub-Commission, in resolution 9 (XXXIII) of 10 September 1980, requested the Secretary-General to bring it to the attention of all Member States and competent United Nations bodies, including the International Court of Justice, in order that they might assess its conclusions, including, in particular, those to the effect that:

(a) *Apartheid,* which was introduced in 1948, as official Government policy, represented a systematization and formalization of controls over the black people of South Africa and was extended to the entire country with a view to maintaining the slavery and slavery-like practices imposed by the white settlers during the early stages of their penetration and settlement of South Africa;

(b) The Goverment of South Africa has continued, through repressive legislation since 1948, to enforce the system of *apartheid* as a slavery-like practice despite the growing resistance of the black population in South Africa;

(c) In agriculture, the conditions of exploitation of black workers similar to those indicated in the Supplementary Convention on the Abolition of Slavery, the Slave Trade, and Institutions and Practices Similar to Slavery of 1956, and in the Forced Labour Convention of 1930, continue to exist on white farms of South Africa.

98.   A second inquiry undertaken as a result of an initiative of the Working Group on Slavery related to the exploitation of child labour. The Economic and Social Council, on 2 May 1980, decided to authorize the Sub-Commission on Prevention of Discrimination and Protection of Minorities to entrust Mr. Abdelwahab Bouhdiba with the preparation of a study on the subject as suggested by the Working Group.

99.   The report[24] was presented to the Sub-Commission at its thirty-fourth session, in 1981. After calling for its wide distribution the Sub-Commission, in resolution 18 (XXXIV) of 10 September 1981, decided to consider at its thirty-fifth session the drawing up of a concrete programme of action to combat violations of human rights of children through the exploitation of child labour. At that session, the Sub-Commission received a note by the Special Rapporteur setting out his proposed programme of action,[25] and decided, in resolution 1982/33 of 10 September 1982, to submit that proposal to the Commission on Human Rights for its consideration.

100.   A third inquiry, on combating the traffic in persons and the exploitation of the prostitution of others, was initiated, at the suggestion of the Working Group, the Commission on the Status of Women and the World Conference of the United Nations Decade for Women, by the Economic and Social Council in resolution 1981/40 of 8 May 1982. The Council requested the Secretary-General to undertake an inquiry among the Governments of Member States and the international organizations concerned on the status of the question of combating the traffic in persons and the exploitation of the prostitution of others and to report thereon to the General Assembly at its thirty-seventh session, "so that, with full knowledge of the facts, joint measures can be envisaged to put an end to this form of slavery".

101.   A report containing all information available to the Secretary-General on the traffic in persons and the exploitation of the prostitution of others[26] was transmitted to the Working Group on Slavery at its eighth session, in 1982. The document was subsequently submitted to the General Assembly at its thirty-seventh session.

102.   In recent years the Working Group on Slavery has reviewed at each session developments relating to slavery and the slave trade, the sale of children, the exploitation of child labour, debt bondage, traffic in persons and exploitation of the prostitution of others, and the slavery-like practices of *apartheid* and colonialism. In addition to summarizing the information made available to it on these subjects, it has formulated recommendations which have subsequently been endorsed by the Sub-Commission and drawn to the attention of the Commission on Human Rights.

103.   In addition, it has initiated studies of special aspects of the problem of slavery and slavery-like practices, such as the reports of the Secretary-General on the sale of children,[27] and on the legal and social problems of sexual minorities,[28] presented to the Sub-Commission at its thirty-ninth session, in 1987, in accordance with Economic and Social Council resolution 1983/30.

104.   The Economic and Social Council, in resolution 1983/30 of 26 May 1983, prepared on the basis of a report on the suppression of the traffic in persons and of the prostitution of others,[29] recommended that Member States should adopt policies aimed, to the extent possible, at (a) preventing prostitution by moral education and civics training, in and out of school; (b) increasing the number of women among the State's personnel having direct contact with the populations concerned; (c) eliminating discrimination that ostracizes prostitutes and makes their reabsorption into society more difficult; (d) curbing the pornography industry and the trade in pornography and penalizing them very severely when minors are involved; (e) punishing all forms of procuring in such a way as to deter it, particularly when it exploits minors; and (f) facilitating occupational training for and the reabsorption into society of persons rescued from prostitution.

105.   The Council further invited Member States to co-operate closely with one another in the search for missing persons and in the identification of international networks of procurers and, if they are members of the International Criminal Police Organization, to co-operate with that organization, requesting it to make the suppression of the traffic in persons one of its priorities.

106.   The General Assembly, in resolution 38/107 of 16 December 1983, expressed the view that prostitution and the accompanying evil of the traffic in persons for the purpose of prostitution are incompatible with the dignity and worth of the human person and endanger the welfare of the individual, the family and the community. The Assembly urged Member States to take all appropriate humane measures, including legislation, to combat prostitution, exploitation of the prostitution of others and all forms of traffic in persons; and appealed to Member States to provide special protection to

---

[24] *Exploitation of child labour* (United Nations publication, Sales No. E.82.XIV.2).

[25] E/CN.4/Sub.2/1982/29.

[26] E/CN.4/Sub.2/AC.2/1982/13 and Add.1.

[27] E/CN.4/Sub.2/1987/28.

[28] E/CN.4/Sub.2/1987/24.

[29] E/1983/7 and Corr.1 and 2.

victims of prostitution through measures including education, social guarantees, and employment opportunities for those victims, with a view to their rehabilitation.

(e) *Study of the situation in Mauritania*

107. The Commission on Human Rights, in resolution 1982/20 of 10 March 1982, decided, pursuant to an invitation by the Government of Mauritania, to authorize the Sub-Commission on Prevention of Discrimination and Protection of Minorities to send a delegation not exceeding two persons, to be appointed by the Chairman of the Sub-Commission in consultation with the Government of Mauritania, to visit that country in order to study the situation and ascertain the country's needs with regard to the question of slavery and the slave trade. The Economic and Social Council noted and endorsed the Commission's decision at its 28th plenary meeting, on 7 May 1982 by decision 1982/129. The Sub-Commission, by decision 1982/7 of 27 August 1982, authorized its Chairman to appoint two of its members, Mr. Bossuyt and Mr. Mudawi, to visit Mauritania for this purpose. Mr. Bossuyt, (Mr. Mudawi being unavailable) visited Mauritania from 14 to 22 January 1984.

108. In his report,[30] Mr. Bossuyt expressed the conviction that he had gathered enough information and had heard a sufficient range of views to be able to assert that slavery as an institution protected by law had been genuinely abolished in Mauritania, although it could not be ruled out that in certain remote corners of the country over which the Administration had little control, certain situations of *de facto* slavery might still persist.

109. The Sub-Commission, in resolution 1984/24 of 11 March 1985, called upon Mr. Bossuyt to submit a final report on the matter at its thirty-ninth session. In the final report,[31] Mr. Bossuyt summarized the action which had been taken as a result of his activities, and indicated that "he remains convinced that the attention the international community has focused on this question, on the initiative of the Anti-Slavery Society and through the Sub-Commission, has—thanks mainly to the positive attitude of the Mauritanian Government—had a beneficial influence in the interest of all those concerned by this question".

C. Abolition of certain types of forced or compulsory labour

1. PROVISIONS OF UNITED NATIONS INSTRUMENTS

110. The Universal Declaration of Human Rights, adopted and proclaimed on 10 December 1948, does not specifically mention forced labour. Article 4 of the Declaration, as stated above, reads as follows:

---

[30] E/CN.4/Sub.2/1984/23.

[31] E/CN.4/Sub.2/1987/27.

No one shall be held in slavery or servitude; slavery and the slave trade shall be prohibited in all their forms.

However, it is clear from the records of discussions which preceded the adoption of article 4 that systems of forced, compulsory or "corrective" labour were considered by the drafters of the Declaration to be new forms of slavery or servitude which were emerging in modern society, and were therefore assumed to be included among the institutions and practices prohibited by the article.

111. The Slavery Convention signed at Geneva on 25 September 1926 and amended by the Protocol approved by General Assembly resolution 794 (VIII) of 23 October 1953, contains a preambular paragraph and one article dealing with the question of forced labour. The preambular paragraph reads:

Considering, moreover, that it is necessary to prevent forced labour from developing into conditions analogous to slavery . . .

Article 5 reads as follows:

The High Contracting Parties recognise that recourse to compulsory or forced labour may have grave consequences and undertake, each in respect of the territories placed under its sovereignty, jurisdiction, protection, suzerainty or tutelage, to take all necessary measures to prevent compulsory or forced labour from developing into conditions analogous to slavery.

It is agreed that:

(1) Subject to the transitional provisions laid down in paragraph (2) below, compulsory or forced labour may only be exacted for public purposes.

(2) In territories in which compulsory or forced labour for other than public purposes still survives, the High Contracting Parties shall endeavour progressively and as soon as possible to put an end to the practice. So long as such forced or compulsory labour exists, this labour shall invariably be of an exceptional character, shall always receive adequate remuneration, and shall not involve the removal of the labourers from their usual place of residence.

(3) In all cases, the responsibility for any recourse to compulsory or forced labour shall rest with the competent central authorities of the territory concerned.

112. Article 8, paragraph 3 of the International Covenant on Civil and Political Rights, adopted and opened for signature, ratification and accession by General Assembly resolution 2200 (XXI) of 16 December 1966, reads as follows:

3. (*a*) No one shall be required to perform forced or compulsory labour;

(*b*) Paragraph 3 (*a*) shall not be held to preclude, in countries where imprisonment with hard labour may be imposed as a punishment for a crime, the performance of hard labour in pursuance of a sentence to such punishment by a competent court;

(*c*) For the purpose of this paragraph the term "forced or compulsory labour" shall not include:

(i) Any work or service, not referred to in subparagraph (*b*), normally required of a person who is under detention in consequence of a lawful order of a court, or of a person during conditional release from such detention;

(ii) Any service of a military character and, in countries where conscientious objection is recognized, any national service required by law of conscientious objectors;

(iii) Any service exacted in cases of emergency or calamity threatening the life or well-being of the community;

(iv) Any work or service which forms part of normal civil obligations.

113. The Supplementary Convention on the Abolition of Slavery, the Slave Trade, and Institutions and Practices Similar to Slavery of 1956 refers to forced labour only in a preambular paragraph which reads:

Having regard to the Forced Labour Convention of 1930 and to subsequent action by the International Labour Organisation in regard to forced or compulsory labour . . .

114. The Convention referred to is the ILO Forced Labour Convention, 1930 (No. 29), which entered into force on 1 May 1932. This Convention provides for the suppression of forced or compulsory labour in all its forms within the shortest possible period subject to exceptions relating to compulsory military service, normal civic obligations, convict labour, work in emergencies and minor communal services. On 25 June 1957 the General Conference of ILO adopted a new Abolition of Forced Labour Convention (No. 105) to abolish "certain forms of forced or compulsory labour constituting a violation of the rights of man referred to in the Charter of the United Nations and enunciated by the Universal Declaration of Human Rights". Under article 1 of this Convention, each member of ILO which ratifies the Convention undertakes to suppress and not to make use of any form of forced or compulsory labour:

(*a*) As a means of political coercion or education or as a punishment for holding or expressing political views or views ideologically opposed to the established political, social or economic system;

(*b*) As a method of mobilising and using labour for purposes of economic development;

(*c*) As a means of labour discipline;

(*d*) As a punishment for having participated in strikes;

(*e*) As a means of racial, social, national or religious discrimination.

Under article 2 each State party undertakes to take effective measures to secure the immediate and complete abolition of forced or compulsory labour as specified in article 1.

115. The International Convention on the Suppression and Punishment of the Crime of *Apartheid*, adopted and opened for signature and ratification or accession by the General Assembly in resolution 3068 (XXVIII) of 30 November 1973, provides, in article II, that the term "the crime of *apartheid*" shall apply to the following inhuman acts committed for the purpose of establishing and maintaining domination by one racial group of persons over any other racial group of persons and systematically oppressing them:

. . . (*e*) Exploitation of the labour of the members of a racial group or groups, in particular by submitting them to forced labour; . . .

2. JOINT UNITED NATIONS/ILO *AD HOC* COMMITTEE ON FORCED LABOUR

116. At its sixth session, in 1948, the Economic and Social Council included in its agenda, at the request of the American Federation of Labor formulated in a letter dated 24 November 1947,[32] an item entitled:

---
[32] E/596.

"Survey on forced labour and measures for its abolition". The American Federation of Labor suggested, in its letter, that the Council should ask ILO to undertake a comprehensive survey on the extent of forced labour in all Member States of the United Nations and to suggest positive measures for eliminating forced labour, including a revised convention and measures for its implementation.

117. At its eighth session the Council adopted resolution 195 (VIII) of 7 March 1949, in which it requested the Secretary-General to co-operate closely with the International Labour Organisation in its work on forced labour questions, to approach all Governments and to enquire whether they would be prepared to co-operate in an impartial investigation on forced labour. The Secretary-General was also requested to inform and consult ILO regarding the progress being made on this question.

118. At its ninth session the Council adopted resolution 237 of 5 August 1949 (IX) in which it took note of the communication of ILO on the conclusions arrived at by the Governing Body of the International Labour Office at its 109th session, recommending that close contact should be established with the Secretary-General with a view to the setting up of an impartial commission of inquiry. The Council considered that the replies received from Governments up to its ninth session did not provide the conditions under which a commission of inquiry could operate effectively, and requested the Secretary-General to ask Governments which had not as yet replied, whether they would be prepared to co-operate in an inquiry.

119. In resolution 350 (XII), adopted on 19 March 1951, the Economic and Social Council, considering the replies furnished by Member States in accordance with resolutions 195 (VIII) and 237 (IX), and taking note of the communications from the International Labour Organisation which set forth the discussions on the question of forced labour at the 111th and 113th sessions of the Governing Gody, decided to establish, in co-operation with ILO, the *Ad Hoc* Committee on Forced Labour, composed of independent persons qualified by their competence and impartiality.

120. The *Ad Hoc* Committee on Forced Labour was requested, in Council resolution 350 (XII), to study the nature and extent of the problem raised by the existence in the world of systems of forced or "corrective" labour, which were employed as a means of political coercion or punishment for holding or expressing political views, and which were on such a scale as to constitute an important element in the economy of a given country, by examining the texts of laws and regulations and their application in the light of the principles set out in the ILO Forced Labour Convention, 1930 (No. 29), the principles of the Charter of the United Nations relating to respect for human rights and fundamental freedoms, and the principles of the Universal Declaration of Human Rights, and if the Committee thought fit, by taking additional evidence into consideration.

121. In its report,[33] the *Ad Hoc* Committee stated that its inquiry had revealed the existence of facts relating to systems of forced labour of so grave a nature that they seriously threatened fundamental human rights and jeopardized the freedom and status of workers in contravention of the obligations and provisions of the Charter of the United Nations. The Committee felt, therefore, that those systems of forced labour, in any of their forms, should be abolished. It suggested that, wherever necessary, international action should be taken, either by framing more conventions or by amending existing conventions.

122. On 7 December 1953, the General Assembly adopted resolution 740 (VIII) in which it affirmed the importance it attached to the abolition of all systems of forced or "corrective" labour and invited the Economic and Social Council and the International Labour Organisation, as a matter of urgency, to give early consideration to the report of the *Ad Hoc* Committee on Forced Labour. At its seventeenth session, the Economic and Social Council examined the report of the *Ad Hoc* Committee and, in resolution 524 (XVII) of 27 April 1954, condemned the systems of forced labour in question and appealed to all Governments to re-examine their laws and administrative practices in the matter. The General Assembly, in resolution 842 (IX) of 17 December 1954, endorsed the Council's condemnation and supported its appeals to Governments.

123. In 1956 the Economic and Social Council considered a second report[34] on forced labour, prepared jointly by the Secretary-General of the United Nations and the Director-General of ILO, pursuant to resolution 524 (XVII) of the Council. On this occasion, the Council in resolution 607 (XXI) of 1 May 1956, again condemned all forms of forced labour and urged that action be taken towards its elimination everywhere. The Council, in the same resolution, commended the ILO for the action it had taken and expressed an interest in further action by the ILO, which had special responsibilities in the field of forced labour. The Council requested the Secretary-General to transmit to the Director-General of the International Labour Office any information which might be received concerning forced labour. ILO was, at the same time, invited to include in its annual report to the Council an account of the action taken in this field.

3. FURTHER ACTION BY THE INTERNATIONAL LABOUR ORGANISATION

124. The question of forced labour was accordingly placed on the agenda of the thirty-ninth session of the International Labour Conference, held at Geneva in June 1956. As a result, the Abolition of Forced Labour Convention, 1957 (No. 105) was adopted by the

Conference the following year. Reference has been made to the provisions of the Convention in section 1, above.

125. The implementation of this Convention, as well as of the ILO Forced Labour Convention of 28 June 1930 (No. 29) has been followed up by the ILO Committee of Experts and the Conference Committee on the Application of Conventions and Recommendations, in accordance with the regular procedure based on examination of reports from ratifying States. In addition, the Committee of Experts prepared general surveys on the application of both Conventions in 1962, 1968 and 1979. Moreover, under the relevant provisions of the ILO Constitution, representations and complaints alleging non-observance of the provisions of these Conventions by ratifying States were examined by the Governing Body of the ILO, including two cases referred to commissions of inquiry, in 1961-1963 and 1981-1982.

D. Protection against torture and other forms of cruel, inhuman or degrading treatment or punishment

126. Over the years United Nations organs and agencies have endeavoured to ensure to everyone adequate protection against torture and other forms of cruel, inhuman or degrading treatment or punishment. They have formulated universal standards applicable to everyone, and codes applicable to those in certain occupations, and have prepared an international declaration and an international convention on the subject—all designed to make a reality of the prohibition which exists, in national and international law, of any form of treament or punishment which violates the human rights or fundamental freedoms of its victims.

1. PROVISIONS OF UNITED NATIONS INSTRUMENTS

127. Article 5 of the Universal Declaration of Human Rights provides that:

No one shall be subjected to torture or to cruel, inhuman or degrading treatment or punishment.

128. The Convention on the Prevention and Punishment of the Crime of Genocide, of 1948, defines "genocide" as meaning "any of the following acts committed with intent to destroy, in whole or in part, a national, ethnical, racial or religious group such as:

. . .

(*b*) Causing serious bodily or mental harm to members of the group;

(*c*) Deliberately inflicting on the group conditions of life calculated to bring about its physical destruction in whole or in part . . .

Similarly article II of the Universal Convention on the Suppression and Punishment of the Crime of *Apartheid,* of 1973, defines the term "the crime of *apartheid*" as applying "to the following inhuman acts committed for the purpose of establishing and maintaining domination by one racial group of persons

---

[33] *Official Records of the Economic and Social Council, Sixteenth Session, Supplement No. 13* (E/2431) and International Labour Office, *Studies and Reports (New Series), Supplement No. 36.*

[34] E/2815 and Add.1-4 and Add.4/Corr.1 and Add.5.

over any other racial group of persons and systematically oppressing them:

(a) Denial to a member of a racial group or groups of the right to life and liberty of person:

(i) By murder of members of a racial group or groups;

(ii) By the infliction upon the members of a racial group or groups of serious bodily or mental harm, by the infringement of their freedom or dignity, or by subjecting them to torture or to cruel, inhuman or degrading treatment or punishment . . .

(b) Deliberate imposition on a racial group or groups of living conditions calculated to cause its or their physical destruction in whole or in part . . .

129.   Article 5 of the Supplementary Convention on the Abolition of Slavery, the Slave Trade, and Institutions and Practices Similar to Slavery, of 1956, provides that:

In a country where the abolition or abandonment of slavery, or of the institutions or practices mentioned in article 1 of this Convention, is not yet complete, the act of mutilating, branding or otherwise marking a slave or a person of servile status in order to indicate his status, or as a punishment, or for any other reason, or of being accessory thereto, shall be a criminal offence under the laws of the States Parties to this Convention and persons convicted thereof shall be liable to punishment.

130.   Article 7 of the International Covenant on Civil and Political Rights, of 1966, reads as follows:

No one shall be subjected to torture or to cruel, inhuman or degrading treatment or punishment. In particular, no one shall be subjected without his free consent to medical or scientific experimentation.

Article 4, paragraph 2, of that Covenant provides against any derogation from article 7.

Article 10 of the same Covenant reads as follows:

1. All persons deprived of their liberty shall be treated with humanity and with respect for the inherent dignity of the human person.

2. (a) Accused persons shall, save in exceptional circumstances, be segregated from convicted persons and shall be subject to separate treatment appropriate to their status as unconvicted persons;

(b) Accused juvenile persons shall be separated from adults and brought as speedily as possible for adjudication.

3. The penitentiary system shall comprise treatment of prisoners the essential aim of which shall be their reformation and social rehabilitation. Juvenile offenders shall be segregated from adults and be accorded treatment appropriate to their age and legal status.

131.   Paragraph 5 of the Declaration on the Protection of Women and Children in Emergency and Armed Conflict, of 1974, reads as follows:

All forms of repression and cruel and inhuman treatment of women and children, including, imprisonment, torture, shooting, mass arrests, collective punishment, destruction of dwellings and forcible eviction, committed by belligerents in the course of military operations or in occupied territories shall be considered criminal.

2. MEASURES TAKEN BY UNITED NATIONS BODIES

(a) *Abolition of corporal punishment in Trust Territories*

132.   In 1949 the Trusteeship Council in the report covering its fourth and fifth sessions,[35] recommended that corporal punishment should be abolished immediately in the Cameroons and Togoland under British administration and that corporal punishment should be

formally abolished in New Guinea. The General Assembly gave its full support to this recommendation and itself recommended, in resolution 323 (IV) of 15 November 1949, "the adoption of strong and effective measures to abolish immediately the corporal punishment of whipping in Ruanda-Urundi". In the following year the General Assembly, in resolution 440 (V) of 2 December 1950, recommended that measures be taken immediately to bring about the complete abolition of corporal punishment in all Trust Territories where it still existed, and requested the Administering Authorities to report on the matter.

133.   Two years later the Assembly reviewed the reports which it had received. It noted that measures had been taken to reduce the number of offences in respect of which corporal punishment was applied, noted the arguments presented by the Administering Authorities concerned to explain why that penalty had not completely disappeared, and expressed the opinion that the considerations presented should not prevent the complete abolition of corporal punishment in the Trust Territories where it still existed. In resolution 562 (VI) of 18 January 1952, the Assembly repeated its previous recommendations and urged Administering Authorities concerned to apply them without delay.

(b) *Standard Minimum Rules for the Treatment of Prisoners*

134.   In 1955 the First United Nations Congress on the Prevention of Crime and the Treatment of Offenders[36] adopted the Standard Minimum Rules for the Treatment of Prisoners[37] worked out by an Advisory Committee of Experts established in accordance with the plan prepared by the Secretary-General and approved by General Assembly resolution 415 (V) of 1 December 1950. In resolution 663 CI (XXIV) of 31 July 1957 the Economic and Social Council approved those Rules and recommended them to States Members.

135.   The purpose of the Standard Minimum Rules for the Treatment of Prisoners is not to describe in detail a model system of penal institutions but, on the basis of the general consensus of contemporary thought and the essential elements of the most adequate systems of today, to set out what is generally accepted as being good principle and practice in the treatment of prisoners and management of institutions. One of the Standard Minimum Rules (Rule 31) is to the effect that corporal punishment, punishment by placing in a dark cell, and all cruel, inhuman or degrading punishment shall be completely prohibited as punishments for disciplinary offences.

---

[35] A/933.

[36] General Assembly resolution 415 (V) of 1 December 1950 and annex on the transfer to the United Nations of the functions of the International Penal and Penitentiary Commission.

[37] *First United Nations Congress on the Prevention of Crime and the Treatment of Offenders: report by the Secretariat* (United Nations publication, Sales No. E.56.IV.4), annex I.A.

136. The General Assembly, in resolution 2858 (XXVI) of 20 December 1971, invited the attention of Member States to the Standard Minimum Rules and recommended that they should be effectively implemented in the administration of penal and correctional institutions and that favourable consideration should be given to their incorporation in national legislation. The Assembly took note with satisfaction of the establishment by the Commission for Special Development of a Working Group on Standard Minimum Rules for the Treatment of Prisoners to advise on methods of strengthening the implementation of the Rules and of improving the reporting procedures thereon.

137. The General Assembly returned to the subject of the Standard Minimum Rules in 1973 when it examined the *Study of Equality in the Administration of Justice* prepared by Mr. Mohammed A. Abu Rannat,[38] Special Rapporteur of the Sub-Commission on Prevention of Discrimination and Protection of Minorities, and the report of the Working Group of Experts established by the Commission for Social Development.[39] In resolution 3144 B (XXVIII) of 14 December 1973, the Assembly recommended that Member States "should make all possible efforts to implement the Standard Minimum Rules for the Treatment of Prisoners in the administration of penal and correctional institutions and take the Rules into account in the framing of national legislation".

138. In resolution 2076 (LXII) of 13 May 1977, the Economic and Social Council decided that a new section E (Rule 95) should be added to the Standard Minimum Rules for the Treatment of Prisoners. The new rule provides that, "without prejudice to the provisions of article 9 of the International Covenant on Civil and Political Rights, persons arrested or imprisoned without charge shall be accorded the same protection" as that accorded under part I of the Rules (Rules of general application), part II, section C (Prisoners under arrest or awaiting trial), and also under the relevant provisions of part II, section A (Prisoners under sentence), "provided that no measures shall be taken implying that re-education or rehabilitation is in any way appropriate to persons not convicted of any criminal offence".

(c) *Declaration on the Protection of All Persons from Being Subjected to Torture and Other Cruel, Inhuman or Degrading Treatment or Punishment*

139. At its thirtieth session, in 1975, the General Assembly considered an analytical summary, prepared by the Secretary-General, of the information received from Member States in accordance with Assembly resolution 3218 (XXIX) of 6 November 1974,[40] and a report by the Secretary-General reflecting the results of the Fifth United Nations Congress on the Prevention of Crime and the Treatment of Offenders and containing the proposal of the Congress for a draft Declaration on the Protection of All Persons from Being Subjected to Torture and Other Cruel, Inhuman or Degrading Treatment or Punishment.[41] By resolution 3452 (XXX) of 9 December 1975, the Assembly adopted the Declaration.

140. The Declaration contains twelve articles. In article 1, "torture" is defined, for the purpose of the Declaration, as meaning "any act by which severe pain or suffering, whether physical or mental, is intentionally inflicted by or at the instigation of a public official on a person for such purposes as obtaining from him or a third person information or confession, punishing him for an act he has committed or is suspected of having committed, or intimidating him or other persons". Torture, the article states further, "does not include pain or suffering arising only from, inherent in or incidental to, lawful sanctions to the extent consistent with the Standard Minimum Rules for the Treatment of Prisoners". It "constitutes an aggravated and deliberate form of cruel, inhuman or degrading treatment or punishment".

141. Article 2 characterizes any act of torture or other cruel, inhuman or degrading treatment or punishment as an offence to human dignity and states that it should be condemned "as a denial of the purposes of the Charter of the United Nations and as a violation of the human rights and fundamental freedoms proclaimed in the Universal Declaration of Human Rights".

142. Article 3 provides that no State may permit or tolerate torture or other cruel, inhuman or degrading treatment or punishment even in exceptional circumstances such as a state of war or a threat of war, internal political instability or any other public emergency. Article 4 calls upon each State to "take effective measures to prevent torture and other cruel, inhuman or degrading treatment or punishment from being practised within its jurisdiction". Article 5 proposes that the prohibition against these practices should be taken fully into account in the training of law enforcement personnel and others involved in the custody or treatment of persons deprived of their liberty. Article 6 calls for systematic review of interrogation methods and practices.

143. Article 7 calls for all acts of torture, as defined in article 1, to be made offences under the criminal law of each State. Article 8 gives the victim of torture or other cruel, inhuman or degrading treatment or punishment "the right to complain to, and to have his case impartially examined by, the competent authorities of the State concerned". Article 9 provides that an impartial investigation should be made by the competent authorities of the State concerned when there is reasonable ground to believe that an act of torture has been committed, even if there has been no formal complaint.

144. Article 10 provides for criminal proceedings to be instituted against an alleged offender or offenders if an investigation establishes that an act of torture appears to have been committed, and for criminal, disciplinary

---

[38] United Nations publication, Sales No. E.71.XIV.3.

[39] See E/AC.57/8, para. 63.

[40] A/10158 and Corr.1 and Add.1.

[41] A/10260.

or other appropriate proceedings to be taken against offenders if the allegations prove to be well-founded. Article 11 calls for redress and compensation to be paid to victims when it has been proved that torture has occurred. Article 12 provides that statements "made as a result of torture or other cruel, inhuman or degrading treatment or punishment may not be invoked as evidence against the person concerned or against any other person in any proceedings".

145.   In resolution 32/64 of 8 December 1977, the General Assembly called upon all Member States "to reinforce their support of the Declaration on the Protection of All Persons from Being Subjected to Torture and Other Cruel, Inhuman or Degrading Treatment or Punishment by making unilateral declarations against torture and other cruel, inhuman or degrading treatment or punishment", along the lines of a text annexed to the resolution, and depositing it with the Secretary-General. Member States were urged to give maximum publicity to such unilateral declarations, and the Secretary-General was requested to inform the General Assembly, in annual reports, of such declarations. The Secretary-General subsequently submitted to the General Assembly reports reproducing the unilateral declarations received.[42]

(d)   Code of Conduct for Law Enforcement Officials

146.   In resolution 34/169 of 17 December 1979, the General Assembly adopted a Code of Conduct for Law Enforcement Officials and transmitted it to Governments with the recommendation that favourable consideration should be given to its use within the framework of national legislation or practice as a body of principles for observance by law enforcement officials.

147.   Article 5 of the Code reads as follows:

No law enforcement official may inflict, instigate or tolerate any act of torture or other cruel, inhuman or degrading treatment or punishment, nor may any law enforcement official invoke superior orders or exceptional circumstances such as a state of war or a threat of war, a threat to national security, internal political instability or any other public emergency as a justification of torture or other cruel, inhuman or degrading treatment or punishment.

148.   In its commentary on article 5, the Assembly points out that "this prohibition derives from the Declaration on the Protection of All Persons from Being Subjected to Torture and Other Cruel, Inhuman or Degrading Treatment or Punishment, according to which '[such an act is] an offence to human dignity and shall be condemned as a denial of the purposes of the Charter of the United Nations and as a violation of the human rights and fundamental freedoms proclaimed in the Universal Declaration of Human Rights [and other international human rights instruments]' ". The Assembly adds that "The term 'cruel, inhuman or degrading treatment or punishment' has not been defined by the General Assembly, but should be interpreted so as to extend the widest possible protection against abuses, whether physical or mental".

---

[42] A/33/197, A/34/145 and Add.1-3, A/37/263.

149.   The Economic and Social Council, in resolution 1986/10 of 21 May 1986, section IX, invited Member States (a) to take into account and respect the Code of Conduct for Law Enforcement Officials within the framework of their national legislation and practice and to bring it to the attention of all persons concerned, particularly law enforcement officials and correctional personnel; (b) to pay particular attention, in informing the Secretary-General of the extent of the implementation and the progress made with regard to the application of the Code, to the use of force and firearms by law enforcement officials; and (c) to provide the Secretary-General with copies of abstracts of laws, regulations and administrative measures concerning the application of the Code, as well as information on possible difficulties in its application.

150.   The Council requested the Secretary-General to prepare every five years, beginning in 1987, an independent report on progress made with respect to the implementation of the Code, and to submit the report to the Committee on Crime Prevention and Control. It further requested him to disseminate the Code and to ensure its use in all relevant United Nations programmes, including technical co-operation activities.

151.   The Committee on Crime Prevention and Control was requested to consider measures for the more effective implementation of the Code.

(e)   Principles of Medical Ethics

152.   In resolution 31/85 of 13 December 1976, the General Assembly invited the World Health Organization to prepare a draft code on medical ethics relevant to the protection of persons subjected to any form of detention or imprisonment against torture and other cruel, inhuman or degrading treatment or punishment.

153.   The Executive Board of the World Health Organization, at its sixty-third session, in January 1979, decided to endorse the principles set forth in a report entitled "Development of codes of medical ethics" containing, in an annex, a draft body of principles prepared by the Council for International Organizations of Medical Sciences and entitled "Principles of medical ethics relevant to the role of health personnel in the protection of persons against torture and other cruel, inhuman or degrading treatment or punishment".

154.   The Economic and Social Council, in resolution 1981/27 of 6 May 1981, recommended that the General Assembly should take measures to finalize the draft Code of Medical Ethics. The Assembly did so at its thirty-seventh session.

155.   In resolution 37/194 of 18 December 1982, the General Assembly took note with appreciation of the "Guidelines for Medical Doctors concerning Torture and other Cruel, Inhuman or Degrading Treatment or Punishment in relation to Detention and Imprisonment", as adopted by the twenty-ninth World Medical Assembly, held in Tokyo in October 1975; and noted

that in accordance with that Declaration "measures should be taken by States and by professional associations and other bodies, as appropriate, against any attempt to subject health personnel or members of their families to threats or reprisals resulting from a refusal by such personnel to condone the use of torture and other forms of cruel, inhuman or degrading treatment".

156. It then went on to set further standards in this field by adopting the "Principles of Medical Ethics relevant to the role of health personnel, particularly physicians, in the protection of prisoners and detainees against torture and other cruel, inhuman or degrading treatment or punishment", as set out in the annex to resolution 37/194. It called upon all Governments to give the Principles of Medical Ethics the widest possible distribution, in particular among medical and paramedical associations, and institutions of detention or imprisonment; and invited all relevant intergovernmental organizations, in particular the World Health Organization, and non-governmental organizations concerned, to bring the Principles to the attention of the widest possible group of individuals, especially those active in the medical and paramedical field.

157. Principle 1 of the Principles of Medical Ethics provides that "health personnel, particularly physicians, charged with the medical care of prisoners and detainees, have a duty to provide them with protection of their physical and mental health and treatment of disease of the same quality and standard as is afforded to those who are not imprisoned or detained".

158. Principle 2 states that "it is a gross contravention of medical ethics, as well as an offence under applicable international instruments, for health personnel, particularly physicians, to engage, actively or passively, in acts which constitute participation in, complicity in, incitement to or attempts to commit torture or other cruel, inhuman or degrading treatment or punishment". A cross-reference is made in the principle, by a footnote, to articles 1 and 7 of the Declaration on the Protection of All Persons from Being Subjected to Torture and Other Cruel, Inhuman or Degrading Treatment or Punishment, where torture is defined as and declared to be a criminal offence.

159. Principles 3, 4 and 5 state that it is a contravention of medical ethics for health personnel, particularly physicians:

To be involved in any professional relationship with prisoners or detainees the purpose of which is not solely to evaluate, protect or improve their physical and mental health;

To apply their knowledge and skills in order to assist in the interrogation of prisoners and detainees in a manner that may adversely affect the physical or mental health or condition of such prisoners or detainees and which is not in accordance with the relevant international instruments;

To certify, or to participate in the certification of, the fitness of prisoners or detainees for any form of treatment or punishment that may adversely affect their physical or mental health and which is not in accordance with the relevant international instruments, or to participate in any way in the infliction of any such treatment or punishment which is not in accordance with the relevant international instruments; or

To participate in any procedure for restraining a prisoner or detainee unless such a procedure is determined in accordance with purely medical criteria as being necessary for the protection of the physical or mental health or the safety of the prisoner or detainee himself, of his fellow prisoners or detainees, or of his guardians, and it presents no hazard to his physical or mental health.

160. Principle 6 states that "there may be no derogation from the foregoing principles on any ground whatsoever, including public emergency".

161. The "relevant international instruments" referred to in the Principles include the Universal Declaration of Human Rights, the International Covenants on Human Rights, the Declaration on the Protection of All Persons from Being Subjected to Torture and Other Cruel, Inhuman or Degrading Treatment or Punishment, and the Standard Minimum Rules for the Treatment of Prisoners.

(f) *Special Rapporteur to examine questions relevant to torture*

162. Seriously concerned about the alarming number of reported cases of torture and other cruel, inhuman or degrading treatment or punishment taking place in various parts of the world, the Commission on Human Rights in resolution 1985/33 of 13 March 1985 decided to appoint for one year a special rapporteur to examine questions relevant to torture. It authorized the Special Rapporteur, in carrying out his mandate, to seek and receive credible and reliable information from Governments, as well as specialized agencies, intergovernmental organizations and non-governmental organizations; and invited him to bear in mind the need to be able to respond effectively to credible and reliable information reaching him and to carry out his work with discretion.

163. The Special Rapporteur thus appointed, Mr. Peter H. Kooijmans, submitted his first report (E/CN.4/1986/15) to the Commission at its forty-second session. The report contained a number of preliminary conclusions and recommendations. The Commission took note of it in resolution 1986/50 of 13 March 1986, and extended his mandate for another year.

164. The Special Rapporteur's second report (E/CN.4/1987/13) indicated that he had received an alarming number of allegations concerning the practice of torture and that in some cases, when he had brought those allegations to the attention of the Governments concerned, the reliability of his sources has been questioned. He explained that he could not disclose the identity of those sources because that might expose them to retaliatory measures; moreover, since torture invariably took place in secluded places, only the Government concerned was in a position either to refute unjustified allegations or, if the information contained an element of truth, to take steps to prevent its recurrence.

165. The report included a chapter on the role of medical personnel in torture, indicating that in many

cases the active or passive assistance of such personnel was an essential element; and a chapter on the question of responsibility for torture, pointing out that in many cases procedures for detecting or punishing it were either missing or deficient. Among the suggestions and recommendations put forward were: the imposition by Governments and medical associations of strict measures against all persons belonging to the medical profession who have in that capacity had a function in the practice of torture; the establishment at the national level of independent authorities empowered to receive and deal with complaints made by individuals; the strict limitation of *incommunicado* detention under national law; and the establishment of international and regional systems, based on periodic visits by committees of experts to places of detention or imprisonment, to monitor the occurrence of torture and other cruel, inhuman or degrading treatment or punishment.

166. The Commission, in resolution 1987/29 of 10 March 1987, noted the Special Rapporteur's conclusions and recommendations, extended his mandate for another year, and requested him to submit a comprehensive report on his activities regarding the practice of torture to its forty-fourth session.

(g) United Nations Voluntary Fund for the Victims of Torture

167. In resolution 33/174 of 20 December 1978 the General Assembly established the United Nations Trust Fund for Chile to receive contributions and distribute, through established channels of assistance, humanitarian, legal and financial aid to persons whose human rights had been violated by detention or imprisonment in Chile, to those forced to leave the country and to relatives of persons in the above-mentioned categories; and requested that annual reports should be submitted to the Assembly and, as appropriate, to the Commission on Human Rights.

168. Two years later the General Assembly, in resolution 35/190 of 15 December 1980, requested the Commission on Human Rights to study the possibility of extending the mandate of the United Nations Trust Fund for Chile to receive voluntary contributions and further to study criteria for their distribution to persons not covered by the mandate of other existing trust funds, whose human rights had been grossly and flagrantly violated, to those who had been forced to leave their countries as a result of gross and flagrant violations of their human rights and to relatives of persons in those categories.

169. The Commission on Human Rights, in resolution 35 (XXXVII) of 11 March 1981, invited the Economic and Social Council to recommend for adoption by the General Assembly a draft resolution which would redesignate the United Nations Trust Fund for Chile as a United Nations voluntary fund for victims of torture.

170. On the recommendation of the Commission and the Council, the General Assembly adopted resolution 36/151 of 16 December 1981, by which it extended the mandate of the United Nations Trust Fund for Chile in order to make it capable of receiving voluntary contributions for distribution, through established channels of assistance, as humanitarian, legal and financial aid to individuals whose human rights had been severely violated as a result of torture and to relatives of such victims; redesignated the Fund as the United Nations Voluntary Fund for Victims of Torture; adopted arrangements for the management of the Fund; and appealed to all Governments to respond favourably to requests for contributions.

171. The Voluntary Fund is administered by the Secretary-General with the advice of a Board of Trustees composed of five members with wide experience in the field of human rights, acting in their personal capacity, who are appointed by the Secretary-General with due regard to equitable geographical distribution. The Secretary-General reports annually to the General Assembly and to the Commission on Human Rights on the administration of the Fund.

172. Since it began operations, in 1983, the Fund has received contributions from 19 governments (the Board expressed the view that it is important for the Fund to receive contributions from as many States as possible), as well as from non-governmental organizations and individuals. Pursuant to recommendations of its Board of Trustees, 96 grants, totalling more than $2 million have been authorized for 57 projects in 27 countries. After taking note of the 1987 report,[43] of the Secretary-General the Assembly in resolution 42/122 of 7 December 1987 expressed its gratitude and appreciation to contributors to the Fund and called upon all Governments, organizations and individuals in a position to do so to make initial as well as further contributions.

(h) Organization and procedures of the Committee against Torture

173. On 26 November 1987, representatives of the States parties to the Convention against Torture and Other Cruel, Inhuman or Degrading Treatment or Punishment held their first meeting at Geneva and elected ten members of the Committee against Torture. The names of five members, to serve for a term of only two years (the normal term of office is four years) were then chosen by lot by the Chairman of the meeting.

174. Under article 19 of the Convention, the States parties submit to the Committee reports on the measures they have taken to give effect to their undertakings under the Convention, the first report within one year after the entry into force of the Convention for the State concerned, and thereafter supplementary reports every four years. Each report is to be considered by the Committee, which may make general comments on them and forward them to the State party concerned. The State party may then respond with its observations.

---

[43] A/42/701.

The comments of the Committee and the observations of the State are then included in the Committee's annual report to the States parties and to the General Assembly.

175. If the Committee receives reliable information which appears to it to contain well-founded indications that torture is being systematically practised in the territory of a State party, it first—under article 20—invites that State to co-operate in the examination of the information. It may then designate one or more of its members to make a confidential inquiry, seeking the co-operation of the State concerned. Such an inquiry may, in agreement with that State, include a visit to its territory. After examining the findings of the inquiry, the Committee transmits them to the State concerned, together with any comments or suggestions which it considers appropriate. All proceedings under article 20 are confidential, but the Committee may decide to include a summary account of them in its annual report.

176. Under article 21, a State party to the Convention may declare that it recognizes the competence of the Committee to receive and consider communications to the effect that a State party claims that another State party is not fulfilling its obligations under the Convention. The provisions of article 21 enter into force only after five States parties have made such declarations. If such a complaint is then brought to the Committee by one State party and directed against another, the Committee first seeks an adjustment of the matter to the satisfaction of both parties. If that proves not to be possible, it then makes its good offices available with a view to a friendly solution of the matter. For this purpose it may set up an *Ad Hoc* Conciliation Commission.

177. Under article 22, a State party to the Convention may declare that it recognizes the competence of the Committee to receive and consider communications from—or on behalf of—individuals subject to its jurisdiction who claim to be victims of a violation by a State party of the provisions of the Convention. Article 22 enters into force only after five States parties have made such declarations. If such a communication is then received by the Committee and is found to be admissible under its rules, the Committee may consider it in the light of information provided by, or on behalf of, the individual and the State party concerned. The Committee's meetings are closed when it considers such communications. At the conclusion of its examination of the facts, the Committee forwards its views to the complainant and to the State party concerned.

E. Protection against arbitrary arrest and detention

178. The competent United Nations bodies have always been concerned with measures to safeguard human liberty, and have examined the rules and practices of various States and legal systems to find new ways of promoting significantly the dignity and security of the human person.

179. The Commission on Human Rights has been particularly concerned with the question of freedom from arbitrary arrest and detention, and has made a comprehensive study of this subject. It has also made a detailed study of a closely related matter, the right of arrested persons to communicate with those whom it is necessary for them to consult in order to ensure their defence or to protect their essential interests.

180. For some time the Commission, having completed these studies, did not take definitive action on either of them. However, recently the studies assumed new importance in connection with the consideration by a number of United Nations bodies, including the General Assembly, of the question of torture and other cruel, inhuman or degrading treatment or punishment. The General Assembly has called for the formulation of a body of principles for the protection of all persons under any form of detention or imprisonment, and that task is nearing completion in the Sixth Committee of the Assembly.

1. PROVISIONS OF UNITED NATIONS INSTRUMENTS

181. Article 9 of the International Declaration of Human Rights provides that:

No one shall be subjected to arbitrary arrest, detention or exile.

182. Article 9 of the International Covenant on Civil and Political Rights reads as follows:

1. Everyone has the right to liberty and security of person. No one shall be subjected to arbitrary arrest or detention. No one shall be deprived of his liberty except on such grounds and in accordance with such procedure as are established by law.

2. Anyone who is arrested shall be informed, at the time of arrest, of the reasons for his arrest and shall be promptly informed of any charges against him.

3. Anyone arrested or detained on a criminal charge shall be brought promptly before a judge or other officer authorized by law to exercise judicial power and shall be entitled to trial within a reasonable time or to release. It shall not be the general rule that persons awaiting trial shall be detained in custody, but release may be subject to guarantees to appear for trial, at any other stage of the judicial proceedings, and, should occasion arise, for execution of the judgement.

4. Anyone who is deprived of his liberty by arrest or detention shall be entitled to take proceedings before a court, in order that that court may decide without delay on the lawfulness of his detention and order his release if the detention is not lawful.

5. Anyone who has been the victim of unlawful arrest or detention shall have an enforceable right to compensation.

183. Article II of the International Convention on the Suppression and Punishment of the Crime of *Apartheid*, adopted and opened for signature and ratification by the General Assembly in resolution 3068 (XXVIII) of 30 November 1973, reads in part as follows:

For the purpose of the present Convention, the term "the crime of *apartheid*", which shall include similar policies and practices of racial segregation and discrimination as practised in southern Africa, shall apply to the following inhuman acts committed for the purpose of establishing and maintaining domination by one racial group of persons over any other racial group of persons and systematically oppressing them:

(*a*) Denial to a member or members of a racial group or groups of the right to life and liberty of person . . .

(iii) By arbitrary arrest and illegal imprisonment of the members of a racial group or groups . . .

2. MEASURES TAKEN BY UNITED NATIONS BODIES

(a) *Study of the right of everyone to be free from arbitrary arrest, detention and exile, and related studies*

184.   At its twelfth session, in 1956, the Commission on Human Rights, in resolution II, recognized that studies of specific rights or groups of rights were "necessary for the purpose of ascertaining the existing conditions, the results obtained and the difficulties encountered in the work of States Members for the wider observance of, and respect for, human rights and fundamental freedoms". It decided to undertake such studies and in them "to stress . . . general developments, progress achieved and measures taken to safeguard human liberty, with such recommendations of an objective and general character as may be necessary". As the first subject for study the Commission decided to select the right of everyone to be free from arbitrary arrest, detention and exile. In resolution 624 B II (XXII) of 1 August 1956 the Economic and Social Council approved the subject.

185.   The Commission appointed a committee composed of four of its States Members to carry out the study. The Committee decided that it would describe the rules and practices under different legal systems in respect of the subject of the study, to the end that nations might share experience and work, individually or jointly, towards the achievement of the standards set forth in the Universal Declaration of Human Rights. The Committee also agreed to pay particular attention to such rules and practices as were found to contribute significantly to the protection and enhancement of the dignity, liberty and security of the human person.

186.   The study of the right of everyone to be free from arbitrary arrest, detention and exile was originally submitted to the Commission on Human Rights in 1961.[44] At its seventeenth session, in 1961, the Commission, in resolution 2 (XVII) of 14 March 1961, requested the four-member Committee on the Right of Everyone to be Free from Arbitrary Arrest, Detention and Exile to undertake a second study, dealing with "the right of arrested persons to communicate with those whom it is necessary for them to consult in order to ensure their defence or to protect their essential interests".

187.   At its eighteenth session, in 1962, the Commission received and examined the revised study of the right of everyone to be free from arbitrary arrest, detention and exile, including draft principles concerning freedom from arbitrary arrest and detention,[45] prepared by the Committee in accordance with the Commission's request in resolution 2 (XVII). It decided, in resolution 2 (XVIII) of 12 April 1962, to transmit the draft principles to Member States and to the specialized agencies, and requested them to submit comments as soon as possible.

188.   At its nineteenth session, in 1963, the Commission received a preliminary report on the study of the right of arrested persons to communicate with those whom it is necessary for them to consult in order to ensure their defence or to protect their essential interests. At its twenty-fifth session, in 1969, the Commission received the final report on the study.[46]

189.   Having considered both studies at its twenty-fifth session, in 1969, the Commission, in resolution 23 (XXV) of 20 March 1969, noted that the new study suggested modifications in some of the draft principles contained in the earlier study of the right of everyone to be free from arbitrary arrest, detention and exile. Desiring to obtain the views of Governments on the new study and the suggested modifications of the draft principles, the Commission requested the Secretary-General to transmit these texts to the Governments of Member States and to specialized agencies for comment.

190.   Further consideration of the two studies was postponed by the Commission for a number of years. However the General Assembly, in resolution 3453 (XXX) of 9 December 1975, requested the Commission at its thirty-second session to study the question of torture and any necessary steps for the formulation of a body of principles for the protection of all persons under any form of detention or imprisonment on the basis of the Study of the right of everyone to be free from arbitrary arrest, detention and exile[47] and the draft principles on freedom from arbitrary arrest and detention contained therein.

(b) *Draft body of principles for the protection of all persons under any form of detention or imprisonment*

191.   The Commission, in resolution 10 (XXXII) of 5 March 1976, requested the Sub-Commission to draw up, on the basis of the Study and other relevant documentation, a body of principles for the protection of all persons under any form of detention or imprisonment. In compliance with this request, the Sub-Commission prepared a draft body of principles, set out in the report of its thirty-first session,[48] which were transmitted to Governments for comment. The principles and comments were forwarded to the General Assembly for consideration by the Economic and Social Council in 1979.

192.   At its thirty-fifth session, the General Assembly established an open-ended Working Group of the Third Committee to elaborate a final version of the draft body of principles. At its thirty-sixth session, the Assembly referred the question to its Sixth Committee and established an open-ended Working Group of that Committee to complete the task. At its thirty-seventh to

---

[44] E/CN.4/813 and Corr.1.

[45] E/CN.4/826 and Corr.1 and 2. The Committee did not deem it necessary or desirable to include in the draft principles provisions regulating exile, which it found had virtually disappeared.

[46] E/CN.4/996.

[47] United Nations publication, Sales No. E.65.XIV.2.

[48] E/CN.4/1296, para. 109.

forty-second sessions, the General Assembly continued its consideration of the item, renewing each year the mandate of the open-ended Working Group of the Sixth Committee. At its forty-second session the Assembly, by decision 42/426, took note of the Working Group and of the progress it had achieved[49] and decided that a Working Group of the Sixth Committee would be established at its forty-third session in order to complete the elaboration of the draft Body of Principles.

193. At its thirty-ninth session the Sub-Commission on Prevention of Discrimination and Protection of Minorities, in decision 1987/108, noted with concern that the Sixth Committee's Working Group had in its most recent revision of the text of the draft Body of Principles (A/C.6/41/L.19) apparently limited the scope of the principles and had made amendments as a result of which the text might fall short of existing norms such as those set out in the International Covenant on Civil and Political Rights. The Sub-Commission requested the Secretary-General to convey its concerns to the Working Group. At the same time it decided to recommend to its parent bodies the adoption of a declaration to the effect that arbitrary or abusive use of force by law-enforcement personnel in any country should be punished as a criminal offence.

(c) *Annual review of developments regarding the human rights of persons subjected to any form of detention or imprisonment*

194. In resolution 7 (XXVII) of 20 August 1974, the Sub-Commission decided to review annually developments regarding the human rights of persons subjected to any form of detention or imprisonment, taking into account any reliably attested information from Governments, the specialized agencies, the regional intergovernmental organizations and the non-governmental organizations in consultative status, provided that such non-governmental organizations acted in good faith and that their information was not politically motivated, contrary to the principles of the Charter of the United Nations. The General Assembly noted the Sub-Commission's decision with appreciation in resolution 3218 (XXIX) of 6 November 1974.

195. The Sub-Commission has since conducted an annual review of developments concerning the human rights of persons subjected to any form of detention or imprisonment, and established sessional working groups to assist in the review at its thirty-fourth to thirty-ninth sessions. The Commission on Human Rights, in resolution 1987/33 of 10 March 1987, requested the Sub-Commission, in carrying out the review, to include in its consideration the work of the Human Rights Committee and the Committee on the Elimination of Racial Discrimination, the developments elsewhere in the human rights programme, and the activities within the United Nations programme on crime prevention and

---

[49] A/C.6/42/L.12.

control bearing on the subject. The Secretary-General was requested to make succinct information on these matters available to the Sub-Commission.

(d) *Enforced or involuntary disappearances*

196. The General Assembly, in resolution 33/173 of 20 December 1978, expressed its deep concern about reports from various parts of the world relating to enforced or involuntary disappearances of persons as a result of excesses on the part of law enforcement or security authorities or similar organizations, often while such persons were subject to detention or imprisonment, as well as unlawful actions or widespread violence. It also expressed concern about reports of difficulties in obtaining reliable information from competent authorities as to the circumstances of such persons, including reports of the persistent refusal of such authorities or organizations to acknowledge that they held such persons in their custody or otherwise to account for them.

197. Deeply moved by the anguish and sorrow which such circumstances caused to the relatives of disappeared persons, especially to spouses, children and parents, the General Assembly called upon Governments:

(*a*) In the event of reports of enforced or involuntary disappearances, to devote appropriate resources to searching for such persons and to undertake speedy and impartial investigations;

(*b*) To ensure that law enforcement and security authorities or organizations are fully accountable, especially in law, in the discharge of their duties, such accountability to include legal responsibilities for unjustifiable excesses which might lead to enforced or involuntary disappearances and to other violations of human rights;

(*c*) To ensure that the human rights of all persons, including those subjected to any form of detention and imprisonment, are fully respected;

(*d*) To co-operate with other Governments, relevant United Nations organs, specialized agencies, intergovernmental organizations and humanitarian bodies in a common effort to search for, locate or account for such persons in the event of reports of enforced or involuntary disappearances.

198. The Assembly requested the Commission on Human Rights to consider the question of enforced or involuntary disappearances with a view to making appropriate recommendations, and urged the Secretary-General to use his good offices in cases of enforced or involuntary disappearances of persons, drawing upon the relevant experience of the International Committee of the Red Cross and other humanitarian organizations.

199. The Commission on Human Rights decided, in resolution 20 (XXXVI) of 29 February 1980, to establish for a period of one year a working group consisting of five of its members, serving as experts in their individual capacities, to examine questions relating to the enforced or involuntary disappearances of persons. The Working Group was authorized to receive information from Governments, intergovernmental organizations, humanitarian organizations, and other reliable sources, and requested to report to the Commission.

200. The establishment and mandate of the Working Group on Enforced or Involuntary Disappearances was approved by the Economic and Social Council, subse-

quently the Group's mandate was extended annually until 1986 and since then for two year periods. Up to 31 December 1987 the Group had held twenty-three sessions, convening normally twice each year at Geneva and once elsewhere in order to hear relatives and witnesses who, otherwise, would not be able to appear before it (1981-1984, New York, 1984 Costa Rica, 1985 Buenos Aires, 1987-1988, New York). At the invitation of the respective Governments it has also undertaken missions to the following countries: Mexico and Cyprus in 1982, Bolivia in 1984, Peru in 1985 and 1986, and Guatemala in 1987.

201. In implementing its mandate, the Working Group receives and examines reports on disappearances submitted by relatives of missing persons or organizations acting on their behalf. After determining whether those reports comply with certain formal criteria, the Working Group transmits individual cases to the Governments concerned, requesting them to carry out investigations and to inform the Group about their results. The Group thus endeavours to establish a channel of communications between the families and Governments, with a view to ensuring that sufficiently documented and clearly identified individual cases of disappearances are investigated and the whereabouts of the missing person clarified. So far, the Working Group has transmitted some 15,000 individual cases to some 40 Governments. The strictly non-accusatory humanitarian approach the Group has adopted in discharging its mandate allows it to deal on a large scale with individual cases of alleged human rights violations of a particularly serious nature. In order to avoid any delays in its endeavours to save human lives, the Group has also initiated a so-called urgent action procedure under which its Chairman is authorized to process cases of recent disappearances in between sessions.

202. Assisting families in determining the fate and whereabouts of their missing relatives who, having disappeared, are placed outside the protective precinct of the law, is the main objective of the Group's activity. Nevertheless, the Group has also examined the phenomenon on a more abstract level by studying, *inter alia,* the extent to which a variety of civil and political, as well as social, economic and cultural rights are being violated by the practice of enforced disappearances of persons. It has also studied preventive and remedial legal or institutional mechanisms on the national level.

(e) *Protection of the human rights of certain categories of detainees or prisoners*

203. On several occasions the General Assembly has adopted special measures for the protection of certain categories of detainees or prisoners, including (i) persons detained or imprisoned as a result of their struggle against violations of human rights; (ii) persons arrested or detained on account of trade union activities; and (iii) persons detained in mental institutions on account of their political beliefs or on other non-medical grounds.

204. The Assembly has recommended that all Governments guarantee to persons within their jurisdiction the full enjoyment of the right of *amparo* (enforcement of constitutional rights), habeas corpus or such other legal remedies to the same effect as may be applicable in their legal systems.

(f) *Persons detained or imprisoned as a result of their struggle against violations of human rights*

205. At its thirty-second session, in 1977, the General Assembly considered the question of the protection of the human rights of certain categories of prisoners. In resolution 32/121 of 16 December 1977, the Assembly recognized "the importance of full respect for the human rights and fundamental freedoms of all persons detained or imprisoned as a result of their struggle against colonialism, aggression and foreign occupation and for self-determination, independence, the elimination of *apartheid* and all forms of racial discrimination and racism, and the termination of all these violations of human rights". Expressing its awareness "of the fact that in many parts of the world numerous persons are detained in respect of offences which they committed, or are suspected of having committed, by reason of their political opinions or convictions", noting that "these persons are often exposed to special dangers as regards the protection of their human rights and fundamental freedoms", and realizing therefore "that special attention should be given to the full respect of the human rights and fundamental freedoms of these persons", the Assembly requested Member States:

(*a*) To take effective measures to safeguard the human rights and fundamental freedoms of the above-mentioned persons;

(*b*) To ensure, in particular, that such persons are not subjected to torture or other cruel, inhuman or degrading treatment or punishment;

(*c*) Also to ensure that such persons, in the determination of any criminal charge against them, receive a fair hearing by a competent, independent and impartial tribunal established by law.

The Assembly further called upon "Member States to examine periodically the possibility of releasing such persons as an act of clemency or by way of conditional release or otherwise".

(g) *Persons arrested or detained on account of trade union activities*

206. At its thirty-third session, in 1978, the General Assembly considered the question of the protection of the human rights of arrested or detained trade union activists. In resolution 33/169 of 20 December 1978, the Assembly reaffirmed the importance of protecting the right to freedom of association as an essential prerequisite for the conduct of any trade union activities, and recommended that special attention should be paid to violations of the right to freedom of association such as the arrest, detention or exile of persons who had engaged in trade union activities consistent with the prin-

ciples of freedom of association. The Assembly requested Member States:

(*a*) To release any persons who, within their jurisdiction and contrary to the provisions of the applicable international instruments, might be under arrest or detention on account of trade union activities;

(*b*) To ensure that, pending the release of such persons, their fundamental rights were fully protected, including the right not to be subjected to torture or other cruel, inhuman or degrading treatment or punishment and the right to receive a fair hearing by a competent, independent and impartial tribunal in the determination of any criminal charge against them; and

(*c*) To take effective measures to safeguard and protect the human rights and fundamental freedoms of trade union leaders who were detained or imprisoned as a result of their struggle against colonialism, aggression and foreign occupation and for self-determination, the elimination of *apartheid* and all forms of racial discrimination and racism, and for the termination of all these violations of human rights.

The General Assembly also recognized the important work done by the International Labour Organisation to promote trade union rights and to take appropriate action in concrete cases of persons arrested, detained or exiled by reason of their trade union activities; and lent its support to the efforts of ILO in that regard.

(h) *Protection of persons detained on grounds of mental ill-health or suffering from mental disorder*

207. The Commission on Human Rights, in resolution 10 A (XXXIII) of 11 March 1977, expressed concern at the consequences that advances in the fields of neuro-surgery, biochemistry and psychiatry might hold for the protection of the human personality and its physical and intellectual integrity, and requested the Sub-Commission on Prevention of Discrimination and Protection of Minorities "to study, with a view to formulating guidelines, if possible, the question of the protection of those detained on the grounds of mental ill-health against treatment that may adversely affect the human personality and its physical and intellectual integrity". The General Assembly endorsed the undertaking of such a study in resolution 33/53 of 14 December 1978.

208. The Sub-Commission on Prevention of Discrimination and Protection of Minorities, by resolution 6 (XXXII) of 5 September 1979, requested the Secretary-General to prepare a report analysing information concerning the subject with a view to the formulation of guidelines regarding: (*a*) the medical measures that might properly be employed in the treatment of persons detained on grounds of mental ill-health, and (*b*) procedures for determining whether adequate grounds existed for detaining such persons and applying such medical measures.

209. After examining the Secretary-General's report on medical measures that may properly be employed in the treatment of persons detained on the grounds of mental ill-health,[50] and taking note of a draft body of principles for the protection of persons suffering from

mental disorder submitted to it by the International Association of Penal Law and the International Commission of Jurists,[51] the Sub-Commission, at its thirty-third session, in 1980, decided to entrust one of its members, Mrs. Erica-Irene A. Daes, with the task of studying the available documentation and submitting to it (*a*) guidelines relating to procedures for determining whether adequate grounds existed for detaining persons on the grounds of mental ill-health, and (*b*) principles for the protection, in general, of persons suffering from mental disorder.

210. At its thirty-fifth session, in 1982, the Sub-Commission received and noted with deepest appreciation and gratitude the report prepared by the Special Rapporteur.[52] The report was considered by a sessional working group established by the Sub-Commission, consisting of five of its members, which prepared a report[53] on the subject. The Sub-Commission, by resolution 1982/34 of 10 September 1982, recommended that the Economic and Social Council should request the Special Rapporteur to supplement her final report, taking into account the views expressed in the Sub-Commission and the Commission on Human Rights, and including any new documentation received from Governments or specialized agencies, and that is should also request the Sub-Commission to submit the revised final report to the Commission on Human rights at its fortieth session. The Sub-Commission further recommended that it be authorized to establish a sessional Working Group to examine the revised report.

211. The definitive report[54] examined in detail the following issues relevant to the topic of the study:

(*a*) Procedures and legal guarantees ensuring respect for the inherent dignity and protection of fundamental freedoms and civil, political, socio-economic, cultural, medical and legal rights of persons diagnosed as "mentally ill" or as "suffering from mental disorder";

(*b*) Questions relating to arbitrary deprivation of the freedoms and human rights of an individual on grounds of his mental condition;

(*c*) Reasons for voluntary and involuntary hospitalization of persons diagnosed as "mentally ill" or "suffering from mental disorder";

(*d*) Right to treatment of the mentally ill;

(*e*) Types of psychiatric institutions;

(*f*) Recommendations for the adoption of legislative and administrative measures or of new or additional procedures and approaches concerning, in particular, the protection of persons detained on grounds of mental ill-health or suffering from mental disorder; and

(*g*) Recommendations for reform of existing mental health laws where inadequate or obsolete, and for medical, socio-economic and administrative measures concerning the improvement and modernization of mental health services and mental institutions.

The report also contained a proposed "Draft body of principles, guidelines and guarantees for the protection of the mentally ill or persons suffering from mental disorder," prepared by the Special Rapporteur.

---

50 E/CN.4/Sub.2/446.

51 E/CN.4/Sub.2/NGO.81.

52 E/CN.4/Sub.2/1982/16.

53 E/CN.4/Sub.2/1982/17.

54 *Principles, Guidelines and Guarantees for the Protection of Persons Detained on Grounds of Mental Ill-health or Suffering from Mental Disorder,* Report prepared by Erica-Irene A. Daes (United Nations publication, Sales No. E.85.XIV.9).

212. The sessional Working Group on the Question of Persons Detained on the Grounds of Mental Ill-health or Suffering from Mental Disorder, composed of five Members of the Sub-Commission acting in their individual capacities, was established by the Sub-Commission on 15 August 1983 and held its first session from 24 August to 1 September 1983, at Geneva. Subsequent sessions were held at Geneva in 1984, 1985 and 1987. At its 1987 session, the Working Group was composed of Mrs. Erica-Irene A. Daes, Chairman/Rapporteur, Mr. A. S. Khasawaneh, Mr. R. V. Baquero, Mr. K. B. S. Simpson and Mr. V.N. Sofinsky.

213. The Working Group undertook two readings of the Draft Body of Principles, Guidelines and Guarantees for the Protection of the Mentally Ill or Persons Suffering from Mental Disorder which had been formulated by the Special Rapporteur.[55] The report of its 1987 session[56] indicated that although considerable progress had been made, the Working Group had not completed its task.

214. The Sub-Commission, in resolution 1987/22 of 3 September 1987, called upon the Working Group to expedite its work, a view reflected also in resolutions of the Commission on Human Rights and the Economic and Social Council. The General Assembly, in resolution 42/98 of 7 December 1987, expressed its deep concern at the repeated evidence of the misuse of psychiatry to detain persons on non-medical grounds, as reflected in the Special Rapporteur's report, and reaffirmed its conviction that detention of persons in mental institutions on account of their political views or on other non-medical grounds is a violation of their human rights. The Assembly urged the Commission on Human Rights and the Sub-Commission to complete the draft body of guidelines, principles and guarantees in time to present it to the Assembly at its forty-fourth session.

(i) *Implications for human rights of states of siege or emergency*

215. The Sub-Commission on Prevention of Discrimination and Protection of Minorities expressed concern, in resolution 10 (XXX) of 31 August 1977, at the manner in which certain countries applied the provisions relating to situations known as states of siege or emergency, and its belief that a comprehensive study of the implications for human rights of recent developments in this sphere would be conducive to the achievement of the aims pursued by the United Nations with respect to human rights.

216. A preliminary oral presentation of the implications for human rights of states of siege or emergency was given at the thirty-first session of the Sub-Commission, in 1978, by Mrs. Nicole Questiaux, one of its members. The Sub-Commission was later authorized by the Economic and Social Council to appoint Mrs. Questiaux as Special Rapporteur to continue the study of the question.

217. After submitting a progress report[57] to the Sub-Commission at its thirty-fourth session, in 1981, Mrs. Questiaux presented her final report[58] at its thirty-fifth session, in 1982. In the report, the Special Rapporteur attempted, first, to recall the basic rules of international law and domestic legislation which set out limitations of State power relating to emergency situations with a view to protecting human rights. She then analysed the *de facto* impact of states of emergency upon the rule of law and respect for human rights. She observed that, too often, evidence showed that the model of guarantees provided by law was deviated from. She further noted that states of emergency tended to become clandestine, permanent or even institutionalized. Increased powers were being granted to the Executive and to military or special courts applying retroactive laws in a summary fashion. The effects were particularly damaging for persons detained on political grounds. She therefore strongly recommended a series of measures to strengthen international monitoring of respect for human rights in such situations.

218. After examining the study and expressing its warmest appreciation to the Special Rapporteur, the Sub-Commission transmitted the study to the Commission on Human Rights by resolution 1982/32 of 10 September 1982. It drew the Commission's attention to the Special Rapporteur's conclusions and recommendations, which it whole-heartedly endorsed; and requested the Commission to arrange for the study to be published and widely disseminated and to be transmitted to the specialized agencies of the United Nations, the Human Rights Committee and the Committee on the Elimination of Racial Discrimination. The Sub-Commission also asked to be authorized to appoint one of its members to undertake a closer study of the advisability of strengthening or extending the inalienability of the rights enumerated in article 4, paragraph 2, of the International Covenant on Civil and Political Rights.

219. The Commission on Human Rights also endorsed the Special Rapporteur's conclusions and shared the Sub-Commission's appreciation of her study. In resolution 1983/18 of 22 February 1983 it requested the Sub-Commission to give the study further consideration and to propose measures which would ensure respect throughout the world for human rights and fundamental freedoms in situations where states of siege or emergency exist, especially of the rights referred to in article 4, paragraph 2, of the International Covenant on Civil and Political Rights which prohibits derogation from certain rights even in time of public emergency.

220. The Sub-Commission decided by resolution 1983/30 that it would aim at submitting an annual report to the Commission containing reliably attested in-

---

[55] E/CN.4/Sub.2/1983/17 and Add.1, and E/CN.4/Sub.2/1987/WG.3/WP.1.

[56] E/CN.4/Sub.2/1987/32.

[57] E/CN.4/Sub.2/490.

[58] E/CN.4/Sub.2/1982/15.

formation on compliance with the rules, internal and international, guaranteeing the legality of the ĩntroduction of a state of emergency and at making reference, in this connection, to the principles defined in the study (proclamation, notification, exceptional threat, proportionality, non discrimination, inalienability of fundamental rights).

221. At the Sub-Commission's request, one of its members, Mr. Leandro Despouy, prepared an explanatory paper on the ways and means of preparing such a report.[59] Later, having been appointed as the Sub-Commission's Special Rapporteur on the subject by Economic and Social Council resolution 1985/37, he prepared the first annual report and a list of States which, since 1 January 1985, had proclaimed, extended, or terminated a state of emergency.[60] The list was based on information and comments submitted to the Special Rapporteur by Governments, competent organs of the United Nations, specialized agencies, regional intergovernmental bodies. It dealt with states of emergency proclaimed, extended or terminated in 27 countries, their duration, the territory involved, the grounds invoked, the measures taken and the rights concerned.

222. Among the initial findings of the Special Rapporteur, the report indicated the rights most often mentioned by Governments as having formed the subject of derogations are those guaranteed by articles 9 (liberty and security of person), 12 (liberty of movement), 17 (prohibition of arbitrary interference with privacy), 19 (freedom of expression and opinion) and 21 (right of peaceful assembly) of the International Covenant on Civil and Political Rights.

223. The Sub-Commission considered the report at its thirty-ninth session, and by resolution 1987/25 expressed its appreciation to the Special Rapporteur. It invited him to continue the work, to update the first report for the Commission on Human Rights at its forty-fourth session,[61] to submit the next annual report and updated list at the fortieth session of the Sub-Commission, in 1988, and to examine it as a matter of high priority under the agenda item "The administration of justice and the human rights of detainees, (b) Question of human rights and states of emergency".

224. By resolution 42/103, the General Assembly stressed the importance of avoiding the erosion of human rights by derogation, and underlined the necessity of strict observance of the agreed conditions and procedures for derogation under article 4 of the International Covenant on Civil and Political Rights, bearing in mind the need for States parties to provide the fullest possible information during states of emergency, so that the justification and appropriateness of measures taken in these circumstances can be assessed.

(j) *The right of* amparo, *habeas corpus, or other legal remedies to the same effect*

225. The General Assembly, noting that the year 1979 marked the three hundredth anniversary of the Act which in 1679 gave statutory force to the remedy of habeas corpus, expressed its conviction, in resolution 34/178 of 17 December 1979, that the application within the legal system of States of *amparo,* habeas corpus or other legal remedies to the same effect was of fundamental importance for: (a) protecting persons against arbitrary arrest and unlawful detention; (b) effecting the release of persons who were detained by reason of their political opinions or convictions, including in pursuance of trade union activities; and (c) clarifying the whereabouts and fate of missing and disappeared persons. The Assembly added that "the use of those remedies may also forestall opportunities for persons exercising power over detainees to engage in torture or other cruel, inhuman or degrading treatment or punishment".

226. Mindful of article 9, paragraph 4, of the International Covenant on Civil and Political Rights, which stipulated that anyone who was deprived of his liberty by arrest or detention should be entitled to take proceedings before a court, in order that the court might decide without delay on the lawfulness of his detention and order his release if the detention was not lawful, the General Assembly called upon all Governments to guarantee to persons within their jurisdiction the full enjoyment of the right of *amparo,* habeas corpus or such other legal remedies to the same effect as might be applicable in their legal system.

(k) *Administrative detention without charge or trial*

227. The Commission on Human Rights, in resolution 1985/16 of 11 March 1985, requested the Sub-Commission on Prevention of Discrimination and Protection of Minorities to analyse available information concerning the practice of administrative detention without charge or trial, and to make recommendations regarding its use. The Sub-Commission requested one of its Members, Mr. Louis Joinet, to prepare an explanatory paper suggesting procedures by which the Sub-Commission might carry out these responsibilities.

228. On the basis of Mr. Joinet's paper,[62] the Sub-Commission, in resolution 1987/24 of 3 September 1987, requested him to draft a questionnaire and send it to all Governments, specialized agencies, regional intergovernmental organizations, and non-governmental organizations in consultative status concerned with a view to obtaining information and views on the subject; and to present the results to the Sub-Commission at its fortieth session.

---

[59] E/CN.4/Sub.2/1985/19.

[60] E/CN.4/Sub.2/1987/19.

[61] E/CN.4/Sub.2/1987/19/Rev.1 and Add.1 and 2.

[62] E/CN.4/Sub.2/1987/16.

(l) Detention of United Nations staff members

229. In resolution 41/205 of 11 December 1986, the General Assembly recalled that, under Article 105 of the Charter of the United Nations, officials of the Organization shall enjoy in the territory of each of its Member States such privileges and immunities as are necessary for the independent exercise of their functions in connection with the Organization, which are indispensable for the proper discharge of their duties; and deplored the growing number of cases where the functioning, safety and well-being of officials had been adversely affected, including cases of detention in Member States and abduction by armed groups and individuals. It also deplored the increasing number of cases in which the lives and well-being of officials had been placed in jeopardy during the exercise of their official functions.

230. The Assembly called upon Member States to respect the privileges and immunities of all United Nations officials and to refrain from any acts that would impede such officials in the performance of their functions; and in particular called upon Member States holding United Nations officials under arrest or detention, or otherwise impeding them in the proper discharge of their duties, to review these cases and coordinate efforts with the Secretary-General to resolve each case with due speed.

231. The Sub-Commission on Prevention of Discrimination and Protection of Minorities expressed its deep concern, in resolution 1987/21 of 3 September 1987, that some 50 staff members were still detained, imprisoned, reported missing or held in a country against their will. Some, it pointed out, had even died in detention. The Sub-Commission appealed to Member States to respect the rights of staff members detained, imprisoned or held in a country against their will, and requested the Secretary-General to redouble and strengthen his efforts to ensure that the human rights and privileges and immunities of United Nations staff members and their families are fully respected. The Sub-Commission further requested the Secretary-General to submit to it a detailed report on the situation of international civil servants and their families detained, imprisoned, missing or held in a country against their will, in order to enable it to consider these cases in the light of the international instruments relating to human rights.

F. Human rights in the administration of justice

232. For a number of years United Nations organs have dealt with various aspects of human rights in the administration of justice. Having incorporated the principle of equality in the administration of justice in the Universal Declaration of Human Rights and many other international instruments, they studied and formulated norms to be applied with a view to eliminating all forms of discrimination in this field, developed strategies for the practical implementation of those norms, and in recent years focused on the issue of the independence and impartiality of the judiciary.

1. PROVISIONS OF UNITED NATIONS INSTRUMENTS

233. Articles 3, 5, 9, 10 and 11 of the Universal Declaration of Human Rights read as follows:

Article 3

Everyone has the right to life, liberty and security of person.

Article 5

No one shall be subjected to torture or to cruel, inhuman or degrading treatment or punishment.

Article 9

No one shall be subjected to arbitrary arrest, detention or exile.

Article 10

Everyone is entitled in full equality to a fair and public hearing by an independent and impartial tribunal, in the determination of his rights and obligations and of any criminal charge against him.

Article 11

1. Everyone charged with a penal offence has the right to be presumed innocent until proved guilty according to law in a public trial at which he has had all the guarantees necessary for his defence.

2. No one shall be held guilty of any penal offence on account of any act or omission which did not constitute a penal offence, under national or international law, at the time when it was committed. Nor shall a heavier penalty be imposed than the one that was applicable at the time the penal offence was committed.

234. Articles 6, 14 and 15 of the International Covenant on Civil and Political Rights read as follows:

Article 6

1. Every human being has the inherent right to life. This right shall be protected by law. No one shall be arbitrarily deprived of his life.

2. In countries which have not abolished the death penalty, sentence of death may be imposed only for the most serious crimes in accordance with the law in force at the time of the commission of the crime and not contrary to the provisions of the present Covenant and to the Convention on the Prevention and Punishment of the Crime of Genocide. This penalty can only be carried out pursuant to a final judgement rendered by a competent court.

3. When deprivation of life constitutes the crime of genocide, it is understood that nothing in this article shall authorize any State Party to the present Covenant to derogate in any way from any obligation assumed under the provisions of the Convention on the Prevention and Punishment of the Crime of Genocide.

4. Anyone sentenced to death shall have the right to seek pardon or commutation of the sentence. Amnesty, pardon or commutation of the sentence of death may be granted in all cases.

5. Sentence of death shall not be imposed for crimes committed by persons below eighteen years of age and shall not be carried out on pregnant women.

6. Nothing in this article shall be invoked to delay or to prevent the abolition of capital punishment by any State Party to the present Covenant.

Article 14

1. All persons shall be equal before the courts and tribunals. In the determination of any criminal charge against him, or of his rights and obligations in a suit law, everyone shall be entitled to a fair and public

hearing by a competent, independent and impartial tribunal established by law. The Press and the public may be excluded from all or part of a trial for reasons of morals, public order (*ordre public*) or national security in a democratic society, or when the interest of the private lives of the parties so requires, or to the extent strictly necessary in the opinion of the court in special circumstances where publicity would prejudice the interests of justice; but any judgement rendered in a criminal case or in a suit at law shall be made public except where the interest of juvenile persons otherwise requires or the proceedings concern matrimonial disputes or the guardianship of children.

2. Everyone charged with a criminal offence shall have the right to be presumed innocent until proved guilty according to law.

3. In the determination of any criminal charge against him, everyone shall be entitled to the following minimum guarantees, in full equality:

(*a*) To be informed promptly and in detail in a language which he understands of the nature and cause of the charge against him;

(*b*) To have adequate time and facilities for the preparation of his defence and to communicate with counsel of his own choosing;

(*c*) To be tried without undue delay;

(*d*) To be tried in his presence, and to defend himself in person or through legal assistance of his own choosing; to be informed, if he does not have legal assistance, of this right; and to have legal assistance assigned to him, in any case where the interests of justice so require, and without payment by him in any such case if he does not have sufficient means to pay for it;

(*e*) To examine, or have examined, the witnesses against him and to obtain the attendance and examination of witnesses on his behalf under the same conditions as witnesses against him;

(*f*) To have the free assistance of an interpreter if he cannot understand or speak the language used in court;

(*g*) Not to be compelled to testify against himself or to confess guilt.

4. In the case of juvenile persons, the procedure shall be such as will take account of their age and the desirability of promoting their rehabilitation.

5. Everyone convicted of a crime shall have the right to his conviction and sentence being reviewed by a higher tribunal according to law.

6. When a person has by a final decision been convicted of a criminal offence and when subsequently his conviction has been reversed or he has been pardoned on the ground that a new or newly discovered fact shows conclusively that there has been a miscarriage of justice, the person who has suffered punishment as a result of such conviction shall be compensated according to law, unless it is proved that the non-disclosure of the unknown fact in time is wholly or partly attributable to him.

7. No one shall be liable to be tried or punished again for an offence for which he has already been finally convicted or acquitted in accordance with the law and penal procedure of each country.

Article 15

1. No one shall be held guilty of any criminal offence on account of any act or omission which did not constitute a criminal offence, under national or international law, at the time when it was committed. Nor shall a heavier penalty be imposed than the one that was applicable at the time when the criminal offence was committed. If, subsequent to the commission of the offence, provision is made by law for the imposition of the lighter penalty, the offender shall benefit thereby.

2. Nothing in this article shall prejudice the trial and punishment of any person for any act or omission which, at the time when it was committed, was criminal according to the general principles of law recognized by the community of nations.

235. Article 7 of the Declaration on the Elimination of All Forms of Racial Discrimination reads as follows:

1. Everyone has the right to equality before the law and to equal justice under the law. Everyone, without distinction as to race, colour or ethnic origin, has the right to security of person and protection by the State against violence or bodily harm, whether inflicted by government officials or by any individual, group or institution.

2. Everyone shall have the right to an effective remedy and protection against any discrimination he may suffer on the ground of race, colour or ethnic origin with respect to his fundamental rights and freedoms through independent national tribunals competent to deal with such matters.

236. **Article 5 of the International Convention on the Elimination of All Forms of Racial Discrimination reads as follows:**

In compliance with the fundamental obligations laid down in article 2 of this Convention, States Parties undertake to prohibit and to eliminate racial discrimination in all its forms and to guarantee the right of everyone, without distinction as to race, colour, or national or ethnic origin, to equality before the law, notably in the enjoyment of the following rights:

(*a*) The right to equal treatment before the tribunals and all other organs administering justice.

237. **Article 16 of the Convention relating to the Status of Refugees entitled "Access to courts", reads as follows:**

1. A refugee shall have free access to the courts of law on the territory of all Contracting States.

2. A refugee shall enjoy in the Contracting State in which he has his habitual residence the same treatment as a national in matters pertaining to access to the courts, including legal assistance and exemption from *cautio judicatum solvi*.

3. A refugee shall be accorded in the matters referred to in paragraph 2 in countries other than that in which he has his habitual residence the treatment granted to a national of the country of his habitual residence.

238. **The corresponding article 16 of the Convention relating to the Status of Stateless Persons provides that:**

1. A stateless person shall have free access to the courts of law on the territory of all Contracting States.

2. A stateless person shall enjoy in the Contracting State in which he has his habitual residence the same treatment as a national in matters pertaining to access to the courts, including legal assistance and exemption from *cautio judicatum solvi*.

3. A stateless person shall be accorded in the matters referred to in paragraph 2 in countries other than that in which he has his habitual residence the treatment granted to a national of the country of his habitual residence.

239. **Article 15 of the Convention on the Elimination of All Forms of Discrimination against Women reads as follows:**

1. States Parties shall accord to women equality with men before the law.

2. States Parties shall accord to women, in civil matters, a legal capacity identical to that of men and the same opportunities to exercise that capacity. In particular, they shall give women equal rights to conclude contracts and to administer property and shall treat them equally at all stages of procedure in courts and tribunals.

3. States Parties agree that all contracts and all other private instruments of any kind with a legal effect which is directed at restricting the legal capacity of women shall be deemed null and void.

4. States Parties shall accord to men and women the same rights with regard to the law relating to the movement of persons and the freedom to choose their residence and domicile.

2. MEASURES TAKEN BY UNITED NATIONS BODIES

(a) Study of equality in the administration of justice

240. At its fifteenth session, in 1963, the Sub-Commission on Prevention of Discrimination and Protection of Minorities decided, in resolution 1 (XV), to undertake a study of equality in the administration of justice, in accordance with article 10 of the Universal Declaration of Human Rights, and appointed one of its members, Mr. Mohammed A. Abu Rannat, as its Special Rapporteur for the study. On the recommendation of the Commission on Human Rights the Economic and Social Council, in resolution 958 (XXXVI) of 12 July 1963, approved the decisions of the Sub-Commission.

241. The Special Rapporteur submitted to later sessions of the Sub-Commission a series of progress reports and a draft report. His final report[63] was examined by the Sub-Commission at its twenty-second session, in 1969, and was transmitted to the Commission on Human Rights by Sub-Commission resolution 3 (XXII) of 9 September 1969. At its twenty-third session, in 1970, the Sub-Commission considered, revised and adopted a series of draft principles on equality in the administration of justice contained in paragraph 596 of the Special Rapporteur's report.[64] The Sub-Commission transmitted the revised principles to the Commission on Human Rights for examination with regard to the advisability of preparing a convention or a declaration, or both, on equality in the administration of justice, or several instruments dealing with various aspects of the problem; and for decision as to subsequent action.

242. The Commission on Human Rights was unable to examine the draft principles until 1973, when it reviewed them in the light of comments received from Governments and forwarded them to the General Assembly. The Assembly, in resolution 3144 (XXVIII) of 14 December 1973, pointed out that those comments had shown a wide diversity of approaches by Governments to the draft principles. The Assembly expressed its deep appreciation to the Special Rapporteur for his study, and called upon Member States "to give due consideration, in formulating legislation and taking other measures affecting equality in the administration of justice, to the above-mentioned draft principles, which may be regarded as setting forth valuable norms, with a view to arriving at the elaboration of an appropriate international declaration or instrument".

(b) Study of discriminatory treatment in the administration of criminal justice

243. At its thirty-second session, in 1979, the Sub-Commission on Prevention of Discrimination and Protection of Minorities considered a preliminary study, prepared by the Secretariat, on the independence and impartiality of the judiciary, jurors and assessors, and the independence of lawyers,[65] and decided to appoint a Special Rapporteur to study the subject further.

244. Mr. Justice Abu Sayeed Chowdhury, a member of the Sub-Commission, was appointed Special Rapporteur. He presented a preliminary study on discriminatory treatment of members of racial, ethnic, religious or linguistic groups at the various levels in the administration of criminal justice, to the Sub-Commission at its thirty-fourth session, in 1981.

245. The Special Rapporteur's final report, entitled "Study on discriminatory treatment of members of racial, ethnic, religious or linguistic groups at the various levels in the administration of criminal justice, such as police, military, administrative and judicial investigations, arrest, detention, trial and execution of sentences, including the ideologies or beliefs which contribute or lead to racism in the administration of criminal justice",[66] was reviewed by the Sub-Commission, the Commission and the Economic and Social Council. The Council, in decision 1984/141, decided that it should be printed and given the widest possible distribution.

(c) Study of amnesty laws

246. At its thirty-sixth session, in 1983, the Sub-Commission on Prevention of Discrimination and Protection of Minorities became aware, in the course of its work relating to the human rights of detainees, of the importance that the promulgation of amnesty laws could have for the safeguard and promotion of human rights. Considering that the preparation of a technical study showing the principal elements of amnesty laws could prove very useful for those considering the elaboration of such laws, the Sub-Commission requested one of its members, Mr. Louis Joinet, to prepare a study of a technical nature on amnesty laws and their role in the safeguard and promotion of human rights.

247. The Special Rapporteur submitted a preliminary report[67] to the Sub-Commission at its thirty-seventh session and a final report at its thirty-eighth session.[68] In the final report he traced the historical evolution of amnesty laws, analysed the legal foundations and purposes of amnesty, and set out the various options available in granting amnesty and the effects of amnesty when granted.

248. On recommendation of the Sub-Commission and the Commission on Human Rights the Economic and Social Council, in decision 1986/38, expressed its appreciation to the Special Rapporteur for the study on amnesty laws and their role in the safeguard and

---

63 E/CN.4/Sub.2/296.

64 For the text of the principles as revised, see United Nations document ST/HR/3, pp. 10-16.

65 E/CN.4/Sub.2/428.

66 E/CN.4/Sub.2/L.766; E/CN.4/Sub.2/1982/7.

67 E/CN.4/Sub.2/1984/15.

68 E/CN.4/Sub.2/1985/16.

promotion of human rights, and decided that the study should be disseminated as widely as possible.

(d) Study on the independence and impartiality of the judiciary, jurors and assessors and the independence of lawyers

249. After considering the preliminary report by the Secretariat on the independence and impartiality of the judiciary, jurors and assessors and the independence of lawyers[69] and taking the action described in (b) above, the Sub-Commission on Prevention of Discrimination and Protection of Minorities recommended to the Economic and Social Council, in resolution 5 (XXXII) of 5 September 1979, that it be authorized to entrust Mr. L. M. Singhvi, one of its members, with the preparation of a report on the subject "to the end that there shall be no discrimination in the administration of justice and that human rights and fundamental freedoms may be maintained and safeguarded".

250. The Council gave the requested authorization in decision 1980/124 of 2 May 1980. The Special Rapporteur submitted a preliminary report[70] to the Sub-Commission in 1980, and progress reports[71] in 1981 and 1982. His final report[72] was placed before the Sub-Commission at its thirty-eighth session, in 1985.

251. In the report, the Special Rapporteur suggested that a Universal Declaration on the Independence of Justice—or, preferably, an international convention on the subject—should be adopted by the United Nations, and presented his own draft of such a Declaration. He pointed out that "With the adoption of a declaration or a convention, the main dimensions of the principles of impartiality and independence would be more directly and effectively reflected in the work of different bodies of the United Nations. A convention would obviously have greater efficacy".

252. The Special Rapporteur presented his study to the Sub-Commission at its thirty-eighth session, in 1985, mentioning the world-wide interest that the question of the independence and impartiality of the judiciary had evoked and the principles that had already been formulated by various intergovernmental and non-governmental conferences. The Sub-Commission however was not able to examine the study in detail until its thirty-ninth session, in 1987.

253. In resolution 1987/23 of 3 September 1987 the Sub-Commission, conscious of the fundamental and far-reaching importance of the principles for safeguarding the independence of justice in all its aspects and bearing in mind the Basic Principles on the Independence of the Judiciary which had been adopted unanimously by the Seventh United Nations Congress on the Prevention of Crime and the Treatment of Of-fenders, expressed its appreciation to the Special Rapporteur for the enduring and valuable contribution he had made to the legal doctrine relating to the independence of justice, which is one of the primary prerequisites for the promotion and protection of human rights. It decided to consider the draft Declaration which the Special Rapporteur had proposed, and called upon the Secretary-General to obtain comments and suggestions on that text from the United Nations Centre for Social Development and Humanitarian Affairs and from Member States. The Special Rapporteur was requested to submit his report on the draft Declaration, in the light of the comments and suggestions received, by 30 May 1988.

(e) Basic principles on the independence of the judiciary

254. The Sixth United Nations Congress on the Prevention of Crime and the Treatment of Offenders, held at Caracas from 25 August to 5 September 1980, called upon the Committee on Crime Prevention and Control to include among its priorities the elaboration of guidelines relating to the independence of judges.[73] The Seventh United Nations Congress on the same subject, convened at Milan from 26 August to 6 September 1985, examined the proposed guidelines drafted by the Committee and, after extensive discussions, adopted the Basic Principles on the Independence of the Judiciary and recommended them for national, regional and interregional action and implementation, taking into account the political, economic, social and cultural circumstances and traditions of each country.[74] The Congress also invited Member States to bring the Basic Principles to the attention of judges, lawyers, members of the executive and the legislature and the public in general, and urged all competent organizations to become actively involved in their implementation. It called upon the Committee on Crime Prevention and Control to consider, as a matter of priority, the effective implementation of the Basic Principles, and requested the Secretary-General to prepare a report on their implementation.

255. The General Assembly, in resolution 40/160 of 13 December 1985, acknowledged the important work accomplished by the Seventh Congress, in particular in relation to the formulation and application of United Nations standards and norms in the administration of justice. The Economic and Social Council, in resolution 1986/10 (V) of 21 May 1986, invited Member States to inform the Secretary-General every five years, beginning in 1988, of the progress achieved in the implementation of the Basic Principles, including their dissemination, their incorporation into national legislation, the

---

[69] E/CN.4/Sub.2/428.

[70] E/CN.4/Sub.2/L.731.

[71] E/CN.4/Sub.2/481 and Add.1 and E/CN.4/Sub.2/1982/23.

[72] E/CN.4/Sub.2/1985/18 and Add.1-6.

[73] Sixth United Nations Congress on the Prevention of Crime and the Treatment of Offenders, Caracas, 25 August-5 September 1980 (United Nations publication, Sales No. E.81.IV.4), chap. I, sect. B, resolution 16.

[74] Seventh United Nations Congress on the Prevention of Crime and the Treatment of Offenders, Milan, 26 August-6 September 1985 (United Nations publication, Sales No. E.86.IV.1), chap. I, sect. D 2.

problems faced in their implementation at the national level and assistance that might be needed from the international community; and requested him to report thereon to the Eighth United Nations Congress on the Prevention of Crime and the Treatment of Offenders.

256. The Commission on Human Rights, in resolution 1987/33 of 10 March 1987, reiterated its call upon Member States to spare no effort in providing for effective legislative and other mechanisms and procedures and adequate resources to ensure more effective implementation of existing international standards relating to human rights in the administration of justice; emphasized the importance of education and public information programmes in the field of human rights for law students, the legal profession and all those responsible for the administration of justice; and recognized the important role that non-governmental organizations, including professional associations of lawyers and judges, can play in promoting human rights in the administration of justice.

257. The Commission requested the Sub-Commission on Prevention of Discrimination and Protection of Minorities to give urgent consideration to the issue of the independence and impartiality of the judiciary and other questions relating to human rights in the administration of justice. It invited the Secretary-General to establish a focal point within the Centre for Human Rights to monitor the aspects relating to human rights in the administration of justice within the various elements of the United Nations human rights programme, the programme on crime prevention and control, and the work of the specialized agencies, regional organizations and non-governmental organizations in consultative status and to provide, as appropriate, advice on co-ordination and other relevant issues in the field.

(f) Standard Minimum Rules for the Administration of Juvenile Justice

258. The Seventh United Nations Congress on the Prevention of Crime and the Treatment of Offenders[75] also prepared, and recommended to the General Assembly for adoption, the United Nations Standard Minimum Rules for the Administration of Juvenile Justice ("The Beijing Rules"). The Rules had been developed by the Committee on Crime Prevention and Control, the Secretary-General, the United Nations Asia and Far East Institute for the Prevention of Crime and the Treatment of Offenders, and other United Nations institutes; and finalized at an Interregional Preparatory Meeting held at Beijing from 14 to 18 May 1984.

259. The Rules relate to such matters as the minimum age of criminal responsibility, the objectives of juvenile justice, the features of effective, fair and humane juvenile justice administration, and the human rights principles to be applied. They also cover matters relating to investigation and prosecution of crimes committed by juveniles, including the question of detention pending trial; and matters relating to the adjudication and disposition of cases against juvenile offenders. In general they recommend the least possible use of institutionalization but set out some essential protections covering juvenile offenders placed in institutions.

260. The General Assembly, in resolution 40/33 of 29 November 1985, adopted the Rules and approved the recommendation of the Congress that they be known as "the Beijing Rules". It invited Member States to adopt, wherever necessary, their national legislation, policies and practices, particularly in training juvenile justice personnel, to the Rules and to bring them to the attention of the relevant authorities and the public in general. It called upon the Committee on Crime Prevention and Control to formulate measures for the effective implementation of the Rules, with the assistance of the United Nations institutes on the prevention of crime and the treatment of offenders; and invited States to inform the Secretary-General of measures taken by them to implement the Rules.

G. The right of everyone to leave any country, including his own, and to return to his country

261. United Nations bodies have recognized the right of everyone to leave any country, including his own, and to return to his country, have provided for the protection of that right in the International Covenant on Civil and Political Rights and other instruments, have studied the problem of discrimination in respect of that right, and have formulated and forwarded to the Governments and organizations concerned draft principles relating to the enjoyment of that right by all. They have also repeatedly reaffirmed the inalienable right of all displaced inhabitants to return to their homes or former places of residence in the territories occupied by Israel since 1967.

1. PROVISIONS OF UNITED NATIONS INSTRUMENTS

262. Paragraph 2 of article 13 of the Universal Declaration of Human Rights provides that:

Everyone has the right to leave any country, including his own, and to return to his country.

263. The International Convention on the Elimination of All Forms of Racial Discrimination states, in article 5, that:

In compliance with the fundamental obligations laid down in article 2 of this Convention, States Parties undertake to prohibit and to eliminate racial discrimination in all its forms and to guarantee the right of everyone, without distinction as to race, colour, or national or ethnic origin, to equality before the law, notably in the enjoyment of the following rights:

. . .

---

[75] Seventh United Nations Congress on the Prevention of Crime and the Treatment of Offenders (United Nations publication, Sales No. E.86.IV.1), chap. I, sect. C 1.

(d) Other civil rights, in particular:

(i) The right to freedom of movement and residence within the border of the State;

(ii) The right to leave any country, including one's own, and to return to one's country;

(iii) The right to nationality.

264. Article 12 of the International Covenant on Civil and Political Rights reads in part as follows:

. . .

2. Everyone shall be free to leave any country, including his own.

3. The above-mentioned rights shall not be subject to any restrictions except those which are provided by law, are necessary to protect national security, public order (*ordre public*), public health or morals or the rights and freedoms of others, and are consistent with the other rights recognized in the present Covenant.

4. No one shall be arbitrarily deprived of the right to enter his own country.

265. Article 15, paragraph 4, of the Convention on the Elimination of All Forms of Discrimination against Women reads as follows:

States Parties shall accord to men and women the same rights with regard to the law relating to the movement of persons and the freedom to choose their residence and domicile.

2. STUDY OF THE RIGHT OF EVERYONE TO LEAVE ANY COUNTRY, INCLUDING HIS OWN, AND TO RETURN TO HIS COUNTRY

266. At its twelfth session, in 1960, the Sub-Commission on Prevention of Discrimination and Protection of Minorities decided, in resolution 5 (XII), to initiate a study of discrimination in the matter of the right of everyone to leave any country, including his own, and to return to his country, as provided in article 13, paragraph 2, of the Universal Declaration of Human Rights. The Sub-Commission appointed one of its members, Mr. José D. Inglés, as Special Rapporteur to carry out the study. The decision to undertake the study was taken in the light of a preliminary investigation of the scope of such a study. At its fifth session, in 1952, the Sub-Commission had established a work programme which provided that among the measures to combat discrimination which it would study would be "those in the field of immigration and travel". The Economic and Social Council, however, in resolution 545 D (XVIII) of 29 July 1954, had requested the Sub-Commission "to take as the objective of its study paragraph 2 of article 13 of the Universal Declaration of Human Rights, namely—the right of everyone to 'leave any country, including his own, and to return to his country' ". Later the Council, in resolution 586 B (XX) of 29 July 1955, had confirmed that this decision "implicitly excluded immigration from the scope of this study".

267. The final report on the study was presented to the Sub-Commission at its fifteenth session, in 1963.[76] At that session the Sub-Commission, after examining a series of draft principles submitted by the Special Rapporteur in chapter VI of the report, formulated draft principles on freedom and non-discrimination in respect of the right of everyone to leave any country, including his own, and to return to his country, and transmitted them to the Commission on Human Rights for further consideration and adoption.[77]

268. The Commission was able to consider the study only at its twenty-ninth session, in 1973. At that time it also considered documentation relating to new developments in the field, prepared by the Secretary-General.[78]

269. On the recommendation of the Commission the Economic and Social Council, in resolution 1788 (LIV) of 18 May 1973, expressed its warm appreciation to the Special Rapporteur, affirmed the need for Governments to bear in mind the relevant decisions and resolutions of the United Nations with respect to the enjoyment of the right of everyone to leave any country, including his own, and to return to his country; and drew the attention of Governments, international and regional intergovernmental organizations and other institutions and bodies concerned to the draft principles which had been prepared and adopted by the Sub-Commission.[79]

270. In 1982 the Sub-Commission reviewed the action which had been taken with regard to the Study and, in resolution 1982/23 of 8 September 1982 requested Mr. Mubanga-Chipoya, one of its members, "to prepare an analysis of current trends and developments in respect of the right of everyone to leave any country, including his own, and to return to his country, and to have the possibility to enter other countries, without discrimination or hindrance, especially of the right to employment, taking into account the need to avoid the phenomenon of the brain drain from developing countries and the question of recompensing those countries for the loss incurred, and to study in particular the extent of restrictions permissible under article 12, paragraph 3, of the International Covenant on Civil and Political Rights". The Rapporteur was requested to present to the Sub-Commission at its thirty-seventh session, in 1984, recommendations for promoting and encouraging respect for and observance of this right.

271. Up to 31 December 1987 the Special Rapporteur had presented to the Sub-Commission a preliminary report (E/CN.4/Sub.2/1984/10), a progress report (E/CN.4/Sub.2/1985/9), and parts of the final report (E/CN.4/Sub.2/1987/10). After examining the preliminary report the Sub-Commission requested him to prepare, for examination at its thirty-ninth session, a final report on: (a) the right of everyone to leave any country, including his own; (b) the extent and effect of restrictions under article 12 (3) of the International Covenant on Civil and Political Rights; (c) the possibility to enter another country; and (d) a preliminary draft of a draft declaration on the right of everyone to leave

---

[76] *Study of Discrimination in Respect of the Right of Everyone to Leave any Country, Including His Own, and to Return to His Country* (United Nations publication, Sales No. E.64.XIV.2).

[77] *Ibid.*, annex I.

[78] E/CN.4/1042 and Add.1-4.

[79] For the text of the draft principles, see ST/HR/3, pp. 6-9.

any country, including his own, and to return to his country. The Special Rapporteur was further requested to continue his work in order to present to the Sub-Commission at its fortieth session (a) a final report on (i) the right to employment; (ii) the right to return to one's own country; and (iii) the phenomenon of the "brain drain" or the outflow of trained personnel from developing countries and the question of recompensing those countries for the loss incurred; and (b) a proposed final draft of the draft declaration on the right of everyone to leave any country, including his own, and to return to his country.

272. Parts of the final report, entitled "Analysis of the current trends and developments regarding the right to leave any country, including one's own, and the right to return to one's own country, and some other rights or considerations arising therefrom", were presented to the Sub-Commission at its thirty-ninth session. The Sub-Commission decided, in decision 1987/105, that it would consider the report and the draft declaration at its fortieth session.

3. THE RIGHT OF RETURN OF DISPLACED INHABITANTS

273. In a number of resolutions adopted since 1967, of which the latest is resolution 42/69 G of 2 December 1987, the General Assembly has repeatedly reaffirmed the inalienable right of all displaced persons to return to their homes or former places of residence in the territories occupied by Israel since 1967; and has repeatedly declared that any attempt to restrict, or to attach conditions to, the free exercise of the right of return by any displaced person is inconsistent with their inalienable right and inadmissible. The Assembly has also repeatedly called upon Israel (a) to take immediate steps for the return of all displaced inhabitants, and (b) to desist from all measures that obstruct the return of the displaced inhabitants, including measures affecting the physical and demographic structure of the occupied territories.

H. The right to own property

1. PROVISIONS OF UNITED NATIONS INSTRUMENTS

274. Article 17 of the Universal Declaration of Human Rights provides that:

1. Everyone has the right to own property alone as well as in association with others.

2. No one shall be arbitrarily deprived of his property.

275. In article 5 of the International Convention on the Elimination of All Forms of Racial Discrimination, States parties undertake to guarantee the right of everyone, without distinction as to race, colour or national or ethnic origin, to equality before the law, notably in the enjoyment of a number of rights including "the right to own property alone as well as in association with others" and "the right to inherit".

276. The Declaration on the Elimination of Discrimination against Women, proclaimed by the General Assembly on 7 November 1967, contains the following provision in article 6:

1. Without prejudice to the safeguarding of the unity and the harmony of the family, which remains the basic unit of any society, all appropriate measures, particularly legislative measures, shall be taken to ensure to women, married or unmarried, equal rights with men in the field of civil law, and in particular:

(a) The right to acquire, administer, enjoy, dispose of and inherit property, including property acquired during marriage. . . .

277. Paragraph 11 of the Declaration on the Rights of Disabled Persons reads as follows:

Disabled persons shall be able to avail themselves of qualified legal aid when such aid proves indispensable for the protection of their persons and property. If judicial proceedings are instituted against them, the legal procedure applied shall take their physical and mental condition fully into account.

278. Article 16 of the Convention on the Elimination of All Forms of Discrimination against Women reads in part as follows:

1. States Parties shall take all appropriates measures to eliminate discrimination against women in all matters relating to marriage and family relations and in particular shall ensure, on a basis of equality of men and women:

. . .

(h) The same rights for both spouses in respect of the ownership, acquisition, management, administration, enjoyment and disposition of property, whether free of charge or for a valuable consideration.

2. MEASURES TAKEN BY UNITED NATIONS BODIES

279. In the course of the consideration by the Commission on Human Rights of the draft covenants on human rights, the question of including an article on the right to own property in the draft covenants was the subject of considerable discussion, particularly at the seventh, eighth and tenth sessions of the Commission. No agreement was reached on a text or on whether the right should be included in the International Covenant on Civil and Political Rights or in the International Covenant on Economic, Social and Cultural Rights or in both.[80] After attempts had been made to come to an agreement through the appointment of a sub-committee of the Commission on Human Rights and the text proposed by the sub-committee had been rejected, the Commission, at its tenth session, decided to adjourn indefinitely consideration of the question of the inclusion of the article on the right of property in the draft covenant on economic, social and cultural rights.

280. During the consideration of the draft covenants by the General Assembly, suggestions for the inclusion of an article on the right of property in one or the other of the two Covenants were made, but none was pressed to the vote. As a consequence, the Covenants as ad-

---

[80] For a summary of the proceedings relating to the inclusion of an article on the right to own property in either Covenant, see *Official Records of the General Assembly, Tenth Session, Annexes*, agenda item 28, part II, chap. VIII, paras. 195-212, and *Official Records of the Economic and Social Council, Eighteenth Session, Supplement No. 7* (E/2573), paras. 40-71.

opted on 16 December 1966, do not contain a provision concerning this right.

281. Aspects of the right of property have repeatedly been considered and dealt with by the General Assembly and the Economic and Social Council in connection with the problem of land reform. To the extent that it deals with nationalization, expropriation and requisitioning, the Declaration on Permanent Sovereignty over Natural Resources of 1962 deals with aspects of the right to own property against the background of the right of peoples and nations to permanent sovereignty over their natural wealth and resources.

282. The General Assembly, in resolution 41/132 of 4 December 1986, recognized that there exist in Member States many forms of legal property ownership, including private, communal and State forms, each of which should contribute to ensuring effective development and utilization of human resources through the establishment of sound bases for political, economic and social justice, invited the United Nations regional commissions to consider the relationship between the full enjoyment of the right of everyone to own property alone as well as in association with others, as set forth in article 17 of the Universal Declaration of Human Rights, and the economic and social development of Member States. The Assembly requested the Secretary-General to prepare a report, taking into account the views of Member States, specialized agencies and other competent bodies of the United Nations system, on (a) the relationship between the full enjoyment by individuals of human rights and fundamental freedoms, in particular the right of everyone to own property alone as well as in association with others, and the economic and social development of Member States; and (b) the role of the right of everyone to own property alone as well as in association with others in ensuring the full and free participation of individuals in the economic and social systems of States.

283. The Commission on Human Rights, in resolution 1987/18 of 10 March 1987, also recognized the existence in Member States of many forms of legal property ownership, and called upon States to ensure that their national legislation with regard to all forms of property precludes any impairment of the enjoyment of human rights and fundamental freedoms, without prejudice to their right freely to choose and develop their political, social, economic and cultural systems. It decided to consider at its forty-fourth session, the influence of various forms of property on the enjoyment of human rights and fundamental freedoms.

284. At its forty-second session, by resolution 42/114 of 7 December 1987, the General Assembly took note of the preliminary oral report on this question made by the Under-Secretary-General for Human Rights and renewed its request to the Secretary-General to report his findings to the Assembly at its forty-third session.

285. By resolution 42/115 of the same date, the General Assembly called upon States to ensure that their national legislation with regard to all forms of property shall preclude any impairment of the enjoyment of human rights and fundamental freedoms, without prejudice to their right freely to choose and develop their political, social, economic and cultural systems. The Assembly requested the Secretary-General, in preparing his report in accordance with resolution 41/132, to take into account resolution 1987/18 of the Commission on Human Rights as well as General Assembly resolution 42/115.

I. Freedom of thought, conscience and religion or belief

286. Freedom of thought, conscience and religion has been recognized by the United Nations bodies concerned as an absolute right; no restrictions of any kind, they have maintained, may be imposed upon man's inner thought or moral consciousness, or his attitude towards the universe or its creator. However, they have agreed that external manifestations of thought, conscience or religion may be subject to legitimate limitations. This approach governed the drafters of the Universal Declaration of Human Rights and of the International Covenant on Civil and Political Rights. It was also adopted by the Sub-Commission on Prevention of Discrimination and Protection of Minorities when it prepared draft principles on freedom and non-discrimination in the matter of religious rights and practices after completing a thorough study of the subject, and by the bodies which prepared the Declaration on the Elimination of All Forms of Intolerance and of Discrimination Based on Religion or Belief.

287. Various United Nations organs were engaged over a nine-year period, from 1962 to 1971, in the preparation of the Declaration, which was adopted and proclaimed by the General Assembly in resolution 36/55 of 25 November 1981.[81] They were engaged even longer in the preparation of the proposed convention, which as at 31 December 1987 had not been completed.

288. The related question of conscientious objection to military service has also been of concern to various United Nations bodies since 1971.

1. PROVISIONS OF UNITED NATIONS INSTRUMENTS

289. In the Charter of the United Nations, Members have pledged themselves to promote universal respect for and observance of human rights and fundamental freedoms for all without discrimination as to religion.

290. Article 18 of the Universal Declaration of Human Rights provides that:

Everyone has the right to freedom of thought, conscience and religion; this right includes freedom to change his religion or belief, and freedom, either alone or in community with others and in public or private, to manifest his religion or belief in teaching, practice, worship and observance.

---

[81] For information concerning the Declaration and measures taken to implement its provisions, see chapter IV, section B, 2 and 3.

291. Article 18 of the International Covenant on Civil and Political Rights reads as follows:

1. Everyone shall have the right to freedom of thought, conscience and religion. This right shall include freedom to have or to adopt a religion or belief of his choice, and freedom, either individually or in community with others and in public or private, to manifest his religion or belief in worship, observance, practice and teaching.

2. No one shall be subject to coercion which would impair his freedom to have or to adopt a religion or belief of his choice.

3. Freedom to manifest one's religion or beliefs may be subject only to such limitations as are prescribed by law and are necessary to protect public safety, order, health, or morals or the fundamental rights and freedoms of others.

4. The States Parties to the present Covenant undertake to have respect for the liberty of parents and, when applicable, legal guardians to ensure the religious and moral education of their children in conformity with their own convictions.

292. Principle 10 of the Declaration of the Rights of the Child provides that:

The child shall be protected from practices which may foster racial, religious and any other form of discrimination. He shall be brought up in a spirit of understanding, tolerance, friendship among peoples, peace and universal brotherhood, and in full consciousness that his energy and talents should be devoted to the service of his fellow men.

2. THE QUESTION OF CONSCIENTIOUS OBJECTION TO MILITARY SERVICE

293. At its twenty-seventh session, in 1971, the Commission on Human Rights considered the question of the education of youth all over the world for the development of its personality and the strengthening of its respect for human rights and fundamental freedoms. In connection with this item of its agenda, the Commission examined in particular the question of conscientious objection to military service, which was recognized to be a matter of increasing concern to young people in certain countries.

294. There was general agreement as to the duty of the individual citizen to defend his family and society when his country was attacked or invaded and to contribute to his country's response to treaty obligations arising, for example, under the Charter of the United Nations or under treaties of collective or mutual defence against aggression. Differences of opinion, however, arose concerning the possibility of permitting exceptions to bearing arms for active military service on grounds of conscientious objection, religious belief or moral conviction.

295. In resolution 11 B (XXVII) of 22 March 1971, the Commission expressed a desire to have more information at its disposal on domestic legislation and practice in this matter with a view to further study of the question, and requested the Secretary-General to make available to the Commission the information on conscientious objection to military service included in the country monographs which had been prepared in connection with the *Study of Discrimination in the Matter of Religious Rights and Practices*.[82] The Sec-

retary-General was also requested to seek up-to-date information on national legislation and other measures and practices relating to conscientious objection to military service and alternative service, and to submit a report on this matter to the Commission as soon as possible.

296. The Secretary-General presented his report on the question of conscientious objection to military service[83] to the Commission at its twenty-ninth session, in 1972. Consideration of the question was, however, repeatedly postponed.

297. In 1978 and 1979, the General Assembly dealt with new aspects of the question of conscientious objection in its consideration of the status of persons refusing service in military or police forces used to enforce *apartheid*. In resolution 33/165 of 20 December 1978 the General Assembly recognized the right of all persons to refuse service in military or police forces which were used to enforce *apartheid*; called upon Member States to grant asylum or safe transit to another State, in the spirit of the Declaration on Territorial Asylum, to persons compelled to leave their country of nationality solely because of a conscientious objection to assisting in the enforcement of *apartheid* through service in military or police forces; urged Member States to consider favourably the granting to such persons of all the rights and benefits accorded to refugees under existing legal instruments; and called upon the appropriate United Nations bodies to provide all necessary assistance to such persons.

298. In resolution 34/93 A of 12 December 1979, the Assembly appealed to the youth of South Africa to refrain from enlisting in the South African armed forces, "which are designed to defend the inhuman system of *apartheid*, to repress the legitimate struggle of the oppressed people and to threaten, and commit acts of aggression against, neighbouring States". Further, the Assembly invited all Governments and organizations to assist, in accordance with resolution 33/165, persons compelled to leave South Africa because of a conscientious objection to assisting in the enforcement of *apartheid* through service in military or police forces. The appeal and invitation were repeated in Assembly resolution 35/206 B of 16 December 1980 (paras. 5 and 6).

299. The Commission on Human Rights resumed consideration of the question of concientious objection to military service in 1980. In resolution 38 (XXXVI) of 12 March 1980, it recognized that the report on the subject which the Secretary-General had submitted to it in 1972 might need updating, and requested the Secretary-General to seek once again from Member States up-to-date information on national legislation and other measures and practices relating to the subject. The Secretary-General prepared a report pursuant to this resolution,[84] and later issued a follow-up report.[85]

---

82 United Nations publication, Sales No. E.60.XIV.2.

83 E/CN.4/1118 and Corr.1 and Add.1-3.

84 E/CN.4/1419 and Add.1-5.

85 E/CN.4/1509.

300. The Commission, in resolution 40 (XXXVII) of 12 March 1981, welcomed the new information and requested the Sub-Commission on Prevention of Discrimination and Protection of Minorities to study the question of conscientious objection to military service in general, and in particular the implementation of Assembly resolution 33/165, with a view to making recommendations to the Commission.

301. The Sub-Commission examined the question of conscientious objection to military service at its thirty-fourth session, in 1981, and in resolution 14 (XXXIV) of 10 September 1981 requested two of its members, Mr. Eide and Mr. Mubanga-Chipoya, to make an analysis of the various dimensions of the question and its interrelationships with the promotion and protection of human rights.

302. The report submitted to the Sub-Commission at its thirty-fifth session by Mr. Eide and Mr. Mubanga-Chipoya[86] summarized, in chapter I, the concept and dimensions of conscientious objection, the relevant international standards, and the approaches to the issue which could be discerned from the views expressed in resolutions and declarations of intergovernmental and non-governmental organizations. Chapter II contained an analysis of the actual situation with respect to conscientious objection under relevant national laws and practices. In chapter III, conclusions were drawn from the material reviewed. A summary of available information on conscription, conscientious objection to military service and alternative service was annexed to the report.

303. In resolution 1982/30 of 10 September 1982, the Sub-Commission requested Mr. Eide and Mr. Mubanga-Chipoya to prepare a final report based on the comments received on their preliminary report and to develop principles related to the question of conscientious objection, with a view to: (a) recognizing the right of all persons to refuse service in military or police forces which were used to enforce *apartheid*, to pursue wars of aggression, or to engage in any other illegal warfare; (b) recognizing the possibility of the right of all persons to refuse service in military or police forces on grounds of conscience or deeply held personal conviction, and their responsibility to offer instead of military service any other service in the social or economic field including work for the economic progress and development of their country; and (c) urging Member States to grant asylum or safe transit to another State to persons compelled to leave their country of nationality solely because of conscientious refusal to serve in the military forces.

304. The final report on the subject,[87] presented to the Sub-Commission at its thirty-sixth session, included an analysis of the information received from all sources on such matters as the grounds recognized as valid reasons for conscientious objection, procedures for obtaining conscientious objection status, the question of

alternative service, the status and experience of conscientious objectors in countries which do not permit conscientious objection or alternative service to military service or which permit it only on limited grounds; and the question of asylum for persons who have fled their country because of their objection to military service.

305. The report also included a set of recommendations for bringing national law and practice into conformity with international standards; summaries of available information on conscription, conscientious objection to military service, and alternative service (annex I), tables listing countries and territories according to their situation with regard to conscription and alternative service (annex III).

306. In resolution 1983/22 of 5 September 1983, the Sub-Commission recognized the great importance of the subject and the need to promote and protect the human rights of conscientious objectors, and expressed the belief that special attention should be given to appropriate avenues of recourse at the national, regional and international levels in order to advance the promotion and protection of those rights. It transmitted the report to the Commission on Human Rights for study of the recommendations, and proposed that it should be printed and given the widest possible distribution.

307. After considering the report, the Commission on Human Rights in resolution 1987/46 of 10 March 1987 recognized that conscientious objection to military service derives from principles and reasons of conscience, including profound convictions, arising from religious, ethical, moral or similar values. It appealed to States to recognize that conscientious objection to military service should be considered a legitimate exercise of the right to freedom of thought, conscience and religion recognized by the Universal Declaration of Human Rights and the International Covenant on Civil and Political Rights, and invited States to take measures aimed at exemption from military service on the basis of genuinely held conscientious objection to armed service.

308. The Commission recommended to States with a system of compulsory military service, where such provision had not already been made, that they consider introducing various forms of alternative service for conscientious objectors which are compatible with the reasons for conscientious objection, bearing in mind the experience of some States in this respect, and that they refrain from subjecting such persons to imprisonment. It also recommended to Member States, if they had not already done so, that they establish within the framework of their national legal system impartial decision-making procedures to determine whether a conscientious objection is valid in any specific case.

309. The Commission, finally, requested the Secretary-General to submit a report to its thirty-fifth session taking into account comments provided by Governments and further information received by him; and decided to resume consideration of the question at that session.

---

[86] E/CN.4/Sub.2/1982/24.

[87] E/CN.4/Sub.2/1983/30.

J. Freedom of opinion and expression

310. At its first session, in resolution 59 (I) of 14 December 1946, the General Assembly stated that:

Freedom of information is a fundamental human right and is the touchstone of all the freedoms to which the United Nations is consecrated;

Freedom of information implies the right to gather, transmit and publish news anywhere and everywhere without fetters. As such it is an essential factor in any serious effort to promote the peace and progress of the world.

Freedom of information requires as an indispensable element the willingness and capacity to employ its privileges without abuse. It requires as a basic discipline the moral obligation to seek the facts without prejudice and to spread knowledge without malicious intent.

Understanding and co-operation among nations are impossible without an alert and sound world opinion which, in turn, is wholly dependent upon freedom of information.

311. At its second session the General Assembly adopted resolutions 110 (II) of 3 November 1947, condemning all forms of propaganda involving a threat to the peace, and resolution 127 (II) of 15 November 1947, inviting the Governments of States Members "to study such measures as might with advantage be taken on the national plane to combat, within the limits of constitutional procedures, the diffusion of false or distorted reports likely to injure friendly relations between States".

312. The United Nations Conference on Freedom of Information, held at Geneva from 23 March to 21 April 1948, endorsed the concepts set out in Assembly resolutions 59 (I), 110 (II) and 127 (II) and endeavoured to reconcile them. Since that time, however, United Nations bodies have experienced difficulty in clarifying and elaborating the concept of freedom of opinion and expression, agreeing upon its legitimate limitations, and recommending effective measures for its realization. The draft convention on freedom of information, prepared by the Conference, had not been adopted as at 31 December 1987; and by that date the Sub-Commission on Freedom of Information had long since been discontinued, efforts to prepare an internationally sanctioned code of ethics for information personnel had been abandoned, and the consideration of periodic reports on freedom of information by the Commission on Human Rights had ended with the termination of the periodic reporting system in 1981.

313. In recent years emphasis on the realization of the right to freedom of opinion and expression has focused upon implementation—through co-operation between the United Nations and the United Nations Educational, Scientific and Cultural Organization and other organizations of the United Nations system, particularly the International Telecommunication Union—of the International Programme for the Development of Communication and the establishment of a new world information and communication order.

1. PROVISIONS OF UNITED NATIONS INSTRUMENTS

314. Article 19 of the Universal Declaration of Human Rights provides that:

Everyone has the right to freedom of opinion and expression; this right includes freedom to hold opinions without interference and to seek, receive and impart information and ideas through any media and regardless of frontiers.

315. Article 19 of the International Covenant on Civil and Political Rights reads as follows:

1. Everyone shall have the right to hold opinions without interference.

2. Everyone shall have the right to freedom of expression; this right shall include freedom to seek, receive and impart information and ideas of all kinds, regardless of frontiers, either orally, in writing or in print, in the form of art, or through any other media of his choice.

3. The exercise of the rights provided for in paragraph 2 of this article carries with it special duties and responsibilities. It may therefore be subject to certain restrictions, but these shall only be such as are provided by law and are necessary:

(a) For respect of the rights or reputations of others;

(b) For the protection of national security or of public order (*ordre public*), or of public health or morals.

Article 20 of the Covenant reads as follows:

1. Any propaganda for war shall be prohibited by law.

2. Any advocacy of national, racial or religious hatred that constitutes incitement to discrimination, hostility or violence shall be prohibited by law.

316. Article 9 of the United Nations Declaration on the Elimination of All Forms of Racial Discrimination reads as follows:

1. All propaganda and organizations based on ideas or theories of the superiority of one race or group of persons of one colour or ethnic origin with a view to justifying or promoting racial discrimination in any form shall be severely condemned.

2. All incitement to or acts of violence, whether by individuals or organizations, against any race or group of persons of another colour or ethnic origin shall be considered an offence against society and punishable under law.

3. In order to put into effect the purposes and principles of the present Declaration, all States shall take immediate and positive measures, including legislative and other measures, to prosecute and/or outlaw organizations which promote or incite to racial discrimination, or incite to or use violence for purposes of discrimination based on race, colour or ethnic origin.

317. Article 4 of the International Convention on the Elimination of All Forms of Racial Discrimination, adopted and opened for signature and ratification by General Assembly resolution 2106 A (XX) of 21 December 1965, reads as follows:

States Parties condemn all propaganda and all organizations which are based on ideas or theories of superiority of one race or group of persons of one colour or ethnic origin, or which attempt to justify or promote racial hatred and discrimination in any form, and undertake to adopt immediate and positive measures designed to eradicate all incitement to, or acts of, such discrimination and, to this end, with due regard to the principles embodied in the Universal Declaration of Human Rights and the rights expressly set forth in article 5 of this Convention, *inter alia*:

(a) Shall declare an offence punishable by law all dissemination of ideas based on racial superiority or hatred, incitement to racial discrimination, as well as all acts of violence or incitement to such acts against any race or group of persons of another colour or ethnic origin, and also the provision of any assistance to racist activities, including the financing thereof;

(b) Shall declare illegal and prohibit organizations, and also organized and all other propaganda activities, which promote and incite racial discrimination, and shall recognize participation in such organization or activities as an offence punishable by law;

(c) Shall not permit public authorities or public institutions, national or local, to promote or incite racial discrimination.

318. Article VII of the Declaration of the Principles of International Cultural Co-operation reads as follows:

1. Broad dissemination of ideas and knowledge, based on the freest exchange and discussion, is essential to creative activity, the pursuit of truth and the development of the personality.

2. In cultural co-operation, stress shall be laid on ideas and values conducive to the creation of a climate of friendship and peace. Any mark of hostility in attitudes and in expression of opinion shall be avoided. Every effort shall be made, in presenting and disseminating information, to ensure its authenticity.

319. Other international instruments dealing with various aspects of freedom of opinion and expression, including the Convention on the International Right of Correction and the UNESCO Declaration on Fundamental Principles concerning the Contribution of the Mass Media to Strengthening Peace and International Understanding, to the Promotion of Human Rights and to Countering Racialism, *Apartheid* and Incitement to War, are described below.

2. THE UNITED NATIONS CONFERENCE ON FREEDOM OF INFORMATION

320. In resolution 59 (I) of 14 December 1946, the General Assembly resolved "to authorize the holding of a conference of all Members of the United Nations on freedom of information". The Economic and Social Council was instructed to undertake the convocation of such a conference, the purpose of which would be to formulate views concerning the rights, obligations and practices that should be included in the concept of freedom of information. The Assembly specified that delegations to the conference should include in each instance persons actually engaged or experienced in press, radio, motion pictures or other media for the dissemination of information.

321. Accordingly the Economic and Social Council, by resolution 74 (V) of 15 August 1947, convened the United Nations Conference on Freedom of Information, which met at Geneva in March-April 1948. The Conference prepared three draft Conventions—on the Gathering and International Transmission of News, on the Institution of an International Right of Correction, and on Freedom of Information—as well as draft articles for inclusion in the Universal Declaration of Human Rights, and a number of resolutions. The Conference referred its Final Act[88] to the Economic and Social Council, which in turn referred it to the General Assembly for action.

322. At its third session, in 1949, the Assembly adopted the draft Convention on the International Transmission of News and the Right of Correction, which consisted of an amalgamation of the provisions of the draft Conventions on the Gathering and International Transmission of News and on the Institution of an International Right of Correction which had been prepared by the Conference. However, the Assembly, in resolution 277 A (III) of 13 May 1949, decided that the Convention it had approved should not be opened for signature until the Assembly had taken definite action on the draft Convention on Freedom of Information.

323. At its seventh session, in 1952, the General Assembly decided to open for signature, as a separate international instrument, the substantive provisions, dealing with the international right of correction, of the Convention that it had approved in 1949. Consequently, it adopted and opened for signature, by resolution 630 (VII) of 16 December 1952, the Convention on the International Right of Correction.

3. CONVENTION ON THE INTERNATIONAL RIGHT OF CORRECTION

324. The Convention on the International Right of Correction, which entered into force on 24 August 1962, attempts to transfer to the international level an institution which has been part of the national law of some countries. Its basic idea is that embodied in the maxim *audiatur et altera pars,* i.e., that the person referred to in a printed report shall have the right to convey to the readers his side of the question. In the Convention the contracting States agree that when a contracting State contends that a news dispatch capable of injuring its relations with other States or its national prestige or dignity, transmitted from one country to another by correspondents or information agencies and published or disseminated abroad is false or distorted, it may submit its version of the facts (called "communiqué") to the contracting States within whose territories such dispatch has been published or disseminated. The receiving State has the obligation to release the communiqué to the correspondents and information agencies operating in its territory through the channels customarily used for the release of news concerning international affairs for publication. The Convention does not impose a legal obligation on the press or other media of information to publish the communiqué. The obligation of the receiving State to release the communiqué arises, however, whatever may be its opinion of the facts dealt with in the news dispatch or in the communiqué which purports to correct it. In the event that the receiving State does not discharge its obligation with respect to a communiqué of another contracting State, the latter may accord, on the basis of reciprocity, similar treatment to a communiqué submitted to it by the defaulting State. The complaining State further has the right to seek relief through the Secretary-General of the United Nations, who shall give appropriate publicity, through the information channels at his disposal, to the communiqué, together with the original dispatch and the comments, if any, submitted to him by the State complained against. The Convention also contains a compromise clause by which disputes not settled by negotiation may be referred to the International Court of Justice.

[88] United Nations publication, Sales No. E.48.XIV.2.

4. DRAFT CONVENTION ON FREEDOM OF INFORMATION

325. A Committee established by the General Assembly in resolution 426 (V) of 14 December 1950 reviewed the draft Convention and prepared a new version.[89] On the basis of the work done by that Committee, the Assembly's Third Committee, at the fourteenth, fifteenth and sixteenth sessions of the Assembly, adopted a preamble and four operative paragraphs.[90]

326. The item, "Draft Convention on Freedom of Information", appeared on the agenda of each regular session of the General Assembly from 1962 to 1980; it did not, however, appear on the agenda of any subsequent session.

5. DRAFT DECLARATION ON FREEDOM OF INFORMATION

327. At its twenty-seventh and twenty-eighth sessions, in 1959, the Economic and Social Council discussed the question of a draft declaration on freedom of information. In resolution 732 (XXVIII) of 30 July 1959, the Council invited the Governments of Member States to comment on the text of such a draft declaration, annexed to the resolution, as well as on the desirability of the adoption by the United Nations of such an instrument.

328. At its twenty-ninth session the Council, in resolution 756 (XXIX) of 21 April 1960, adopted a draft Declaration on Freedom of Information and transmitted it to the General Assembly "with the hope that it will promote the realization of freedom of information and assist the General Assembly in the completion of its work in this field". The draft Declaration prepared by the Council reaffirms the principles which, in the Council's view, "should be upheld and observed and which domestic law and international conventions and other instruments for the protection of freedom of information should support and endeavour to promote", among them the following:

Article 1. The right to know and the right freely to seek the truth are inalienable and fundamental rights of man. Everyone has the right, individually and collectively, to seek, receive and impart information.

Article 2. All Governments should pursue policies under which the free flow of information, within countries and across frontiers, will be protected. The right to seek and transmit information should be assured in order to enable the public to ascertain facts and appraise events.

Article 3. Media of information should be employed in the service of the people. No Government or public or private body or interests should exercise such control over media for disseminating information as to prevent the existence of a diversity of sources of information or to deprive the individual of free access to such sources. The

development of independent national media of information should be encouraged. . . .

Article 4. Those who disseminate information must strive in good faith to ensure the accuracy of the facts reported and respect the rights and the dignity of nations, and of groups and individuals without distinction as to race, nationality or creed.

329. The item, "Draft Declaration on Freedom of Information", appeared on the agenda of each regular session of the General Assembly from 1962 to 1980; it did not, however, appear on the agenda of any subsequent session.

6. MEASURES INITIATED BY THE UNITED NATIONS CONFERENCE ON FREEDOM OF INFORMATION

330. In addition to preparing the draft Convention on the Gathering and International Transmission of News, the draft Convention on the Institution of an International Right of Correction, and the draft Convention on Freedom of Information, mentioned above, the United Nations Conference on Freedom of Information adopted 43 resolutions grouped under the following headings: General principles (resolutions 1 to 4); Measures to facilitate the gathering and international transmission of information (resolutions 5 to 24); Measures concerning the free publication and reception of information (resolutions 25 to 38); Continuing machinery to promote the free flow of information (resolution 39); Miscellaneous (resolutions 40 and 41); Possible modes of action by means of which the recommendations of the Conference can best be put into effect (resolutions 42 and 43).

331. The Conference referred all its decisions to the Economic and Social Council, which examined them over a period of several years and prepared recommendations for the General Assembly. On the basis of these recommendations and proposals put forward by Member States, the Assembly adopted a number of important resolutions on various aspects of freedom of information at its fourth, fifth, seventh, eighth and ninth sessions.

(a) *Access for news personnel to United Nations meetings and public information sources and services*

332. In resolution 314 (IV) of 21 October 1949, the General Assembly urged all States Members of the United Nations to grant news personnel of all countries who had been accredited to the United Nations or to the specialized agencies, as the case might be, free access:

(*a*) To countries where meetings of the United Nations or specialized agencies or any conferences convened by them take place, for the purpose of covering such meetings . . .

(*b*) To all public information sources and services of the United Nations and the specialized agencies and to all meetings and conferences of the United Nations or of the specialized agencies which are open to the Press, equally and without discrimination.

---

[89] A/AC.42/7 and Corr.1, annex.

[90] See *Official Records of the General Assembly, Fourteenth Session, Third Committee, Annexes,* agenda item 35, document A/4341; *ibid., Fifteenth Session, Third Committee, Annexes,* agenda item 35, document A/4636; *ibid., Sixteenth Session, Third Committee, Annexes,* agenda item 36, document A/5041.

(b) *Interference with the right to freedom of information*

333. In resolution 424 (V) of 14 December 1950, the General Assembly, finding that duly authorized radio operating agencies in some countries were deliberately interfering with the reception by people of those countries of certain radio signals originating beyond their territories, condemned measures of this nature as a denial of the right of all persons to be fully informed concerning news, opinions and ideas regardless of frontiers. The Assembly invited the Governments of all Member States to refrain from such interference with the right of their peoples to freedom of information, and invited all Governments to refrain from radio broadcasts what would mean unfair attacks or slanders against other peoples anywhere and in so doing to conform strictly to an ethical conduct in the interest of world peace by reporting facts truly and objectively.

(c) *Freedom of information and of the press in emergencies*

334. In resolution 425 (V) of 14 December 1950, the General Assembly, considering that limitations might be placed on freedom of information and of the press in emergencies or on the pretext of emergencies, recommended to all Member States that, when they were compelled to declare a state of emergency, measures to limit freedom of information and of the press should be taken only in the most exceptional circumstances and then only to the extent strictly required by law.

(d) *Question of false and distorted information*

335. In resolution 634 (VII) of 16 December 1952, the General Assembly expressed the view that the "dissemination of false or distorted information by national as well as international information enterprises is one of the causes of the lack of mutual understanding among nations, to the detriment of international harmony", and recommended "that United Nations bodies studying the problems of freedom of information should consider appropriate measures for avoiding the harm done to international understanding by the dissemination of false and distorted information".

(e) *Technical assistance in promoting freedom of information*

336. In resolution 839 (IX) of 17 December 1954, the General Assembly authorized the Secretary-General "to render, at the request of Member States, services which do not fall within the scope and objectives of existing technical assistance programmes; in order to assist these States in promoting freedom of information".

(f) *Use of broadcasting in the cause of peace*

337. In resolution 841 (IX) of 17 December 1954, the General Assembly expressed the view that the International Convention concerning the Use of Broadcasting in the Cause of Peace (Geneva, 1936)[91] constituted an important element in the field of freedom of information, and decided to request States parties to that Convention to indicate whether they wished to transfer to the United Nations the functions which had been performed, under the terms of that Convention, by the League of Nations. The General Assembly requested the Secretary-General to prepare for this purpose a draft protocol and to include in it new articles which would provide that each party should refrain from radio broadcasts that would mean unfair attacks or slanders against other peoples anywhere and also that each party should not interfere with the reception within its territory of foreign radio broadcasts. An appropriate draft protocol was prepared by the Secretary-General and circulated to the States parties to the Convention of 1936. Final action has not yet been taken on the draft; however, in resolution 1903 (XVIII) of 18 November 1963, on participation in general multilateral treaties concluded under the auspices of the League of Nations, the General Assembly listed the International Convention concerning the Use of Broadcasting in the Cause of Peace, 1936, among those which might be of interest for accession by additional States.

7. SUB-COMMISSION ON FREEDOM OF INFORMATION AND OF THE PRESS

338. The Commission on Human Rights at its first session, in 1947, decided to establish a Sub-Commission on Freedom of Information and of the Press, to be composed of twelve persons selected by the Commission in consultation with the Secretary-General and subject to the consent of the Governments of which the persons were nationals. As the Commission did not have the time at that session to select the members of the Sub-Commission, they were appointed by the Economic and Social Council. The Council resolved that the functions of the Sub-Commission would be, in the first instance, to examine what rights, obligations and practices should be included in the concept of freedom of information and to report to the Commission on Human Rights on any issues that might arise from such examination; and to perform any other functions entrusted to it by the Council or by the Commission.

339. Following the General Assembly's decision on the calling of an International Conference on Freedom of Information, the Sub-Commission was requested by the Council to prepare a draft documented agenda for the Conference and suggestions as to the Governments, specialized agencies and organizations to be invited.

---

[91] League of Nations, *Treaty Series,* vol. CLXXXVI, p. 301.

340. The Sub-Commission held its first session in 1947. After preparing detailed recommendations concerning the Conference, it began an examination of what rights, obligations and practices should be included in the concept of freedom of information. By and large, the substantive and procedural recommendations of the Sub-Commission concerning the Conference were accepted by the Council without major modifications.

341. At its second session, in 1948, the Sub-Commission drafted articles on freedom of information for inclusion in the draft Declaration and the draft Covenant on Human Rights. The Sub-Commission also outlined certain principles upon which its drafting of the articles had been based.

342. At its third session, in 1949, the Sub-Commission considered its future work and priorities. At its fourth session, in 1950, it prepared recommendations on such matters as interference with radio signals, measures limiting freedom of information in a state of emergency, governmental interference in the supply and control of newsprint, and the preparation of an international code of ethics for information personnel.

343. The Economic and Social Council reviewed the organization and operation of its commissions at its thirteenth sesion and decided, in resolution 414 B I (XIII) of 18-20 September 1951, "To continue the Sub-Commission on Freedom of Information and of the Press in order to enable it, at a final session convened for this purpose when the Secretary-General is in possession of all the necessary documentation, to complete its work on the draft International Code of Ethics for Journalists".

8. INTERNATIONAL CODE OF ETHICS FOR THE USE OF
INFORMATION PERSONNEL

344. At its fifth and last session, the Sub-Commission redrafted the Code of Ethics in the light of the comments which had been received. Later the Economic and Social Council, in resolution 442 (XIV) of 13 June 1952, requested the Secretary-General to communicate the draft Code and the relevant documentation to national and international professional associations and information enterprises for such action as they might deem appropriate, informing then that, if they thought it desirable, the United Nations might co-operate with them in organizing an international conference for the purpose of drawing up an International Code of Ethics.

345. The General Assembly, in resolution 635 (VII) of 16 December 1952, expressed the view that "all further work connected with the draft Code should be undertaken by professional members of information enterprises with no interference from Governments, either on the national or the international level". The Assembly requested the Secretary-General, if a representative group of information enterprises and of national and international professional associations expressed a desire to do so, to co-operate with it in organizing an international professional conference for the purpose of preparing and adopting a final text of an International Code of Ethics, and taking such further steps concerning implementation of the Code as it might deem advisable.

346. The Secretary-General presented his report on the question of organizing an international professional conference to prepare the final text of an International Code of Ethics for the Use of Information Personnel[92] to the General Assembly at its ninth session, in 1954. After examining the report, the Assembly came to the conclusion that the information enterprises and national and international associations which favoured the organization of a conference did not appear to constitute a sufficiently representative group, and accordingly decided to take no further action, for the time being, in regard to the organization of such a conference. The Secretary-General was requested, however, to transmit the text of the draft International Code, together with his report, to the enterprises and associations with which he had been in communication regarding the matter, for their information and for such action as they might deem proper.

9. STUDIES AND REPORTS ON FREEDOM OF
INFORMATION

347. The Rapporteur appointed by the Economic and Social Council in resolution 442 C (XIV) of 13 June 1952, Mr. Salvador P. López, presented his report, entitled "Freedom of information, 1953" to the Council at its seventeeth session, in 1954.[93] The report dealt with contemporary problems and developments in the field of freedom of information, and contained a series of recommendations for action. After considering the report, the Council, in resolution 522 A (XVII) of 29 April 1954, requested the Secretary-General, in conjunction with the specialized agencies (particularly UNESCO and ITU), and in consultation with professional associations and information enterprises, to prepare a number of reports on various aspects of freedom of information.

348. On the basis of recommendations made by the Rapporteur, the Council, in resolutions 522 B to I, K and L (XVII), also of 29 April 1954, dealt with such matters as the transmission of outgoing news dispatches, the status and movement of foreign correspondents, copyright, independence of information personnel, professional training, press rates and priorities, international broadcasting, tariff and trade practices, the encouragement and development of independent domestic information enterprises and the production and distribution of newsprint. The Council also, in resolution 522 J (XVII), recommended that due consideration should be given by specialized agencies and by

---

[92] See *Official Records of the General Assembly, Ninth Session, Annexes,* agenda item 29, documents A/2691 and Add.1 and 2.

[93] E/2426 and Add.1-5.

the United Nations Technical Assistance Administration to requests which Governments might submit for aid which would be useful in promoting freedom of information. The General Assembly later, in resolution 926 (X) of 14 December 1955, authorized the Secretary-General to render advisory services in the field of human rights, including assistance in promoting freedom of information.

349. At its resumed nineteenth session, in 1955, the Council received the following reports prepared by the Secretary-General pursuant to Council resolution 522 A (XVII) of 29 April 1954:

(a) Programme to promote among new personnel wider knowledge of United Nations, foreign countries and international affairs;[94]

(b) Current principles and practices involved in the censorship of outgoing news dispatches;[95]

(c) Legal aspects of the rights and responsibilities of the media of information;[96]

(d) The problem of protecting sources of information of news personnel;[97] and

(e) Public and private information monopolies and their effects on freedom of information.[98]

At the same session, the Council received a joint UNESCO/ITU study on the problem of transmitting press messages,[99] and a report by ITU on the unrestricted transmission of news.[100]

350. After considering these reports, the Council, in resolution 574 B (XIX) of 26 May 1955, took note of them and urged all States to cease censoring outgoing news dispatches in peacetime and to facilitate the unrestricted transmission of news by telecommunication services. The Council requested the Secretary-General to transmit the study on the legal aspects of the rights and responsibilities of the media of information to information enterprises and professional associations for their information.

351. The Commission on Human Rights, at its twelfth session, in 1956 (resolution X), decided that at its thirteenth session it would consider the question: "Review of the progress made in the field of freedom of information and consideration of measures for the effective promotion of that right, with such recommendations as may be necessary". At its thirteenth session it appointed a Committee on Freedom of Information to examine and review the recommendations and decisions on the subject of freedom of information already made in the various organs of the United Nations and the work done in that field by the specialized agencies, particularly UNESCO. After receiving the report of the Committee[101] at its fourteenth session, in 1958, the Commission requested UNESCO and other specialized agencies concerned to initiate action to consider and implement the suggestions of the Committee concerning underdeveloped countries wherever possible and as expeditiously as possible, with the object of assisting them to build up adequate media of information and their use for the free flow of information.

352. A second substantive report on freedom of information was prepared, in accordance with Council resolution 718 II (XXVII) of 24 April 1959, by Mr. Hilding Eek, a consultant appointed by the Secretary-General. Entitled "Report on developments in the field of freedom of information since 1954",[102] the report dealt with such matters as facilities for the free flow of information, obstacles to the free flow of information, the content and quality of information, and the extent to which people receive news of the United Nations and of its specialized agencies.

353. Thereafter, for several years, the Secretary-General prepared and submitted to the Commission on Human Rights annual reports on developments affecting freedom of information.[103] The series was discontinued, however, in 1965.

10. PERIODIC REPORTS ON FREEDOM OF INFORMATION

354. At its twenty-ninth session, in 1973, the Commission on Human Rights considered, with the assistance of its *Ad Hoc* Committee on Periodic Reports on Human Rights, the reports on freedom of information for the period from 1 July 1967 to 30 June 1970 received from States and specialized agencies in accordance with Economic and Social Council resolution 1074 C (XXXIX) of 28 July 1965.[104] In resolution 23 (XXIX) of 4 April 1973, the Commission noted with regret that a number of countries had not submitted such reports, expressed the hope that an increasing number of Governments would report in the future, and deplored the absence of information on the exercise of freedom of expression and freedom of information in some territories still under colonial rule. The Commission noted a number of trends revealed in the reports received, including the continuing efforts on the part of Governments to facilitate freedom of information, the continuing expansion of information facilities in all parts of the world, and the growing role of the mass media as an instrument for the promotion of the economic, social and cultural policies of States. The Commission recommended that Member States should intensify their individual and joint efforts to raise the standards of gathering and disseminating information, to widen the participation of the population as a whole in the enjoyment of freedom of information, and to promote and protect this freedom as defined in the Universal Declaration of Human Rights.

---

94 E/2705 and Corr.1 and Add.1 and 2.

95 E/2683 and Add.1-3.

96 E/2698 and Add.1.

97 E/2693 and Add.1-3.

98 E/2687 and Add.1-3.

99 E/2686 and Corr.1 and 2.

100 E/2681.

101 E/CN.4/762 and Corr.1.

102 E/3443.

103 E/CN.4/822 and Add.1-3; E/CN.4/838 and Add.1-3; E/CN.4/862 and Add.1 and 2.

104 E/CN.4/1066; E/CN.4/1067 and Add.1 and 2.

355. After repeatedly postponing consideration of periodic reports on human rights, including reports on freedom of information, the Commission adopted decision 10 (XXXVII) of 13 March 1981 in which it decided to discontinue its consideration of the item "Periodic reports on human rights", and to recommend to the Economic and Social Council that it terminate the periodic reporting system. The Council decided in decision 1981/151 of 8 May 1981 to terminate the periodic reporting system established by Council resolution 1074 C (XXXIX) of 28 July 1965.

11. DETENTION OF PERSONS WHO EXERCISE THE RIGHT TO FREEDOM OF OPINION AND EXPRESSION

356. The Sub-Commission on Prevention of Discrimination and Protection of Minorities, in resolution 1983/32 of 6 September 1983, expressed the hope that States will do all in their power to avoid threats to peace and security by promoting and protecting human rights and fundamental freedoms within their borders, including releasing all persons detained for their views who have not used or advocated violence.

357. Taking note of this decision, the Commission on Human Rights in resolution 1984/26 of 12 March 1984 expresssed its concern at the extensive detention in many parts of the world of persons who exercise the right to freedom of opinion and expression, and appealed to all States to ensure respect and support for the rights of such persons. In particular it called upon States detaining anyone solely for exercising the right to freedom of expression as laid down in the International Covenant on Civil and Political Rights to release them immediately; while in general it called upon States that had not yet done so to take steps to allow the full realization of the right to freedom of opinion and expression in their territory.

358. The Commission reiterated these views in resolutions 1985/17 of 11 March 1985, 1986/46 of 12 March 1986, 1987/32 of 10 March 1987. In the latter resolution it requested the Sub-Commission to continue to consider, within the framework of its mandate, the right to freedom of opinion and expression as laid down in the International Covenant on Civil and Political Rights.

12. DEVELOPMENT OF INFORMATION MEDIA IN DEVELOPING COUNTRIES

359. The development of information media in developing countries is an aspect of freedom of information which, with the special co-operation of UNESCO, the United Nations has considered in some detail.

360. In resolution 1778 (XVII) of 7 December 1962, the Assembly invited the Governments concerned to include adequate provision in their economic plans for the development of national information media and recommended that the Governments of the more developed countries should co-operate with developing countries with a view to meeting the urgent needs of the latter in connection with programmes for the development of independent national information media, with due regard for the culture of each country. The Technical Assistance Board, the Special Fund, the specialized agencies concerned, the regional economic commissions and other public and private agencies and institutions were invited to assist, as appropriate, the developing countries in strengthening their national information media.

361. UNESCO was requested by the Assembly to continue to further the programme for the development of information media, including the application of new techniques of communication for achievement of rapid progress in education; to keep up to date, as far as possible, its survey on this subject; and to report, as appropriate, to the Commission on Human Rights and to the Economic and Social Council.

362. Since that time UNESCO has endeavoured to encourage a free flow and wider and better-balanced dissemination of information through increased exchanges of news and media programmes. Four instruments have been drawn up for that purpose: an agreement for facilitating the international circulation of visual and auditory materials of an educational, scientific or cultural character; an agreement on the importation of educational, scientific and cultural materials; a convention concerning the international exchange of publications; and a convention concerning the exchange of official publications and government documents between States. UNESCO has also provided aid to Member States in the training of information personnel and in the development of radio, television and cinema facilities.

363. The General Conference of UNESCO, in 1976, decided that priority should be given, in the execution of UNESCO's free flow of information and communication policies, to assisting developing countries to establish and strengthen their information systems in line with their needs. It further decided that assistance should be given to those countries with a view to liberating them from dependence on the developed countries for their communication and information systems.

364. The General Assembly, in resolution 31/139 of 16 December 1976, noted these decisions with satisfaction and requested UNESCO to continue and intensify its programme for the development of mass communication systems, especially for the benefit of developing countries. UNESCO has since continued to provide assistance to Member States, with priority to developing countries, for the development of their communication systems.

13. MEASURES TO ENSURE A FREE AND BALANCED FLOW OF INFORMATION AND THE RIGHTS OF INDIVIDUALS AND COMMUNITIES TO COMMUNICATE

365. As the specialized agency responsible for promotion of the use of the mass media and the study of its roles in society, UNESCO has undertaken a wide range of activities dealing with the promotion of human rights

in the field of communication in implementation of article 19 of the Universal Declaration of Human Rights and the corresponding article 19 of the International Covenant on Civil and Political Rights, both of which provide that the right to freedom of opinion and expression includes freedom to seek, receive and impart information and ideas through any media regardless of frontiers. Over the years, the work of UNESCO has been adapted to meet the challenge of the vastly increased volume of international communication and exchange of information and to develop the means and structures for the transmission and reception of information and ideas in all countries. Implicit in all these activities is the fundamental concept of communication as a basis human right.

366. Concern for the free flow of information has always been of central importance in the work of UNESCO; its unique contribution to this principle has been to broaden progressively its approach to embrace the concept that the flow of information must be "balanced" as well as "free". In so doing, UNESCO has sought to meet the challenge of the vastly increased volume of international communication and exchange of information in a world of serious imbalance as regards the means and structures for the transmission and reception of information and ideas.

367. Because communication is a phenomenon which must be considered not only in absolute but also in relative terms—i.e., in relation to the diverse situations in which it takes place—the gap which exists in this field between different nations, and between different social groups within each nation, produces an imbalance and inequality in the exercise of the right to intercommunication and mutual exchange of information and ideas, and ultimately to the data on which decisions affecting the destiny of societies and the fate of individuals are based. In recent years there has been a sharpening awareness of these disparities and inequalities in the realm of information and communication, both on the international level—notably between industrialized and developing countries—and on the national level, between regions, collectivities and social groups.

368. As a contribution to remedying this imbalance, UNESCO has undertaken, through training and other programmes, to assist developing countries in establishing effective communication policies and infrastructures. These efforts reflect the view that communications play in integral part in development.

369. As part of this programme, UNESCO organized a series of regional intergovernmental conferences on communication policies: the Intergovernmental Conference on Communication Policies in Latin America and the Caribbean (San José, Costa Rica, 1976), the Intergovernmental Conference on Communication Policies in Asia and Oceania (Kuala Lumpur, Malaysia, 1979), the Intergovernmental Conference on Communication Policies in Africa (Yaoundé, Cameroon, 1980), and the Intergovernmental Conference on Communication Policies in the Arab States (Khartoum, Sudan, 1987).

370. A number of human rights principles are set out in the San José Declaration: the right of access to all cultural property and the right to free and democratic participation in various forms of expression; the duty to use all means of communications for peaceful purposes; the joint responsibility of the State and its citizens to set up programmes for broad and positive means of communication within the framework of development policy; and the obligation to base national communication policy on national realities, freedom of expression and respect for individual and social rights.

371. The Kuala Lumpur Declaration stressed many human rights principles: the right to acquire an objective picture of reality by means of accurate and comprehensive information through a diversity of sources; the vital importance of communication for survival, liberation and growth; the need for countries to develop comprehensive national communication policies based on a global vision of communication and of the goals of economic and social development; opportunities for increased participation of citizens in the communication process and for more freedom and autonomy for the mass media; the recognition of freedom of expression and freedom of information as prerequisites for effective communication between peoples and individuals and the belief that a new world information and communication order is an integral part of the efforts to achieve a new international economic order and a manifestation of the ideals of justice, independence and equality between individuals and nations.

372. The Yaoundé Declaration, among other things, stressed the need to develop the continent's communications within a framework of collective self-reliance so as to lessen the dependence on foreign information mechanisms. It also affirmed that communication and access to communication constituted an individual and collective right, and that every nation had the right to become the subject and originator of its own communication activities. The Declaration reaffirmed that every people had the right freely to inform and be informed; and called for international co-operation to eliminate the obstacles to the affirmation of the continent's identity. In particular it appealed to UNESCO and other agencies of the United Nations system for support in the quest for a new world information and communication order to pave the way to peace, justice and freedom.

14. DECLARATION ON FUNDAMENTAL PRINCIPLES CONCERNING THE CONTRIBUTION OF THE MASS MEDIA TO STRENGTHENING PEACE AND INTERNATIONAL UNDERSTANDING, TO THE PROMOTION OF HUMAN RIGHTS AND TO COUNTERING RACISM, *APARTHEID* AND INCITEMENT TO WAR

373. The Declaration, adopted by the General Conference of UNESCO by acclamation on 22 November 1978, endeavours to define a set of principles which all creators and distributors of information may be able to

endorse, taking into account the variety and development of communication systems, the complexity of the problems of information in modern society, the diversity of solutions which have been offered to those problems, the aspirations of the developing countries for the establishment of a new, more just and more effective world information and communication order, and the legitimate desire of all parties concerned that their aspirations, points of view and cultural identity be taken into consideration. At the same time, it seeks to underpin the efforts of United Nations bodies, particularly UNESCO, to create the conditions necessary for a freer, broader and more balanced flow of information, including assistance to journalists and news reporters in the exercise of their functions.

374. The Declaration is a singular testimony of the commitment of the mass media to promoting the values of peace and the advancement of international understanding. So far translated into 26 languages, it has also been discussed at several international meetings and many professional organizations have reaffirmed their agreement with its principles.

15. NEW WORLD INFORMATION AND COMMUNICATION ORDER

375. Bearing in mind the above-mentioned UNESCO Declaration, article 19 of the Universal Declaration of Human Rights, articles 19 and 20 of the International Covenant on Civil and Political Rights, and other decisions which it had adopted on information and mass communication, the General Assembly, in resolution 33/115 B of 18 December 1978, affirmed the need to establish a new, more just and more effective world information and communication order, intended to strengthen peace and international understanding and based on the free circulation and wider and better-balanced dissemination of information.

376. One year later, in resolution 34/182 of 18 December 1979, the Assembly affirmed its primary role in elaborating, co-ordinating and harmonizing United Nations policies and activities in the field of information towards the establishment of a new, more just and more effective world information and communication order, and recognized the central and important role of the United Nations Educational, Scientific and Cultural Organization in the field of information and mass communications and in the implementation of the relevant decisions adopted by the General Conference of that organization at its twentieth session and by the General Assembly in resolutions 33/115 A to C. The Assembly requested the Director-General of UNESCO to submit to it a progress report on the establishment of a new world information and communication order, and requested the Secretary-General to continue to take the necessary measures to ensure the close collaboration of organizations within the United Nations system in promoting United Nations policies and programmes in the field of information and mass communications

towards the establishment of a new world information and communication order.

377. The General Conference of UNESCO, at its twenty-first session (Belgrade, October-November 1980) adopted resolution 21 C/4.19 by consensus, which provided for the first time the following set of considerations upon which a new world information and communication order could be based:

(a) Elimination of the imbalances and inequalities which characterize the present situation;

(b) Elimination of the negative effects of certain monopolies, public or private, and excessive concentrations;

(c) Removal of the internal and external obstacles to a free flow and wider and better balanced dissemination of information and ideas;

(d) Plurality of sources and channels of information;

(e) Freedom of the press and information;

(f) Freedom of journalists and all professionals in the communication media, a freedom inseparable from responsibility;

(g) The capacity of developing countries to achieve improvement of their own situations, notably by providing their own equipment, by training their personnel, by improving their infrastructures and by making their information and communication media suitable to their needs and aspirations;

(h) The sincere will of developed countries to help them attain these objectives;

(i) Respect for each people's cultural identity and for the right of each nation to inform the world public about its interests, its aspirations and its social and cultural values;

(j) Respect for the right of all peoples to participate in international exchanges of information on the basis of equality, justice and mutual benefit; and

(k) Respect for the right of the public, ethnic and social groups and of individuals to have access to information sources and to participate actively in the communication process.

Resolution 21 C/4.19 also pointed out that:

(a) the new world information and communication order should be based on the fundamental principles of international law, as laid down in the Charter of the United Nations, and (b) diverse solutions to information and communication problems are required because social, political, cultural and economic problems differ from one country to another and, within a given country, from one group to another.

378. Resolution 21 C/4.20 of the UNESCO General Conference encouraged professional organizations of journalists to examine the practical application and implementation of the Declaration on Fundamental Principles concerning the Contribution of the Mass Media to Strengthening Peace and International Understanding, to the Promotion of Human Rights and to Countering Racialism, *Apartheid* and Incitement to War, mentioned in subsection 14 above. Since its adoption meetings of journalists have been held for this purpose in Latin America, the Caribbean, and Africa.

379. Resolution 21 C/4.21 of the General Conference reflected the desire of UNESCO member States for operational activities to ensure that tomorrow's means of communication did not reproduce today's inequalities; it approved the implementation of the International Programme for the Development of Communication as decided upon by the second session of the Programme's Intergovernmental Council held from 18 to 25 January 1982 at Acapulco, as well as the efforts of

UNESCO for the establishment of a new world information and communication order. Since then, the IPDC has received requests for financing amounting to $US 79,210,000. Financing has been assured through a Special Account amounting to $US 11,710,000, which covers only 14.7 per cent of expressed needs. In addition to this, IPDC has awarded 470 fellowships under its training programme.

380. UNESCO has continued in-depth studies on the notion of "the right to communicate" within the context of a new world information and communication order, as requested by the General Conference in 1978. The studies have dealt with different aspects of the notion, in particular: the democratization of communication, communication and human rights, obstacles to a free flow of information and the legal implications of an international instrument. A status report on the subject was published in 1982 in the UNESCO series "Reports and Papers on Mass Communication", followed by the Director-General's report on the right to communicate, submitted to the twenty-third session of the General Conference, in 1985. This was followed by a case-study on the Portuguese information law and its implications for the right to communicate, which is to be published in 1989.

381. With regard to the concept of a new world information and communication order, qualified as "an evolving and continuous process" since the twenty-second session of the General Conference (1983), two round-tables were held, organized jointly by the United Nations and UNESCO: the first at Igls, Austria, in September 1983, the second at Copenhagen, Denmark, in April 1986. The reports of each of the round-tables were presented to the General Assembly. In addition, UNESCO undertook to produce a chronological survey of all conclusive documents regarding a new world information and communication order adopted by international governmental and non-governmental meetings in the period from 1976 to 1986.

382. Reports of the Director-General of UNESCO on the implementation of the International Programme for the Development of Communication and the establishment of a new world information and communication order, and on the social, economic and cultural effects of the accelerated development of communication technologies, have been submitted regularly to the General Assembly since 1980. The latest report bearing this title[105] was noted by the Assembly in resolution 41/68 B of 3 December 1986. The most recent Director-General's report, submitted to the Assembly's forty-second session, bears only on the International Programme for the Development of Communication, as requested by the Assembly.

383. After taking note of the 1987 report of the Director-General of UNESCO[106] the General Assembly, in resolution 42/162 B of 8 December 1987, expressed the view that UNESCO's International Programme for

---

[105] A/41/582.
[106] A/42/571.

the Development of Communication represents a significant step towards the gradual elimination of existing imbalances in the field of information and communications, and expressed its appreciation to all Member States that had made or pledged a contribution towards the implementation of that Programme. The Assembly further reaffirmed the ongoing efforts of UNESCO, which retains the central role in the field of information, gradually to eliminate existing imbalances, particularly with respect to the development of infrastructures and production capacities, and to encourage a free flow and wider and better-balanced dissemination of information with the view to the establishment of a new world information and communication order, seen as an evolving and continuous process, in accordance with the relevant UNESCO consensus resolutions.

K. Freedom of association, including trade union rights

384. Freedom of association, including trade union rights, is unique in that it is dealt with not only in the International Covenant on Civil and Political Rights as a civil right but also in the International Covenant on Economic, Social and Cultural Rights as an economic and social right.

385. The International Labour Organisation has as one of its objectives the promotion and protection of freedom of association for occupational purposes, and it has adopted the international instruments and established the international machinery required to deal effectively with this matter. Its competence in the field, in so far as States members of ILO are concerned, has been recognized by the United Nations organs concerned; when allegations of violations of trade union rights are received by the United Nations, they are automatically transmitted to the Governing Body of ILO for consideration if they relate to a State member of ILO.

386. In the case of allegations of violations of trade union rights relating to States members of the United Nations but not of ILO, the Economic and Social Council in recent years has referred such allegations to the *Ad Hoc* Working Group of Experts on Southern Africa of the Commission on Human Rights for investigation and report. The Working Group has been given extensive authority to look into such complaints by the Council. With the consent of the Government concerned, such complaints may be referred to the ILO Fact-Finding and Conciliation Commission on Freedom of Association.

1. PROVISIONS OF UNITED NATIONS INSTRUMENTS

387. Article 20 of the Universal Declaration of Human Rights provides that:

1. Everyone has the right to freedom of peaceful assembly and association.

2. No one may be compelled to belong to an association.

Article 23 of the Declaration reads in part as follows:

...

4. Everyone has the right to form and to join trade unions for the protection of his interests.

388. Article 8 of the International Covenant on Economic, Social and Cultural Rights reads as follows:

1. The States Parties to the present Covenant undertake to ensure:

(a) The right of everyone to form trade unions and join the trade union of his choice, subject only to the rules of the organization concerned, for the promotion and protection of his economic and social interests. No restrictions may be placed on the exercise of this right other than those prescribed by law and which are necessary in a democratic society in the interests of national security or public order or for the protection of the rights and freedoms of others;

(b) The right of trade unions to establish national federations or confederations and the right of the latter to form or join international trade-union organizations;

(c) The right of trade unions to function freely subject to no limitations other than those prescribed by law and which are necessary in a democratic society in the interests of national security or public order or for the protection of the rights and freedoms of others;

(d) The right to strike, provided that it is exercised in conformity with the laws of the particular country.

2. This article shall not prevent the imposition of lawful restrictions on the exercise of these rights by members of the armed forces or of the police or of the administration of the State.

3. Nothing in this article shall authorize States Parties to the International Labour Organisation Convention of 1948 concerning Freedom of Association and Protection of the Right to Organise to take legislative measures which would prejudice, or apply the law in such a manner as would prejudice, the guarantees provided for in that Convention.

389. Article 22 of the International Covenant on Civil and Political Rights reads:

1. Everyone shall have the right to freedom of association with others, including the right to form and join trade unions for the protection of his interests.

2. No restrictions may be placed on the exercise of this right other than those which are prescribed by law and which are necessary in a democratic society in the interests of national security or public safety, public order (ordre public), the protection of public health or morals or the protection of the rights and freedoms of others. This article shall not prevent the imposition of lawful restrictions on members of the armed forces and of the police in their exercise of this right.

3. Nothing in this article shall authorize States Parties to the International Labour Organisation Convention of 1948 concerning Freedom of Association and Protection of the Right to Organise to take legislative measures which would prejudice, or to apply the law in such a manner as to prejudice, the guarantees provided for in that Convention

390. The Right to Organise and Collective Bargaining Convention, 1949 (No. 98), came into force on 18 July 1951. The Convention requires States parties to provide adequate protection for workers against acts of anti-union discrimination (article 1), and for workers' and employers' organizations against mutual acts of interference in their establishment, functioning or administration (article 2). States parties must establish appropriate machinery to ensure respect for these rights (article 3) and take measures to encourage and promote voluntary negotiation between employers or employers' organizations and workers' organizations (article 4).

391. The Workers' Representatives Convention, 1971 (No. 135), came into force on 18 July 1951. Supplementing the terms of the Right to Organise and Collective Bargaining Convention, 1949 (No. 98), the new Convention provides that "workers' representatives in

the undertaking shall enjoy effective protection against any act prejudicial to them, including dismissal, based on their status or activities as a workers' representative or on union membership or participation in union activities, in so far as they act in conformity with existing laws or collective agreements or other jointly agreed arrangements" (article 1). Workers' representatives will be afforded such facilities in the undertaking "as may be appropriate in order to enable them to carry out their functions promptly and efficiently" (article 2). For the purpose of the Convention the term "workers' representatives" means persons recognized as such under national law and practice whether they are trade union representatives or representatives freely elected by workers in the undertaking (article 3).

2. PROVISIONS OF ILO INSTRUMENTS

392. The principal instruments of the International Labour Organisation in the fields of freedom of association and trade union rights are the Freedom of Association and Protection of the Right to Organise Convention, 1948 (No. 87), the Right to Organise and Collective Bargaining Convention, 1949 (No. 98), the Workers' Representatives Convention, 1971 (No. 135), the Rural Workers' Organizations Convention, 1975 (No. 141), the Labour Relations (Public Service) Convention, 1978 (No. 151), and the Collective Bargaining Convention, 1981 (No. 154). The Freedom of Association and Protection of the Right to Organise Convention, 1948 (No. 87), came into force on 4 July 1950. The guarantees to which it requires States parties to give effect include the following: "workers and employers, without distinction whatsoever, shall have the right to establish and, subject only to the rules of the organisation concerned, to join organisations of their own choosing without previous authorisation" (article 2). "Workers' and employers' organisations shall have the right to draw up their constitutions and rules, to elect their representatives in full freedom, to organise their administration and activities and to formulate their programmes. The public authorities shall refrain from any interference which would restrict this right or impede the lawful exercise thereof" (article 3). "Workers' and employers' organisations shall not be liable to be dissolved or suspended by administrative authority" (article 4). They "shall have the right to establish and join federations and confederations" which shall "have the right to affiliate with international organisations of workers and employers" (article 5). In exercising the rights provided for in the Convention, "workers and employers and their respective organisations, like other persons or organised collectivities, shall respect the law of the land. The law of the land shall not be such as to impair, nor shall it be so applied as to impair, the guarantees provided for in this Convention" (article 8).

393. The Rural Workers' Organisations Convention, 1975 (No. 141), came into force on 24 November 1977. According to this Convention, all categories of rural

workers, whether wage-earners or self-employed, have the right to establish and, subject only to the rules of the organization concerned, to join organizations of their own choosing without previous authorization. Rural workers' organizations shall be independent and voluntary in character and shall remain free from all interference, coercion or repression. In order to enable rural workers to play their role in economic and social development, States which ratify the Convention must pursue a policy of active encouragement to rural workers' organizations, particularly with a view to eliminating obstacles to their establishment, their growth and the pursuit of their lawful activities.

394. The Labour Relations (Public Service) Convention, 1978 (No. 151) came into force on 25 February 1981. The Convention requires States parties to provide protection for public employees against acts of anti-union discrimination, and to ensure that public employees' organizations enjoy complete independence from public authorities. States parties must establish appropriate facilities for the representatives of recognized public employees' organizations in order to enable them to carry out their functions promptly and efficiently, both during and outside their hours of work. Public employees, as other workers, are to be ensured the civil and political rights which are essential for the normal exercise of freedom of association, subject only to the obligations arising from their status and the nature of their functions.

395. The Collective Bargaining Convention, 1981 (No. 154) came into force on 11 August 1983 and covers all branches of economic activity. States parties are required to take measures to promote collective bargaining (article 5) after prior consultation and, wherever possible, agreement between public authorities and employers' and workers' organizations (article 7).

3. MEASURES TAKEN BY UNITED NATIONS BODIES AND BY THE INTERNATIONAL LABOUR ORGANISATION

396. At its fourth session, in 1947, the Economic and Social Council placed on its agenda, at the request of the World Federation of Trade Unions, the item, "Guarantees for the exercise and development of trade union rights". In considering the item, the Council took into account memoranda submitted by the World Federation of Trade Unions[107] and by the American Federation of Labor.[108] In resolution 52 (IV) of 24 March 1947, the Council transmitted these documents to the International Labour Organisation and requested it to consider the question at its forthcoming session. The Council also transmitted the documents to the Commission on Human Rights in order that it might consider those aspects of the subject which might appropriately form part of the bill or declaration on human rights.

397. The question was considered at the thirtieth session of the International Labour Conference, which adopted a report describing the action which it had taken, and two resolutions. The resolutions related to freedom of association and protection of the right to organize and to bargain collectively, and international machinery for safeguarding freedom of association. The first concerned the fundamental principles on which freedom of association must be based. The second visualized the embodiment of these principles in one or several international labour conventions.

398. The Economic and Social Council, after considering the report of the Conference, decided, in resolution 84 (V) of 8 August 1947, (a) to recognize the principles proclaimed by the International Labour Conference, (b) to request ILO to continue its efforts to prepare one or several international conventions; and (c) to transmit the report to the General Assembly. The Assembly, in resolution 128 (II) of 17 November 1947, approved the Council's resolutions 52 (IV) and 84 (VI), stated its view that the inalienable right of trade union freedom of association is essential to the improvement of the standard of living of workers and to their economic well-being, and endorsed the principles proclaimed by the International Labour Conference and the principles recognized in the Constitution of the International Labour Organisation and the Declaration of Philadelphia. The Assembly recommended that ILO "pursue urgently, in collaboration with the United Nations and in conformity with the resolution of the International Labour Conference concerning international machinery for safeguarding trade union rights and freedom of association, the study of the control of their practical application". The Assembly also transmitted the report of ILO to the Commission on Human Rights.

399. As stated above, on 9 July 1948 the International Labour Conference adopted the Freedom of Association, and Protection of the Right to Organise Convention (No. 87). The Conference also adopted a resolution requesting the ILO Governing Body to enter into consultation with the competent organs of the United Nations for the purpose of examining what developments to existing international machinery were necessary to ensure the safeguarding of freedom of association.

400. The General Assembly, in resolution 279 (III) of 13 May 1949, expressed the earnest hope that Governments would take prompt action for the early ratification of the Freedom of Association and Protection of the Right to Organise Convention.

401. At its ninth session, in 1949, the Economic and Social Council considered a report prepared by the Secretary-General after consultation with the Director-General of ILO, in which he recommended the setting up of a joint United Nations/ILO commission of inquiry and conciliation;[109] and a letter from the Director-General of ILO informing the Secretary-General that the Governing Body of ILO had adopted a resolution in

---

[107] E/C.2/28.
[108] E/C.2/32.

[109] E/1405.

233

which it approved the establishment of a fact-finding and conciliation commission on freedom of association for the purpose of international supervision of that freedom.

402. The Council, in resolution 239 (IX) of 2 August 1949, noted the report of the Secretary-General and the communication from the Director-General of ILO and requested ILO to proceed, on behalf of the United Nations in accordance with its relationship agreement, as well as on its own behalf, with the establishment of the Fact-Finding and Conciliation Commission on Freedom of Association; and requested the Secretary-General and the Director-General to consult together with a view to exchanging information and formulating a procedure for making the services of the Commission available to the appropriate organs of the United Nations with respect to Members of the United Nations which were not members of the International Labour Organisation.

403. At its tenth session, in 1950, the Council laid down the basic procedure for dealing with allegations regarding infringements of trade union rights which has since been followed by the United Nations and ILO. In resolution 277 (X) of 17 February 1950, the Council decided that it would forward to the Governing Body of the International Labour Office, for its consideration as to referral to the Fact-Finding and Conciliation Commission, all allegations regarding infringements of trade union rights received from Governments or trade union or employers' organizations against States members of ILO; and invited ILO to refer, in the first instance, to the Council any allegations regarding infringements of trade union rights against a Member of the United Nations which was not a member of ILO. At the same time the Council requested the Secretary-General to bring allegations regarding infringements of trade union rights received from Governments or trade union or employers' organizations to the attention of the Council, and recommended that the General Assembly should also refer such allegations to the Council for action in accordance with the procedures which it had established.

404. In 1951, the Governing Body of the International Labour Office decided to establish a Governing Body Committee on Freedom of Association for the preliminary examination of allegations concerning violations of trade union rights received from Governments, trade union or employers' organizations and to consider the appropriateness of referral of particular cases to the Fact-Finding and Conciliation Commission.[110]

405. The Economic and Social Council, in resolution 474 (XV) of 9 April 1953, requested the Secretary-General to forward to the Governing Body of ILO all such allegations, directed against members of ILO, in the future.

406. Since its establishment, the Governing Body Committee on Freedom of Association has examined more than 1,100 cases. In the course of this work, it has established an important body of principles on the manner in which international standards concerning trade union rights should be applied in specific situations.[111] In the early 1980s the number of new complaints received each year by the Committee increased dramatically, but it has since levelled off. At any given time the Committee has about 60 cases pending, and cases have been presented over the years against the majority of member States of the ILO. The complexity of the cases has also increased, from both a legal and a political point of view; one recent survey, for example, found that for the eight-year period 1974-1982 almost one half of the cases involved alleged violations of the civil liberties of trade unionists, including deaths, disappearances, arrests and cases of forced exile.

407. A few cases have been referred to the Fact-Finding and Conciliation Commission on Freedom of Association. They have concerned trade union rights of persons employed in the public sector in Japan (report issued in 1965), Greece (1966), Chile (1975), Lesotho (1975), and the United States of America (Puerto Rico) (1981).

4. ALLEGATIONS CONCERNING INFRINGEMENTS OF TRADE UNION RIGHTS IN SOUTHERN AFRICA

408. The question of what action to take in regard to allegations concerning infringements of trade union rights in States not members of ILO assumed great practical importance when South Africa ceased to be a member of that specialized agency. The solution adopted by the Economic and Social Council, in resolutions 1216 (XLII) of 1 June 1967 and 1302 (XLIV) of 28 May 1968, was to authorize the *Ad Hoc* Working Group of Experts established by the Commission on Human Rights under resolution 2 (XXIII) to deal also with allegations concerning the infringement of trade union rights in South Africa, Namibia, and Southern Rhodesia. In resolution 1302 (XLIV), the Council requested the *Ad Hoc* Working Group to report to the Council on its findings and to submit its recommendations for any action to be taken in specific cases.

409. At its forty-sixth session, in 1969, the Economic and Social Council received the report prepared by the *Ad Hoc* Working Group of Experts in accordance with Council resolution 1302 (XLIV).[112] The report analysed the evidence which the *Ad Hoc* Working Group had received concerning trade union rights and related matters in the Republic of South Africa, Namibia and Southern Rhodesia, and contained the conclusions and recommendations of the Working Group.

410. In resolution 1412 (XLVI) of 6 June 1969, the Council noted with appreciation the report of the *ad Hoc* Working Group and a report prepared by the

---

[110] For information on the special procedure of the ILO relating to freedom of association, see chap. XIV, section D (1) (h).

[111] See *Freedom of Association: Digest of Decisions of the Freedom of Association Committee of the Governing Body of the ILO.* Third edition, ILO, 1985.

[112] E/4646.

Committee on Freedom of Association of the International Labour Organisation.[113] The Council called upon the Government of the Republic of South Africa to conform to the generally accepted international standards pertaining to the right to freedom of association, and in particular to permit trade unionists of all races, and regardless of whether they belonged to registered or non-registered organizations in South Africa, to benefit from the facilities offered by the major international trade unions regarding educational and other assistance in the trade union field.

411. The Economic and Social Council has since transmitted to the *Ad Hoc* Working Group of Experts a number of allegations regarding infringements of trade union rights in South Africa, and has requested it to continue to study such infringements. The mandate of the *Ad Hoc* Working Group has been regularly renewed and broadened by the Commission on Human Rights and the Council. In 1983, allegations of infringements of trade union rights, addressed recpectively by the International Confederation of Free Trade Unions and the World Federation of Trade Unions to the Director-General of the ILO, were referred to the Council in accordance with resolution 277 (X).

412. The Council, on the recommendation of the Commission, has noted and endorsed the conclusions and recommendations formulated by the *Ad Hoc* Working Group in a number of resolutions, in which it has expressed the view that the repressive legislation adopted in South Africa and the practices pursued in accordance with that legislation were in flagrant contradiction with the international standards governing trade union rights, and that South Africa had consistently and deliberately violated trade union freedoms; condemned the continued infringement of trade union rights and, in particular, the repression of African workers and their trade unions in South Africa and Namibia; called for the immediate repeal of banning orders issued against African and other trade unionists and an end to the use of torture and cruel and inhuman treatment of those detained for their political and trade union activities; demanded the immediate and complete abolition of all restrictions on the trade union rights of African workers, including migrant workers, and the immediate and unconditional recognition of all existing African trade unions; demanded the cessation of all government and police interference in labour disputes; and called for the immediate release of all imprisoned trade unionists and the lifting of the ban on fund-raising drives by the Federation of South African Trade Unions.

413. In resolution 1982/40, and again in resolution 1985/43, the Council requested the *Ad Hoc* Working Group to continue to study the situation of trade union rights in South Africa and to report thereon to the Commission and to the Council. The Working Group has since included such information in its reports. In its progress report submitted to the Commission in 1986,[114] for example, it included information on the conditions of black workers, the treatment of workers on trial, the incidence and results of strikes, the activities of the industrial courts and the results of consumer boycotts initiated by trade unions.

414. The Secretary-General was informed in November 1971 that the Governing Body of the ILO had decided, on recommendation of its Committee on Freedom of Association, to refer to the Economic and Social Council for consideration, in accordance with Council resolution 277 (X) of 17 February 1950, certain allegations regarding infringements of trade union rights in Lesotho. Subsequently, the ILO transmitted to the Secretary-General a communication from the Government of Lesotho containing its comments on the allegations. As the allegations were against a State Member of the United Nations which was not a member of ILO, the Secretary-General requested the consent of the Government of Lesotho to have them referred to the Fact-Finding and Conciliation Commission on Freedom of Association of ILO. Once the Government had informed the Secretary-General that it had no objection to having the complaint so referred, this was done and the Commission's report on the question[115] was examined by the Council in 1976.

5. ALLEGATIONS CONCERNING INFRINGEMENTS OF TRADE UNION RIGHTS IN OTHER STATES NOT MEMBERS OF ILO

415. The Secretary-General was informed in November 1971 that the Governing Body of the ILO had decided, on recommendation of its Committee on Freedom of Association, to refer to the Economic and Social Council for consideration, in accordance with Council resolution 277 (X) of 17 February 1950, certain allegations regarding infringements of trade union rights in Lesotho. Subsequently, the ILO transmitted to the Secretary-General a communication from the Government of Lesotho containing its comments on the allegations. As the allegations were against a State Member of the United Nations which was not a member of ILO, the Secretary-General requested the consent of the Government of Lesotho to have them referred to the Fact-Finding and Conciliation Commission of Freedom of Association of ILO. Once the Government had informed the Secretary-General that it had no objection to having the complaint so referred, this was done and the Commission's report on the question[115] was examined by the Council in 1976.

416. In resolution 1996 (LX) of 12 May 1976, the Council requested the Government of Lesotho to inform the Secretary-General of any steps taken to implement the recommendations contained in the Conciliation Commission's report; and requested the Secretary-General to transmit any communications received from

[113] E/4610, annex.

[114] E/CN.4/1986/9, chap. IV.

[115] ILO document GB.197/3/5.

that Government on the matter to the Director-General of ILO for the information of the Governing Body of ILO.

417. At its sixtieth session, in 1976, the Economic and Social Council also considered, under a procedure governed by resolution 277 (X), allegations of infringements of trade union rights in the Bahamas,[116] submitted by the trade unions in that country; and a reply from the Government concerned, which rejected the allegations.[117] In decision 150 (LX) of 12 May 1976, the Council decided to defer consideration of the subject and requested the Secretary-General to ascertain from the complainant unions whether they would clarify the nature of their allegations, as had been requested by the Government of the Bahamas, or preferred to withdraw their complaint.

418. At its sixty-second session, in 1977, the Council, having received clarifications of the allegations from the complainant unions pursuant to decision 150 (LX),[118] (a) noted, in decision 235 (LXII) of 13 May 1977, that the Bahamas had become a member of the International Labour Organisation on 25 May 1976, and (b) decided to request the Secretary-General to transmit, on its behalf, the documentary material which had been before the Council to ILO for appropriate action.

419. With regard to allegations regarding infringements of trade union rights in Bahrain, the Council, in decision 238 (LXII) of 13 May 1977, (a) noted that Bahrain had become a member of the International Labour Organisation on 18 April 1977, and (b) took note of the communication from the World Federation of Trade Unions[119] as well as of the reply of the Government of Bahrain.[120]

420. On 18 November 1977, the World Federation of Trade Unions addressed a complaint to the Director-General of ILO alleging infringement of trade union rights in Puerto Rico, a Territory under United States administration. The United States had withdrawn from membership of ILO with effect from 5 November 1977. At its 205th session (February-March 1978), the Governing Body of ILO decided to refer the complaint to the Economic and Social Council, in accordance with Council resolution 277 (X). Following a communication from the Government of the United States consenting to referral of the complaint to the Fact-Finding and Conciliation Commission, the Council decided on 21 July 1978 to transmit the case to the Commission. The United States rejoined ILO on 13 February 1980. The Commission's report was issued in September 1981.

---

[116] E/5645.
[117] E/5765.
[118] E/5928.
[119] E/5932.
[120] E/5932/Add.1.

6. PROTECTION OF THE HUMAN RIGHTS OF ARRESTED OR DETAINED TRADE UNION ACTIVISTS

421. In resolution 32/121 of 16 December 1977 the General Assembly adopted measures for the protection of the human rights of persons who "are detained in respect of offences which they committed, or are suspected of having committed, by reason of their political opinions or convictions". One year later, in resolution 33/160 of 20 December 1978, the Assembly noted that one important category of prisoners falling within the ambit of resolution 32/121 were those arrested or detained in connection with their trade union activities. Citing the provisions of articles 5, 10, 19 and 20 of the Universal Declaration of Human Rights, article 8 of the International Covenant on Economic, Social and Cultural Rights and article 22 of the International Covenant on Civil and Political Rights, the Assembly reaffirmed the importance of protecting the right to freedom of association as an essential prerequisite for the conduct of trade union activities and recommended that special attention should be paid to such violations of the right to freedom of association as the arrest, detention or exile of persons who had engaged in trade union activities consistent with the principles of freedom of association. The Assembly requested Member States:

(a) To release any persons who, within their jurisdiction and contrary to the provisions of the above-mentioned international instruments, may be under arrest or detention on account of trade union activities;

(b) To ensure that, pending the release of such persons, their fundamental rights are fully protected, including the right not to be subjected to torture or other cruel, inhuman or degrading treatment or punishment and the right to receive a fair hearing by a competent, independent and impartial tribunal in the determination of any criminal charge against them;

(c) To take effective measures to safeguard and protect the human rights and fundamental freedoms of trade union leaders who are detained or imprisoned as a result of their struggle against colonialism, aggression and foreign occupation and for self-determination, independence, the elimination of *apartheid* and all forms of racial discrimination and racism, and for the termination of all these violations of human rights.

7. FREEDOM OF ASSOCIATION FOR JUDGES AND LAWYERS

422. On 11 September 1980 the Sub-Commission on Prevention of Discrimination and Protection of Minorities discussed freedom of association as a matter of particular importance in the cases of judges and lawyers. In resolution 13 (XXXIII) of 11 September 1980, the Sub-Commission, mindful of the essential role played by judges and lawyers in the protection and promotion of human rights, and considering that associations of judges and lawyers reinforced their individual professional competence and independence and thus aided them in fulfilling that role, called upon all States fully to respect and guarantee the right of all judges and lawyers freely and without interference to form or participate in professional organizations of their own.

L. The right of everyone to take part in the government of his country

423. The political rights set out in article 21 of the Universal Declaration of Human Rights differ from other rights set out in the Declaration in that they may be enjoyed by the individual only in "his country"—i.e., the country of which he is a national or citizen. Article 25 of the International Covenant on Civil and Political Rights makes the corresponding legal obligation more precise by its use of the opening words, "every citizen . . .".

424. The Sub-Commission on Prevention of Discrimination and Protection of Minorities has completed a *Study of Discrimination in the Matter of Political Rights*[121] and has prepared draft general principles on freedom and non-discrimination in the matter of political rights which have been forwarded to the Governments and organizations concerned. The Sub-Commission has also completed a study entitled *Racial Discrimination*[122] which deals among other things with racial discrimination in the political sphere.

425. Other competent bodies of the United Nations system have taken action to promote the enjoyment of political rights, particularly by women (see chapter VI above) and by the peoples of dependent Territories and developing countries.

1. PROVISIONS OF UNITED NATIONS INSTRUMENTS

426. Article 21 of the Universal Declaration of Human Rights provides that:

1. Everyone has the right to take part in the government of his country, directly or through freely chosen representatives.

2. Everyone has the right of equal access to public service in his country.

3. The will of the people shall be the basis of the authority of government; this will shall be expressed in periodic and genuine elections which shall be by universal and equal suffrage and shall be held by secret vote or by equivalent free voting procedures.

427. Article 25 of the International Covenant on Civil and Political Rights reads as follows:

Every citizen shall have the right and the opportunity, without any of the distinctions mentioned in article 2 and without unreasonable restrictions:

(a) To take part in the conduct of public affairs, directly or through freely chosen representatives;

(b) To vote and to be elected at genuine periodic elections which shall be by universal and equal suffrage and shall be held by secret ballot, guaranteeing the free expression of the will of the electors;

(c) To have access, on general terms of equality, to public service in his country.

428. The United Nations Declaration on the Elimination of All Forms of Racial Discrimination provides, in article 6, that:

No discrimination by reason of race, colour or ethnic origin shall be admitted in the enjoyment by any person of political and citizenship rights in his country, in particular the right to participate in elections through universal and equal suffrage and to take part in the government. Everyone has the right of equal access to public service in his country.

429. By article 5 of the International Convention on the Elimination of All Forms of Racial Discrimination States parties undertake "to guarantee the right of everyone, without distinction as to race, colour, or national or ethnic origin, to equality before the law", notably in the enjoyment of a series of rights including:

(c) Political rights, in particular the right to participate in election—to vote and to stand for election—on the basis of universal and equal suffrage, to take part in the Government as well as in the conduct of public affairs at any level and to have equal access to public service.

430. The Convention on the Political Rights of Women contains the following articles designed to equalize the status of men and women in the enjoyment and exercise of political rights:

Article I

Women shall be entitled to vote in all elections on equal terms with men, without any discrimination.

Article II

Women shall be eligible for election to all publicly elected bodies, established by national law, on equal terms with men, without any discrimination.

Article III

Women shall be entitled to hold public office and to exercise all public functions, established by national law, on equal terms with men, without any discrimination.

431. Part II of the Convention on the Elimination of All Forms of Discrimination against Women contains the following articles relating to political rights:

Article 7

States Parties shall take all appropriate measures to eliminate discrimination against women in the political and public life of the country and, in particular, shall ensure to women, on equal terms with men, the right:

(a) To vote in all elections and public referenda and to be eligible for election to all publicly elected bodies;

(b) To participate in the formulation of government policy and the implementation thereof and to hold public office and perform all public functions at all levels of government;

(c) To participate in non-governmental organizations and associations concerned with the public and political life of the country.

Article 8

States Parties shall take all appropriate measures to ensure to women, on equal terms with men and without any discrimination, the opportunity to represent their Governments at the international level and to participate in the work of international organizations.

2. STUDY OF DISCRIMINATION IN THE MATTER OF POLITICAL RIGHTS

432. A study of discrimination in the matter of political rights was suggested to the Sub-Commission on Prevention of Discrimination and Protection of Minorities at its fifth session, in 1952, and was included by the Sub-Commission in its list of projected studies. The list

---

[121] United Nations publication, Sales No. E.63.XIV.2.

[122] United Nations publication, Sales No. E.76.XIV.2.

was subsequently approved, with slight modifications, by the Commission on Human Rights and the Economic and Social Council.

433. At its sixth session, in 1956, the Sub-Commission decided to proceed with the study, and appointed one of its members, Mr. Hernán Santa Cruz, as Special Rapporteur. The study was completed in 1962, and was considered by the Sub-Commission at its fourteenth session.

434. On the basis of draft principles formulated by the Special Rapporteur, the Sub-Commission prepared a series of general principles on freedom and non-discrimination in the matter of political rights. In resolution 1 (XIV), the Sub-Commission transmitted to the Commission on Human Rights the *Study of Discrimination in the Matter of Political Rights*,[123] the records of its consideration of the study and the draft principles, and the general principles which it had prepared, "in the belief that the formulation of international and regional instruments based upon these principles and their adoption by States Members of the United Nations would be a fitting culmination to the study".

435. The draft general principles on freedom and non-discrimination in the matter of political rights formulated by the Sub-Commission include the following:[124]

Every national of a country is entitled within that country to full and equal political rights without distinction of any kind, such as race, colour, sex, language, religion, political or other opinion, national or social origin, property, birth or other status;

No one shall be denied nationality, or deprived of nationality, as a means of denying him or depriving him of political rights;

The age, length of residence and other conditions prescribed by law for the exercise of any particular political right shall be the same for all nationals of a country or inhabitants of a political unit, as the case may be;

Every national is entitled to vote in any national election, referendum or plebiscite held in his country, and in any such public consultation held in the political or administrative unit thereof in which he resides;

The right to vote shall not be dependent upon literacy or any other educational qualifications;

Every national is entitled to vote in any election, or other public consultation for which he is eligible, on equal terms, and each vote shall have the same weight;

Every voter shall be able to vote in such a manner as not to involve disclosure of how he has voted or intends to vote;

Every national shall be eligible on equal terms for election to any elective public office in his country or in any political or administrative unit thereof in which he resides;

Every national shall be eligible on equal terms to hold any non-elective public office in his country, or any political or administrative unit thereof in which he resides.

436. In the general principles, reference is made to the right of all peoples to self-determination, by virtue of which they freely determine their political status and freely pursue their economic, social and cultural development; and to freedom of opinion and expression and freedom of peaceful assembly and association, which are essential to the enjoyment of political rights.

Reference is also made to the question of ensuring the periodicity and the genuine character of elections. A few measures which, if prescribed by law, should not be considered discriminatory, are listed; these include reasonable requirements for the exercise of the right to vote or the right of access to public office, reasonable qualifications for appointment to public office which stem from the nature of the duties of the office, measures which establish a reasonable period which must elapse before naturalized persons may exercise their political rights, and special measures taken to ensure the adequate representation of an element of the population of a country whose members are in fact prevented by political, economic, religious, social, historical or cultural conditions from enjoying equality with the rest of the population in the matter of political rights.

437. The Special Rapporteur introduced his study at the eighteenth session of the Commission on Human Rights, in 1962. However, it was not until the twenty-ninth session of the Commission, in 1973, that it was able to consider the study and take action on it. At that session the Commission also had before it a note by the Secretary-General containing a comparative chart of the provisions of the general principles and the related provisions of the International Covenant on Civil and Political Rights,[125] and information from Governments concerning new developments in the matter of political rights.[126]

438. The Commission, in resolution 6 (XXIX) of 20 March 1973, recommended to the Economic and Social Council a draft resolution which the Council subsequently adopted as resolution 1786 (LIV) of 18 May 1973. In that resolution the Council expressed its warm appreciation to the Special Rapporteur and to the Sub-Commission, drew the attention of Governments, international and regional intergovernmental organizations, non-governmental organizations and other institutions and bodies concerned to the draft general principles on freedom and non-discrimination in the matter of political rights and expressed the hope that they would take them into account, together with the relevant provisions of the International Covenant on Civil and Political Rights, when considering the question of discrimination in the matter of political rights.

M. Machinery to monitor the implementation of civil and political rights

HUMAN RIGHTS COMMITTEE

439. Special bodies have been set up by the United Nations to monitor the implementation of civil and political rights: the Human Rights Committee, estab-

---

[123] United Nations publication, Sales No. E.63.XIV.2.

[124] For the full text of the draft principles, see ST/HR/3, pp. 1-5.

[125] E/CN.4/1013.

[126] E/CN.4/1013/Add.1-5.

lished in 1977 in accordance with article 28 of the International Covenant on Civil and Political Rights and the Committee against Torture, established in 1987 in accordance with article 17 of the Convention against Torture and Other Cruel, Inhuman or Degrading Treatment or Punishment.

440. Article 28 of the International Covenant on Civil and Political Rights provides that:

1. There shall be established a Human Rights Committee (hereafter referred to in the present Covenant as the Committee). It shall consist of eighteen members and shall carry out the functions hereinafter provided.

2. The Committee shall be composed of nationals of the States Parties to the present Covenant who shall be persons of high moral character and recognized competence in the field of human rights, consideration being given to the usefulness of the participation of some persons having legal experience.

3. The members of the Committee shall be elected and shall serve in their personal capacity.

441. The Human Rights Committee accordingly consists of 18 members of high moral character and recognized competence in the field of human rights, elected for four-year terms by secret ballot at meetings of the States parties to the Covenant, and serve in their personal capacity. The Committee's initial membership was elected from a list of persons nominated by the States parties at a meeting of States parties held at United Nations Headquarters on 20 September 1976. The Committee held its first session from 21 March to 1 April 1977 and has held a total of 31 sessions through 31 December 1987.

(a) *Functions of the Committee*

442. The tasks of the Committee, as set out in articles 40 to 45 of the Covenant, are: to study reports on the measures States parties have adopted to give effect to the rights recognized in the Covenant, and on the progress made in the enjoyment of those rights and to formulate and transmit to the States parties such general comments as it may consider appropriate. Under article 41 of the Covenant, a State party may at any time declare that it recognizes the competence of the Committee to receive and consider communications to the effect that a State party claims that another State party is not fulfilling its obligations under the Covenant. Should such a communication be received and provided that both parties have recognized the Committee's competence, the Committee can perform certain functions with a view to settling disputes and when necessary establish an *ad hoc* conciliation commission to make available its good offices to States parties involved in a dispute concerning the application of the Covenant, with a view to a friendly solution of the matter on the basis of respect for the Covenant. Such a commission must submit a report to the Committee Chairman, not later than 12 months after having been seized of the matter, for communication to the States parties concerned.

443. Under the Optional Protocol to the International Covenant on Civil and Political Rights, individuals who claim that any of their rights enumerated in the Covenant have been violated and who have exhausted all available domestic remedies may submit written communications to the Human Rights Committee for consideration. No communication can be received by the Committee if it concerns a State party to the Covenant which is not also a party to the Optional Protocol. The Committee considers communications in the light of all written information made available to it by the individual and by the State party concerned, and forwards its views to the State party concerned and to the individual.

444. States parties to the International Covenant on Civil and Political Rights are invited to send representatives to be present at the meetings of the Human Rights Committee when their reports are examined. Such representatives should be able to answer questions put by the Committee. The Committee may also request States parties to submit additional information.

445. The Committee normally holds three sessions each year, and reports annually to the General Assembly, through the Economic and Social Council.

446. At each session, the Committee examines reports from States parties to the Covenant on the measures taken by them to give effect to the rights recognized in the Covenant, on the progress made in the enjoyment of those rights and on any factors and difficulties affecting the implementation of the Covenant. It considers the reports in public meetings in the presence of representatives of the reporting States. A summary of the consideration of each State report is included in the Committee's annual report.

447. In accordance with article 40, paragraph 4 of the Covenant and on the basis of its consideration of State party reports, the Committee also elaborates general comments relating to various articles of the Covenant and their implementation.

448. The Committee also considers communications received under the Optional Protocol, with the assistance of a working group established at every session on communications, consisting of not more than five of its members. All documents pertaining to the Committee's work under the Protocol are confidential, and they are examined in closed meetings. The texts of final decisions of the Committee, however, are made public. The Committee includes a summary of its activities under the Protocol in its annual report.

449. The Committee also regularly establishes a working group to assist it in the drafting of lists of issues in connection with the consideration of periodic States' reports and in the preparation of general comments. This working group is made up of not more than five members of the Committee.

450. By the end of 1987, there were 87 States parties to the International Covenant on Civil and Political Rights, 40 of which had also ratified or acceded to the Optional Protocol, and 21 States had made the declara-

tion under article 41 of the Covenant recognizing the competence of the Human Rights Committee to consider communications relating to inter-State disputes.

(b) *Activities of the Committee*

451. Article 40 of the International Covenant on Civil and Political Rights provides that:

1. The States Parties to the present Covenant undertake to submit reports on the measures they have adopted which give effect to the rights recognized herein and on the progress made in the enjoyment of those rights:

(a) Within one year of the entry into force of the present Covenant for the States Parties concerned;

(b) Thereafter whenever the Committee so requests.

2. All reports shall be submitted to the Secretary-General of the United Nations, who shall transmit them to the Committee for consideration. Reports shall indicate the factors and difficulties, if any, affecting the implementation of the present Covenant.

3. The Secretary-General of the United Nations may, after consultation with the Committee, transmit to the specialized agencies concerned copies of such parts of the reports as may fall within their field of competence.

4. The Committee shall study the reports submitted by the States Parties to the present Covenant. It shall transmit its reports, and such general comments as it may consider appropriate, to the States Parties. The Committee may also transmit to the Economic and Social Council these comments along with the copies of the reports it has received from States Parties to the present Covenant.

5. The States Parties to the present Covenant may submit to the Committee observations on any comments that may be made in accordance with paragraph 4 of this article.

452. In order to assist States parties in submitting initial reports as required under paragraph 1 (a), the Human Rights Committee, at its second session, approved general guidelines regarding the form and contents of those reports.[127] Later, at its thirteenth session, it adopted a decision calling upon States to submit subsequent reports, as required under paragraph 1 (b), every five years[128] and also approved appropriate general guidelines for the preparation of such periodic reports.[129] At each session, the Committee is informed of, and considers, the status of submission of reports.

453. The Committee follows two distinct procedures in considering initial reports and periodic reports. In the case of initial reports, members of the Committee pose a series of questions concerning the implementation of most or all of the articles of the Covenant. Once all the questions have been raised, the representative of the State party responds *en bloc* to the questions that had been raised.

454. In considering periodic reports, the Committee entrusts a working group with responsibility for reviewing the reports and other relevant information in order to identify the matters requiring discussion with the State party representatives of the reporting State. The

working group prepares a list of issues to be taken up with State party representatives during the report's consideration and such lists when approved by the Committee are transmitted to the representatives of the States parties concerned prior to their appearance before the Committee together with the appropriate explanations on the procedure to be followed. The lists of issues are not exhaustive, and members of the Committee are free to raise other matters or to request additional information. The various issues are discussed, one by one, with the State party's representatives providing immediate responses to members' questions in a process of dialogue.

455. In addition to its systematic review of reports received from States parties to the Covenant, the Human Rights Committee deals with written communications received from individuals who claim that any of their rights enumerated in the Covenant have been violated and who indicate that they have exhausted all available domestic remedies. Of the 87 States that had ratified or acceded to the Covenant as at 31 December 1987, 40 accepted the competence of the Committee to deal with individual complaints by ratifying or acceding to the Optional Protocol to the Covenant.

456. Since the Committee started its work under the Optional Protocol at its second session in 1977, 260 communications concerning 24 States were placed before it for consideration. As at 31 December 1987 the status of those communications was as follows;

(a) Concluded by views under article 5, paragraph 4, of the Optional Protocol which provides that after examining communications "The Committee shall forward its views to the State Party concerned and to the individual": 81;

(b) Concluded in another manner (inadmissible, discontinued, suspended or withdrawn): 113;

(c) Declared admissible, but not yet concluded: 16; and

(d) Pending at the pre-admissibility stage: 50.

457. A volume containing selected decisions under the Optional Protocol, from the second to the sixteenth session (July 1982) was published in 1985.[130] The Committee's annual reports for 1984, 1985, 1986 and 1987[131] contain a summary of the procedural and substantive issues considered by the Committee and of the decisions taken. In addition, the *Official Records of the Human Rights Committee* are published in two volumes, with volume 1 containing the Committee's summary records of its meetings and volume 2 the documents of the various sessions. The *Yearbook of the Human Rights Committee 1977-1978*,[132] covering the Committee's first to fifth sessions, was published in 1987.

---

127 See *Official Records of the General Assembly, Thirty-second Session, Supplement No. 44* (A/32/44 and Corr.1), annex IV.

128 *Ibid., Thirty-sixth session, Supplement No. 40* (A/36/40), annex V.

129 *Ibid.*, annex VI.

130 United Nations publication, Sales No. E.84.XIV.2.

131 See *Official Records of the General Assembly, Thirty-ninth session, Supplement No. 40* (A/39/40); ibid., *Fortieth session, Supplement No. 40* (A/40/40), ibid., *Forty-first session, Supplement No. 40* (A/41/40), and ibid., *Forty-second session, Supplement No. 40* (A/42/40).

132 United Nations publication, Sales No. E.85.XIV.5 (vol.1) and E.85.XIV.10 (vol.2).

458. In the 10 years that have passed since the Committee was established, its efforts to fulfil its obligations under the International Covenant on Civil and Political Rights have consistently met with the approval of the General Assembly and other organs of the United Nations concerned with human rights. The Committee has also enjoyed the general support of States parties to the Covenant.

459. At its forty-second session, in 1987, the General Assembly considered and noted with appreciation the annual report of the Human Rights Committee on the work of its twenty-ninth and thirtieth sessions, held at Geneva from 23 March to 10 April and from 6 to 24 July 1987 respectively.[133] In resolution 42/103 of 7 December 1987 the Assembly expressed its satisfaction with the serious and constructive manner in which the Committee is continuing to undertake its functions; expressed its appreciation to the States parties to the International Covenant on Civil and Political Rights that submitted their reports to the Committee and urged States parties that had not done so to submit their reports as speedily as possible; and urged the States parties that had been requested by the Committee to provide additional information to comply with that request. It noted with satisfaction that the majority of States parties to the Covenant had been represented by experts for the presentation of their reports, and expressed the hope that all States parties would arrange such representation in the future.

460. The Assembly, further, stressed the importance of avoiding the erosion of human rights by derogation, and underlined the necessity of strict observance of the agreed conditions and procedures for derogation under article 4 of the International Covenant on Civil and Political Rights, bearing in mind the need for States parties to provide the fullest possible information during states of emergency, so that the justification and appropriateness of measures taken in these circumstances can be assessed.

(c) *Problems faced by the Committee*

461. In its report to the forty-second session of the General Assembly, the Committee referred to its problem of overdue reports, which has been a matter of growing concern for some years, and proposed a number of possible remedies. It noted in particular that less than one half of the initial reports due for submission during a recent five-year period (7 out of 18), and only about 30 per cent of the second periodic reports that had become due (22 out of 58), had been received. The Committee emphasized that the submission of such reports was an international legal obligation under article 40, paragraph 1 (*a*), of the International Covenant on Civil and Political Rights. It noted, however, that the problem of overdue reports was not confined to the Committee but also affected other human rights supervisory bodies, and that the General Assembly had been discussing the matter since 1984. As an interim measure the Chairman of the Committee sent special letters to States parties whose initial reports were overdue for more than a year, and whose second reports were overdue since 1983.

462. In 1986, because of the financial crisis of the United Nations, the Committee was able to hold only two, instead of the customary three, sessions; and both were convened at Geneva. Only one, instead of the customary two pre-sessional working groups was established at each session. However, in view of the cancellation of the Committee's fall session and the need to deal on an urgent basis with certain communications received under the Optional Protocol, a special three-member working group met at Geneva from 8 to 10 December 1986.

---

[133] *Official Records of the General Assembly, Forty-second Session, Supplement No. 40* (A/42/40).

IX. PROTECTION OF AND ASSISTANCE TO VULNERABLE GROUPS OF PERSONS

Introduction

1. Some groups of persons are known to be particularly vulnerable to violations of their human rights and fundamental freedoms, among them children, persons belonging to ethnic, religious or linguistic minorities, the aging, members of indigenous populations, aliens, migrant workers and disabled persons.

2. Competent organs and agencies within the United Nations sytem have from time to time adopted special measures of protection and assistance to benefit members of such disadvantaged groups of persons. Such special measures, when necessary to ensure equality in the realization of the human rights and fundamental freedoms of those groups or of their individual members, are not considered to be discriminatory as long as they do not lead to the maintenance of separate rights for different groups or individuals and are not continued once the objectives for which they were taken have been achieved.

3. A few examples of such special measures are set out below.

A. The rights of the child

4. The concern of the United Nations with the rights of the child dates back to 1946, when the Temporary Social Commission of the Economic and Social Council stated that the terms of the Declaration of Geneva, adopted by the Assembly of the League of Nations, should be as binding on the peoples of the world of that time as they had been in 1924. Subsequently the Social Commission in 1950 adopted a draft Declaration on the Rights of the Child and transmitted it to the Economic and Social Council with the recommendation that the Commission on Human Rights be requested to inform the Council of its observations on the draft with a view to its approval by the General Assembly.

5. The Economic and Social Council, in resolution 309 C (XI) of 13 July 1950, noted the close relationship between the draft Declaration and the Universal Declaration of Human Rights and requested the Commission on Human Rights to submit its observations on the principle and contents of the draft Declaration. The Commission discussed the question at its thirteenth and fifteenth session, in 1957 and 1959, and transmitted its observations to the Council in the form of a revised draft Declaration. The Council forwarded the revised draft, and other relevant documentation, to the General Assembly.

1. DECLARATION OF THE RIGHTS OF THE CHILD

6. In resolution 1386 (XIV) of 20 November 1959,the General Assembly proclaimed the Declaration of the Rights of the Child "to the end that he may have a happy childhood and enjoy for his own good and for the good of society the rights and freedoms herein set forth". The Assembly called upon "parents, upon men and women as individuals, and upon voluntary organizations, local authorities and national Governments" to recognize the rights set out in the Declaration and to strive for their observance by legislative and other measures.

7. The Declaration presents, in a series of principles, a code for the well-being of every child "without any exception whatsoever" and "without distinction or discrimination on account of race, colour, sex, language, religion, political or other opinion, national or social origin, property, birth or other status, whether of himself or of his family". Among the principles proclaimed are the following:

Principle 2

The child shall enjoy special protection, and shall be given opportunities and facilities, by law and by other means, to enable him to develop physically, mentally, morally, spiritually and socially in a healthy and normal manner and in conditions of freedom and dignity. In the enactment of laws for this purpose, the best interests of the child shall be the paramount considerations.

Principle 3

The child shall be entitled from his birth to a name and a nationality.

Principle 4

The child shall enjoy the benefits of social security. He shall be entitled to grow and develop in health; to this end, special care and protection shall be provided both to him and to his mother, including adequate pre-natal and post-natal care. The child shall have the right to adequate nutrition, housing, recreation and medical services.

Principle 5

The child who is physically, mentally or socially handicapped shall be given the special treatment, education and care required by his particular condition.

Principle 6

The child, for the full and harmonious development of his personality, needs love and understanding. He shall, wherever possible, grow up in the care and under the responsibility of his parents, and, in any case, in an atmosphere of affection and of moral and material security; a child of tender years shall not, save in exceptional circumstances, be separated from his mother. Society and the public authorities shall have the duty to extend particular care to children without a family and to those without adequate means of support. Payment of State and other assistance towards the maintenance of children of large families is desirable.

Principle 7

The child is entitled to receive education, which shall be free and compulsory, at least in the elementary stages. He shall be given an education which will promote his general culture, and enable him, on a basis of equal opportunity, to develop his abilities, his individual judgement, and his sense of moral and social responsibility, and to become a useful member of society.

The best interest of the child shall be the guiding principle of those responsible for his education and guidance; that responsibility lies in the first place with his parents.

The child shall have full opportunity for play and recreation, which should be directed to the same purposes as education; society and the public authorities shall endeavour to promote the enjoyment of this right.

Principle 8

The child shall in all circumstances be among the first to receive protection and relief.

Principle 9

The child shall be protected against all forms of neglect, cruelty and exploitation. He shall not be the subject of traffic, in any form.

The child shall not be admitted to employment before an appropriate minimum age; he shall in no case be caused or permitted to engage in any occupation or employment which would prejudice his health or education, or interfere with his physical, mental or moral development.

Principle 10

The child shall be protected from practices which may foster racial, religious and any other form of discrimination. He shall be brought up in a spirit of understanding, tolerance, friendship among peoples, peace and universal brotherhood, and in full consciousness that his energy and talents should be devoted to the service of his fellow men.

2. UNITED NATIONS CHILDREN'S FUND

8. The United Nations International Children's Emergency Fund (UNICEF) was established by General Assembly resolution 57 (I) of 11 December 1946, to be utilized for the benefit of children and adolescents of countries which had been the victims of aggression; its assistance was to be provided on the basis of need, without discrimination because of race, creed, national status or political belief. Subsequently, the Assembly recognized the need for continued action to relieve the sufferings of children, particularly in developing countries and countries that had been subject to the devastations of war and other calamities. Accordingly, in resolution 802 (VIII) of 6 October 1953, the Assembly decided to continue the organization indefinitely, but changed its name to the United Nations Children's Fund while retaining the symbol UNICEF. The Economic and Social Council was requested to continue to review its work periodically and to make recommendations to the Assembly.

9. The basic function of UNICEF is to help the Governments of developing countries to improve the quality of life of their children. Its approach to development aid is the conviction that children are the means, as well as the beneficiaries, of national development, and that enlightened social policies benefiting children are a prerequisite for sustained economic and social progress. UNICEF assists programmes for children in more than 100 countries in Africa, the Americas, Asia and the Eastern Mediterranean, with a combined population which includes approximately 960 million children.

10. Operations of the Fund are directed by an Executive Board, composed of 41 States elected by the Economic and Social Council for terms of three years.

11. Noting that the year 1986 marked the fortieth anniversary of the Fund, the General Assembly, in resolution 40/120 of 17 December 1985, reaffirmed the principles and guidelines for programme activities established by the Executive Board in its efforts to bring about a major world-wide improvement in child survival and child development, and noted that the fortieth anniversary of the Fund presented a unique opportunity for advancing those principles which, in its terms, "have the potential for a virtual revolution in child survival". It requested the Fund to continue to develop and promote appropriate means by which Governments, the United Nations and other international organizations, as well as individuals, may express their commitment for the survival and development of children, and appealed for increased support, assistance and contributions to the Fund.

3. INTERNATIONAL YEAR OF THE CHILD (1979)

12. In resolution 31/169 of 21 December 1976, the General Assembly proclaimed the year 1979 International Year of the Child, and decided that the Year should have the following general objectives:

(a) To provide a framework for advocacy on behalf of children and for enhancing the awareness of the special needs of children on the part of decision-makers and the public;

(b) To promote recognition of the fact that programmes for children should be an integral part of economic and social development plans, with a view to achieving, in both the long term and the short term, sustained activities for the benefit of children at the national and international levels.

13. The year 1979—the twentieth anniversary of the adoption of the Declaration on the Rights of the Child—was essentially a year of action at the national level to improve the situation of children, supported by activities and consultations at the regional and international levels. Leadership was provided by UNICEF, with the assistance of an Inter-Agency Advisory Group.

4. PRINCIPLES OF GOOD FOSTER PLACEMENT AND ADOPTION PRACTICE

14. Soon after the Declaration on the Rights of the Child was adopted, the World Conference on Adoption and Foster Placement, held at Milan from 16 to 19 September 1971, drew attention to a number of serious problems relating to the adoption and foster placement of children, and the General Assembly in resolution 3028 (XXVII) of 18 December 1972 requested the Commission on Social Development to examine this question and to make recommendations which would include

principles of good adoption and foster placement practice.

15. The Economic and Social Council, in resolution 1925 (LVIII) of 6 May 1975, noted that there was a wide diversity of views on adoption and foster placement, reflecting the broad range of social and cultural values prevailing in different parts of the world, and recognized the problems which can arise in the case of intercountry movement of children and the need to safeguard the rights of all concerned, particularly those of the child. It affirmed the desirability of drawing up a declaration on principles of good adoption practice in the light of which countries could examine their own laws according to their own traditions, and requested the Secretary-General to prepare a draft declaration on social and legal principles relating to adoption and foster placement of children nationally and internationally and to draft guidelines for the use of Governments in the implementation of those principles.

16. The Secretary-General prepared these texts with the assistance of a group of experts in family and child welfare representative of all geographical regions. After review by the Commission for Social Development they were transmitted to the General Assembly, where they were examined by the Third and Sixth Committees with the assistance of open-ended informal consultations between Member States representing different legal systems.

17. The General Assembly, in resolution 41/85 of 3 December 1986, adopted the Declaration on Social and Legal Principles relating to the Protection and Welfare of Children, with Special Reference to Foster Placement and Adoption Nationally and Internationally. The Declaration proclaims nine principles relating to general family and child welfare, three relating to foster placement and twelve relating to adoption, bearing in mind that in all foster placement and adoption procedures the best interests of the child should be the paramount consideration. The principles reflect relevant provisions of the Universal Declaration of Human Rights, both International Covenants on Human Rights, the International Convention on the Elimination of All Forms of Racial Discrimination and the Convention on the Elimination of All Forms of Discrimination against Women. In particular, they reaffirm and elaborate principle 6 of the Declaration on the Rights of the Child, which states that the child shall, wherever possible, grow up in the care and under the responsibility of his parents and, in any case, in an atmosphere of affection and moral and material security.

18. The principles are as follows:

A. *General family and child welfare*

1. Every State should give a high priority to family and child welfare.

2. Child welfare depends upon good family welfare.

3. The first priority for a child is to be cared for by his or her own parents.

4. When care by the child's own parents is unavailable or inappropriate, care by relatives of the child's parents, by another substitute—foster or adoptive—family or, if necessary, by an appropriate institution should be considered.

5. In all matters relating to the placement of a child outside the care of the child's own parents, the best interests of the child, particularly his or her need for affection and right to security and continuing care, should be the paramount consideration.

6. Persons responsible for foster placement or adoption procedures should have professional or other appropriate training.

7. Governments should determine the adequacy of their national child welfare services and consider appropriate actions.

8. The child should at all times have a name, a nationality and a legal representative. The child should not, as a result of foster placement, adoption or any alternative régime, be deprived of his or her name, nationality or legal representatives unless the child thereby acquires a new name, nationality or legal representative.

9. The need of a foster or an adopted child to know about his or her background should be recognized by persons responsible for the child's care, unless this is contrary to the child's best interests.

B. *Foster placement*

10. Foster placement of children should be regulated by law.

11. Foster family care, though temporary in nature, may continue, if necessary, until adulthood but should not preclude either prior return to the child's own parents or adoption.

12. In all matters of foster family care the prospective foster parents and, as appropriate, the child and his or her own parents should be properly involved. A competent authority or agency should be responsible for supervision to ensure the welfare of the child.

C. *Adoption*

13. The primary aim of adoption is to provide the child who cannot be cared for by his or her own parents with a permanent family.

14. In considering possible adoption placements, persons responsible for them should select the most appropriate environment for the child.

15. Sufficient time and adequate counselling should be given to the child's own parents, the prospective adoptive parents and, as appropriate, the child in order to reach a decision on the child's future as early as possible.

16. The relationship between the child to be adopted and the prospective adoptive parents should be observed by child welfare agencies or services prior to the adoption. Legislation should ensure that the child is recognized in law as a member of the adoptive family and enjoys all the rights pertinent thereto.

17. If a child cannot be placed in a foster or an adoptive family or cannot in any suitable manner be cared for in the country of origin, intercountry adoption may be considered as an alternative means of providing the child with a family.

18. Governments should establish policy, legislation and effective supervision for the protection of children involved in intercountry adoption. Intercountry adoption should, wherever possible, only be undertaken when such measures have been established in the States concerned.

19. Policies should be established and laws enacted, where necessary, for the prohibition of abduction and of any other act for illicit placement of children.

20. In intercountry adoption, placements should, as a rule, be made through competent authorities or agencies with application of safeguards and standards equivalent to those existing in respect of national adoption. In no case should the placement result in improper financial gain for those involved in it.

21. In intercountry adoption through persons acting as agents for prospective adoptive parents, special precautions should be taken in order to protect the child's legal and social interests.

22. No intercountry adoption should be considered before it has been established that the child is legally free for adoption and that any pertinent documents necessary to complete the adoption, such as the consent of competent authorities, will become available. It must also be established that the child will be able to migrate and to join the prospective adoptive parents and may obtain their nationality.

23. In intercountry adoption, as a rule, the legal validity of the adoption should be assured in each of the countries involved.

24. Where the nationality of the child differs from that of the prospective adoptive parents, all due weight shall be given to both the law of the State of which the child is the national and the law of the prospective adoptive parents. In this connection due regard shall be given to the child's cultural and religious background and interests.

5. DRAFT CONVENTION ON THE RIGHTS OF THE CHILD

19. At its thirty-fourth session, in 1978, the Commission on Human Rights, taking into consideration the draft convention on the rights of the child submitted by Poland, requested the Secretary-General to prepare a report containing the views, observations and suggestions on the draft received from Member States, the competent specialized agencies, regional intergovernmental organizations and non-governmental organizations.

20. At its thirty-fifth to forty-fourth sessions, the Commission continued to examine the draft convention, establishing an open-ended Working Group to meet for this purpose one week prior to each session.

21. Concerned that the situation of children in many parts of the world remains critical as a result of inadequate social conditions, natural disasters, armed conflicts, exploitation, hunger and disability, and convinced that urgent and effective national and international legislation is called for, the General Assembly, in resolution 42/101 of 7 December 1987, requested the Secretary-General to authorize convening the Commission's open-ended Working Group for an additional week at its January 1988 session in order to complete a draft convention so as to facilitate its conclusion in 1989, the year of the thirtieth anniversary of the Declaration on the Rights of the Child and of the tenth anniversary of the International Year of the Child (1979). The Assembly also called upon the Commission on Human Rights to make every effort to complete the draft convention and to submit it to the Assembly in 1989.

B. The rights of persons belonging to ethnic, religious or linguistic minorities

22. When the Third Committee of the General Assembly was preparing the final text of the Universal Declaration of Human Rights in Paris in 1948, several delegations wished to have included in the Declaration not only a non-discrimination article but also provisions regarding positive measures taken for the protection of minorities. Some representatives argued that the problem of minorities was greatly complicated by the different structures of the various States; they felt that some countries might not be able to agree to the inclusion of minorities provisions in a declaration which was of universal scope because, should they try to apply them, they might find their national unity disrupted. Others took the view that it would not be possible in a single article to effect a compromise between the views of the New World, which in general wished to assimilate immigrants, and the Old World, in which racial and national minorities existed. In addition, one representative pointed out that the rights of all minorities were already fully protected in the proposed Declaration: thus, article 18 guaranteed them freedom of religion, article 19 freedom of opinion and expression, article 20 freedom of assembly, article 26 the choice of education, and article 27 the right to participate in cultural life; in addition, article 2, on non-discrimination, expressly protected all minorities.

23. In resolution 217 C (III) of 10 December 1948 the General Assembly, considering that the United Nations could not remain indifferent to the fate of minorities, and that it was difficult to adopt a uniform solution for this complex and delicate question, which had special aspects in each State in which it arose, and considering the universal character of the Universal Declaration of Human Rights, decided not to deal in a specific provision with the question of minorities in the text of the Declaration. Instead, it referred to the Economic and Social Council several proposals which had been submitted by various delegations and requested the Council to ask the Commission on Human Rights and the Sub-Commission on Prevention of Discrimination and Protection of Minorities to make a thorough study of the problem of minorities, in order that the United Nations might be able to take effective measures for the protection of racial, national, religious and linguistic minorities.

24. The Economic and Social Council, in resolution 191 (VIII) of 9 February 1949, transmitted the matter to the Commission on Human Rights, which referred it to the Sub-Commission.

25. At its second session, in 1949, the Sub-Commission decided to place on the agenda of its next session the item, "Definition and classification of minorities". In order to facilitate its discussion of this item the Secretary-General submitted to the Sub-Commission a memorandum entitled "Definition and classification of minorities",[1] presenting, in an organized fashion, the principal elements to be taken into consideration in any attempt to define or to classify minorities.

26. At its fourth session, in 1951, the Sub-Commission prepared a draft article on the rights of persons belonging to minorities for inclusion in the International Covenant on Civil and Political Rights. The article, as amended by the Commission on Human Rights at its eighth session, in 1952, was later adopted as article 27 of the Covenant, and reads as follows:

In those States in which ethnic, religious or linguistic minorities exist, persons belonging to such minorities shall not be denied the right, in community with other members of their group, to enjoy their own culture, to profess and practise their own religion, or to use their own language.

---

[1] E/CN.4/Sub.2/85.

27. On the recommendation of the Sub-Commission, the Commission on Human Rights, at its ninth session, in 1953, transmitted two draft resolutions to the Economic and Social Council for consideration, one relating to the protection of newly created minorities and the other to the abolition of discriminatory measures affecting minorities. After considering the former the Council adopted resolution 502 F (XVI) of 3 August 1953, in which it recommended that, "in the preparation of any international treaties, decisions of international organs, or other acts which establish new States, or new boundary lines between States, special attention should be paid to the protection of any minority which may be created thereby".

28. After considering the latter proposal, however, the Council, in resolution 502 B II (XVI) of the same date, expressed the view that before adopting recommendations concerning the application of special measures for the protection of minorities, it was necessary to undertake a more thorough study of the whole question, including definition of the term "minority" for the purpose of such recommendations. The Council accordingly requested the Commission on Human Rights and the Sub-Commission to continue their work on the protection of minorities with this consideration in mind, and to submit revised recommendations to the Council.

29. At its sixth session, in 1954, the Sub-Commission, in resolution F, pointed out to the Commission on Human Rights that on three separate occasions (at its third, fourth and fifth sessions) it had submitted to the Commission "a draft resolution containing a definition of minorities for purposes of protection by the United Nations", and that the Commission had on each occasion referred that draft back to the Sub-Commission for further study. The Sub-Commission accordingly had decided "to initiate a study of the present position as regards minorities throughout the world" and had decided that for the purpose of such a study the term "minority" would include "only those non-dominant groups in a population which possess and wish to preserve ethnic, religious or linguistic traditions or characteristics markedly different from those of the rest of the population"; and that no further work on the problem of definition could serve any useful purpose at that stage.

30. At its tenth session the Commission, in resolution IV, requested the Sub-Commission "to give further study to the whole question, including the definition of the term 'minority', and to report thereon" to a later session of the Commission.

31. It was not until 1961 that the Sub-Commission returned to the question of the protection of minorities. In resolution 7 (XIII), the Sub-Commission requested the Secretary-General "to compile the texts of those international instruments which were of contemporary interest and which provide special protective measures for ethnic, religious or linguistic groups and to present such a compilation, together with an analysis of these special measures, for consideration by the Sub-Commission at its fourteenth session".

32. At its fourteenth session, in 1962, the Sub-Commission received and noted the compilation prepared by the Secretary-General[2] and in resolution 4 (XIV) requested the Secretary-General to prepare another document, "listing and classifying special protective measures of an international character for ethnic, religious or linguistic groups". Pursuant to that request, the Secretary-General prepared and submitted a memorandum[3] to the Sub-Commission at its fifteenth session, in 1963. In resolution 6 (XV) the Sub-Commission noted the memorandum as "an instructive addition" to the earlier compilation. The Economic and Social Council, in resolution 1161 (XLI) of 5 August 1966, authorized the Secretary-General to print, circulate and make available for sale to the public the memorandum and the compilation as one publication.[4]

33. At its twentieth session, in 1967, the Sub-Commission in resolution 9 (XX) decided "to include in the programme of its future work, and to initiate, as soon as possible, a study of the implementation of the principles set out in article 27 of the International Covenant on Civil and Political Rights, with special reference to analysing the concept of minority taking into account the ethnic, religious and linguistic factors and considering the position of ethnic, religious or linguistic groups in multinational societies". On the recommendation of the Commission on Human Rights the Economic and Social Council, in resolution 1418 (XLVI) of 6 June 1969, approved the Sub-Commission's decision and authorized it to designate a Special Rapporteur to carry out the study.

34. At its twenty-fourth session, in 1971, the Sub-Commission appointed one of its members, Mr. Francesco Capotorti, as Special Rapporteur for the study on the rights of persons belonging to ethnic, religious and linguistic minorities. The Special Rapporteur submitted to the Sub-Commission a preliminary report, two progress reports, a draft report and a final report. The final report[5] was considered by the Sub-Commission at its thirtieth session, in 1977.

35. In his report, the Special Rapporteur formulated a tentative definition of the term "minority" drawn up solely with the application of article 27 of the International Covenant on Civil and Political Rights in mind. In that precise context, he suggested, the term "minority" may be taken to mean:

A group numerically inferior to the rest of the population of a State, in a non-dominant position, whose members—being nationals of the State—possess ethnic, religious or linguistic characteristics differing from those of the rest of the population and show, if only implicitly, a sense of solidarity, directed towards preserving their culture, traditions, religion or language.

Among the recommendations made by the Special Rapporteur were: (*a*) full use of the procedures of implementation contained in the International Covenant on

[2] E/CN.4/Sub.2/124.

[3] E/CN.4/Sub.2/221.

[4] *Protection of Minorities* (United Nations publication, Sales No. E.67.XIV.3).

[5] E/CN.4/Sub.2/384 and Add.1-6.

Civil and Political Rights with regard to article 27 thereof, (b) provision of appropriate procedures on the national level to deal effectively with violations of the rights granted to members of minority groups under article 27, and (c) preparation of a draft declaration on the rights of members of minority groups, within the framework of the principles set forth in article 27. The Special Rapporteur further expressed the strong belief that bilateral agreements dealing with minority rights concluded between States where minorities lived and states from which such minorities orginated (especially between neighbouring countries) would be extremely useful, provided that co-operation with regard to the rights of members of minority groups was based on mutual respect for the principles of the sovereignty and territorial integrity of the States concerned and non-interference in their internal affairs.

36. The Sub-Commission, in resolution 5 (XXX) of 31 August 1977, recommended that the Commission on Human Rights consider drafting a declaration on the rights of members of minorities, within the framework of the principles set forth in article 27 of the International Covenant on Civil and Political Rights.

37. The Commission, at its thirty-fourth session, in 1978, established an informal working group, open to all its members, to consider questions connected with the drafting of such a declaration. A draft declaration, proposed by Yugoslavia,[6] was referred to the Working Group. Similar open-ended working groups were established by the Commission at its thirty-fifth to forty-fourth sessions. In resolution 1988/64 of 10 March 1987, the Commission decided to establish at its forty-fifth session an open-ended working group to continue consideration of the revised draft declaration proposed by Yugoslavia.

38. At one point in its consideration of this question, the Sub-Commission requested one of its members, Mr. Jules Deschênes, to prepare guidelines on the question to serve as a basis for its discussion. At the thirty-eighth session of the Sub-Commission, in 1985, Mr. Deschênes submitted a study[7] which concluded with his proposed definition of the term "minority" as follows:

A group of citizens of a State, constituting a numerical minority and in a non-dominant position in that State, endowed with ethnic, religious or linguistic characteristics which differ from those of the majority of the population, having a sense of solidarity with one another, motivated, if only implicity, by a collective will to survive and whose aim is to achieve equality with the majority in fact and in law.

39. However, differing views were expressed by the members of the Sub-Commission with regard to the definition of the term "minority", and the proposed definition did not command general approval. The Sub-Commission accordingly transmitted Mr. Deschênes's study and proposal to the Commission on Human Rights together with the records[8] of the discussion in the Sub-Commission.

C. The rights of the aging

40. Various United Nations bodies have been concerned with the question of aging since 1948, when a draft Declaration of Old Age Rights was submitted to the General Assembly by Argentina.[9] In resolution 213 (III) of 4 December 1948, the Assembly communicated the draft Declaration to the Economic and Social Council. In resolution 198 (VIII) of 2 March 1949 the Council requested the Secretary-General to prepare documentation on the subject and submit it to the Social Commission and the Commission on Human Rights; the Commissions were requested to study and report on the subject.

41. The question remained on the agendas of the two Commissions for a number of years without definitive action. In 1969 an item entitled "Question of the elderly and the aged" was included in the agenda of the twenty-fourth session of the General Assembly at the request of Malta. It was considered at the twenty-sixth, twenty-eighth and thirty-second sessions of the Assembly, and resulted in the adoption of resolutions 2842 (XXVI), 3137 (XXVIII), 32/131 and 32/132. At its thirty-third session, the Assembly decided to organize a World Assembly on the Elderly in 1982. The title was later changed to World Assembly on Aging.

42. The World Assembly on Aging was held at Vienna from 26 July to 6 August 1982. The General Assembly considered and took note of its report[10] in resolution 37/51 of 3 December 1982. The Assembly endorsed the Vienna International Plan of Action on Aging, which had been adopted by consensus at the World Assembly, and called upon Governments to make continuous efforts to implement the principles and recommendations contained in that Plan. The Secretary-General was requested to report to the Assembly at its thirty-eighth session on the progress achieved in implementing and following up the Plan.

43. The States gathered in the World Assembly on Aging reaffirmed their belief that the fundamental and inalienable rights enshrined in the Universal Declaration of Human Rights apply fully and undiminishedly to the aging, and recognized that the quality of life was no less important than longevity, and that the aged should therefore, as far as possible, be enabled to enjoy in their own families and communities a life of fulfilment, health, security and contentment, appreciated as an integral part of society.[11]

44. Endorsing this viewpoint, the General Assembly in resolution 37/51 called upon Governments to make continuous efforts to implement the principles and recommendations contained in the Plan of Action in accordance with their national structures, needs and ob-

---

[6] E/CN.4/L.1367/Rev.1.

[7] E/CN.4/Sub.2/1985/31, para. 181.

[8] E/CN.4/Sub.2/1985/SR.13 to 16.

[9] A/C.3/213/Rev.1.

[10] *Report of the World Assembly on Aging, Vienna, 26 July to 6 August 1982* (United Nations publication, Sales No. E.82.1.16).

[11] *Report of the World Assembly on Aging, Vienna, 26 July to 6 August 1982* (United Nations publication, Sales No. E.82.I.16, chap. VI).

jectives; and requested the Secretary-General (*a*) to take the necessary steps to ensure that sufficient resources within reasonable limits are made available for the effective implementation of, and follow-up action to, the Plan of Action; (*b*) to take such steps as may be appropriate for the necessary strengthening of activities in the field of aging at the central and regional levels of the United Nations; (*c*) to strengthen the international network of existing information, research and training centres in the field of aging; (*d*) to implement the recommendations of the Assembly concerning international co-operation with respect to aging; and (*e*) to continue to use the United Nations Trust Fund for the World Assembly on Aging to meet the needs of the aging in the developing countries.

45. On the initiative of the Government of Malta, an Expert Group Meeting on the Feasibility of Establishing an Institute on Aging was held at Malta from 15 to 19 December 1986. In resolution 1987/41 of 28 May 1987 the Council thanked the Government of Malta for its continuing efforts in the field of aging and recommended to the Secretary-General the conclusions contained in the report of the Expert Group Meeting on the understanding that the proposed institute in Malta would essentially be a training institute to fulfil the training needs of developing countries in implementing the Plan of Action and that the proposed institute would not preclude the establishment of other institutes or training centres related to the United Nations in other countries or regions of the world. The Secretary-General was further requested to consider additional ways of solving the great need for world-wide training of staff in the gerontological area.

D. The rights of indigenous populations

46. The Economic and Social Council, in resolution 1589 (L) of 21 May 1971, authorized the Sub-Commission on Prevention of Discrimination and Protection of Minorities to make a complete and comprehensive study of the problem of discrimination against indigenous populations, and to suggest the necessary national and international measures for eliminating such discrimination. Later that year the Sub-Commission appointed one of its members, Mr. José R. Martinez Cobo, as Special Rapporteur to carry out the study.

47. At various sessions held between 1973 and 1984, the Sub-Commission examined portions of the Special Rapporteur's report. In 1984 it was able to consider the report as a whole[12] and adopted resolution 1984/35 of 30 August 1984 in which it characterized the study as constituting ''an invaluable contribution to the clarification of the basic legal, social, economic and cultural problems of indigenous populations''.

48. On recommendation of the Sub-Commission and the Commission on Human Rights, the Economic and

Social Council in decision 1985/137 of 30 May 1985 requested the Secretary-General to issue the full report in consolidated form and to circulate it widely;[13] and to print its conclusions and recommendations.[14]

49. The Special Rapporteur's conclusions called for principles to be formulated for use as guidelines by Governments of all States in their activities concerning indigenous populations, on a basis of respect for the ethnic identity of such populations and for the rights and freedoms to which they are entitled; a thorough and careful study of the provisions of treaties concluded by indigenous peoples with present nation-States or with countries acting as colonial administering Powers at the time in question, to determine the official force of such provisions at present, the observance or lack of effective observance of such provisions, and the consequences of all this for the peoples and nations concerned; and the development of measures, in consultation with the indigenous populations concerned, to improve the situation of those populations in such special areas as health, housing, education, language, culture, employment, the right of ownership of land, political rights, religious rights and practices, and equality in the administration of justice.

50. Before the Special Rapporteur had concluded his study, the Sub-Commission had adopted the practice, authorized by Economic and Social Council resolution 1982/34 of 7 May 1982, of establishing at each annual session a Working Group on Indigenous Populations to review developments pertaining to the promotion and protection of the human rights and fundamental freedoms of the indigenous populations and to give special attention to the evolution of standards concerning the rights of those populations.

51. The Working Group held its first session at Geneva from 9 to 13 August 1982, immediately prior to the 1982 session of the Sub-Commission. It has since met annually except in 1986, when the sessions of the Sub-Commission and of its subsidiary bodies were postponed because of the financial crisis facing the United Nations.

52. In order to assist representatives of indigenous communities and organizations to participate in the deliberations of the Working Group, the General Assembly in resolution 40/131 of 13 December 1985 established the United Nations Voluntary Fund for Indigenous Populations, funded by voluntary contributions from Governments and non-governmental organizations and administered with the advice of a five-member Board of Trustees appointed by the Secretary-General.

53. The Working Group has undertaken to give first priority to the preparation of a draft international declaration on indigenous rights, to be adopted and proclaimed by the General Assembly. In performing this

---

[12] E/CN.4/Sub.2/476 and Add.1-6; E/CN.4/Sub.2/1982/2 and Add.1-7; and E/CN.4/Sub.2/1983/21 and Add.1-8.

[13] E/CN.4/Sub.2/1986/7 and Add.1-4 (five volumes).

[14] *Study of the Problem of Discrimination against Indigenous Populations,* by José R. Martinez Cobo. United Nations publication, Sales No. E.86.XIV.3.

task its attention was drawn, at the 1987 session, to many situations where the human rights of indigenous populations were being seriously infringed. The description of these situations presented not as complaints but as examples of factual situations of deep concern to indigenous peoples, were welcomed by the Working Group which considered that such information would facilitate its efforts to formulate standards through the identification of the issues involved and the clarification of the relevant legal and political concepts.

E. The rights of aliens

54. At the twenty-eighth session of the Commission on Human Rights, in 1972, reference was made by one representative to violations of human rights involved in the massive expulsion of nationals of his own country by the Government of a neighbouring country. He noted that such massive expulsions, revealing clearly the pursuance of a policy of collective vengeance against innocent and defenceless people of a specific ethnic group, were premeditated and were carried out in defiance of the most elementary human rights and the most tested practices of international law. Although he acknowledged that under legal doctrine and in judicial practice the right of expulsion was recognized, this right was not discretionary, in his view, and could be exercised only within clearly defined limits. He presented documentary evidence in support of the allegations made on the appalling conditions endured by those expelled from the country in which they had peacefully and legally resided for many years.

55. The Commission took no action on the matter at its twenty-eighth session. However, at its twenty-ninth session it prepared a draft resolution for consideration by the Economic and Social Council. On its recommendation the Council, in resolution 1790 (LIV) of 18 May 1973, requested the Commission and the Sub-Commission on Prevention of Discrimination and Protection of Minorities "to consider as a matter of priority the problem of the applicability of existing international provisions for the protection of human rights to individuals who are not citizens of the country in which they live, to consider what measures in the field of human rights, including the possibility of a declaration, would be desirable", and to submit appropriate recommendations to the Council. The Council urged States, "pending the adoption of further measures in this field, to accord the highest practicable level of protection to all individuals who are not their citizens but who are nevertheless under their jurisdiction".

56. At its twenty-seventh session, in 1974, the Sub-Commission decided, in resolution 10 (XXVII) of 21 August 1974, to appoint one of its members, Baroness Elles, as Special Rapporteur to prepare a report supplementing the Secretary-General's survey on the subject. The Special Rapporteur submitted the first four chapters of her report to the Sub-Commission at its twenty-eighth session, in 1975. The full report was submitted to the Sub-Commission at its twenty-ninth session, in 1976[15] but was considered only at its thirtieth session, in 1977.

57. The report[16] contained (a) a brief historical outline of the development of the protection granted to aliens, of the status of aliens and of their treatment; (b) consideration of international protection of the human rights of aliens, including the stateless and refugees, provided for in contemporary human rights instruments, in the constitutions of international organizations and in international law; (c) an examination of (i) those rights which States guarantee to aliens and those rights which by their nature are attributable only to nationals or citizens, and (ii) those rights which by their nature are related exclusively to citizens; (d) an analysis of the restrictions, reservations, limitations and derogations which may be made on human rights on the ground of nationality, for which provision is made in human rights instruments; (e) a review and evaluation of the machinery available to non-citizens for redress of injuries and other remedies for the enforcement of their human rights; (f) conclusions drawn from the above research, examination and considerations; and (g) recommendations and proposals to the Sub-Commission concerning measures which are required for the more effective protection of the human rights of individuals who are not citizens of the country in which they live. A draft declaration on the human rights of individuals who are not citizens of the country in which they live was annexed to the report (annex I).

58. At its thirtieth session, in 1977, the Sub-Commission examined the Special Rapporteur's report and, in resolution 4 (XXX) of 31 August 1977, expressed its grateful appreciation to the Special Rapporteur for the excellent study she had submitted. The Sub-Commission requested the Secretary-General to submit the draft declaration contained in annex I to Governments for their consideration and comments and requested the Special Rapporteur, taking into account the replies of Governments and the views expressed during the discussion of the item in the Sub-Commission, to present a new draft declaration to the Sub-Commission at its thirty-first session.

59. The Sub-Commission transmitted the study and a revised draft declaration to the Commission on Human Rights by resolution 9 (XXXI) of 13 September 1978. After consideration by the Commission the study, a revised draft declaration[17] and the comments thereon received from Governments[18] were transmitted through the Economic and Social Council to the General Assembly.

60. At its thirty-fifth session, in 1980, the Assembly decided to establish an open-ended Working Group entrusted with elaborating a final version of the draft declaration. Similar Working Groups were established at

---

[15] E/CN.4/Sub.2/392 and Corr.1.

[16] Now a United Nations publication, Sales No. E.80.XIV.2.

[17] E/CN.4/1336.

[18] E/CN.4/1354 and Add.1-6.

the thirty-sixth, thirty-seventh, thirty-eighth, thirty-ninth and fortieth sessions.

61. The General Assembly adopted and proclaimed the Declaration on the Human Rights on Individuals who are not Nationals of the Country in which They Live in resolution 40/144 of 13 December 1985. The Declaration recognizes that the protection of human rights and fundamental freedoms provided for in international instruments should not be limited to nationals but should also be ensured for individuals who are not nationals of the country in which they live, i.e., for aliens as well as for citizens.

62. The Declaration provides that every State shall make public its national legislation or regulations affecting aliens, and that aliens must observe the laws of the State in which they live and respect the customs and traditions of the people of that State. It then lists the particular human rights which they are entitled to enjoy in accordance with domestic law and subject to the relevant international obligations of the State; these include the right to life and security of person; the right to protection against arbitrary or unlawful interference with privacy, family, home or correspondence; the right to be equal before the courts and tribunals; the right to choose a spouse, to marry and to found a family; the right to freedom of thought, opinion, conscience and religion; the right to retain their own language, culture, and tradition; the right to transfer monetary assets abroad, subject to domestic currency restrictions; and —subject to restrictions prescribed by law—the right to leave the country, the right to freedom of expression, the right to peaceful assembly and the right to own property alone as well as in association with others.

63. The Declaration further provides that, subject to their obligation with respect to the customs and traditions of the people of the State in which they live, aliens shall also enjoy the right to safe and healthy working conditions, the right to join trade unions and other organizations and associations of their choice, the right to health protection, medical care, social security, social service, education, rest and leisure.

64. Further provisions state that no alien shall be subjected to torture or to cruel, inhuman or degrading treatment or punishment; that aliens lawfully in the territory of a State may be expelled therefrom only in pursuance of a decision reached in accordance with law; that no alien shall be arbitrarily deprived of his lawfully acquired assets; and that any alien may be free at any time to communicate with the consulate or diplomatic mission of the State of which he is a national or of any other State entrusted with representing the State of which he is a national.

F. The rights of migrant workers

65. Migrant workers and their families, who are usually, non-citizens of the country in which they live and work, have for some years been of particular con-cern to the United Nations and to the International Labour Organisation.

66. In resolution 1706 (LIII) of 28 July 1972, the Economic and Social Council noted with alarm and indignation reports of incidents involving the illegal transportation, organized or undertaken by criminal elements, to some European countries and the exploitation of workers from some African countries in conditions akin to slavery or forced labour. Deeply concerned over malpractices involving inequality and discrimination and unlawful forms of recruitment and treatment of such workers, and deploring the fact that advantage was being taken of conditions of mass poverty, ignorance and unemployment in the countries of origin to exploit and profit from such labour through illicit and clandestine trafficking, the Council condemned these malpractices, appealed to the Governments concerned to apprehend and bring to justice those responsible for them, and called for the adoption of measures aimed at combating and preventing them. The Council instructed the Commission on Human Rights to consider the question and to prepare appropriate recommendations for further action. It took note of steps which had been taken by ILO to reinforce its action for the protection of migrant workers and invited it to pursue energetically its examination of the matter and to report thereon to the Council.

67. The General Assembly also expressed its deep concern, in resolution 2920 (XXVII) of 15 November 1972, over the *de facto* discrimination of which foreign workers were the victims in certain countries of Europe and of other continents despite the efforts made by certain Governments to prevent and repress it. The Assembly called upon the Governments concerned to take or supervise the application of measures to put an end to the discriminatory treatment of which migrant workers in their territory were the victims, and particularly to ensure the improvement of arrangements for receiving such workers, and invited all Governments to ensure respect for the provisions of the International Convention on the Elimination of All Forms of Racial Discrimination. It recommended that the Commission on Human Rights should consider the question of the exploitation of labour through illicit and clandestine trafficking at its next session, and invited ILO to continue the studies on the subject which it had begun. In particular the Assembly urged Governments, which had not done so to give high priority to ratification of the ILO Migration for Employment Convention (Revised), 1949 (No. 97) in the context of their efforts to eliminate illicit trafficking in foreign labour.

68. As recommended by the Council and the General Assembly, the Commission on Human Rights considered the question as a matter of priority at its twenty-ninth session, in 1973. On the recommendation of the Commission, the Council, in resolution 1789 (LIV) of 18 May 1973, urged States to ratify the relevant ILO Conventions and to conclude bilateral agreements relating to migration for employment as appropriate. The Council further requested the Sub-Commission on Pre-

vention of Discrimination and Protection of Minorities and the Commission on the Status of Women to study the question in depth on the basis of materials, studies and suggestions to be submitted by Member States, and to recommend what further measures might be necessary for the protection, without distinction, of the human rights of foreign workers. The Council requested Member States to submit to the Secretary-General such materials, studies and suggestions as they deemed relevant, for transmission to the Sub-Commission and to the Commission on the Status of Women.

69.   In the debate in the Sub-Commission, members generally agreed that there were two aspects to be taken into account in dealing with the matter: (i) the illicit and clandestine operations, and (ii) the discriminatory treatment of migratory workers in host countries. In resolution 6 (XXVI) of 19 September 1973, the Sub-Commission expressed the view that a preliminary study should be undertaken and entrusted one of its members, Mrs. Halima Warzazi, with this task. The Commission on Human Rights decided, on 6 March 1974, to take note of the Sub-Commission's decision and to inform the Economic and Social Council of the action.

70.   In 1974 the Sub-Commission considered a preliminary report prepared by Mrs. Warzazi[19] and in 1975 it examined her final report.[20] It requested the Secretariat to consolidate in a single document the preliminary report, the final report, the Special Rapporteur's introductory remarks and the draft recommendations which she had prepared with the help of an informal working group. In 1976 it examined the consolidated report.[21] It took note of that report with appreciation and forwarded it to the Commission on Human Rights. It further drew the attention of the Commission to the report of the United Nations seminar on the human rights of migrant workers, held at Tunis from 12 to 24 November 1975.[22]

71.   On 16 December 1976 the General Assembly, after considering the item "Measures to improve the sitation and ensure the human rights and dignity of all migrant workers", adopted resolution 31/127 on this subject. In that resolution it expressed serious concern at the *de facto* discrimination frequently suffered by alien workers in some countries, despite the legislative and other efforts exerted to prevent and punish it, and called upon all States to take measures to prevent and put an end to such discrimination against migrant workers, and to ensure the implementation of such measures. In particular the Assembly invited all States:

(*a*) To extend to migrant workers having regular status in their territories treatment equal to that enjoyed by their own nationals with regard to the protection of human rights and to the provisions of their labour legislation and their social legislation;

(*b*) To promote and facilitate by all means in their power the implementation of the relevant international instruments and the adoption

of bilateral agreements designed, *inter alia,* to eliminate the illicit traffic in alien workers;

(*c*) To adopt, pending the conclusion of such agreements, the appropriate measures to ensure that the fundamental human rights of all migrant workers, irrespective of their immigration status, are fully respected under their national legislation.

Governments of host countries were invited to make arrangements for information and reception facilities and to put into effect policies relating to training, health, housing and educational and cultural development for migrant workers and their families, and to guarantee the free exercise by them of activities calculated to preserve their cultural values. Governments of countries of origin were invited to give the widest possible dissemination to information calculated to pre-advise and protect migrants.

72.   At its thirty-second session the General Assembly, in resolution 32/120 of 16 December 1977, recommended that the Commission on Human Rights and the Economic and Social Council should consider the question of migrant workers fully and in depth at their next sessions on the basis of the instruments adopted and the documents and studies prepared by the United Nations and the specialized agencies.

73.   At its thirty-third session, the Assembly, in resolution 33/163 of 20 December 1978, called upon all States to consider ratifying the Migrant Workers (Supplementary Provisions) Convention, 1975 (No. 143), adopted by the General Conference of the International Labour Organisation; and requested the Secretary-General to explore with Member States, and in co-operation with ILO in particular, the possibility of drawing up an international convention on the rights of migrant workers.

74.   At its thirty-fourth session the General Assembly decided, by resolution 34/172 of 17 December 1979, to create at its thirty-fifth session a working group open to all Member States to elaborate an international convention on the protection of the rights of all migrant workers and their families; and invited the international organizations concerned to participate in its work and to co-operate with a view to the elaboration of such a convention.

75.   The Assembly established the Working Group at its thirty-fifth session, in 1980. Similar Working Groups were established at the thirty-sixth to forty-second sessions, but were unable to conclude their task although some of the Working Groups held an inter-sessional meeting as well as a meeting during the General Assembly's regular session.

76.   In resolution 42/140 of 7 December 1987, the Assembly took note of the two most recent reports of the Working Group[23] and of the progress made on the drafting, in second reading, of the draft convention; and decided that the Working Group should again hold an inter-sessional meeting of two weeks' duration in New York, immediately after the first regular session of 1988 of the Economic and Social Council, in order to

[19] E/CN.4/Sub.2/351.

[20] E/CN.4/Sub.2/L.629.

[21] E/CN.4/L.640.

[22] ST/TAO/HR.50.

[23] A/C.3/42/1 and A/C.3/42/6.

enable it to complete its task as soon as possible. It further decided that the Working Group should meet during the Assembly's forty-third session, preferably at the beginning of the session, to continue the second reading of the draft international convention on the protection of the rights of all migrant workers and their families.

77. Earlier the Economic and Social Council received and took note, in resolution 1985/24 of 29 May 1985, of a report by the Secretary-General on the social situation of migrant workers. While noting with appreciation the progress made by the Working Group on the Drafting of an International Convention on the Protection of the Rights of all Migrant Workers and Their Families, the Council recognized the need for further efforts at the national, bilateral, regional and international levels to improve the social situation of migrant workers and their families.

78. The Council accordingly invited Member States to establish and/or expand programmes and services designed to improve the welfare of migrant workers and their families and to meet the new needs and problems emerging as a result of the changing circumstances of the international migration of labour. It emphasized that such programmes should give major attention to the protection of families of migrant workers and to a substantial improvement in the conditions for genuine integration of members of migrants' families, particularly women, children and youth, into the host society; and called for special care to be paid to the education of children so that they maintain and develop the knowledge of their maternal language and their cultural heritage.

79. The Council, further, affirmed the need for the Governments of the Member States concerned to enact or strictly apply legislation to prevent or punish discriminatory or xenophobic activities against migrants, to enable the migrant workers to enjoy the benefits of association within the law. The Secretary-General was requested to encourage operational activities to achieve results in this field, and to consider the implementation of other measures to benefit migrant workers and their families.

G. The rights of disabled persons

1. DECLARATION ON THE RIGHTS OF DISABLED PERSONS

80. By resolution 3447 (XXX) of 9 December 1975, the General Assembly proclaimed the Declaration on the Rights of Disabled Persons and called for national and international action to ensure that it would be used as a common basis and frame of reference for the protection of the rights set forth therein. In doing so the Assembly bore in mind "the necessity of preventing physical and mental disabilities and of assisting disabled persons to develop their abilities in the most varied fields of activities and of promoting their integration as far as possible in normal life".

81. The Declaration defines the term "disabled person" as meaning "any person unable to ensure by himself or herself, wholly or partly, the necessities of a normal individual and/or social life, as a result of a deficiency, either congenital or not, in his or her physical or mental capabilities". It provides that organizations of disabled persons may be usefully consulted in all matters regarding the rights of such persons; and calls for disabled persons, their families and communities, to be fully informed by all appropriate means of the rights contained in the Declaration.

82. The Declaration sets out the following principles:

2. Disabled persons shall enjoy all the rights set forth in this Declaration. These rights shall be granted to all disabled persons without any exception whatsoever and without distinction or discrimination on the basis of race, colour, sex, language, religion, political or other opinions, national or social origin, state of wealth, birth or any other situation applying either to the disabled person himself or herself or to his or her family.

3. Disabled persons have the inherent right to respect for their human dignity. Disabled persons, whatever the origin, nature and seriousness of their handicaps and disabilities, have the same fundamental rights as their fellow-citizens of the same age, which implies first and foremost the right to enjoy a decent life, as normal and full as possible.

4. Disabled persons have the same civil and political rights as other human beings; paragraph 7 of the Declaration on the Rights of Mentally Retarded Persons applies to any possible limitation or suppression of those rights for mentally disabled persons.

5. Disabled persons are entitled to the measures designed to enable them to become as self-reliant as possible.

6. Disabled persons have the right to medical, psychological and functional treatment, including prosthetic and orthetic appliances, to medical and social rehabilitation, education, vocational training and rehabilitation, aid, counselling, placement services and other services which will enable them to develop their capabilities and skills to the maximum and will hasten the process of their social integration or reintegration.

7. Disabled persons have the right to economic and social security and to a decent level of living. They have the right, according to their capabilities, to secure and retain employment or to engage in a useful, productive and remunerative occupation and to join trade unions.

8. Disabled persons are entitled to have their special needs taken into consideration at all stages of economic and social planning.

9. Disabled persons have the right to live with their families or with foster parents and to participate in all social, creative or recreational activities. No disabled person shall be subjected, as far as his or her residence is concerned, to differential treatment other than that required by his or her condition or by the improvement which he or she may derive therefrom. If the stay of a disabled person in a specialized establishment is indispensable, the environment and living conditions therein shall be as close as possible to those of the normal life of a person of his or her age.

10. Disabled persons shall be protected against all exploitation, all regulations and all treatment of a discriminatory, abusive or degrading nature.

11. Disabled persons shall be able to avail themselves of qualified legal aid when such aid proves indispensable for the protection of their persons and property. If judicial proceedings are instituted against them, the legal procedure applied shall take their physical and mental condition fully into account.

83. In resolution 31/82 of 13 December 1976, the General Assembly recommended "that all Member States should take account of the rights and principles laid down in the Declaration on the Rights of Disabled Persons in establishing their policies, plans and programmes"; and recommended "that all international

organizations and agencies concerned should include in their programmes provisions ensuring the effective implementation of those rights and principles''. The Secretary-General was requested to inform the General Assembly of the measures taken with a view to implementing the rights and principles laid down in the Declaration.

2. INTERNATIONAL YEAR OF DISABLED PERSONS (1981)

84.   In resolution 31/123 of 16 December 1976 the General Assembly proclaimed the year 1981 International Year for Disabled Persons and decided to devote that year to a set of objectives, including:

(*a*) Helping disabled persons in their physical and psychological adjustment to society;

(*b*) Promoting all national and international efforts to provide disabled persons with proper assistance, training, care and guidance, to make available to them opportunities for suitable work and to ensure their full integration in society;

(*c*) Encouraging study and research projects designed to facilitate the practical participation of disabled persons in daily life, for example by improving their access to public buildings and transportation systems:

(*d*) Educating and informing the public of the rights of disabled persons to participate in and contribute to various aspects of economic, social and political life;

(*e*) Promoting effective measures for the prevention of disability and for the rehabilitation of disabled persons.

85.   The Assembly established a 15-member Advisory Committee for the International Year for Disabled Persons at its thirty-second session, and increased the membership to 23 at its thirty-third session. In resolution 34/154 of 17 December 1979, the Assembly approved the Advisory Committee's recommendations,[24] and adopted them as the Plan of Action for the Year. It decided to expand the theme of the Year to "Full participation and equality", and changed the name of the Year in English to the International Year of Disabled Persons.

86.   The World Programme of Action concerning Disabled Persons, as formulated by the Advisory Committee,[25] was adopted by the General Assembly in resolution 37/52 of 3 December 1982. In that resolution the Assembly expressed its deep concern that no less than five hundred million persons were estimated to suffer from disability of one form or another, of whom four hundred million were estimated to be in developing countries, and its conviction that the International Year of Disabled Persons had given a genuine and meaningful impetus to activities related to equalization of opportunities for disabled persons, as well as prevention and rehabilitation at all levels. The Assembly called upon Member States and all organizations, organs and agencies of the United Nations system to ensure early implementation of the World Programme of Action.

3. DECLARATION ON THE RIGHTS OF MENTALLY-RETARDED PERSONS

87.   By resolution 2856 (XXVI) of 20 December 1971, the General Assembly proclaimed the Declaration on the Rights of Mentally-Retarded Persons and called for national and international action to ensure that the Declaration would be used as a common basis and frame of reference for the protection of the rights set forth therein. In doing so the Assembly bore in mind the necessity of assisting mentally retarded persons to develop their abilities in various fields of activity and of promoting their integration as far as possible in normal life.

88.   The Declaration sets out the following principles:

1. The mentally retarded person has, to the maximum degree of feasibility, the same rights as other human beings.

2. The mentally retarded person has a right to proper medical care and physical therapy and to such education, training, rehabilitation and guidance as will enable him to develop his ability and maximum potential.

3. The mentally retarded person has a right to economic security and to a decent standard of living. He has a right to perform productive work or to engage in any other meaningful occupation to the fullest possible extent of his capabilities.

4. Whenever possible, the mentally retarded person should live with his own family or with foster parents and participate in different forms of community life. The family with which he lives should receive assistance. If care in an institution becomes necessary, it should be provided in surroundings and other circumstances as close as possible to those of normal life.

5. The mentally retarded person has a right to a qualified guardian when this is required to protect his personal well-being and interests.

6. The mentally retarded person has a right to protection from exploitation, abuse and degrading treatment. If prosecuted for any offence, he shall have a right to due process of law with full recognition being given to his degree of mental responsibility.

7. Whenever mentally retarded persons are unable, because of the severity of their handicap, to exercise all their rights in a meaningful way or it should become necessary to restrict or deny some or all of these rights, the procedure used for that restriction or denial of rights must contain proper legal safeguards against every form of abuse. This procedure must be based on an evaluation of the social capability of the mentally retarded person by qualified experts and must be subject to periodic review and to the right of appeal to higher authorities.

4. DECLARATION ON THE RIGHTS OF DEAF-BLIND PERSONS

89.   The Economic and Social Council, in decision 1979/24 adopted at its 14th plenary meeting on 9 May 1979, took note of a Declaration on the Rights of Deaf-Blind Persons, which had been prepared and adopted by the Helen Keller World Conference on Services to Deaf-Blind Youths and Adults on 16 September 1977, and brought it to the attention of the General Assembly as part of the documentation submitted to the Assembly in connection with the International Year.

90.   The definition of deaf-blind persons attached to the Declaration was as follow: "Persons who have substantial visual and hearing losses such that the combination of the two causes extreme difficulty in pursuit of educational, vocational, avocational, or social skills".

---

[24] A/34/158 and Corr.1, annex.

[25] A/37/351/Add.1 and Add.1/Corr.1, para. 99.

Article 1 of the Declaration sets out its basic principle, namely that:

Every deaf-blind person is entitled to enjoy the universal rights that are guaranteed to all people by the Universal Declaration of Human Rights and the rights provided for all disabled persons by the Declaration on the Rights of Disabled Persons.

5. UNITED NATIONS DECADE OF DISABLED PERSONS

91. The General Assembly, in resolution 37/53 of 3 December 1982, proclaimed the period 1983-1992 the United Nations Decade of Disabled Persons, and encouraged Member States to utilize this period as one of the means to implement the World Programme of Action Concerning Disabled Persons. The proclamation was made on the understanding that no additional resources from the United Nations system would be used for this purpose, and that the Decade would be funded by the United Nations Trust Fund for the International Year of Disabled Persons which would be continued throughout the Decade.

92. In 1985, the Secretary-General submitted a report to the General Assembly and the Economic and Social Council on the implementation of the World Programme of Action and the United Nations Decade of Disabled Persons.[26] The report described an extensive programme of activities but pointed out that progress towards the improvement of the situation of the disabled had been slow, particularly in Africa, Latin America and the least-developed countries. The Assembly, in resolution 40/31 of 29 November 1985, expressed its appreciation to Member States and organizations that had made donations to the Fund, and invited all countries to give high priority to projects concerning the prevention of disabilities and the rehabilitation and equalization of the opportunities of disabled persons. It called upon Member States, national committees and non-governmental organizations to assist in publicizing the objectives and achievements of the Decade.

---

[26] A/40/728 and Corr.1.

6. STUDY OF HUMAN RIGHTS VIOLATIONS AND DISABLED PERSONS

93. The Economic and Social Council, in resolution 1984/26 of 24 May 1984, expressed its deep concern that serious violations of human rights remain a significant cause of temporary and permanent disability, and encouraged the Secretary-General to obtain the views of concerned international organizations on ways and means of preventing serious violations of human rights which may cause disabilities.

94. At the request of the Council, the Sub-Commission on Prevention of Discrimination and Protection of Minorities, by resolution 1984/20 of 29 August 1984, appointed a Special Rapporteur, Mr. Leandro Despouy, to undertake a thorough study of the causal connection between serious violations of human rights and fundamental freedoms and disability, as well as the progress made to alleviate problems.

95. In a preliminary report submitted to the Sub-Commission at its thirty-eighth session, in 1985, the Special Rapporteur pointed out that:

The precariousness of the disabled person's physical situation is compounded by a degree of precariousness in his legal position, with respect to the specific rights granted to him and the lack of precision as to the extent to which rights already established are guaranteed. In addition, disabled persons are often subjected to serious *de facto* violations which must be prevented and eliminated through the strengthening of legal instruments and the establishment of control mechanisms to stop such violations.

The United Nations must pay particular attention to human rights violations causing disability, such as military conflicts, torture, cruel and inhuman treatment, and others.

Penalties (whether based on internal law or religion) which have the deliberate effect of disabling the individual should be regarded as contrary to international law. . . . Amputation is the classic example of that kind of penalty . . . since it deliberately brings about disability. . . .

The discrimination to which disabled persons are subjected not only constitutes a violation of human rights but also, in most cases, aggravates the disability and, by making disabled persons a class apart, is prejudicial to society as a whole. It has a disruptive, negative effect on society at large by creating two parallel worlds, which in some cases are at odds with each other. . . .

96. The Sub-Commission, after reviewing the preliminary report, requested the Special Rapporteur to continue his work and to submit a progress report for consideration at its fortieth session.

X. PROTECTION AND ASSISTANCE TO REFUGEES AND STATELESS PERSONS

Introduction

1. The United Nations has been concerned since its inception with the situation confronting refugees, displaced persons, stateless persons and "returnees", and has adopted a number of measures to protect their human rights and to find appropriate and durable solutions for their problems.

2. At its third session, in 1948, the General Assembly initiated United Nations assistance to Palestine refugees, and in 1949 it established the United Nations Relief and Works Agency for Palestine Refugees in the Near East. Since May 1950 this Agency, which is supported by voluntary contributions, has been providing relief, education, training, health and other services to Arab refugees from Palestine. In 1967 and 1982, the functions of the Agency were widened to include humanitarian assistance, as far as practicable, on an emergency basis and as a temporary measure, to other displaced persons in serious need of immediate assistance, as a result of the 1967 and subsequent hostilities. In 1986, the Agency's mandate was extended until 30 June 1990.

3. At its fourth session, in 1949, the General Assembly established the Office of the United Nations High Commissioner for Refugees. The original three-year mandate of the High Commissioner was extended periodically, and the current term ends on 31 December 1993.

4. In recent years the international community has been particularly concerned about mass exoduses of refugees and displaced persons from areas of armed conflict, and in particular about the growing number of refugees in Africa. With the assistance of governmental experts, the General Assembly has endeavoured to find ways and means of preventing new massive flows of refugees which often have given rise to adverse consequences for the countries of origin as well as for the receiving States.

A. United Nations Relief and Works Agency for Palestine Refugees in the Near East

5. The Agency is headed by a Commissioner-General, assisted by an Advisory Commission composed of 10 Member States. The Commissioner-General reports annually to the General Assembly on the work of the Agency, and to the Secretary-General on matters to be brought to the attention of the United Nations or its appropriate organs.

6. Although the Agency is doing all it can within the limits of available resources, its financial situation has deteriorated seriously in recent years. In 1970, the General Assembly established a Working Group on the Financing of the United Nations Relief and Works Agency for Palestine Refugees in the Near East and requested it to study all aspects of the financing of the Agency. The Working Group submitted to the Assembly, at every subsequent session, recommendations to help solve the financial problems. However the continuing critical financial situation of the Agency permits the provision of only minimum services to the Palestine refugees.

7. In resolution 42/69 A of 2 December 1987, the Assembly noted with profound concern that, despite the commendable and successful efforts of the Commissioner-General to collect additional contributions, this increased level of income was still insufficient to cover essential budget requirements and that, at the foreseen levels of giving, deficits will recur each year.

B. Office of the United Nations High Commissioner for Refugees

8. The United Nations High Commissioner for Refugees serves as the spearhead of the international community's current efforts to solve the problems of refugees, displaced persons, stateless persons and "returnees" in the spirit of the Charter of the United Nations and the provisions of article 14 of the Universal Declaration of Human Rights, which reads as follows:

1. Everyone has the right to seek and to enjoy in other countries asylum from persecution.

2. This right may not be invoked in the case of prosecutions genuinely arising from non-political crimes or from acts contrary to the purposes and principles of the United Nations.

9. The Office of the United Nations High Commissioner for Refugees was established for a three-year term by the General Assembly in resolution 319 (IV) of 3 December 1949. The High Commissioner's work is entirely humanitarian and non-political. In 1954 and again in 1981, this work won for the Office the Nobel Peace prize. The 1 million Swedish kroner awarded with the 1981 prize was used to establish a Trust Fund for Handicapped Refugees.

10. The Office of the United Nations High Commissioner for Refugees replaced the International Refugee Organization (IRO), an agency established by General Assembly resolution 62 (I) of 15 December 1946 to assist victims of the nazi, fascist or falangist régimes and others unable or unwilling to avail themselves of the protection of the Government of their country of nationality. The IRO terminated its activities on 30 June 1950, leaving about 180,000 refugees to be repatriated or resettled.

11. The terms of reference of the Office were first set out in General Assembly resolution 319 (IV) of 3 December 1949 and further elaborated in Assembly resolution 428 (V) of 14 December 1950. According to paragraph 8 of the annex to the latter resolution, which annex constitutes the Statute of the Office, the High Commissioner shall provide for the protection of refugees falling under the competence of his Office by:

(a) Promoting the conclusion and ratification of international conventions for the protection of refugees, supervising their application and proposing amendments thereto;

(b) Promoting through special agreements with Governments the execution of any measures calculated to improve the situation of refugees and to reduce the number requiring protection;

(c) Assisting governmental and private efforts to promote voluntary repatriation or assimilation within new national communities;

(d) Promoting the admission of refugees, not excluding those in the most destitute categories, to the territories of States;

(e) Endeavouring to obtain permission for refugees to transfer their assets and especially those necessary for their resettlement;

(f) Obtaining from Governments information concerning the number and conditions of refugees in their territories and the laws and regulations concerning them;

(g) Keeping in close touch with the Governments and intergovernmental organizations concerned;

(h) Establishing contact in such manner as he may think best with private organizations dealing with refugee questions;

(i) Facilitating the co-ordination of the efforts of private organizations concerned with the welfare of refugees.

Paragraph 9 of the annex stipulates that the High Commissioner shall engage in such additional activities, including repatriation and resettlement, as the General Assembly may determine, within the limits of the resources placed at his disposal.

12. The Office concerns itself with persons who come within its competence under the terms of its Statute. Through subsequent resolutions of the General Assembly, its mandate has been widened to include also displaced persons who are in a refugee-like situation.

13. By resolution 3274 (XXIX) of 10 December 1974, the General Assembly requested the Office of the High Commissioner "provisionally to undertake the functions foreseen under the Convention on the Reduction of Statelessness [of 28 August 1961] in accordance with its article 11 . . .;" and by resolution 31/36 of 30 November 1976, the Assembly requested the High Commissioner "to continue to perform these functions".

14. In accordance with paragraph 2 of its Statute, "The work of the High Commissioner shall be of an entirely non-political character; it shall be humanitarian and social . . .".

1. ORGANIZATIONAL AND PROCEDURAL ARRANGEMENTS

15. The High Commissioner is elected by the General Assembly on nomination of the Secretary-General. He appoints, for the same term as his own mandate, a Deputy High Commissioner of a nationality other than his own.

16. The Office of the High Commissioner is located in Geneva, Switzerland. In accordance with paragraph 16 of the Statute of his Office, the High Commissioner maintains a number of representatives in areas or countries where there are significant refugee problems.

17. The High Commissioner reports annually to the General Assembly through the Economic and Social Council. By a decision of 27 October 1969, the Economic and Social Council arranged that in future the annual report of the United Nations High Commissioner for Refugees would be retained on the agenda of the Council's summer session on the understanding that the report would be transmitted to the General Assembly without debate, unless the Council were to decide otherwise, at the specific request of one or more of its members or of the High Commissioner, at the time of the adoption of the agenda.

18. Assistance provided by the High Commissioner is normally channelled through Governments or governmental bodies or non-governmental organizations. Assistance programmes are submitted for authorization to the Executive Committee of the High Commissioner's Programme and a report on the implementation of these programmes is also submitted to this body.

19. Pursuant to paragraph 4 of the Statute, an Advisory Committee on Refugees was established by Economic and Social Council resolution 393 (XIII) B of 10 September 1951. The Committee was reconstituted as the Executive Committee of the United Nations Refugee Fund, which was in turn replaced by the Executive Committee of the Programme of the United Nations High Commissioner for Refugees, established by Council resolution 672 (XXV) of 30 April 1958. The terms of reference of the Executive Committee were set out in General Assembly resolution 1166 (XII) of 26 November 1957 as follows:

(a) To give directives to the High Commissioner for the liquidation of the United Nations Refugee Fund;

(b) To advise the High Commissioner, at his request, in the exercise of his functions under the Statute of his Office;

(c) To advise the High Commissioner as to whether it is appropriate for international assistance to be provided through his Office in order to help to solve specific refugee problems remaining unsolved after 31 December 1958 or arising after that date;

(d) To authorize the High Commissioner to make appeals for funds to enable him to solve the refugee problems referred to in subparagraph (c) above;

(e) To approve projects for assistance to refugees coming within the scope of subparagraph (c) above;

(f) To give directives to the High Commissioner for the use of the emergency fund to be established under the terms set out in paragraph 7 of resolution 1166 (XII).

20. The Executive Committee meets once a year at Geneva. The Committee consists of 40 representatives of States Members of the United Nations or members of any of the specialized agencies, elected by the Economic and Social Council on the widest geographical basis from those States with a demonstrated interest in, and devotion to, the solution of the refugee problem.

2. INTERNATIONAL PROTECTION AND ASSISTANCE

21.   In accordance with paragraph 1 of the Statute of his Office, the United Nations High Commissioner for Refugees, acting under the authority of the General Assembly, shall assume the function of providing international protection, under the auspices of the United Nations, to refugees who fall within the scope of the present Statute . . . The provisions of paragraph 8 of the Statute, reproduced in paragraph 11 above, determine the means whereby the High Commissioner provides for the protection of refugees falling under the competence of his Office.

22.   The protection activity of the High Commissioner has developed in accordance with the provisions of the Statute, particularly within the framework of international legal instruments such as the 1951 United Nations Convention and its 1967 Protocol relating to the Status of Refugees, the Convention on the Reduction of Statelessness and the Convention relating to the Status of Stateless Persons. In his report to the forty-second session of the General Assembly,[1] the High Commissioner pointed out that there is widespread recognition that persons who have been displaced from their countries as a result of armed conflicts, foreign aggression, occupation or internal upheavals should also be protected from danger through the granting, as a minimum, of temporary asylum, i.e. until such time as conditions in the country of origin permit their safe return.

23.   Paragraph 1 of the Statute provides that the United Nations High Commissioner for Refugees, acting under the authority of the General Assembly, shall assume the function . . . of seeking permanent solutions for the problem of refugees by assisting governments and, subject to the approval of the governments concerned, private organizations to facilitate the voluntary repatriation of such refugees, or their assimilation within new national communities.

24.   Furthermore, paragraphs 9 and 10 of the Statute of his Office provide that:

The High Commissioner shall engage in such additional activities, including repatriation and resettlement, as the General Assembly may determine, within the limits of the resources placed at his disposal.

The High Commissioner shall administer any funds, public or private, which he receives for assistance to refugees, and shall distribute them among the private and, as appropriate, public agencies which he deems best qualified to administer such assistance.

25.   At the time when the Statute of the Office of the High Commissioner was adopted it was considered that its principal function would be to provide international protection for refugees and that its activities in the field of material assistance would assume less prominence. The Office's functions in regard to material assistance were subsequently, however, extended. In resolution 538 (VI) of 2 February 1952, the General Assembly authorized the High Commissioner, under paragraph 10 of the Statute of his Office, to appeal for funds to enable emergency aid to be given to the most needy groups of refugees within his mandate.

26.   In resolution 832 (IX) of 21 October 1954, the General Assembly authorized the High Commissioner to undertake a programme designed to achieve permanent solutions for refugees and authorized him to make appeals for funds for this purpose. Finally, in resolution 1166 (XII) of 26 November 1957, the General Assembly requested the Economic and Social Council to establish the Executive Committee of the High Commissioner's Programme, the functions of which include approving projects for assistance to refugees and authorizing the High Commissioner to make appeals for funds for the financing of such assistance. The Executive Committee of the Programme of the United Nations High Commissioner for Refugees approves the expenditures of the Office of the High Commissioner.

27.   The ever-increasing number of refugee situations throughout the world, and the requests for assistance directed to the High Commissioner by the Governments concerned, have contributed to a considerable development of the activities of the United Nations High Commissioner for Refugees with respect to facilitating voluntary repatriation, resettling refugees in countries of durable asylum and various forms of material assistance to refugees, aimed primarily at durable solutions in the country of asylum.

28.   In recent years, the High Commissioner has also provided assistance, in accordance with the relevant resolutions of the General Assembly, to an increasing number of displaced persons. Thus, in 1986, he was obliged to respond to urgent assistance needs of refugees with whom he was concerned in Somalia, in the Sudan, in Djibouti, and to help voluntary returnees and displaced persons in Ethiopia and Chad.

29.   In accordance with the Statute of his Office, the High Commissioner reports annually to the General Assembly through the Economic and Social Council. He is entitled to present his views to the Assembly, the Council, and their subsidiary bodies. The mandate of the Office is extended by the General Assembly for periods of five years. Most recently, in resolution 42/108 of 7 December 1987, the Assembly decided to continue the Office for a further period of five years from 1 January 1989.

30.   After examining the 1987 report of the High Commissioner on the activities of his Office,[2] the General Assembly in resolution 42/109 of 7 December 1987 noted with satisfaction that 103 States had ratified or acceded to the 1951 Convention and/or the 1967 Protocol relating to the Status of Refugees, and appealed to all States to consider acceding to these instruments in order to enhance their universal character. It condemned all violations of the rights and safety of refugees and asylum-seekers, in particular those perpetrated by military or armed attack against refugee camps and settlements and other forms of violence; recognized

---

[1] *Official Records of the General Assembly, Forty-second Session, Supplement No. 12* (A/42/12).

[2] *Ibid.*

the importance of attaining durable solutions to refugee problems and, in particular, the need to address in this process the causes that force refugees and asylum-seekers to flee their countries of origin in the light of the report of the Group of Governmental Experts on International Co-operation to Avert New Flows of Refugees; and urged all States to support the High Commissioner in his efforts to achieve durable solutions to the problem of refugees and displaced persons of concern to his Office, primarily through voluntary repatriation or return, including assistance to returnees, as appropriate or, whenever appropriate, through integration into countries of asylum or through resettlement in third countries.

31. The Assembly, further, expressed deep appreciation for the valuable material and humanitarian response of receiving countries, in particular those developing countries which, despite limited resources, continue to admit, on a permanent or temporary basis, large numbers of refugees and asylum-seekers; and urged the international community to assist those countries in order to enable them to cope with the additional burden that the care for refugees and asylum-seekers represents.

32. As an integral part of the United Nations system, UNHCR participates fully in all arrangements for co-operation established within that system.

33. With regard to international protection, the High Commissioner maintains direct contact with the Centre for Human Rights, the Commission on Human Rights and the Human Rights Committee and with intergovernmental organizations such as the Council of Europe, the League of Arab States, OAU and the Organization of American States (OAS). In addition, close contact is maintained with the International Committee of the Red Cross (ICRC) and other non-governmental organizations directly concerned with the problems of refugees, displaced persons and stateless persons.

34. With regard to assistance activities, a number of United Nations agencies and programmes have provided help to the High Commissioner, ranging from the implementation of specific sectors of assistance projects to the provision of technical advice and expertise. For example, UNICEF has carried out activities in the fields of health, education and community development; UNDP has assigned United Nations Volunteers in various areas of need; UNFPA has helped in the taking of censuses in refugee camps; and WFP has provided most of the basic food needs of refugees either from its own resources or by channelling bilateral contributions.

35. Of the specialized agencies, ILO has provided technical expertise in such areas as vocational training and income-generating activities for refugee settlements and for women refugees. UNESCO has helped to ascertain, and provide for, the educational needs of refugees, and WHO has provided health co-ordinators for several countries, as well as health supplies.

3. CONVENTION RELATING TO THE STATUS OF REFUGEES

36. In accordance with General Assembly resolution 429 (V) of 14 December 1950, a Conference of Plenipotentiaries met in Geneva in 1951 to consider a draft convention relating to the status of refugees and a draft protocol relating to the status of stateless persons, prepared by an *ad hoc* Committee on Refugees and Stateless Persons which had been established by the Economic and Social Council. On 28 July 1951 the Conference adopted the Convention relating to the Status of Refugees, revising and consolidating previous international agreements on the status of refugees and extending the scope of, and the protection accorded by, such instruments.

37. The Convention sets out, in article 1, a definition of the term "refugee" for the purposes of the Convention. Articles 2 to 11 contain general provisions and provide for non-discrimination as to race, religion, or country of origin; religious freedom, at least to the extent granted to nationals; safeguarding of rights apart from the Convention; equal treatment with aliens unless the Convention contains more favourable provisions, and exemption from legislative reciprocity after three years' residence; exemption from exceptional measures which might be taken against the person, property or interests of nationals of a foreign State solely on account of such nationality; recognition of continuity of residence; and sympathetic consideration of the position of refugee seamen.

38. Articles 12 to 16 pertain to the juridical status of the refugee, articles 17 to 19 concern the rights of refugees to engage in gainful employment, articles 20 to 24 concern the welfare of the refugee in regard to such matters as rationing, housing, public education, public relief, labour legislation and social security. Article 25 deals with the provision of administrative assistance to refugees and article 26 with their freedom of movement. Articles 27 and 28 deal respectively with the issue of identity papers to refugees and of travel documents to enable them to travel outside their country of lawful residence. (The Schedule to the Convention contains detailed provisions regarding the issue of such travel documents, their period of validity, their renewal or extension, etc.) Article 29 deals with the applicability of fiscal charges to refugees and article 30 with the right of refugees to transfer their assets from the territory of a Contracting State to another country where they have been admitted for resettlement. Articles 31 to 33 contain important provisions which are relevant to the question of asylum. According to these articles, a refugee requesting asylum in the territory of a contracting State may not be subjected to penalties on account of his illegal entry or presence provided he presents himself without delay to the competent authorities; if he has resided in the territory of a contracting State he may not be expelled save on grounds of national security and public order and in any event he may not be expelled or returned in any manner whatsoever to the frontiers of

territories where his life or freedom would be threatened on account of his race, religion, nationality, membership of a particular social group or political opinion.[3] Article 34 of the Convention requires contracting States as far as possible to facilitate the assimilation and naturalization of refugees and in particular to make every effort to expedite naturalization proceedings and to reduce the charges and costs of such proceedings. Article 35 of the Convention requires the contracting States to co-operate with the Office of the United Nations High Commissioner for Refugees in the exercise of its functions and in particular to facilitate its duty of supervising the application of the provisions of the Convention.

4. PROTOCOL RELATING TO THE STATUS OF REFUGEES

39. As a result of a dateline contained in the definition of the term "refugee" the Convention relating to the Status of Refugees only applied to persons who had become refugees "as a result of events occurring before 1 January 1951". In order to remove this dateline and to make the Convention applicable in all new refugee situations, a Protocol relating to the Status of Refugees was prepared and submitted to the General Assembly at its twenty-first session. In resolution 2198 (XXI) of 16 December 1966 the Assembly took note of the Protocol and requested the Secretary-General to transmit its text to States with a view to enabling them to accede. The Protocol was opened for signature on 31 January 1967 and upon accession thereto by six States, came into force on 4 October 1967.

5. DECLARATION AND DRAFT CONVENTION ON TERRITORIAL ASYLUM

40. Proposals for the inclusion of a provision on the right of asylum were put forward at various stages in the preparation of the International Covenants on Human Rights, but were rejected because of the difficulty of reaching agreement on the categories of persons who should be granted asylum. While there was a general understanding that States should be generous in granting asylum it was not found possible to translate this principle into a positive obligation in the Covenants.

41. As no article on asylum had been included in the draft covenants, the Government of France submitted to the Commission on Human Rights, in 1957, a draft declaration on the right of asylum.[4] The Commission, after considering the comments of Governments, the United Nations High Commissioner for Refugees, and non-governmental organizations concerned, adopted the

draft declaration at its sixteenth session, in 1960, and transmitted it to the Economic and Social Council, which in turn forwarded it to the General Assembly.

42. The Third Committee of the General Assembly considered the draft declaration at its fifteenth, sixteenth, and seventeenth sessions, held in 1960, 1961 and 1962. In 1965 the Assembly referred the question to the Sixth (Legal) Committee. In 1966, a Working Group of that Committee prepared a revised draft declaration on the basis of the work which had been done by the Commission on Human Rights and the Third Committee.

43. By resolution 2312 (XXII) of 14 December 1967, the General Assembly adopted the Declaration on Territorial Asylum. The Declaration lays down a series of fundamental principles in regard to territorial asylum. It states in the first place that the granting of asylum "is a peaceful and humanitarian act and that, as such, it cannot be regarded as unfriendly by any other State". Moreover, where a State finds difficulty in granting or continuing to grant asylum, other States "individually or jointly or through the United Nations shall consider, in a spirit of international solidarity, appropriate measures to lighten the burden on that State". Finally the Declaration gives expression to the basic humanitarian principles of *non-refoulement* according to which no person shall be rejected at the frontier, expelled, or returned to a country where he may be subjected to persecution.

44. At its thirtieth session the General Assembly, in resolution 3456 (XXX) of 9 December 1975, requested the Secretary-General, in consultation with the United Nations High Commissioner for Refugees, to convene a conference of plenipotentiaries on territorial asylum from 10 January to 4 February 1977, to consider and adopt a convention on territorial asylum.

45. The United Nations Conference on Territorial Asylum met at Geneva as scheduled but did not succeed in adopting the proposed draft convention. It recommended that the General Assembly consider the question of convening, at an appropriate time, a resumed session of the Conference. As at 31 December 1982 a resumed session had not been convened.

6. ASSISTANCE TO STUDENT REFUGEES IN SOUTHERN AFRICA

46. In resolution 31/126 of 16 December 1976, the General Assembly expressed its concern about the continuing influx of large numbers of South African student refugees to Botswana, Lesotho and Swaziland, which imposed a heavy burden on the limited resources of those countries; and requested the Secretary-General to consult with the three Governments and the liberation movements concerned with a view to organizing and providing appropriate emergency financial and other forms of assistance for the care, subsistence and education of these refugee students.

---

[3] This prohibition of expulsion or return contained in article 33 may, however, he made the subject of an exception in the case of a refugee who is a danger to the security of the country in which he is or who, having been convicted by a final judgement of a particularly serious crime, constitutes a danger to the community of that country.

[4] E/CN.4/L.454/Rev.1.

47. At its thirty-second and thirty-third sessions the General Assembly endorsed the measures taken by the Secretary-General and the United Nations High Commissioner for Refugees to mobilize assistance to the South African student refugees, and urged the international community to contribute generously to the assistance programme. At its thirty-fourth session, in resolution 34/174 of 17 December 1979, the Assembly decided to enlarge the assistance programme for South African student refugees to include student refugees from Namibia and Zimbabwe, and reiterated its appeals for increased and sustained assistance.

48. At recent sessions the General Assembly continued its annual review of assistance to student refugees in southern Africa. In resolution 42/138 of 7 December 1987 it noted with concern that the discriminatory and repulsive practices that continue to be applied in South Africa and Namibia cause a continued and increased influx of student refugees into Botswana, Lesotho, Swaziland and Zambia; and expressed its appreciation to the Governments of those countries for granting asylum and making educational and other facilities available to the student refugees in spite of the pressure that the continuing influx of those refugees exerts on facilities in their countries.

49. The Assembly requested the High Commissioner, in co-operation with the Secretary-General, to continue to organize and implement an effective programme of educational and other appropriate assistance for student refugees from Namibia and South Africa granted asylum in the countries mentioned above, and appealed for contributions to the assistance programme for such students.

7. INTERNATIONAL CO-OPERATION TO AVERT NEW FLOWS OF REFUGEES

50. The item, "International co-operation to avert new flows of refugees", was included on the agenda of the General Assembly at the request of the Federal Republic of Germany.[5] In resolution 35/124 of 11 December 1980, the Assembly, deeply disturbed by the human suffering affecting millions of men, women and children who fled or were forcibly expelled from their homelands and sought refuge in other countries, expressed the view that the United Nations was called upon to consider, in addition to humanitarian and social relief, suitable means to avert new flows of refugees. Strongly condemning all policies and practices of oppressive and racist régimes as well as aggression, alien domination and foreign occupation, which in its view were primarily responsible for the massive flows of refugees throughout the world and which resulted in inhuman suffering, the Assembly invited all Member States to convey to the Secretary-General their comments and suggestions on international co-operation to avert new flows of refugees and to facilitate the return of those refugees who wished to do so. The Secretary-General was requested to report to the Assembly on this question.

51. At its thirty-sixth session, in 1981, the General Assembly examined the Secretary-General's report,[6] and adopted resolution 36/148 of 16 December 1981, in which it reaffirmed the inviolability of the provisions of the Charter of the United Nations and the Universal Declaration of Human Rights and of other existing international instruments, norms and principles relevant to responsibilities of States with regard to averting new massive flows of refugees, as well as to the status and the protection of refugees; and noted that, in addition to creating individual human misery, massive flows of refugees could impose great political, economic and social burdens upon the international community as a whole, with dire effects on developing countries. The Assembly further emphasized the right of refugees to return to their homes in their homelands and reaffirmed the right of those who did not wish to return to receive adequate compensation.

52. Under resolution 36/148 the General Assembly established a group of governmental experts of 17 members and requested it to undertake as soon as possible a comprehensive review of the problem in all its aspects. The Group of Governmental Experts on International Co-operation to Avert New Flows of Refugees was called upon to take into account the comments and suggestions which had been communicated to the Secretary-General, the views expressed in the Assembly and the Commission on Human Rights, and the study on human rights and mass exoduses which a Special Rapporteur was preparing for submission to the Commission.

53. The final report of the Group of Governmental Experts[7] was examined by the General Assembly at its forty-first session, in 1986. In the report, the Group analysed the circumstances causing new massive flows of refugees and the appropriate means to improve international co-operation to avert such massive flows.

54. The analysis of causes and factors led to the conclusion that the emergence of massive flows of refugees is a result of a number of complex and often interrelated economic and social problems related to, and influenced by, the overall international situation; it may affect the political and social stability, as well as the economic development, of the receiving States, and also carry adverse consequences for the economies of the countries of origin and entire regions, thus endangering international peace and security. Moreover, in view of its complex nature and magnitude, as well as its potentially destabilizing effects, averting massive flows of

[5] A/35/242.

[6] A/36/582 and Corr.1 and Add.1.

[7] A/41/324.

refugees is a matter of serious concern to the international community as a whole.

55.   In its recommendations, the Group proposed that the General Assembly should call upon Member States, for the purpose of averting new massive flows of refugees, to respect a number of obligations, among them:

. . .

(c) In view of their responsibilities under the Charter of the United Nations and consistent with their obligations under the existing international instruments in the field of human rights, States, in the exercise of their sovereignty, should do all within their means to prevent new massive flows of refugees. Accordingly, States should refrain from creating or contributing by their policies to causes and factors which generally lead to massive flows of refugees;

(d) States should promote civil, political, economic, social and cultural rights and accordingly refrain from denying them to, and from discriminating against, groups of their population because of their nationality, ethnicity, race, religion or language, thus directly or indirectly forcing them to leave their country;

(e) States should co-operate with one another in order to prevent future massive flows of refugees. They should promote international co-operation in all its aspects, in particular at the regional and sub-regional levels, as an appropriate and important means to avert such flows;

(f) States should, wherever new massive flows of refugees occur, respect the existing generally recognized norms and principles of international law governing the rights and obligations of States and refugees directly concerned, including those pertaining to the rights of refugees to be facilitated in returning voluntarily and safely to their homes in their homelands and to receive adequate compensation therefrom, where so established, in cases of those who do not wish to return;

. . .

56.   The Group further recommended that Member States should be called upon to co-operate with one another and with the Security Council, the General Assembly, the Economic and Social Council, the Secretariat and other relevant organs of the United Nations in a fuller and more timely manner for the prevention of new massive flows of refugees, and that the main organs of the United Nations, and the Secretary-General, should make fuller use of their respective competences to prevent such massive flows.

57.   The General Assembly, in resolution 41/70 of 3 December 1986, endorsed the conclusions and recommendations of the Group of Governmental Experts, called upon Member States to respect the recommendations, and requested the main organs of the United Nations, and the Secretary-General, to make fuller use of their respective competences for the prevention of new massive flows of refugees.

8. HUMAN RIGHTS AND MASS EXODUSES

58.   In resolution 30 (XXXVI) of 11 March 1980, the Commission on Human Rights noted the continuing great distress of refugees and displaced persons in various regions of the world and the immense burden imposed on the first host countries and territories which received the victims of these sudden and massive movements of population, which were frequently the result of violations of human rights. The Commission requested the Secretary-General, in cases where any

large-scale exoduses became a matter of international concern, to consider establishing direct contacts with appropriate Governments, to assess the relationships between the situation and full enjoyment of human rights and to make concrete recommendations for ameliorating such situations.

59.   Later that year the General Assembly, in resolution 35/196 of 15 December 1980, also expressed deep concern at the continued incidence of large-scale exoduses and displacements and the resulting hardships and problems for the persons and States concerned, expressed its determination to facilitate solutions to those problems, and requested the Commission on Human Rights to make recommendations for further action.

60.   At its thirty-seventh session, in resolution 29 (XXXVII) of 11 March 1981, the Commission decided to appoint a special rapporteur to study the question of human rights and mass exoduses, and invited its Chairman to appoint an individual of recognized international standing as special rapporteur. The Council approved that action in decision 1981/145 of 8 May 1981.

61.   The Special Rapporteur, Sadruddin Aga Khan, presented his study on human rights and massive exoduses[8] to the Commission at its thirty-eighth session. In resolution 1982/32 of 11 March 1982, the Commission commended him for the study and requested the Secretary-General to transmit it to the General Assembly and to bring it to the attention of the Group of Governmental Experts on International Co-operation to Avert New Flows of Refugees established by Assembly resolution 36/148 of 16 December 1981.

62.   At its forty-second session, in 1987, the General Assembly reviewed the Special Rapporteur's Study, together with the report of the Group of Governmental Experts on International Co-operation to Avert New Flows of Refugees[9] and the Secretary-General's report on human rights and mass exoduses.[10] In addition, its attention was drawn to the Secretary-General's decision to establish an office for research and the collection of information responsible, inter alia, for the provision of early warning of developing situations requiring his attention and the monitoring of factors related to possible flows of refugees and displaced persons and comparable emergencies and the preparation of plans for possible responses, as mentioned in his report on the work of the Organization to the General Assembly.[11]

63.   The Assembly, in resolution 42/144 of 7 December 1987 welcomed the steps taken by the Secretary-General and other steps taken within the United Nations to examine and deal with the problem. Conscious of the fact that human rights violations are one of the multiple and complex factors causing mass exoduses of refugees and

---

[8] E/CN.4/1503.

[9] A/41/324.

[10] A/38/538.

[11] *Official Records of the General Assembly, Forty-first Session, Supplement No. 1* (A/41/1).

displaced persons, as indicated in each of the studies and report, the Assembly invited the Commission on Human Rights to keep the question of human rights under review.

C. International Conferences on Assistance to Refugees in Africa

64. The General Assembly, in resolution 35/42 of 25 November 1980, noted with deep regret the inadequacy of the assistance provided to the growing number of African refugees, and requested the international community to contribute substantially to programmes designed to help them. It requested the Secretary-General, in close co-operation with the Secretary-General of the Organization of African Unity and the United Nations High Commissioner for Refugees, to convene at Geneva on 9 and 10 April 1981, at the ministerial level, an International Conference on Assistance to Refugees in Africa.

65. The report of the Secretary-General on the Conference[12] was considered by the General Assembly at its thirty-sixth session. In resolution 36/124 of 14 December 1981, the Assembly expressed its appreciation and gratitude to all donor countries and to the international community at large for their very positive response to the appeal for assistance to African refugees and for their contribution to such assistance, and urged them to continue to support programmes undertaken on behalf of refugees in Africa.

66. As requested in paragraph 6 of resolution 36/124, the Secretary-General submitted a report[13] to the Economic and Social Council at its second regular session of 1982, providing detailed information on post-conference activities, including data on pledges and contributions made at the Conference as known at 3 May 1982. He submitted information on activities after 3 May 1982 to the General Assembly.[14] These reports indicated that one of the results of the Conference had been the receipt of pledges of approximately $573 million.

67. In resolution 37/197 of 18 December 1982 the General Assembly expressed its appreciation to all donor countries, the United Nations High Commissioner for Refugees and the international community for their continued support and assistance to African refugees, and its concern that the assistance available fell short of the urgent needs of refugees and returnees in Africa. It requested the Secretary-General, in close co-operation with the Secretary-General of the Organization of African Unity and the United Nations High Commissioner for Refugees, to convene a second International Conference on Assistance to Refugees in Africa at Geneva in 1984.

68. A second International Conference on Assistance to Refugees in Africa was held at Geneva from 9 to 11 July 1984 to launch collective action by the international community aimed at achieving lasting solutions. The report of the Conference[15] was examined by the General Assembly at its thirty-ninth session, in 1984.

69. The Declaration and Programme of Action adopted by the Conference pointed out the persistent and serious problem of large numbers of refugees on the African continent and the economic and social burden borne by African countries of asylum on account of the presence of those refugees. On the basis of these findings the General Assembly, in resolution 39/139 of 14 December 1984 recognized the universal collective responsibility of sharing the urgent and overwhelming burden of the problem of African refugees through effective mobilization of resources to meet the urgent and long-term needs of the refugees and to strengthen the capacity of countries of asylum to provide adequately for them, as well as to assist the countries of origin in the rehabilitation of voluntary returnees. It thanked all who had contributed to alleviating the plight of the refugees and urged the international community to maintain the momentum created by the Conference and to translate its principles and programmes into action.

70. However in 1987 the Assembly, after reviewing a later report by the Secretary-General on assistance to refugees in Africa[16] noted with deep concern in resolution 42/107 of 7 December 1987 that many of the projects submitted to the Second International Conference on Assistance to Refugees in Africa had yet to be funded and implemented, and called upon all Member States and organizations of the United Nations system to intensify their support for the speedy implementation of the recommendations and pledges made at the Conference.

D. Group of Governmental Experts on International Co-operation to Avert New Flows of Refugees

71. Taking into account paragraph 4 of General Assembly resolution 40/166 of 16 December 1985, in which the Assembly called upon the Group of Governmental Experts on International Co-operation to Avert New Flows of Refugees which it had established by resolution 36/148 of 16 December 1981 "to work expeditiously on the fulfilment of its mandate", the Group concluded its study in May 1986.[17]

72. In its conclusions, the Group of Experts stated that its analysis of causes and factors showed that the emergence of massive flows of refugees is a result of a number of complex and often interrelated political, economic and social problems related to, and influenced by, the overall international situation. It added that massive flows of refugees may affect the political and

---

[12] A/36/534, annex I.

[13] E/1982/76.

[14] A/37/522.

[15] A/CONF. 125/2 and Add.1.

[16] A/42/491.

[17] A/41/254, annex.

social stability, as well as the economic development, of receiving States, and may also have adverse consequences for the economies of the countries of origin or even entire regions, thus undermining international peace and security. In its recommendations, the Group expressed the view that States, in the exercise of their sovereignty, should do all within their means to prevent new massive flows of refugees, and should refrain from creating, or contributing to, such massive flows.

73. On the basis of the Group's report, the Assembly in resolution 41/70 of 3 December 1986 urged the main organs of the United Nations to make fuller use of their competences under the Charter of the United Nations to prevent new massive flows of refugees, and requested the Secretary-General to bring the report of the Group of Governmental Experts to the attention of Member States and all relevant organizations, organs and programmes of the United Nations system.

XI. THE SITUATION OF HUMAN RIGHTS IN PARTICULAR AREAS AND COUNTRIES

Introduction

1. In a resolution adopted on 18 June 1965, the Special Committee on the Situation with regard to the Implementation of the Declaration on the Granting of Independence to Colonial Countries and Peoples drew the attention of the Commission on Human Rights to evidence submitted by petitioners concerning violations of human rights committed in certain Non-Self Governing Territories.

2. After discussing the Special Committee's resolution the Economic and Social Council, in resolution 1102 (XL) of 4 March 1966, invited the Commission to consider, as a matter of importance and urgency, "the question of the violation of human rights and fundamental freedoms, including policies of racial discrimination and segregation and of *apartheid* in all countries, with particular reference to colonial and other dependent countries and territories", and to submit its recommendations on measures to halt those violations to the Council at its forty-first session.

3. The Commission considered this question at its twenty-second session, in 1966, and adopted resolution 2 (XXII) on 25 March 1966. In part B of that resolution the Commission informed the Council that, in order completely to deal with the question of violations of human rights and fundamental freedoms in all countries, it would be necessary for the Commission to consider the means by which it might be more fully informed of such violations, with a view to devising recommendations for measures to halt them.

4. The General Assembly, in resolution 2144 A (XXI) of 26 October 1966, invited the Economic and Social Council and the Commission on Human Rights to give urgent consideration to "ways and means of improving the capacity of the United Nations to put a stop to violations of human rights wherever they may occur".

5. At its nineteenth session, in 1967, the Sub-Commission on Prevention of Discrimination and Protection of Minorities, in resolution 5 (XIX) of 18 January 1967 recommended that the Commission should adopt an appropriate method for the gathering, collation and evaluation of relevant information on the violation of human rights and fundamental freedoms.

6. In resolution 8 (XXIII) of 16 March 1967 the Commission decided to give annual consideration to the item, "Question of violations of human rights and fundamental freedoms, including policies of racial discrimination and segregation and of *apartheid*, in all countries, with particular reference to colonial and other dependent countries and territories". The Commission requested the Sub-Commission to prepare, for the use of the Commission in examining this question, a report containing information on violations of human rights and fundamental freedoms from all available sources, and invited the Sub-Commission to bring to the attention of the Commission any situation which it had reasonable cause to believe revealed a consistent pattern of violation of human rights and fundamental freedoms in any country. In this connection the Commission requested the Economic and Social Council to authorize the Commission and the Sub-Commission to examine information relevant to gross violations of human rights and fundamental freedoms contained in communications concerning human rights received by the United Nations. The Commission further requested authority, in appropriate cases, to make a thorough study and investigation of situations which revealed a consistent pattern of violations of human rights, and to report with recommendations thereon to the Council.

7. The Economic and Social Council, in resolution 1235 (XLII) of 6 June 1967, authorized the Commission and the Sub-Commission to examine information relevant to gross violations of human rights contained in the communications, and further decided "that the Commission on Human Rights may, in appropriate cases . . . make a thorough study of situations which reveal a consistent pattern of violations of human rights . . . and report, with recommendations thereon, to the Economic and Social Council".

8. Three years later, the Council adopted resolution 1503 (XLVIII) of 27 May 1970, in which it authorized the Sub-Commission on Prevention of Discrimination and Protection of Minorities to appoint a working group, to meet in private once a year to consider all communications, including replies of Governments thereon, received by the Secretary-General "with a view to bringing to the attention of the Sub-Commission those communications, together with replies of Governments, if any, which appear to reveal a consistent pattern of gross and reliably attested violations of human rights and fundamental freedoms within the terms of reference of the Sub-Commission".[1]

9. In resolution 32/130 of 16 December 1977, the General Assembly decided that:

In approaching human rights questions within the United Nations system, the international community should accord, or continue to accord, priority to the search for solutions to the mass and flagrant violations of human rights of peoples and persons affected by situations, such as those resulting from *apartheid*, from all forms of racial

---

[1] For information on the procedures established for the handling of communications concerning violations of human rights, see chapter XIV, section C.

discrimination, from colonialism, from foreign domination and occupation, from aggression and threats against national sovereignty, national unity and territorial integrity, as well as from the refusal to recognize the fundamental rights of peoples to self-determination and of every nation to the exercise of full sovereignty over its wealth and natural resources.

10. In a number of resolutions adopted later, and most recently in resolution 42/119 of 7 December 1987, the Assembly reiterated this approach, reaffirmed its responsibility for achieving international co-operation in promoting and encouraging respect for human rights and fundamental freedoms for all, and expressed its concern about serious violations of human rights, particularly mass and flagrant violations of those rights, wherever they may occur.

A. The situation of human rights in particular areas

1. SOUTHERN AFRICA

11. On the basis of reports submitted annually by its *Ad Hoc* Working Group of Experts on southern Africa,[2] the Commission on Human Rights has reviewed at each session since 1976 the constant and flagrant violations of human rights in southern Africa, and in particular the policies of *apartheid* and racial discrimination in South Africa, Namibia and Southern Rhodesia.

12. In resolution 8 (XXXII) of 4 March 1976, the Commission deplored that policies of *apartheid* and racial discrimination persisted in southern Africa and that South Africa was continuing its illegal occupation of the territory of Namibia. In later resolutions the Commission has condemned the massacres committed by the South African police during the demonstrations at Soweto in June 1976, denounced with indignation the inhuman treatment of the freedom fighters arrested by the régimes in South Africa and Southern Rhodesia, vehemently condemned the criminal acts committed by the South African authorities on children protesting against *apartheid*, and expressed its deep indignation at the continuing widespread and inhuman violations of human rights in South Africa and in Namibia.

13. Most recently the Commission, in resolution 1987/7 of 19 February 1987, referred to "the worsening of the situation in southern Africa as a result of South Africa's racist policies of oppression, aggression and occupation, which constitutes a clear threat to world peace and security", and condemned "the continuing breach by South Africa of the obligations assumed by it under the Charter of the United Nations and its persistent non-compliance with the relevant resolutions and decisions of the United Nations".[3]

2. THE OCCUPIED ARAB TERRITORIES

14. On the basis of reports submitted by its Special Committee to Investigate Israeli Practices Affecting the Population of the Occupied Territories, the General Assembly adopted a series of resolutions concerning Israeli violations of the human rights of the people of those territories,[4] reaffirming that occupation itself constitutes a grave violation of their human rights, condemning Israeli policies and practices giving rise to these and other violations, and demanding that it cease and desist forthwith.

15. The Security Council also adopted a number of resolutions referring to Israeli violation of the human rights of the people of the occupied territories.[5] In addition, the International Conference on the Question of Palestine, held at Geneva from 29 August to 7 September 1983, adopted the Geneva Declaration which touched on the subject.[6]

16. Recalling these decisions, as well as its own previous resolutions,[7] the Commission on Human Rights, in resolution 1986/1 A of 20 February 1986, urged Israel to refrain from the policies and practices violating human rights in the occupied territories, and to report, through the Secretary-General, to the Commission at its forty-third session on the implementation of the resolution. At the same time the Commission requested the General Assembly to recommend to the Security Council the adoption against Israel of the measures referred to in Chapter VII of the Charter of the United Nations for its persistent violation of the human rights of the population of the Palestinian and other occupied Arab territories.

17. In resolution 1986/2 of the same date, the Commission directed its attention to the Syrian territory occupied by Israel. It strongly condemned Israel for its persistent disregard for, and defiance of, the provisions of Security Council resolution 497 (1981) and other resolutions relating to that territory, and strongly deprecated Israel's failure to implement the provisions of those resolutions by ending its occupation and ceasing its repressive measures and violations of human rights. In particular it deplored "the inhuman treatment, terror and practices contrary to human rights which the Israeli occupation authorities continue to apply against Syrian citizens in the occupied Syrian Golan Heights by reason

---

[2] E/CN.4/1187, E/CN.4/1222 and Corr.1, E/CN.4/1270, E/CN.4/1311, E/CN.4/1365, E/CN.4/1429, E/CN.4/1485 and 1486, E/CN.4/1983/10, E/CN.4/1984/8, E/CN.4/1985/8, E/CN.4/1986/9 and E/CN.4/1987/8.

[3] For information concerning the situation of human rights in South Africa and Namibia, see chapter V.

[4] Resolutions ES-7/2 of 29 July 1980, 37/88 A to G of 10 December 1982, 37/123 A to F of 16 and 20 December 1982, 38/58 A to E of 13 December 1983, 38/79 A to H of 15 December 1983, 39/49 A to D of 11 December 1984, 39/95 A to H of 14 December 1984 and 40/161 A to G of 16 December 1985.

[5] Resolutions 237 (1967) of 14 June 1967, 465 (1980) of 1 March 1980, 468 (1980) of 8 May 1980, 469 (1980) of 20 May 1980, 471 (1980) of 5 June 1980, 476 (1980) of 30 June 1980, 478 (1980) of 20 August 1980 and 484 (1980) of 10 December 1980.

[6] *Report of the International Conference on the Question of Palestine, Geneva, 29 August-7 September 1983* (United Nations publication, Sales No. E.83.I.21), part one, chap. I, sect. A.

[7] Resolutions 1982/1 A and B of 11 February 1982, 1983/1 A and B and 1983/2 of 15 February 1983, 1984/1 A and B and 1984/2 of 20 February 1984 and 1985/1 A and B of 19 February 1985.

of their refusal of Israeli nationality and in order to force them to carry Israeli identity cards, which practices constitute a flagrant violation of the Universal Declaration of Human Rights, the Geneva Convention relative to the Protection of Civilian Persons in Time of War of 12 August 1949, and the relevant resolutions adopted by the Security Council, the General Assembly and other international bodies, and also constitute a threat to peace and international security''.

B. The situation of human rights in particular countries

1. AFGHANISTAN

18. On 3 January 1980, a number of Member States addressed a letter to the President of the Security Council requesting an urgent meeting of the Council to consider the situation in Afghanistan and its implications for international peace and security. The Council met from 5 to 9 January and decided, in view of the lack of unanimity of its permanent members, to call an emergency special session of the General Assembly to examine that matter.

19. At its sixth emergency special session, held in January 1980, the General Assembly, in resolution ES-62, of 14 January 1980, strongly deplored the armed intervention in Afghanistan, called for the withdrawal of foreign troops from that country, and urged all parties concerned to assist in bringing about conditions necessary for the voluntary return of the Afghan refugees to their homes.

20. The Commission on Human Rights considered the situation in Afghanistan at its thirty-sixth session, and, in resolution 3 (XXXVI) of 14 February 1980, condemned the Soviet military aggression against the Afghan people, denounced and deplored it as a flagrant violation of international laws, covenants, and norms, primarily the Charter of the United Nations, and called upon all peoples and Governments throughout the world to persist in condemning that aggression and denouncing it as an aggression against human rights and a violation of the freedoms of peoples. The Commission demanded the immediate and unconditional withdrawal of all Soviet troops stationed on Afghan territories, reiterated that Soviet troops should refrain from acts of oppression and tyranny against the Afghan people until the complete withdrawal of Soviet forces from Afghan territory, called upon all Member States to refrain from providing assistance to the imposed régime of Afghanistan, and urged all States and people throughout the world to provide generous assistance and succour to the refugees from Afghanistan who had been driven away from their homes.

21. Later the Economic and Social Council, in resolution 1984/37 of 24 May 1984, requested the Chairman of the Commission to appoint a Special Rapporteur to examine the situation of human rights in Afghanistan.

The Special Rapporteur, Mr. Felix Ermacora, reported to the Commission at its forty-first session, in 1985.[8]

22. After examining the report the Commission, in resolution 1985/38 of 13 March 1985, expressed its profound concern at the grave and massive human rights violations in Afghanistan as reflected in that report; and expressed its distress, in particular, at the widespread violations of the right to life, liberty and security of person, including the commonplace practice of torture against the régime's opponents, indiscriminate bombings of the civilian population and the deliberate destruction of crops. It called on the parties to the conflict to apply fully the principles and rules of international humanitarian law and to admit international humanitarian organizations, in particular the International Committee of the Red Cross, and to facilitate their operations for the alleviation of the suffering of the people in Afghanistan; and urged the authorities in Afghanistan to put a stop to the grave and massive violations of human rights and in particular to the military repression being conducted against the civilian population of Afghanistan.

23. The General Assembly, after examining an interim report of the Special Rapporteur,[9] also expressed profound concern that disregard for human rights was more widespread than had been recognized before and that the conflict continued to engender human rights violations on a large scale with the result that not only the lives of individuals but the existence of whole groups of persons and tribes were endangered. In resolution 40/137 of 13 December 1985 it noted that such widespread violations of human rights, that had already caused millions of people to flee their homes and country, were still giving rise to large flows of refugees and displaced persons. It urged the authorities in Afghanistan to co-operate with the Commission on Human Rights and its Special Rapporteur.

24. The mandate of the Special Rapporteur has been renewed annually since then, and he has continued to report to each annual session of the General Assembly and the Commission. His 1987 report to the Commission[10] indicated that a situation of armed conflict continued to exist in Afghanistan, leaving large numbers of victims without protection or assistance, but that the International Committee of the Red Cross had resumed its activities in that country and that the Afghan authorities had made promising declarations on national reconciliation.

25. The Commission, in resolution 1987/58 of 11 March 1987, expressed deep concern that the Afghan authorities, with heavy support from foreign troops, were acting with great severity against their opponents and suspected opponents without any respect for the international human rights obligations which they had assumed; that the methods of warfare used were contrary to humanitarian standards; that the civilian pop-

---

[8] E/CN.4/1985/21.

[9] A/40/843, annex.

[10] E/CN.4/1987/22.

266

ulation suffered severe consequences as a result of indiscriminate bombardments and military operations primarily targeted on villages and the agricultural structure; that the widespread violations of the right to life, liberty and security of person continued; that numbers of persons were detained for seeking to exercise their fundamental rights and freedoms under conditions contrary to internationally-recognized standards; that the educational system did not appear to respect the liberty of parents to ensure the religious and moral education of their children in conformity with their own convictions; and that such widespread violations of human rights were still giving rise to large flows of refugees and displaced persons.

26. The General Assembly, after examining an interim report prepared by the Special Rapporteur,[11] expressed its own concern about these situations in resolution 42/135 of 7 December 1987, and welcomed the cooperation that the Afghan authorities had begun to extend to the Commission by permitting its Special Rapporteur access to facilities for conducting his investigation when he visited Afghanistan from 30 July to 9 August 1987.

2. BOLIVIA

27. In resolution 23 (XXXIII) of 12 September 1980, the Sub-Commission on Prevention of Discrimination and Protection of Minorities expressed deep concern about serious and reliable reports of gross violations of human rights in Bolivia. The Sub-Commission made an urgent appeal to the Government of Bolivia to respect the Universal Declaration of Human Rights and to take all necessary steps to restore and safeguard basic human rights and fundamental freedoms in Bolivia, particularly when there were threats to human life and liberty, and recommended that the Commission on Human Rights should study the reported violations and take urgent measures aimed at the restoration of human rights in that country. It requested Governments, specialized agencies, other intergovernmental organizations and non-governmental organizations in consultative status, to submit information on the subject to the Secretary-General and called upon one of its members, Mrs. Halima Embarek Warzazi, to prepare an analysis of the information and to present it to the Commission on Human Rights.

28. The General Assembly, in resolution 35/185 of 15 December 1980, took note of a letter addressed to the Secretary-General by the Bolivian authorities indicating their readiness to fix a date on which a delegation from the Commission on Human Rights might visit Bolivia,[12] urged those authorities to ensure respect for human rights and fundamental freedoms, including freedom of expression and trade union rights, and requested the Commission on Human Rights to accept the invitation by the Bolivian authorities, in order to study the human rights situation at first hand.

29. The analysis of the information received by the Secretary-General, prepared by Mrs. Warzazi,[13] was presented to the Commission on Human Rights at its thirty-seventh session. In the analysis, she pointed out that "it must first be recognized that no thorough and comprehensive investigation of the human rights situation in that country by an impartial international body has yet been made. However, the information ... contains allegations of serious violations perpetrated during and after the *coup d'état* in 1980". The analysis of the material, she added, "appears to establish a direct relationship between the violations of human rights and the events that took place in the country after the military *coup*". After reviewing the main allegations of violations relating to the Government of Bolivia, Mrs. Warzazi concluded that they consisted of accusations concerning violations of the rights enumerated in articles 3, 5, 21 and 23, paragraph 4, of the Universal Declaration of Human Rights.

30. The Commission, in resolution 34 (XXXVII) of 11 March 1981, requested its Chairman to appoint a Special Envoy of the Commission to make a thorough study of the human rights situation in Bolivia. Pursuant to that resolution, Mr. Héctor Gros Espiell was appointed as the Commission's Special Envoy, and visited Bolivia between 20 and 27 October 1981. His study,[14] together with the comments of the Government of Bolivia[15] was presented to the Commission at its thirty-eighth session. In the study, the Special Envoy concluded that, following 17 June 1980, grave, massive and persistent violations of human rights had been committed in Bolivia, but that since 4 September 1981, there had been an improvement in the situation.

31. Having extended the mandate of the Special Envoy, the Commission examined a further study by him,[16] and the comments of the Government of Bolivia thereon,[17] at its thirty-ninth session, and noted with satisfaction the Special Envoy's conclusion that since 10 October 1982 the constitutional Government of Bolivia had demonstrated complete respect for human rights. It also welcomed the creation of a national commission to investigate cases of disappearances, and noted the determination of the Government to take the necessary measures to ensure that a thorough investigation of all past violations of human rights would be undertaken with a view to establishing responsibility through due process of law. The Commission decided to conclude its consideration of the human rights situation in Bolivia and requested the Secretary-General to provide advisory services and other appropriate human rights assistance as might be requested by the Government.[18]

---

[11] A/42/667 and Corr.1, annex.

[12] A/C.3/35/9.

[13] E/CN.4/1441.

[14] E/CN.4/1500 and Corr.1.

[15] E/CN.4/1500/Add.1.

[16] E/CN.4/1983/22.

[17] E/CN.4/1983/22/Add.1.

[18] Commission on Human Rights resolution 1983/33.

32. An its fortieth session the Commission considered a memorandum submitted by the Special Envoy[19] in which he suggested that the most effective co-operation would consist of assistance in channelling and promoting the resolution of the basic economic and social situations which condition the genuine existence of human rights, and that for this purpose it would be necessary for a team from the Centre for Human Rights, subsequently broadened and supplemented to an adequate extent, to plan and organize all-round assistance from the United Nations system so as to co-operate in the economic and social rehabilitation of Bolivia. The Commission, in resolution 1984/43 of 13 March 1984, endorsed the suggestion.

33. On recommendation of the Commission, the Economic and Social Council, in resolution 1984/32 of 24 May 1984, requested the Secretary-General, under the programme of advisory services in the field of human rights and in consultation with the Government of Bolivia, to examine ways and means and possible resources for rapid implementation of the projects suggested by the Special Envoy in his report, and invited the Member States, United Nations organizations, and humanitarian and non-governmental organizations to provide support and assistance to the Government of Bolivia in its efforts to strengthen the enjoyment of human rights and fundamental freedoms in that country. On its recommendation the Economic and Social Council, in resolution 1984/32 of 24 May 1984, requested the Secretary-General, under the programme of advisory services in the field of human rights, and in consultation with the Government of Bolivia, to examine ways and means and possible resources for rapid implementation of the projects suggested by the Special Envoy.

3. CHILE

34. In resolution 3219 (XXIX) of 6 November 1974, the General Assembly endorsed the recommendation made by the Sub-Commission on Prevention of Discrimination and Protection of Minorities, in resolution 8 (XXVII) of 21 August 1974, that the Commission on Human Rights should study the reported violations of human rights in Chile at its thirty-first session.

35. In resolution 8 (XXXI) of 27 February 1975, the Commission decided to appoint an *Ad Hoc* Working Group of five of its members to inquire into the situation of human rights in Chile on the basis of oral and written evidence, to be gathered from all relevant sources, and of a visit to Chile. The Group was requested to report the results of its inquiries to the Commission at its thirty-second session and to submit a progress report on its findings to the Secretary-General for inclusion in his report to the General Assembly at its thirtieth session.

36. The General Assembly considered the question of the protection of human rights in Chile at its thirtieth, thirty-first and thirty-second sessions, and on each occasion expressed distress at the continuation of the violations of human rights in that country and invited the Commission on Human Rights to extend the mandate of the *Ad Hoc* Working Group so as to enable it to continue its inquiries and report both to the Assembly and to the Commission. The Commission accordingly extended the Working Group's mandate at its thirty-second, thirty-third and thirty-fourth sessions, in 1976, 1977 and 1978.

37. The *Ad Hoc* Working Group submitted its report[20] to the General Assembly at its thirty-third session. In resolution 33/175 of 20 December 1978, the Assembly invited the Commission to appoint, in consultation with the Chairman of the *Ad Hoc* Working Group, from among members of the Group, a Special Rapporteur on the situation of human rights in Chile. The Assembly also invited the Commission to consider at its thirty-fifth session the most effective ways of clarifying the whereabouts and fate of missing persons in Chile, urged the Chilean authorities to co-operate with the Special Rapporteur, and requested the Commission to submit a progress report on action taken in compliance with the resolution.

38. The General Assembly further, in resolution 33/174 of 20 December 1978, decided to establish a voluntary United Nations Trust Fund for Chile. In resolution 33/176 of the same date it welcomed the fact that the *Ad Hoc* Working Group had finally been able to travel to Chile and carry out, on the spot, an investigation of the human rights situation in that country in accordance with its mandate, and drew the attention of the Commission on Human Rights to the importance of the *Ad Hoc* Working Group's experience in view of the Commission's future action, when dealing with consistent patterns of gross violations of human rights.

39. At its thirty-third session the General Assembly also considered a study of the impact of foreign economic aid and assistance on respect for human rights in Chile, prepared by Mr. Antonio Cassese, a Special Rapporteur of the Sub-Commission on Prevention of Discrimination and Protection of Minorities.[21]

40. The Assembly had invited the Commission on Human Rights to consider this question in resolution 31/124 of 16 December 1976, and the Commission had requested the Sub-Commission to undertake a study of the subject in resolution 9 (XXXIII) of 9 March 1977. The Sub-Commission, in appointing Mr. Cassese to prepare the study, had requested him to analyse the volume, origins, development and significance of the assistance given to the régime in Chile, and to study whether a quantitative or qualitative change in such aid might contribute to restoring respect for human rights in Chile. The Special Rapporteur's general conclusion was that foreign economic assistance to Chile helped to

---

[19] E/CN.4/1984/46, para. 7.

[20] A/33/331.

[21] E/CN.4/Sub.2/412, vols. I-IV and Corr.1.

maintain human rights violations and to uphold the oppressive political system.

41. At its first regular session in 1979, the Economic and Social Council endorsed the decision of the Commission on Human Rights in resolution 11 (XXXV) of 6 March 1976 to appoint Mr. Abdoulaye Dieye as Special Rapporteur on the situation of human rights in Chile, and Mr. Felix Ermacora and Mr. Waleed M. Sadi, as experts in their individual capacity, to study the fate of missing and disappeared persons in Chile.[22] Mr. Sadi subsequently resigned his appointment.

42. At its thirty-fourth session, in 1980, the General Assembly considered the reports of the Special Rapporteur[23] and of the Expert on the Question of the Fate of Missing and Disappeared Persons in Chile.[24] In resolution 34/179 of 17 December 1979 it noted that both reports clearly indicated that generally the situation of human rights had not improved, and in a number of areas had even deteriorated, compared with that described by the *Ad Hoc* Working Group.

43. Since that time, the General Assembly and the Commission on Human Rights have considered reports submitted by the Special Rapporteur[25] annually. The mandate of the Special Rapporteur has been renewed each year. In 1983 Mr. R. Lallah was appointed by the Chairman of the Commission to succeed Mr. Abdoulaye Dieye as Special Rapporteur, and in 1985 Mr. Fernando Volio Jimenez was appointed upon Mr. Lallah's resignation.

44. After examining the report submitted to its forty-third session,[26] the Commission, in resolution 1987/60 of 12 March 1987, expressed its deep concern:

At the persistence of serious violations of human rights in Chile, as described in the report of the Special Rapporteur, which refers to such violations as murders, deaths in alleged confrontations, abductions, temporary disappearances, torture and ill-treatment by the security forces, the climate of insecurity and extreme violence, the maintenance of exile and the discriminatory character of the announced, but not yet published, register of citizens authorized to return to the country, the attacks on international humanitarian organizations and the denial of fundamental rights and freedoms through the maintenance of arbitrary executive powers during the prolonged period in which states of emergency have been in force;

At the systematic and continuing restrictions imposed by the Chilean Government on the exercise of the rights to freedom of expression, assembly and association through the use of repressive methods and violent responses to social and political opposition demonstrations, in particular military searches of marginal settlements and university premises and acts of intimidation against religious and lay human rights bodies;

At the persistent ineffectiveness of the Chilean Government in respecting human rights and restoring legality in conformity with the Universal Declaration of Human Rights which is essential for the effective enjoyment and exercise of human rights and fundamental freedoms and in the best democratic tradition of Chile;

At the continued acts of extreme violence from all sources in Chile which have exacerbated the climate of insecurity, which is one of the factors that make a peaceful return to democracy difficult; and

At the ineffectiveness of the government authorities in preventing the ill-treatment of individuals by the military, police and security forces, particularly at the failure of the competent judicial authorities to take the necessary steps to conduct full investigations and prosecute those responsible for the numerous unresolved cases of murder, abduction, disappearance and torture, and for serious injuries through the use of further repressive methods of inhuman cruelty.

45. The Commission emphasized the need for the Government of Chile to restore and respect human rights in conformity with the principles of the Universal Declaration of Human Rights and in compliance with the obligations it had assumed under various international instruments, so that the principle of legality, democratic institutions and the effective enjoyment and exercise of human rights and fundamental freedoms may be restored.

46. The General Assembly, in resolution 40/145 of 13 December 1985, expressed its indignation at the persistence of serious and systematic violations of human rights in Chile, in particular the suppression of acts of social protest which has caused a considerable number of deaths and injuries and mass and individual arrests, at the intimidation of national human rights organizations, at the frequent reports of torture and ill-treatment, and at the treacherous crimes in which the police forces are judicially implicated. It once again called urgently on the Chilean authorities to restore and respect human rights, and in particular:

(*a*) To put an end not only to the state of siege, as was done in June 1985, but also to the régime of exception and especially the practice of declaring "constitutional states of emergency" under which serious and continuing violations of human rights are committed;

(*b*) To investigate and clarify without delay the fate of persons who were arrested for political reasons and later disappeared, to assist and inform their families of the results of such investigation and to bring to trial and punish those responsible for their disappearance;

(*c*) To respect the right to life and the right to physical and moral integrity by putting an end to the practice of torture and other cruel, inhuman or degrading treatment or punishment and to put an immediate end to intimidation and persecution as well as to kidnappings, arbitrary or abusive detention and imprisonment in secret places:

---

[22] See Economic and Social Council decision 1979/32 of 10 May 1979.

[23] A/34/583.

[24] A/34/583/Add.1

[25] A/35/522, E/CN.4/1428; A/36/594, E/CN.4/1484; A/37/564, E/CN.4/1983/9; A/38/385 and Add.1, E/CN.4/1984/7; A/39/631, E/CN.4/1985/38; A/40/647 and Corr.1, E/CN.4/1986/2; A/41/719, E/CN.4/1987/7 and A/42/556 and Corr.1.

[26] E/CN.4/1987/7.

(*d*) To respect the right of nationals to live in and freely enter and leave their country, without arbitrary restrictions or conditions, and to cease the practices of *relegación* (assignment to forced residence) and forced exile;

(*e*) To restore the full enjoyment and exercise of labour rights, including the rights to organize trade unions, the right to collective bargaining and the right to strike, and to put an end to the suppression of the activities of trade union leaders and their organizations and comply with the provisions of the international agreements of the International Labour Organisation to which Chile has subscribed;

(*f*) To respect and, where necessary, restore economic, social and cultural rights, in particular the rights intended to preserve the cultural identity and improve the economic and social status of the indigenous populations, including the right to their land;

. . .

4. CYPRUS

47. In recent years several United Nations organs have expressed concern about persons missing in Cyprus as a result of armed conflict there. The General Assembly, in resolution 3212 (XXIX) of 1 November 1974, expressed the view that all refugees in Cyprus should return to their homes in safety, and called upon the parties concerned to take urgent measures to that end. The Commission on Human Rights, in resolution 4 (XXXI) of 13 February 1975, called upon "all parties concerned to adhere strictly to the principles of the United Nations, international instruments in the field of human rights, and the relevant resolutions of the General Assembly and the Security Council . . . and to undertake urgent measures for the return of all refugees" in Cyprus to their homes in safety. The Sub-Commission on Prevention of Discrimination and Protection of Minorities, in resolution 1 (XXVIII) of 10 September 1975, also expressed concern at the continuing plight of the displaced persons in Cyprus, and invited the parties concerned to do their utmost for a just solution and the return of the displaced persons to their homes in safety.

48. The Assembly returned to the subject in 1975. In resolution 3450 (XXX) of 9 December 1975, it expressed its grave concern about the fate of a considerable number of Cypriots who were missing as a result of armed conflict in Cyprus, and requested the Secretary-General to make every effort, in close co-operation with the International Committee of the Red Cross, to assist in tracing and accounting for persons missing as a result of armed conflict in that country.

49. Again, in 1977, the General Assembly took up the question of missing persons in Cyprus. In resolution 32/128 of 16 December 1977, the Assembly expressed its concern at the lack of progress towards the tracing and accounting for missing persons in Cyprus and expressed the hope that the informal discussions which were then taking place, to establish a joint committee to trace those missing persons, would be successful.

50. On 22 April 1981 the establishment of the Committee on Missing Persons in Cyprus was announced. However, the Committee was unable to overcome procedural difficulties or to achieve any progress towards the commencement of its investigative work. Noting that fact, and emphasizing the need for a speedy solution of the humanitarian problem, the General Assembly, in resolution 37/181 of 17 December 1982, invited the Working Group on Enforced or Involuntary Disappearances of the Commission on Human Rights to follow developments and to recommend ways and means to the parties concerned with a view to overcoming the procedural difficulties of the Committee on Missing Persons in Cyprus and, in co-operation with it, to facilitate the effective implementation of its investigative work. The Assembly also called upon all parties concerned to facilitate such investigation in a spirit of co-operation and good will, and requested the Secretary-General to continue to provide his good offices with a view to facilitating the work of the Committee on Missing Persons in Cyprus.

51. The question of violations of human rights in Cyprus has since been examined, from time to time, by the Commission on Human Rights and the Sub-Commission on Prevention of Discrimination and Protection of Minorities, but without results.

52. The Commission, in resolution 1987/50 of 11 March 1987, reiterated its previous calls for the full restoration of human rights to the population of Cyprus, and called for the tracing of, and accounting for, missing persons without delay.

53. The Sub-Commission, in resolution 1987/19 of 2 September 1987, likewise demanded full restoration of all human rights to the whole population of Cyprus, including the freedom of movement, the freedom of settlement and the right to property. In addition to expressing its concern about the fate of the missing persons, the Sub-Commission also expressed concern about "the policy and practice of the implantation of settlers from Turkey in the occupied territories of Cyprus, which constitute a form of colonialism and an attempt to change illegally the demographic structure of Cyprus".

5. DEMOCRATIC KAMPUCHEA

54. In decision 9 (XXXIV) of 8 March 1978, the Commission on Human Rights requested the Secretary-General to transmit to the Government of Democratic Kampuchea the documents and summary records of the thirty-fourth session of the Commission relating to the human rights situation in that country, with a view to inviting that Government to send its comments and observations, and to transmit the response of the Government, together with all the information that might be available about the situation, to the Commission through the Sub-Commission on Prevention of Discrimination and Protection of Minorities. Having considered the materials and information thus placed before it, the Sub-Commission requested its Chairman to analyse these materials on its behalf and to present his analysis to the Commission.

55. The Chairman of the Sub-Commission, Mr. A. Bouhdiba, introduced the analysis he had prepared[27] to

---

[27] E/CN.4/1335.

the Commission at its 1510th meeting. Consideration of the analysis was however postponed until the Commission's thirty-sixth session. Meanwhile the Sub-Commission, in resolution 4 B (XXXII) of 5 September 1979, urged the Government of Democratic Kampuchea to take urgent measures to restore full respect for human rights and fundamental freedoms in that country and to take such measures as might be necessary in order to prevent such violations from occurring in the future.

56. The General Assembly considered the situation in Kampuchea at its thirty-fourth session, and, in resolution 34/22 of 14 November 1979, it expressed its deep regret concerning the armed intervention by outside forces in the internal affairs of Kampuchea and called for the immediate withdrawal of all foreign forces from that country. In resolution 34/175 of 17 December 1979 it urged the Commission to take timely and effective action in cases of mass and flagrant violations of human rights.

57. Noting that in January 1979 Democratic Kampuchea had been invaded by foreign forces, leading to further human suffering and a large-scale exodus of refugees, the Commission on Human Rights, in resolution 29 (XXXVI) of 11 March 1980, expressed serious concern that Kampuchea was still under foreign occupation and that the conflict was continuing, thus preventing the people of Kampuchea from exercising their right to self-determination. The Commission condemned the gross and flagrant violations of human rights which had occurred in Kampuchea and urged the parties to observe fully the fundamental principles of human rights pending cessation of hostilities. Further, the Commission recommended that the people of Kampuchea be granted their fundamental freedoms and human rights, including the right to decide their own future through free and fair elections without outside interference, subversion or coercion.

58. The General Assembly, in resolution 35/6 of 22 October 1980, called for the convening of an international conference to discuss the total withdrawal of foreign troops from Kampuchea and measures by the United Nations to ensure law and order and the observance of fundamental principles of human rights in Kampuchea.

59. The International Conference on Kampuchea, held at United Nations Headquarters from 13 to 17 July 1981, adopted a Declaration on Kampuchea in which it reaffirmed resolutions 34/22 and 35/6, and called for their full implementation. In resolution 1 (I), the Conference established the *Ad Hoc* Committee of the International Conference on Kampuchea.

60. The General Assembly considered the report of the Conference[28] at its thirty-sixth session. In resolution 36/5 of 21 October 1981 the Assembly adopted the Declaration on Kampuchea and resolution 1 (I), by which the Conference had established the *Ad Hoc* Committee. It emphasized that it was the inalienable right of the Kampuchean people, who had sought refuge in neigh-

bouring countries, to return safely to their homeland; and reiterated its view that, to bring about a durable peace in South-East Asia, there was an urgent need for a comprehensive political solution to the Kampuchean problem which would provide for the withdrawal of all foreign forces and ensure respect for the sovereignty, independence, territorial integrity and neutral and non-aligned status of Kampuchea, as well as the right of the Kampuchean people to self-determination free from outside interference.

61. The Sub-Commission on Prevention of Discrimination and Protection of Minorities at its thirty-fourth session, in 1981, and the Commission on Human Rights at its thirty-eighth session, in 1982, continued to consider the human rights situation in Kampuchea on the basis of a review of further materials on the subject prepared by Mr. Asbjørn Eide, one of its members.[29] At its thirty-fifth session, in 1982, the Sub-Commission again reviewed the situation on the basis of a report presented orally by Mr. Eide. In resolution 1982/22 of 8 September 1982, it called upon the Commission on Human Rights to affirm the need for a political settlement based on the self-determination of the people of Kampuchea and on respect for all other human rights.

62. The General Assembly continued its consideration of this question at its thirty-seventh to forty-second sessions, and adopted resolutions 37/6 of 28 October 1982, 38/3 of 27 October 1983, 39/5 of 30 October 1984, 40/7 of 5 November 1985, 41/6 of 21 October 1986 and 42/3 of 14 October 1987. In resolution 42/3, it reaffirmed the earlier resolutions and called for their full implementation, and reaffirmed its conviction that the withdrawal of all foreign forces from Kampuchea, the restoration and preservation of its independence, sovereignty and territorial integrity, the right of the Kampuchean people to determine their own destiny and the commitment by all States to non-interference and non-intervention in the internal affairs of Kampuchea are the principal components of any just and lasting resolution of the Kampuchean problem. It reiterated its hope that, following a comprehensive political solution, an intergovernmental committee will be established to consider a programme of assistance to Kampuchea for the reconstruction of its economy and for the economic and social development of all States in the region.

63. The Commission on Human Rights also continued to consider the question annually, and adopted resolutions 1983/5 of 15 February 1983, 1984/12 of 29 February 1984, 1985/12 of 27 February 1985, 1986/25 of 10 March 1986 and 1987/6 of 19 February 1987. In resolution 1987/6, it reiterated its condemnation of the persistent occurrence of gross and flagrant violations of human rights in Kampuchea as expressed in its earlier resolutions, deplored the continued violations of fundamental human rights, the principles of international law and the Charter of the United Nations, and further deplored the reported forced demographic changes and displacement of the Kampuchean population.

---

[28] United Nations publication, Sales No. E.81.I.20.

[29] E/CN.4/Sub.2/L.780.

64. In the resolution the Commission strongly reaffirmed its call to the parties to the conflict in Kampuchea to cease all hostilities forthwith and for the immediate and unconditional withdrawal of foreign forces from Kampuchea, in order that (*a*) the Kampuchean people, free from any foreign interference, aggression and coercion, will be able to exercise their fundamental and inalienable human rights in their totality and indivisibility; (*b*) the United Nations may be able to offer its services effectively in the field of human rights and fundamental freedoms in Kampuchea; (*c*) in the exercise of their fundamental freedoms and inalienable rights, the Kampuchean people will then be able to choose and determine their own future through free and fair elections under United Nations supervision; (*d*) the exercise of the right of all Kampuchean refugees to return to their homeland in safety may be possible; and (*e*) efforts towards a comprehensive political solution to the Kampuchean problem, within the framework of the Declaration on Kampuchea of 17 July 1981 and the relevant United Nations resolutions, may be pursued with a view to establishing an independent, free and non-aligned Kampuchea and thereby achieving durable peace in South-East Asia.

65. The Commission, finally, requested the Secretary-General to continue to monitor closely the developments in Kampuchea and urgently to intensify efforts, including the use of his good offices, to bring about a comprehensive political settlement and the restoration of the fundamental human rights of the Kampuchean people.

6. EL SALVADOR

66. The World Conference of the United Nations Decade for Women, which met in Copenhagen from 14 to 30 July 1980, adopted a resolution entitled "Situation of women in El Salvador".[30] In the resolution the Conference expressed the view that the serious violations of human rights and fundamental freedoms which had taken place in El Salvador as a result of attempts to curb popular unrest had led to the deaths of thousands of persons, including women and children, that the serious events taking place in that country were creating a climate of insecurity, and that the civilian population and, in particular, women and children, lacked the most basic guarantees. Deeply shocked by reports of the degrading and humiliating conditions to which women and children were being subjected and by the practice of harassing the families of persons who were being sought with a view to forcing the latter to give themselves up, the Conference expressed deep concern about the serious situation of human rights and fundamental freedoms in El Salvador. It urged the Salvadorian authorities to adopt the necessary measures to guarantee

full respect for human rights and fundamental freedoms in that country, and to provide information on the situation of persons who had disappeared and, in particular, that of women and children detained for political reasons.

67. As requested by the Conference, the General Assembly considered the situation of human rights and fundamental freedoms in El Salvador at its thirty-fifth session. In resolution 35/192 of 15 December 1980, the Assembly expressed its deep concern at the grave violations of human rights and fundamental freedoms in El Salvador, deplored the murders, disappearances and other violations of human rights reported in that country, and urged the Government of El Salvador to take the necessary steps to ensure full respect for human rights and fundamental freedoms in that country. Further, it requested the Commission on Human Rights to examine the situation of human rights in El Salvador at its thirty-seventh session.

68. Having done this, the Commission in resolution 32 (XXXVII) of 11 March 1981 reiterated the views and recommendations of the General Assembly and requested its Chairman to appoint a Special Representative of the Commission (*a*) to investigate the reports about murders, abductions, disappearances, terrorist acts and all grave violations of human rights and fundamental freedoms which had taken place in El Salvador, based on information from all relevant sources, and (*b*) to make recommendations as to what steps the Commission could take to help to secure the enjoyment of human rights and fundamental freedoms in El Salvador.

69. The General Assembly at its thirty-sixth session studied the interim report prepared by the Commission's Special Representative, Mr. José Antonio Pastor Ridruejo,[31] and found that it confirmed the seriousness of the situation prevailing in El Salvador and, among other things, provided evidence on the general attitude of passiveness and inactivity of the Salvadorian authorities with respect to constant human rights violations in that country. After reaffirming the views and recommendations which the Commission had expressed in resolution 32 (XXXVII), the Assembly, in resolution 36/155 of 16 December 1981, requested the Commission on Human Rights to examine the situation in El Salvador on the basis of the Special Representative's final report.

70. The Commission carefully examined that report[32] at its thirty-eighth session. In resolution 1982/28 of 11 March 1982, it found that the report confirmed the persistence of murders, abductions, terrorist acts and all grave violations of human rights and fundamental freedoms in El Salvador, perpetrated by governmental paramilitary organizations and other armed groups, and noted that the Special Representative had underlined the general attitude of passivity and inactivity on the part of the Salvadorian authorities with regard to constant violations of human rights in that country.

---

[30] *Report of the World Conference of the United Nations Decade for Women: Equality, Development and Peace* (United Nations publication, Sales No. E.80.IV.3), chap. 1, sect. B., resolution 19, p. 82.

[31] A/36/608, annex.

[32] E/CN.4/1502.

71. Since that time, the Commission on Human Rights has considered the Special Representative's reports on the situation of human rights in El Salvador[33] annually, and has renewed the Special Representative's mandate each year.

72. In his report to the Commission's 1987 session,[34] the Special Representative noted that respect for human rights continued to be an important element in the policy of the constitutional Government of El Salvador, a policy which—within the process of democratic normalization—was achieving increasingly significant and commendable results in the crucial area of respect for the life of persons both in non-combat situations and in or as a result of combat. At the same time he pointed out that serious violations of human rights continued to be committed in the country and that these were still a cause of concern.

73. After examining the report the Commission, in resolution 1987/51 of 11 March 1987, applauded the advances made but nevertheless expressed its deep concern at the fact that serious and numerous violations of human rights continued to take place in El Salvador owing, *inter alia*, to non-compliance with the humanitarian rules of war. Accordingly, it requested the Government of El Salvador and the insurgent forces to adopt measures conducive to the humanization of the conflict by observing scrupulously the Geneva Conventions of 1949 and the Additional Protocols thereto of 1977; and called upon both sides to do their utmost in all measures intended to avoid death or harm to the physical integrity of the non-combatant population as a result of warfare and the placing of contact mines.

74. The Commission, further, deplored the fact that the capacity of the judicial system in El Salvador to investigate, prosecute and punish violations of human rights continued to be patently unsatisfactory, and urged the competent authorities to hasten the adoption of the forceful measures necessary to investigate, in the most rapid, exemplary and effective manner, the violations of those rights.

75. In his report to the 1987 session of the General Assembly,[35] the Special Representative summarized a number of new developments affecting the situation of human rights in El Salvador, among them the signature in Guatemala on 7 August 1987 by the Central American Governments of the Agreement on "Procedure for the establishment of a firm and lasting peace in Central America", the assassination of the Co-ordinator of the Commission on Human Rights (non-governmental), and the conclusion of agreements between the Government and the *Frente Farabundo Marti para la Liberacion Nacional* covering evacuations of war-wounded for medical attention.

76. The General Assembly, in resolution 42/137 of 7 December 1987, expressed its trust that the fulfilment of the undertaking assumed in the Agreement would lead to an improvement of the situation of human rights and fundamental freedoms in El Salvador, expressed its consternation at the assassination of the Co-ordinator of the Commission on Human Rights (non-governmental) and its faith that the authorities of El Salvador would continue investigations leading to the punishment of those responsible, and recognized that the resumption of the dialogue between the Government and the *Frente Farabundo Marti para la Liberacion Nacional-Frente Democratico Revolucionario*, in the context of the Guatemala Agreement, constitutes one of the best ways of achieving a solution that will help to improve the situation of human rights of the Salvadorian people. It urged the two sides to continue that dialogue, within the framework of the Guatemala Agreement, until the achievement of a global political solution that will end the armed conflict and promote the broadening and strengthening of and democratic, pluralistic and participatory process that will involve the promotion of social justice, respect for human rights and the full exercise of the right of the Salvadorian people to determine freely and without external interference of any kind its economic, political and social system.

7. GUATEMALA

77. The Commission on Human Rights, meeting in Geneva in 1979 for its thirty-fifth session, took note with profound regret of the assassination on 25 January of that year of a Deputy of the Guatemalan Congress and former member of the United Nations Secretariat, and of the communication received from the Government of Guatemala declaring that it condemned "the unspeakable crime" and that it was "acting with all necessary diligence to apprehend those responsible and to elucidate the matter". In a telegram to the Government, the Commission stated that it would welcome some information on the matter before the beginning of its thirty-sixth session.[36]

78. The response of the Government of Guatemala[37] was noted by the Commission in resolution 32 (XXXVI) of 11 March 1980, in which the Commission expressed its profound concern at the situation of human rights and fundamental freedoms in Guatemala, urged the Government of that country to take the necessary measures to ensure full respect for the human rights and fundamental freedoms of the people of Guatemala, and took note with satisfaction of the decision of the Government of Guatemala to invite the Inter-American Commission on Human Rights to visit the country and to prepare a report on the situation of human rights.

79. As requested by the Commission, the Secretary-General brought this resolution to the attention of the

---

[33] E/CN.4/1983/20, E/CN.4/1984/25 and Corr.1, E/CN. 4/1985/18, E/CN.4/1986/22 and E/CN.4/1987/21.

[34] E/CN.4/1987/21.

[35] A/42/641 and Corr.1, annex.

---

[36] See Commission on Human Rights decision 12 (XXXV) of 14 March 1979.

[37] E/CN.4/1387.

Government of Guatemala and reported on the results of that contact to the Commission at its thirty-seventh session.[38] The Commission, in resolution 33 (XXXVII) of 11 March 1981, expressed its profound concern at the deterioration in the situation of human rights and fundamental freedoms in Guatemala and requested the Secretary-General to continue his efforts to establish direct contacts with the Government concerned and to report both to the General Assembly and to the Commission. The Assembly received the Secretary-General's report[39] and, in decision 36/435 of 16 December 1981, requested the Secretary-General to continue his efforts to establish direct contacts with the Government of Guatemala and requested that Government to co-operate further with the Secretary-General in his efforts to establish such contacts.

80. The Commission on Human Rights, at its thirty-eighth session, took note of the General Assembly's decision and took into account information on the human rights situation in Guatemala contained in a note presented by the Secretary-General.[40] Expressing its profound concern at the continuing deterioration in the situation of human rights and fundamental freedoms in Guatemala, the Commission in resolution 1982/31 of 11 March 1982 requested its Chairman to appoint a Special Rapporteur to make a thorough study of the human rights situation in Guatemala and to present it to the Commission at its thirty-ninth session.

81. The Sub-Commission on Prevention of Discrimination and Protection of Minorities, at its thirty-fifth session, noted that the information which had come to its attention revealed a pattern of gross and persistent violations of human rights in Guatemala. In resolution 1982/17 of 7 September 1982, it expressed the hope that the Government of Guatemala would take steps to put an end to such violations, and noted in this regard that, in its letter to the Sub-Commission,[41] the Government had indicated its willingness to guarantee and ensure in the future the legitimate rights of all citizens of Guatemala.

82. The General Assembly considered the situation of human rights and fundamental freedoms in Guatemala at its thirty-seventh session, in 1982. In resolution 37/184 of 17 December 1982, it expressed its satisfaction at the declared willingness of the Government of Guatemala to co-operate with a Special Rapporteur to be appointed under Commission on Human Rights resolution 1982/31 with a mandate to make a thorough study of the human rights situation in Guatemala; indicated that it was disturbed about the large number of missing persons who remained unaccounted for; and noted with concern the state of siege in force in Guatemala since 1 July 1982, under which basic human rights were abrogated and serious violations of human rights were reported to have occurred.

83. The appointment of a Special Rapporteur was delayed and had not been made when the Commission on Human Rights held its thirty-ninth session, in 1983. In resolution 1983/37, the Commission reiterated its profound concern at the continuing reports of massive violations of human rights taking place in Guatemala, called upon its Chairman to appoint the Special Rapporteur with the shortest possible delay, and requested the Special Rapporteur to make an interim report to the General Assembly as well as a final report to the Commission.

84. Later in 1983 Viscount Colville of Culross was appointed as Special Rapporteur, and submitted an interim report to the General Assembly.[42] After examining and noting the report, the Assembly welcomed the lifting of the state of siege in Guatemala and the abolition of the ''special tribunals'' which had been active there, but expressed its concern about the large number of persons who had disappeared, including those reported to have been tried by the ''special tribunals'', and who, despite appeals from various international organizations, remained unaccounted for.

85. In resolution 38/100 of 16 December 1983, the Assembly expressed its deep concern at the continuing massive violations of human rights in Guatemala, particularly the violence against non-combatants, the widespread repression, killing and massive displacement of rural and indigenous populations; and called upon the Government of Guatemala to refrain both from forcefully displacing people belonging to rural and indigenous populations and from the practice of coercive participation in civilian patrols, leading to human rights violations. It also requested the Government to investigate and clarify the fate of persons who had disappeared and were still unaccounted for, including those reported to have been tried by the special tribunals. Further, it called upon the Government to establish a system for the revocation of convictions and sentences passed by the special tribunals, and appealed to it to allow international humanitarian organizations to render their assistance in investigating the fate of persons who had disappeared. Finally, it appealed to all parties concerned in Guatemala to ensure the application of the relevant norms of international humanitarian law applicable in armed conflicts of a non-international character to protect the civilian population and to seek an end to all acts of violence.

86. At its fortieth session, in 1984, the Commission on Human Rights examined the Special Rapporteur's report,[43] as well as his interim report to the General Assembly.[44] Thanking the Special Rapporteur for the report, which revealed in some detail the suffering of the people of Guatemala due to violations of human rights, the Commission in resolution 1984/53 of 14 March 1984, echoed the profound concern which the General Assembly had expressed, and urged the Gov-

---

[38] E/CN.4/1438.

[39] A/36/705.

[40] E/CN.4/1501.

[41] E/CN.4/Sub.2/1982/38.

[42] A/38/485.

[43] A/38/485.

[44] E/CN.4/1984/30.

ernment to take effective measures to ensure that all its authorities and agencies, including its security forces, fully respect human rights and fundamental freedoms. In addition, it called upon Governments to refrain from supplying arms and other military assistance to Guatemala as long as serious human rights violations continued to be reported there.

87. At the request of the Commission the General Assembly received a second interim report from the Special Rapporteur at its thirty-ninth session, in 1984.[45] On the basis of that report and other reliable information it noted in resolution 39/120 of 14 December 1984 that elections to the Constituent Assembly of Guatemala had been held in July 1984, thus fulfilling the first stage of the electoral process for the installation of a new constitutional Government according to the timetable proposed by the existing Government, and affirmed the importance of creating conditions in which the electoral process could be pursued in a climate free from intimidation and terror. It welcomed the fact that many of the persons who had been tried by the special tribunals had been released, and urged the Government to establish the necessary conditions to ensure the independence of the judicial system and to enable the judiciary to uphold the rule of law, including the right of habeas corpus, and to prosecute and punish speedily and effectively those, including members of the military and security forces, found responsible for violations of human rights.

88. The Commission on Human Rights examined a further report by the Special Rapporteur at its forty-first session, in 1985,[46] which indicated that although improvements had been noted in some areas, serious and systematic violations of human rights continued to occur in Guatemala. In resolution 1985/36 of 13 March 1985 the Commission welcomed the dialogue which had developed between the Government and the Mutual Support Group of the families of the disappeared, and the subsequent establishment of a commission to investigate and clarify the fate of persons who had been subjected to involuntary or forced disappearances and were still unaccounted for; and urged the commission to act with vigour and expediency. It appealed to the Government to adhere to its new timetable for the return to democracy, and to ensure conditions which would allow the full participation of all in the political process. It also appealed to all parties in the conflict to create a climate free from intimidation and terror.

89. The Special Rapporteur's final report, presented to the Commission in 1986,[47] indicated a return to constitutionality in Guatemala with the establishment of a popularly-elected civilian Government, the entry into force of the new Constitution of the Republic as from 14 January 1986, and the Government's declared intention of promoting respect for human rights.

90. The Commission, in resolution 1986/62 of 13 March 1986, welcomed these developments, as well as the establishment, in accordance with the provisions of the Constitution, of the National Human Rights Commission and the office of the Attorney for Human Rights. It also took into account the fact that the new Guatemalan *Amparo*, Habeas Corpus and Constitutionality Act established guarantees and means of defence of the constitutional order and of the individual human rights protected by the Constitution, and that this Act provided a means of monitoring effective compliance with the provisions of the Constitution.

91. Expressing its gratitude to Viscount Colville of Culross for the manner in which he had discharged his mandate as Special Rapporteur, and taking note with satisfaction of the willingness of the Government of Guatemala to continue co-operating with the Commission by providing full and detailed information on the implementation of the new legal order for the protection of human rights and its efforts to guarantee the full enjoyment of fundamental freedoms in Guatemala, the Commission decided to terminate the mandate of the Special Rapporteur and requested its Chairman to appoint a Special Representative to receive and evaluate the information forwarded by the Government and other relevant information from reliable sources.

92. Appointed as the Commission's Special Representative, Viscount Colville of Culross reported to the Commission,[48] at its 1987 session, on the situation existing at that time, and in particular on such matters as abolition of the death penalty for ordinary offences connected with political offences, establishment of the National Commission on Human Rights within the Congress of the Republic, establishment of the Procurator for Human Rights and definition of the powers of this office, contacts with the International Committee of the Red Cross concerning an ICRC presence in the country, control and reform of the Security Forces, the establishment of inter-institutional co-ordinating bodies under civilian control at the departmental level, and the relaxation of military controls over rural populations. In this connection he pointed out that the civilian self-defence patrols, although renamed Voluntary Committees for Civil Defence, were still active despite the stated policy of the URNG (the combined guerrilla movement) that they should be abolished.

93. The Commission, in resolution 1987/53 of 11 March 1987, expressed its appreciation to the Government of Guatemala for its collaboration and for the facilities and co-operation afforded to the Special Representative, and noted with satisfaction that measures had been taken by the Government to guarantee the protection of human rights and fundamental freedoms. It welcomed the process of democratization and return to constitutionality; encouraged the Government to continue to take effective measures to ensure that its authorities and agencies, civilian as well as military, including law enforcement officials, fully respect human rights and fundamental freedoms; and took note with satisfaction of the willingness of the Government to

[45] A/39/635.
[46] E/CN.4/1985/19.
[47] E/CN.4/1986/23.

[48] E/CN.4/1987/24.

continue co-operating with the Commission. Terminating the mandate of the Special Representative, the Commission called upon the Secretary-General to provide such advisory services and other appropriate forms of assistance in the field of human rights as may be requested by the Government, and to appoint an expert with a view to assisting the Government, through direct contacts, in taking the necessary action for the further restoration of human rights.

8. THE ISLAMIC REPUBLIC OF IRAN

94.   Having heard statements regarding the serious violation of human rights and fundamental freedoms being experienced by the Baha'i community of Iran, the Sub-Commission on Prevention of Discrimination and Protection of Minorities, in resolution 10 (XXXIII) of 10 September 1980, expressed its profound concern for the safety of the members of the elected National Administrative Council of the Baha'i of Iran, who had been arrested, as well as for the safety of all members of that community, both as individuals and collectively. It requested the Secretary-General to transmit its concern to the Government of the Islamic Republic of Iran and to invite that Government to express its commitment to the guarantees provided in the International Covenant on Civil and Political Rights by granting full protection of fundamental rights and freedoms to the Baha'i religious community in Iran, and by protecting the life and liberty of the members of that community.

95.   At its thirty-fourth session, the Sub-Commission heard further statements "clearly demonstrating the systematic persecution of the Baha'is in Iran, including summary arrests, torture, beatings, executions, murders, kidnappings, disappearances, abductions, and many other forms of harassment. In resolution 8 (XXXIV) of 9 September 1981, the Sub-Commission expressed its conviction that the treatment of the Baha'is was motivated by religious intolerance and a desire to eliminate the Baha'i Faith from the land of its birth, and its concern that the Government of Iran appeared to have ignored all previous approaches made on behalf of that community. It expressed its profound concern for the perilous situation facing the community, and its appreciation of the efforts of the Secretary-General on its behalf. It urged the Secretary-General to continue those efforts, and drew the situation to the attention of the Commission on Human Rights.

96.   The Commission at its thirty-eighth session considered resolution 8 (XXXIV) of the Sub-Commission and the note by the Secretary-General pursuant to that resolution.[49] It joined the Sub-Commission in expressing concern about grave violations of human rights and fundamental freedoms in Iran. In resolution 1982/27 of 11 March 1982 the Commission urged the Government of Iran, as a State party to the International Covenant

on Civil and Political Rights, to respect and ensure to all individuals within its territory and subject to its jurisdiction the rights recognized in that Covenant, without distinction of any kind. Further, it requested the Secretary-General to establish direct contacts with the Government of Iran on the human rights situation prevailing in that country, to continue his efforts to endeavour to ensure that the Baha'is were guaranteed full enjoyment of their human rights and fundamental freedoms, and to submit a report to the Commission at its thirty-ninth session on the general human rights situation prevailing in Iran.

97.   Recalling the Commission's resolution, the Sub-Commission, in resolution 1982/25 of 8 September 1982, expressed its concern at the reports of continued violations of human rights in Iran and its hope that the Secretary-General's direct contacts would produce positive improvements. In that connection it determined that the human rights situation in Iran was sufficiently serious to merit continuing scrutiny by all concerned United Nations bodies, including the Commission on Human Rights.

98.   Bearing in mind the Sub-Commission's resolution, the Commission on Human Rights examined, in 1983 and 1984, reports on the human rights situation in the Islamic Republic of Iran prepared by the Secretary-General (E/CN.4/1983/19 and E/CN.4/1984/32), as well as information contained in the report of its Special Rapporteur on summary or arbitrary executions (E/CN.4/1983/16). In expressing its appreciation to the Secretary-General for the efforts deployed by him in the framework of his ongoing contacts with the Government of the Islamic Republic of Iran, the Commission expressed regret at the refusal of that Government to receive a mission which had been arranged by the Secretary-General in agreement with the Government.

99.   In resolution 1984/54 of 14 March 1984, the Commission requested its Chairman to appoint a Special Representative of the Commission to establish contact with the Government concerned and to make a thorough study of the human rights situation in Iran.

100.   The Special Representative, Mr. Andres Aguilar, presented a preliminary report[50] to the Commission at its forty-first session, in 1985, in which he indicated that he had been unable to establish dialogue and co-operation with the Government of the Islamic Republic of Iran. The Commission extended his mandate, and in 1985 he submitted interim reports to the General Assembly[51] and to the Commission.[52] After examining these reports the Assembly, in resolution 40/141 of 13 December 1985, and the Commission, in resolution 1986/41 of 12 March 1986, expressed their deep concern over the specific and detailed allegations of violations of human rights in the Islamic Republic of Iran to which the Special Representative referred, and, in particular,

---

[49] E/CN.4/1517.

[50] E/CN.4/1985/20.

[51] A/40/874.

[52] E/CN.4/1986/25.

those related to the right to life, such as summary and arbitrary executions; the right to freedom from torture or cruel, inhuman or degrading treatment or punishment; the right to liberty and security of person and to freedom from arbitrary arrest or detention; the right to a fair trial; the right to freedom of thought, conscience and religion and to freedom of expression; and the right of religious minorities to profess and practise their own religion.

101. Having informed the Commission that he was not in a position to continue serving as its Special Representative on the human rights situation in the Islamic Republic of Iran, Mr. Andres Aguilar was succeeded by Mr. Reynaldo Galindo Pohl in that office. The new Special Representative presented an interim report to the General Assembly[53] at its forty-second session, in 1987.

102. Taking note of that report, the Assembly in resolution 42/136 of 7 December 1987 expressed again its deep concern about the numerous and detailed allegations of grave human rights violations in the Islamic Republic of Iran, and its concern in particular that, although the Special Representative indicated that the number of alleged violations of the right to life had dimished over a two-year period, information made available to the Special Representative alleged the execution of some one hundred persons in the period October 1986-September 1987 because of their political and religious convictions. It also expressed concern at allegations that maltreatment and torture, both physical and psychological, were common in Iranian prisons during interrogation and before and after the final verdict, and at the existence of extremely summary and informal proceedings, the unawareness of specific accusations, the lack of legal counsel and other irregularities in respect to fair trial.

103. The Assembly shared the opinion of the Special Representative that the denial by the Government of the Islamic Republic of Iran of the allegations of violations of human rights as a whole, without details, was not sufficient for a sensible assessment of the situation on human rights in that country; and endorsed his conclusion that acts continued to occur in the Islamic Republic of Iran that are inconsistent with international instruments to which the Government of that country is bound, and that the persistence of certain facts continues to justify continuing international concern.

104. The Assembly urged the Government of the Islamic Republic of Iran, as a State party to the International Covenant on Civil and Political Rights, to respect and ensure to all individuals within its territory and subject to its jurisdiction the rights recognized in that Covenant; and called upon it to extend its full cooperation to the Special Representative of the Commission on Human Rights and, in particular, to permit him to visit that country.

9. MALAWI

105. From 1977 to 1980 the Commission on Human Rights examined the situation regarding the alleged persecution of Jehovah's Witnesses in Malawi. The Government of Malawi did not co-operate with the Commission or reply to the communication addressed to it regarding this matter.

106. On the recommendation of the Commission, the Economic and Social Council adopted resolution 1980/31 of 2 May 1980, in which it regretted the failure of that Government of Malawi to co-operate with the Commission in the examination of a situation said to have deprived thousands of Jehovah's Witnesses in Malawi of their basic human rights and fundamental freedoms between 1972 and 1975, which constrained the Council to publicize the matter; and expressed the hope that the human rights of all citizens of Malawi had been fully restored and, in particular, that adequate measures were being taken to provide a remedy to those who might have suffered injustices.

10. NICARAGUA

107. At its thirty-third session, in 1978, the General Assembly heard a statement by the President of the Republic of Costa Rica on the violations of his country's sovereignty by military aircraft of Nicaragua[54] and took note of a message concerning the matter sent to the President of the Assembly by the President of the Republic of Colombia and the President of the Republic of Venezuela on 27 September 1978.[55] Considering the extreme gravity of the events that had taken place and were continuing to occur in Nicaragua, which had caused the death of thousands of people, incalculable destruction of property and repeated violations of the most basic rights, the General Assembly, in resolution 33/76 of 15 December 1978, censured the repression of the civilian population of Nicaragua and urged the Nicaraguan authorities to ensure respect for the human rights of the citizens of Nicaragua, in accordance with their international commitments and the provisions of the Charter of the United Nations.

108. The Commission on Human Rights considered the situation of human rights in Nicaragua at its thirty-fifth session, bearing in mind that indiscriminate repression had continued against the civilian population, which lacked the most elementary safeguards, since the adoption of General Assembly resolution 33/76. In resolution 14 (XXXV) of 13 March 1979, the Commission condemned the violation of human rights and fundamental freedoms by the Nicaraguan authorities, expressed its deep concern that the Government of Nicaragua had taken no steps to respect the human rights and fundamental freedoms of the population, and de-

---

[53] A/42/648, annex.

[54] *Official Records of the General Assembly, Thirty-third Session, Plenary Meetings*, 11th meeting, paras. 72-126.

[55] A/33/275, annex.

manded that the Nicaraguan authorities put an end to the existing grave situation and ensure respect for the human rights and fundamental freedoms of the citizens of Nicaragua. The Commission requested the Secretary-General to keep the development of the situation in Nicaragua under continuing review and to report to the Commission through the Sub-Commission on Prevention of Discrimination and Protection of Minorities.

109. The Secretary-General's report, containing information received from three Governments, one specialized agency and five non-governmental organizations was presented to the Sub-Commission at its thirty-second session.[56] The Sub-Commission, in resolution 4 C (XXXII) of 5 September 1979, requested the Secretary-General to supplement it for presentation to the Commission on Human Rights. It urged the Government of Nicaragua to take urgent measures to restore full respect for human rights and fundamental freedoms in that country and to take such measures as might be necessary in order to prevent such violations from occurring in the future.

110. The Secretary-General presented his report and the addendum thereto[57] concerning the situation of human rights in Nicaragua to the Commission on Human Rights at its thirty-sixth session. The Commission did not adopt a resolution on this question.

11. POLAND

111. Aware of the fact that recent events in Poland had given rise to considerable humanitarian problems, the Commission on Human Rights, in resolution 1982/26 of 10 March 1982, expressed its deep concern at the continued reports of widespread violations of human rights and fundamental freedoms in Poland, including the arbitrary arrest and detention of thousands of persons, denial of the right to freedom of expression and the right of peaceful assembly, suspension of the right to form and join independent trade unions, and at the imposition of severe punishment on persons accused of violating martial law. The Commission affirmed the right of the Polish people to pursue its political, economic, social and cultural development, free from outside interference, noted that the Polish authorities had stated their intention to terminate the restrictive measures imposed on the exercise of human rights and fundamental freedoms, and expressed the hope that its stated intention would be realized in the very near future, particularly in relation to the release of all persons detained without charge, the review of severe prison sentences imposed in the context of the state of martial law in Poland, and the lifting of restrictions on the free flow of information. The Commission requested the Secretary-General or a person designated by him to undertake a thorough study of the human rights situa-

tion in Poland, and decided to review that situation, on the basis of the study, at its thirty-ninth session.

112. The Secretary-General followed the situation of human rights in Poland as required by the resolution and on 21 December 1982 announced that he had designated Under-Secretary-General Hugo Gobbi to continue to follow the situation in Poland on his behalf.

113. In a report presented to the Commission on Human Rights,[58] at its thirty-ninth session, Under-Secretary-General Hugo Gobbi pointed out that in Poland two distinct human rights problems might be distinguished: on the one hand, the problem of implementing all the rights and freedoms set out in the International Covenants on Human Rights, and on the other hand, the problem of the recognition and enjoyment of freedom of association and trade union rights, which were dealt with in article 8 of the International Covenant on Economic, Social and Cultural Rights and article 22 of the International Covenant on Civil and Political Rights, but also in the ILO Freedom of Association and Protection of the Right to Organize Convention, 1948 (No. 87) and in the ILO Right to Organize and Collective Bargaining Convention, 1949 (No. 98). Of these problems, Mr. Gobbi wrote:

55. Inasmuch as the specific problem of freedom of association is concerned, as governed by article 22 of the International Covenant on Civil and Political Rights and article 8 of the International Covenant on Economic, Social and Cultural Rights and by the ILO Conventions Nos. 87 and 98, the Government of Poland adopted a new law on trade unions on 18 October 1982. The new law gives a new trade union structure to the country, abolishing all the existing organizations, because of the "political actions contrary to the statutes of the trade union and to national legislation", undertaken by some of them.

56. The new trade union law is the subject of a thorough analysis by the ILO.[59] In that analysis doubts are expressed concerning the compatibility of the new trade-union law with the above-mentioned ILO Conventions. The procedures followed in the ILO in regard to the complaints to the effect that Convention No. 87 governing Freedom of Association and Protection of the Right to Organize has not been complied with, have yet to be completed.

. . .

58. As regards allegations concerning the situation of political prisoners, it is not possible to make any evaluation without a verification *in loco* in direct consultation with those concerned and primarily the Polish authorities.

59. A number of positive steps have been taken by the Government of Poland, such as the adoption of specific legal regulations during the period of suspension of martial law that eliminates most of the rigours of life under martial law. These regulations considerably limited the competence of military courts with respect to civilians, lifted most of the restrictions on freedom of movement and, in particular, completely lifted internments. Notwithstanding such indications I would hope that further measures for normalization will be taken in order to satisfy all the requirements established by international instruments ratified by Poland in pursuance of the aspirations of the Polish people.

114. After examining the report, the Commission, in resolution 1983/30 of 8 March 1983, reaffirmed the right of the Polish people to pursue its political, social and cultural development free from outside interference, and called upon the Polish authorities to realize fully and without further delay their stated intention to

---

[56] E/CN.4/Sub.2/426.

[57] E/CN.4/Sub.2/426/Add.1, E/CN.4/1372.

[58] E/CN.4/1983/18.

[59] See document GB 221/6/19 of the Governing Body of the ILO.

terminate the restrictive measures imposed on the exercise of human rights and fundamental freedoms, particularly in relation to a review of the severe prison sentences imposed in the context of the state of martial law, the lifting of restrictions on the free flow of information, and the repeal of the new restrictions imposed on the Polish people. Further, the Commission decided to request the Secretary-General or a person designated by him to update and complete the thorough study of the human rights situation in Poland and to present a comprehensive report to the Commission at its fortieth session.

115.   At that session, the Commission received a further report on the situation presented by Under-Secretary-General Patricio Ruedas at the request of the Secretary-General.[60] After summarizing the available information on new legislative and other developments, Mr. Ruedas set out the following conclusions:

38. A difficult economic and social situation has existed, and continues to exist, since 1981 in Poland, taxing to the utmost the resources and the stamina of the Polish people and of the Polish Government. Poland is in the process of change. Martial law, imposed in December 1981, lasted formally for 19 months. During that period, numerous arrests were made, including those for political reasons. Furthermore, some Polish citizens died as a result of clashes between demonstrators and the police: at least two, in 1981; at least one in 1982 and at least two in 1983. That the figures are under dispute is not so important as that deaths actually occurred, for one single case is one too much. This is also the view of the Polish authorities, as reported to the Secretary-General.

39. The suspension and, thereafter, the lifting of martial law, as well as the enactment and implementation of the clemency measures and, subsequently, the amnesty law, have produced conditions favourable to a reconciliation between different sectors of Polish society. The figures quoted above are significant in this regard—particularly if comparison is made between the figure of about 1,500 persons detained for political reasons as of 4 January 1983 (E/CN.4/1983/18, para. 35) and that of 281 detainees—most of them on a temporary basis—as of 18 February 1984. These are certainly encouraging developments, to be seen as such by any independent observer.

40. Some questions can nevertheless be entertained regarding some of the recent (1983) legislation, be it only temporary. Thus, for example, the amendment to the Polish penal code, seems to perpetuate a similar provision which existed in Article 46 (1) of the now defunct martial law. Also the "Special Legal Regulations in the Period of Overcoming the Socio-Economic Crisis", referred to in paragraph 20 above, while temporary in nature, provide for extensive powers to the authorities in several domains, including education. As regards the possible exercise of these powers, the writer of this report is impressed by the spirit of moderation evidenced by all members of the Polish Government who met with him, and is authorized by the Secretary-General to say that he, too, noted favourably that spirit. This has permitted the Secretary-General to state that what he heard in Poland was "very encouraging on all fronts".

41. In operative paragraph 4 of its resolution 1983/30, the Commission on Human Rights called upon the Polish authorities "to realize fully and without further delay their stated intention to terminate the restrictive measures imposed on the exercise of human rights and fundamental freedoms, particularly in relation to a review of the severe prison sentences imposed in the context of the state of martial law, the lifting of restrictions on the free flow of information, and the repeal of the new restrictions imposed on the Polish people". In the light of the information contained in this report, it seems clear that in at least one very important aspect—the review of prison sentences—effect has been given to the resolution through enactment and implementation of the clemency measures and the amnesty law".

---

60 E/CN.4/1984/26.

116.   A draft resolution relating to the situation of human rights in Poland was presented to the Commission by France, the Federal Republic of Germany, Italy and the Netherlands (E/CN.4/1984/L.66), but by decision 1984/110 the Commission postponed consideration of it to a later session.

12. SRI LANKA

117.   In decision 1984/111 of 14 March 1984, the Commission on Human Rights took note of information concerning terrorist violence in Sri Lanka which had been voluntarily submitted to it by the Government of that country,[61] and appealed to the parties to take all necessary measures to strengthen and maintain peace and restore harmony among the people of the country. Welcoming all measures for rehabilitation and reconciliation and expressing the hope that they would succeed in achieving a lasting solution, the Commission decided that further consideration of the matter was not necessary.

118.   However, the Commission re-opened the subject in 1987, when its Special Rapporteur on torture described the situation in Sri Lanka as a matter of great concern and its Working Group on Enforced or Involuntary Disappearances reported that it had transmitted more than a hundred new cases to the Government of that country.

119.   In resolution 1987/61, the Commission took note of the reports of the Special Rapporteur[62] and of the Working Group,[63] and called upon all parties and groups to respect fully the universally-accepted rules of humanitarian law, to renounce the use of force and acts of violence and to pursue a negotiated political solution based on principles of respect for human rights and fundamental freedoms. The Commission, further, invited the Government of Sri Lanka to intensify its co-operation with the International Committee of the Red Cross in the fields of dissemination and promotion of international humanitarian law and to consider favourably the offer of the services of the ICRC to fulfil its functions of protection of humanitarian standards, including the provision of assistance and protection to victims of all affected parties.

C. Assistance to Governments in their efforts to ensure the realization of human rights

120.   Under the programme of advisory services in the field of human rights, established by the General Assembly in resolution 926 (X) of 14 December 1955, the Secretary-General is authorized "to make provision at the request of Governments, and with the co-operation of the specialized agencies where appropriate and with-

---

61 E/CN.4/1984/10.

62 E/CN.4/1987/13.

63 E/CN.4/1987/15 and Corr.1 and Add.1.

out duplication of their existing activities, for the following forms of assistance with respect to the field of human rights: (*a*) advisory services of experts; (*b*) fellowships and scholarships; and (*c*) seminars". Later an additional form of assistance, namely, regional training courses, was included in the programme.

121. Resolution 926 (X) provides that the Secretary-General may undertake such assistance in agreement with, and on the basis of requests from, Governments. As regards the services of experts, the type of assistance to be rendered to each country is determined by the Governments concerned.

122. In recent years, a few Governments had availed themselves of such services. The amount of assistance provided, and the conditions under which it is to be rendered, are decided by the Secretary-General with due regard to the greater needs of underdeveloped areas and in conformity with the principle that each requesting Government is expected to assume responsibility, as far as possible, for all or a considerable part of the expenses involved.

1. EQUATORIAL GUINEA

123. At its thirty-fifth session, the Commission in its resolution 15 (XXXV), bearing in mind ECOSOC resolution 1235 (XLII) authorizing the Commission to conduct studies of situations where gross and systematic human rights violations occur, decided to appoint a Special Rapporteur to study the human rights situation in Equatorial Guinea. The Commission considered the report of the Special Rapporteur, Mr. Volio Jiménez, at its thirty-sixth session.

124. In resolution 33 (XXXVI) of 11 March 1980, the Commission on Human Rights expressed the view that important changes that had occurred in Equatorial Guinea since 3 August 1979 indicated a desire on the part of the new régime to restore and guarantee enjoyment of human rights in that country. Noting with appreciation the interest of the Government in co-operating with the United Nations in order to ensure the effective enjoyment of fundamental rights by the citizens of Equatorial Guinea, the Commission decided, in response to the Government's request, to request the Secretary-General to appoint, as an expert in his individual capacity, a person with wide experience of the situation in Equatorial Guinea with a view to assisting the Government of that country in taking the action necessary for the full restoration of human rights and fundamental freedoms there. The Commission's decision was endorsed by the Economic and Social Council in decision 1980/137 of 2 May 1980.

125. The Commission received the report submitted by the expert, Mr. Fernando Volio Jiménez,[64] at its thirty-seventh session, and took note of it with approval. On its recommendation the Economic and Social Council adopted resolution 1981/38 of 8 May 1981, in which it

expressed its appreciation to the expert and to the Government of Equatorial Guinea and reiterated its readiness to assist that Government, at its request, in the task of restoring human rights in Equatorial Guinea. Bearing in mind the need for co-ordination with other assistance activities, the Council requested the Secretary-General to draw up, in consultation with the expert and the Government, a draft plan of action for implementing those recommendations of the expert which he considered to be feasible. The Secretary-General was further requested, in drawing up the plan of action, to consult Governments, other United Nations organs and the relevant parts of the United Nations Secretariat, specialized agencies, non-governmental organizations and the Organization of African Unity, with a view to determining in what ways they might be able to contribute towards implementing the plan.

126. The Secretary-General submitted to the thirty-eighth session of the Commission on Human Rights a draft plan of action for the restoration of human rights and fundamental freedoms in Equatorial Guinea.[65] The Commission, in resolution 1982/34 of 11 March 1982, took note of the report. On the recommendation of the Commission, the Economic and Social Council, in resolution 1982/36 of 7 May 1982, took note of the plan of action, expressed regret at the delay in its implementation, and requested the Secretary-General to discuss with the Government of Equatorial Guinea the role that the United Nations could play in carrying it out.

127. By a letter dated 4 May 1982 the President of Equatorial Guinea informed the Secretary-General that the Equatorial Guinea National Commission was engaged in the drafting of a new constitution and requested the United Nations to provide the Government with two qualified constitutional experts to assist in the task. Welcoming the request, the Secretary-General, with the co-operation and assistance of the expert who had prepared the report on Equatorial Guinea, recruited two constitutional experts to assist the National Commission.

128. The experts stayed in Equatorial Guinea from 14 to 28 July 1982, reviewing the draft constitution prepared by the National Commission and making their comments on its provisions. A number of their suggestions were incorporated in the final text, which was promulgated on 3 August 1982. Subsequently, a referendum was held and the new Constitution was approved.

129. At its forty-second session, in 1986, the Commission on Human Rights was informed by the Secretary General that two legal experts had undertaken a mission to Equatorial Guinea in January of that year to assist in the codification of certain basic legal texts. The jurists had remained in the country for two weeks and had met with a number of officials of the Government, but had not been able to overcome a number of serious difficulties which had adversely affected the results of their mission. The Secretary-General had transmitted their re-

---

[64] E/CN.4/1439.

[65] E/CN.4/1495.

ports and recommendations to the Government for comment.

130. At its forty-third session, in 1987, the Commission was informed by the Secretary-General that he still had not received the requested comments.[66] In resolution 1987/36 of 10 March 1987, the Commission expressed the hope that the Government of Equatorial Guinea would react as soon as possible to the Secretary-General's communication. It requested the Government of Equatorial Guinea to give appropriate consideration to the implementation of the plan of action proposed by the United Nations.

2. HAITI

131. Between 1981 and 1986, the Commission on Human Rights examined materials concerning the human rights situation in Haiti within the framework of the procedure established under Economic and Social Council resolution 1503 (XLVIII), together with materials and observations received from the Government of the country. Because these communications concerned a number of allegations of violations of human rights, the Commission endeavoured to pursue a dialogue with representatives of the Government of Haiti in the hope of encouraging improvements in the situation. Confidential reports on direct contacts were presented to the Commission in 1982, 1983 and 1984.

132. At the request of the Commission, the Secretary-General examined ways and means whereby advisory services in the field of human rights could be made available to the Government of Haiti. As part of this process, experts designated by the Secretary-General visited Haiti for discussions with Government officials.

133. In the light of its consideration of the human rights situation then prevailing in Haiti, the Commission on Human Rights adopted on 13 March 1986 a confidential decision by which it requested its Chairman to appoint a special representative (a) to collect any information concerning the human rights situation in Haiti and to evaluate the development of the situation as regards political, civil, economic, social and cultural rights and freedoms, including the holding of free elections; (b) to study, with the Government of Haiti, any assistance that might be given as part of the advisory services in the field of human rights; and (c) to report to the Commission at its forty-third session. The Commission adopted this decision after having examined available materials concerning the human rights situation in Haiti and having taken note of the change in government which had occurred in that country on 5 February 1986.

134. Having heard a statement by the representative of the new Government concerning its intention to restore human rights and fundamental freedoms in Haiti, including the holding of free elections, the Commission stated that it was encouraged by that statement and was desirous of following the development of the human rights situation in the country. The Commission considered that it would be useful for it to be further informed by the new Government of Haiti before its forty-third session, about the implementation of measures for the promotion and protection of human rights and about those aspects of the human rights situation in the country which required further clarification.

135. At its forty-third session, in 1987, the Commission examined the confidential report of its Special Representative, Mr. Michel Gauvin, and other material relating to the human rights situation in Haiti, in a closed meeting. In resolution 1987/13 of 2 March 1987 it expressed its appreciation to the Special Representative and to the Government of Haiti for its unreserved co-operation with the Special Representative and with the Commission, and invited that Government to continue in its endeavours to develop full respect for human rights and fundamental freedoms in Haiti. It decided that resolution 1987/13 should be made public, and on its recommendation the Economic and Social Council, by decision 1987/140, released to the public the report of the Special Representative.

136. In resolution 1987/13, the Commission called upon the Government of Haiti to give consideration to the adoption of measures in areas of need indicated by the Special Representative, particularly (a) training and instruction of the police, military and prison personnel in respect for human rights and fundamental freedoms; (b) adoption of measures to strengthen the independence of the judiciary; (c) absolute prohibition of torture; (d) establishment of a panel of eminent Haitian personalities to investigate and report on past human rights abuses in the country; and (e) possibility of inviting international observers to the forthcoming legislative and presidential elections.

137. The Commission, further, invited the Secretary-General to proceed to award three fellowships to qualified Haitian nationals for training in the following areas indicated by the Special Representative: (a) role of the police in the promotion and protection of human rights; (b) human rights of prisoners and detainees; and (c) human rights in the administration of justice. It also urged him, in co-operation with the Government, to finalize the dates and arrangements for a training course on human rights in Haiti; and requested him to appoint an expert with a view to assisting the Government, through direct contacts, in taking the necessary action for the full restoration of human rights. One function of the expert so appointed will be to formulate recommendations for the full restoration of human rights in Haiti.

138. In view of the findings of the Special Representative and the information provided by the Government, the Commission decided to discontinue its consideration of the situation in Haiti under the procedure established by Economic and Social Council resolution 1503 (XLVIII). However, it planned to review the report of the expert appointed by the Secretary-General at its forty-fourth session under the agenda item entitled "Advisory services in the field of human rights".

---

[66] E/CN.4/1987/33/Add.2.

3. UGANDA

139. In resolution 34/122 of 14 December 1979 the General Assembly expressed its deep concern at the tragic loss of life, widespread destruction of property and severe damage to the economic and social infrastructure of Uganda, and urgently appealed to the international community to contribute generously to the reconstruction, rehabilitation and development needs of the country. In resolution 35/103 of 5 December 1980, the Assembly expressed its appreciation to the Secretary-General for the steps he had taken to mobilize assistance for Uganda, and requested him to ensure that adequate financial and budgetary arrangements were made for the organization of an effective international programme of assistance to Uganda and for the mobilization of international assistance.

140. Considering the need to take account of the importance of assistance designed to help the Government of Uganda to restore human rights and fundamental freedoms in the implementation of Assembly resolution 35/103, and noting with satisfaction the efforts made by that Government to restore a democratic system respectful of human rights and fundamental freedoms, the Commission on Human Rights, in resolution 30 (XXXVII) of 11 March 1981, requested the Secretary-General to provide advisory services and other forms of appropriate assistance to help the Government of Uganda in taking appropriate measures to continue to guarantee the enjoyment of human rights and fundamental freedoms. This decision was subsequently approved by the Economic and Social Council in decision 1981/146 of 8 May 1981.

141. In decision 1982/139, adopted by the Economic and Social Council in response to the interest expressed by the Government of Uganda, the Council requested the Secretary-General to provide advisory services and other forms of appropriate assistance to help the Government of Uganda to continue guaranteeing the enjoyment of human rights and fundamental freedoms, paying particular attention to the following areas: (*a*) the need for appropriate assistance to restore a law library for the High Court and Ministry of Justice; (*b*) the need for the revision of Ugandan laws, in conformity with recognized norms of human rights and fundamental freedoms, and the printing of consolidated volumes of the revised laws; (*c*) the need for the training of prison officers with a view to securing the application of recognized norms on treatment of prisoners; and (*d*) the need for the training of police officials, particularly investigative and scientific experts.

142. The Secretary-General accordingly developed contacts with the Government of Uganda and various sectors and agencies of the United Nation system. In the light of these exchanges of views, the Government submitted a statement of needs and projects. The Commission on Human Rights, in resolution 1983/47, authorized the Secretary-General to provide Uganda with all appropriate assistance to help it to continue guaranteeing the enjoyment of human rights, and all States, specialized agencies and United Nations organs, as well as humanitarian and non-governmental organizations, were invited to lend their assistance to the Government of Uganda in such efforts.

143. The Commission on Human Rights, in resolution 1984/45 of 13 March 1984, noted with satisfaction the efforts of the Government and people of Uganda to restore in that country a democratic system respectful of human rights and fundamental freedoms, and requested the Secretary-General to continue his contacts with the Government and, while providing all possible assistance, also to identify and bring to the attention of that Government external sources of assistance which it could possibly draw upon.

XII. PROTECTION OF HUMAN RIGHTS IN ARMED CONFLICTS

Introduction

1. The protection of human rights in armed conflicts has been a matter of particular concern to the international community for many years. Traditionally the International Committee of the Red Cross has taken the initiative in codifying rules of international humanitarian law, and under the auspices of the ICRC the Geneva Conventions of 12 August 1949,[1] as well as the earlier Hague Conventions of 1899 and 1907,[2] and the Geneva Protocol of 1925[3] were prepared. However, the compliance of some States parties with the obligations they assumed in ratifying these instruments has been questioned by some international human rights bodies which have expressed concern about the amount of protection afforded by them to the safety, welfare and security of the inhabitants of areas of armed conflicts.

A. International co-operation to reduce the violence and brutality of armed conflicts

2. In dealing with the Middle East conflict the Security Council, in resolution 237 (1967), first emphasized that essential and inalienable human rights should be respected even during the vicissitudes of war. It recommended that Governments scrupulously respect the humanitarian principles governing the treatment of prisoners of war and the protection of civilian persons in time of war set forth in the Geneva Conventions.

3. The Council's resolution was welcomed with great satisfaction by the General Assembly in resolution 2252 (ES-V) of 4 July 1967, and has since been repeatedly recalled and reaffirmed.[4]

4. The International Conference on Human Rights, held in 1968, during the International Year for Human Rights, observed that[5] armed conflicts continued to plague humanity, that the widespread violence and brutality of the times—including massacres, summary executions, torture, inhuman treatment of prisoners, killing of civilians in armed conflicts and the use of

chemical and biological means of warfare including napalm bombing—eroded human rights and engendered brutality, and that it was essential for humanitarian principles to prevail even during periods of armed conflict. The Conference accordingly recommended remedial action. It requested the Secretary-General, "after consultation with the International Committee of the Red Cross, to draw the attention of all States Members of the United Nations system to the existing rules of international law on the subject and to urge them, pending the adoption of new rules, to ensure that in all armed conflicts the inhabitants and belligerents are protected in accordance witht 'the principles of the law of nations derived from the usages established among civilized peoples, from the laws of humanity and from the dictates of the public conscience''. The Conference also called upon all States which had not done so to become parties to the Hague Conventions of 1899 and 1907, the Geneva Protocol of 1925 and the Geneva Conventions of 1949.

5. On recommendation of the Conference, the General Assembly, in resolution 2444 (XXIII) of 19 December 1968, invited the Secretary-General, in consultation with the International Committee of the Red Cross and other appropriate international organizations, to study (a) steps which could be taken to secure the better application of existing humanitarian international conventions and rules in all armed conflicts, and (b) the need for additional humanitarian international conventions or for other appropriate legal instruments to ensure the better protection of civilians, prisoners and combatants in all armed conflicts and the prohibition and limitation of the use of certain methods and means of warfare. At the same time if affirmed resolution XXVIII of the Twentieth International Conference of the Red Cross, held at Vienna in 1965, which laid down the following principles for observance by all governmental and other authorities responsible for action in armed conflicts:

That the right of the parties to a conflict to adopt means of injuring the enemy is not unlimited;

That it is prohibited to launch attacks against the civilian populations as such;

That distinction must be made at all times between persons taking part in the hostilities and members of the civilian population to the effect that the latter be spared as much as possible.

1. REPORTS ON RESPECT FOR HUMAN RIGHTS IN ARMED CONFLICTS

6. At its twenty-fifth session, in 1969, the General Assembly considered two reports on the subject presented by the Secretary-General (A/7720 and A/8052). The

---

[1] United Nations, *Treaty Series*, vol. 75, Nos. 970-973.

[2] International Committee of the Red Cross, *Protocols additional to the Geneva Conventions of 12 August 1949* (Geneva, 1977).

[3] Carnegie Endowment for International Peace, *The Hague Conventions and Declarations of 1899 and 1907* (New York, Oxford University Press, 1915).

[4] See Security Council resolutions 248 (1968) and 497 (1981), General Assembly resolutions 2443 (XXIII), 2452 B (XXIII), 2535 B (XXIV), 2546 (XXIV), 2727 (XXV), 2851 (XXVI), 3005 (XXVII), 32/44, 34/51, 37/116, 39/77 and 41/72.

[5] *Final Act of the International Conference on Human Rights*, United Nations publication, Sales No. E.68.XIV.2, p. 18.

first report included an historical survey of international instruments of a humanitarian character relating to armed conflict, examined the relationship between the Geneva Conventions of 1949 and certain United Nations human rights instruments, and raised the question of the humanitarian law applicable to conflicts not of an international character. The second report examined in greater detail the extent to which United Nations instruments protected human rights in armed conflicts, and pointed out that the protection ensured by those instruments was more far-reaching in some instances than that provided by the Geneva Conventions and other humanitarian instruments. It emphasized, in particular, that the International Covenant on Civil and Political Rights contained provisions from which no derogation was permitted: provisions intended to apply at all times and everywhere, in time of peace as well as in time of war, and to the full range of conceivable conflicts whether or not of an international character. Thus the protection to be derived from the Covenant might in some respects be wider and more extensive than that provided by the Geneva Conventions.

7. The reports also contained a number of observations, suggestions and recommendations concerning many aspects of the protection of human rights in armed conflicts, both *de lege lata* and *de lege ferenda*. These included observations relating to the establishment of civilian sanctuaries and concerning the prohibition of the use of certain weapons such as chemical and bacteriological weapons, suggestions for the possible extension of the scope of the Geneva Conventions of 1949 to include rules applicable in conflicts not of an international character, and observations on the persons to be protected in internal conflicts and in situations involving guerrilla warfare, on conditions for privileged belligerency, and on the applicability of the fourth Geneva Convention (on civilian persons) to freedom fighters.

8. At its twenty-fifth session, the General Assembly considered the question of human rights in armed conficts and on 9 December 1970 adopted five resolutions relating to it.

9. In resolution 2673 (XXV), the General Assembly initiated work on a draft international agreement ensuring the protection of journalists engaged in dangerous missions. The action taken pursuant to this resolution is summarized in section A, 3, below.

10. In resolution 2674 (XXV) the General Assembly affirmed that the participants in resistance movements and freedom fighters should be treated, in case of their arrest, as prisoners of war. It also strongly condemned bombardments of civilian populations and the use of chemical and bacteriological weapons.

11. In resolution 2675 (XXV), the General Assembly affirmed certain basic principles for the protection of civilian populations in armed conflicts, the first of which was that fundamental human rights, as accepted in international law and laid down in international instruments, continued to apply fully in situations of armed conflict.

12. In resolution 2676 (XXV), the General Assembly addressed itself in particular to the treatment of prisoners of war. The Assembly noted resolution XI adopted by the XXIst International Conference of the Red Cross held at Istanbul in 1969. Considering that "the direct repatriation of seriously wounded and seriously sick prisoners of war and the repatriation or internment in a neutral country of prisoners of war who have undergone a long period of captivity constituted important aspects of human rights as advanced and preserved under the Geneva Convention of 1949 and the Charter of the United Nations", the Assembly called upon "all parties to any armed conflict to comply with the terms and provisions of the Geneva Convention relative to the Treatment of Prisoners of War, of 12 August 1949, so as to ensure the humane treatment of all persons entitled to the protection of the Convention and, *inter alia*, to permit regular inspection, in accordance with the Convention, of all places of detention of prisoners of war by a protecting Power or humanitarian organization such as the International Committee of the Red Cross".

13. In resolution 2677 (XXV), the General Assembly laid down a programme for further work in this field. In particular it welcomed the decision of the International Committee of the Red Cross to convene in 1971 a conference on the reaffirmation and development of international humanitarian law applicable to armed conflicts, to be attended by government experts, and expressed the view that one or more plenipotentiary diplomatic conferences might be convened in order to adopt international legal instruments for the reaffirmation and development of humanitarian law applicable to armed conflicts. It emphasized the importance of continued close co-operation between the United Nations and the International Committee of the Red Cross.

14. Between 1971 and 1977 the Secretary-General presented to the General Assembly, at its request, seven additional reports on various aspects of the protection of human rights in armed conflicts, reviewing the ongoing work of the International Committee of the Red Cross in this field as well as that of the Diplomatic Conference on the Reaffirmation and Development of International Humanitarian Law Applicable in Armed Conflicts convened at Geneva in 1974, 1975, 1976 and 1977 by the Swiss Federal Council. In addition, the Secretary-General presented reports to the Assembly on existing rules of international law concerning the prohibition or restriction of the use of specific weapons (A/9215, vols. I and II), on the protection of journalists engaged in dangerous missions in areas of armed conflict (A/10147), and on napalm and other incendiary weapons and all aspects of their possible use (A/8803).

15. The fourth session of the Diplomatic Conference on the Reaffirmation and Development of International Humanitarian Law Applicable to Armed Conflicts, held at Geneva from 17 March to 10 June 1977, resulted in the adoption of two Protocols Additional to the Geneva Conventions of 12 August 1949, namely, Protocol I relating to the Protection of Victims of International

Armed Conflicts and Protocol II relating to the Protection of Victims of Non-International Armed Conflicts. In addition, the Diplomatic Conference recommended that a special conference be called on the issue of prohibition of use for humanitarian reasons of specific conventional weapons and adopted a series of resolutions and a Final Act.

16. In resolution 32/44 of 8 December 1977, the General Assembly welcomed the successful conclusion of the Diplomatic Conference and noted its recommendation concerning a special conference to be called on the issue of prohibition or restriction of use for humanitarian reasons of specific conventional weapons. It expressed its appreciation to the Swiss Federal Council for acting as host to the four sessions of the Diplomatic Conference and to the International Committee of the Red Cross for preparing the basis for discussion and for its constant assistance to the Conference. The Assembly urged States to consider without delay the matter of signing and ratifying or acceding to the two Protocols, opened for signature on 12 December 1977 in Berne; and appealed to all States which had not done so to become parties to the Geneva Conventions of 1949.

2. PROTOCOLS ADDITIONAL TO THE GENEVA CONVENTIONS OF 12 AUGUST 1949[6]

17. Protocol I reaffirms and develops the provisions of the Geneva Conventions of 1949 protecting the victims of armed conflicts of an international nature, and supplements the measures intended to secure the application of those provisions. Protocol II does the same with respect to conflicts which are not of an international nature.

18. Part I of Protocol I sets out certain general principles and definitions, and provides (article 5) for the appointment of a Protecting Power, for the purpose of supervising the application of the Conventions and Protocol, by each party to a conflict.

19. Part II contains provisions to ameliorate the condition of the wounded, sick and shipwrecked when an international armed conflict occurs (articles 8 to 34); and provides for the collection and provision of information concerning persons missing or dead as a result of such a conflict (articles 33 and 34).

20. Part III deals with methods and means of warfare (articles 35 to 42) and combatant and prisoner-of-war status (articles 43 to 47). Article 35 prohibits the employment of methods or means of warfare which may cause superfluous injury, unnecessary suffering, or widespread, long-term and severe damage to the environment. Article 44 provides that any combatant who falls into the power of an adverse party shall be considered to be a prisoner of war, and article 45 sets out measures for the protection of such prisoners. Articles

---

6 For the texts of these Protocols, see International Committee of the Red Cross, *Protocols additional to the Geneva Conventions of 12 August 1949*. Geneva, 1977.

46 and 47 provide that neither spies nor mercenaries shall have the right to the status of prisoner of war.

21. Part IV (articles 48 to 79) provides protection for members of the civilian population who have fallen into the hands of an adverse Party. Articles 48 to 71 supplement the provisions of the Third Geneva Convention relating to the protection of the civilian population and civilian objects against the dangers arising from military operations, and lay down a series of rules for this purpose, the basic rule being (article 48) that parties to a conflict shall at all times distinguish between the civilian population and combatants and shall direct their operations only against military objectives. Starvation of civilians and attacks against the natural environment, as methods of warfare, are specifically prohibited. Articles 72 to 79 deal with the treatment of persons in the power of a party to the conflict. Articles 76 to 78 set out special measures for the protection of women and children, in particular against rape, forced prostitution and any other form of indecent assault. Article 79 provides that journalists engaged in dangerous professional missions in areas of armed conflict shall be considered as civilians, and shall be protected under the Conventions and Protocol provided that they take no action adversely affecting their civilian status. It further provides for an identity card to be issued to such journalists by their Government, attesting to their status as journalists.

22. Parts V and VI (articles 80 to 102) set out measures for the execution of the Conventions and the Protocol and for repression of breaches of their provisions, including the establishment of an International Fact-Finding Commission (article 90) to inquire into allegations that those provisions have been violated; and include the usual final provisions.

23. The non-international conflicts to which Protocol II applies include conflicts between the armed forces of a Government and dissident armed forces or other organized armed groups which exercise control over part of its territory. It does not, however, apply to situations of internal disturbances and tensions, such as riots and other isolated and sporadic acts of violence.

24. Article 4 calls for humane treatment, without adverse distinction, of all persons who do not take a direct part, or who have ceased to take part, in hostilities, whether or not their liberty has been restricted. It lists a number of acts, such as murder, torture, mutilation and corporal punishment, which are totally prohibited. Article 5 establishes minimum standards with regard to persons deprived of their liberty for reasons related to armed conflict, and lays down rules protecting those prosecuted or punishment for criminal offences related to armed conflict.

25. Articles 7 to 12 provide for the protection and care of persons wounded, sick or shipwrecked as a result of a non-international conflict. Articles 13 to 18 set out special measures for the protection of the civilian population against acts or threats of violence (article 13), against starvation as a method of combat (article 14),

and against forced movement from their own territory (article 17). In addition, acts of hostility directed against historical monuments, works of art or places of worship—or their use in support of military objectives—are prohibited (article 16).

26. At the request of the General Assembly, the Secretary-General reports periodically on the state of acceptance of the Protocols. In resolutions 34/51 of 23 November 1979, 37/116 of 16 December 1982, 39/77 of 13 December 1984 and 41/72 of 3 December 1986, the Assembly has noted that although the Geneva Conventions of 1949 are almost universally accepted, the number of States that have become parties to the Protocols is more limited. The Assembly has repeatedly called upon all States parties to the Geneva Conventions to become parties to the Protocols and to consider making the declaration provided for under article 90 of Protocol I accepting the competence of an International Fact-Finding Commission. As at 31 December 1987, 62 States had signed, 26 had ratified and 45 had acceded to Protocol I, and 58 States had signed, 24 had ratified and 40 had acceded to Protocol II. Ten States had made the declaration provided for under article 90 of Protocol I.

3. PROTECTION OF JOURNALISTS ENGAGED IN DANGEROUS MISSIONS IN AREAS OF ARMED CONFLICT

27. The initiative to provide for the protection of journalists engaged in dangerous missions in areas of armed conflict was taken by the General Assembly at its twenty-fifth session when, in resolution 2673 (XXV) of 9 December 1970, it stated that it was essential for the United Nations to obtain complete information concerning armed conflicts and that journalists, whatever their nationality, had an important role to play in that regard. The Assembly noted with regret that journalists engaged in missions in areas where an armed conflict was taking place sometimes suffered as a result of their professional duty. It enumerated the provisions of the Geneva Conventions of 1949 under which certain types of protection might be granted to journalists, but added that those provisions did not cover some categories of journalists engaged in dangerous missions and did not correspond to their needs. Convinced of the need for an additional humanitarian international instrument to ensure the better protection of journalists engaged in dangerous missions, the Assembly invited the Economic and Social Council to request the Commission on Human Rights to consider the possibility of preparing a draft international agreement on the question which would provide for the creation of a universally recognized and guaranteed identification document.

28. The Commission on Human Rights at its twenty-eighth session, in 1972, approved as a basis for further work the draft articles of an international convention on the protection of journalists engaged in dangerous missions in areas of armed conflict.[7] It also decided to transmit the draft articles to the second session of the Conference of Government Experts convened by the International Committee of the Red Cross in order that they might be brought to the notice of the Conference for its observations.

29. In his report on the question to the General Assembly at its thirty-second session,[8] the Secretary-General indicated that the Diplomatic Conference on Reaffirmation and Development of International Humanitarian Law Applicable in Armed Conflicts had adopted Protocol I to the Geneva Convention of 1949 containing an article (article 79) on measures of protection for journalists. The article reads as follows:

1. Journalists engaged in dangerous professional missions in areas of armed conflict shall be considered as civilians within the meaning of Article 50, paragraph 1.

2. They shall be protected as such under the Conventions and this Protocol, provided that they take no action adversely affecting their status as civilians, and without prejudice to the right of war correspondents accredited to the armed forces to the status provided for in Article 4 A (4) of the Third Convention.

3. They may obtain an identity card similar to the model in Annex II of this Protocol. This card, which shall be issued by the government of the State of which the journalist is a national or in whose territory he resides or in which the news medium employing him is located, shall attest to his status as a journalist.

The identity card approved by the Conference for journalists on dangerous professional missions, constituting annex II to Protocol I, was reproduced in annex I of the Secretary-General's report.

4. LEGAL STATUS OF COMBATANTS STRUGGLING AGAINST COLONIAL AND ALIEN DOMINATION AND RACIST RÉGIMES

30. Between 1968 and 1973 the General Assembly made numerous appeals to the colonial Powers and those occupying foreign territories, as well as to various racist régimes[9] to ensure the application to the fighters for freedom and self-determination of the provisions of the Geneva Convention relative to the Treatment of Prisoners of War of 12 August 1949 and the Geneva Convention relative to the Protection of Civilian Persons in Time of War of the same date.

31. In resolution 3103 (XXVIII) of 12 December 1973 the Assembly recalled these appeals and expressed its deep concern that compliance with the provisions of the said Conventions had not been ensured. Noting that the treatment of the combatants struggling against colonial and alien domination and racist régimes captured as prisoners remained inhuman, the Assembly proclaimed a series of basic principles of the legal status of the combatants struggling against colonial and alien domination

---

[7] *Official Records of the Economic and Social Council, Fifty-second Session, Supplement No. 7* (E/5113), chap. XIII, resolution 6 (XXVIII), annex.

[8] A/32/144 and Add.1.

[9] General Assembly resolutions 2383 (XXIII) of 7 November 1968, 2508 (XXIV) of 21 November 1969, 2547 (XXIV) of 11 December 1969, 2652 (XXV) of 3 December 1970, 2678 (XXV) of 9 December 1971, 2796 (XXVI) of the same date, and 2871 (XXVI) of 20 December 1971.

and racist régimes "without prejudice to their elaboration in future within the framework of the development of international law applying to the protection of human rights in armed conflicts".

32. The principles so proclaimed were:

1. The struggle of peoples under colonial and alien domination and racist régimes for the implementation of their right to self-determination and independence is legitimate and in full accordance with the principles of international law.

2. Any attempt to suppress the struggle against colonial and alien domination and racist régimes is incompatible with the Charter of the United Nations, the Declaration on Principles of International Law concerning Friendly Relations and Co-operation among States in accordance with the Charter of the United Nations, the Universal Declaration of Human Rights and the Declaraion on the Granting of Independence to Colonial Countries and Peoples and constitutes a threat to international peace and security.

3. The armed conflicts involving the struggle of peoples against colonial and alien domination and racist régimes are to be regarded as international armed conflicts in the sense of the 1949 Geneva Conventions, and the legal status envisaged to apply to the combatants in the 1949 Geneva Conventions and other international instruments is to apply to the persons engaged in armed struggle against colonial and alien domination and racist régimes.

4. The combatants struggling against colonial and alien domination and racist régimes captured as prisoners are to be accorded the status of prisoners of war and their treatment should be in accordance with the provisions of the Geneva Convention relative to the Treatment of Prisoners of War, of 12 August 1949.

5. The use of mercenaries by colonial and racist régimes against the national liberation movements struggling for their freedom and independence from the yoke of colonialism and alien domination is considered to be a criminal act and the mercenaries should accordingly be punished as criminals.

6. The violation of the legal status of the combatants struggling against colonial and alien domination and racist régimes in the course of armed conflicts entails full responsibility in accordance with the norms of international law.

5. ASSISTANCE AND CO-OPERATION IN ACCOUNTING FOR PERSONS MISSING OR DEAD IN ARMED CONFLICTS

33. The concern of the United Nations for the solution of legal difficulties arising from the absence, due to armed conflict, of persons whose death cannot be conclusively established dates back to 1948, when the Economic and Social Council, in resolution 158 (VII) of 24 August 1948, requested the Secretary-General to prepare a draft convention on the subject. After examination and revision by an *ad hoc* committee, the draft convention was considered by the General Assembly. In resolution 369 (IV) of 3 December 1949, the Assembly decided to convene an international conference of government representatives to conclude work on the convention.

34. The Convention on the Death of Missing Persons[10] was opened for acceptance on 6 April 1950, and entered into force on 24 January 1952. It ceased to be valid on 23 January 1957 in accordance with its article 17, but its validity was twice extended, each time for a five-year period.

35. In his report on respect for human rights in armed conflicts to the General Assembly at its thirty-second session,[11] the Secretary-General pointed out that Protocol I additional to the Geneva Conventions of 1949 contained an article (article 33) on missing persons which stated the general principle that "as soon as circumstances permit, and at the latest from the end of active hostilities, each Party to the conflict shall search for the persons who have been reported missing by an adverse Party. Such adverse Party shall transmit all relevant information concerning such persons in order to facilitate such searches."

B. International action to prohibit or restrict the use of certain weapons

36. Organs of the United Nations primarily concerned with disarmament, and with the prohibition or restriction of the use of certain weapons, have adopted a number of measures which protect human rights, particularly the right to life. Some of the important measures in this category are described below.

1. PROHIBITION OF THE USE OF NUCLEAR AND THERMONUCLEAR WEAPONS

37. In resolution 1653 (XVI) of 24 November 1961, the General Assembly adopted the Declaration on the Prohibition of the Use of Nuclear and Thermonuclear Weapons, in which it declared that:

(*a*) The use of nuclear and thermonuclear weapons is contrary to the spirit, letter and aims of the United Nations and, as such, a direct violation of the Charter of the United Nations;

(*b*) The use of nuclear and thermonuclear weapons would exceed event the scope of war and cause indiscriminate suffering and destruction to mankind and civilization and, as such, is contrary to the rules of international law and to the laws of humanity;

(*c*) The use of nuclear and thermonuclear weapons is a war directed not against an enemy or enemies alone but also against mankind in general, since the peoples of the world not involved in such a war will be subjected to all the evils generated by the use of such weapons;

(*d*) Any State using nuclear and thermonuclear weapons is to be considered as violating the Charter of the United Nations, as acting contrary to the laws of humanity and as committing a crime against mankind and civilization.

38. The Declaration was reaffirmed by General Assembly resolutions 33/71 B of 14 December 1978, 34/83 G of 11 December 1979, 35/152 D of 12 December 1980 and 36/92 I of 9 December 1981. Since 1984, the Assembly has repeatedly requested the Conference on Disarmament to commence negotiations with a view to achieving agreement on an international convention which would prohibit the use or threat of use of nuclear weapons under any circumstances, but the Conference has advised it each year that it was unable to undertake such negotiations.

---

[10] United Nations, *Treaty Series*, vol. 119, No. 1610, p. 122.

[11] A/32/144 and Add.1.

2. Banning of Nuclear Weapon Tests in the Atmosphere, in Outer Space and Under Water

39. In 1963 the Treaty Banning Nuclear Weapon Tests in the Atmosphere, in Outer Space and Under Water[12] was signed. It entered into force on 10 October 1963. This Treaty was not concluded under direct United Nations auspices. It was however noted with approval by the General Assembly in resolution 1910 (XVIII) of 27 November 1963.

40. In the preamble to the Treaty the parties state that they seek to achieve the discontinuance of all test explosions of nuclear weapons for all time, are determined to continue negotiations to that end, and desire to put an end to the contamination of man's environment by radioactive substances. In the Treaty itself, each of the parties undertakes to prohibit, to prevent and not carry out any nuclear weapon test explosion or any other nuclear explosion at any place under its jurisdiction or control in the atmosphere, in outer space or under water.

3. Principles Governing the Activities of States in the Exploration and Use of Outer Space, Including the Moon and Other Celestial Bodies

41. In resolution 2222 (XXI) of 19 December 1966, the General Assembly commended the Treaty on Principles Governing the Activities of States in the Exploration and Use of Outer Space, including the Moon and Other Celestial Bodies. In that Treaty the States parties "undertake not to place in orbit around the Earth any objects carrying nuclear weapons or any other kinds of weapons of mass destruction, [not to] install such weapons on celestial bodies, or station weapons in outer space in any other manner". The moon and other celestial bodies are to be used exclusively for peaceful purposes.

4. Non-Proliferation of Nuclear Weapons

42. By resolution 2373 (XXII) of 12 June 1968 the General Assembly commended the Treaty on the Non-Proliferation of Nuclear Weapons. By that Treaty each nuclear-weapon State party "undertakes not to transfer to any recipient whatsoever nuclear weapons or other nuclear explosive devices or control over such weapons or explosive devices, directly or indirectly; and not in any way to assist, encourage, or induce any non-nuclear-weapon State to manufacture or otherwise acquire nuclear weapons or other nuclear explosive devices . . .".

5. Convention on Prohibitions or Restrictions on the Use of Certain Conventional Weapons Which May Be Deemed to Be Excessively Injurious or to Have Indiscriminate Effects, and Protocols Thereto

43. In his second report on respect for human rights in armed conflicts,[13] presented to the General Assembly at its twenty-fifth session, in 1970, the Secretary-General recalled that the International Conference on Human Rights, in resolution XXIII, had referred to the question of napalm bombing and had added that the question called for study. The idea of undertaking a study of the legality or otherwise of napalm bombing had received the support of a number of experts consulted by the Secretary-General and of those of the International Committee of the Red Cross. The Secretary-General suggested that if the General Assembly accepted the merit of such a study, it might consider requesting him to prepare, with the assistance of qualified consultants, a report on napalm weapons and the effects of their possible use.

44. In resolution 2852 (XXVI) of 20 December 1971, the General Assembly made such a request and the report, entitled *Napalm and Other Incendiary Weapons and All Aspects of Their Possible Use*,[14] was submitted to the Assembly at its twenty-seventh session, in 1972. The report concluded that the massive spread of fire through incendiary weapons was largely indiscriminate in its effects on military and civilian targets and that a number of injuries, whether directly from the action of incendiary weapons or as a result of fires initiated by them, were intensely painful and required exceptional resources, far beyond the reach of most countries, for their medical treatment.

45. The General Assembly, in resolution 2932 A (XXVII) of 29 November 1972, commended the Secretary-General's report to the attention of all Governments and peoples and requested the Secretary-General to circulate it to the Governments of Member States for their comments.

46. Later, in resolution 32/44 of 8 December 1977, the General Assembly noted the recommendation, adopted by the Diplomatic Conference on the Reaffirmation and Development of International Humanitarian Law Applicable in Armed Conflicts, that a special conference be called on the issue of prohibition or restriction of use for humanitarian reasons of specific conventional weapons.

47. Subsequently, the General Assembly adopted a number of resolutions concerning the use of weapons which may be deemed to be excessively dangerous or to have indiscriminate effects, including resolutions 3076 (XXVIII), 3255 A and B (XXIX), 3464 (XXX), 31/64, 32/152, 33/70, 34/82 and 35/153.

48. In resolution 35/153 of 12 December 1980, the General Assembly took note of the Final Report of the United Nations Conference on Prohibitions and Restrictions of Use of Certain Conventional Weapons Which May Be Deemed to Be Excessively Injurious or to Have Indiscriminate Effects, held at Geneva from 10 to 28 September 1979 and from 15 September to 10 October 1980,[15] and welcomed the successful conclusion of the Conference, which had resulted in the adoption, on 10 October 1980, of the following instruments:

---

[12] United Nations, *Treaty Series*, vol. 480, No. 6964, p. 43

[13] A/8052.

[14] United Nations publication, Sales No. E.73.I.3.

[15] A/CONF.95/15.

(*a*) Convention on Prohibitions or Restrictions on the Use of Certain Conventional Weapons Which May Be Deemed to Be Excessively Injurious or to Have Indiscriminate Effects:

(*b*) Protocol on Non-Detectable Fragments (Protocol I);

(*c*) Protocol on Prohibitions or Restrictions on the Use of Mines, Booby Traps and Other Devices (Protocol II); and

(*d*) Protocol on Prohibitions or Restrictions on the Use of Incendiary Weapons (Protocol III).

The General Assembly commended the Convention and the three annexed Protocols to all States, with a view to achieving the widest possible adherence to those instruments.

49. The Secretary-General informed the General Assembly, as its fortieth session, on the state of adherence to the Convention and its Protocols (A/40/550). In resolution 41/50 of 3 December 1986, the Assembly noted with satisfaction that an increasing number of States had either signed, ratified, accepted or acceded to those instruments, all of which had entered into force on 2 December 1983.

6. PROHIBITION OF THE DEVELOPMENT AND MANUFACTURE OF NEW TYPES OF WEAPONS OF MASS DESTRUCTION AND NEW SYSTEMS OF SUCH WEAPONS

50. The General Assembly, in resolution 3479 (XXX) of 11 December 1975 and 31/74 of 10 December 1976, requested the Conference of the Committee on Disarmament to work out an agreement on the prohibition of the development and manufacture of new types of weapons of mass destruction and new systems of such weapons. After noting the discussion of this subject which had taken place at the Conference the Assembly, in resolution 32/84 B of 12 December 1977, urged States to refrain from developing new weapons of mass destruction based on new scientific principles, called upon States to apply scientific discovery for the benefit of mankind, and welcomed the active continuation of negotiations relating to the prohibition and limitation of identified weapons of mass destruction. The Assembly has defined "weapons of mass destruction" as "atomic explosive weapons, radioactive material weapons, lethal chemical and biological weapons and any weapons developed in the future which have characteristics comparable in destructive effects to those of the atomic bomb or other weapons mentioned above".

51. Since 1977, there has been little change in the situation although the General Assembly has considered the question at every regular session. On 12 December 1984 the Assembly, in resolution 39/62, called upon States Members of the Security Council, as well as other militarily significant States, to make declarations of their refusal to create new types of weapons of mass destruction and new systems of such weapons. On 3 December 1986 the Assembly, in resolution 41/56, once again requested the Conference on Disarmament to keep the question constantly under review with a view to making, when necessary, recommendations on undertaking specific negotiations on the identified types of such weapon. Also, in that resolution, the Assembly called upon all States, immediately following the identification of any new type of weapon of mass destruction, to commence negotiations on its prohibition with the simultaneous introduction of a moratorium on its practical development; and urged States to refrain from any action that could adversely affect the efforts aimed at preventing the emergence of new types of weapons of mass destruction and new systems of such weapons.

7. PROHIBITION OF THE EMPLACEMENT OF NUCLEAR WEAPONS AND OTHER WEAPONS OF MASS DESTRUCTION ON THE SEA-BED AND THE OCEAN FLOOR AND IN THE SUBSOIL THEREOF

52. The Treaty on the Prohibition of the Emplacement of Nuclear Weapons and Other Weapons of Mass Destruction on the Sea-Bed and the Ocean Floor and in the Subsoil Thereof was commended by the General Assembly in resolution 2660 (XXV) of 7 December 1970, and opened for signature on 11 February 1971. Parties to the Treaty are bound not to emplant or emplace nuclear weapons or other weapons of mass destruction—or facilities designed for launching or testing of such weapons—on the sea-bed and the ocean floor and in the subsoil thereof beyond the outer limit of the sea-bed zone. The prohibitions do not apply either to the coastal State or to the sea-bed beneath its territorial waters.

8. PROHIBITION OF THE USE OF CHEMICAL AND BACTERIOLOGICAL WEAPONS

53. Over the years the General Assembly has repeatedly dealt with the question of chemical and bacteriological (biological) weapons and has strongly recommended the accession of States not yet parties to it to the Protocol for the Prohibition of the Use in War of Asphyxiating, Poisonous or Other Gases, and of Bacteriological Methods of Warfare, signed at Geneva on 17 June 1925.[16]

54. It was only at its twenty-sixth session, in 1971, that the Assembly was in a position to consider and to commend, by its resolution 2826 (XXVI) of 16 December 1971, the Convention on the Prohibition of the Development, Production and Stockpiling of Bacteriological (Biological) and Toxin Weapons and on Their Destruction. In this Convention each State party undertakes never in any cirumstances to develop, produce, stockpile or otherwise acquire or retain:

(1) Microbial or other biological agents, or toxins whatever their origin or method of production, of types and in quantities that have no justification for prophylactic, protective or other peaceful purposes;

(2) Weapons, equipment or means of delivery designed to use such agents or toxins for hostile purposes or in armed conflict.

Each State party further

---

[16] League of Nations, *Treaty Series*, vol. XCIV, No. 2138.

undertakes to destroy, or to divert to peaceful purposes, as soon as possible but not later than nine months after the entry into force of the Convention, all agents, toxins, weapons, equipment and means of delivery specified in article 1 of the Convention, which are in its possession or under its jurisdiction or control. In implementing the provisions of this article all necessary safety precautions shall be observed to protect populations and the environment.

The Convention, opened for signature and ratification on 10 April 1972, entered into force on 26 March 1975.

55. At its tenth special session, in 1978, the General Assembly decided that the conclusion of a convention prohibiting the development, production and stockpiling of all chemical weapons—and their destruction—was one of the most urgent tasks of the international community (resolution S-10/2, paras. 72, 73 and 75). Since that time, it has repeatedly urged the Conference on Disarmament to accelerate its negotiations on such a convention, and has called upon all States, pending the conclusion of such a comprehensive ban, to co-operate in efforts to prevent the use of chemical weapons (resolution 41/58 C of 3 December 1986).

9. PREVENTION OF NUCLEAR CATASTROPHE

56. The General Assembly stated, in the Declaration on the Prevention of Nuclear Catastrophe contained in resolution 36/100 of 9 December 1981, that States and statesmen that resort first to the use of nuclear weapons would be committing the gravest crime against humanity. "There will never be any justification or pardon for statesmen who take the decision to be the first to use nuclear weapons", the Declaration stipulates. "Any doctrines allowing the first use of nuclear weapons and any actions pushing the world towards a catastrophe are incompatible with human moral standards and the lofty ideals of the United Nations". Nuclear energy, the Declaration concludes, should be used exclusively for peaceful purposes and only for the benefit of mankind.

57. Convinced that the prevention of nuclear war and the reduction of the risk of such war are matters of the highest priority and of vital interest to all people of the world, the Assembly has repeatedly called upon the Conference on Disarmament to undertake negotiations with a view to achieving agreement on appropriate and practical measures to prevent nuclear war. However it was compelled to note with regret, in resolution 41/86 G of 4 December 1986, that the Conference up to that time had not even been able to establish a subsidiary body to consider steps which could be taken to prevent nuclear war.

C. International co-operation to prevent and punish crimes against peace, war crimes, and crimes against humanity

58. In 1950 the International Law Commission, as directed by the General Assembly, completed a formulation of the principles of international law recognized in the Charter of the Nürnberg Tribunal and in the judge-

ment of the Tribunal. By resolution 488 (V) of 12 December 1950, the Assembly decided to send the formulation, which consisted of seven principles, to the Governments of Member States for comments, and requested the Commission, in preparing a draft code of offences against the peace and security of mankind (which the Assembly had also requested), to take account of the observations on the formulation of the Nürnberg principles made in the Assembly or received later from Governments.

1. THE NÜRNBERG PRINCIPLES[17]

59. Principle I, as formulated by the International Law Commission, states that "Any person who commits an act which constitutes a crime under international law is responsible therefor and liable to punishment".

60. Principles II to V, and Principle VII, read as follows:

Principle II

The fact that internal law does not impose a penalty for an act which constitutes a crime under international law does not relieve the person who committed the act from responsibility under international law.

Principle III

The fact that a person who committed an act which constitutes a crime under international law acted as Head of State or responsible Government official does not relieve him from responsibility under international law.

Principle IV

The fact that a person acted pursuant to order of his Government or of a superior does not relieve him from responsibility under international law, provided a moral choice was in fact possible to him.

Principle V

Any person charged with a crime under international law has the right to a fair trial on the facts and law.

Principle VII

Complicity in the commission of a crime against peace, a war crime, or a crime against humanity as set forth in Principle VI is a crime under international law.

61. Principle VI provides that the following are punishable as crimes under international law:

(*a*) Crimes against peace:

(i) Planning, preparation, initiation or waging of a war of aggression or a war in violation of international treaties, agreements or assurances;

(ii) Participation in a common plan or conspiracy for the accomplishment of any of the acts mentioned under (i).

(*b*) War crimes: violations of the laws or customs of war which include, but are not limited to, murder, ill-treatment or deportation to slave-labour or for any other purpose of civilian population of or in occupied territory: murder or ill-treatment of prisoners of war, of

---

[17] For the text of the Nürnberg principles, see *The Work of the International Law Commission*, third edition (United Nations publications, Sales No. E.80.V.II), pp.116 and 117.

persons on the seas, killing of hostages, plunder of public or private property, wanton destruction of cities, towns, or villages, or devastation not justified by military necessity.

(c) Crimes against humanity: murder, extermination, enslavement, deportation and other inhuman acts done against any civilian population, or persecutions on political, racial or religious grounds, when such acts are done or such persecutions are carried on in execution of or in connection with any crime against peace or any war crime.

2. DRAFT CODE OF OFFENCES AGAINST THE PEACE AND SECURITY OF MANKIND

62. In the same resolution that requested it to formulate the Nürnberg principles, the General Assembly called upon the International Law Commission to prepare a draft code of offences against the peace and security of mankind. On the basis of a report prepared by Jean Spiropoulos, its Special Rapporteur, the Commission completed a draft Code at its third session, in 1951, and submitted it to the General Assembly.

63. The Commission decided to limit the scope of the draft Code to offences containing a political element and endangering or disturbing the maintenance of international peace and security; it therefore omitted such matters as slavery and traffic in women and children. It also decided to deal only with the criminal responsibility of individuals and not to include provisions on crimes committed by abstract entities. In doing so it accepted the view expressed in the judgement of the Nürnberg Tribunal that "crimes against international law are committed by men, not by abstract entities, and only by punishing individuals who commit such crimes can the provisions of international law be enforced".

64. The Commission revised the draft Code at its fifth session, in 1953, in the light of observations received from Governments. In 1954 the General Assembly postponed further consideration of the draft Code until its special Committee on the Question of Defining Aggression had submitted its report.

65. The Definition of Aggression was finally approved by the General Assembly in resolution 3314 (XXIX) of 14 December 1974. On the recommendation of the International Law Commission, the Assembly, at the 105th plenary meeting of its thirty-second session, in 1977, decided to add the item, "Draft Code of Offences against the Peace and Security of Mankind", to the agenda of its thirty-third session.

66. In resolution 33/97 of 16 December 1978, the General Assembly requested the Secretary-General to invite Member States and relevant international intergovernmental organizations to submit their comments on the draft Code, including comments on the procedure to be adopted; and decided to consider the question further at its thirty-fifth session. In resolution 36/106 of 10 December 1981, it invited the International Law Commission to resume its work on the draft Code, taking into account the results achieved by the process of the progressive development of international law.

67. At its thirty-seventh session, the General Assembly considered the report of the Commission[18] and, in resolution 37/102 of 16 December 1982, noted with satisfaction that the Commission had appointed a special rapporteur for the draft Code. It invited the Commission to continue its work and to submit a preliminary report to the Assembly at its thirty-eighth session on the scope and structure of the draft Code.

68. The draft Code adopted by the Commission at its sixth session[19] in 1954, and submitted to the General Assembly, states in article 1 that:

Offences against the peace and security of mankind, as defined in this Code, are crimes under international law, for which the responsible individuals shall be punished.

69. Article 2 lists the following acts as offences against the peace and security of mankind:

(1) Any act of aggression, including the employment by the authorities of a State of armed force against another State for any purpose other than national or collective self-defence or in pursuance of a decision or recommendation of a competent organ of the United Nations.

(2) Any threat by the authorities of a State to resort to an act of aggression against another State.

(3) The preparation by the authorities of a State of the employment of armed force against another State for any purpose other than national or collective self-defence or in pursuance of a decision or recommendation of a competent organ of the United Nations.

(4) The organization, or the encouragement of the organization, by the authorities of a State, of armed bands within its territory or any other territory for incursions into the territory of another State, or the toleration of the organization of such bands in its own territory, or the toleration of the use by such armed bands of its territory as a base of operations or as a point of departure for incursions into the territory of another State, as well as direct participation in or support of such incursions.

(5) The undertaking or encouragement by the authorities of a State of activities calculated to foment civil strife in another State, or the toleration by the authorities of a State of organized activities calculated to foment civil strife in another State.

(6) The undertaking or encouragement by the authorities of a State of terrorist activities in another State, or the toleration by the authorities of a State of organized activities calculated to carry out terrorist acts in another State.

(7) Acts by the authorities of a State in violation of its obligations under a treaty which is designed to ensure international peace and security by means of restrictions or limitations on armaments, or on military training, or on fortifications, or of other restrictions of the same character.

(8) The annexation by the authorities of a State of territory belonging to another State, by means of acts contrary to international law.

(9) The intervention by the authorities of a State in the internal or external affairs of another State, by means of coercive measures of an economic or political character in order to force its will and thereby obtain advantages of any kind.

(10) Acts by the authorities of a State or by private individuals committed with intent to destroy, in whole or in part, a national, ethnic, racial or religious group as such, including:

(i) Killing members of the group;

---

[18] *Official Records of the General Assembly, Thirty-seventh Session, Supplement No. 10* (A/37/10).

[19] For the text of the draft Code, see *The Work of the International Law Commission*, third edition (United Nations publication, Sales No. E.80.V.11), pp. 117-119.

(ii) Causing serious bodily or mental harm to members of the group;

(iii) Deliberately inflicting on the group conditions of life calculated to bring about its physical destruction in whole or in part;

(iv) Imposing measures intended to prevent births within the group;

(v) Forcibly transferring children of the group to another group.

(11) Inhuman acts such as murder, extermination, enslavement, deportation or persecutions, committed against any civilian population on social, political, racial, religious or cultural grounds by the authorities of a State or by private individuals acting at the instigation or with the toleration of such authorities.

(12) Acts in violation of the laws or customs of war.

(13) Acts which constitute:

(i) Conspiracy to commit any of the offences defined in the preceding paragraphs of this article; or

(ii) Direct incitement to commit any of the offences defined in the preceding paragraphs of this article; or

(iii) Complicity in the commission of any of the offences defined in the preceding paragraphs of this article; or

(iv) Attempts to commit any of the offences defined in the preceding paragraphs of this article.

70.   Article 3 provides that:

The fact that a person acted as Head of State or as responsible government official does not relieve him of responsibility for committing any of the offences defined in this Code.

71.   Article 4, which concludes the draft Code, provides that:

The fact that a person charged with an offence defined in this Code acted pursuant to an order of his Government or of a superior does not relieve him of responsibility in international law if, in the circumstances at the time, it was possible for him not to comply with that order.

72.   At its thirty-seventh to forty-second sessions, the General Assembly considered the annual reports of the Commission[20] and, in resolutions 37/102, 38/10, 39/80, 40/69, 41/75 and 42/156, invited the Commission to continue its work on the elaboration of the draft Code. As tentatively outlined by the Commission's Special Rapporteur, the Code would consist of two parts:[21] Part I, relating to the scope of the draft articles, the definition of an offence against the peace and security of mankind, and the general principles governing the subject; and Part II, dealing specifically with acts constituting offences against the peace and security of mankind. In the view of the Special Rapporteur,[22] such an offence is constituted by the breach of obligations intended to protect the most fundamental interests of mankind, namely, those which reflect mankind's basic needs and concerns and on which the preservation of the human race depends. Such interests include the maintenance of peace, the protection of fundamental human rights, the safeguarding of the right of self-determination of peoples and the safeguarding and preservation of the human environment.

3. Convention on the Non-Applicability of Statutory Limitations to War Crimes and Crimes against Humanity

73.   On the basis of a draft prepared by the Secretary-General[23] the draft convention on the non-applicability of statutory limitations to war crimes and crimes against humanity was prepared by the Commission on Human Rights and the Economic and Social Council and submitted to the General Assembly at its twenty-second session, in 1967. Although it was unable to complete the preparation of the proposed convention at that session, owing to lack of time, the Assembly, in resolution 2338 (XXII) of 18 December 1967, recommended that no legislative or other action be taken which might be prejudicial to the aims and purposes of a convention on the non-applicability of statutory limitations to war crimes and crimes against humanity, pending the adoption of a convention by the General Assembly.

74.   The Convention was adopted and opened for signature, ratification and accession by the General Assembly in resolution 2391 (XXIII) of 26 November 1968, and entered into force on 11 November 1970. As at 31 December 1987 the Convention had been ratified or acceded to by 30 States.

75.   Article I of the Convention provides that:

No statutory limitation shall apply to the following crimes, irrespective of the date of their commission:

(a) War crimes as they are defined in the Charter of the International Military Tribunal, Nürnberg, of 8 August 1945 and confirmed by resolutions 3 (I) of 13 February 1946 and 95 (I) of 11 December 1946 of the General Assembly of the United Nations, particularly the "grave breaches" enumerated in the Geneva Convention of 12 August 1949 for the protection of war victims.

(b) Crimes against humanity whether committed in time of war or in time of peace as they are defined in the Charter of the International Military Tribunal, Nürnberg, of 8 August 1945 and confirmed by resolutions 3 (I) of 13 February 1946 and 95 (I) of 11 December 1946 of the General Assembly of the United Nations, eviction by armed attack or occupation and inhuman acts resulting from the policy of *apartheid*, and the crime of genocide as defined in the 1948 Convention on the Prevention and Punishment of the Crime of Genocide, even if such acts do not constitute a violation of the domestic law of the country in which they were committed.

76.   Under article II, provisions of the Convention "apply to representatives of the State authority and private individuals who, as principals or accomplices, participate in or who directly incite others to the commission of any of those crimes, or who conspire to commit them, irrespective of the degree of completion, and to representatives of the State authority who tolerate their commission".

77.   Under article III, States parties to the Convention "undertake to adopt all necessary domestic measures, legislative or otherwise, with a view to making possible the extradition, in accordance with international law, of the persons referred to in article II . . .". Article IV provides that the States parties "undertake to adopt, in accordance with their respective constitutional process, any legislative or other measures necessary to ensure

---

[20] *Official Records of the General Assembly, Thirty-seventh to Forty-second Sessions, Supplement No. 10* (A/37-42/10).

[21] *Ibid., Fortieth Session* (A/40/10), para. 43.

[22] *Ibid., Thirty-seventh Session* (A/37/10), para. 69.

[23] E/CN.4/928.

that statutory or other limitations shall not apply to the prosecution and punishment of the crimes referred to in articles I and II . . . and that, where they exist, such limitations shall be abolished''.

4. PRINCIPLES OF INTERNATIONAL CO-OPERATION IN THE DETECTION, ARREST, EXTRADITION AND PUNISHMENT OF PERSONS GUILTY OF WAR CRIMES AND CRIMES AGAINST HUMANITY

78. In 1969, a year after the adoption of the Convention on the Non-Applicability of Statutory Limitations to War Crimes and Crimes against Humanity, the General Assembly once again turned its attention to the general question of the punishment of war criminals and of persons who had committed crimes against humanity. In resolution 2583 (XXIV) of 15 December 1969, the Assembly set out its conviction that ''the thorough investigation of war crimes and crimes against humanity, and the detection, arrest, extradition and punishment of persons responsible for war crimes and crimes against humanity, constitute an important element in the prevention of such crimes, the protection of human rights and fundamental freedoms, the encouragement of confidence, the furtherance of international co-operation among peoples and the promotion of international peace and security''. The Assembly called upon ''all the States concerned to take the necessary measures for the thorough investigation of war crimes and crimes against humanity, as defined in article I of the Convention on the Non-Applicability of Statutory Limitations to War Crimes and Crimes against Humanity, and for the detection, arrest, extradition and punishment of all war criminals and persons guilty of crimes against humanity who have not been brought to trial or punished''. It called upon all States which had not done so to ratify the Convention on the Prevention and Punishment of the Crime of Genocide and drew attention to the special need for international action to ensure the prosecution and punishment of persons guilty of war crimes and crimes against humanity.

79. At its twenty-seventh session, in 1972, the General Assembly considered a report prepared by the Secretary-General in accordance with Economic and Social Council resolution 1691 (LII) of 2 June 1972,[24] containing an analytical survey of the comments, observations and proposals received from States on the question of the punishment of war criminals and of persons who had committed crimes against humanity; a note prepared by the Secretary-General on conclusions and recommendations of United Nations bodies and of the International Committee of the Red Cross relating to grave breaches of the fourth Geneva Convention,[25] and draft principles on the question proposed by the Byelorussian Soviet Socialist Republic, Czechoslovakia and Democratic Yemen.[26]

---

[24] A/8823 and Add.1.

[25] A/8837.

[26] *Official Records of the General Assembly, Twenty-seventh Session, Annexes,* agenda item 52, document A/8939, para. 7.

80. In resolution 3020 (XXVII) of 18 December 1972 the Assembly took note of the draft principles, transmitted them to the Commission on Human Rights, and requested the Commission to submit to the Assembly, through the Economic and Social Council, draft principles for its consideration. The Commission, after examining the relevant documentation, prepared and adopted a set of draft principles in resolution 13 (XXIX) of 29 March 1973. The Economic and Social Council endorsed these draft principles in resolution 1791 (LIV) of 18 May 1973 and recommended them to the General Assembly for adoption.

81. The General Assembly adopted, in resolution 3074 (XXVIII) of 3 December 1973, nine principles of international co-operation in the detection, arrest, extradition and punishment of persons guilty of war crimes and crimes against humanity, as follows:

1. War crimes and crimes against humanity, wherever they are committed, shall be subject to investigation and the persons against whom there is evidence that they have committed such crimes shall be subject to tracing, arrest, trial and, if found guilty, to punishment.

2. Every State has the right to try its own nationals for war crimes or crimes against humanity.

3. States shall co-operate with each other on a bilateral and multilateral basis with a view to halting and preventing war crimes and crimes against humanity, and shall take the domestic and international measures necessary for that purpose.

4. States shall assist each other in detecting, arresting and bringing to trial persons suspected of having committed such crimes and, if they are found guilty, in punishing them.

5. Persons against whom there is evidence that they have committed war crimes and crimes against humanity shall be subject to trial and, if found guilty, to punishment, as a general rule in the countries in which they committed those crimes. In that connexion, States shall co-operate on questions of extraditing such persons.

6. States shall co-operate with each other in the collection of information and evidence with would help to bring to trial the persons indicated in paragraph 5 above and shall exchange such information.

7. In accordance with article 1 of the Declaration on Territorial Asylum of 14 December 1967,[27] States shall not grant asylum to any person with respect to whom there are serious reasons for considering that he has committed a crime against peace, a war crime or a crime against humanity.

8. States shall not take any legislative or other measures which may be prejudicial to the international obligations they have assumed in regard to the detection, arrest, extradition and punishment of persons guilty of war crimes and crimes against humanity.

9. In co-operating with a view to the detection, arrest and extradition of persons against whom there is evidence that they have committed war crimes and crimes against humanity and, if found guilty, their punishment, States shall act in conformity with the provisions of the Charter of the United Nations and of the Declaration on Principles of International Law concerning Friendly Relations and Co-operation among States in accordance with the Charter of the United Nations.[28]

5. WAR CRIMES FILES: ACCESS AND GUIDELINES

82. At its thirty-ninth session, in 1987, the Sub-Commission on Prevention of Discrimination and Protection of Minorities adopted two resolutions relating to the de-

---

[27] Resolution 2312 (XXII).

[28] Resolution 2625 (XXV), annex.

tention and punishment of war criminals and persons who have committed crimes against mankind.

83. In resolution 1987/2 of 31 August 1987, the Sub-Commission took note of recent efforts at bringing suspected war criminals to justice, more particularly in Canada, France, the Federal Republic of Germany, Israel, the United States of America and the Union of Soviet Socialist Republics, and welcomed the prospect of a decision to broaden access to War Crimes Commission files. In a draft resolution prepared for consideration by the Commission on Human Rights, the Sub-Commission proposed that the Commission should recognize the importance of broader access to those files and should encourage the Secretary-General to pursue his efforts at setting new guidelines for such access, in consultation with the 17 Member States which formerly composed the War Crimes Commission.

84. In resolution 1987/4 of the same date, the Sub-Commission, considering that according to consistent evidence a large number of war criminals and persons guilty of crimes against mankind live in the territories of States Members of the United Nations, and concerned about the resurgence of Nazi ideas and their diffusion, urged all States to secure the just punishment of such criminals and called upon all Governments to take all possible initiatives, in conformity with internal and international law, to put an end to neo-Nazi propaganda and other activities.

6. DRAFTING OF AN INTERNATIONAL CONVENTION AGAINST THE RECRUITMENT, USE, FINANCING AND TRAINING OF MERCENARIES

85. In considering the implementation of the Declaration on the Granting of Independence to Colonial Countries and Peoples, the General Assembly on several occasions declared that the practice of using mercenaries against national liberation movements in colonial States constitutes a criminal act, and called upon all States to take the measures necessary to prevent the recruitment, financing and training of mercenaries in their territory and to prohibit their nationals from serving as mercenaries.[29]

86. The Security Council also, on several occasions, condemned any State which persisted in permitting or tolerating the recruitment of mercenaries, or which provided facilities to them, with the objective of overthrowing the Governments of States Members of the United Nations.[30]

87. Recognizing "that mercenarism is a threat to international peace and security and, like murder, piracy and genocide, is a universal crime against humanity", the Assembly, in resolution 34/140 of 14 December 1979, urged all States to consider effective measures to prohibit the recruitment, training, assembly, transit or use of mercenaries within their territories, and decided to prepare an international convention which would outlaw mercenarism in all its manifestations. In resolution 35/48 of 4 December 1980 it established the *Ad Hoc* Committee on the Drafting of an International Convention Against the Recruitment, Use, Financing and Training of Mercenaries to undertake this task.

88. The *Ad Hoc* Committee, composed of thirty-five Member States appointed by the President of the General Assembly with due regard for equitable geographical distribution and representation of the principal legal systems of the world, held annual sessions between 1981 and 1985, and reported to the thirty-sixth to the fortieth sessions of the General Assembly.[31] The Committee's scheduled 1986 session was deferred pursuant to General Assembly decision 40/472 of 9 May 1986.

89. In each of its reports the *Ad Hoc* Committee indicated that although it had achieved substantial progress, it had not been able to complete its work. After examining each report, the General Assembly extended its mandate.

90. The Commission on Human Rights considered the item, "The Use of Mercenaries as a Means to Impede the Exercise of the Right of Peoples to Self-determination" at its forty-second session, held in 1986. In resolution 1986/26 of 10 March 1986, the Commission expressed its deep concern about the increasing menace which the activities of mercenaries represent for all States, particularly African States and other developing States of the world, and about the loss of life, the substantial damage to property and the long-term negative effects on the economy of southern African countries resulting from mercenary aggressions.

91. On recommendation of the Commission, the Economic and Social Council, in resolution 1986/43 of 23 May 1986, and the General Assembly, in resolution 41/102 of 4 December 1986, condemned the increased recruitment, financing, training, assembly, transit and use of mercenaries, as well as all other forms of support to mercenaries for the purpose of destabilizing and overthrowing the Governments of Southern Africa, Central America and other developing States and fighting against the national liberation movements of peoples struggling for the exercise of their right to self-determination; denounced any State that persists in the recruitment, or permits or tolerates the recruitment, of mercenaries and provides facilities to them for launching armed aggression against other States; called upon all States to exercise the utmost vigilance against the menace posed by the activities of mercenaries and to en-

---

[29] Resolutions 2395 (XXIII) of 29 November 1968, 2465 (XXIII) of 20 December 1968, 2548 (XXIV) of 11 December 1969, 2708 (XXV) of 14 December 1970 and 3103 (XXVIII) of 12 December 1973.

[30] Resolutions 239 (1967) of 10 July 1967, 405 (1977) of 14 April 1977, 419 (1977) of 24 November 1977, 496 (1981) of 15 December 1981 and 507 (1982) of 28 May 1982.

[31] *Official Records of the General Assembly, Thirty-sixth Session, Supplement No. 43* (A/36/43) and *ibid., Thirty-seventh Session, Supplement No. 43* (A/37/43 and Corr.1), and *ibid., Thirty-eighth Session, Supplement No. 43* (A/38/43), and *ibid., Thirty-ninth Session, Supplement No. 43* (A/39/43 and Corr.1), and *ibid., Fortieth Session, Supplement No. 43* (A/40/43), and *ibid., Forty-second Session, Supplement No. 43* (A/42/43).

sure that their territories were not used for such activities; and urged all States to take the necessary measures under their respective domestic laws to prohibit the recruitment, financing, training and transit of mercenaries on their territory.

92.   In its resolution, the Economic and Social Council urged the Commission on Human Rights to appoint a Special Rapporteur to study the subject further. Accordingly the Commission, in resolution 1987/16 of 9 March 1987, decided to appoint for one year a Special Rapporteur to examine the question of the use of mercenaries as a means of violating human rights and of impeding the exercise of the right of peoples to self-determination. On 1 September 1987, the Chairman of the Commission, after consultation with the other members of the Bureau, appointed Mr. Enrique Bernales Ballesteros (Peru) as Special Rapporteur of the Commission on the question of mercenaries.

93.   The General Assembly, in resolution 42/96 of 7 December 1987, welcomed the Commission's decision and requested that the Special Rapporteur's report be transmitted to it at its forty-third (1988) session.

XIII. HUMAN RIGHTS, PEACE AND DEVELOPMENT

Introduction

1. The interrelationship between the enjoyment of human rights, the maintenance of peace and security and the achievement of international development goals is extremely close; indeed, the interdependance of these programmes is inherent in their nature. On the one hand, gross violations of human rights and inequitable economic relations between developed and developing countries adversely affect international peace and security. On the other hand, it is only in an atmosphere of peace and security that everyone can enjoy his rights and freedoms; as long as there is hunger, disease, or lack of opportunities to participate in the government of one's country there can be neither lasting peace nor significant development. Moreover, it is increasingly being realized that human rights, peace and development can only be achieved when the arms race has been put to an end and when the use of new scientific and technological developments is limited in the interests of peace and for the benefit of mankind.

2. The relations that exist between human rights, peace and development were thoroughly explored by a seminar on that subject held at United Nations Headquarters, New York, from 3 to 14 August 1981, in accordance with General Assembly resolution 35/174 of 15 December 1980. The Seminar adopted a number of conclusions and recommendations by consensus, among them the following:[1]

(1) The Seminar agrees that human rights, peace and development are interrelated and interdependent and that the fostering of one promotes the enhancement of the others. The absence of peace, or the achievement of development by a people, can never exempt a State from its obligation to ensure respect for the human rights of its nationals and of the persons residing in its territory;

. . .

(3) The maintenance of international peace and security for all peoples and individuals is vital for social and economic progress and for the full realization of human rights and vice versa;

. . .

(5) The advancement of development is related to the promotion of peace. The great resources which would be released by disarmament could contribute in a major way to the development of all States, especially those which are presently developing;

. . .

(8) (a) The appropriate human rights organs, particularly the Commission on Human Rights and the Sub-Commission on Prevention of Discrimination and Protection of Minorities, should examine practical issues arising from the interrelationship between human rights, peace and development. In particular, the relationship between militarization and human rights should be studied;

---

[1] *Report of the Seminar on the Relations that Exist between Human Rights, Peace and Development* (ST/HR/SER.A/10), chap. IV.

A. International peace and security as an essential condition for the realization of human rights

3. The importance of international peace to the realization of human rights and fundamental freedoms is made clear in several provisions of the Charter of the United Nations, among them the first words of the Preamble which read:

WE THE PEOPLES OF THE UNITED NATIONS DETERMINED

to save succeeding generations from the scourge of war, which twice in our lifetime has brought untold sorrow to mankind, and

to reaffirm faith in fundamental human rights, in the dignity and worth of the human person, in the equal rights of men and women and of nations large and small . . .

4. Article 1 of the Charter sets out the purposes of the United Nations in the following terms:

1. To maintain international peace and security, and to that end: to take effective collective measures for the prevention and removal of threats to the peace, and for the suppression of acts of aggression or other breaches of the peace, and to bring about by peaceful means, and in conformity with the principles of justice and international law, adjustment or settlement of international disputes or situations which might lead to a breach of the peace;

2. To develop friendly relations among nations based on respect for the principle of equal rights and self-determination of peoples, and to take other appropriate measures to strengthen universal peace;

3. To achieve international co-operation in solving international problems of an economic, social, cultural, or humanitarian character, and in promoting and encouraging respect for human rights and for fundamental freedoms for all without distinction as to race, sex, language or religion; . . .

5. The interdependence between peace and human rights is also affirmed in other provisions of the Charter, notably in Article 55, which reads as follows:

With a view to the creation of conditions of stability and well-being which are necessary for peaceful and friendly relations among nations based on respect for the principle of equal rights and self-determination of peoples, the United Nations shall promote:

. . .

c. universal respect for, and observance of, human rights and fundamental freedoms for all without distinction as to race, sex, language, or religion.

The Charter also states, in Article 56, tht "all Members pledge themselve to take joint and separate action in co-operation with the Organization for the achievement of the purposes set forth in Article 55".

6. It should be borne in mind that the prohibition of the threat or use of force in international relations is not an absolute one; only those threats or uses of force which are contrary to the Charter of the United Nations may be said to constitute a violation of international law. Threats or uses of force in self-defence against an armed attack, in achieving freedom and independence,

and in rebelling against tyranny and oppression, are legitimate at least until the Security Council has taken measures necessary to maintain or restore international peace and security.

7. The right to self-defence is set out in the Charter itself. Article 51 reads as follows:

> Nothing in the present Charter shall impair the inherent right of individual or collective self-defence if an armed attack occurs against a Member of the United Nations, until the Security Council has taken measures necessary to maintain international peace and security. Measures taken by Members in the exercise of this right of self-defence shall be immediately reported to the Security Council and shall not in any way affect the authority and responsibility of the Security Council under the present Charter to take at any time such action as it deems necessary in order to maintain or restore international peace and security.

8. The legitimacy of the struggle of colonial peoples to achieve freedom and independence has been recognized by the General Assembly, the Security Council, and other organs of the United Nations, and has been affirmed and reaffirmed in many resolutions and decisions. Most recently the General Assembly, in resolution 37/35 of 23 November 1982, affirmed once again its recognition of the legitimacy of the struggle of the peoples under colonial and alien domination to exercise their right to self-determination and independence by all the necessary means at their disposal.

9. The legitimacy of rebellion against tyranny and oppression is recognized in the third preambular paragraph of the Universal Declaration of Human Rights, which reads as follows:

> Whereas it is essential, if man is not to be compelled to have recourse, as a last resort, to rebellion against tyranny and oppression, that human rights should be protected by the rule of law . . .

10. Records of the discussion which took place in the Third Committee of the General Assembly at the time when this clause was under debate[2] indicate that, in the view of one of its co-sponsors, the right to resist oppression was a fundamental human right which any truly democratic State must respect since it was at the very basis of its existence. He pointed out, in response to objections that the adoption of the clause might encourage subversive movements against legitimately established order, that there was nothing in the clause to encourage rebellion against a really democratic régime based upon universal suffrage and respect for human rights; it was concerned only with the right to rise up against a system of tyranny and oppression. Such a right, he felt, was legitimate and sacred.[3]

1. UNITED NATIONS RESOLUTIONS LINKING HUMAN RIGHTS AND PEACE

11. From time to time United Nations bodies have adopted resolutions linking the enjoyment of human rights with the maintenance of international peace and security. One of the first of these was resolution 110 (II), adopted by the General Assembly on 3 November 1947, in which the Assembly, while recalling that all Member States had pledged themselves to take joint and separate action to promote universal respect for, and observance of, fundamental freedoms, including freedom of expression, condemned "all forms of propaganda . . . designed or likely to provoke or encourage any threat to the peace, breach of the peace, or act of aggression". The Assembly further called upon the Government of each Member State, within its constitutional limits, to encourage the dissemination of all information designed to give expression to the undoubted desire of all peoples for peace.

12. Another early resolution of the General Assembly linking human rights and peace was resolution 290 (IV) of 1 December 1949, entitled "Essentials of peace". In that resolution the Assembly called upon every nation "to refrain from any threats or acts, direct or indirect, aimed at impairing the freedom, independence or integrity of any State, or at fomenting civil strife and subverting the will of the people in any State"; and further called upon every nation "to promote, in recognition of the paramount importance of preserving the dignity and worth of the human person, full freedom for the peaceful expression of political opposition, full opportunity for the exercise of religious freedom and full respect for all the other fundamental rights expressed in the Universal Declaration of Human Rights".

13. The General Assembly, in resolution 37/199 of 18 December 1982, clearly recognized "that international peace and security are essential elements for the full realization of human rights, including the right to development," and reaffirmed "that it is of paramount importance for the promotion of human rights and fundamental freedoms that Member States should undertake specific obligations through accession to, or ratification of, international instruments in this field and, consequently, that the standard-setting work within the United Nations system in the field of human rights and the universal acceptance and implementation of the relevant international instruments should be encouraged".

14. The Commission on Human Rights and its Sub-Commission on Prevention of Discrimination and Protection of Minorities have also stressed the importance of international peace and security to the realization of human rights. The Commission has considered this question regularly since 1976 under the agenda item entitled "Human rights and scientific and technological developments".

15. In resolution 5 (XXXII) of 27 February 1976, the Commission expressed its firm conviction that unqualified respect for and promotion of human rights and fundamental freedoms required the existence of international peace and security, and welcomed every effort made by States to strengthen world peace and to reduce international tension. The Commission affirmed that flagrant and massive violations of human rights, including economic, social and cultural rights, might lead the world into armed conflicts.

---

[2] *Official Records of the General Assembly, Third Session, part 1, Summary Records of Meetings of the Third Committee*, pp. 748-788.
[3] *Ibid.*, p. 774.

16. In resolutions 1982/7 of 19 February 1982, 1983/43 of 9 March 1983, 1984/28 of 12 March 1984, and 1986/10 of 10 March 1986, the Commission reaffirmed that all peoples and all individuals have an inherent right to life and that the safeguarding of this cardinal right is an essential condition for the enjoyment of the entire range of economic, social and cultural as well as civil and political rights. In those resolutions the Commission also expressed its profound concern that international peace and security continue to be threatened by the arms race in all its aspects, and stressed the urgent need for the international community to make every effort to strengthen peace, remove the growing threat of war, particularly nuclear war, halt the arms race and achieve general and complete disarmament under effective international control and prevent violations of the principles of the Charter of the United Nations regarding the sovereignty and territorial integrity of States and the self-determination of peoples.

17. In resolution 1982/7, the Commission requested its Sub-Commission to carry out a study of the negative consequences of the arms race, particularly the nuclear arms race in all its aspects, for the implementation of economic, social, cultural as well as civil and political rights. Pursuant to that request the Sub-Commission, at its 1982 session, examined the question and reached the conclusion that serious infringements of the principles of the Charter of the United Nations and of other relevant international instruments, in particular such odious crimes as aggression, invasion, military occupation, genocide, *apartheid* and other crimes against humanity constituted gross violations of human rights which had an effect on international peace and security. The Sub-Commission prepared a draft resolution for consideration by the Economic and Social Council in which the Council was to draw the attention of the Security Council and the General Assembly to the fact that in many instances such mass and flagrant violations of human rights resulted in threats to, or breaches of, international peace and security, and was to request the Security Council to consider how such violations could be dealt with as effectively as possible. Under the draft resolution, the Council was also to request the Assembly to invite the International Law Commission to take mass and flagrant violations of human rights into account when elaborating the draft code of offences against the peace and security of mankind; and was to request the Sub-Commission to continue its consideration of the item with a view to preparing principles, and, in particular, establishing criteria to govern situations which could be considered as constituting gross and flagrant violations of human rights, the effect of which had an impact on international peace and security.

18. Although the Commission did not take the action proposed by the Sub-Commission, the wish was expressed for further study of the subject. The Sub-Commission accordingly requested the Secretary-General to prepare an analysis on the subject based on replies from Governments and intergovernmental and non-governmental organizations. After examining the analysis (E/CN.4/Sub.2/1984/11), the Sub-Commission, in resolution 1984/30, expressed its conviction that the maintenance of international peace and security for all peoples and individuals was vital for social and economic progress and for the full realization of human rights and vice versa, and stressed the threat that the arms race, particularly the nuclear arms race, posed for the achievement of social and economic progress and for the universal realization of all human rights. In the same resolution, the Sub-Commission also requested the Secretary-General to prepare a progress report, taking into consideration all the replies received and the comments made by the members of the Commission and the Sub-Commission. The Secretary-General was also requested to submit a guide to United Nations conventions, resolutions and reports on the adverse consequences of the arms race for the universal realization of human rights. The Sub-Commission further decided to consider gross violations of human rights and international peace as a separate item. The two abovementioned documents were submitted to the Sub-Commission at its thirty-eighth session (E/CN.4/Sub.2/1985/10 and E/CN.4/Sub.2/1985/11).

19. After considering these and other relevant documents the Sub-Commission, in resolution 1985/2 of 27 August 1985, recognized that respect for human rights and fundamental freedoms was one of the important conditions for securing international peace, and that peace, independence, disarmament and development, the central issues of our time, were all necessary for securing in full measure human dignity and basic human rights and fundamental freedoms, requested the Secretary-General to provide the Sub-Commission at its fortieth session with a report on the interrelationship between human rights and international peace in all its aspects and dimensions, including the adverse impact of escalating military expenditures, particularly those of the nuclear-weapon States, on the international social and economic situation and the right to development, and in particular to examine the adverse consequences of the extension and dissemination of nuclear arms in non-nuclear regions for international peace and security, the social and economic development of the countries of the region, and the enjoyment of human rights and fundamental freedoms.

20. The Sub-Commission also recommended to the Commission on Human Rights that an item entitled "The adverse consequences of the arms race, especially the dissemination of nuclear arms in non-nuclear regions, for international peace and security and for the protection of human rights and fundamental freedoms" be included in its agenda at its forty-third session. It further decided in resolution 1985/1 that item 7 of its own agenda should be entitled "International peace and security as an essential condition for the enjoyment of human rights, above all the right to life".

21. The Sub-Commission considered the Secretary-General's report entitled "International Peace and Security as an Essential Condition for the Enjoyment of Human Rights, Above All the Right to Life", at its

thirty-ninth session, and took note of it with appreciation in decision 1987/101 of 31 August 1987.

2. INTERNATIONAL INSTRUMENTS LINKING HUMAN RIGHTS AND PEACE

22. A number of international instruments adopted by United Nations bodies contain clauses linking human rights generally, or one or more particular human rights, with international peace and security.

23. The first preambular paragraph of the Universal Declaration of Human Rights, adopted and proclaimed by the General Assembly on 10 December 1948, reads as follows:

Whereas recognition of the inherent dignity and of the equal and inalienable rights of all members of the human family is the foundation of freedom, justice and peace in the world, . . .

24. In the Declaration on Principles of International Law concerning Friendly Relations and Co-operation among States in accordance with the Charter of the United Nations, adopted by the General Assembly in resolution 2625 (XXV) of 24 October 1970, the third preambular paragraph stresses "the importance of maintaining and strengthening international peace founded upon freedom, justice and respect for human rights", while the thirteenth preambular paragraph expresses the conviction "that the subjection of peoples to alien subjugation, domination and exploitation constitutes a major obstacle to the promotion of international peace and security".

25. The Declaration on the Use of Scientific and Technological Progress in the Interests of Peace and for the Benefit of Mankind, adopted by the General Assembly in resolution 3384 (XXX) of 10 November 1975, solemnly proclaims, in article 1, that

All States shall promote international co-operation to ensure that the results of scientific and technological developments are used in the interests of strengthening international peace and security, freedom and independence, and also for the purpose of the economic and social development of peoples and the realization of human rights and freedoms in accordance with the Charter of the United Nations.

(a) *Declaration on the Preparation of Societies for Life in Peace*

26. In the Declaration on the Preparation of Societies for Life in Peace, adopted by the General Assembly in resolution 33/73 of 15 December 1978, the Assembly reaffirms the right of individuals, States and all mankind to life in peace.

27. Principle 1, set out in the Declaration, provides that:

Every nation and every human being, regardless of race, conscience, language or sex, has the inherent right to life in peace. Respect for that right, as well as for other human rights, is in the common interest of all mankind and an indispensable condition of advancement of all nations, large and small, in all fields.

Principles 5, 7 and 8 deal with the duties of States in ensuring enjoyment of the right to life in peace, and read as follows:

5. Every State has the duty to respect the right of all peoples to self-determination, independence, equality, sovereignty, the territorial integrity of States and the inviolability of their frontiers, including the right to determine the road of their development, without interference or intervention in their internal affairs.

. . .

7. Every State has the duty to discourage all manifestations and practices of colonialism, as well as racism, racial discrimination and *apartheid*, as contrary to the right of peoples to self-determination and to other human rights and fundamental freedoms.

8. Every State has the duty to discourage advocacy of hatred and prejudice againt other peoples as contrary to the principles of peaceful coexistence and friendly co-operation.

28. Part II of the Declaration calls upon all States, in order to implement the above principles, (*a*) to act perseveringly and consistently, with due regard for the constitutional rights and the role of the family, the institutions and the organizations concerned: (i) to ensure that their policies relevant to the implementation of the Declaration, including educational processes and teaching methods as well as media information activities, incorporate contents compatible with the task of the preparation for life in peace of entire societies and, in particular, the young generations; (ii) therefore, to discourage and eliminate incitement to racial hatred, national or other discrimination, injustice or advocacy of violence and war.

(b) *Declaration on the Participation of Women in Promoting International Peace and Understanding*

29. The basic principle set out in the Declaration on the Participation of Women in Promoting International Peace and Understanding, adopted by the General Assembly in resolution 37/63 of 3 December 1982, is formulated in article 1 thereof, which reads:

Women and men have an equal and vital interest in contributing to international peace and co-operation. To this end women must be enabled to exercise their right to participate in the economic, social, cultural, civil and political affairs of society on an equal footing with men.

(c) *Declaration on the Right of Peoples to Peace*

30. In the Declaration on the Right of Peoples to Peace, approved by the General Assembly in resolution 39/11 of 12 November 1984, the conviction is expressed "that life without war serves as the primary prerequisite for the material well-being, development and progress of countries, and for the full implementation of the rights and fundamental human freedoms proclaimed by the United Nations". The Declaration solemnly proclaims that the peoples of our planet have a sacred right to peace, and declares that the preservation of that right, and the promotion of its implementation, constitute a fundamental obligation of each State. It emphasizes that ensuring the exercise of the right demands that the policies of States be directed towards the elimination of the threat of war, particularly nuclear war, the renunciation of the use of force in international relations, and the settlement of international disputes by

peaceful means on the basis of the Charter of the United Nations.

31. The General Assembly then appeals to all States and international organizations to do their utmost to assist in implementing the right of peoples to peace through the adoption of appropriate measures at both the national and the international level.

(d) *Declaration on the Inadmissibility of Intervention and Interference in the Internal Affairs of States*

32. In the Declaration on the Inadmissibility of Intervention and Interference in the Internal Affairs of States, approved by General Assembly resolution 36/103 of 9 December 1981, the Assembly solemnly declares that the principle of non-intervention and non-interference in the internal and external affairs of States comprehends the following rights and duties:

I . . . (c) The right of States and peoples to have free access to information and to develop fully, without interference, their system of information and mass media and to use their information media in order to promote their political, social, economic and cultural interests and aspirations, based, *inter alia*, on the relevant articles of the Universal Declaration of Human Rights and the principles of the new international information order;

II . . . (d) The duty of a State to refrain from any forcible action which deprives peoples under colonial domination or foreign occupation of their right to self-determination, freedom and independence;

. . .

(g) The duty of a State to prevent on its territory the training, financing and recruitment of mercenaries, or the sending of such mercenaries into the territory of another State, and to deny facilities, including financing, for the equipping and transit of mercenaries;

. . .

(l) The duty of a State to refrain from the exploitation and the distortion of human rights issues as a means of interference in the internal affairs of States, of exerting pressure on other States or creating distrust and disorder within and among States or groups of States;

. . .

(n) The duty of a State to refrain from organizing, training, financing and arming political and ethnic groups on their territories or the territories of other States for the purpose of creating subversion, disorder or unrest in other countries;

. . .

III . . . (b) The right and duty of States fully to support the right to self-determination, freedom and independence of peoples under colonial domination, foreign occupation or racist régimes, as well as the right of these peoples to wage both political and armed struggle to that end, in accordance with the purposes and principles of the Charter;

(c) The right and duty of States to observe, promote and defend all human rights and fundamental freedoms within their own national territories and to work for the elimination of massive and flagrant violations of the rights of nations and peoples, and, in particular, for the elimination of *apartheid* and all forms of racism and racial discrimination;

(d) The right and duty of States to combat, within their constitutional prerogatives, the dissemination of false or distorted news which can be interpreted as interference in the internal affairs of other States or as being harmful to the promotion of peace, co-operation and friendly relations among States and nations.

33. The Declaration further provides that nothing in it shall prejudice the right to self-determination, freedom and independence of peoples under colonial domination, foreign occupation or racist régimes, and the right to seek and receive support in accordance with the purposes and principles of the Charter, the provisions of the Charter, or action taken by the United Nations under Chapters VI and VII of the Charter.

3. University for Peace

34. By resolution 33/109 of 18 December 1978, the General Assembly took note with appreciation of the proposal submitted by Costa Rica for the establishment of a University for Peace within the system of the United Nations University, and requested the Secretary-General to transmit that proposal to Member States, the United Nations Educational, Scientific and Cultural Organization, the Rector and Council of the United Nations University and to other appropriate agencies for comment.

35. The General Assembly approved the idea of establishing a University for Peace by resolution 34/111 of 14 December 1979, and decided that it should serve as an international centre of higher learning for postgraduate studies, research and the dissemination of knowledge specifically aimed at training for peace and have its headquarters in Costa Rica.

36. An International Agreement for the Establishment of the University for Peace and the Charter of the University for Peace were approved by the General Assembly in resolution 35/55 of 5 December 1980. The Charter provides, in Article 17, paragraph 1, that:

Irenology, which shall comprise the study of peace, education for peace and human rights, shall be the main concern of the University. The studies carried out at the University shall focus on the topic of international peace. Completion of a programme of studies, including irenology as a compulsory subject, shall be required for obtaining any degree granted by the University.

4. International Year of Peace (1986)

37. The year 1986 was declared to be the International Year of Peace by the General Assembly in resolution 37/16 of 16 November 1982, and was formally proclaimed as such in resolution 40/3 of 24 October 1985, the fortieth anniversary of the United Nations.

38. In the Proclamation, the Assembly referred to peace as a universal ideal, the promotion of which is the primary purpose of the United Nations. It stated that

. . . the promotion of international peace and security requires continuing and positive action by States and peoples aimed at the prevention of war, removal of various threats to peace—including the nuclear threat—respect for the principle of non-use of force, the resolution of conflicts and peaceful settlement of disputes, confidence-building measures, disarmament, maintenance of outer space for peaceful uses, development, the promotion and exercise of human rights and fundamental freedoms, decolonization in accordance with the principle of self-determination, elimination of racial discrimination and *apartheid*, the enhancement of the quality of life, satisfaction of human needs and protection of the environment,

and called upon all peoples to join with the United Nations in resolute efforts to safeguard peace and the future of humanity.

39. The International Year of Peace was observed on a world-wide basis during 1986 by States Members of the United Nations, intergovernmental and non-governmental organizations, educational, scientific, cultural and research institutions and their communication media. Most of the observances highlighted the role of the United Nations in the promotion and maintenance of international peace and security.

B. Economic, social and cultural development and the realization of human rights

40. A close link between economic, social and cultural development and the realization of human rights is also evident in resolutions and international instruments adopted by United Nations bodies.

41. On 26 November 1957 the General Assembly, in resolution 1161 (XII), expressed the view "that a balanced and integrated economic and social development would contribute towards the promotion and maintenance of peace and security, social progress and better standards of living, and the observance of and respect for human rights and fundamental freedoms".

42. This theme was elaborated upon by the International Conference on Human Rights, held at Teheran from 22 April to 13 May 1968. In resolution XVII, the Conference expressed its belief "that the enjoyment of economic and social rights is inherently linked with any meaningful enjoyment of civil and political rights and that there is a profound inter-connexion between the realization of human rights and economic development". It noted "that the vast majority of mankind continues to live in poverty, suffer from squalor, disease and illiteracy and thus leads a sub-human existence, constituting in itself a denial of human dignity"; that there was an "ever-widening gap between the standards of living in the economically developed and developing countries"; and recognized "that universal enjoyment of human rights and fundamental freedoms would remain a pious hope unless the international community succeeds in narrowing this gap". It further recognized "the collective responsibility of the international community to ensure the attainment of the minimum standard of living necessary for the enjoyment of human rights and fundamental freedoms by all persons throughout the world".

43. In the operative paragraphs of the resolution the Conference invited "all members of the international community to comply with their Charter obligations by regarding implementation of the Charter provisions on human rights and fundamental freedoms not only as a matter of national obligation but also as a matter of international obligation"; called upon "the developing States to continue to make every effort to raise the standard of living of their people through effective use of all available resources and to reduce economic disparities within their jurisdiction"; and called upon the "competent organs of the United Nations to give high priority to assistance programmes having a direct bear-

ing on a universal realization of human rights and fundamental freedoms".

44. The Commission on Human Rights, at its twenty-fifth session, in 1969, adopted resolution 15 (XXV) of 13 March 1969, in which it affirmed:

(a) That the universal enjoyment of the economic, social, and cultural rights set forth in the Universal Declaration of Human Rights depends to a very large degree on the rapid economic and social development of the developing countries which are inhabited by more than one-half of the world's population, whose lot continues to deteriorate as a result of the tendencies which characterize international economic relations;

(b) That the ultimate objective of any effort to promote economic development should be social development of peoples, the welfare of every human being and the full development of his personality.

1. DECLARATION ON SOCIAL PROGRESS AND DEVELOPMENT

45. The Declaration on Social Progress and Development, prepared by the Commission for Social Development and adopted by the General Assembly in resolution 2542 (XXIV) of 11 December 1969, states (article 10) that social progress and development shall aim at the continuous raising of the material and spiritual standards of living of all members of society, with respect for and in compliance with human rights and fundamental freedoms, through the attainment of the following main goals:

(a) The assurance at all levels of the right to work and the right of everyone to form trade unions and workers' associations and to bargain collectively; promotion of full productive employment and elimination of unemployment and under-employment; establishment of equitable and favourable conditions of work for all, including the improvement of health and safety conditions; assurance of just remuneration for labour without any discrimination as well as a sufficiently high minimum wage to ensure a decent standard of living; the protection of the consumer;

(b) The elimination of hunger and malnutrition and the guarantee of the right to proper nutrition;

(c) The elimination of poverty; the assurance of a steady improvement in levels of living and of a just and equitable distribution of income;

(d) The achievement of the highest standards of health and the provision of heatlh protection for the entire population, if possible free of charge;

(e) The eradication of illiteracy and the assurance of the right to universal access to culture, to free compulsory education at the elementary level and to free education at all levels; the raising of the general level of life-long education;

(f) The provision for all, particularly persons in low income groups and large families, of adequate housing and community services.

46. Additional goals set out in the Declaration include the protection of the rights of the mother and the child, of the aged and disabled, and of the physically or mentally handicapped; the guarantee that all individuals, without discrimination of any kind, are made aware of their rights and obligations and receive the necessary aid in the exercise and safeguarding of their rights; the limitation of all forms of discrimination and exploitation; and the protection and improvement of the human environment. The achievement of these objectives, the Declaration states, requires the mobilization of the necessary resources by national and international action.

The Assembly recommended that all Governments should take the Declaration's principles, objectives and means and methods into consideration in formulating their policies, plans and programmes.

47. Fifteen years after its adoption, the General Assembly found that the main objectives of the Declaration still had not been universally realized. In resolution 41/142 of 4 December 1986 the Assembly reaffirmed the lasting validity of the Declaration's principles and urged all Governments to take them into account in their bilateral and multilateral relations in the field of development.

2. POPULAR PARTICIPATION AS AN IMPORTANT FACTOR IN DEVELOPMENT AND IN THE REALIZATION OF HUMAN RIGHTS

48. The International Development Strategy for the Third United Nations Development Decade, annexed to General Assembly resolution 35/56 of 5 December 1980, declares that the ultimate aim of development is the constant improvement of the well-being of the entire population on the basis of its full participation in the process of development and a fair distribution of the benefits therefrom.

49. At its thirty-seventh session, the General Assembly considered the report of the Secretary-General on the International Seminar on Popular Participation, held at Ljubljana, Yugoslavia, from 17 to 25 May 1982,[4] and took note of it with appreciation.

50. In resolution 37/55 of 3 December 1982, the Assembly requested the Commission on Human Rights to consider at its thirty-ninth session the question of popular participation in its various forms as an important factor in development and in the realization of human rights, taking into account, *inter alia*, the results of the deliberations of the Seminar, and to submit to it appropriate suggestions for more complete realization of human rights. On recommendation of the Commission in its resolution 1984/15 of 6 March 1984, the Economic and Social Council, by decision 1984/131 of 24 May 1984, endorsed the Commission's request to the Secretary-General to prepare a study on the right to popular participation in its various forms as an important factor in development and in the full realization of all human rights.

51. The study (E/CN.4/1985/10 and Add.1 and 2) was received and noted with appreciation by the Commission in resolution 1985/44 of 14 March 1985, and subsequently by the General Assembly in resolution 40/99 of 13 December 1985. The Assembly invited Governments, the concerned specialized agencies and organs of the United Nations system and the relevant non-governmental organizations to comment on the study and requested the Commission to continue consideration of the question.

C. Use of science and technology in the interests of peace and for the benefit of mankind

52. Although both the International Covenants on Human Rights and the Universal Declaration of Human Rights contain provisions relating to various aspects of the effect of scientific and technological developments upon the enjoyment of human rights and fundamental freedoms, this question was not considered in detail until 1968, when it was the subject of debate at the International Conference on Human Rights.

53. In paragraph 18 of the Proclamation of Teheran,[5] adopted by the Conference on 13 May 1968, the Conference expressed the view that:

While recent scientific discoveries and technological advances have opened vast prospects for economic, social and cultural progress, such developments may nevertheless endanger the rights and freedoms of individuals and will require continuing attention.

In resolution XI,[6] the Conference recommended "that the organizations of the United Nations family should undertake a study of the problems with respect to human rights arising from developments in science and technology".

54. On the basis of this recommendation, the General Assembly, in resolution 2450 (XXIII) of 19 December 1968, invited the Secretary-General to undertake, with the assistance, *inter alia*, of the Advisory Committee on the Application of Science and Technology to Development and in co-operation with the executive heads of the competent specialized agencies, a study of the problems in connection with human rights arising from developments in science and technology, in particular from the following standpoints:

(a) Respect for the privacy of individuals and the integrity and sovereignty of nations in the light of advances in recording and other techniques;

(b) Protection of the human personality and its physical and intellectual integrity, in the light of advances in biology, medicine and biochemistry;

(c) Uses of electronics which may affect the rights of the person and the limits which should be placed on such uses in a democratic society;

(d) More generally, the balance which should be established between scientific and technological progress and the intellectual, spiritual, cultural and moral advancement of humanity.

The Assembly also requested the Secretary-General "to prepare, on a preliminary basis, a report comprising a summary account of studies already made or in progress on the aforementioned subjects, emanating in particular from governmental and inter-governmental sources, the specialized agencies and the competent non-governmental organizations, and a draft programme of work which might be undertaken in fields in which subsequent surveys would be necessary for the attainment of the objectives of the . . . resolution."

55. At its twenty-sixth session in 1970, the Commission on Human Rights received the preliminary report[7]

---

[4] A/37/442.

[5] *Final Act of the International Conference on Human Rights* (United Nations publication, Sales No. E.68.XIV.2), p. 3.

[6] *Ibid.*, p. 12.

[7] E/CN.4/1028, and Add.1-3 and Add.3/Corr.1 and 2 and Add.4-6.

requested by the General Assembly. At that session, however, it did not have the time necessary to study the substantial documentation compiled and examined in that report. The Commission proceeded to a thorough examination of the whole problem at its twenty-seventh session in 1971.

56. In resolution 10 (XXVII) of 18 March 1971, the Commission on Human Rights recognized the need during the Second United Nations Development Decade to concentrate its attention on the most important and basic problems of protecting human rights and fundamental freedoms in the context of scientific and technological progress, and in particular on:

(a) Protection of human rights in the economic, social and cultural fields in accordance with the structure and resources of States and the scientific and technological level they have reached, as well as protection of the right to work in conditions of the automation and mechanization of production;

(b) The use of scientific and technological developments to foster respect for human rights and the legitimate interests of other peoples and respect for generally recognized moral standards and standards of international law;

(c) Prevention of the use of scientific and technological achievements to restrict fundamental democratic rights and freedoms.

1. REPORTS ON HUMAN RIGHTS AND SCIENTIFIC AND TECHNOLOGICAL DEVELOPMENTS

57. During the period between 1971 and 1976, a number of reports on various aspects of human rights and scientific and technological developments were prepared by the Secretary-General and the specialized agencies concerned, and considered by the Commission on Human Rights and the General Assembly. Among the major reports were:

The report on respect for the privacy of individuals and the integrity and sovereignty of nations in the light of advances in recording and other techniques,[8] which deals with beneficial uses of new devices and methods of auditory and visual surveillance, personality assessment techniques ("personality tests"), polygraphs ("lie detectors"), narco-analysis and certain blood, breath and other bodily tests for non-medical purposes, and communication and observation satellites.

The report on uses of electronics which may affect the rights of the person and the limits which should be placed on such uses in a democratic society,[9] which deals with beneficial uses of computerized personnel data systems, benefits derived from computers in various areas of their use, beneficial applications of electronic automation from the point of view of human rights, and benefits derived from electronic communications techniques in various fields of their application.

The report on protection of the human personality and its physical and intellectual integrity, in the light of advances in biology, medicine and biochemistry,[10] which deals with the beneficial use of artificial insemination, psychotropic drugs, procedures of prenatal diagnosis, and chemicals introduced into food production, processing, packaging and storage.

Reports on the impact of scientific and technological developments on economic, social and cultural rights,[11] which deal with the use in the modern world of scientific and technological progress to in-

crease the availability and improve the quality of food and clothing. These reports also contain information concerning the realization of the rights to food and clothing, just and favourable remuneration, equal pay for equal work, housing, rest and leisure, and social security under conditions of scientific and technological progress.

The report on protection of broad sectors of the population against social and material inequalities, as well as other harmful effects which might arise from the use of scientific and technological developments,[12] which deals with the harmful effects of automation and mechanization of production, deterioration of the human environment, the population explosion, and the hazards arising from the increasingly destructive power of modern weapons and from atomic radiation.

The report on the balance which should be established between scientific and technological progress and the intellectual, spiritual, cultural and moral advancement of humanity,[13] which deals with the effects of scientific and technological progress upon the enjoyment of particular human rights and fundamental freedoms, including those set out in articles 1, 2, 3, 5, 10, 11 (1), 12, 16 (1), 17 (1), 18, 19, 20 (1), 21, 23, 24, 25, 26 (1) and (2), and 27 of the Universal Declaration of Human Rights; and which outlines possible international action to assess new technologies, give warning of the possible dangers to human rights which they may present, and possibly even control new developments if threats to human rights seem likely.

58. In addition, Special Rapporteurs appointed by the Sub-Commission on Prevention of Discrimination and Protection of Minorities prepared studies relating to various aspects of the impact of scientific and technological developments on the realization of human rights, including:

(a) The study on *Principles, Guidelines and Guarantees for the Protection of Persons Detained on Grounds of Mental Ill-health or Suffering from Mental Disorder*,[14] which deals with the protection of the fundamental freedoms, human and legal rights of persons who are mentally ill or suffering from mental disorder;

(b) The abolition of psychiatric abuses;

(c) The promotion of mental health law and medical practice; and

(d) The improvement of mental health care and mental institutions, and the study of the "Relevant guidelines in the field of computerized personnel files",[15] which deals with the effect upon human rights caused by the computerization of personal data.

59. In resolution 3026 B (XXVII) of 18 December 1972 the General Assembly requested the Commission on Human Rights to examine the possibility of preparing draft instruments designed to strengthen respect for human rights proclaimed in the Universal Declaration of Human Rights in the light of developments in science and technology. The following year, in resolution 3150 (XXVIII) of 14 December 1973, the Assembly called upon all States to develop further international co-operation to ensure that the results of scientific and technological developments are used in the interests of strengthening international peace and security, the reali-

---

[8] E/CN.4/1116 and Add.1-3 and Add.3/Corr.1 and Add.4.

[9] E/CN.4/1142 and Add.1 and 2.

[10] E/CN.4./1172 and Corr.1 and Add.1-3.

[11] E/CN.4/1084, E/CN.4/1115, E/CN.4/1141 and E/CN.4/1198.

[12] A/10146.

[13] E/CN.4/1199 and Add.1.

[14] United Nations publication, Sales No. E.85.XIV.9.

[15] E/CN.4/Sub.2/18.

zation of the people's right to self-determination and respect for national sovereignty, freedom and independence and for the purpose of economic and social development and improving the quality of life for the entire population. The Assembly recommended all States to pursue a policy of utilizing all scientific and technological achievements to satisfy the material and spiritual needs of all sectors of the population. At the same time, it recognized that, where it exists, the use of scientific and technological achievements for the purpose of violating the sovereignty of States, interfering in their internal affairs, waging aggressive wars, suppressing national liberation movements or pursuing a policy of racial discrimination not only is a flagrant violation of the Charter of the United Nations and other principles of international law, but constitutes an inadmissible distortion of the purposes that should guide scientific and technological developments for the benefit of mankind. The Secretary-General was requested to submit, in co-operation with the competent international agencies and organizations, a report on the subject to the Assembly.

60. The report,[16] presented in 1975, dealt with such matters as the harmful effect of automation and mechanization of production on the enjoyment of the right to work, the harmful effect of scientific and technological developments on the enjoyment of the right to adequate food, and problems of equality of treatment in relation to the impact of scientific and technological development on the right to health. In addition, it analysed the problem of the deterioration of the human environment as a result of scientific and technological development, the problem of the harmful effect of the population explosion on conditions of life, and the problem of the increasingly destructive power of modern weapons and the special public health problems of atomic radiation.

1. All States shall promote international co-operation to ensure that the results of scientific and technological developments are used in the interests of strengthening international peace and security, freedom and independence, and also for the purpose of the economic and social development of peoples and the realization of human rights and freedoms in accordance with the Charter of the United Nations.

. . .

3. All States shall take measures to ensure that scientific and technological achievements satisfy the material and spiritual needs of all sectors of the population.

4. All States shall refrain from any acts involving the use of scientific and technological achievements for the purposes of violating the sovereignty and territorial integrity of other States, interfering in their internal affairs, waging aggressive wars, suppressing national liberation movements or pursuing a policy of racial discrimination. Such acts are not only a flagrant violation of the Charter of the United Nations and principles of international law, but constitute an inadmissible distortion of the purposes that should guide scientific and technological developments for the benefit of mankind.

5. All States shall co-operate in the establishment, strengthening and development of the scientific and technological capacity of developing countries with a view to accelerating the realization of the social and economic rights of the peoples of those countries.

6. All States shall take measures to extend the benefits of science and technology to all strata of the population and to protect them, both socially and materially, from possible harmful effects of the misuse of scientific and technological developments, including their misuse to infringe upon the rights of the individual or of the group, particularly with regard to respect for privacy and the protection of the human personality and its physical and intellectual integrity.

7. All States shall take the necessary measures, including legislative measures, to ensure that the utilization of scientific and technological achievements promotes the fullest realization of human rights and fundamental freedoms without any discrimination whatsoever on grounds of race, sex, language or religious beliefs.

8. All States shall take effective measures, including legislative measures, to prevent and preclude the utilization of scientific and technological achievements to the detriment of human rights and fundamental freedoms and the dignity of the human person.

9. All States shall, whenever necessary, take action to ensure compliance with legislation guaranteeing human rights and freedoms in the conditions of scientific and technological developments.

2. DECLARATION ON THE USE OF SCIENTIFIC AND TECHNOLOGICAL PROGRESS IN THE INTERESTS OF PEACE AND FOR THE BENEFIT OF MANKIND

61. On 10 November 1975 the General Assembly, in resolution 3384 (XXX) of 10 November 1975, solemnly proclaimed the Declaration on the Use of Scientific and Technological Progress in the Interests of Peace and for the Benefit of Mankind. Among other things the Declaration provided (para. 2) that "All States shall take appropriate measures to prevent the use of scientific and technological developments, particularly by State organs, to limit or interfere with the enjoyment of human rights and fundamental freedoms of the individual as enshrined in the Universal Declaration of Human Rights, the International Covenants on Human Rights and other relevant international instruments."

62. Additional principles set out in the Declaration were as follows:

3. IMPLEMENTATION OF THE DECLARATION

63. Before the proclamation of the Declaration, consideration was given to the possibility of establishing special international technology assessment machinery which would assess new technologies from the point of view of human rights, drawing attention to possible dangers to human rights which they may present and possibly even calling for controls upon new developments which represented threats to human rights; and which would also assess the potential benefits to mankind of such developments. A group of eminent international experts convened at Geneva in September 1975 recommended that international machinery should be entrusted with technological assessment for mankind as a whole; this assessment would include the evaluation of possible side effects and long-range effects of particular innovations and would aim at determining whether the time is right for such innovations and whether their advantages outweigh the discernable disadvantages. All such decisions, it was agreed, must be made on the basis of the considered opinion of bodies of experts and

---

[16] A/10146.

laymen, representing the interests of all the people as well as of future generations.

64. However, in resolution 31/128 of 16 December 1976, the General Assembly put aside these suggestions and requested the Commission on Human Rights to give special attention to the implementation of the Declaration. Later, in resolution 35/130 of 11 December 1980, the Assembly requested the Secretary-General to submit to the Assembly a report prepared on the basis of information received from Member States regarding the implementation of the provisions of the Declaration. The Secretary-General has since 1982 submitted annual reports on the subject,[17] which the General Assembly has noted with satisfaction.[18]

65. The General Assembly and the Commision on Human Rights continued to deal with matters relating to implementation of the Declaration under the agenda item, "Human rights and scientific and technological developments". The General Assembly adopted resolutions 37/189 A and B of 18 December 1982, 38/113 of 16 December 1983, 40/111 of 13 December 1985, and 41/115 of 4 December 1986, all on the subject, while the Commission on Human Rights expressed its views in resolutions 1982/7 of 19 February 1982, 1983/43 of 9 March 1983, 1984/28 of 12 March 1984 and 1986/10 of 10 March 1986.

66. In these resolutions, the Assembly and the Commission repeatedly reaffirmed that all peoples and all individuals have an inherent right to life and that the safeguarding of this cardinal right is an essential condition for the enjoyment of the entire range of economic, social and cultural, as well as civil and political, rights. They stress again and again the urgent need for the international community to make every effort to strengthen peace, remove the growing threat of war, particularly nuclear war, halt the arms race and achieve general and complete disarmament under effective international control and prevent violations of the principles of the Charter of the United Nations regarding the sovereignty and territorial integrity of States and the self-determination of peoples, thus contributing to ensuring the right to life. They further stress the foremost importance of the implementation of practical measures of disarmament for releasing substantial additional resources, which should be utilized for social and economic development, particularly for the benefit of the developing countries. They call upon all States, appropriate organs of the United Nations, specialized agencies and intergovernmental and non-governmental organizations concerned to take the necessary measures to ensure that the results of scientific and technological progress are used exclusively in the interests of international peace, for the benefit of mankind and for promoting and encouraging universal respect for human rights and fundamental freedoms. In addition, they call upon all States that have not yet done so to take effective measures with a view to prohibiting, in accordance with the International Covenant on Civil and Political Rights, any propaganda for war, in particular the formulation, propounding and dissemination of any propaganda for doctrines and concepts aimed at unleashing nuclear war.

67. In connection with a related agenda item, "Implications of scientific and technological developments for human rights", the General Assembly in resolution 33/53 of 14 December 1978 requested the Commission on Human Rights to urge the Sub-Commission on Prevention of Discrimination and Protection of Minorities to undertake, as a matter of priority, a study of the question of the protection of those detained on grounds of mental ill-health, with a view to formulating guidelines. The Commission requested such a study in resolution 10 A (XXXIII) of 11 March 1977, and the report prepared by the Sub-Commission's Special Rapporteur, Mrs. Erica-Irene A. Daes—containing detailed evidence of the misuse of psychiatry to detain persons on non-medical grounds—was completed in 1985. A body of principles, guidelines and guarantees, aimed at preventing the detention of persons in mental institutions on account of their political views or on other non-medical grounds, is under preparation by the Sub-Commission for future consideration by the General Assembly.

4. CONCERN OF UNESCO FOR HUMAN AND CULTURAL IMPLICATIONS OF SCIENTIFIC AND TECHNOLOGICAL ADVANCES

68. Member States of UNESCO have shown concern for the human and cultural implications of scientific and technological advances. Among the industrialized countries, some have established or are planning to create machinery to study and deal with the situation. While most of the developing countries have not yet reached this stage, many have become keenly aware of the fact that the introduction of new scientific and technological advances can have an adverse effect upon their national and local cultures and values.

69. The Ministers Responsible for the Application of Science and Technology to Development in Latin America and the Caribbean, at a conference organized by UNESCO at Brasilia in 1985, called for fostering "appreciation of scientific and technological methods and practices in the culture of our peoples", and urged "the use of science and technology for peaceful ends" while rejecting "any application that places the survival of humanity in jeopardy".

70. Various meetings of experts, convened under the UNESCO interdisciplinary programme for the study of the impact of science on society, have also considered the problem of the effect of the transmission of science and technology on local and national cultures. One such meeting, held in Nairobi in 1976, addressed itself pri-

---

[17] A/37/330 and Add.1, A/38/195, A/39/422 and Add.1, A/40/493 and Add.1 and 2, A/41/463 and Add.1; and A/42/392 and Add.1 and 2.

[18] General Assembly resolutions 37/189, 38/112, 39/133, 40/112, 41/115 and 42/100.

marily to the impact of technology of the western world upon the culture of the developing countries, particularly those in Africa. The experts attending implicitly agreed on the importance of the development of technological innovations adapted to the societies which are to receive them, and on the need for a more profound study of the problem.

71.   In 1981, UNESCO convened a symposium to examine pseudo-scientific theories invoked to justify racism and racial discrimination, held in Athens from 30 March to 3 April. The symposium resulted in the Athens Appeal which denounced the invocation of pseudo-scientific theories, on the basis of different disciplines such as biology, genetics, psychology, sociology, history and philosophy.

72.   In 1982, a symposium with the theme of human rights, new human rights, and scientific and technological progress was convened in Trieste under the auspices of the International Institute for the Study of Human Rights, in order to study the positive and negative consequences of certain scientific and technological advances, particularly in the field of informatics, telematics and genetic manipulations.

5. Concern of the World Health Organization for Medical Implications of Scientific and Technological Advances

73.   Reference has been made above to the Principles of Medical Ethics relevant to the role of health personnel in the protection of persons against torture and other cruel, inhuman or degrading treatment or punishment. The Code was formulated by the Council for International Organizations of Medical Sciences as a result of a request to the World Health Organization from the General Assembly of the United Nations. The Code was endorsed by the Executive Board of the World Health Organization at its sixty-third session, in January 1979, and transmitted to the General Assembly through the Secretary-General.

74.   The World Health Organization, jointly with the Council for International Organizations of Medical Sciences, prepared and published in 1982 the International Guidelines for Biomedical Research Involving Human Subjects. The Guidelines have particular relevance to externally sponsored research undertaken in third world countries. Most importantly, they stress the need for peer review within the country in which the research is to be undertaken. The Guidelines were dis-

tributed to all ministries of health, to medical research councils, medical facilities, concerned non-governmental organizations and medical journals, as well as to research-based pharmaceutical companies.

75.   In addition the World Health Organization cosponsored, with the Council for International Organizations of Medical Sciences, a series of round-table discussions on bioethics covering the following subjects:

Medical Ethics and Medical Education, Mexico, 1980;

Human Experimentation and Medical Ethics, Manila, 1981;

Health Policy, Ethics and Human Values—an International Dialogue, Athens, 1984;

Battered Children and Child Abuse, Berne, 1985; and

Health Policy, Ethics and Human Values: European and North American Perspectives, Noordwijk, 1987.

These meetings constitute an important element in ongoing comprehensive programmes concerning medical ethical issues related to both biomedical research and the delivery of health services.

76.   In addition, the World Health Organization cosponsored, with the Council of International Organizations of Medical Sciences, round-table discussions on medical ethics and medical education, held in Mexico in 1980, and on human experimentation and medical ethics, held at Manila in 1981. These meetings constitute an important element in ongoing comprehensive programmes concerning ethical issues related to both biomedical research and the delivery of health services.

77.   The World Health Organization is also cosponsoring a programme initiated by the Council for International Organizations of Medical Sciences on Health Policy, Ethics and Human Values: an International Dialogue, of which the main objectives are:

To strengthen national capacities for addressing and making decisions about the ethical and human-values issues involved in health policy;

To contribute to improved understanding of the concepts inherent in WHO's goal of health for all, particularly in terms of its value content;

To develop transcultural and transdisciplinary approaches and methods for working in this field; and

To use improved understanding of the approaches of various societies to the ethical and human-values aspects of health policy, as a way to promote deeper human understanding of human values across cultural and political lines.

PART TWO

PART TWO

XIV. SETTING AND IMPLEMENTING INTERNATIONAL HUMAN RIGHTS STANDARDS

Introduction

1. In 1986 the General Assembly reviewed the extensive network of international standards in the field of human rights which it and other United Nations bodies, including the specialized agencies, had established, reaffirmed that effective implementation of these international standards is of fundamental importance, and recognized the value of continuing efforts to identify specific areas where further international action is required to develop the existing international legal framework in the field of human rights pursuant to Article 13, paragraph 1 a, of the Charter of the United Nations.

2. In resolution 41/120 of 4 December 1986, the Assembly called upon Member States and United Nations bodies to accord priority to the implementation of existing international standards in the field of human rights and urged broad ratification of, or accession to, existing treaties in this field. It urged Member States and the United Nations bodies engaged in developing new international human rights standards to pay due regard in this work to the established international legal framework, and reaffirmed the important role of the Commission on Human Rights in the development of international human rights instruments.

3. The Assembly, further, invited Member States and United Nations bodies to bear in mind the following guidelines in developing such instruments: They should, *inter alia*, (a) be consistent with the existing body of international human rights law; (b) be of fundamental character and derive from the inherent dignity and worth of the human person; (c) be sufficiently precise to give rise to identifiable and practicable rights and obligations; (d) provide, where appropriate, realistic and effective implementation machinery; and (e) attract broad international support.

4. The setting and implementation of international standards in the field of human rights has developed rapidly since the basic standards were established in the Charter of the United Nations, the Universal Declaration of Human Rights, and the International Covenants on Human Rights. Within the United Nations system alone, these major instruments have been supplemented by more than 60 declarations, conventions and protocols dealing with particular human rights issues, while many others have been brought into effect by regional intergovernmental organizations. This proliferation of standards, and of international machinery to implement them, has naturally given rise to some confusion, which the Assembly's guidelines are intended to correct.

A. Setting international standards

5. United Nations bodies formulate international standards in the field of human rights either by preparing and adopting or proclaiming recommendations—sometimes called "declarations"—which are usually of broad and even universal application, or by preparing and opening for signature, ratification and accession multilateral conventions—sometimes called "covenants"—which are legally binding upon States accepting them as such. The practice as to the use of the terms "Declaration" and "Recommendation" was described in the following terms in a memorandum prepared in 1962 by the Office of Legal Affairs and submitted to the Commission on Human Rights at its eighteenth session:

3. In United Nations practice, a "declaration" is a formal and solemn instrument, suitable for rare occasions when principles of great and lasting importance are being enunciated, such as the Universal Declaration of Human Rights. A recommendation is less formal.

4. Apart from the distinction just indicated, there is probably no difference between a "recommendation" and a "declaration" in United Nations practice as far as strict legal principle is concerned. A "declaration" or a "recommendation" is adopted by resolution of a United Nations organ. As such, it cannot be made binding upon Member States, in the sense that a treaty or convention is binding upon the parties to it, purely by the device of terming it a "declaration" rather than a "recommendation". However, in view of the greater solemnity and significance of a "declaration", it may be considered to impart, on behalf of the organ adopting it, a strong expectation that members of the international community will abide by it. Consequently, in so far as the expectation is gradually justified by State practice, a declaration may by custom become recognized as laying down rules binding upon States.

5. In conclusion, it may be said that, in United Nations practice, a "declaration" is a solemn instrument resorted to only in very rare cases relating to matters of major and lasting importance where the maximum compliance is expected.[1]

6. It may be added that, in United Nations practice, a treaty is simply a formal agreement between two or more States. Human rights treaties are those international agreements containing provisions to promote or to protect one or more human rights or fundamental freedoms. They are normally prepared by a body within the United Nations system or by a special conference of plenipotentiaries convened for the purpose, and are opened for signature and ratification or accession by the States specified therein. Such treaties are normally called conventions. Instruments revising the terms of conventions, or adding further provisions, generally are known as protocols. Certain conventions have been

---

[1] *Official Records of the Economic and Social Council, Thirty-fourth Session, Supplement No. 8* (E/3616/Rev.1), para. 105.

termed "covenants" to stress their great overall importance. A convention, protocol or covenant enters into force only after it has been ratified or acceded to by the number of States specified in one of its articles, and is legally binding only upon those States which have become parties to it by ratification, accession, succession or otherwise.

7. In the field of human rights, United Nations bodies have frequently adopted both a declaration or recommendation, and a convention, on a particular subject. In most cases, the declaration or recommendation, which is universally applicable, sets out general principles or general standards of human rights, while the convention defines specific rights and the limitations or restrictions on the use thereof, and sets out the obligations to be assumed by the States which ratify or accede to it.

8. Thus, in the preparation of the International Bill of Human Rights, the Universal Declaration of Human Rights was adopted first, in 1948, and was followed by the International Covenants on Human Rights in 1966. Similarly, the United Nations Declaration on the Elimination of All Forms of Racial Discrimination, adopted in 1963, was followed by the International Convention on the Elimination of All Forms of Racial Discrimination, adopted and opened for signature in 1965. In the same way, the Declaration on the Elimination of Discrimination against Women, adopted in 1967, was followed by the Convention on the Elimination of All Forms of Discrimination against Women, adopted in 1979. In one case, the procedure was reversed; the adoption and opening for signature and ratification of the Convention on Consent to Marriage, Minimum Age for Marriage and Registration of Marriages in 1962 was followed by the adoption, in 1965, of the Recommendation on Consent to Marriage, Minimum Age for Marriage and Registration of Marriages.

9. The specialized agencies concerned with human rights matters frequently adopt a Convention and a Recommendation on a single subject simultaneously. Thus, the International Labour Conference at its 1958 session adopted both the Discrimination (Employment and Occupation) Convention (No. 111) and the Recommendation (No. 111) on the same subject. Similarly the General Conference of UNESCO at its 1960 session adopted both the Convention and the Recommendation against Discrimination in Education. In this connection, it should be noted that under the ILO Constitution a Recommendation adopted by the International Labour Conference has a special legal effect involving, as in the case of an ILO Convention, the obligation for all States Members to submit the instrument to the competent national legislative authorities and to report on national law and practice in regard to the instrument when requested.

1. PREPARATION OF STANDARD-SETTING INSTRUMENTS

10. There is no single established procedure for the preparation of international instruments in the field of

human rights; each is prepared in whatever manner the bodies concerned consider to be appropriate.

11. In the case of the recently adopted Declaration on the Elimination of All Forms of Intolerance and of Discrimination Based on Religion or Belief, for example, the process of preparation began when the Sub-Commission on Prevention of Discrimination and Protection of Minorities initiated a study of discrimination in the matter of religious rights and practices at its 1953 session. The study was completed in 1960, at which time the Sub-Commission prepared a series of draft principles relating to discrimination in respect of the right to freedom of thought, conscience and religion and transmitted them to the Commission on Human Rights.

12. In 1962, the General Assembly requested the Commission to prepare a draft declaration on the elimination of all forms of religious intolerance and a draft convention on the same subject. In 1972, the Assembly decided to accord priority to the preparation of the declaration. The Commission on Human Rights began drafting the declaration in 1974. By 1978, it had adopted texts for the title and the preamble. In 1981, it finally adopted the text of a draft Declaration on the Elimination of All Forms of Intolerance and of Discrimination Based on Religion or Belief. By the end of 1981—28 years after the first study was initiated—the General Assembly was able to adopt and proclaim the Declaration on the Elimination of All Forms of Intolerance and of Discrimination Based on Religion or Belief.

13. In the case of the Convention on the Elimination of All Forms of Discrimination against Women, nine years were required for the elaboration of the instrument from the time the item was first placed on the agenda of the Commission on the Status of Women, in 1970, to the adoption of the completed Convention by the General Assembly in 1979. The World Plan of Action for the Implementation of the Objectives of the International Women's Year, prepared in 1975 by the World Conference of the International Women's Year, called for high priority to be given to the preparation and adoption of the convention on the elimination of discrimination against women, with effective procedures for its implementation. The Commission on the Status of Women devoted large parts of its twenty-fifth and twenty-sixth sessions to the convention in 1975 and 1976, and held a resumed twenty-sixth session in December 1976, in order to complete a draft of the convention. The draft had to be considered at three successive sessions of the General Assembly before agreement could be reached on a final text. The Convention on the Elimination of All Forms of Discrimination against Women was finally adopted and opened for signature and ratification or accession on 18 December 1979.

14. In the preparation of such instruments, most of the bodies concerned have found it advantageous first to secure the comments of Governments and interested international organizations on the drafts submitted to them, and then to call upon the Secretariat to prepare a working paper presenting and analysing the replies re-

ceived. In recent years, many bodies called upon to draft an international instrument have found it advantageous to set up a working group or drafting committee to attempt to reconcile the various texts and proposals under consideration. Informal working groups, open to all members of the body concerned, have been favoured in some instances.

15. It has also been found advantageous, in many cases, to reach agreement on the title, general provisions and substantive articles of a proposed instrument before taking up the preamble or remaining articles. However, in the case of the two instruments mentioned above, considerable time had to be devoted to finding titles before further work could be profitably undertaken.

16. Almost invariably, a Style Committee is established to review from the linguistic point of view the versions of the draft instrument in the various languages before it is adopted, in order to ensure the concurrence of all the versions.

17. On several occasions, several United Nations bodies have collaborated in the preparation of an international human rights instrument, using a variety of techniques for consultation, co-operation and co-ordination. For example, in the preparation of the International Covenants on Human Rights, the specialized agencies concerned were consulted and proposals which they submitted were taken into account.

2. ACCEPTANCE OF CONVENTIONS

18. All multilateral conventions in the field of human rights concluded by United Nations bodies provide that the consent of a State to be bound by their terms must be expressed either by ratification or accession, and that the instruments of ratification or accession must be deposited with the Secretary-General of the United Nations. They are open for ratification or accession either by all States or by all Member States. In the latter case, provision is usually made for ratification or accession by non-member States upon the invitation of the General Assembly.

19. Human rights conventions adopted by specialized agencies are usually open for ratification or acceptance only to States members of the organization concerned, and provide for the deposit of instruments of ratification with its Director-General. In accordance with Article 102 of the Charter of the United Nations, the Directors-General communicate particulars of all ratifications, declarations and acts of denunciation to the Secretary-General of the United Nations for registration.

20. The General Assembly and the Economic and Social Council have repeatedly appealed to eligible States to become parties to the conventions which deal with human rights, including those prepared by United Nations organs and those prepared under the auspices of the specialized agencies concerned.

21. The Sub-Commission on Prevention of Discrimination and Protection of Minorities decided, in res-

olution 1 B (XXIII) of 5 September 1979, to establish each year a sessional working group to meet during its annual session in order to consider ways and means of encouraging Governments to ratify or accede to international human rights instruments. The Sub-Commission requested the Secretary-General to write, well before each of its sessions, to the Governments which had not accepted the instruments in question, requesting them to inform the Sub-Commission of the circumstances which had not enabled them to do so, and to explain any particular difficulties they had faced in respect of which the United Nations might be able to offer assistance. The Working Group was invited to examine the replies received and, if necessary, to discuss them with representatives of the Governments concerned; and to consider, in appropriate cases, what forms of assistance could be provided to those Governments with a view to assisting them to ratify or adhere to the conventions.

22. The Working Group examined the replies received from 3 States at its first session, in 1980; 8 at its second session, in 1981; 22 at its third session, in 1982; and 17 at its fourth session, in 1983. At its fourth session, it also considered a draft resolution proposed by its Chairman-Rapporteur suggesting the appointment by the Sub-Commission of a Special Rapporteur to undertake a study entitled "Ways and Means of Encouraging the Universal Acceptance of International Human Rights Instruments" in the light of the findings of the Working Group.

23. The sessional Working Group established by the Sub-Commission in 1984 completed the examination of replies received from Governments. In resolution 1984/36 of 30 August 1984, the Sub-Commission took note of the Working Group's report,[2] requested the Secretary-General to hold informal discussions concerning prospects for ratification of human rights instruments with government delegations as appropriate, and decided to suspend the work of the Working Group and to request the Chairman of the Sub-Commission to appoint at its 1985 session one of its members to report to it at that session on the basis of information made available by the Secretary-General.

24. On 9 August 1985 the Sub-Commission appointed Mr. Marc Bossuyt as an expert to report to it at that session on information received under resolution 1984/36.[3] However, the Sub-Commission was unable to consider the item at that session and decided, in resolution 1985/34 of 30 August 1985 to consider the question, "Encouragement of universal acceptance of human rights instruments" on a biennial basis, starting at its thirty-ninth session.

25. At its thirty-ninth session, held in 1987, the Sub-Commission adopted resolution 1987/1 containing a draft resolution intended for eventual adoption by the General Assembly entitled "Enhancing universal respect for human rights". The draft resolution proposed that the Assembly should launch a world-wide campaign

---

[2] E/CN.4/Sub.2/1984/26.

[3] Decision 1985/104.

aimed at universal ratification of all international human rights instruments, and suggested that 1988, the fortieth anniversary of the adoption of the Universal Declaration of Human Rights, would provide a unique opportunity to enhance interest in, and improve respect for, human rights and the relevant international instruments.

3. RESERVATIONS TO CONVENTIONS, AND OBJECTIONS THERETO

26. A number of States, in ratifying or acceding to a particular international human rights instrument, have made reservations concerning some of the provisions of that instrument. Other States parties to the same instrument have subsequently raised objections to the reservation or stated that they do not accept it.[4] The Secretary-General receives such reservations, and objections thereto, and forwards them to the interested parties without ruling on their legal effect. The reservations, in some cases, have aroused concern because they appear to be incompatible with the object and purpose of the instrument to which they apply.

27. In 1950, the General Assembly requested an advisory opinion from the International Court of Justice regarding reservations which had been made concerning the Convention on the Prevention and Punishment of the Crime of Genocide by certain States parties, and at the same time referred the general question of reservations concerning multilateral treaties to the International Law Commission.

28. The International Law Commission, in its 1951 report, stated that the criterion of compatibility with the object and purpose of a convention, applied by the Court to the Genocide Convention, would not be suitable for application to multilateral conventions in general; while no single rule uniformly applied could be wholly satisfactory, the rule suitable for application in the majority of cases was that which the Secretary-General had followed theretofore.

29. The General Assembly, in resolution 598 (VI) of 12 January 1952, endorsed the International Law Commission's recommendation that clauses on reservations should be inserted in future conventions; stated that the Court's advisory opinion should be followed in regard to the Genocide Convention; and requested the Secretary-General, in respect of future United Nations conventions, to act as depositary for documents containing reservations or objections thereto without passing on the legal effect of such documents, which were to be communicated to all States concerned, to whom it would be left to draw the legal consequences. In 1959, the Secretary-General was requested to follow the same practice with respect to United Nations conventions

concluded before, as well as after, the Assembly's 1952 decision.

B. Supervising the realization of international human rights standards

30. Most of the many United Nations bodies concerned with human rights provide a continuing supervision of the realization of international human rights standards under a general system of periodic routine review of information received from all reliable sources, including reports from Member States, intergovernmental and non-governmental organizations and communications alleging violations of human rights received from, or on behalf of, the victims of such violations. Among such bodies are the Commission on Human Rights, the Sub-Commission on Prevention of Discrimination and Protection of Minorities and the Commission on the Status of Women.

31. In addition, there are now a number of special bodies, established in accordance with international conventions dealing with particular aspects of human rights, which devote full time and attention to monitoring the implementation of the provisions of those conventions. Among such bodies are the Committee on the Elimination of Racial Discrimination, the Human Rights Committee, the Committee on Economic, Social and Cultural Rights, the Committee on the Elimination of Discrimination against Women, the Group of Three and the Committee against Torture.

32. The general supervisory and the specialized monitoring systems are closely interlinked, function harmoniously without conflict, and serve to complement one another. Together they combine to ensure that everyone, without distinction, may fully enjoy his human rights and fundamental freedoms.

1. REVIEWS OF REPORTS

33. The presentation of reports to an international authority is an implementation procedure of long standing, utilized for many years before the establishment of the United Nations.[5]

34. Article 64 of the United Nations Charter provides that the Economic and Social Council may take appropriate steps to obtain regular reports from the specialized agencies, and may make arrangements with the Members of the United Nations and with the specialized agencies to obtain reports on the steps taken to give effect to its own recommendations and to recommendations on matters falling within its competence made by the General Assembly. Further, the Council may communicate its observations on these reports to the Assembly.

---

[4] For the texts of States parties' reservations, and relevant objections, concerning international human rights instruments, see *Human Rights—Status of International Instruments* (ST/HR/5, Sales No. E.87.XIV.2).

[5] See, for example, Article 22 of the Convenant of the League of Nations; articles 19 and 22 of the Constitution of ILO; see also Articles 73 e, 87 a and 88 of the Charter of the United Nations and article VIII of the Constitution of UNESCO.

35. The Council has exercised its power under Article 64 by including requests for such reports in individual resolutions or by setting up procedures for obtaining general reports on the implementation of certain categories of resolutions, such as those on human rights matters.

36. The General Assembly, in resolution 119 (II) of 31 October 1947, recommended that, in fulfilment of Article 64 of the Charter, the Secretary-General should report annually to the Economic and Social Council, and that the Council should report to the General Assembly, on steps taken by the Governments of Member States to give effect to the recommendations of the Council, as well as to the recommendations of the Assembly on matters falling within the Council's competence.

37. At its eighth session, the Council, after considering General Assembly resolution 119 (II), adopted resolution 210 (VIII) on 18 March 1949, dealing with the establishment of regular procedures and schedules for reports by Governments on lists of recommendations to be transmitted to them by the Secretary-General. The Council set up a timetable for annual reports by Governments and by the Secretary-General, and requested Governments to arrange their reports in such form as to assist the Secretary-General in compiling "a fully annotated list to serve as an index to all the reports received".

38. At its ninth session, by resolution 255 (IX) of 14 July 1949, the Council established an *Ad Hoc* Committee to examine the replies from Governments and the report of the Secretary-General. At its tenth session, the Council, having examined the report of the *Ad Hoc* Committee, decided, by resolution 283 (X) of 8 February 1950, to follow the procedures recommended by the Committee, and amended resolution 210 (VIII) accordingly. In resolution 283 (X), the Council established arrangements for a general biennial reporting procedure, and indicated certain points on which the Secretary-General should request Governments to make statements.

39. The Secretary-General submitted a report under the biennial procedure to the Council at its fourteenth session. At that session, the Council, by resolution 450 (XIV) of 29 July 1952, noted that the Assembly and the Council had shown an increasing tendency to adopt resolutions which required specific reports within specified time-limits and that the record of replies to such resolutions had been satisfactory. It therefore discontinued the general biennial reporting procedure and decided to include in its resolutions, wherever practicable, indications as to the timing of the reports expected from Governments in implementation of the resolutions concerned, and to include each year in its annual report to the General Assembly information regarding replies received from Governments on the implementation of recommendations of the Assembly and the Council on economic and social matters.

2. SYSTEM OF PERIODIC REPORTS ON HUMAN RIGHTS

40. On the recommendation of the Commission on Human Rights, the Economic and Social Council adopted resolution 624 B (XXII) of 1 August 1956, establishing a system of periodic reports on human rights. It requested "States Members of the United Nations and of the specialized agencies to transmit to the Secretary-General, every three years, a report describing developments and the progress achieved during the preceding three years in the field of human rights, and measures taken to safeguard human liberty in their metropolitan area and Non-Self-Governing and Trust Territories; the report to deal with the rights enumerated in the Universal Declaration of Human Rights and with the right of peoples to self-determination".

41. In resolution 1074 C (XXXIX) of 28 July 1965, the Council revised the system of reporting so as to call for the submission of information not on an annual basis but within a continuing three-year cycle scheduled as follows: (*a*) in the first year, on civil and political rights; (*b*) in the second year, on economic, social and cultural rights; and (*c*) in the third year, on freedom of information.

42. The Secretary-General was requested to forward the information received from Member States and specialized agencies under the terms of the resolution in full, together with a subject and country index, to the Commission on Human Rights, the Commission on the Status of Women and the Sub-Commission on Prevention of Discrimination and Protection of Minorities. The observations received from non-governmental organizations, as well as any comments that might be made on them by the Member State concerned, were also to be made available by the Secretary-General to the two Commissions and the Sub-Commission.

43. The Sub-Commission was requested to undertake the initial study of the materials, to report thereon to the Commission on Human Rights, and to submit comments and recommendations for consideration by the Commission. The Commission on the Status of Women was invited to inform the Commission on Human Rights of its comments and of any recommendations it might wish to make.

44. After examining the periodic reports at regular intervals from 1957 to 1977, the Commission on Human Rights postponed consideration of the item at its thirty-third session, in 1977, and at several later sessions. The General Assembly, in resolution 35/209 of 17 December 1980, decided to terminate certain activities which the Secretary-General had identified as obsolete, ineffective or of marginal usefulness, which included the system of periodic reports on human rights. The Commission concurred in this, in decision 10 (XXXVII) of 13 March 1981.

3. INTEGRATED REPORTING SYSTEM ON THE STATUS OF WOMEN

45. The Economic and Social Council, in resolution 1677 (LII) of 2 June 1972, requested States Members of the United Nations, starting in the period 1972-1973, to submit information on the implementation of the Dec-

laration on the Elimination of Discrimination against Women according to a four-year cycle in which in the first period of two years information would be submitted on the implementation of the civil and political rights set out in articles 2, 4, 5, 6, 7 and 8 of the Declaration and in the second period of two years on the implementation of the economic, social and cultural rights set out in articles 2, 9 and 10 of the Declaration.

46. Additional reporting procedures were subsequently established by General Assembly resolutions 3490 (XXX) and 3520 (XXX), of 12 and 15 December 1975 respectively, which called for biennial system-wide reviews and appraisals of the implementation of the World Plan of Action for the Implementation of the Objectives of the International Women's Year and of progress made under the International Development Strategy for the Second United Nations Development Decade.

47. The General Assembly decided, in resolution 33/186 of 29 January 1979, to integrate the three reporting systems. The Economic and Social Council, in resolution 1980/38 of 2 May 1980, expressed the view that the Commission on the Status of Women should continue its fundamental functions of monitoring the situation with regard to the status of women and of developing proposals and recommendations to the Council on the basis of all relevant information, and decided to continue the integrated reporting system on the status of women as the means of monitoring the realization during 1980-1985 of the World Plan of Action for the Implementation of the Objectives of the International Women's Year and of the programme of action for the second half of the United Nations Decade for Women.

4. REPORTING OBLIGATIONS OF STATES UNDER CERTAIN INSTRUMENTS

48. A principal function of the bodies mentioned above established to monitor the implementation of human rights instruments, including the Committee on the Elimination of Racial Discrimination, the Human Rights Committee, the Committee on Economic, Social and Cultural Rights, the Commission on the Elimination of Discrimination against Women, the Committee against Torture and the Group of Three, is to examine reports submitted at regular intervals by States parties to the respective instruments.

49. In this connection the General Assembly considered at its forty-first session a report by the Secretary-General containing information as at 1 June 1986 on the problem of overdue reports by States parties to United Nations human rights instruments,[6] and noted with concern that the situation was critical with regard to overdue reports under the International Convention on the Elimination of All Forms of Racial Discrimination and that a significant backlog of reports had developed in relation to other instruments.

50. In resolution 41/121 of 4 December 1986 the Assembly recognized the burden that coexisting reporting systems placed upon Member States that are parties to various instruments and noted that the burden could become more onerous as further instruments entered into force, but nevertheless reiterated the fundamental importance it attaches to the fulfilment of reporting obligations under international human rights instruments.

51. The Assembly drew attention to the need for States parties to submit reports to the various bodies that have been set up to supervise such instruments in a timely manner, and to co-operate as fully as possible with those bodies to make the best use of their meeting time. It urged States parties with overdue reports to make every effort to present their reports as soon as possible and to take advantage of opportunities whereby such reports could be consolidated. Further, it invited the Chairmen of the various supervisory bodies to maintain communication and dialogue with each other on common issues and problems, requested the Secretary-General to consider making provision in his proposed programme budget for 1988-1989 for a meeting of the Chairmen of these bodies, and endorsed the Secretary-General's proposal to arrange training courses for those regions experiencing the most serious difficulties in relation to meeting reporting obligations.

52. The following year, in resolution 42/105 of 7 December 1987, the Assembly requested the Secretary-General to propose a draft agenda for the meeting of the persons chairing treaty bodies to be held at Geneva in October 1988 reflecting the following objectives: (*a*) to give priority attention to consideration of remedial measures, including co-ordinated action when appropriate, to deal with the problems highlighted in the reports of the Secretary-General;[7] (*b*) to give further consideration to harmonizing and consolidating reporting guidelines on the basis of the suggestions made in the above-mentioned reports, with a view to providing clearer and more comprehensive guidelines for more concise reporting by States parties; (*c*) to identify and develop possible projects for technical advisory services with a view to assisting States parties upon their request in fulfilling their reporting obligations; and (*d*) to explore ways of expediting consideration of periodic reports, such as by envisaging time-limits on oral interventions, avoiding duplication in questioning, requesting supplementary written material and encouraging States parties to submit reports that are as succinct as possible.

C. Handling of communications concerning human rights

53. Several organs of the United Nations have established procedures for handling communications concerning human rights received from individuals and organizations in Trust and Non-Self-Governing Territories.

---

[6] A/41/510.

[7] A/40/600 and Add.1; A/41/510.

54. For example, the Trusteeship Council, which is empowered by Article 87 of the Charter of the United Nations to accept petitions and examine them in consultation with the administering authority, did so for many years under procedures which have since been discontinued because of the reduction in the number of Trust Territories and consequently in the number of petitions.

55. The Special Committee on the Situation with regard to the Implementation of the Declaration on the Granting of Independence to Colonial Countries and Peoples decided, at its eighth meeting on 5 March 1962, that it would hear petitioners and receive written petitions, and it has since done so frequently. It maintains a standing Sub-Committee on Petitions, Information and Assistance which screens written petitions and arranges for petitioners to be heard.

56. In addition, the Special Committee against *Apartheid* receives and considers communications received from non-governmental sources opposed to the policies of *apartheid* of the Government of South Africa, and maintains a standing Sub-Committee on Petitions and Information to assist it in this task.

57. With regard to communications and petitions concerning human rights received from the vast majority of independent countries and territories, however, the situation is not the same. The handling of such communications and petitions by United Nations bodies was a controversial issue for many years.

58. At its first session, in 1947, the Commission on Human Rights established a Sub-Committee on the Handling of Communications, the function of which was to consider how communications concerning human rights, addressed to the Commission or to other organs of the United Nations, should be handled. The report of the Sub-Committee to the Commission[8] contained, in paragraph 3, the statement that "the Commission has no power to take any action in regard to any complaints regarding human rights". Following the unanimous adoption by the Commission of that paragraph of the report of the Sub-Committee, one member of the Commission proposed that it be amended by adding the following: "The Commission draws the Economic and Social Council's attention to the serious gap which results from the absence of this power". The member of the Commission in question did not make any proposal for bridging the gap, but hoped that the Economic and Social Council would instruct the Commission to do so. The Chairman of the Commission suggested that no mention of the gap should be made in the Commission's report but that the Rapporteur should be asked to explain the situation orally to the Economic and Social Council. This suggestion was accepted by the member concerned, who withdrew his proposed amendment.

59. The Commission on the Status of Women also considered the problem of communications at its first session. It appointed a Sub-Committee with the task (*a*) to deal with communications concerning the status of women already received and to bring forward to the Commission such communications as might be of special interest; (*b*) to consider how the Commission should deal with such communications in the future. The Sub-Committee divided the communications into two categories, namely, those which express interest, give information or suggestions or offer co-operation and those which contain protests and requests for action. The Sub-Committee summarized the latter communications and drew the attention of the Commission thereto and assumed "that the subject matter therein contained would receive further discussion in the course of the development of the Commission's programme, since all of it is truly related to such a programme".

60. With respect to future communications, the Sub-Committee recommended and the Commission subsequently approved a procedure for handling them. Unlike the corresponding recommendations of the Commission on Human Rights, the recommendations of the Commission on the Status of Women did not contain a statement to the effect that the Commission on the Status of Women had no power to take any action in regard to any complaints relating to matters within its competence. In other respects, the recommendations of the Commission on the Status of Women did not substantially differ from the corresponding recommendations of the Commission on Human Rights.

1. Economic and Social Council resolutions 75 (V) and 76 (V)

61. The Economic and Social Council considered the reports of both Commissions at its fifth session. On the recommendation of its Social Committee, the Council adopted on 5 August 1947 resolutions 75 (V) and 76 (V) dealing respectively with communications concerning human rights and communications concerning the status of women. In resolution 75 (V), the Council approved the statement that the Commission on Human Rights "recognized that it has no power to take any action in regard to any complaints concerning human rights". In resolution 76 (V), the Council stated that it recognized that, as in the case of the Commission on Human rights, the Commission on the Status of Women had no power to take any action in regard to any complaints concerning the status of women.

62. The statement that the Commission on Human Rights had no power to take any action in regard to any complaints concerning human rights has, in subsequent years, repeatedly been the subject of consideration by the Commission and by principal organs. In 1949, the Secretary-General submitted to the Commission on Human Rights a comprehensive report "on the present situation with regard to communications concerning human rights", in which he made a series of technical observations including comments on the statement on the Commission's lack of power.[9]

---

[8] E/CN.4/14/Rev.2.

[9] E/CN.4/165.

2. ECONOMIC AND SOCIAL COUNCIL RESOLUTION 728 F (XXVIII)

63. Numerous attempts were made, between 1947 and 1959, to alter the "self-denying" rule contained in resolution 75 (V) and to establish a procedure for the handling of communications concerning human rights better calculated to promote respect for, and the observance of, those rights. None was successful, however, and when the Economic and Social Council finally consolidated human rights communications procedures in resolution 728 F (XXVIII) of 30 July 1959, it registered in paragraph 1 of the resolution its continued approval of the statement that "the Commission on Human Rights recognizes that it has no power to take any action in regard to any complaints concerning human rights". In paragraph 2 of the resolution, the Secretary-General was requested:

(a) To compile and distribute to members of the Commission on Human Rights before each session a non-confidential list containing a brief indication of the substance of each communication, however addressed, which deals with the principles involved in the promotion of universal respect for, and observance of, human rights and to divulge the identity of the authors of such communications unless they indicate that they wish their names to remain confidential;

(b) To compile before each session of the Commission a confidential list containing a brief indication of the substance of other communications concerning human rights, however addressed, and to furnish this list to members of the Commission, in private meeting, without divulging the identity of the authors of communications except in cases where the authors state that they have already divulged or intend to divulge their names or that they have no objection to their names being divulged;

(c) To enable the members of the Commission, upon request, to consult the originals of communications dealing with the principles involved in the promotion of universal respect for, and observance of, human rights;

(d) To inform the writers of all communications concerning human rights, however addressed, that their communications will be handled in accordance with this resolution, indicating that the Commission has no power to take any action in regard to any complaint concerning human rights;

(e) To furnish each Member State concerned with a copy of any communication concerning human rights which refers explicitly to that State or to territories under its jurisdiction, without divulging the identity of the author, except as provided for in subparagraph (b) above;

(f) To ask Governments sending replies to communications brought to their attention in accordance with subparagraph (e) whether they wish their replies to be presented to the Commission in summary form or in full.

64. In the resolution, the Council further provided that members of the Sub-Commission on Prevention of Discrimination and Protection of Minorities should have, with respect to communications dealing with discrimination and minorities, the same facilities as were enjoyed by members of the Commission on Human Rights. The Council also suggested to the Commission on Human Rights, as it had earlier, in resolution 75 (V), that it should at each session appoint an *ad hoc* committee to meet shortly before its following session for the purpose of reviewing the non-confidential list of communications prepared by the Secretary-General in accordance with paragraph 2 (a) of the resolution. An *ad hoc* committee of this nature has only been set up

by the Commission on three occasions, in 1948, 1949 and 1950 (at the Commission's third, fifth and sixth sessions) but never after the adoption of Council resolution 728 F (XXVIII), and a non-confidential list of communications has not been issued since the Commission's thirty-third session, in 1977.

3. COMMUNICATIONS REGARDING INFRINGEMENTS OF TRADE UNION RIGHTS, AND FORCED LABOUR

65. In accordance with Economic and Social Council resolutions 277 (X) of 17 February 1950 and 474 A (XV) of 9 April 1953, communications containing allegations of infringements of trade union rights received from Governments, or from trade union or employers' organizations, are forwarded by the Secretary-General, if they are against member States of the International Labour Organisation (ILO), to the ILO Governing Body, which considers whether or not to refer them to the Fact- Finding and Conciliation Commission.

66. In the event of the State concerned not being a member of ILO, the Secretary-General must submit the communication to the Council and, on its behalf, seek the consent of the Government concerned to having it forwarded to ILO. In the event of such consent not being forthcoming, the Council decides upon the alternative action to be taken. On several occasions in recent years, the Council has transmitted such communications to the *Ad Hoc* Working Group of Experts on Southern Africa of the Commission on Human Rights, which has investigated and reported on them.

67. Economic and Social Council resolution 607 (XXI) of 1 May 1956 provides that the Secretary-General transmit any information received on forced labour to the Director-General of the International Labour Office.

4. COMMUNICATIONS RELATING TO GROSS VIOLATIONS OF HUMAN RIGHTS

68. In resolution 1102 (XL) of 4 March 1966, the Economic and Social Council, acting upon the initiative of the Special Committee on the Situation with regard to the Implementation of the Declaration on the Granting of Independence to Colonial Countries and Peoples, invited the Commission on Human Rights "to consider as a matter of importance and urgency the question of the violation of human rights and fundamental freedoms, including policies of racial discrimination and segregation and of *apartheid* in all countries, with particular reference to colonial and other dependent countries and territories, and to submit to the Council . . . its recommendations on measures to halt those violations". The Commission considered the question at its twenty-second session and, in resolution 2 B (XXII), informed the Council that, in order for it to deal completely with the question of violations of human rights in all countries, it would first have to consider the

means whereby it might be more fully informed of such violations. The Council, in resolution 1164 (XLI) of 5 August 1966, concurred in that view, and shortly thereafter the General Assembly, in resolution 2144 A (XXI) of 26 October 1966, invited the Council and the Commission to give urgent consideration to ways and means of improving the capacity of the United Nations to put a stop to violations of human rights wherever they might occur.

69. At its twenty-third session, in 1967, the Commission on Human Rights undertook a comprehensive examination of the problems involved in giving effect to the directives it had received from the General Assembly and the Economic and Social Council.[10] By resolution 6 (XXIII) of 22 March 1967, the Commission set up an *Ad Hoc* Study Group "to study in all its aspects the proposal to establish regional commissions on human rights within the United Nations system". In paragraph 2 of resolution 9 (XXIII) of 16 March 1967 it instructed the same Study Group "to study in all its aspects the question of the ways and means by which the Commission might be enabled or assisted to discharge functions in relation to violation of human rights . . . whilst maintaining and fulfilling its other functions". By resolution 7 (XXIII) of 16 March 1967, the Commission decided to appoint a Special Rapporteur to survey United Nations past action in its efforts to eliminate *apartheid* and to study the legislation and practices in South Africa, South West Africa and Southern Rhodesia instituted to establish and maintain *apartheid*, racial discrimination and related phenomena.

70. In resolution 8 (XXIII) of 16 March 1967, the Commission requested the Economic and Social Council to authorize the Commission and the Sub-Commission on Prevention of Discrimination and Protection of Minorities "to examine information relevant to gross violations of human rights . . . contained in the communications [concerning human rights] listed . . . pursuant to Council resolution 728 F (XXVIII). In the same resolution, the Commission further requested authority, in appropriate cases, and after careful consideration of the information thus made available to it, to make a thorough study and investigation of situations revealing a consistent pattern of violations of human rights. In paragraph 1 of resolution 9 (XXIII), the Commission recommended that the Council should confirm the inclusion in the terms of reference of the Commission of "the power to recommend and adopt general and specific measures to deal with violations of human rights".

5. ECONOMIC AND SOCIAL COUNCIL RESOLUTION 1235 (XLII)

71. Noting Commission resolutions 8 (XXIII) and 9 (XXIII), the Economic and Social Council, in resolu-

tion 1235 (XLII) of 6 June 1967, granted the Commission and the Sub-Commission the authority they had sought, "to examine information relevant to gross violations of human rights and fundamental freedoms . . . in all countries . . .". The Council thus took a decision of principle that in certain situations the Commission and the Sub-Commission might take action concerning complaints in the matter of human rights. In the resolution, the Council decided that the Commission could, in appropriate cases and after careful consideration of the information thus made available to it, "make a thorough study of situations which reveal a consistent pattern of violations of human rights . . . and report, with recommendations thereon, to the Council".

72. Work on the problem of preparing new procedures for the handling of human rights communications was undertaken by the Sub-Commission on Prevention of Discrimination and Protection of Minorities. On the basis of a draft prepared by the Sub-Commission, the Commission, at its twenty-fifth session, in 1968, submitted to the Council a draft resolution entitled "Procedure for dealing with communications relating to violations of human rights and fundamental freedoms". The main provisions of the draft resolution were adopted by the Council in resolution 1503 (XLVIII) of 27 May 1970.

6. ECONOMIC AND SOCIAL COUNCIL RESOLUTION 1503 (XLVIII)

73. At its resumed forty-eighth session, in 1970, the Economic and Social Council, acting on the recommendation of the Commission on Human Rights, adopted resolution 1503 (XLVIII) of 27 May 1970, entitled "Procedure for dealing with communications relating to violations of human rights and fundamental freedoms". The main features of the procedure—the rules concerning the question of admissibility of communications, the application of the procedure by the implementing bodies, the rule of confidentiality and the question of the review of the procedure—will be dealt with below.

(a) *Main features*

74. In accordance with paragraph 1 of the resolution, a five-member working group of the Sub-Commission on Prevention of Discrimination and Protection of Minorities, the Working Group on Communications, meets annually for two weeks, immediately before the session of the Sub-Commission, to consider all communications and Government replies thereon received by the Secretary-General under Council resolution 728 F (XXVIII) of 30 July 1959, with a view to bringing to the attention of the Sub-Commission those communications, together with replies from Governments, if any, which appear to reveal a consistent pattern of gross and

---

[10] *Official Records of the Economic and Social Council, Forty-second Session, Supplement No. 6*, chap. V, resolutions 5 (XXIII), 6 (XXIII), 7 (XXIII), 8 (XXIII) and 9 (XXIII).

reliably attested violations of human rights and fundamental freedoms. A decision to refer a communication to the Sub-Commission requires the support of a majority of the members of the Working Group on Communications. No further action is taken under the procedure in respect of communications which are not referred to the Sub-Commission.

75. Under paragraph 5 of the resolution, the role of the Sub-Commission on Prevention of Discrimination and Protection of Minorities is to consider the selection of communications, and the Government replies relating thereto, brought before it by the Working Group on Communications, with a view to determining whether to refer to the Commission on Human Rights any particular situations which appear to reveal a consistent pattern of gross and reliably attested violations of human rights.

76. Substantive examination of the particular situations then takes place in the Commission on Human Rights, which, as provided in paragraph 6 of the resolution, is called on to determine (a) whether a particular situation requires a thorough study and a report and recommendations thereon to the Economic and Social Council, in accordance with the authority granted in Council resolution 1235 (XLII) (see para. 71 above), or (b) whether a particular situation may be a subject of an investigation by an *ad hoc* committee to be appointed by the Commission. The latter alternative, however, is subject to the express consent of the State concerned. To assist it in its task under the resolution, the Commission on Human Rights has every year since 1974 set up a working group of its own (see (c) Application of the procedures, paras. 88-94 below).

77. A number of basic functions are assigned to the Secretary-General in paragraph 4 of the resolution. He is called on (a) to furnish to the members of the Sub-Commission every month a list of communications prepared by him in accordance with Council resolution 728 F (XXVIII) and a brief description of them, together with the text of any replies received from Governments; (b) to make available to the members of the Working Group on Communications at their meetings the originals of such communications listed as they may request, having due regard to the provisions of paragraph 2 (b) of Council resolution 728 F (XXVIII) concerning the divulging of the identity of the authors of communications; and (c) to circulate to the members of the Sub-Commission, in the working languages, the text of such communications as are referred to the Sub-Commission by the Working Group on Communications. Acting on a recommendation from the Commission (Commission decision 7 (XXXI) of 24 February 1975), the Council further requested the Secretary-General, in decision 79 (LVIII) of 6 May 1975, to furnish the monthly lists of communications also to the members of the Commission.

(b) *Admissibility of communications*

78. As an initial step in the implementation of the resolution, the Economic and Social Council requested the Sub-Commission on Prevention of Discrimination and Protection of Minorities to devise appropriate procedures for dealing with the question of admissibility of communications. Provisional procedures for this purpose were adopted by the Sub-Commission in resolution 1 (XXIV) of 13 August 1971.

79. The Sub-Commission's provisional procedure provides, under the heading "Standards and criteria", that the object of the communication must not be inconsistent with the relevant principles of the Charter, the Universal Declaration of Human Rights or of other applicable instruments in the field of human rights. It then paraphrases the provisions of Council resolutions 1235 (XLII) and 1503 (XLVIII) in providing that communications shall be admissible only if, after consideration thereof, together with the replies, if any, of the Governments concerned, there are reasonable grounds to believe that they may reveal a consistent pattern of gross and reliably attested violations of human rights and fundamental freedoms, including policies of racial discrimination and segregation and *apartheid* of any country, including colonial and other dependent countries and peoples.

80. On the question of the source of communications, the provisional procedure provides that admissible communications may originate from a person or group of persons who, it can be reasonably presumed, are victims of the violations and also from any person or group of persons who have direct and reliable knowledge of those violations. Communications from non-governmental organizations are admissible if the organization concerned acts in good faith in accordance with recognized principles of human rights, not resorting to politically motivated stands contrary to the provisions of the Charter, and has direct and reliable knowledge of such violations. Communications are not inadmissible solely because the knowledge of the individual authors is second-hand, provided that they are accompanied by clear evidence. Anonymous communications are inadmissible.

81. The author of a communication, whether an individual, a group of individuals or an organization, must be clearly identified. This, however, is, pursuant to paragraph 4 (b) of resolution 1503 (XLVIII) and paragraph 2 (b) of the provisional procedure, subject to the provision of Council resolution 728 F (XXVIII), which provides that the identity of the authors must not be divulged, except in cases where the authors state that they have already divulged or intend to divulge their names or that they have no objection to their names being divulged.

82. Under the heading "Contents of communications and nature of allegations", the provisional procedure provides for a series of further conditions governing the admissibility of communications. The communication must contain a description of the facts and must indicate the purpose of the petition and the rights that have been violated. Communications are inadmissible if

their language is essentially abusive and in particular if they contain insulting references to the State against which the complaint is directed. Such communications may, however, be considered if they meet the other criteria for admissibility after deletion of the abusive language.

83. Elaborating upon the general requirement that the subject of the communication must not be inconsistent with the relevant principles of the Charter, the provisional procedure further provides that a communication shall be inadmissible if it has manifestly political motivations and its subject is contrary to the provisions of the Charter.

84. While, as already indicated, communications are not inadmissible solely because the author's knowledge is second-hand, a communication is inadmissible if it appears to be based exclusively on reports disseminated by mass media.

85. Under the heading "Existence of other remedies", the provisional procedure makes provision for the avoidance of the overlapping with other existing procedures, for the exhaustion of domestic remedies and for the exclusion of the repeated submission to United Nations organs of communications already settled in accordance with human rights principles.

86. It is provided, in particular, that communications shall be inadmissible if their admission would prejudice the functions of the specialized agencies of the United Nations. Communications shall be inadmissible if domestic remedies have not been exhausted, unless it appears that such remedies would be ineffective or unreasonably prolonged. Any failure to exhaust remedies must be satisfactorily explained.

87. Having adopted the procedure concerning the question of admissibility of communications, the Sub-Commission adopted resolution 2 (XXIV) of 16 August 1971 concerning the establishment of the Working Group on Communications envisaged in paragraph 1 of Council resolution 1503 (XLVIII). Thus, the stage was set for the application of the new procedure.

(c) *Application of the procedures*

88. The Working Group on Communications has met every year since 1972, except in 1986 when the annual sessions of the Sub-Commission and its pre-sessional working group were cancelled. From 1972 to 1987 the Working Group has had before it for consideration over 350,000 communications and several thousand Government replies relating thereto. Any decision to refer a communication to the Sub-Commission requires the affirmative vote of at least three members of the Working Group. Although the number of communications referred to the Sub-Commission is relatively small in comparison with the total number of communications reviewed by the Working Group, the material thus brought to the Sub-Commission's attention is often voluminous, in some years adding up to between 1,000 and 2,000 pages in document form. In accordance with paragraph 2 of Sub-Commission resolution 2 (XXIV), and in conformity with paragraph 8 of Council resolution 1503 (XLVIII), the decisions of the Working Group are communicated to the Sub-Commission annually in a confidential report. The text of the communications referred to the Sub-Commission is reproduced in addenda to the report.

89. At its twenty-fifth session, in 1972, the Sub-Commission on Prevention of Discrimination and Protection of Minorities had before it the first report of the Working Group on Communications, including the full text, in the working languages, of the communications brought to its attention, as provided in paragraph 4 (c) of Council resolution 1503 (XLVIII). After consideration of the material brought before it, the Sub-Commission adopted a public resolution, requesting the Secretary-General to inform Governments of the importance it attached to such replies as Governments might wish to submit in respect of the communications channelled into the procedure and suggesting that the Working Group on Communications might, at its second session in 1973, re-examine the communications singled out in its first report, in the light of Government replies which might subsequently be received. No particular situations were referred to the Commission on Human Rights at that time.

90. At its twenty-sixth session, in 1973, the Sub-Commission had before it the second report of the Working Group on Communications and took action thereon under paragraph 5 of Council resolution 1503 (XLVIII) by referring a number of particular human rights situations to the Commission on Human Rights for consideration. Since then, the Sub-Commission has every year (except in 1986 when its annual session was cancelled) referred particular human rights situations to the Commission for consideration under the 1503 procedure. As of the thirty-ninth session of the Sub-Commission, held from 10 August to 4 September 1987, particular human rights situations in 42 countries have been referred to the Commission on Human Rights under the procedure.

91. At its thirtieth session, in 1974, the Commission on Human Rights was for the first time seized of material referred to it by the Sub-Commission under Council resolution 1503 (XLVIII). After consideration of a number of procedural and substantive questions relating to the application of the procedure, the Commission decided, in decision 3 (XXX) of 6 March 1974, to refer the relevant documents to the Governments concerned with the request that they make written observations thereon in time for the Commission's next session. As a standing instruction for the future, the Commission requested the Sub-Commission, whenever it decides to refer a particular situation to the Commission, to so inform the Government concerned and, at the same time, to invite the Government to make its written observations on the material in question in order to enable the Commission to take them into account when examining the situation. In the same decision, the

Commission also decided to establish, with the approval of the Economic and Social Council, a working group of five Commission members, to meet for one week before its next session, in 1975, to examine the material which had been transmitted to the Commission by the Sub-Commission, together with any observations which might have been received by then from the Governments concerned and such further material as might be transmitted to the Commission by the following session of the Sub-Commission. With the approval of the Council, the Commission has every year since 1974 set up such a working group to assist it in the implementation of the 1503 procedure. This working group, which by now must be regarded as a permanent feature in the application of the procedure, has become known as the Working Group on Situations. It places before the Commission every year a recommendation for the course of action to take on each particular situation which the Commission has before it, both those referred for the first time to the Commission and those which the Commission has decided to keep pending before it under the procedure.

92.   In the course of the years, the Commission has adopted a number of further procedural decisions concerning the general application of the procedure. By decisions 3 to 5 (XXXIV) of 3 March 1978, the Commission decided (a) that the Chairman/Rapporteur of the Sub-Commission's Working Group on Communications should be invited to attend the relevant closed meetings of the Commission; (b) that the Sub-Commission and the Working Group on Communications would have access to the records of the Commission relating to the 1503 procedure, together with all other confidential Commission documents pertaining thereto; and (c) that the Governments concerned should be invited to attend and participate in the relevant closed meetings of the Commission. To facilitate a meaningful participation and co-operation by the Governments concerned, the Commission decided, by decision 14 (XXXV) of 12 March 1979, that the Working Group on Situations should transmit the text of its recommendations to the Governments concerned, as soon as possible, and, by decision 9 (XXXVI) of 7 March 1980, that the Government representatives, invited to participate, should have the right to be represented not only during the substantive debate concerning the human rights situation in their country, but also during the adoption of the Commission's decision thereon.

93.   In the practical application of the procedure governed by Economic and Social Council resolution 1503 (XLVIII), the Commission on Human Rights has devised its own working methods, not explicitly spelled out in the resolution. The method of conducting a thorough study under paragraph 6 (a) of the resolution has only been applied once and the method of setting up an *ad hoc* investigatory body, with the consent of the Government concerned, has never been used. Instead, the Commission has strived for establishing a meaningful dialogue with the Governments of the countries concerned, through direct contacts, conducted between

Commission sessions, either by the Secretary-General or by special representatives or independent experts, who are appointed by the Commission and requested to report to the following session. Government co-operation in exercises of this nature has steadily grown through the years, as the procedure itself has become more readily accepted and recognized. On a number of occasions, the Commission has had the occasion to compliment Governments for the unreserved co-operation given to its special representatives or independent experts in connection with on-the-spot visits, during which they had free access to people from all walks of life, both government officials and private persons of all shades of opinion.

94.   Wishing to be regularly informed about the implementation of its decisions under Council resolution 1503 (XLVIII), the Commission, in resolution 15 (XXXIV) of 7 March 1978, requested the Secretary-General to report thereon, quarterly, to the members of the Commission.

(d) *Confidentiality*

95.   Paragraph 8 of Council resolution 1503 (XLVIII) lays down the rule of confidentiality which governs the functions of the bodies involved in its implementation. It stipulates that "all actions" envisaged in the implementation of the resolution by the Sub-Commission or the Commission "shall remain confidential until such time as the Commission may decide to make recommendations to the Economic and Social Council". This rule of confidentiality applies also to the working groups of the Commission and the Sub-Commission. The meetings of all these bodies are, accordingly, held in private and their records and all other documents relating thereto remain confidential until such time as the Council may decide otherwise. However, since the Commission's thirty-fourth session, in 1978, the Chairman has each year, after the closed meetings, made a public statement indicating which countries have been under examination under the procedure. In the interest of equity, the Chairman has in recent years made a distinction between the country situations that remain under consideration within the procedure and the situations in respect of which the Commission has decided to take no further action under the procedure.

96.   Acting on recommendations from the Commission, or upon its own initiative (after examination of a particular situation has been concluded), the Economic and Social Council has on a number of occasions decided that confidential material which the Commission has had before it under the procedure should no longer be restricted. By decision 1979/35 of 10 May 1979 the Council decided that the relevant material concerning Equatorial Guinea should no longer be restricted, by decision 1985/139 of 30 May 1985 that the material concerning Uruguay should no longer be restricted, by decision 1985/156 of 30 May 1985 that the material concerning Argentina should no longer be restricted, by

decision 1986/147 of 23 May 1986 that the material concerning the Philippines should no longer be restricted, and by decision 1987/140 of 29 May 1987 that the confidential report of the Special Representative of the Commission on the human rights situation in Haiti should be made public.

(e) *Review of the procedure*

97. Paragraph 10 of Council resolution 1503 (XLVIII) envisaged that the procedure set out in it for dealing with communications relating to violations of human rights should be reviewed "if any new organ entitled to deal with such communications should be established within the United Nations or by international agreement".

98. Following the entry into force on 23 March 1976 of the International Covenant on Civil and Political Rights and the Optional Protocol thereto and the establishment of the Human Rights Committee, which, under the Optional Protocol, receives and considers communications from individuals claiming to be victims of violations of the rights enumerated in the Covenant, the Commission on Human Rights, in resolution 16 (XXXIV) of 7 March 1978, requested the Secretary-General to prepare for its thirty-fifth session "an analysis of existing United Nations procedures for dealing with communications concerning violations of human rights, to assist the Commission in studying measures to avoid possible duplication and overlapping of work in the implementation of these procedures". A public document of this nature (E/CN.4/1317) was placed before the thirty-fifth session by the Secretary-General, as requested. The document basically concluded, after a detailed comparison of the two procedures, that there might not be any substantive duplication or overlapping in their implementation (see further paragraph 114 below, concerning the basic differences between the two procedures). It offered, however, some practical suggestions of a technical nature, aimed at avoiding any duplication and overlapping at the initial Secretariat stage (having mainly to do with the sorting out of the incoming mail), with a view to ensuring proper channelling of material into each procedure.

99. No further action has been taken by the Commission or the Council under paragraph 10 of Council resolution 1503 (XLVIII). However, at the thirty-ninth session of the Sub-Commission on Prevention of Discrimination and Protection of Minorities, in 1987, a draft resolution was introduced concerning the advisability of reviewing the procedure (E/CN.4/Sub.2/1987/L.27). After an exchange of views and the submission of two amendments (E/CN.4/Sub.2/1987/L.43 and E/CN.4/Sub.2/1987/L.47), the Sub-Commission decided, in decision 1987/102 of 31 August 1987, to postpone consideration of the draft resolution and the amendments thereto to its fortieth session in 1988.

7. OPTIONAL PROTOCOL PROCEDURE

100. Under article 1 of the Optional Protocol to the International Covenant on Civil and Political Rights, a State party to the Covenant that becomes party to the Protocol recognizes the competence of the Human Rights Committee to receive and consider communications from individuals subject to its jurisdiction who claim to be victims of a violation by that State of any of the rights set forth in the Covenant. Article 2 specifies that individuals who claim that any of their rights have been violated and who have exhausted all available domestic remedies may submit a written communication to the Committee for consideration. Forty of the 87 States which have acceded to or ratified the Covenant have accepted the competence of the Committee to deal with individual complaints by ratifying or acceding to the Optional Protocol. These States are: Argentina, Austria, Barbados, Bolivia, Cameroon, Canada, Central African Republic, Colombia, Congo, Costa Rica, Denmark, Dominican Republic, Ecuador, Equatorial Guinea, Finland, France, Iceland, Italy, Jamaica, Luxembourg, Madagascar, Mauritius, Netherlands, Nicaragua, Niger, Norway, Panama, Peru, Portugal, Saint Vincent and the Grenadines, San Marino, Senegal, Spain, Suriname, Sweden, Trinidad and Tobago, Uruguay, Venezuela, Zaire and Zambia. No communication can be received by the Committee if it concerns a State party to the Covenant which is not also a party to the Optional Protocol. Consideration of communications under the Optional Protocol takes place in closed meetings and the documents pertaining to the work of the Committee under the Optional Protocol (submissions from the parties and other working documents of the Committee) are confidential.

(a) *Admissibility*

101. Once a communication has been registered, the Committee must decide whether it is admissible under the Optional Protocol. The requirements for admissibility, which are contained in articles 1, 2, 3 and 5 (2) of the Optional Protocol, are listed in rule 90 of the Committee's provisional rules of procedure, pursuant to which the Committee shall ascertain:

(*a*) That the communication is not anonymous and that it emanates from an individual, or individuals, subject to the jurisdiction of a State party to the Protocol;

(*b*) That the individual claims to be a victim of a violation by that State party of any of the rights set forth in the Covenant. Normally, the communication should be submitted by the individual himself or by his representative; the Committee may, however, accept to consider a communication submitted on behalf of an alleged victim when it appears that he is unable to submit the communication himself;

(*c*) That the communication does not constitute an abuse of the right of submission under the Protocol;

(*d*) That the communication is not incompatible with the provisions of the Covenant;

(*e*) That the same matter is not being examined under another procedure of international investigation or settlement;

(*f*) That the individual has exhausted all available domestic remedies.

102.   Under rule 91 (1) the Committee or its Working Group on Communications[11] may request the State party concerned or the author of the communication to submit, within a time-limit which is indicated in each such decision (normally six weeks or two months), additional written information or observations relevant to the question of admissibility of the communication. Such a request does not imply that any decision has been taken on the question of admissibility (rule 91 (3)). If the case is referred to the State party at this stage, any reply received from it is transmitted to the author to give him an opportunity to comment thereon. If the case is only referred back to the author for clarifications under rule 91 and is subsequently declared inadmissible, no transmittal to the State party may have taken place. The Committee may also decide to discontinue consideration of a communication without the adoption of a written decision (e.g. when it is withdrawn or when the author otherwise indicates that he does not wish to pursue the matter). A decision to declare a communication admissible or inadmissible rests with the Committee itself, not with the Working Group on Communications.

(b) *Merits*

103.   If a communication is declared admissible, the Committee proceeds to consider the substance of the complaint. In accordance with article 4 of the Optional Protocol, it requests the State party concerned to submit to the Committee "explanations or statements clarifying the matter and the remedy, if any, which may have been taken" by it. Under article 4 (2), the State party has a time-limit of six months in which to submit its observations. When these observations are received by the Secretariat, the author is given an opportunity to comment thereon. The Committee then normally formulates its views and forwards them to the State party and to the author of the communication, in accordance with article 5 (4) of the Optional Protocol. Before the adoption of final views, further information may be sought from the State party or the author by means of an interim decision. Throughout the proceedings, the principle of equality of arms prevails. Unless a communication is declared inadmissible without referral to the State party, both parties are given an opportunity to comment on each other's submissions.

---

[11] Rule 91 simply refers to "a Working Group" having this competence. The Committee has in practice institutionalized this Working Group, which is generally referred to as the Working Group on Communications.

(c) *Interim measures*

104.   Rule 86 of the Committee's provisional rules of procedure provides that the Committee may, prior to the forwarding of its final views on a communication, inform the State party whether interim measures of protection may be desirable to avoid irreparable damage to the victim of the alleged violation. Such request for interim measures does not imply a determination of the merits of the communication. The Committee has had occasion to request interim measures in a number of cases, e.g. where it informed the State party of the view of the Committee "that pending further consideration of the case, the alleged victim, having sought refuge in S., should not be handed over or expelled to Country X". In an interim decision relating to another case, the Committee expressed concern over the state of health of the alleged victim and requested the State party "as a matter of urgency to arrange for him to be examined by a competent medical board and . . . to furnish the Committee with a copy of the board's report". The Committee has also adopted a number a decisions requesting a State party to refrain from carrying out a death sentence pending further examination of the communication.

(d) *Evidence and burden of proof*

105.   Thus far the Committee has not developed any independent fact-finding functions under the Optional Protocol, but it is required pursuant to article 5 (1) of the Optional Protocol to consider "all written information made available to it" by the parties.

106.   With respect to the burden of proof, the Committee has established in a number of cases dealing with alleged violations of articles 6 (right to life), 7 (torture and ill-treatment) and 9 (arbitrary arrest, disappeared persons), that

this cannot rest alone on the author of the communication, especially considering that the author and the State party do not always have equal access to the evidence and that frequently the State party alone has access to relevant information. It is implicit in article 4 (2) of the Optional Protocol that the State party has the duty to investigate in good faith all allegations of violation of the Covenant made against it and its authorities, especially when such allegations are corroborated by evidence submitted by the author of the communication, and to furnish to the Committee the information available to it. In cases where the author has submitted to the Committee allegations supported by substantial witness testimony, as in this case, and where further clarification of the case depends on information exclusively in the hands of the State party, the Committee may consider such allegations as substantiated in the absence of satisfactory evidence and explanations to the contrary from the State party.

Furthermore, the Committee has held that "a refutation of [the author's] allegation in general terms is not sufficient".

(e) *Individual opinions*

107.   The Committee in practice works by consensus without resorting to voting as provided for in article 39

(2) (*b*) of the Covenant. However, pursuant to rule 94 (3) of the Committee's provisional rules of procedure, members can append their individual opinions to the Committee's views. Such individual opinions have been appended to the Committee's views in seven cases. Individual opinions have also been appended in three cases to decisions declaring communications inadmissible.

(f) *Duration of the procedure*

108.   Since the Committee, which meets three times a year, must allow both the author and the State party sufficient time to prepare their submissions, a decision on admissibility can only be taken between six months and a year after the initial submission; views under Article 5 (4) of the Optional Protocol may follow one year later. The entire procedure normally may be completed within two to three years. The committee tries to deal expeditiously with all communications.

(g) *Progress of work*

109.   Since the Committee started its work under the Optional Protocol at its second session, in 1977, at the closure of its thirty-first session (October/November 1987), 260 communications relating to 24 States parties had been placed before it for consideration. The status of registered communications is as follows:

(*a*) Concluded by the adoption of views under article 5 (4) of
the Optional Protocol................................ 81

(*b*) Concluded by decision of inadmissibility 61

(*c*) Discontinued (without a written decision) or withdrawn ... 52

(*d*) Declared admissible, not yet concluded 16

(*e*) Pending at pre-admissibility stage..................... 50

Violations of the provisions of the Covenant have been found by the Committee in 72 of the 81 communications concluded with the adoption of views.

(h) *Publicity*

110.   As indicated in paragraph 100 above, consideration of communications under the optional Protocol takes place in closed meetings and the documents pertaining to the procedure are confidential. Accordingly, the rule of confidentiality prevails while a communication is under consideration. A summary of the Committee's work under the Optional Protocol is, however, included in its annual report to the General Assembly, as provided in article 6 of the Protocol.

111.   Notwithstanding the confidentiality of the proceedings while a communication is under consideration, the Committee has from the outset followed the practice of making public the text of its decisions of a final nature, both views adopted under article 5 (4) of the Optional Protocol and decisions declaring communications

inadmissible. These decisions have been reproduced in annexes to the Committee's annual reports.[12]

112.   At its fifteenth session, held in 1982, the Committee decided to proceed with the periodical publication of a selection of its decisions under the Optional Protocol, including, in addition to decisions of a final nature, certain important decisions declaring communications admissible and other decisions of an interlocutory nature. Volume I of this series, covering decisions taken from the second to the sixteenth sessions inclusive, was published in 1985 in English.[13] Volume II, covering decisions taken from the seventeenth to the thirty-second sessions inclusive, is to be published late in 1988.

8. DIFFERENCES BETWEEN THE 1503 PROCEDURE AND THE OPTIONAL PROTOCOL PROCEDURE

113.   The main features and application of the procedures governed, on the one hand, by Economic and Social Council resolution 1503 (XLVIII) and, on the other hand, by the procedure set out in the Optional Protocol to the International Covenant on Civil and Political Rights, have been dealt with in paragraphs 73 to 112 above. It emerges that there are some basic differences between these two procedures, which, in general, would apply also in a comparison between the former procedure and other existing treaty-based procedures (see paragraphs 115 *et seq.* below).

114.   The fundamental difference between the procedure under resolution 1503 (XLVIII) and the procedure under the Optional Protocol is that the former is concerned with the examination of situations, whereas the latter is concerned with the examination of individual complaints, i.e., isolated instances of alleged violations of human rights. The Human Rights Committee has adopted the view that, in principle, there is no overlapping or duplication of work between the two procedures, because of the different mandates given to the bodies entrusted with their implementation.

115.   Other differences between the procedure under Council resolution 1503 (XLVIII) and that established under the Optional Protocol include the following:

(*a*) The former is based on a resolution of a United Nations organ, and its implementation is to a high degree dependent on the voluntary co-operation of States,

---

[12] See *Official Records of the General Assembly, Thirty-fourth Session, Supplement No. 40* (A/34/40); *Thirty-fifth Session, Supplement No. 40* (A/35/40); *Thirty-sixth Session, Supplement No. 40* (A/36/40); *Thirty-seventh Session, Supplement No. 40* (A/37/40); *Thirty-eighth Session, Supplement No. 40* (A/38/40); *Thirty-ninth Session, Supplement No. 40* (A/39/40); *Fortieth Session, Supplement No. 40* (A/40/40); *Forty-first Session, Supplement No. 40* (A/41/40); *Forty-second Session, Supplement No. 40* (A/42/40).

[13] CCPR/C/OP/1, United Nations publication, Sales No. E.84.XIV.2. French and Spanish versions of volume I will be published in 1988.

whereas the latter is based on a binding international treaty under which States parties have accepted the application of a specific procedure for the examination of certain claims brought against them;

(*b*) The former is applicable with regard to all States, whereas the latter is applicable only with regard to States parties to the Optional Protocol;

(*c*) The former embraces violations of all human rights and fundamental freedoms, whereas the latter is restricted to those civil and political rights which are protected by the International Covenant on Civil and Political Rights;

(*d*) The former is applicable to communications from any person, group of persons or non-governmental organizations that claim to have reliable knowledge, direct or second-hand, of the alleged violations, whereas the latter requires a certain standing by the author, i.e., the communication must either be signed by the alleged victim or by his duly appointed representative, or by someone having the authority to act on behalf of the alleged victim; in this connection, the Committee regards close family connection as a sufficient link to justify an author acting on behalf of an alleged victim, but has declined to consider communications where the authors have failed to establish any link between themselves and the alleged victim;

(*e*) Under the former procedure the authors of communications have no standing. They are not involved at any stage in the implementation of the procedure and are not privy to any action taken by the implementing bodies, unless it is made public in accordance with paragraph 8 of the procedure. The authors are merely informed by the Secretariat that their communications have been received, that copies of them have been furnished to the Member States concerned and that summaries of their contents will be made available to the members of the Sub-Commission on Prevention of Discrimination and Protection of Minorities and the members of the Commission on Human Rights in accordance with the procedure. Under the latter procedure the author of a communication placed before the Human Rights Committee has full standing at all stages in the implementation of the procedure. He is informed of all actions taken by the Committee, or its Working Group on Communications, as is the State party concerned, and is given, at all stages, an opportunity to comment on any written submission made by the State party.

9. OTHER TREATY-BASED PROCEDURES

116. Since the entry into force of the International Covenant on Civil and Political Rights and the Optional Protocol thereto on 23 March 1976, two other treaty-based procedures for dealing with communications have come into force, i.e., the procedure governed by article 14 of the International Convention on the Elimination of All Forms of Racial Discrimination and the procedure governed by article 22 of the Convention against

Torture and Other Cruel, Inhuman or Degrading Treatment or Punishment.

(a) *Article 14 of the International Convention on the Elimination of All Forms of Racial Discrimination*

117. Under article 14 of the International Convention on the Elimination of All Forms of Racial Discrimination, individuals or groups of individuals who claim that any of their rights enumerated in the Convention have been violated by a State party and who have exhausted all available domestic remedies may submit written communications to the Committee on the Elimination of Racial Discrimination for consideration. Twelve of the 124 States that have ratified or acceded to the Convention have declared that they recognize the competence of the Committee to receive and consider communications under article 14 of the Convention. These States are Costa Rica, Denmark, Ecuador, France, Iceland, Italy, Netherlands, Norway, Peru, Senegal, Sweden and Uruguay. No communication can be received by the Committee if it concerns a State party to the Convention which has not recognized the competence of the Committee to receive and consider communications.

118. Consideration of communications under article 14 of the Convention takes places in closed meetings (rule 88 of the Committee's rules of procedure). All documents pertaining to the work of the Committee under article 14 (submissions from the parties and other working documents of the Committee) are confidential.

119. In carrying out its work under article 14 of the Convention, the Committee may be assisted by a working group of not more than five of its members, which submits recommendations to the Committee regarding the fulfilment of the conditions of admissibility of communications (rule 87) or on the action to be taken in respect of communications which have been declared admissible (rule 95, para. 1).

120. The competence of the Committee to exercise the functions provided for in article 14, paragraph 9, of the Convention became effective on 3 December 1982, and the Committee commenced its work under article 14 of the Convention at its thirteenth session, in 1984. Under article 14, paragraph 8, of the Convention, the Committee shall include in its annual report a summary of the communications considered by it and of the explanations and statements of the States parties concerned, together with the Committee's own suggestions and recommendations thereon. The Committee's work under article 14 of the Convention has not yet reached that reporting stage.

(b) *Article 22 of the Convention against Torture*

121. Under article 22 of the Convention against Torture and Other Cruel, Inhuman or Degrading Treatment or Punishment, individuals who claim to be victims of a

violation by a State party of the provisions of the Convention and who have exhausted all available domestic remedies may submit written communications to the Committee against Torture for consideration. By the end of 1987, 10 of the 28 States that had ratified or acceded to the Convention had declared that they recognized the competence of the Committee to receive and consider communications under article 22 of the Convention. These States are Argentina, Austria, Denmark, France, Luxembourg, Norway, Spain, Sweden, Switzerland and Togo. No communication can be received by the Committee if it concerns a State party to the Convention which has not recognized the competence of the Committee to receive and consider comuications. Consideration of communications takes place in closed meetings, in accordance with paragraph 6 of article 22 of the Convention.[14]

10. COMMUNICATIONS FROM NON-GOVERNMENTAL ORGANIZATIONS ALLEGING VIOLATIONS OF HUMAN RIGHTS

122. Under the rules governing the Economic and Social Council's consultation with non-governmental organizations which are concerned with matters within its competence, set out in Council resolution 1296 (XLIV) of 23 May 1968, such organizations have certain rights to make submissions, in written or oral form, to the Council and its subsidiary bodies.

123. In 1952, some difficulty arose regarding the circulation of written statements, submitted by non-governmental organizations in consultative status, which consisted of or contained complaints of alleged violations of human rights. The Secretary-General consulted the Council's Committee on Non-Governmental Organizations on the matter, and requested guidance as to the procedure to be followed in regard to such statements.

124. In its report on the question, the Committee suggested that the Secretary-General should handle such communications in accordance with Council resolution 75 (V), subsequently replaced by resolution 728 F (XXVIII). This recommendation was approved by the Economic and Social Council in resolution 454 (XIV) of 28 July 1952.

125. At its thirty-first session, in 1975, the Commission on Human Rights adopted resolution 7 (XXXI) of 24 February 1975, containing a draft resolution for consideration by the Economic and Social Council relating to written and oral statements by non-governmental organizations in consultative status. On the recommendation of the Commission, the Council, in resolution 1919 (LVIII) of 5 May 1975, recalled that in resolution 454 (XIV) it had decided "that all communications emanating from non-governmental organizations in

consultative status containing complaints of alleged violations of human rights should be dealt with not under the rules of consultative relationship but under the decisions for the inclusion of such material in confidential lists of communications prepared for the Commission on Human Rights, as further set out in paragraph 2 (*b*) of Council resolution 728 F (XXVIII)". The Council confirmed, that communications from non-governmental organizations containing complaints of alleged violations of human rights should be handled according to the provisions of Council resolutions 454 (XIV) and 728 F (XXVIII), paragraph 2 (*b*).

11. COMMUNICATIONS CONCERNING THE STATUS AND ADVANCEMENT OF WOMEN

126. Reference has been made above[15] to Economic and Social Council resolution 76 (V) of 5 August 1947, dealing with communications concerning the status of women. That procedure, as amended by Council resolution 304 I (XI) of 17 July 1950, is essentially the same as the one established by Council resolution 728 F (XXVIII) of 30 July 1959.

127. Council resolution 76 (V), as amended, calls for two separate lists to be prepared for the Commission on the Status of Women: a non-confidential list containing summaries of communications dealing with the principles relating to the promotion of the status of women in the political, economic, social, civil and educational fields, and a confidential list containing summaries of "other communications", i.e., communications containing allegations of violations of human rights affecting the status of women. A summary of all these communications is, however, also included in the lists prepared for the Commission on Human Rights and the Sub-Commission on Prevention of Discrimination and Protection of Minorities under Council resolutions 728 F (XXVIII) and 1503 (XLVIII).

128. The procedure provided for in Council resolution 76 (V) was in suspense from 1974 to 1980, after the Commission had decided to delete consideration of communications from its work programme, in view of the expanded procedure for dealing with communications established by Council resolution 1503 (XLVIII). However, at its twenty-eighth session, in 1980, the Commission on the Status of Women appointed an *Ad Hoc* Working Group on Communications consisting of five representatives, which considered in private meetings a confidential list of communications, a non-confidential list of communications, and a note by the Secretariat entitled "Relevant resolutions and procedures dealing with communications concerning human rights and the status of women". On the basis of its consideration of this question, the Commission prepared two draft resolutions for the Economic and Social Council, one on fundamental freedoms guaranteed to individuals, calling upon Governments to ensure that no

---

[14] The rules of procedure relating to the functions of the Committee against Torture under article 22 of the Convention were adopted at its first session, held from 8 to 22 April 1988.

[15] Section C, 1, of the present chapter.

one can be prosecuted, persecuted or harassed simply because of a familly or social relationship with an accused or convicted person, and the other calling upon Governments to pay particular attention to the conditions in which women are detained, especially concerning respect for their dignity and corporal integrity. Both resolutions later were adopted by the Council (resolutions 1980/40 and 1980/41 of 2 May 1980).

129. In resolution 1980/39, of the same date, the Council recalled that the Commission on the Status of Women was entitled to receive communications relating to the status of women but had no mandate to act upon them. It requested the Commission on the Status of Women to consider, at its twenty-ninth session, procedures for handling communications relating to the status of women, and to submit its views to the Council at its first regular session of 1982.

130. At its twenty-ninth session, the Commission on the Status of Women again appointed an *Ad Hoc* Working Group on Communications. The Commission, after hearing an oral report by a member of the Working Group, adopted a draft resolution for consideration by the Economic and Social Council. In the draft resolution, it was proposed that the Council should reaffirm the mandate of the Commission to consider confidential and non-confidential communications on the status of women, and should request the Secretary-General to solicit the co-operation of the specialized agencies, regional commissions and other United Nations bodies in compiling a report on such communications.

131. After consultation with the Commission on Human Rights, the Economic and Social Council, in resolution 1983/27 of 26 May 1983, reaffirmed the mandate of the Commission on the Status of Women to consider confidential and non-confidential communications on the status of women, requested the Secretary-General to submit a report on such communications to the Commission, and authorized the Commission thenceforth to appoint a Working Group consisting of not more than five of its members, selected with due regard for geographical distribution, to meet in closed meetings during each session of the Commission to perform the following functions:

(a) Consideration of all communications, including the replies of Governments thereon, if any, with a view to bringing to the attention of the Commission those communications, including the replies of Governments, which appear to reveal a consistent pattern of reliably attested injustice and discriminatory practices against women; and

(b) Preparation of a report, based on its analysis of the confidential and non-confidential communications, which will indicate the categories in which communications are most frequently submitted to the Commission.

132. The Council requested the Commission to examine the report of the Working Group and to avoid duplication of the work undertaken by other organs of the Economic and Social Council. It empowered the Commission only to make recommendations to the Council, which is then to decide what action may appropriately be taken on the emerging trends and patterns of communications. Further, it decided that all actions envisaged in the implementation of the resolution by the Commission should remain confidential until such time as the Commission may decide to make recommendations to the Council.

D. Handling of communications by the specialized agencies

133. Supervisory machinery also exists in respect of international human rights instruments adopted under the auspices of the International Labour Organisation and the United Nations Educational, Scientific and Cultural Organization and mentioned under the relevant headings of the present publication.

134. The implementation of these instruments by the specialized agency concerned is subject to periodic routine supervision, carried out by a committee of experts, on the basis of reports submitted by the Governments of the contracting States. Procedures have also been established to deal with complaints or disputes concerning the application or interpretation of ratified conventions. In the case of freedom of association, a special procedure has been established, under which complaints can be brought against States, even though they are not bound by conventions on the subject.

1. INTERNATIONAL LABOUR ORGANISATION

135. Ever since its establishment in 1919, ILO has established machinery and procedures to secure the implementation, on the widest possible scale, of the principles which it advocates and which have been given concrete expression in the 166 International Labour Conventions and 174 Recommendations adopted up to 31 December 1987, most of which affect human rights as laid down also in the Universal Declaration of Human Rights.

136. Some of these procedures were established from the start in the Constitution of ILO. Since then, important developments have occurred as a result of gradually evolving practice and of amendments to the ILO Constitution made in 1946.

137. In 1950, parallel procedures were established, in agreement with the United Nations, to deal with complaints in the field of freedom of association.

138. In the successive stages of these developments, the established procedures have been actuated in particular by the following considerations: in the first place, to ensure that the Conventions adopted by the Conference are ratified on the widest possible scale and that, once ratified, they are applied; secondly, in the case of Conventions which have not been ratified (and also in the case of Recommendations, which are not

open to ratification), to ensure that the question of their implementation is re-examined from time to time, both by the States and by ILO; in addition, in particularly important cases, to supplement the general machinery by additional procedures; and finally, in cases where divergencies of view or disputes arise in regard to questions within the province of ILO, whether between States or between a State and one or several organizations of employers or workers, to deal with the dispute on the basis of an impartial examination of the facts and a search for a settlement of the matter.

139. Because of these considerations, it has been found necessary to establish different procedures to meet varying situations. In certain cases, the question concerns formal obligations under the Constitution of ILO and Conventions ratified by a member State (the total number of ratifications of Conventions amounted to over 5,300 at the end of 1987). In other cases, no such obligations exist but the procedure permits the examination of the situation in a field covered by a Convention, even if the latter has not been ratified, or by a Recommendation, or more generally within the province of ILO.

140. There exist provisions for the examination of complaints by member States or by employers' or workers' organizations alleging that a given State is not implementing a Convention. In addition, there is periodic and routine supervision of the application of Conventions and Recommendations, based on the examination of Governments' reports and not dependent on the presentation of complaints; this ensures continuity of supervision and, because of its automatism, removes from this procedure any element of dispute.

(a) *Submission of Conventions and Recommendations to the competent authorities*

141. Since its adoption in 1919, the Constitution of ILO has provided in article 19 that Conventions and Recommendations must, within a period of from 12 to 18 months after their adoption, be submitted to the national authorities which are competent to enact legislation or take other action to give effect to these instruments. Special provisions are applicable to federal States in respect of Conventions and Recommendations for which action on the part of the constituent States is appropriate in whole or in part.

142. This obligation does not require Governments to propose ratification of a Convention or acceptance of a Recommendation; they retain complete freedom as to the nature of the proposals to be made to the competent authorities. However, Conventions and Recommendations must be submitted to the competent authorities in all cases and not only when the ratification of a Convention appears possible or when it is deemed advisable to give effect to the provisions of a Recommendation.

143. By virtue of a constitutional amendment adopted in 1946, member States must communicate to the Director-General of the International Labour Office information on the measures taken to submit Conventions and Recommendations to the competent authorities, on the authorities considered as competent and on the decisions taken by the latter. Copies of this information must be communicated to representative organizations of employers and workers of the countries concerned.

144. The fulfilment of the obligations relating to submission to the competent authorities is supervised by the Committee of Experts on the Application of Conventions and Recommendations and by the Conference (see below, (e) and (f)).

(b) *The general system for periodic, routine supervision on the basis of Governments' reports*

145. The system of periodic routine supervision operates on the basis of reports from Governments. The Constitution of ILO from its inception in 1919 (article 22) has required States which have ratified Conventions to make an annual report on the measures taken to give effect to them. It soon became apparent that the sending of reports was not sufficient in the absence of machinery for examining the reports and supervising the application of ratified Conventions. Following the adoption of a resolution by the International Labour Conference in 1926, machinery was set up consisting of two components: on the one hand, a committee of independent experts responsible for examining Governments' reports from a legal and technical point of view; on the other, the establishment, at each session of the Conference, of a committee responsible for examining the question of the application of Conventions.

146. The Director-General is required by the Constitution (article 23, paragraph 1) to lay before each annual session of the International Labour Conference a summary of the information and reports which have been communicated to him by member States.

(c) *Reports on ratified Conventions*

147. The reports must be made in such form and contain such particulars as the Governing Body may request. The Governing Body adopts for each Convention a report form calling for detailed information on the relevant national laws and regulations and on the measures taken to ensure the practical application of the Convention (labour inspection, judicial decisions, statistical information, observations from employers' and workers' organizations).

148. Under arrangements adopted by the Governing Body in 1976, "detailed" reports on the application of ratified Conventions are requested at yearly, two-yearly or four-yearly intervals, depending on the importance of the subject covered, the recency of ratification, and the existence of problems in their application. States are required to communicate copies of their reports to the representative organizations of employers and workers

in their country (article 23, paragraph 2, of the Constitution). The organizations concerned may make observations on the application of the provisions of a Convention. States are requested to supply information in their reports on any such observations received and to add any comments that they may consider useful.

(d) *Reports on unratified Conventions and on Recommendations*

149. The Constitution of ILO has, since 1946, provided in article 19, paragraphs 5, 6 and 7, that States members must, at the request of the Governing Body, submit reports indicating the position of their law and practice in regard to the matters dealt with in Conventions which they have not ratified or in Recommendations, showing the extent to which effect had been given or is proposed to be given to their provisions. In the case of a Convention, States members must also indicate the difficulties which prevent or delay ratification. In the case of a Recommendation, they must indicate the modifications which have been found necessary in applying the instrument. Copies of these reports also must be communicated to representative organizations of employers and workers.

150. In application of the provisions of article 19, the Governing Body chooses each year a limited number of Conventions and Recommendations of current interest and requests States to supply reports on them.

(e) *The Committee of Experts on the Application of Conventions and Recommendations*

151. As indicated above, the reports supplied by Governments have been subject, since 1927, to technical examination by the Committee of Experts on the Application of Conventions and Recommendations. This Committee is composed of independent members, who are appointed in their personal capacity by the Governing Body of the International Labour Office, on the proposal of the Director-General.

152. At the time of the creation of the Committee, it was stressed (Governing Body, thirty-third session, 1926) that the experts should be selected from among persons of recognized technical competence, whose complete impartiality could not be challenged, that they should in no sense be considered as representatives of Governments, and that they must therefore be persons of independent standing, not directly connected with a government service or a trade organization.

153. These requirements of impartiality and independence, and of eminent qualifications in the legal or social fields, have remained the basic criteria in the appointment of members of the Committee. The experts are drawn mainly from the judiciary, from academic circles (professors of international or labour law) and from among persons with considerable experience in public administration.

154. In 1987, on the occasion of the sixtieth anniversary of its establishment, the Committee reaffirmed its fundamental principles of "independence, objectivity and impartiality in pointing out the extent to which the position in each State appears to be in conformity with the terms of Conventions and obligations which that State has undertaken by virtue of the Constitution of the ILO".

155. The Committee, when first set up, was composed of six experts, and the gradual increase in its membership to the present figure of twenty has been imposed partly by the progressive increase in its work load (more member States, more Conventions, more ratifications, etc.) and by the desire to ensure a wider geographical representation among its members. At present, the Committee is composed of five experts from Western European countries, three from Eastern European countries, four from Asian countries, three from African countries, three from South American countries and two from countries in North and Central America.

156. The experts are appointed for renewable periods of three years. In practice, the mandates of the experts are generally extended for successive periods. Continuity of membership not only enables the experts to become thoroughly familiar with the often complex standards for which they are responsible, but also facilitates discussion within the Committee, which must rely on the cumulative experience of its members in shaping and formulating its views on a collective basis.

157. The Committee examines the situation of the States by studying the reports supplied by the Governments, official journals, and compilations of legislation, etc., and also any available information on practical application and comments submitted by employers' or workers' organizations.

158. The comments made by the Committee on the basis of this examination take various forms. In the case of ratified Conventions, the Committee's comments may take the form of "observations" or "direct requests". The former are set out in the Committee's published reports. Direct requests are communicated to Governments on behalf of the Committee, without being reproduced in its report; they are, however, available to interested parties. Direct requests are used when the point at issue is technical or relates to a discrepancy of minor importance, or when the object is to obtain more detailed information.

159. The Committee follows the same procedure in matters relating to the obligation on States to submit Conventions and Recommendations to the competent authorities.

160. In the case of reports requested on unratified Conventions and on Recommendations, the Committee makes a general survey indicating, in regard to the Conventions and Recommendations selected for reporting, the situation in the various member States, whether or not the latter have ratified the Conventions in question. In recent years, several such surveys have related to instruments in the field of basic human rights, such

as those concerning forced labour (1979) and equal remuneration (1986).

161. In accordance with a decision adopted by the ILO Governing Body in November 1976, the Committee of Experts has been entrusted also with the task of examining the reports and other available information on the implementation of the provisions of the International Covenant on Economic, Social and Cultural Rights falling within the scope of the activities of ILO, for the purpose of reporting to the Economic and Social Council on behalf of ILO, under the provisions of article 18 of the Covenant.

162. In 1968, the procedure of direct contacts was established, under which, at the request or with the agreement of the Government concerned, a representative of the Director-General of the International Labour Office may visit a country for discussions aimed at overcoming difficulties in the application of ratified conventions and the discharge of standards-related obligations.

(f) The Conference Committee on the Application of Conventions and Recommendations

163. The Conference, at each session, has before it a summary of the information and reports on the application of Conventions sent by Governments and the report of the Committee of Experts mentioning the discrepancies noted by it.

164. Since 1927 the Conference has, at each session, appointed a committee consisting of government, employers' and workers' representatives, to examine the question of the application of Conventions and Recommendations.

165. This committee bases its work on reports by the Committee of Experts. It invites the Governments concerned to participate in its work, with a view to providing additional information with regard to the discrepancies noted by the Committee of Experts and with reference to the measures which they have taken or may contemplate to eliminate these discrepancies. Governments are thus able to explain their position during the Committee's discussions.

166. In these discussions, employers' and workers' representatives can express their views on the manner in which Conventions are applied, whether in their own country or in other countries, and can supplement the particulars given in the reports by further information drawn from the experience of the organizations which they represent.

167. The Conference Committee summarizes its discussions and any conclusions which it may reach in a report which it submits to the Conference and which is discussed by the latter in plenary session. The Conference Committee, in its report, draws the special attention of the Conference to cases in which Governments appear to encounter serious difficulties in fulfilling obligations under the Constitution of ILO or under ratified Conventions.

(g) Procedures based on the presentation of complaints

168. The Constitution of ILO, from the outset, established procedures for the presentation of representations and complaints concerning non-observance of ratified Conventions. They are laid down in articles 24 to 34 of the Constitution. They are applicable generally to all Conventions adopted by ILO. In addition, special procedures were set up in 1950 in the field of freedom of association, not limited to cases where formal obligations exist under ratified Conventions.

169. The Constitution of ILO (articles 24 and 25) provides that employers' and workers' organizations may make a representation to the International Labour Office that "any of the members has failed to secure in any respect the effective observance within its jurisdiction of any Convention to which it is a party". Any such representation is brought before the Governing Body of ILO and is examined, in the first place, by a committee composed of members of the Governing Body, chosen in equal numbers from government, employers' and workers' representatives. The representation may be communicated to the Government concerned for it "to make such statement on the subject as it may think fit". If it does not make a statement within a reasonable time or if the statement made is not deemed to be satisfactory, the Governing Body has the right to publish the representation and the statement, if any, made in reply to it.

170. The Constitution (article 26, paragraph 1) provides that a member State may file a complaint if it is not satisfied that any other member "is securing the effective observance of any Convention which both have ratified . . .".

171. The complaints procedure may also be adopted by the Governing Body on its own motion, or on receipt of a complaint from a delegate to the Conference (article 26, paragraph 4).

172. When a complaint is brought before it, the Governing Body may either communicate the complaint in the first instance to the Government, as in the case of a representation or, if this is not deemed necessary or if no satisfactory reply has been received within a reasonable time, it may appoint a Commission of Inquiry to make a thorough examination of the complaint and to report thereon. The Commission prepares a report embodying its findings on all facts relevant to determining the issue between the parties and containing its recommendations as to the steps which should be taken to meet the complaint and the time within which they should be taken (article 28).

173. Under article 29 of the Constitution of ILO, the Governments concerned are required, within a period of three months, to inform the Director-General of the International Labour Office whether or not they accept the recommendations of the Commission of Inquiry and, if not, whether they propose to refer the complaint to the International Court of Justice. The Court may affirm, vary or reverse any of the findings or recom-

mendations of the Commission of Inquiry (article 32); the decision of the Court is final (article 31). If any member failing to carry out within the time specified the recommendations in the report of the Commission of Inquiry, or in the decision of the International Court of Justice, as the case may be, the Governing Body may recommend to the International Labour Conference such action as it may deem wise and expedient to secure compliance therewith (article 33).

(h) Special procedure relating to freedom of association

174. In the field of freedom of association, the Governing Body set up, in 1950, a special procedure to examine complaints presented either by Governments or by employers' or workers' organizations. These complaints are submitted, in the first place, to the Governing Body Committee on Freedom of Association, composed of representatives of Governments, employers and workers. With the consent of the Government concerned, they may be referred to the Fact-Finding and Conciliation Commission on Freedom of Association, which is composed of independent members. The procedure was set up by the Governing Body in agreement with the Economic and Social Council. Complaints relating to freedom of association may be presented even against States which have not ratified the Conventions on freedom of association.

(i) The Governing Body Committee on Freedom of Association

175. In 1951, the Governing Body established the Committee on Freedom of Association and entrusted it with the preliminary examination of the above-mentioned complaints. This Committee is composed of three Government members, three employers' members and three workers' members of the Governing Body.

176. No representative or national of the State against which a complaint has been made, nor any person occupying an official position in the national association of employers or workers which has made the complaint, may participate in the Committee's deliberations or be present during the examination of the complaint in question.

177. Rules have been established for the working of this procedure, particularly as regards the receivability of complaints and regarding communication with complainants and with the Governments concerned. The latter are given every opportunity to present their observations in regard to the complaints concerning them.

178. In cases presenting a greater degree of urgency, that is, those involving human life or personal freedom, or new or changing conditions affecting the freedom of action of a trade-union movement as a whole, and cases arising out of a continuing state of emergency or involving the dissolution of an organization, the Director-General may, under the procedure, with the consent of the Government concerned and having obtained the prior approval of the Chairman of the Committee, send a representative to the country involved in the complaint.

179. As a general rule, the Committee examines the complaints on the basis of written texts presented to it (on the one hand, complaints, and on the other, observations of the Governments concerned). In certain cases, however, it has also made use of the report drawn up following an on-the-spot mission by a representative of the Director-General, sent by the latter at the request or with the consent of the Government concerned, with a view to establishing the facts at the source of the complaint.

180. The Committee always endeavours to reach unanimous decisions, and in fact is reports have been unanimous in all cases.

181. The Committee submits its reports to the Governing Body[16] and indicates to the latter the reasons for which it considers either that a case does not call for further examination or recommends that its conclusions and recommendations should be communicated to the Governments concerned. In exceptional cases involving particularly grave situations, it may recommend that the case be referred to the Fact-Finding and Conciliation Commission on Freedom of Association.

182. Since 1951, the Committee, which meets three times a year, has examined more than 1400 cases. On many occasions, the Governing Body, on the proposal of the Committee, has addressed recommendations to Governments to amend their national law or practice. In an appreciable number of cases, the Governments of the countries concerned have had regard to these recommendations. In particular, effect has been given to recommendations of the Governing Body in the following ways: legislation which was criticized has been repealed or amended, practices considered to be incompatible with the principles of freedom of association have been abandoned, factual situations which gave rise to complaints have been remedied, imprisoned trade-union leaders have been released, and death sentences passed on trade unionists have been commuted.

(ii) The Fact-Finding and Conciliation Commission on Freedom of Association

183. In agreement with the Economic and Social Council, the Governing Body set up, in 1950, a Fact-Finding and Conciliation Commission on Freedom of Association, composed of nine independent members appointed by the Governing Body on the proposal of the Director-General, which may work in panels of not less than three or more than five members. This Commission is authorized to deal with complaints made either by Governments or by employers' or workers' organizations, alleging infringements in the exercise of trade-union rights. The Commission is essentially a fact-finding body which may discuss with the Government concerned situations referred to it for investigation,

---

[16] The reports of the Committee on Freedom of Association are published in the *Official Bulletin* of the International Labour Office.

with a view to settling difficulties by means of agreement. As a rule, no case may be submitted to the Commission without the consent of the Government concerned.

184. It is for the Governing Body to decide whether the Government concerned should be invited to give its consent to the referral of a case to the Fact-Finding and Conciliation Commission. If the Government concerned does not give its consent for the referral of the case to the Commission or does not reply within four months to the invitation addressed to it in this connection, the Governing Body considers what measures should be taken in this regard.

185. Complaints of violations of trade union rights involving States which are not members of ILO, but which are Members of the United Nations, may also, with the consent of the Government concerned, be referred to the Commission.

(i) *Discrimination (Employment and Occupation) Convention, 1958 (No. 111)*

186. The Discrimination (Employment and Occupation) Convention, 1958 (No. 111), requires States parties (article 2) "to declare and pursue a national policy designed to promote, by methods appropriate to national conditions and practice, equality of opportunity and treatment in respect of employment and occupation, with a view to eliminating any discrimination in respect thereof". Article 3 of the Convention enumerates the measures to be taken for the application of the national policy declared in pursuance of article 2.

187. The reports of States parties on the application of the Discrimination (Employment and Occupation) Convention are examined by the Committee of Experts and the Conference Committee on the Application of Conventions and Recommendations in accordance with the procedure applicable to all ratified Conventions, described above. In addition, the Governing Body decided, at its 208th and 209th sessions (November 1978 and March 1979), that countries which have not ratified the Convention should report every four years, under article 19 of the Constitution, on the state of their law and practice and the prospects of ratification. These reports also are examined by the Committee of Experts and the Conference Committee on the Application of Conventions and Recommendations.

188. In 1972-1973 the Governing Body decided to make provision for the preparation of special surveys in the field of discrimination in employment designed to contribute to the evaluation of the facts and the search for solutions in certain national situations. The Director-General was authorized "to examine the effect to be given to any request for a special survey submitted by a member State, or a workers' or employers' organization, on specific questions of concern to them, and, if the Government concerned agrees to such a survey, to settle the arrangements for carrying it out in agreement with the Government".

189. In addition, the ILO is conducting a programme of practical activities to promote the implementation of the ILO standards for the elimination of discrimination. These activities include the holding of regional, sub-regional and national tripartite seminars, the elaboration and dissemination of guides of practice, and other information and guidance.

2. UNITED NATIONS EDUCATIONAL, SCIENTIFIC AND CULTURAL ORGANIZATION

190. The General Conference of the United Nations Educational, Scientific and Cultural Organization (UNESCO) has adopted several conventions and recommendations relating to human rights and, in particular, to those specified in articles 19, 26 and 27 of the Universal Declaration of Human Rights. The adoption by the General Conference of a convention or recommendation imposes on the member States of UNESCO specific legal obligations which have been defined in the Constitution. Moreover, the General Conference has adopted rules of procedure and decisions of various kinds to govern the implementation of conventions and recommendations.

(a) *Submission of instruments to the competent national authorities*

191. Under article IV, paragraph 4, of the UNESCO Constitution, each State is obliged to "submit recommendations or conventions to its competent authorities within a period of one year from the close of the session of the General Conference at which they were adopted". Moreover, under article VIII, as amended by the General Conference, "each Member State shall submit to the Organization, at such times and in such manner as shall be determined by the General Conference, reports on the laws, regulations, and statistics relating to its educational, scientific and cultural institutions and activities, and on the action taken upon the recommendations and conventions referred to in article IV, paragraph 4".

192. The Rules of Procedure concerning Recommendations to Member States and International Conventions, which were adopted in 1950, stipulate that initial special reports relating to any convention or recommendation adopted shall be transmitted not less than two months prior to the opening of the first ordinary session of the General Conference following that at which such recommendation or convention was adopted (article 16, paragraph 2).

193. At its tenth session, held in 1958, the General Conference determined the substance of the initial reports. They have to include (*a*) a statement indicating whether the convention or recommendation has been submitted to the competent national authorities, (*b*) the name of that authority, (*c*) a statement indicating whether such authorities have taken any steps to give

effect to the convention or recommendation, (*d*) the nature of such steps.

(b) *Submission and examination of the reports of member States*

194.   The 1950 Rules of Procedure provide that, in addition to the initial special reports which are the subject of the developments described above, the General Conference may further request member States to submit, by prescribed dates, additional reports giving such further information as may be necessary. As stipulated in article VII of the UNESCO Constitution, as amended, cited above, additional reports are to include information on the laws, regulations and statistics regarding the State's educational, scientific and cultural institutions and activities.

195.   The obligation to report periodically, in a manner determined by the General Conference, is, as indicated above, constitutional. It covers both recommendations and conventions and applies to all member States without making any distinction, in the case of a convention, concerning whether or not they have ratified it.

196.   Furthermore, several UNESCO conventions provide that States parties thereto should submit periodic reports on their application and implementation.

197.   According to the 1950 Rules of Procedure, the General Conference, having considered the reports of member States, has to submit its observations in one or more general reports to be circulated to member States, to the national commissions and to all other authorities designated by the General Conference. Thus, the observations are certain to receive wide publicity.

198.   Article 7 of the UNESCO Convention against Discrimination in Education (adopted on 14 December 1960) specifies that the States parties shall in their periodic reports submitted to the General Conference give information on the legislative and administrative provisions which they have adopted and other action which they have taken for the application of the Convention. The Recommendation against Discrimination in Education contains similar provisions.

199.   At its thirteenth session, the General Conference invited the Executive Board of UNESCO to put into effect, by 1965, a procedure for the submission and examination of such reports. The Board decided that the reports should be elaborated on the basis of a questionnaire and should be presented at regular intervals. It further decided that the reports, after analysis by the Secretariat of UNESCO, should be examined by a special Committee of the Board (the Committee on Conventions, and Recommendations in Education), and transmitted with the comments of the Executive Board to the General Conference.

200.   At its 21st session (1980) the General Conference, having noted that UNESCO procedures to monitor the implementation of its normative instruments involved a variety of organs and that they were characterized by the participation of a very small number of member States, invited the Director-General and the Executive Board to undertake a study of these diverse procedures, with the aim of securing better co-ordination and making the procedures more effective and efficient. At its twenty-third session the General Conference, having examined the in-depth study, recommended to the Director-General that (*a*) the draft questionnaires or forms sent to Member States with a view to the preparation of their "additional reports" on the application of the standard-setting instruments should be as simple as possible and should be submitted to the Executive Board's Committee on Conventions and Recommendations (CR) for harmonization, so that the Committee can carry out its functions in the best possible way, (*b*) the said questionnaires or forms should gradually, and as far as possible, be prepared in such a way that they can be analysed with data-processing methods, and (*c*) a survey of Member States should be conducted, relating to any difficulties they might encounter in drawing up their reports and in actually applying standard-setting instruments.

(c) *Conciliation and Good Offices procedure*

201.   Unlike ILO, UNESCO has no constitutional or statutory provision for appeals or for reviewing complaints concerning the implementation of its conventions. Consequently, no general procedure has been established for that purpose.

202.   However, as indicated in chapter I, section H, 3, above, the General Conference of UNESCO, desirous of facilitating the implementation of the Convention against Discrimination in Education, adopted on 10 December 1962 the Protocol Instituting a Conciliation and Good Offices Commission to be responsible for seeking a settlement of any disputes which may arise between States parties to that Convention.

203.   The Commission instituted by the Protocol is a permanent one. It consists of members elected by the General Conference of UNESCO after nomination by States parties to the Protocol. Members serve in their personal capacity. They must be nationals of States parties to the Protocol, but not more than one national of a State may serve on the Commission.

204.   In electing members, the General Conference endeavours to include persons of recognized competence in the field of education, as well as persons having judicial or legal experience, and to give consideration to equitable geographical distribution of membership and to the representation of the different forms of civilization, as well as of the principal legal systems. Members are elected for six years and are eligible for re-election if renominated.

205.   The members of the Conciliation and Good Offices Commission were elected by the General Conference at its sixteenth session, in 1970. The Commission held its first meeting from 1 to 3 February 1971.

206. For the time being, recourse to the Commission is limited to States parties to the Protocol. If one of those States considers that another of those States is not giving effect to the provisions of the Convention, it may, by written communication, bring the matter to the attention of that State. The receiving State has three months in which to reply. If the matter is not adjusted to the satisfaction of both States within six months, either State has the right to refer it to the Commission.

207. The Protocol entered into force on 24 October 1968. From the beginning of the sixth year after that date, the Commission may also be made responsible for seeking the settlement of any dispute arising between States which are parties to the Convention but are not parties to the Protocol, if those States agree.

208. The Commission's competence is limited (a) to disputes arising between States, and (b) to disputes concerning the application or interpretation of the Convention. In any matter referred to it, the Commission may call upon the States parties to the dispute to provide it with all pertinent information. However, it cannot deal with a matter until all available domestic remedies have been exhausted, within the meaning attributed to that expression in international law.

209. The function of the Commission, after it has obtained the information which it deems necessary, is essentially to ascertain the facts and make available its good offices to the States concerned, with a view to an amicable solution of the matter "on the basis of respect for the Convention".

210. In every case, the Commission has to draw up a report. If a solution has been reached, the report has to be brief and confine itself to a statement of the facts and of the solution agreed upon. If, on the other hand, a solution to the dispute is not reached, the report has to indicate, in addition to stating the facts, the recommendations of the Commission. Separate opinions are permitted.

(d) Communications procedure

211. In 1967, the Executive Board of UNESCO adopted a decision to the effect that communications received by the Organization relating to individual cases concerning human rights, and falling within the competence of UNESCO are considered—after having been communicated to the Government concerned for its observations, if any—by a Committee of the Board, which reports to the Board.

212. The UNESCO General Conference at its nineteenth session, in 1976, invited the Director-General and the Board "to study the procedures which should be followed in the examination of cases and questions which might be submitted to UNESCO concerning the exercise of human rights in the spheres of its competence, in order to make its action more effective".

213. The procedure followed by UNESCO in the examination of communications relating to cases and questions concerning the exercise of human rights in the spheres of its competence is laid down in decision 3.3, adopted by the Executive Board at its 104th session (1978 spring session), the text of which is reproduced in part below:

Conditions

(a) Communications shall be deemed admissible if they meet the following conditions:

(i) The communication must not be anonymous;

(ii) The communication must originate from a person or a group of persons who, it can be reasonably presumed, are victims of an alleged violation of any of the human rights referred to in paragraph (iii) below. It may also originate from any person, group of persons or non-governmental organization having reliable knowledge of those violations;

(iii) The communication must concern violations of human rights falling within the competence of UNESCO in the fields of education, science, culture and information and must not be motivated exclusively by other considerations;

(iv) The communication must be compatible with the principles of the Organization, the Charter of the United Nations, the Universal Declaration of Human Rights, the International Covenants on Human Rights and other international instruments in the field of human rights;

(v) The communication must not be manifestly ill-founded and must appear to contain relevant evidence;

(vi) The communication must be neither offensive nor an abuse of the right to submit communications. However, such a communication may be considered if it meets all other criteria of admissibility, after the exclusion of the offensive or abusive parts;

(vii) The communication must not be based exclusively on information disseminated through the mass media;

(viii) The communication must be submitted within a reasonable time-limit following the facts which constitute its subject-matter or within a reasonable time-limit after the facts have become known;

(ix) The communication must indicate whether an attempt has been made to exhaust available domestic remedies with regard to the facts which constitute the subject-matter of the communication and the result of such an attempt, if any;

(x) Communications relating to matters already settled by the States concerned in accordance with the human rights principles set forth in the Universal Declaration of Human Rights and the International Covenants on Human Rights shall not be considered;

Procedures

(b) The Director-General shall:

(i) Acknowledge receipt of communications and inform the authors thereof of the above-mentioned conditions governing admissibility;

(ii) Ascertain that the author of the communication has no objection to his communication, after having been communicated to the government concerned, being brought to the notice of the Committee and to his name being divulged;

(iii) Upon receipt of an affirmative answer from the author of the communication, transmit the communication to the government concerned, informing it that the communication will be brought to the notice of the Committee, together with any reply the government may wish to make;

(iv) Transmit the communication to the Committee, together with the reply, if any, of the government concerned and additional relevant information from the author, taking into account the need to proceed without undue delay;

(c) The Committee shall examine in private session the communications transmitted to it by the Director-General;

(d) The Committee shall decide on the admissibility of communications in accordance with the above-mentioned conditions;

(e) Representatives of the governments concerned may attend meetings of the Committee, in order to provide additional information or to answer questions from members of the Committee on either admissibility or the merits of the communication;

(f) The Committee may avail itself of the relevant information at the disposal of the Director-General;

(g) In consideration of a communication, the Committee may, in exceptional circumstances, request the Executive Board to authorize it under Rule 29 of the Rules of Procedure to take appropriate action;

(h) The Committee may keep a communication submitted to it on its agenda while seeking additional information it may consider necessary for the disposition of the matter;

(i) The Director-General shall notify the author of the communication and the government concerned of the Committee's decision on the admissibility of the communication;

(j) The Committee shall dismiss any communication which, having been found admissible, does not, upon examination of the merits, appear to warrant further action. The author of the communication and the government concerned shall be notified accordingly;

(k) Communications which warrant further consideration shall be acted upon by the Committee, with a view to helping to bring about a friendly solution designed to advance the promotion of the human rights falling within the fields of competence of UNESCO;

. . .

XV. PROMOTING RESPECT FOR, AND OBSERVANCE OF, HUMAN RIGHTS AND FUNDAMENTAL FREEDOMS

Introduction

1. Extensive public relations and educational activities are essential to the promotion of universal respect for, and observance of, human rights and fundamental freedoms, and are used extensively by the United Nations Centre for Human Rights, in co-operation with the Department of Public Information, with this end in view. Such activities include the encouragement and facilitation of media coverage of the work of international human rights organs and the dissemination to the public of texts, studies, publications and information materials.

2. In addition, the teaching of human rights in schools, institutions of higher learning and special training courses is constantly stimulated, and Governments are provided with such advisory services and expert assistance in human rights matters as they may request. Further, United Nations bodies such as the Commission on Human Rights and the Human Rights Committee sometimes make use of public relations and educational activities to induce support for policies adopted and programmes undertaken in this field.

3. UNESCO has played a major role in the development of human rights teaching, and has issued a textbook on the subject for use by law and political science faculties. The Secretary-General is in the process of issuing and of widely distributing a teaching booklet on human rights to serve as a broad and flexible framework within which teaching could be structured and developed in accordance with national circumstances. And all other relevant elements of the United Nations system, including the specialized agencies and regional commissions, have been called upon by the General Assembly to facilitate the dissemination of the human rights materials of the United Nations and to improve the co-ordination of their activities in this field.

A. Awareness and public information

4. The United Nations Centre for Human Rights and the Department of Public Information work closely in generating public awareness and disseminating basic information on human rights matters. To that end, they rely also on the co-operation and assistance of United Nations information centres scattered throughout the world. Through the recent establishment of a section on external relations, publications and documentation, the Centre for Human Rights endeavours to enhance yet further co-operation with that wider human rights community made up of national and international governmental and non-governmental organizations, academic and research communities, the media and concerned individuals.

5. Basically, the Centre for Human Rights is responsible for increasing public interest in, and knowledge of, all questions relating to the promotion and protection of human rights. It elaborates and implements programmes for this purpose, maintains contacts with interested organizations, academic and research institutions, arranges for the publication and distribution of the *Yearbook on Human Rights*, the *Bulletin of Human Rights*, *Fact Sheets*, *Newsletters* and other information materials. It organizes regional workshops and seminars, round-tables, it answers public inquiries, and in general provides the public with substantive information on human rights.

6. The Department of Public Information, among its other activities, covers the debates on human rights in United Nations organs through press releases and radio and television programmes; it produces films, photographs and exhibits on the subject, and it regularly organizes briefings and programmes for representatives of the media. Human rights publications, wallsheets, posters and exhibits are displayed and distributed through its United Nations information centres, which are kept abreast of activities relating to human rights at all times.

7. Although these activities to improve public knowledge of human rights concerns have continued and expanded since the General Assembly, in adopting the Universal Declaration of Human Rights, called for its text to be disseminated among all peoples throughout the world, there are still many individuals, in various regions and at different levels of society, who have not yet been made aware of their human rights and fundamental freedoms nor of the extensive international machinery deployed to protect their enjoyment of those rights and freedoms.

8. The Commission on Human Rights has considered the development of public information activities relating to human rights at each session for a number of years. In 1985, the Secretary-General's report on the subject[1] included a number of comments and proposals for enhancing the promotional activities of the United Nations in the field of human rights submitted by Governments, United Nations agencies and nongovernmental organizations. After examining them, the Commission, in resolution 1985/49 of 14 March 1985:

---

[1] E/CN.4/1985/16.

Requested the Secretary-General to issue as soon as practicable the personalized version of the Universal Declaration of Human Rights[2] in the six official languages of the United Nations, to complete this task by the end of 1986 and to proceed thereafter, in co-operation with regional organizations and Governments, to the production of personalized versions of the Declaration in national and local languages;

Requested the Secretary-General to build up the collection of reference works within each United Nations Information Centre and in particular to dispatch existing United Nations material to each Centre immediately;

Requested the Secretary-General to make greater use of audio-visual techniques designed for both children and adults and of computer technology in the preparation an distribution of United Nations material in the field of human rights;

Requested the Secretary-General to collect relevant material already prepared by specialized agencies, regional bodies, groups, non-governmental organizations and individuals, with a view to preparing a basic human rights teaching booklet in the six official languages of the United Nations;

Requested the Secretary-General to examine ways in which the potential of the entire United Nations system, including the specialized agencies, might be used to assist in the dissemination of human rights material; and

Requested the regional commissions to assist in the dissemination of human rights material prepared by the United Nations to Governments, non-governmental organizations and individuals, in particular in the distribution of copies of the Universal Declaration of Human Rights, the International Covenants on Human Rights and other international human rights instruments in the languages of the regions, and to investigate ways of promoting co-operation within the regions to that end.

9. These suggestions were welcomed and endorsed by the General Assembly in resolution 40/125 of 13 December 1985, in which it recognized the fundamental importance of national and regional public information activities in the field of human rights and the catalytic effect that initiatives of the United Nations could have on these activities. The Assembly called upon all relevant elements of the United Nations system, including the specialized agencies and regional commissions, to assist further in the dissemination of United Nations materials on human rights.

10. In 1987 both the Commission on Human Rights and the General Assembly received and noted a further report by the Secretary-General on the development of public information activities in the field of human

rights.[3] The Assembly, in resolution 42/118 of 7 December 1987, noted, *inter alia*, that, despite its repeated appeals, these activities continued to be denied adequate resources, and called upon the Secretary-General to prepare a report on the advisability of launching a World Public Information Compaign on Human Rights in 1989, and to include in the report an outline of the planned activities. In this connection the Assembly reaffirmed the need for materials on human rights to be made available in simplified, attractive and accessible form, in national and local languages, and for effective use to be made of the mass media, in particular radio and television and audio-visual technologies, in order to reach a wider audience, with priority given to children, other young people and the disadvantaged, including those in isolated areas.

B. Studies of various aspects of human rights

11. Article 13 of the Charter of the United Nations authorizes the General Assembly to initiate studies and make recommendations for the purpose, *inter alia*, of "promoting international co-operation in the economic, social, cultural, educational, and health fields, and assisting in the realization of human rights and fundamental freedoms for all without distinction as to race, sex, language, or religion".

12. Under article 62, the Economic and Social Council "may make or initiate studies and reports with respect to international economic, social, cultural, educational, health, and related matters, and may make recommendations with respect to any such matters to the General Assembly, to the Members of the United Nations, and to the specialized agencies concerned".

13. Both the Assembly and the Council, as well as many of their subsidiary bodies including the Commission on Human Rights, the Sub-Commission on Prevention of Discrimination and Protection of Minorities, and the Commission on the Status of Women, have undertaken studies of various aspects of human rights with a view to the preparation of standard-setting instruments and effective programmes of action to promote and protect particular rights or freedoms. Once the studies have served their original purpose, they are normally published and widely disseminated as a means of enlightening public opinion and stimulating public interest in the area which they cover.

1. PURPOSES AND PROCEDURES OF STUDIES

14. A number of studies have been undertaken for the purpose of providing the United Nations organ concerned with information on the situation existing, in law and in fact, in respect of a wide variety of human rights questions. One of the main objectives of such studies is to obtain detailed information on a particular subject

---

[2] The personalized version is reproduced in annex III of the report, E/CN.4/1985/16. Each copy contains the inscription, "These are the human rights of _____ as set forth in the Universal Declaration of Human Rights".

---

[3] E/CN.4/1987/16.

before deciding upon a course of action. Another is the enlightenment of public opinion on a particular human rights issue. For example, the study of forced labour undertaken by the joint United Nations/ILO *Ad Hoc* Committee on Forced Labour in 1953[4] exposed to public attention the problems raised by the existence in the world of vast systems of forced or "corrective" labour, employed as a means of political coercion or as punishment for holding or expressing political views; and on such a scale as to constitute an important element in the economy of the countries concerned. Public reaction to this exposure led to the disappearance of such systems in a number of countries, and eventually to the adoption by the International Labour Conference, in 1957, of the Abolition of Forced Labour Convention.

15. More recently, studies of gross violations of human rights in several countries, involving the use of torture, "disappearances" and summary or arbitrary executions, established the urgent need for international remedial measures and thus paved the way for adoption by the General Assembly in 1984, and entry into force in 1987, of the Convention against Torture and Other Cruel, Inhuman or Degrading Treatment or Punishment.

16. In this connection, it may be noted that the Commission on Human Rights, when approving at its tenth session, in 1954, the procedures which had been formulated by the Sub-Commission on Prevention of Discrimination and Protection of Minorities for carrying out its studies on discrimination, specified that the studies should be draw up "not only to serve as a basis for the Sub-Commission's recommendations, but also with a view to educating world opinion".[5]

2. Organs entrusted with the preparation of studies

17. Many of the studies on human rights matters initiated by United Nations bodies have been entrusted to the Secretary-General. Others have been carried out by committees or working groups, or by Special Rapporteurs.

18. In recent years, the Secretary-General has been called upon to prepare two comprehensive studies on human rights questions. One, requested by the General Assembly in resolution 2444 (XXIII) of 19 December 1968, dealt with respect for human rights in armed conflicts, including (*a*) steps which could be taken to secure the better application of existing humanitarian international conventions and rules in all armed conflicts, and (*b*) the need for additional humanitarian international conventions or for other appropriate legal instruments to ensure the better protection of civilians, prisoners and combatants in all armed conflicts and the prohibi-

tion and limitation of the use of certain methods and means of warfare. The second, authorized in Assembly resolution 2450 (XXIII) of the same date, dealt with the human rights problems arising from new developments in science and technology.

19. Several human rights studies authorized by the Economic and Social Council were carried out by Special Rapporteurs; one was prepared by a consultant appointed by the Secretary-General in agreement with the Council.

20. Of the studies initiated by the Commission on Human Rights, several were carried out by its *Ad Hoc* Committee of Experts on southern Africa, several by *ad hoc* committees appointed by the Commission or by its Chairman, and the remainder by Special Rapporteurs. Of the studies initiated by the Sub-Commission on Prevention of Discrimination and Protection of Minorities, all have been carried out by Special Rapporteurs.

21. In some instances, specialized agencies, particularly ILO and UNESCO, have prepared studies on human rights questions at the request of the Economic and Social Council.

22. A list of studies in the field of human rights, undertaken for the Economic and Social Council, the Commission on Human Rights and the Sub-Commission on Prevention of Discrimination and Protection of Minorities, follows.[6] The list includes completed studies and some still in progress. It does not include the numerous studies and reports prepared by the Secretary-General.

(a) *Studies prepared for the Economic and Social Council*

1. *Report of the* Ad Hoc *Committee on Forced Labour, 1953.*[7]

2. *Freedom of information, 1953,*[8] report submitted by Mr. Salvador P. López, Rapporteur on freedom of information.

3. *Report on developments in the field of freedom of information since 1954,*[9] prepared by Mr. Hilding Eek, consultant appointed by the Secretary-General in agreement with the Council.

4. *Concise summary of information on slavery,*[10] report prepared by Mr. Hans Engen, Rapporteur appointed by the Council in accordance with Council resolution 525 A (XVII) of 29 April 1954.

---

[4] See *Report of the* Ad Hoc *Committee on Forced Labour, 1953 (Official Records of the Economic and Social Council, Sixteenth Session, Supplement No. 13* (E/2431) and No. 36 in the *Studies and Reports (New Series)* of the International Labour Office).

[5] See E/2573, para. 377.

[6] United Nations publications which have been printed bear a sales number and are kept in stock for a minimum of 10 years, after which they are available on microfiche only. Mimeographed documents are kept in stock for 2 years, after which they are available on microfiche only.

[7] *Official Records of the Economic and Social Council, Sixteenth Session, Supplement No. 13* (E/2431).

[8] *Ibid., Supplement No. 12* (E/2426).

[9] *Official Records of the Economic and Social Council, Thirty-first Session, Annexes,* agenda item 10 (Part II), document E/3443.

[10] *Ibid., Nineteenth Session, Annexes,* agenda item 8, document E/2673 and Add.1-4.

5. *Report on Slavery,*[11] report prepared by Mr. Mohamed Awad, Special Rapporteur appointed by the Secretary-General in accordance with Council resolution 960 (XXXVI) of 12 July 1963.

(b) *Studies prepared for the Commission on Human Rights*

1. *Study of the Right of Everyone to be Free from Arbitrary Arrest, Detention and Exile,*[12] prepared by the Committee on the Right of Everyone to be Free from Arbitrary Arrest, Detention and Exile, consisting of four members of the Commission on Human Rights, elected by the Commission.

2. *Study of the right of arrested persons to communicate with those whom it is necessary for them to consult in order to ensure their defence or to protect their essential interests,*[13] prepared by the Committee on the Right of Everyone to be Free from Arbitrary Arrest, Detention and Exile.

3. *Study of* apartheid *and racial discrimination in southern Africa,*[14] prepared by Mr. Manouchehr Ganji, Special Rapporteur appointed by the Commission in resolution 7 (XXIII) of 16 March 1967.

4. *The Realization of Economic, Social and Cultural Rights: Problems, Policies, Progress,*[15] prepared by Mr. Manouchehr Ganji, Special Rapporteur appointed by the Commission in resolution 14 (XXV) of 13 March 1969.

5. *Study concerning the question of* apartheid *from the point of view of international penal law,*[16] prepared by the *Ad Hoc* Working Group of Experts on Human Rights in southern Africa.

6. *Study on ways and means of ensuring the implementation of international instruments such as the International Convention on the Suppression and Punishment of the Crime of* Apartheid, *including the establishment of the international jurisdiction envisaged by the Convention,*[17] prepared by the *Ad Hoc* Working Group of Experts on Human Rights in southern Africa.

7. *Study on assistance to racist régimes in southern Africa,*[18] prepared by the Special Rapporteur of the Sub-Commission on Prevention of Discrimination and Protection of Minorities, Mr. Ahmed M. Khalifa, at the request of the Commission in resolution 7 (XXXIII) of 4 March 1977.

(c) *Studies prepared for the Sub-Commission on Prevention of Discrimination and Protection of Minorities*

1. *Study of Discrimination in Education,*[19] prepared by Mr. Charles D. Ammoun, Special Rapporteur appointed by the Sub-Commission at its sixth session, in 1954.

2. *Study of Discrimination in the Matter of Religious Rights and Practices,*[20] prepared by Mr. Arcot Krishnaswami, Special Rapporteur appointed by the Sub-Commission at its eighth session, in 1956.

3. *Study of Discrimination in the Matter of Political Rights,*[21] prepared by Mr. Hernán Santa Cruz, Special Rapporteur appointed by the Sub-Commission at its eighth session, in 1956.

4. *Study of Discrimination in Respect of the Right of Everyone to Leave any Country, Including his Own, and to Return to his Country,*[22] prepared by Mr. José D. Inglés, Special Rapporteur appointed by the Sub-Commission at its twelfth session, in 1960.

5. *Study of Discrimination Against Persons Born out of Wedlock,*[23] prepared by Mr. Vieno Voitto Saario, Special Rapporteur appointed by the Sub-Commission at its fourteenth session, in 1962.

6. *Study of Equality in the Administration of Justice,*[24] prepared by Mr. Mohammed Ahmed Abu Rannat, Special Rapporteur appointed by the Sub-Commission at its fifteenth session, in 1963.

7. *Racial Discrimination,*[25] prepared by Mr. Hernán Santa Cruz, Special Rapporteur appointed by the Sub-Commission at its eighteenth session, in 1966. This is a revised and updated version of the *Special Study on Racial Discrimination in the Political, Economic, Social and Cultural Spheres,*[26] prepared by the same Special Rapporteur and published in 1971.

8. *Question of slavery and the slave trade in all their practices and manifestations, including the slavery-like practices of* apartheid *and colonialism,*[27] prepared by Mr. Mohamed Awad, Special Rapporteur appointed by the Sub-Commission at its twenty-second session, in 1969.

9. *Study of the rights of persons belonging to ethnic, religious and linguistic minorities,*[28] prepared by Mr. Francesco Capotorti, Special Rapporteur appointed by the Sub-Commission at its twenty-fourth session, in 1971.

---

[11] United Nations publication, Sales No. E.67.XIV.2.

[12] United Nations publication, Sales No. E.65.XIV.2.

[13] E/CN.4/996.

[14] E/CN.4/979, E/CN.4/979/Add.1 and Corr.1 and E/CN.4/979/Add.2-8.

[15] United Nations publication, Sales No. E.75.XIV.2.

[16] E/CN.4/1075.

[17] E/CN.4/1426.

[18] United Nations publication, Sales No. E.79.XIV.3.

[19] United Nations publication, Sales No. E.57.XIV.3.

[20] United Nations publication, Sales No. E.60.XIV.2.

[21] United Nations publication, Sales No. E.63.XIV.2.

[22] United Nations publication, Sales No. E.64.XIV.2.

[23] United Nations publication, Sales No. E.68.XIV.3.

[24] United Nations publication, Sales No. E.71.XIV.3.

[25] United Nations publication, Sales No. E.76.XIV.2.

[26] United Nations publication, Sales No. E.71.XIV.2.

[27] E/CN.4/Sub.2/322.

[28] United Nations publication, Sales No. E.78.XIV.1.

10. *Study of the problem of discrimination against indigenous populations,*[29] prepared by the Special Rapporteur, Mr. Jose R. Martinez Cobo, appointed by the Sub-Commission at its twenty-fourth session, in 1971.

11. *Study of the question of the prevention and punishment of the crime of genocide,*[30] prepared by the Special Rapporteur, Mr. Nicodème Ruhashyankiko, appointed by the Sub-Commission at its twenty-fourth session, in 1971.

12. *Study of the exploitation of labour through illicit and clandestine trafficking,*[31] prepared by the Special Rapporteur, Mrs. Halima Embarek Warzazi, appointed by the Sub-Commission at its twenty-sixth session, in 1973.

13. *Study of the adverse consequences for the enjoyment of human rights of political, military, economic and other forms of assistance given to the colonial and racist régimes in southern Africa,*[32] prepared by Mr. Ahmed M. Khalifa, Special Rapporteur appointed by the Sub-Commission at its twenty-seventh session, in 1974. The study has since been revised several times, most recently in 1982.[33]

14. *Study of international provisions protecting the human rights of non-citizens,*[34] prepared by the Special Rapporteur, Baroness Elles, appointed by the Sub-Commission at its twenty-seventh session, in 1974.

15. *Study on the implementation of United Nations resolutions relating to the right of peoples under colonial and alien domination to self-determination,*[35] prepared by Mr. Héctor Gros Espiell, Special Rapporteur appointed by the Sub-Commission at its twenty-seventh session, in 1974.

16. *Study of the individual's duties to the community and the limitations on human rights and freedoms under article 29 of the Universal Declaration of Human Rights: A contribution to the freedom of the individual under law,*[36] prepared by the Special Rapporteur, Mrs. Erica-Irene A. Daes, appointed by the Sub-Commission at its twenty-seventh session, in 1974.

17. *Study of the historical and current development of the right to self-determination on the basis of the Charter of the United Nations and other instruments adopted by United Nations organs, with particular reference to the promotion and protection of human rights and fundamental freedoms,*[37] prepared by the Special Rapporteur, Mr. Aureliu Cristescu, appointed by the Sub-Commission at its twenty-seventh session, in 1974.

18. *Study on the question of the human rights of persons subjected to any form of detention or imprisonment,*[38] prepared by the Special Rapporteur, Mrs. Nicole Questiaux, appointed by the Sub-Commission at its thirtieth session, in 1977.

19. *Updating of the Report on Slavery submitted to the Sub-Commission in 1966,*[39] prepared by the Special Rapporteur, Mr. Benjamin Whitaker, appointed by the Sub-Commission at its thirty-first session, in 1978.

20. *Study on the independence and impartiality of the judiciary, jurors and assessors and the independence of lawyers,*[40] prepared by Mr. L. M. Singhvi, Special Rapporteur, appointed by the Sub-Commission at its thirty-second session, in 1979.

21. *Study of the new international economic order and the promotion of human rights,*[41] prepared by the Special Rapporteur, Mr. Raul Ferrero, appointed by the Sub-Commission at its thirty-third session, in 1980.

22. *Study on the exploitation of child labour,*[42] prepared by Mr. A. Bouhdiba, Special Rapporteur, appointed by the Sub-Commission at its thirty-third session, in 1980.

23. *Study on guidelines, principles and guarantees for the protection of persons suffering from mental disorder,*[43] prepared by Mrs. Erica-Irene A. Daes, Special Rapporteur, appointed by the Sub-Commission at its thirty-third session, in 1980.

24. *Study on the status of the individual in contemporary international human rights law,*[44] prepared by Mrs. Erica-Irene A. Daes, appointed by the Sub-Commission at its thirty-third session, in 1980.

25. *Study on the question of conscientious objection to military service,*[45] prepared by Mr. Asbjørn Eide and Mr. L. C. Mubanga-Chipoya, Special Rapporteurs, appointed by the Sub-Commission at its thirty-fourth session, in 1981.

26. *Analysis of current trends and developments in respect of the right of everyone to leave any country, including his own, and to return to his country, and to have the possibility to enter other countries,*[46] prepared by Mr. L. C. Mubanga-Chipoya, Special Rapporteur, appointed by the Sub-Commission at its thirty-fifth session, in 1982.

[29] E/CN.4/Sub.2/1986/7 and Add.1-4. Addendum 4, containing the conclusions, proposals and recommendations of the Special Rapporteur, issued as United Nations publication, Sales No. E.86.XIV.3.

[30] E/CN.4/Sub.2/416.

[31] United Nations publication, Sales No. E.86.XIV.1.

[32] E/CN.4/Sub.2/383.

[33] E/CN.4/Sub.2/1987/8 Rev.1 and Add.1, Parts I and II.

[34] United Nations publication, Sales No. E.80.XIV.2.

[35] United Nations publication, Sales No. E.79.XIV.5.

[36] United Nations publication, Sales No. E.82.XIV.1.

[37] E/CN.4/Sub.2/404.

[38] E/CN.4/Sub.2/1982/15.

[39] E/CN.4/Sub.2/1982/20 and Add.1.

[40] E/CN.4/Sub.2/1985/18 and Add.1-6.

[41] E/CN.4/Sub.2/1983/24 and Add.1 and 2.

[42] E/CN.4/Sub.2/479.

[43] E/CN.4/Sub.2/1983/13.

[44] E/CN.4/Sub.2/1983/30.

[45] E/CN.4/Sub.2/1983/30.

[46] E/CN.4/Sub.2/1985/9.

27. *Report of the Working Group on Traditional Practices Affecting the Health of Women and Children,*[47] established by Commission resolution 1984/84.

28. *Study of the relevant guidelines in the field of computerized personnel files,*[48] prepared by Mr. Louis Joinet, Special Rapporteur, appointed by the Sub-Commission at its thirty-third session, in 1980.

29. *Study of the right to adequate food as a human right,*[49] prepared by Mr. Asbjørn Eide, Special Rapporteur, appointed by the Sub-Commission at its thirty-sixth session, in 1983.

30. *Study on amnesty laws and their role in the safeguard and promotion of human rights,*[50] prepared by Mr. Louis Joinet, Special Rapporteur, appointed by the Sub-Commission at its thirty-sixth session, in 1983.

31. *Study of the current dimensions of the problems of intolerance and of discrimination on grounds of religion or belief,*[51] prepared by Mrs. Elizabeth Odio Benito, Special Rapporteur, appointed by the Sub-Commission at its thirty-sixth session, in 1983.

32. *Study on the question of the prevention and punishment of the crime of genocide,* prepared by Mr. B. Whitaker, Special Rapporteur, appointed by the Sub-Commission at its thirty-sixth session, in 1983 (resolution 1983/2).[52]

23. A number of additional studies, for which various members of the Sub-Commission have been appointed as Special Rapporteurs, are under way, with reports to be presented to the Sub-Commission at its sessions in 1988 and 1989.

C. Yearbook on Human Rights

24. In resolution 9 (II) of 21 June 1946, the Economic and Social Council requested the Secretary-General to make arrangements for the compilation and publication of a yearbook on law and usage relating to human rights, "the first edition of which should include all declarations and bills of rights now in force in the various countries".

25. From 1946 onwards, the *Yearbook on Human Rights* has been published by the Secretary-General with the co-operation of Governments of Member States. From 1946 to 1972, the *Yearbook* was issued annually. From 1973 to 1978 it was issued every two years. In resolution 1979/37 of 10 May 1979, the Economic and Social Council decided that, beginning as soon as possible, the *Yearbook* should again be issued annually.

26. In that resolution, the Council altered the contents of the *Yearbook*, with a view to reflecting human rights

developments in a maximum number of States, bearing in mind that States parties to such international instruments as the International Covenants on Human Rights the International Convention on the Elimination of All Forms of Racial Discrimination and the International Convention on the Suppression and Punishment of the Crime of *Apartheid* submit reports on an established basis in accordance with the requirements of those instruments. The Council also decided that States would no longer be invited to submit separate contributions either directly or through correspondents for inclusion in the *Yearbook*; however, individual States wishing to provide a contribution intended specifically for the *Yearbook* would be free to do so.

27. Under the guidelines annexed to resolution 1979/37, Part I of the *Yearbook* consists of material reflecting legislative, administrative, judicial and other national measures and court decisions. The material is selected from government reports submitted under the international human rights instruments or contributions submitted by States intended specifically for the *Yearbook*. It also contains information relating to the exercise, in certain Trust and Non-Self-Governing Territories, to the right to self-determination, based on reports of the Special Committee on Decolonization.

28. Part II consists of two separate sections. Section A reflects the practice of the supervisory bodies concerning the examination of government reports and, as appropriate, reports from specialized agencies, and other tasks entrusted to those bodies under the relevant international instruments. Section B includes relevant decisions, general recommendations, general comments and observations made by the supervisory bodies in connection with their examination of reports submitted by Governments and the specialized agencies concerned, and other tasks entrusted to those bodies under international instruments.

29. Part III consists of an account of other international developments and activities in the field of human rights in the United Nations system, excluding activities covered in Part II. Part III also includes extracts from important documents adopted by the competent organs of the United Nations system or submitted in accordance with the decisions of such organs, selected with a view to their wider dissemination, and statements of policy or principle by the Secretary-General on questions of human rights. In addition, selected material is included in annexes.

30. Changes in content and format have delayed publication of the *Yearbook* in recent years. The *Yearbook on Human Rights for 1979,*[53] the first one to be prepared in accordance with the directives laid down by the Economic and Social Council in resolution 1979/37, was issued only in 1986. The French edition of the *Yearbook on Human Rights for 1980* was published in 1987; the English version for 1980 will be issued in spring 1988.

---

[47] E/CN.4/Sub.2/1986/42.

[48] E/CN.4/Sub.2/1983/18.

[49] E/CN.4/Sub.2/1987/23.

[50] E/CN.4/Sub.2/1984/15.

[51] E/CN.4/Sub.2/1987/27.

[52] E/CN.4/Sub.2/1985/6.

---

[53] United Nations publication, Sales No. E.85.XIV.7.

D. Advisory services in the field of human rights

31. On 23 October 1953, the General Assembly adopted two resolutions concerning technical assistance in the field of human rights. In resolution 729 (VIII), the Assembly approved a decision by the Economic and Social Council authorizing the Secretary-General to render, at the request of Member States, services which did not fall within the scope of the technical assistance programmes of that time, in order to assist those States in promoting and safeguarding the rights of women. In resolution 730 (VIII), the Assembly authorized the Secretary-General to render similar services at the request of any Member State, in order to assist the Government of that State within its territory in the eradication of discrimination or in the protection of minorities, or both.

32. One year later, in resolution 839 (IX) of 17 December 1954, the Assembly authorized the Secretary-General to render similar services at the request of Member States, in order to assist those States in promoting freedom of information.

33. In 1955, the Assembly decided, in resolution 926 (X) of 14 December 1955, to consolidate these technical assistance programmes with a broad programme of assistance in the field of human rights, the entire programme to be known as "advisory services in the field of human rights", and authorized the Secretary-General to make provision at the request of Governments, and with the co-operation of the specialized agencies where appropriate, for the following forms of assistance with respect to the field of human rights:

(*a*) Advisory services of experts;

(*b*) Fellowships and scholarships;

(*c*) Seminars.

34. The Assembly specified that the assistance was to be provided in agreement with the Governments concerned, on the basis of requests received from Governments; that the kind of service should be determined by the Government concerned; that the selection of persons to receive scholarships and fellowships should be made by the Secretary-General on the basis of proposals received from Governments; and that the amount of assistance and the conditions under which it was to be rendered should be decided by the Secretary-General, with due regard to the greater needs of the under-developed areas and in conformity with the principle that each requesting Government should assume responsibility, as far as possible, for all or a considerable amount of the expenses connected with the assistance furnished to it, either by making a contribution in cash, or in the form of services for the purpose of carrying out the programme. It stated further that the assistance should be applicable to any subject in the field of human rights, unless adequate advisory assistance was available elsewhere.

35. The Assembly recommended that the specialized agencies should continue to develop their technical assistance activities with a view to aiding member States to further the effective observance of human rights, and expressed the hope that international and national non-governmental organizations, universities, philanthropic foundations and other private groups would supplement the new United Nations programme with similar programmes designed to further research and studies, the exchange of information, and assistance in the field of human rights.

36. A number of Member States have responded favourably to the programme of advisory services in the field of human rights either by acting as host to seminars or regional training courses (a fourth form of assistance added in 1967), by nominating qualified nationals for fellowships or scholarships, or by receiving scholars from other countries. However, the financial resources provided for the programme were not always adequate, and the number of seminars that could be organized each year was reduced for this and other reasons.

37. From 1957 to 1973, seminars on subjects related to the advancement of women were organized as part of the programme of advisory services in the field of human rights. Since 1973, however, such seminars have been separated from the programme, and are now administered by the Advancement of Women Branch of the Centre for Social Development and Humanitarian Affairs.

38. In resolution 1978/14 of 5 May 1978, the Economic and Social Council requested that the financing of the programme of advisory services in the field of human rights should be arranged as a part of the budget of the human rights programme, and reiterated its request to the Secretary-General to organize at least two seminars and one training course annually, and to grant at least twenty-five scholarships each year, giving special attention to the needs of the developing countries.

39. The Commission on Human Rights, in resolution 1986/52 of 13 March 1986, requested the Secretary-General to submit to it relevant information on the possible role of an eventual trust fund on advisory services in the field of human rights and, if it were established, the manner in which it could function. The Secretary-General's report, submitted in pursuance of that resolution,[54] indicated that the establishment and operation of such a trust fund could broaden the scope of the advisory services programme.

40. In resolution 1987/38 of 10 March 1987, the Commission requested the Secretary-General to establish and administer, in accordance with the Financial Regulations and Rules of the United Nations, a voluntary fund for advisory services and technical assistance in the field of human rights. It emphasized that the objective of the trust fund would be to provide additional financial support for practical activities focused on the implementation of international conventions and other international instruments on human rights promulgated by the United Nations, its specialized agencies or regional organizations.

---

[54] E/CN.4/1987/33 and Add.1, Add.1/Corr.1 and Add.2

41. The Commission authorized the Secretary-General to receive voluntary contributions to the fund from Governments, intergovernmental and non-governmental organizations and individuals in a position to make such contributions, and to solicit contributions, or to make such representations or appeals for contributions, as he deems appropriate. It called upon all Governments, intergovernmental and non-governmental organizations and individuals to consider making voluntary contributions to the fund, and encouraged Governments in need of technical assistance in the field of human rights to avail themselves of the services of experts in the field.

42. After the Commission's resolution had been endorsed by the Economic and Social Council in decision 1987/147 of 29 May 1987, the Secretary-General established the Voluntary Fund for Advisory Services and Technical Assistance in the Field of Human Rights.

1. ADVISORY SERVICES OF EXPERTS

43. Until recently, few Governments had availed themselves of the advisory services of experts under the programme. However, in recent years the demand for such services has increased.

44. Reference has been made in chapter XI, section C, above, to expert assistance provided to the Governments of Equatorial Guinea, Haiti and Uganda in their efforts to restore, in their countries, a democratic system respectful of human rights and fundamental freedoms. The number of requests by Governments for services of this nature in the years 1980 to 1982 was greater than in any previous three-year period.

45. For example, before 1970 two Governments received advice concerning elections, electoral laws, procedures and techniques, while others utilized assistance relating to the advancement of women. In 1970-1971 the Secretary-General, at the request of the Government of Cameroon, provided the services of an expert to advise on promotion of the participation of women in national affairs and development, with special emphasis on community development. After the Commission on Human Rights had expressed the view, in resolution 1983/33, that the United Nations should be prepared to consider providing assistance to any nation emerging from a period of human rights violations, upon its request, such assistance was extended to several countries in this position. For example, in 1982 a mission was undertaken by two constitutional experts, recruited by the Secretary-General at the request of the Government of Equatorial Guinea, to assist the National Commission in that country in the drafting of a new constitution. And in 1983 the Secretary-General sent experts to Uganda, at the request of the Government, to assist in the review of legislation and in the training of law librarians, legal clerks, penitentiary staff and police officers.

46. The Sub-Commission on Prevention of Discrimination and Protection of Minorities, in resolution 1984/19 of 29 August 1984, requested the Secretary-General to invite Governments receiving aid from the United Nations Development Programme to indicate their specific needs in such areas as (*a*) the establishment or strengthening of law faculties, (*b*) the development of adequate law libraries, (*c*) the training of judges, (*d*) the drafting of legal texts in conformity with the provisions of international human rights instruments, (*e*) the publication of official law journals, and (*f*) the collection and classification of legal material, including legislation and digests of court decisions. In response, 14 States indicated their need for the establishment or strengthening of law faculties, 32 for the development of adequate law libraries, 20 for the training of judges, 9 for the drafting of legal texts in conformity with the provisions of international human rights instruments, 13 for the publication of official law journals and 20 for the classification of legal material.[55] The requests were to be drawn to the attention of the Commission on Human Rights at its 1988 session.

47. In resolution 1987/37 of 10 March 1987, the Commission on Human Rights encouraged Governments to avail themselves of the advisory services of experts in the field of human rights, for example for drafting basic legal texts in conformity with international human rights conventions.

2. HUMAN RIGHTS SEMINARS

48. Up to 31 December 1987, 26 world-wide and 40 regional seminars had been organized under the programme of advisory services in the field of human rights. Such seminars provided government-nominated experts with opportunities to exchange ideas, experience, and the knowledge gained in solving—or attempting to solve—human rights problems; they brought together key people for short periods to stimulate their thinking and to encourage greater awareness of matters relating to the promotion and protection of human rights.

49. In the case of world-wide seminars, normally 32 Governments, in addition to the host Government, are invited to nominate participants; and the geographical distribution of those selected to participate is the same as that of the Commission on Human Rights: eight from African States, six from Latin American States, eight from Western European and other States, four from Eastern European States, and six from Asian States. In the case of regional seminars, all States within a particular region (such as Asia or Latin America) are invited to nominate participants.

50. Participants, although nominated by Governments, attend the seminar in their personal capacity and do not represent Governments. Nominations of participants are accompanied by brief *curriculum vitae*. As these nominations are received from Governments, the Secretary-General confirms them and issues a formal invitation. On occasion, the Secretary-General has ex-

---

[55] E/CN.4/Sub.2/1985/24 and Add.1 and 2, and E/CN.4/Sub.2/1987/7.

ercised his prerogative of questioning a nomination —usually on the ground that the person concerned is not an expert in the field covered by the seminar—and proposing reconsideration.

51. Each participant is invited to write, in one of the working languages of the seminar, a paper dealing with the seminar topic from the point of view of the situation in his country. These "country monographs" are reproduced and circulated in their original language.

52. In addition, two or three expert consultants are invited by the Secretary-General to prepare basic background papers to elucidate the topics on the agenda of the seminar and to highlight pertinent problems with a view to stimulating discussion. These papers are translated into all languages used at the seminar.

53. United Nations bodies and specialized agencies which have an interest in the topic of the seminar are invited to designate representatives. Non-governmental organizations in consultative relationship with the Economic and Social Council whose aims and purposes are closely related to the seminar topic are invited to send observers.

54. The atmosphere at human rights seminars is as informal as possible. Participants are discouraged from imitating the debates which take place in United Nations organs. They are also discouraged from making formal recommendations or attempting to vote on resolutions or decisions. This, of course, does not prevent the seminar from embodying in its report any significant consensus of opinion, or from requesting that its views be communicated to the appropriate United Nations body.

55. A draft report for each seminar is prepared by a Rapporteur elected by the participants. The draft report is normally presented by the Rapporteur at the last meeting of the seminar, at which time drafting changes may be proposed. The final report is then adopted by the seminar.

56. A list of human rights seminars follows.

(i) *World-wide seminars*

1. Ljubljana, Yugoslavia, 8-21 June 1965—Seminar on the multinational society.
   Report: ST/TAO/HR/23

2. Brasilia, Brazil, 23 August-4 September 1966—Seminar on *apartheid*.
   Report: ST/TAO/HR/27

3. Helsinki, Finland, 1-14 August 1967—Seminar on the civic and political education of women.
   Report: ST/TAO/HR/30

4. London, United Kingdom, 18 June-1 July 1968—Seminar on freedom of association.
   Report: ST/TAO/HR/32

5. New Delhi, India, 27 August-9 September 1968—Seminar on the elimination of all forms of racial discrimination.
   Report: ST/TAO/HR/34

6. Nicosia, Cyprus, 26 June-9 July 1969—Seminar on special problems relating to human rights in developing countries.
   Report: ST/TAO/HR/36

7. Belgrade, Yugoslavia, 2-12 June 1970—Seminar on the role of youth in the promotion and protection of human rights.
   Report: ST/TAO/HR/39

8. Moscow, USSR, 8-21 September 1970—Seminar on the participation of women in the economic life of their countries (with reference to the implementation of article 10 of the Declaration on the Elimination of Discrimination against Women).
   Report: ST/TAO/HR/41

9. Yaoundé, Cameroon, 16-29 June 1971—Seminar on measures to be taken on the national level for the implementation of United Nations instruments aimed at combating and eliminating racial discrimination and for the promotion of harmonious race relations.
   Report: ST/TAO/HR/42

10. Nice, France, 24 August-6 September 1971—Seminar on the dangers of a recrudescence of intolerance in all its forms and the search for ways of preventing and combating it.
    Report: ST/TAO/HR/44

11. Vienna, Austria, 19 June-1 July 1972—Seminar on human rights and scientific and technological developments.
    Report: ST/TAO/HR/45

12. Istanbul, Turkey, 11-24 July 1972—Seminar on the status of women and family planning.
    Report: ST/TAO/HR/46

13. San Remo, Italy, 28 August-10 September 1973—Seminar on youth and human rights.
    Report: ST/TAO/HR/47

14. Ohrid, Yugoslavia, 25 June-8 July 1974—Seminar on the promotion and protection of human rights of national, ethnic and other minorities.
    Report: ST/TAO/HR/49

15. Tunis, Tunisia, 12-24 November 1975—Seminar on the human rights of migrant workers.
    Report: ST/TAO/HR/50

16. Maseru, Lesotho, 17-22 July 1978—Seminar on the Exploitation of Blacks in South Africa and Namibia and on Prison Conditions in South African Jails.
    Report: ST/HR/SER.A/1

17. Geneva, Switzerland, 18-29 September 1978—Seminar on National and Local Institutions for the Promotion and Protection of Human Rights.
    Report: ST/HR/SER.A/2

18. Geneva, Switzerland, 5-9 November 1979—Round Table of University Professors and Directors of Race Relations Institutions on the Teaching of Problems of Racial Discrimination.
    Report: ST/HR/SER.A/5

19. Geneva, Switzerland, 30 June-11 July 1980—Seminar on the Effects of the Existing Unjust International Economic Order on the Economies of the Developing Countries and the Obstacle that this Represents for the Implementation of Human Rights and Fundamental Freedoms.

Report: ST/HR/SER.A/8

20. Geneva, Switzerland, 29 June-3 July 1981—Seminar on Effective Measures to Prevent Transnational Corporations and Other Established Interests from Collaborating with the Racist Régime of South Africa.

Report: ST/HR/SER.A/9

21. United Nations Headquarters, New York, 3-14 August 1981—Seminar on the Relations that Exist between Human Rights, Peace and Development.

Report: ST/HR/SER.A/10

22. Geneva, Switzerland, 29 November-3 December 1982—Seminar on violations of human rights in the Palestinian and other Arab territories occupied by Israel.

Report: ST/HR/SER.A/14

23. Geneva, Switzerland, 20 June-1 July 1983—Seminar on the experience of different countries in the implementation of international standards in human rights.

Report: ST/HR/SER.A/15

24. Geneva, Switzerland, 3-14 December 1984—Seminar on the encouragement of understanding, tolerance and respect in matters relating to freedom of religion or belief.

Report: ST/HR/SER.A/16

25. Geneva, Switzerland, 9-20 September 1985—Seminar on community relations commissions and their functions.

Report: ST/HR/SER.A/17

26. Geneva, Switzerland, 28 October-8 November 1985—Seminar on ways and means of achieving the elimination of the exploitation of child labour in all parts of the world.

Report: ST/HR/SER.A/18

27. Yaoundé, Cameroon, 28 April-9 May 1986—Seminar on international assistance and support to peoples and movements struggling against colonialism, racism, racial discrimination and *apartheid*.

Report: ST/HR/SER.A/19

(ii) *Regional seminars*

1. Bangkok, Thailand, 5-16 August 1957—Seminar on the civic responsibilities and increased participation of Asian women in public life.

Report: ST/TAA/HR/1

2. Baguio City, Philippines, 17-28 February 1958—Seminar on the protection of human rights in criminal law and procedure.

Report: ST/TAA/HR/2

3. Santiago, Chile, 19-30 May 1958—Seminar on the protection of human rights in criminal law and procedure.

Report: ST/TAA/HR/3

4. Peradeniya (Kandy), Ceylon, 4-15 May 1959—Seminar on judicial and other remedies against the illegal exercise or abuse of administrative authority.

Report: ST/TAO/HR/4

5. Bogotá, Colombia, 18-29 May 1959—Seminar on the participation of women in public life.

Report: ST/TAO/HR/5

6. Buenos Aires, Argentina, 31 August-11 September 1959—Seminar on judicial and other remedies against the illegal exercise or abuse of administrative authority.

Report: ST/TAO/HR/6

7. Tokyo, Japan, 10-24 May 1960—Seminar on the role of substantive criminal law in the protection of human rights, and the purposes and legitimate limits of penal sanctions.

Report: ST/TAO/HR/7

8. Vienna, Austria, 20 June-4 July 1960—Seminar on the protection of human rights in criminal procedure.

Report: ST/TAO/HR/8

9. Addis Ababa, Ethiopia, 12-23 December 1960—Seminar on the participation of women in public life.

Report: ST/TAO/HR/9

10. Wellington, New Zealand, 6-20 February 1961—Seminar on the protection of human rights in the administration of criminal justice.

Report: ST/TAO/HR/10

11. Bucharest, Romania, 19 June-3 July 1961—Seminar on the status of women in family law.

Report: ST/TAO/HR/11

12. Mexico City, Mexico, 15-28 August 1961—Seminar on *amparo,* habeas corpus and other similar remedies.

Report: ST/TAO/HR/12

13. New Delhi, India, 20 February-5 March 1962—Seminar on freedom of information.

Report: ST/TAO/HR/13

14. Tokyo, Japan, 8-21 May 1962—Seminar on the status of women in family law.

Report: ST/TAO/HR/14

15. Stockholm, Sweden, 12-25 June 1962—Seminar on judicial and other remedies against the abuse of administrative authority, with special emphasis on the role of parliamentary institutions.

Report: ST/TAO/HR/15

16. Canberra, Australia, 29 April-13 May 1963—Seminar on the role of the police in the protection of human rights.

Report: ST/TAO/HR/16

17. Warsaw, Poland, 6-19 August 1963—Seminar on the rights of the child.

Report: ST/TAO/HR/17

18. Bogotá, Colombia, 3-16 December 1963—Seminar on the status of women in family law.

Report: ST/TAO/HR/18

19. Rome, Italy, 7-20 April 1964—Seminar on freedom of information.

Report: ST/TAO/HR/20

20. Kabul, Afghanistan, 12-25 May 1964—Seminar on human rights in developing countries.

Report: ST/TAO/HR/21

21. Lomé, Togo, 18-31 August 1964—Seminar on the status of women in family law.

Report: ST/TAO/HR/22

22. Ulan Bator, Mongolia, 3-17 August 1965—Seminar on the participation of women in public life.

Report: ST/TAO/HR/24

23. Dakar, Senegal, 8-22 February 1966—Seminar on human rights in developing countries.

Report: ST/TAO/HR/25

24. Budapest, Hungary, 14-27 June 1966—Seminar on the participation in local administration as a means of promoting human rights.

Report: ST/TAO/HR/26

25. Manila, Philippines, 6-19 December 1966—Seminar on measures required for the advancement of women, with special reference to the establishment of a long-term programme.

Report: ST/TAO/HR/28

26. Kingston, Jamaica, 25 April-8 May 1967—Seminar on the effective realization of civil and political rights at the national level.[56]

Report: ST/TAO/HR/29

27. Warsaw, Poland, 15-28 August 1967—Seminar on the realization of economic and social rights contained in the Universal Declaration of Human Rights.

Report: ST/TAO/HR/31

28. Accra, Ghana, 19 November-2 December 1968—Seminar on the civic and political education of women.

Report: ST/TAO/HR/35

29. Iasi, Romania, 5-18 August 1969—Seminar on the effects of scientific and technological developments on the status of women.

Report: ST/TAO/HR/37

30. Cairo, Egypt, 2-15 September 1969—Seminar on the establishment of regional commissions on human rights, with special reference to Africa.

Report: ST/TAO/HR/38

31. Lusaka, Zambia, 23 June-4 July 1970—Seminar on the realization of economic and social rights, with particular reference to developing countries.

Report: ST/TAO/HR/40

32. Libreville, Gabon, 27 July-9 August 1971—Seminar on the participation of women in economic life (with reference to the implementation of article 10 of the Declaration on the Elimination of Discrimination against Women and of General Assembly resolution 2716 (XXV)).

Report: ST/TAO/HR/43

33. Dar-es-Salaam, United Republic of Tanzania, 23 October-5 November 1973—Seminar on the study of new ways and means for promoting human rights, with special attention to the problems and needs of Africa.

Report: ST/TAO/HR/48

34. Geneva, Switzerland, 9-20 July 1979—Seminar on recourse procedures available to victims of racial discrimination and activities to be undertaken at the regional level.

Report: ST/HR/SER.A/3

35. Monrovia, Liberia, 10-21 September 1979—Seminar on the establishment of regional commissions on human rights, with special reference to Africa.

Report: ST/HR/SER.A/4

36. The Hague, Netherlands, 14-25 April 1980—Symposium on the role of the police in the protection of human rights.

Report: ST/HR/SER.A/6

37. Nairobi, Kenya, 19-30 May 1980—Seminar on political, economic, cultural and other factors underlying situations leading to racism, including a survey of the increase or decline of racism and racial discrimination.

Report: ST/HR/SER.A/7

38. Managua, Nicaragua, 14-22 December 1981—Seminar on recourse procedures and other forms of protection available to victims of racial discrimination and activities to be undertaken at the national and regional levels.

Report: ST/HR/SER.A/11

39. Colombo, Sri Lanka, 21 June-2 July 1982—Seminar on national, local and regional arrangements for the promotion and protection of human rights in the Asian region.

Report: ST/HR/SER.A/12

40. Bangkok, Thailand, 2-13 August 1982—Seminar on recourse procedures and other forms of protection available to victims of racial discrimination and activities to be undertaken at the national and regional levels, with special reference to Asia and the Pacific.

Report: ST/HR/SER.A/13

---

[56] In accordance with Economic and Social Council resolutions 1123 (XLI) of 26 July 1966 and 1125 (XLI) of 26 July 1966, the Secretary-General made arrangements for the attendance at this seminar of four participants from countries outside the Western hemisphere.

3. FELLOWSHIPS

57. Human rights fellowships are intended to give persons entrusted with functions important to the promotion and protection of human rights in their countries the opportunity to broaden their professional knowledge and experience by acquainting themselves with advanced methods and techniques in this field. Most fellowships are awarded for relatively short periods of time, usually from two to three months. They are given to candidates nominated by their Governments, on the basis of the candidate's qualifications, his position in his home country, his proposed field of study and the practical use he expects to make of the knowledge and experience gained on his return home. In the selection of candidates, preference is given to persons having direct responsibilities in the field of the implementation of human rights in their respective countries. While undergoing their training abroad, the recipients of fellowships are under the general supervision of the competent United Nations agencies; but in each host country, a governmental or semi-governmental department or agency agrees beforehand to be responsible for the direct supervision of the training.

58. At the conclusion of the training programme and before returning home, fellows submit a report on their work. Later, information on how the fellow has utilized the fellowship experience in his home country is obtained by means of a questionnaire.

59. Most of the candidates nominated by Governments and awarded fellowships have been government officials of a high standing, ranging from 25 to 50 years of age. Among the recipients of the awards have been judges; prosecutors; senior police officials; instructors at police academies; officials responsible for drafting legislation; officials of national development boards; officials of ministries of justice, interior, labour and social affairs; members of legislatures; officials of national non-governmental organizations; members of the bar; and university teachers.

60. As regards the areas of study or training to be undertaken, the majority of requests for awards of human rights fellowships have related to national activities and projects concerned with the improvement of the existing judiciary or administrative procedures, the drafting of new legislation, the modification of existing laws, or the observation in other countries of the experience gained from the establishment of new institutions and the application of new techniques in the promotion and protection of human rights. The requests generally fall into one of three categories: (a) for study and observation of comparable procedures abroad; (b) for on-the-spot comparative analysis of legislation; and (c) for on-the-spot observation of the working of a technique or institution which is being examined from the standpoint of adoption or adaptation in the fellow's own country.

61. The greatest number of requests received have been for study and observation of existing procedures of various facets of the administration of justice. Thus,

Governments have at times requested that their prosecutors, judges and officials of ministries of justice be given the opportunity to observe abroad such matters as the use of writs of habeas corpus, techniques for ensuring the right of the accused to a speedy trial, protection of human rights in the preliminary investigation of criminal offences, methods of interrogation of suspected or accused persons, and ways of protecting the right of such persons to communicate with lawyers, family members and friends.

62. As to the type of fellowship which involves on-the-spot comparative analysis related to the drafting or modification of legislation in the candidate's own country, Governments have often proposed members of their legislatures, members of committees charged with legislative reform, officials of ministries of justice and government draftsmen who are responsible for drawing up laws and regulations. The protection of the human rights of certain categories of persons, such as refugees, new immigrants and resident aliens, were among the subjects studied under this type of fellowship.

63. For the third type of fellowship, Governments have nominated judges, prosecutors, police officials and other officials of ministries of justice to observe the working of judicial and other remedies against the abuse of administrative authority, including the operation of *conseils d'état*, administrative tribunals and the role of the ombudsman.

64. In response to Economic and Social Council resolution 1680 (LII) of 2 June 1972, the Secretary-General has in recent years given special attention to securing the appointment, as human rights fellows, of women and persons involved in activities designed to eliminate discrimination against women; and Governments have nominated greater numbers of women among their candidates for awards under the programme.

65. In 1982, the Secretary-General received 63 governmental nominations for individual human rights fellowships. Bearing in mind the importance of ensuring a broad distribution of the fellowships among the nationalities of the applicants, 32 fellowships were awarded to candidates from 32 countries.

66. In 1987, the Secretary-General received 64 governmental nominations for individual human rights fellowships. Bearing in mind the importance of ensuring a broad distribution of the fellowships among the nationalities of the applicants, recommendations were made for awarding 30 individual fellowships to candidates from 28 countries.

4. REGIONAL TRAINING COURSES

67. In resolution 959 (XXXVI) of 12 July 1963, the Economic and Social Council requested the Secretary-General to consider the organization—from savings available under part V of the United Nations budget and on an experimental basis—of one or more regional courses in human rights.

68. No such savings were available from 1964 to 1971. However, pilot projects in group training for human rights fellows were held in 1967 in Japan and in 1968 in Poland. The first pilot project was held at the United Nations Asia and Far East Institute for the Prevention of Crime and Treatment of Offenders, Fuchu, Tokyo, Japan, in co-operation with the Government of Japan, from 15 June to 26 July 1967, with participants from Asia and the Far East, and was concerned with human rights in the administration of justice. The second, organized in co-operation with the Government of Poland, was held at Warsaw from 8 July to 3 August 1968, with participants from French-speaking countries of Africa, and dealt with the realization of the rights of the child in planning and administration at the national and local levels.

69. In resolution 17 (XXIII) of 22 March 1967, the Commission on Human Rights requested the Secretary-General to consider the organization, from 1969 onwards, of one or more regional training courses in human rights. As at 31 December 1987, eight such training courses had been organized. The first four were concerned with human rights in the administration of criminal justice. The first was held at Tokyo, Japan, from 14 August to 13 September 1982, for participants from English-speaking countries in Africa for participants from countries members of the Economic Commission for Africa, as well as for participants from Asia and the Far East. The second was held at the Centre for Social and Criminological Research, Cairo, Egypt, from 18 June to 7 July 1973, for participants or nationals from African countries members of the Economic Commission for Africa and from Arabic-speaking countries outside Africa. The third was held at San José, Costa Rica, from 24 November to 12 December 1975, for participants from countries members of the Economic Commission for Latin America. The fourth was held at the Australian Institute of Criminology, Canberra, Australia, from 27 November to 17 December 1976, for candidates from countries members of the Economic and Social Commission for Asia and the Pacific. The fifth, which dealt with the subject "Safeguards against deprivation of the right to liberty and security of person", was held at the United Nations Asia and Far East Institute for the Prevention of Crime and Treatment of Offenders, Fuchu, Tokyo, Japan, from 5 to 22 December 1977, for candidates from countries members of the Economic and Social Commission for Asia and the Pacific. The sixth, which dealt with the subject "Human rights guarantees in the administration of criminal justice", was held at the Australian Institute of Criminology, Canberra, from 30 November to 18 December 1981, also for candidates from countries members of the Economic and Social Commission for Asia and the Pacific.

70. The seventh training course was national rather than regional in nature; it was held at La Paz from 19 to 30 May 1986, for government personnel in that country concerned with the provisions of international human rights standards and the experience of relevant

international organs. Forty-five persons, including magistrates, officials of the Ministries of Foreign Affairs, Interior and Education, and representatives of the *Assemblea Permanente de Derechos Humanos* (a non-governmental organization to which the Government delegated many of the organizational tasks), took part in the course, which included lectures on international, regional and national systems of protection of human rights as well as a series of practical exercises in the drafting of national reports for consideration by international human rights monitoring bodies.

71. The eighth training course was held at the Headquarters of the Economic and Social Commission for Asia and the Pacific, at Bangkok, from 12 to 23 October 1987, for participants from countries members of that Commission. Its purpose was to familiarize senior officials responsible for the preparation of educational materials in their respective countries with the various international human rights instruments, the experience of countries in the region in their implementation, and the ways and means of incorporating them in the curricula of national educational systems at both the elementary and secondary school levels. Nineteen participants nominated by their Governments participated in the training course, at which regional experts and staff members of the Centre for Human Rights presented lectures and led discussions.

72. The common objective of the regional training courses has been to familiarize senior and experienced government officials, responsible for various aspects of the administration of justice, with the relevant legislation and administrative practices and procedures of other countries as these affect human rights, and thus to provide for an exchange of views on the law and practice relating to the protection of human rights in criminal procedures. The courses have included lectures by experts and officials provided by the United Nations and the host Government, followed by discussions amongst participants guided by the experts. Visits have been arranged to local institutions such as police headquarters, courts, prisons and other facilities. Participants, for the most part, have been judges, public prosecutors, police officials and jurists, i.e., individuals in a position to influence and implement policies and programmes in related human rights matters in their respective countries on their return home.

E. National human rights institutions

73. The question of the establishment of commissions on human rights at the national level has been of concern to various United Nations bodies since the inception of the Organization.

74. In resolution 9 (II) of 21 June 1946, the Economic and Social Council, on the recommendation of the "nuclear" Commission on Human Rights, invited Members of the United Nations to consider "the desirability of establishing information groups or local human rights committees within their respective countries

to collaborate with them in furthering the work of the Commission on Human Rights''.

75. The question of national commissions on human rights was considered only sporadically, in connection with the preparation of measures of implementation for inclusion in the International Covenants on Human Rights, until 1960, when a former Chairman of the Commission on Human Rights submitted to it a memorandum in which he expressed the view that national advisory committees on human rights, properly instituted and consisting of outstanding personalities, would be of great assistance to Governments in solving national or local human rights problems.

76. On the recommendation of the Commission, the Economic and Social Council, in resolution 772 B (XXX) of 25 July 1960, recognized the importance of the contribution which could be made towards the promotion of respect for and observance of human rights by bodies representing, in each country, informed opinion on questions relating to human rights.

77. Expressing the view that the studies and opinions of such bodies on questions of human rights could be of great value to Governments in the promotion of respect for and observance of human rights, the Council invited the Governments of Member States to favour, in such manner as might be appropriate, the formation of such bodies, or to encourage them where they already existed. The Council further invited Governments to communicate to the Secretary-General all relevant information on this subject, and requested the Secretary-General to prepare a report thereon, to be circulated to Governments and submitted to the Commission on Human Rights.

78. The Secretary-General's report on the subject[57] was considered by the Commission on Human Rights at its eighteenth session, in 1962. On the recommendation of the Commission, the Economic and Social Council, in resolution 888 F (XXXIV) of 24 July 1962, requested the Secretary-General to transmit the report to Member States and again invited Governments to favour, in the light of conditions in their countries, the formation of national advisory committees on human rights. It suggested that such bodies could, for example, study questions relating to human rights, consider the situation as it existed nationally, offer advice to the Government, and assist in the formation of public opinion in favour of respect for human rights.

79. One year later, the Council, in resolution 961 F (XXXVI) of 12 July 1963, adopted on the recommendation of the Commission on the Status of Women, drew the attention of member States "to the value of appointing national commissions on the status of women, composed of leading men and women with experience in government service, education, employment, community development and other aspects of public life, to develop plans and make recommendations for improving the position of women in their respective countries''.

80. In resolution 1961 (XVIII) of 12 December 1963, the General Assembly invited all Member States to intensify their domestic efforts in the field of human rights, with the assistance of their appropriate organizations. In resolution 2200 C (XXI) of 16 December 1966, by which it adopted the International Covenants on Human Rights, the Assembly invited the Economic and Social Council to request the Commission on Human Rights to examine in all its aspects the advisability of the establishment of national commissions on human rights or the designation of other appropriate institutions to perform certain functions pertaining to the observance of the Covenants.

81. For a few years the Commission on Human Rights was concerned primarily about the setting up of national commissions on human rights. However, in the report on its twenty-sixth session, held in 1970, the Commission recorded its agreement that the question of whether or not to establish national commissions was one to be decided by each Government in the light of the traditions and institutions of its country.

82. The Commission, by resolution 23 (XXXIV) of 8 March 1978, recognized the importance of action by Member States to develop and utilize their national machinery for the effective realization of human rights and repeated the invitation addressed to Member States by the General Assembly and the Economic and Social Council, to set up such national institutions. The Commission decided that a seminar on national and local institutions in the field of human rights should be held in 1978 to suggest possible guidelines for the structure and functioning of national institutions.

83. The Seminar on National and Local Institutions for the Promotion and Protection of Human Rights was held at Geneva from 18 to 29 September 1978, and approved by consensus a series of guidelines for the structure and functioning of national institutions.[58]

84. The guidelines suggested that the functions of national institutions in the field of human rights should include (a) acting as a source of relevant information for the Government and for the people of the country regarding matters connected with human rights, (b) assisting in the education of public opinion towards an awareness of and respect for human rights, (c) considering, deliberating upon, and making recommendations regarding any particular state of affairs that may exist nationally and that the Government may wish to refer to them, (d) advising on any questions regarding human rights matters referred to them by the Government, (e) studying and keeping under review the status of legislation, judicial decisions and administrative arrangements for the promotion of human rights, and preparing and submitting periodic reports to the appropriate authorities, and (f) performing any other function which the Government may wish to assign to them in connection with its duties under those international conventions in the field of human rights to which it is a State party.

---

[57] E/CN.4/828 and Add.1.

[58] ST/HR/SER.A/2, chap. V.

85.   As for the structure of such national institutions, the guidelines recommended that they should be so designed as to reflect in their composition wide cross-sections of the population of the nation and bring all parts of that population into the decision-making process in regard to human rights, that they should function regularly, and that immediate access to them should be available to any member of the public or public authority. In appropriate cases, it was added, national institutions should have local or regional advisory organs to assist them in discharging their functions.

86.   The guidelines were endorsed by the General Assembly in resolution 33/46 of 14 December 1978 and by the Commission on Human rights in resolution 24 (XXXV) of 14 March 1979. The Commission invited all Member States to take appropriate steps for the establishment, where they did not already exist, of national institutions for the promotion and protection of human rights, and requested the Secretary-General to submit to the General Assembly a report providing detailed information on existing national institutions.

87.   The Secretary-General presented further substantive reports on the subject to the General Assembly in 1981 and 1983.[59] In 1987 he submitted to the Assembly, through the Commission on Human Rights and the Economic and Social Council, a consolidated report,[60] intended for eventual publication as a United Nations handbook on national institutions for the use of Governments, which included information on the various types and models of national and local institutions for the protection and promotion of human rights, taking into account differing social and legal systems. All of the reports recognize that nearly all national institutions have a bearing upon both the protection and the promotion of human rights, and contribute to the full realization of these rights in a closely related manner.

88.   The consolidated report deals with legislative organs and organs established to examine the constitutionality of laws; judicial organs, such as courts of general jurisdiction, constitutional courts, special courts and tribunals, administrative courts and tribunals, and other organs established within the framework of the judicial system; and administrative organs, such as human rights commissions, agencies for the protection of specific groups, and equal employment agencies. It also outlines the variety of functions assigned to, and procedures used by, ombudsmen in some countries, whose primary role is to protect the rights of the individual who believes himself to be the victim of unjust acts on the part of the public administrator. In addition, it stresses the important role and significant successes of non-governmental organizations in promoting and protecting human rights at the national level, mainly by educational activities and by attracting attention to human rights violations.

89.   The General Assembly, in resolution 42/116 of 7 December 1987, welcomed the consolidated report and requested the Secretary-General to bring it up to date, bearing in mind the practical needs of those engaged in the development of national institutions. In particular it called upon him to include in the updated report all the information provided by Governments and any additional information Governments may wish to provide, with particular emphasis on the functioning of various models of national institutions in implementing international standards on human rights, as well as a list of existing national institutions with contact points and a bibliography of relevant materials. The updated report is to be transmitted to the Assembly at its forty-fourth session, in 1989, for wide distribution as a United Nations handbook on national institutions.

90.   The Assembly, further, affirmed the role of national institutions as focal points for the dissemination of human rights materials and other public relations activities under the auspices of the United Nations, and encouraged the development of funding and other strategies to facilitate the establishment of such institutions.

F. Regional arrangements for the promotion and protection of human rights

91.   The Commission on Human Rights, in resolution 6 (XXIII) of 22 March 1967, noted that two regional intergovernmental commissions on human rights, the Commission on Human Rights of the Council of Europe and the Inter-American Commission on Human Rights had existed for some time outside the United Nations system, and expressed the belief that it was timely to give encouragement to the formation of regional commissions on human rights within or outside the United Nations system. The Commission set up an *ad hoc* group of eleven of its members to study in all its aspects a proposal to establish regional commissions on human rights within the United Nations system, in the light of discussions held on this proposal during the session of the Commission. The *Ad Hoc* Study Group was requested to pay particular attention to (*a*) the basis on which regional commissions on human rights might be established in those areas where such bodies did not exist, (*b*) the terms of reference of such commissions and the method of appointing their members, and (*c*) the relationship between the Commission on Human Rights, on the one hand, and the existing regional commissions and those that might subsequently be established, on the other.

92.   The report of the *Ad Hoc* Study Group[61] to the Commission gave an account of the Group's deliberations on the questions assigned to it, but contained no generally agreed conclusions or recommendations. The Commission, in resolution 7 (XXIV) of 1 March 1968, requested the Secretary-General to transmit it to Mem-

---

[59] A/36/440 and A/38/416.

[60] A/42/395.

[61] E/CN.4/966 and Add.1.

349

ber States, and to regional intergovernmental organizations, for their comments.

93. The Commission further requested the Secretary-General to consider the possibility of arranging suitable regional seminars under the programme of advisory services in the field of human rights in those regions where no regional commission on human rights existed, for the purpose of discussing the usefulness and advisability of establishing such commissions.

94. The United Nations Seminar on the Establishment of Regional Commissions on Human Rights, with Special Reference to Africa, was held at Cairo from 2 to 15 September 1969. The Commission on Human Rights noted the report[62] and the conclusions of the Seminar in resolution 6 (XXVI) of 10 March 1970, and requested the Secretary-General to arrange for appropriate consultation and exchange of information between the Commission and the Organization of African Unity (OAU) as regards the possibility of the establishment of an African regional commission on human rights.

95. The United Nations Seminar on the Study of New Ways and Means for Promoting Human Rights, with Special Attention to the Problems and Needs of Africa, was held at Dar es Salaam from 23 October to 5 November 1973, and recommended that OAU should consider appropriate steps, including the convening of a preparatory committee, with a view to establishing such a commission. In resolution 24 (XXXIV) of 8 March 1978, the Commission on Human Rights took note of the conclusions of the Seminar and requested the Secretary-General to give OAU such assistance as it might require for the establishment of an African commission on human rights.

96. The United Nations Seminar on the Establishment of Regional Commissions on Human Rights with Special Reference to Africa, held at Monrovia from 10 to 20 September 1979, adopted the Monrovia Proposal for the setting up of an African Commission on Human Rights, contained in annex I to its report.[63]

97. The Proposal, which included draft provisions for a possible model African commission on human rights, was to be submitted to OAU for consideration. It suggested that the commission should promote and protect human rights in Africa by a variety of methods and procedures, including the study of African human rights issues and of situations involving alleged violations of human rights, the provision of its good offices to States members of OAU in relation to such situations, the formulation and elaboration of standards to serve as bases for the adoption of legislation by African Governments to deal with legal issues related to the enjoyment of human rights and fundamental freedoms, and the establishment of co-operation with other African institutions and organizations concerned with the promotion and protection of human rights.

98. In resolution 34/171 of 17 December 1979, the General Assembly noted the report of the Seminar and expressed the hope that its recommendations would be given due consideration by the Governments and organizations concerned, and reiterated its appeal to States in areas where regional arrangements in the field of human rights did not exist to consider the establishment of such arrangements. In resolution 35/197 of 15 December 1980, it noted with satisfaction the efforts within OAU to elaborate an African charter of human rights and to establish an African commission on human rights. In resolution 36/154 of 16 December 1981, it commended OAU on the adoption of the African Charter of Human and People's Rights. In resolution 37/172 of 17 December 1982, it commended OAU for its continuing efforts to promote respect for the guarantees and norms of human rights and fundamental freedoms, and noted with interest the African Charter of Human and People's Rights[64] and the efforts to obtain its early entry into force.

99. The Seminar on National, Local and Regional Arrangements for the Promotion and Protection of Human Rights in the Asian Region, held at Colombo from 21 June to 2 July 1982, adopted no conclusions or recommendations concerning regional arrangements for the promotion and protection of human rights. However, participants identified some of the problems and needs which should be taken into account should such arrangements be contemplated, and considered the relevance of the experience of other regions to the countries of Asia and the Pacific. Discussion of the desirability, feasibility and timeliness of establishing such arrangements in the Asian region produced no consensus of opinion.

100. The General Assembly, in resolution 37/171 of 17 December 1982, took note of the report of the Seminar[65] and requested the Secretary-General to transmit it to States members of the Economic and Social Commission for Asia and the Pacific, to invite their comments thereon, and to submit the report and comments to the Commission on Human Rights at its fortieth session for its consideration.

101. Although Asia remains without a regional Commission on Human Rights or similar body, the Regional Council of the Association of Southeast Asian Nations (Brunei Darussalem, Indonesia, Malaysia, the Philippines, Singapore and Thailand) adopted, on 9 December 1983, the Declaration of the Basic Duties of Asean Peoples and Governments, in which human rights and fundamental freedoms are spelled out in terms of duties of governments, of peoples, of the military, and of civilian leaders. In the Declaration the Regional Council, a non-governmental advisory body established by the Association, "urges all governments and peoples of the region to incorporate these duties in their national constitutions and laws, and to faithfully

---

[62] ST/TAO/HR/38.

[63] ST/HR/SER.A/4; see also A/34/359/Add.1, annex I.

[64] See American Society of International Law, *International Legal Materials*, vol. XXI, No. 1, January 1982, p. 59.

[65] A/37/422.

implement and enforce them forthwith". However, no provision is made for supervisory or monitoring activity.

G. Right and responsibility of individuals, groups and organs of society to promote and protect human rights

102. In a study prepared by Mrs. Erica-Irene A. Daes, Special Rapporteur of the Sub-Commission on Prevention of Discrimination and Protection of Minorities, and entitled *Study of the individual's duties to the community and the limitations on human rights and freedoms under article 29 of the Universal Declaration of Human Rights: A contribution to the freedom of the individual under law*[66] it was recommended that the Sub-Commission should prepare a draft declaration on the principles governing the reponsibilities of the individual in connection with, in particular, the promotion and observance of human rights and fundamental freedoms in a contemporary community.

103. After an examination of the question by the Sub-Commission and the Commission on Human Rights, the Commission, in resolution 1982/30 of 11 March 1982, reiterated the right and responsibility of individuals, groups and organs of society to promote and protect the rights recognized in relevant international instruments; emphasized that in the exercise of those rights the individual should be subject only to the limitations set out in those instruments, and pointed out that the imposition of additional limitations or the persecution of anyone exercising his rights is at variance with the obligations of States, under those instruments, to work for the full and effective enjoyment of human rights and fundamental freedoms. The Commission requested the Secretary-General to present to the Sub-Commission elements for a draft body of principles on the right and responsibility of individuals, groups and organs of society to promote and protect human rights and fundamental freedoms.

104. The report of the Secretary-General[67] suggested that the proposed body of principles should contain elements relating to (*a*) the right of individuals, groups, and organs of society to promote and protect human rights and fundamental freedoms, and elements relating to (*b*) the responsibility of individuals, groups and organs of society to promote and protect those rights and freedoms.

105. The Sub-Commission, in resolution 1982/24 of 8 September 1982, noted the report with appreciation and requested its Special Rapporteur, Mrs. Daes, to prepare the draft principles and to submit them for consideration by the Sub-Commission at its thirty-sixth session, in 1983. The Commission in turn, in resolution 1982/24 of 8 September 1982, welcomed the Sub-Commission's action and decided to undertake work on the draft dec-

laration at its forty-first session on the basis of the Sub-Commission's report and as a matter of priority.

106. The Commission however found it impossible to establish such a working group at its forty-first session, and the working groups established at its forty-second and forty-third sessions continued the elaboration of the draft declaration. Consideration of the question was accordingly postponed to the Commission's forty-fourth session, in 1988.

H. Popular participation as an important factor in the realization of human rights

107. The Declaration on Social Progress and Development, proclaimed by the General Assembly in resolution 2542 ((XXIV) of 11 December 1969, called, *inter alia*, for the adoption of measures to ensure the effective participation, as appropriate, of all elements of society in the preparation and execution of national plans and programmes of social and economic development.

108. The Economic and Social Council, in resolution 1746 (LIV) of 16 May 1973, recommended to Governments that appropriate measures should be taken at all levels to ensure more active participation by the entire population, including the labour force, in the production, preparation and execution of economic and social development policies and programmes. Later, in resolution 1929 (LVIII) of 6 May 1975, the Council noted that, to be effective, popular participation should be consciously promoted by Governments, with full recognition of civil, political, social, economic and cultural rights and through innovative measures, including structural changes and institutional reform and development, as well as through the encouragement of all forms of education, particularly compulsory primary education, designed to involve actively all segments of society.

109. The General Assembly considered the question of popular participation at its thirty-second, thirty-fourth and thirty-seventh sessions, and adopted resolutions 32/130, 34/46 and 37/55 on the subject. In resolution 37/55 of 3 December 1982 it recognized that social progress and development are founded on respect for the dignity and value of the human person and should ensure the promotion of human rights and social justice; and requested the Commission on Human Rights to consider the question of popular participation in its various forms as an important factor in the development and realization of human rights, taking into account the report of the International Seminar on Popular Participation which had been held at Ljubljana from 17 to 25 May 1982.[68]

110. On recommendation of the Commission, the Economic and Social Council, in resolution 1983/31 of 27 May 1983, requested the Secretary-General to undertake a comprehensive analytical study of the right to popular participation in its various forms as an impor-

---

[66] United Nations publication, Sales No. E.82.XIV.1.

[67] E/CN.4/Sub.2/1982/12.

[68] A/37/442.

tant factor in the full realization of all human rights, taking into account the concept and practice of popular participation that had been caried out by relevant United Nations organs, specialized agencies and other bodies, the views expressed in the Commission, and the relevant national experiences of Governments.

111. A preliminary report containing a provisional outline was presented to the Commission at its fortieth session by the Secretary-General.[69] The final study[70] was examined by the Commission at its forty-first session, and was noted with appreciation in resolution 1985/44 of 14 March 1985.

112. In that resolution the Commission requested the Secretary-General to circulate the study to Governments, United Nations organs and specialized agencies, and non-governmental organizations, and to prepare a further report setting out those comments. The Secretary-General submitted such reports to the Commission at its forty-second and forty-third session,[71] but in each case the Commission called for additional comments and a further report. In resolution 1987/21 of 10 March 1987 the Commission requested the Secretary-General to prepare a study of laws and practices by countries regarding the question of the extent to which the right to participation has been established and has evolved at the national level.

I. The search for ways and means of improving the effective enjoyment of human rights and fundamental freedoms

113. In resolution 3221 (XXIX) of 6 November 1974, the General Assembly requested the Secretary-General "to solicit the views of member States, the specialized agencies and regional intergovernmental organizations on alternative approaches and ways and means within the United Nations system for improving the effective enjoyment of human rights and fundamental freedoms", and invited "appropriate non-governmental organizations in consultative status with the Economic and Social Council to submit to the Secretary-General any relevant material on the subject". The Secretary-General was asked to submit a concise analytical report, based on the views and materials received and any other relevant material, to the Assembly at its thirtieth sessions.

114. The Secretay-General's report[72] was considered by the General Assembly at its thirtieth session. In resolution 3451 (XXX) of 9 December 1975, the Secretary-General was requested to submit to the Assembly at its thirty-second session an updated version of the report, prepared in the light of further replies received from Member States and non-governmental organizations and of the views expressed on the subject at the thirtieth session.

115. The Secretary-General's updated report[73] was submitted to the General Assembly at its thirty-second session, in 1977. In the course of the debate in the Third Committee of the Assembly a draft resolution submitted by a number of States[74] proposed *inter alia* the establishment, under the authority of the Secretary-General, of a United Nations High Commissioner for Human Rights, and set out the proposed mandate of the High Commissioner.

116. The Third Committee decided not to vote on the draft resolution, on the understanding that it would be transmitted to the Commission on Human Rights, together with all related documentation, for consideration at the Commission's thirty-fourth session in connection with an overall analysis of alternative approaches and ways and means for improving the effective enjoyment of human rights and fundamental freedoms.

117. The General Assembly, after considering the Secretary-General's reports, took note of the Third Committee's decision. In resolution 32/130 of 16 December 1977, it expressed the view "that the thirtieth anniversary of the Universal Declaration of Human Rights should be marked by an overall analysis of existing problems in the field of human rights and by increased efforts to find appropriate solutions for the effective promotion and protection of human rights and fundamental freedoms, taking into account the experiences and contributions of both developed and developing countries, and requested the Commission on Human Rights to undertake such an overall analysis at its thirty-fourth session as a matter of priority.

118. Having considered the reports submitted by the Secretary-General, the Assembly decided that the approach to the future work within the United Nations system with respect to human rights questions should take into account the following concepts:

(*a*) All human rights and fundamental freedoms are indivisible and interdependent; equal attention and urgent consideration should be given to the implementation, promotion and protection of both civil and political, and economic, social and cultural rights;

(*b*) The full realization of civil and political rights without the enjoyment of economic, social and cultural rights is impossible; the achievement of lasting progress in the implementation of human rights is dependent upon sound and effective national and international policies of economic and social development", as recognized by the Proclamation of Teheran of 1968;

(*c*) All human rights and fundamental freedoms of the human person and of peoples are inalienable;

(*d*) Consequently, human rights questions should be examined globally, taking into account both the overall context of the various societies in which they present themselves, as well as the need for the promotion of the full dignity of the human person and the development and well-being of the society;

(*e*) In approaching human rights questions within the United Nations system, the international community should accord, or continue to accord, priority to the search for solutions to the massive and flagrant violations of human rights of peoples and persons affected by situations such as those resulting from *apartheid*, from all forms of racial discrimination, from colonialism, from foreign domination and occupation, from aggression and threats against national sovereignty,

---

69 E/CN.4/1984/12 and Add.1.

70 E/CN.4/1985/10 and Add.1 and 2.

71 E/CN.4/1986/11 and Add.1, and E/CN.4/1987/11.

72 A/10235.

73 A/32/178 and A/32/179.

74 A/C.3/32/L.25/Rev.1

national unity and territorial integrity, as well as from the refusal to recognize the fundamental rights of peoples to self-determination and of every nation to the exercise of full sovereignty over its wealth and natural resources;

(*f*) The realization of the new international economic order is an essential element for the effective promotion of human rights and fundamental freedoms and should also be accorded priority;

(*g*) It is of paramount importance for the promotion of human rights and fundamental freedoms that Member States undertake specific obligations through accession to or ratification of international instruments in this field; consequently, the standard-setting work within the United Nations system in the field of human rights and the universal acceptance and implementation of the relevant international instruments should be encouraged;

(*h*) The experience and contribution of both developed and developing countries should be taken into account by all organs of the United Nations system in their work related to human rights and fundamental freedoms.

119. At its thirty-sixth session, in 1980, the Commission on Human Rights decided to establish, at the very beginning of its thirty-seventh session, an open-ended sessional working group to continue the overall analysis and to elaborate recommendations based on that analysis for consideration by the Commission.

120. The Working Group submitted its report[75] to the Commission at its thirty-seventh session. The Commission noted, in resolution 23 (XXXVII) of 10 March 1981, that the Working Group has formulated a number of ideas which merited further study, and decided to establish a similar working group for this purpose at its thirty-eighth session, to continue the analysis. By decision 6 (XXXVII) of the same date, the Commission advised the General Assembly that it had not reached a decision on the establishment of a United Nations High Commissioner for Human Rights.

121. After reviewing information relating to the promotion and protection of human rights in the world at its thirty-fifth session, in 1981, the Sub-Commission on Prevention of Discrimination and Protection of Minorities concluded that it was essential for the United Nations to develop ways and means of responding urgently to violations of human rights and fundamental freedoms. In resolution 12 (XXXIV) of 10 September 1981, the Sub-Commission informed its parent body of its conviction that the number and scale of gross violations of human rights occurring in many parts of the world required urgent and effective forms of action by the United Nations, and expressed the view that the establishment of a post of United Nations High Commissioner for Human Rights would be most valuable in advancing the promotion and protection of human rights in the world. The Sub-Commission also decided that it would consider at its thirty-fifth session the positive role a High Commissioner could play in ensuring the full enjoyment of human rights and fundamental freedoms.

122. In resolution 36/135 of 14 December 1981, the General Assembly noted that the Commission on Human Rights had been considering the question of the desirability of the establishment of a post of United Nations High Commissioner for Human Rights since 1978,

and called upon it to give this matter the attention it deserved.

123. The Commission, by resolution 1982/22 of 10 March 1982, requested the Sub-Commission on Prevention of Discrimination and Protection of Minorities to formulate a first study on possible terms of reference for the mandate of a United Nations High Commissioner for Human Rights, taking into account the provisions of the Charter of the United Nations and of pertinent international instruments concluded under United Nations auspices, the concepts contained in General Assembly resolution 32/130 of 16 December 1977, as well as the practice of the United Nations system for the promotion and protection of human rights.

124. At its thirty-fifth session, in 1982, the Sub-Commission discussed the positive role a United Nations Commissioner for Human Rights could play in promoting the full enjoyment of human rights and fundamental freedoms, and submitted to the Commission a series of detailed proposals concerning the possible terms of reference for the mandate of such a High Commissioner.

125. The General Assembly, by resolution 37/200 of 18 December 1982, requested the Commission to continue its efforts to improve the capacity of the United Nations system to take urgent action in cases of serious violations of human rights, bearing in mind the proposals of the Sub-Commission.

126. The Commission, in resolution 1983/49 of 10 March 1983, characterized the proposals as a valuable contribution to the further consideration of the question, and invited the Sub-Commission to re-submit them the following year after reviewing them in the light of views expressed in the Commission and any further comments or recommendations drawn to its attention.

127. The Sub-Commission, in resolution 1983/36 of 6 September 1983, recommended to the Commission the adoption of a draft resolution under which the Economic and Social Council would suggest to the General Assembly that the United Nations High Commissioner for Human Rights should, if the post were to be established, assume the following functions and responsibilities:[76]

(*a*) Carry out specific mandates and tasks assigned by the General Assembly, the Economic and Social Council, and the Commission on Human Rights;

(*b*) Consult as appropriate with other elements of the United Nations system, including the Secretary-General and the Centre for Human Rights, and appropriate specialized agencies, with may have or share responsibilities for promoting or safeguading specific human rights for the purpose of exchanging information and of collaborating with them in developing and implementing appropriate co-ordinated action;

(*c*) Initiate direct contacts with Governments, whenever such action appears necessary or desirable, to safeguard or assist in restoring respect for human rights, bearing in mind the following principles:

(i) Such contacts shall be prompt, confidential and exclusively humanitarian in purpose;

(ii) In undertaking such action, the High Commissioner shall pay particular attention to urgent situations;

---

[75] E/CN.4/L.1577.

[76] E/CN.4/1984/3, chap. I A, draft resolution XVI, annex.

(iii) Direct contacts shall have the specific purpose of ascertaining the facts and, when appropriate in the light of the facts, of assisting the parties concerned with a view to ensuring full respect for the human rights of individuals or groups on whose behalf the contacts were undertaken;

(iv) Such assistance may include, *inter alia*, technical advice on measures which could be taken to promote the effective observance of human rights, offers to conciliate or mediate in situations and provision of information on the availability of appropriate assistance from other elements of the United Nations system, including the Centre for Human Rights and the specialized agencies;

(*d*) Report annually to the General Assembly, the Economic and Social Council and the Commission on Human Rights on his or her activities. These reports should constitute a separate item on the agenda of these bodies. These reports might, with the consent of the Government concerned, include a summary of the results of the High Commissioner's direct contacts with the Government. With the consent of the Government concerned, the Commissioner might also announce the results of such direct contacts at other times during the year;

(*e*) Promote and protect the observance of human rights and fundamental freedoms for all, as defined in the Universal Declaration of Human Rights, without distinction as to race, colour, sex, language, religion, political or other opinion, national or social origin, property, birth or other status;

(*f*) Give special attention to the importance of ensuring the effective enjoyment by all of their civil and political rights and their economic, social and cultural rights and such other rights as are recognized by the Charter of the United Nations and by the General Assembly, bearing in mind that all human rights and fundamental freedoms are indivisible and interdependent;

(*g*) Accord priority to such massive violations of human rights as *apartheid*, racism and racial discrimination, colonial domination, foreign occupation and alien subjugation;

(*h*) Consider as situations of special concern those resulting from aggression and threats against national sovereignty and also from the denial of the fundamental and inalienable rights of peoples to self-determination and from the refusal to recognize the right of every nation to the exercise of full sovereignty over its wealth and resources.

128. The Sub-Commission proposed, further, that the General Assembly should be called upon to decide:

That the Bureau of the Commission on Human Rights should act as an advisory committee to the High Commissioner, advising him or her on any aspect of the latter's responsibilities; such advice to be given on the initiative of the Bureau or at the request of the High Commissioner;

That the High Commissioner should be elected by the General Assembly; that the period of his or her mandate should be five years; that he or she should not serve for two consecutive terms; and that the High Commissioner should be elected on the principle of regional rotation to ensure that every United Nations geographical region gets the post of High Commissioner; and

That the work of the High Commissioner shall be humanitarian in character, guided solely by an impartial concern for the promotion and protection of human rights and fundamental freedoms and not directed towards obtaining political advantage for any State.

129. The Sub-Commission also put forward a number of suggestions concerning the administrative arrangements under which the Office of the High Commissioner might function if its establishment is decided upon.

130. At its fortieth and subsequent sessions, the Commission on Human Rights did not give further consideration to the Sub-Commission's proposals and suggestions on this subject.

J. Commemorative observances of human rights anniversaries

131. The first anniversary of the Universal Declaration of Human Rights was marked by an anniversary concert on 10 December 1949 at Carnegie Hall in New York City. Since that time, a number of concerts, programmes of entertainment featuring artists from all parts of the world, and other commemorative observances, have been arranged to mark important human rights anniversaries.

132. The Commission on Human Rights, at its twelfth session, in 1956, expressed a desire in resolution VI that plans should be developed for the widest possible celebration of the tenth anniversary of the Universal Declaration on Human Rights on 10 December 1958. The Commission appointed a Committee to prepare such plans, which were later transmitted to the Economic and Social Council.

133. The Council, in resolution 651 B (XXIV) of 24 July 1957, urged all Member States to join in observing the tenth anniversary of the Declaration, making use of the plans which it annexed to the resolution. The Council recommended that all States should consider the desirability of setting up national committees for the purpose of planning the observance of the anniversary, and invited the specialized agencies and other international governmental and non-governmental organizations to co-operate.

134. On 10 December 1958, the General Assembly held a special meeting to commemorate the tenth anniversary of the adoption of the Universal Declaration of Human Rights. The Assembly was addressed by Mrs. Eleanor Roosevelt (United States of America), former Chairman of the Commission on Human Rights; Mr. Guillaume Georges-Picot (France) on behalf of Mr. René Cassin, also a former Chairman of the Commission; Mr. R.S.S. Gunewardene (Sri Lanka), Chairman of the Commission at that time; and Mr. Charles Malik (Lebanon), Chairman of the Third Committee of the General Assembly at its third session, in 1948.

135. Special meetings of the General Assembly have since been convened from time to time to commemorate significant anniversaries of the Declaration.

136. Such celebrations demonstrate to the world the importance attached to the adoption of the Universal Declaration of Human Rights and its unique character as an international instrument and a "standard of achievement for all peoples and all nations". They have afforded opportunities for publicizing the Declaration, for making known the human rights and fundamental freedoms which it proclaims, and for awakening new interest in, and understanding of those rights and

freedoms. They may also be said to have had the indirect effect of associating the public at large with the activities of the United Nations system in the field of human rights and of promoting at the grassroots level the effective realization and enjoyment of human rights and fundamental freedoms.

1. HUMAN RIGHTS DAYS

137. The General Assembly, in resolution 423 (V) of 4 December 1950, invited "all States and interested organizations to adopt 10 December of each year as Human Rights Day, to observe this day to celebrate the proclamation of the Universal Declaration of Human Rights by the General Assembly on 10 December 1948, and to exert increasing efforts in this field of human progress".

138. The Assembly expressed the view that the anniversary of the adoption of the Declaration should be appropriately celebrated in all countries as part of a common effort to bring the Declaration to the attention of the peoples of the world, and expressed its appreciation to those countries which had begun to celebrate this anniversary even before the adoption of the resolution.

139. Since 1950, Human Rights Day has been observed in many countries throughout the world. At United Nations Headquarters, the Secretary-General usually issues a special Human Rights Day message on 10 December.

2. OTHER HUMAN RIGHTS-RELATED ANNIVERSARIES

140. In resolution 2142 (XXI) of 26 October 1966, the General Assembly proclaimed 21 March as the International Day for the Elimination of Racial Discrimination. The first observance of the Day took place on 21 March 1967.

141. The date selected for the world-wide observance commemorates the anniversary of the tragic incident which occurred on 21 March 1960 in Sharpeville, South Africa, when many peaceful demonstrators against racial discrimination were fired upon and killed by the authorities. The incident focused the attention of the world upon the inherent dangers of racial discrimination, segregation, and *apartheid*, and upon the evils of the philosophy of racial superiority often invoked to support such policies.

142. Since 1967, the International Day for the Elimination of Racial Discrimination has been observed annually in many countries and at the Headquarters of the United Nations. These observances have provided opportunities for reconsidering the need to put an end to racial discrimination, segregation and *apartheid*, and to put into motion the forces of enlightened public opinion which are required to reach this goal.

143. In 1976, following the uprising in Soweto and other areas of South Africa on 16 June, the General Assembly proclaimed that date as International Day of Solidarity with the Struggling People of South Africa. In the same year, the Assembly proclaimed 11 October as a Day of Solidarity with South African Political Prisoners.

144. In addition, the following anniversaries are observed by United Nations bodies and national communities: the Week of Solidarity with the Colonial Peoples of Southern Africa Fighting for Freedom, Independence and Equal Rights (25-31 May); the International Day of Solidarity with the Struggle of Women of South Africa and Namibia (9 August); Namibia Day (26 August); the Week of Solidarity with the People of Namibia and its Liberation Movement (beginning 27 October); and the International Day of Solidarity with the Palestinian People (29 November).

K. Teaching about human rights

145. In resolution 217 D (III) of 10 December 1948, the General Assembly expressed the view that the adoption of the Universal Declaration of Human Rights was an historic act, destined to consolidate world peace through the contribution of the United Nations towards the liberation of individuals from the unjustified oppression and constraint to which they were too often subjected, and that the text of the Declaration should be disseminated among all peoples throughout the world.

146. The Assembly recommended Governments of Member States to show their adherence to Article 56 of the Charter of the United Nations by using every means within their power solemnly to publicize the text of the Declaration and to cause it to be disseminated, displayed, read and expounded principally in schools and other educational institutions, without distinction based on the political status of countries or territories.

147. The Economic and Social Council, in resolution 314 (XI) of 24 July 1950, invited the United Nations Educational, Scientific and Cultural Organization (UNESCO) to encourage and facilitate teaching about the Universal Declaration of Human Rights in schools and adult education programmes and through the press, radio and film services. Later, the Council, in resolution 958 D II (XXXVI) of 12 July 1963, invited "universities, institutes, learned societies, trade unions and other organizations which are concerned with human rights to make available their contribution to a wider knowledge and the advance of human rights through education, research and discussion, and also through publications, newspapers and periodicals, particularly with regard to measures giving effect to human rights".

148. The International Conference on Human Rights, in resolution XX of 12 May 1968, called upon States "to ensure that all means of education shall be employed so that youth grows up and develops in a spirit of respect for human dignity and for equal rights of all men and all peoples without discrimination as to race, colour, language, sex or faith".

149. The Conference invited UNESCO to develop its programmes aimed at making children aware, from the time they start school, of respect for the dignity and rights of man and at making the principles of the Universal Declaration of Human Rights prevail at all levels of education, particularly in institutions of higher learning, where the future cadres are trained. It recommended that youth organizations should pay special attention to international gatherings and exchanges which should lead to better knowledge and better exchanges of views among the young, in order to arouse in them an active interest in the cause of human rights and fundamental freedoms.

150. The General Assembly, in resolution 2445 (XXIII) of 19 December 1968, requested Member States to take steps, as appropriate and according to the scholastic system of each State, to introduce or encourage the regular study of the United Nations and the specialized agencies, and of the principles proclaimed in the Universal Declaration of Human Rights and in other declarations on human rights, in the training of teaching staff for primary and secondary schools. It further called for progressive instruction on those subjects in the curricula of primary and secondary schools, and invited teachers to seize every opportunity to draw the attention of their pupils to the increasing role of the United Nations system in peaceful co-operation among nations and in joint efforts to promote social justice and economic and social progress in the world.

151. Measures to stimulate teaching about human rights in schools have formed an integral part of the UNESCO programme of education for international understanding and teaching about the United Nations. Principal methods of work have included studies of teaching methods, materials and programmes; seminars and conferences; publications; action for the improvement of textbooks; promotion of experimental activities in schools and teacher-training institutions; and the provision of consultative services to Member States and to teacher-training institutions assisted under the United Nations Development Programme.

152. Among the first steps taken by UNESCO was the execution in 1951 of a survey, carried out in collaboration with several international non-governmental organizations, of teachers, of methods, materials and programmes of teaching about human rights. The resulting reports provided the main basis for work at an international seminar on teaching about human rights held in the Netherlands in 1952. The seminar was in turn followed by a UNESCO publication, *The Universal Declaration of Human Rights: A Guide for Teachers* (1953), containing practical suggestions on teaching about human rights.

153. In 1953 UNESCO initiated the Associated Schools Project in Education for International Understanding. The objective was to stimulate the organization of pilot programmes in selected schools of member States of UNESCO which would further the development of education for international understanding. Human rights was chosen at the outset as one of three main themes of these experimental activities which have continued up to the present. Many of the pre-schools, primary schools, secondary schools and teacher-training institutions (which numbered 2,158 in 97 countries in 1987) concentrate their work on human rights. The results have been disseminated through several UNESCO publications and documents such as *Education for International Understanding; Examples and suggestions for Classroom Use* (1959); *Some suggestions on Teaching about Human Rights* (1968); *World Problems in the Classroom; The Role of the United Nations* (1973); *Education for international co-operation and peace at the primary-school level* (1983); *Synopsis of the Inter-regional experimental project on the study of contemporary World Problems* (1983); *World Concerns and the United Nations* (United Nations, 1983); *Seeds for Peace: The Role of Pre-School Education in International Understanding and Education for Peace* (1985); *Partners in Promoting Education for International Understanding: For participation in the UNESCO Associated School project* (1986). The reports of activities carried out in the field of human rights are also published in the bi-annual circular, *International Understanding at School*. Teaching about human rights has also been a subject of discussion at national, regional and international seminars organized as part of the Associated Schools Project.

154. Parallel with these activities are those looking to the improvement of textbooks and teaching materials from the point of view of their contribution to international understanding and respect for the principles of human rights.

155. Several bilateral and multilateral consultations concerning the revision of history, geography and social sciences textbooks for primary, secondary and higher education have been organized in recent years in various countries belonging to different regions of the world.

156. The Intergovernmental Conference on Education for International Understanding, Co-operation and Peace and Education relating to Human Rights and Fundamental Freedoms, with a View to Developing a Climate of Opinion favourable to the Strengthening of Security and Disarmament, held in Paris in April 1983, recommended to Member States to ". . . take the necessary steps to extend the scope of the 1974 Recommendation to the education system as a whole" and with a view to, *inter alia*, ". . . extending them to higher education". In accordance with this recommendation, the International Consultation on ways of improving educational action at the level of higher education, to provide students with the necessary knowledge of problems relating to peace and respect for human rights and the rights of peoples, was convened in Athens in 1986. Nineteen eminent scientists, specialists in human and social sciences and higher education made a number of recommendations concerning the general approach, aims, content and forms of international education at the higher education level.

157. As the follow-up of this consultation, a practical seminar was organized in Belgium in 1987 to draw up

experimental projects in the fields recommended by the consultation which resulted in practical suggestions for higher educational institutions with a view to launching experimental projects aimed at improving education for peace, disarmament, respect for human rights and the rights of people.

158. A Sub-Regional Workshop to Establish a Framework for Evaluation of Textbooks in Social Sciences, History and Geography was held in Bridgetown, Barbados, from 27 to 30 April 1987. It was followed by an analysis of the context of history, geography and social studies textbooks in the English-speaking sub-region.

1. DEVELOPMENT OF THE TEACHING OF HUMAN RIGHTS

159. The Commission on Human Rights, in resolution 17 (XXIX) of 3 April 1973, requested UNESCO "to continue to extend its activities in these fields and, in particular, to encourage teaching and research in human rights in universities and to this end to accelerate the preparation of appropriate material for the teaching of human rights in universities, for the guidance of universities and institutes in which the various legal, scientific, technical and other disciplines are taught".

160. As regards teaching materials at the university level, a textbook entitled *The International Dimensions of Human Rights* has been designed in particular for use by law and political science faculties. Steps have been taken for the preparation of a second textbook, on science, technology, and human rights, for use in teaching at university faculties of natural sciences and medicine.

161. In addition, UNESCO has provided financial assistance to institutions in developing countries for the preparation of programmes in the field of international law and human rights. It has also begun the preparation of a programme designed to intensify teaching and research in international humanitarian law.

162. The Commission on Human Rights, in resolution 3 (XXXIII) of 21 February 1977, took note of the Recommendation Concerning Education for International Understanding, Co-operation and Peace and Education Relating to Human Rights and Fundamental Freedoms which the General Conference of UNESCO had adopted at its eighteenth session.

163. The International Congress on the Teaching of Human Rights, a joint initiative of UNESCO and the Federal Republic of Austria, was held at Vienna from 12 to 16 September 1978. The final document of the Congress comprises two parts and an annex, which contains recommendations and proposals formulated by the Rapporteurs on the basis of proposals by participants and observers.

164. The first part, after referring to the Recommendation concerning Education for International Understanding, Co-operation and Peace and Education Relating to Human Rights and Fundamental Freedoms,

enumerates the principles and considerations which should guide the teaching of human rights. The second part suggests (*a*) the establishment of a six-year plan for human rights education, (*b*) the setting up of a voluntary fund for the development of knowledge of human rights through education and information, and (*c*) the making of a preliminary study, with a view to the preparation of a UNESCO convention on human rights teaching and education.

165. Pursuant to the recommendations adopted at this Congress, a meeting of experts, held at the headquarters of UNESCO, in Paris, from 25 to 28 June 1979, prepared a draft seven-year plan for the development of the teaching of human rights. The draft plan is addressed partly to UNESCO, partly to member States, and partly to non-governmental organizations and specialized institutions. It covers a number of measures relating to the structures, material, curricula and ways and means of human rights teaching. The plan was accepted by the General Conference of UNESCO in resolution 3/03, adopted at its twenty-first session.

166. The activities selected for the development of the teaching of human rights were essentially aimed at broadening or developing, where necessary:

(*a*) National, regional and international structures for the teaching of human rights, so as to foster the exchange of information in this field;

(*b*) Teaching materials;

(*c*) Curricula for both formal and non-formal educational systems;

(*d*) Teaching methods and the facilities available in this connection.

The programme for human rights teaching includes humanitarian law.

167. In addition, a Voluntary Fund for the development of knowledge of human rights through teaching and information was adopted by the Executive Board at its 108th session. This was designed to provide funds, supplementary to those available under the UNESCO Regular Programme and Budget, for financing the implementation of the Plan for the Development of the Teaching of Human Rights.

168. At its twenty-second session, in 1983, the General Conference of UNESCO adopted resolution 13.5, in which it recognized that UNESCO's Plan for the Development of Human Rights Teaching was one of the organization's major contributions to the promotion of human rights and pointed out that education, teaching and access to education are of particular importance to the promotion of human rights and the rights of peoples. The Conference invited the Director-General to organize a meeting to examine the Plan and the progress made in implementing it.

169. Pursuant to the resolution, the UNESCO Secretariat undertook a survey of progress by addressing a questionnaire to Member States, international organizations and institutes specialized in human rights research and teaching. To evaluate the state of implementation of the Plan, an Informal Consultation of Experts was

organized at UNESCO Headquarters from 9 to 12 July 1985. The view of the experts was that the Plan, originally scheduled for completion in seven years, should be extended and that regional meetings should be organized to assess the progress made.

2. Encouragement of Human Rights Institutes

170. In order to encourage the establishment of institutions capable of sustained teaching and research activities relating to human rights, and in order to prepare the establishment of a network of institutions, UNESCO has provided assistance to several international or regional meetings of human rights experts.

171. At the international level, UNESCO has established regular co-operation with the International Institute of Human Rights (Strasbourg). UNESCO assists in the organization of the annual training sessions of this Institute, and especially in the programme that enables university teachers and professionals to acquire practical knowledge about international protection of human rights.

172. In addition, UNESCO has taken various measures to enable teachers and students to acquire specific knowledge about human rights;

(a) Fellowships have been awarded under the Participation Programme for the initial and advanced training of students;

(b) Each year, at UNESCO headquarters, about fifteen trainees work for a month in the field of human rights. This training enables them to acquire valuable experience, particularly in UNESCO's fields of competence;

(c) A UNESCO Prize for the Teaching of Human Rights was established by decision of the Executive Board at its 104th session. Its purpose is to encourage such teaching and stimulate interest in it. The Prize was awarded for the first time in 1978 and was awarded thereafter in 1979, 1981 and 1983.

173. With regard to the creation of an international clearing house for teaching human rights and for the exchange of information on the curricula and on existing courses and specialized research in the field of human rights, a feasibility study was undertaken by an international non-governmental organization specialized in the field of social science documentation.

174. Another means of international co-operation and exchange of information on human rights teaching is UNESCO's bulletin *Teaching of Human Rights* which is published with a view to providing liaison between all those involved in teaching and research regarding human rights. UNESCO has published this bulletin since 1980. The topics covered have included: the place of human rights in different cultural and religious traditions; the problems of information in the field of human rights; new issues and concerns in the field of human rights, and new forms of regional co-operation; and reflections on the Universal Declaration of Human Rights

which retrace UNESCO's research activities on the meaning of human rights. The most recent issue is a collection of curricula and a compilation of teaching material at all levels of education and on in-and-out of school contexts which will serve as a guidebook for human rights teaching. News from human rights teaching, research and professional associations figures as a regular feature in this bulletin.

175. At the regional level, conferences on the teaching of human rights at university level were organized regularly with a view to encouraging the initiatives taken by national, sub-regional or regional institutes of human rights: for Asia in 1981 (New Delhi) in co-operation with the Indian National Centre for Human Rights Research and Education, as well as the Human Rights Documentation and Research Centre at Jawarharlal Nehru University; for Latin America in Quito, in 1982 and 1984, in co-operation with the Latin American Association for Human Rights (ALDHU); for Africa in Kinshasa in 1982, 1983 and 1985 in co-operation with the "Centre de recherche interdisciplinaire pour la promotion et protection des droits de l'homme en Afrique centrale" (CRIDHAC). Two interregional symposia on human rights were held in Turkey (Istanbul in March 1979 and Ankara in June 1980), in conjunction with the Faculty of Political Science of the University of Ankara.

176. In March 1982, a regional seminar on Human Rights in African Cultural Traditions was organized with the assistance of UNESCO, in co-operation with the Institute of Human Rights and Peace in Dakar, Senegal. In October 1982, UNESCO, under contract to the Association of Young African Lawyers, organized a regional meeting in Lomé on human rights within African traditions.

177. At the national level, UNESCO co-operated with professional organizations such as Bar Associations (Paris and Dakar) and research institutes such as the National Institute for Pedagogical Research (Paris), the International Centre of Sociological, Penal and Penitentiary Research Studies (Messina), and the International Institute for Human Rights Studies (Trieste). Several National Commissions were associated with activities to promote the insertion of human rights education in different disciplines and at various levels of education.

3. Preparation and Dissemination of Teaching Materials

178. A textbook entiled *International Dimensions of Human Rights*, intended for the teaching of human rights at the university level, was published in French in 1978 and in Portuguese in 1983. An updated version was published in English in 1982, and in Spanish and Japanese in 1984. The book describes international and regional procedures which existed for the promotion and protection of human rights, and explains how they operated.

179. In addition, UNESCO published a booklet entitled *Human Rights: Questions and Answers*, elaborated by Leah Levin and illustrated by a famous cartoonist. The booklet provides answers to a number of questions about the meaning of the rights proclaimed in the Universal Declaration of Human Rights and about the instruments which exist to guarantee respect for them. The booklet was published in English, French and Spanish. It was issued in Finnish by the UNESCO Finnish National Commission in 1983, and a German-language version was issued in 1984. Portuguese and Spanish versions are being prepared.

180. With regard to human rights teaching for specific professional groups, a manual for medical students, entitled *Le médecin et les droits de l'homme*, written by Mr. Maurice Torelli, was published with the assistance of UNESCO. A manual of humanitarian law, *The International Dimensions of Humanitarian Law*, was published in 1986.

181. The anthology of human rights, *The Birthright of Man*, edited by Jeanne Hersch, which appeared in French in 1968, in English in 1969 and in Spanish in 1973, was out of stock for many years. This publication was re-edited in French in 1984 (Editions J.-C. Lattès).